HANDBOOK OF PROGRAMMING LANGUAGES, VOLUME III

Little Languages and Tools

Peter H. Salus, Series Editor in Chief

Handbook of Programming Languages, Volume III: Little Languages and Tools

Peter H. Salus, Series Editor in Chief

Published by:
Macmillan Technical Publishing
201 West 103rd Street
Indianapolis, IN 46290 USA

FIRST EDITION

International Standard Book Number: 1-57870-010-8

Library of Congress Catalog Card Number: 97-81204

01 00 99 98 4 3 2 1

Interpretation of the printing code: The rightmost double-digit number is the year of the book's printing; the rightmost single-digit, the number of the book's printing. For example, the printing code 98-1 shows that the first printing of the book occurred in 1998.

Composed in Sabon and MCPdigital by Macmillan Technical Publishing

Printed in the United States of America

Warning and Disclaimer

This book is designed to provide information about little languages and tools. Every effort has been made to make this book as complete and as accurate as possible, but no warranty or fitness is implied.

The information is provided on an as-is basis. The authors and Macmillan Technical Publishing shall have neither liability nor responsibility to any person or entity with respect to any loss or damages arising from the information contained in this book or from the use of the discs or programs that may accompany it.

Permissions

Chapter 1 is reprinted with the permission of AT&T Bell Laboratories from Bentley, J. 1988. More programming pearls: Confessions of a coder. Reading, MA: Addison-Wesely. Copyright © ACM.

Chapter 2 is reprinted with permission from Kernighan, B.W., and L. L. Cherry. 1977. A System for typesetting mathematics. Computing Sience Technical Report No. 17. Murray Hill, NJ: Bell Laboratories. Revision based on the 1975 publication A System for Typesetting Mathematics. CACM 18 (3) : 151. New York: AVM Publications.

Chapter 5 is derived from Arnold Robbin's book Effective AWK Programming, published by SSC (Seattle, WA) and the Free Software Foundation (Boston, MA). Copyright © by the Free Software Foundation.

Chapter 6 is reprinted with permission from Dougherty, D., and Robbins, A. 1997. sed & awk. Cambridge, MA: O'Reilly.

Associate Publisher
Jim LeValley

Managing Editor
Caroline Roop

Executive Editors
Linda Engelman
Tom Stone

Acquisitions Editors
Jane K. Brownlow
Karen Wachs

Development Editor
Kitty Wilson Jarrett

Project Editor
Brad Herriman

Copy Editor
Kristine Simmons

Indexers
Chris Cleveland
Bront Davis

Team Coordinator
Amy Lewis

Manufacturing Coordinator
Brook Farling

Book Designer
Gary Adair

Cover Designer
Karen Ruggles

Production Team Supervisor
Daniela Raderstorf

Production
Mary Hunt
Laura A. Knox

Overview

Table of Contents

Foreword to the *Handbook of Programming Languages*

The aim of the *Handbook of Programming Languages* is to provide a single, comprehensive source of information concerning a variety of individual programming languages and methodologies for computing professionals. The *Handbook* is published in multiple volumes and covers a wide range of languages, organized by type and functionality.

The *Handbook* includes four volumes:

Volume I: Object-Oriented Programming Languages

This volume contains chapters on Smalltalk, C++, Eiffel, Ada95, Modula-3, and Java.

Volume II: Imperative Programming Languages

This volume contains chapters on Fortran, Pascal, Icon, and C, as well as a chapter on intermediate languages by Ron Cytron.

Volume III: Little Languages and Tools

This volume contains chapters on little languages and domain-specific languages, such as troff, awk, sed, Perl, Tcl and Tk, Python, and SQL. It also contains seminal work by Brian Kernighan and Lorinda Cherry as well as Jon Bentley and essays by Paul Hudak and Peter Langston.

Volume IV: Functional and Logic Programming Languages

This volume contains chapters on functional (Lisp, Scheme, Guile, and Emacs Lisp) and logic (Prolog) programming languages.

Natural, or human, languages appear to be about 10,000 years old. Symbolic, or formal, languages began in Sumer (a civilization of southern Iraq from about 3800 to 2300 BCE), where we find the oldest writing system, cuneiform. It was followed by Egyptian hieroglyphics (about 3000 BCE), the language of the Harappa in the Indus valley, the Chinese shell and bone inscriptions, and (in the Western hemisphere) the language of the Maya.

Writing systems abstract from speech and formalize that abstraction in their symbols. This may be done semantically (for example, hieroglyphs, English numerals, and symbols such as &) or phonologically (for example, alphabetic spelling).

In more recent times, further abstractions have become necessary: warning beacons, flags on sailing vessels, railway telegraph/semaphore, Morse code, and so forth.

Mechanical methods for calculating are very old, but they all involve symbolic abstraction. The abacus is probably the oldest of such constructions. The Chinese and Egyptians had this device nearly four millennia ago. The Mayans possessed it when the Spanish arrived. It was only a few years after Napier's discovery of logarithms (1614), and the use of his "bones" (marked ivory rods) for multiplication, that the slide rule was invented.

In 1642, at the age of 18, Blaise Pascal invented a calculator that could add and carry to aid his father, a tax collector. Almost 30 years later, in 1671, Leibniz took Pascal's machine a step further and built a prototype machine that could multiply using an ingenious device called the *stepped wheel*, which was still in use in mechanical calculators manufactured in the late 1940s. Leibniz demonstrated his calculator to the Royal Society in London in 1676.

The first commercially successful calculator was invented by Charles Xavier Thomas in 1820. By 1878, an astounding 1,500 had been sold—nearly 30 per year. They were still being manufactured by Darras in Paris after World War I. The Brunsviga adding machine, based on an 1875 patent by Frank Stephen Baldwin, which substituted a wheel with a variable number of protruding teeth for the Leibniz stepped wheel, sold an incredible 20,000 machines between 1892 and 1912—1,000 per year.

The first keyboard-driven calculator was patented in 1850 by D. D. Parmalee, and Dorr Eugene Felt's Comptometer—the first successful key-driven, multiple-order calculating machine—was patented in 1887.

In 1812, Charles Babbage came up with a notion for a different type of calculator, which he termed a *difference engine*. He was granted support by the British government in 1823. Work stopped in 1833, and the project was abandoned in 1842, the government having decided the cost was too great. From 1833 on, though, Babbage devoted himself to a different sort of machine, an analytical engine, that would automatically evaluate any mathematical formula. The various operations of the analytical engine were to be controlled by punched cards of the type used in the

Jacquard loom. Though only a fraction of the construction appears to have been effected, Babbage's notes, drawings, and portions of the engine are in the Victoria and Albert Museum (as is the set of Napier's bones that belonged to Babbage).

The Jacquard loom, a successful attempt at increasing production through automation, was itself the result of several prior innovations: In 1725 Bouchon substituted an endless paper tape with perforations for the bunches of looped string. In 1728 Falcon substituted perforated cards, but attached them to strings, and in 1748, Jacques de Vaucanson combined the bands of perforated paper and the cards. The patterns on the cards were perforated by machines that cut on designs painted on by stencils. The programmed machine was born.

Over 100 years later, Herman Hollerith, a graduate of Columbia College in New York, recalled the existence of those perforated cards. Hollerith had just started work at the Census Bureau at a generous salary of $600 per year. There he was put to work on a survey of power and machinery used in manufacturing. But he also met John Shaw Billings, who was in charge of "vital statistics." One night at dinner, Billings complained about the recently invented but inadequate tabulating device of Charles Seaton, which had been used for the census of 1870. Billings felt that given the increased population, the 1880 census might not be completed in less than seven or eight years, and the 1890 census would still be incomplete in 1900. "There ought to be a machine for doing the purely mechanical work of tabulating population and similar statistics," Billings said. "We talked it over," Hollerith recalled 30 years later, "and I remember...he thought of using cards with the description of the individual shown by notches punched in the edge of the card." Hollerith thought about constructing a device to record and read such information and asked Billings to go into business with him. Billings was a cautious man and said no.

In 1882 Hollerith went to MIT as an instructor in mechanical engineering (he was then 22). Teaching at MIT gave him the time to work on his machine. He first considered putting the information on long strips of paper, but this proved impractical. In the summer of 1883, Hollerith took a train trip west. On the train he saw the "punch photograph," a way for conductors to punch passengers' descriptions onto tickets so they could check that the same individual was using the ticket throughout the trip; in this system things like gender and hair and eye color were encoded.

Hollerith patented his first machine in 1884 and an improved design in 1886, when he performed a trial by conducting the Baltimore census. On the basis of reports of the trial, New Jersey and New York placed orders for machines (to tally mortality rates). Hollerith and some business colleagues bid for the contract for the 1890 census and won it. The government of Austria ordered machines in 1890. Canada ordered five the next year. Italy and Norway followed, and then Russia. The machines were a clear success. Hollerith incorporated his Hollerith Electric Tabulating System as the Tabulating Machine Company in 1896; he reincorporated it in 1905.

Nearly 80 years passed before the computer industry moved beyond several of Hollerith's insights. First, so that operators would have no problem orienting the cards, he cut a corner from the upper right. Second, he *rented* the machines at a reasonable rate (the rental fees for the 1890 census were $750,000; the labor cost in 1880 had been $5 million), but *sold* the patented cards (more than 100 million between 1890 and 1895). Third, he adapted the census-counting to tally freight and passenger data for railroads. Hollerith effectively invented reusability.

Despite the fact that Thomas Watson said (in 1945), "I think there is a world market for about five computers," the first completed was one he had funded. Howard Aiken of Harvard, along with a small team, began in 1939 to put together a machine that exploited Babbage's principles. It consisted, when completed in 1944, of a 51-foot by 8-foot panel on which tape readers, relays, and rotary switches were mounted. Nearly all of the operations of the Harvard Mark I Calculator were controlled by mechanical switches, driven by a 4-horsepower motor.

The first all-electronic computer was the Electronic Numerical Integrator and Calculator. Completed by J. W. Mauchly and J. P. Eckert of the University of Pennsylvania in late 1945 and installed in 1946, it was commissioned by the Ballistics Research Laboratory (BRL) at the Aberdeen (Maryland) Proving Ground. It was—and will remain, I expect—the largest computing machine ever built: It was made up of 18,000 tubes and 1,500 relays. ENIAC was the electronic analogue of the Mark I, but ran several hundred times faster.

ENIAC had offspring in England, too. Maurice V. Wilkes and his group began planning their Electronic Delay Storage Automatic Calculator (EDSAC) in late 1946, on Wilkes's return from Pennsylvania, and began work at the University Mathematical Laboratory in Cambridge early in the new year. It was one fifth the size of ENIAC and based on ideas that John von Neumann had presented in a paper. When it performed its first fully automatic calculation in May 1949, EDSAC became the first electronic machine to be put into operation that had a high-speed memory (store) and I/O (input/output) devices. Within a few years, EDSAC's library contained more than 150 subroutines, according to Wilkes.

At virtually the same time, in Manchester, a team under M. H. A. Newman began work on a machine that was to embody the EDVAC concepts. F. C. Williams, who invented cathode ray tube storage, I. J. Good, who had worked on the Colossus code-breaking machine with Alan M. Turing, and Turing himself, joined the team. The Manchester Automatic Digital Machine prototype was built in 1948, and the definitive machine ran its first program in June 1949. MADM introduced to computing both the index register and pagination.

In the meantime, IBM had begun work on its Selective-Sequence Electronic Calculator (SSEC). It is important to remember that while EDSAC was the first electronic computer, the SSEC was the first *computer*—it combined computation with a stored program. It was put into operation at IBM headquarters in Manhattan early in 1948, cleverly placed behind plate glass windows at street level so that pedestrians could see it operate. It was a large machine with 13,000 tubes and 23,000 relays. Because all the arithmetic calculations were carried out by the tubes, it was more than 100 times as fast as the Mark I. It also had three different types of memory: a high-speed tube store, a larger capacity in relays, and a vastly larger store on 80-column paper tape. Instructions and input were punched on tape and there were 66 heads arranged so that control was transferred automatically from one to the other. "It was probably the first machine to have a conditional transfer of control instruction in the sense that Babbage and Lady [Ada] Lovelace recommended," wrote B. W. Bowden in 1953. It did work for, among other things, the Atomic Energy Commission, before being dismantled in August 1952.

That very June, von Neumann and his colleagues completed Maniac at the Institute for Advanced Studies in Princeton, New Jersey. It employed the electrostatic memory invented by F. C. Williams and T. Kilburn, which required a single cathode ray tube, instead of special storage tubes.

The next advance in hardware came at MIT's Whirlwind project, begun by Jay Forrester in 1944. Whirlwind performed 20,000 single-address operations per second on 16-digit words, employing a new type of electrostatic store in which 16 tubes each contained 256 binary digits. The Algebraic Interpreter for the Whirlwind and A-2—developed by Grace Murray Hopper for the UNIVAC—are likely the most important of the machine-oriented languages.

The 704, originally the 701A, was released in 1954. It was the logical successor to the IBM 701 (1952, 1953). The evolution of the 701 into the 704 was headed up by Gene Amdahl. The direct result of the 701/704 was the beginning of work on Fortran (which stands for *formula translator*) by John Backus at IBM in 1953. Work on the Fortran translator (we would call it a compiler) began in 1955 and was completed in 1957. Fortran was, without a doubt, the first programming language.

In December 1959, at the Eastern Joint Computer Conference at the Statler Hotel in Boston, the three-year-old DEC unveiled the prototype of its PDP-1 (Programmed Data Processor-1). It was priced at $120,000 and deliveries began in November 1960.

The PDP-1 was an 18-bit machine with a memory capacity between 4,096 and 32,768 words. The PDP-1 had a memory cycle of 5 microseconds and a computing speed of 100,000 computations per second. It was the result of a project led by Benjamin Gurley and was composed of 3,500 transistors and 4,300 diodes. It had an editor, a macroassembler, and an ALGOL compiler, DECAL. It employed a paper tape reader for input and an IBM typewriter for output. The PDP-1 had the best cost/performance of any real-time computer of its generation. It was also the first commercial computer to come with a graphical display screen.

Just over 40 years ago there were no programming languages. In 1954 programming was still a function of hardware. Fortran was invented in 1957. It was soon being taught. By 1960, not only had COBOL and Lisp joined the roster, but so had others, many now thankfully forgotten. Over the past 40 years, nearly 4,000 computer languages have been produced. Only a tithe of these are in use today, but the growth and development of them has been progressive and organic.

There are a number of ways such languages can be taxonomized. One frequent classification is into machine languages (the natural language of a given device), assembly languages (in which common English words and abbreviations are used as input to the appropriate machine language), and high-level languages (which permit instructions that more closely resemble English instructions). Assembly languages are translators; high-level languages require conversion into machine language: These translators are called *compilers*. Among the high-level languages currently in use are C, C++, Eiffel, and Java.

Yet there is no guide for the overwhelmed programmer, who merely wants to get her job done. This *Handbook of Programming Languages* is intended to serve as an instant reference, a life-preserver, providing information to enable that programmer to make intelligent choices as to which languages to employ, enough information to enable him to program at a basic level, and references to further, more detailed information.

Peter H. Salus
Boston, February 1998

General Bibliography

Histories of Programming Languages

Bergin, T. J., and R. G. Gibson (Eds.). 1996. *History of programming languages*. Reading, MA: Addison-Wesley. Proceedings of ACM's Second History of Programming Languages Conference.

Sammet, J. A. 1969. *Programming languages: History and fundamentals*. Englewood Cliffs, NJ: Prentice Hall. An indispensable work.

Wexelblat, R. L. (Ed.). 1981. *History of programming languages*. New York: Academic Press. The proceedings of ACM's First History of Programming Languages Conference.

Reader on Programming Languages

Horowitz, E. 1987. *Programming languages: A grand tour* (3rd ed.). Rockville, MD: Computer Science Press.

Surveys and Guides to Programming Languages

Appleby, D. 1991. *Programming languages: Paradigm and practice*. New York: McGraw-Hill.

Bal, H. E., and D. Grune. 1994. *Programming language essentials.* Wokingham, England: Addison-Wesley.

Cezzar, R. 1995. *A guide to programming languages.* Norwood, MA: Artech House.

Sethi, R. 1996. *Programming languages: Concepts & constructs* (2nd ed.). Reading, MA: Addison-Wesley.

Stansifer, R. 1995. *The study of programming languages.* Englewood Cliffs, NJ: Prentice Hall.

Foreword to This Volume: Little Languages and Tools

Fortran, Ada, C, C++, etc. are big production systems. But many other languages that (as Jon Bentley points out in the article reprinted below) are "specialized to a particular problem domain" and "took only a few days to implement." Although Bentley's article appeared only a little more than a dozen years ago, it was based on work that was then already a decade old. Kernighan and Cherry's eqn paper, originally published in 1975, is reproduced (in its 1978 revision) next. The final "introduction" is an essay by Paul Hudak on "special domain languages," bringing everything up to the present.

With this material as introduction, we move on to a detailed article on troff (the UNIX typesetting language) by Akkerhuis. eqn is a "little language" that serves (as do tbl, pic, grap, chem, refer, etc.) as a preprocessor for troff, written by Joe Ossanna and maintained since his untimely death in 1977 by Brian Kernighan. troff was based on RUNOFF, the text formatter of Corbato's CTSS (1964).

eqn is written in AWK, a pattern-matching language developed in 1977 by Aho, Weinberger and Kernighan, and the next chapter is devoted to AWK, followed by an introduction to sed, a non-interactive streams editor.

SQL is a database query tool or great utility. Perl, created by Larry Wall, is the foremost tool for Web development and for system administration. Python, an object-oriented scripting language, can be used for a vast variety of tasks. Tcl/Tk — the Tool control language and its Toolkit — is a language designed to be used specifically with the X Windows System, and thus has become one of the most useful tools where the Web is concerned.

As a demonstration of just how tools and little languages can be used in special domains, Peter Langston has written an enchanting piece on "Little Languages for Music."

There are many more tools (e.g., lex, yacc) and even more little languages (e.g. LOGO, BDMP, SASS), but this volume is already long enough.

Peter H. Salus

Boston, February 1998

Trademark Acknowledgments

All terms mentioned in this book that are known to be trademarks or service marks have been appropriately capitalized. Macmillan Technical Publishing cannot attest to the accuracy of this information. Use of a term in this book should not be regarded as affecting the validity of any trademark or service mark.

Dedication

This *Handbook* is dedicated to John Backus, James Gosling, Adele Goldberg, Ralph Griswold, Brian Kernighan, John McCarthy, Bertrand Meyer, Dennis Ritchie, Bjarne Stroustrup, and the memory of Joe Ossanna, without whose efforts most of these languages wouldn't exist.

Acknowledgments

Many individuals deserve mention where this enormous *Handbook* is concerned. First of all, Tom Stone, who abetted my thinking and then effected a contract prior to deserting me for another publisher; next, Jim LeValley and Don Fowley at Macmillan, for being willing to take a chance on this project. I'd also like to thank Linda Engelman, Tracy Hughes, Amy Lewis, Jane Brownlow, Karen Wachs, and Kitty Jarrett at Macmillan.

In addition to the many authors, I'd like to thank Lou Katz, Stuart McRobert, Len Tower, and Brent Welch for their advice, patience, and friendship.

My gratitude to the ACM, to Addison-Wesley Longman, to MIT Press, to O'Reilly & Associates, and to the Waite Group for permissions to reprint various materials is enormous.

The errors and omissions are mine.

About the Series Editor

Peter H. Salus

Peter H. Salus is the author of *A Quarter Century of UNIX* (1994) and *Casting the Net: From ARPANET to Internet and Beyond* (1995). He is an internationally recognized expert and has been the keynote speaker at Uniforum Canada, the UKUUG, the NLUUG, and the OTA (Belgium) in the past few years. He has been executive director of the USENIX Association and of the Sun User Group and vice president of the Free Software Foundation. He was the managing editor of *Computing Systems* (MIT Press) from 1987 to 1996. He writes on a variety of computing topics in a number of magazines. His Ph.D. in linguistics (New York University, 1963) has led him from natural languages to computer languages.

About the Authors

Jaap Akkerhuis

After graduation from the Hogere Technische School, Amsterdam, with an electrical engineering degree, Jaap Akkerhuis served a brief stint at the phonetical institute of the University of Amsterdam. There he built an interface between a standard commercial tape recorder and a Data General Eclipse in order to digitize sound material.

After that, he joined the Mathematisch Centrum in Amsterdam, where he was introduced to UNIX 6th Edition. He became system administrator for the fast-growing number of UNIX installations and especially for the prepress facilities and equipment for the in-house printing facilities for its scientific publications. In 1981, he was one of the key people who built the European part of Usenet and the Internet. At the same time, he was active in the European and Dutch UNIX users groups.

In 1988, he was asked to join the software release engineering group at Carnegie Mellon University. Soon he joined the text interchange research group.

With Jonathan Rosenberg, Mark Sherman, and Ann Marks, he co-authored a book about text format translation and the Office Documentation Standard (ODA): *Multi-media Document Translation: ODA and the EXPRESS Project*. In 1989, the project was terminated and he joined mt Xinu (Berkeley, CA). He was responsible for the development of the Macintosh file server running under UNIX, a commercial product now marketed by Xinet.

In 1991, he joined AT&T Bell Labs (Murray Hill, NJ), where he worked once again on documentation format translation problems. One of the questions to be answered was how documents could be interchanged between the internal standard and an industry standard and how these formats could be expressed in SGML. He was also part of the group that was responsible for the 3.4 Release of the Documenter's WorkBench. Akkerhuis also helped to popularize WWW services on the internal internet.

In 1995, he returned to the Netherlands as member of the technical staff at NLnet, and leader of the development group.

Jon Bentley

Jon Bentley is a member of the technical staff at Bell Laboratories (Lucent Technologies). Previously he was with AT&T Bell Laboratories, and before that he was associate professor of computer science at Carnegie Mellon University, where he received a Dean's Award for Excellence in Undergraduate Education. Bentley holds a B.S. from Stanford University and M.S. and Ph.D. degrees from the University of North Carolina. He began writing "Programming Pearls" for CACM in 1983.

Lorinda L. Cherry

Lorinda L. Cherry holds a B.A. in mathematics from the University of Delaware and an M.S. in computer science from Stevens Institute of Technology. She has been employed at AT&T since 1966. She has been working on graphics, word processing, and language design for more than 25 years. Cherry is the author of Writer's Workbench, bc, and dc, as well as co-author of eqn.

Dale Dougherty

Dale Dougherty is president and CEO of Songline Studios, an affiliate of O'Reilly & Associates specializing in the development of online content. The founding editor of the Nutshell series, Dale has written *sed & awk* (with Arnold Robbins), *DOS Meets UNIX* (with Tim O'Reilly), *Using UUCP & Usenet* (with Grace Tudino), and *Guide to the Pick System* (all published by O'Reilly).

Mike Glover

Mike Glover has been working as a computer consultant in the greater Toronto area for the past four years. His specialty is UNIX system administration, system programming, and mission-critical installations. Although he does everything from network installations to kernel hacking and vacuuming—if he's asked nicely—he doesn't do windows! Mike got his start with UNIX systems at the University of Toronto Erindale College computer center, where he learned how to maintain and repair UNIX systems and angry users. Mike is still working on trying to fix angry users. In his off time he teaches karate, but if you were to ask Christina, she would tell you that Mike doesn't have "off" time.

Paul Hudak

Paul Hudak joined the faculty at Yale University in 1982, having received his B.S. at Vanderbilt, M.S. at MIT, and Ph.D. from the University of Utah.

Professor Hudak is interested in functional programming, theory of programming languages, and application of programming language principles to multimedia software development. Hudak believes that programming languages should be pushed further in the direction of high-level abstractions in which the programmer says less about the details of a computation and more about the problem specification itself. At the same time he recognizes the need for smart compilation techniques to make such languages practical. His most recent interest is in applying these principles to multimedia technology, including computer music, graphics and animation, and robotics.

Hudak was instrumental in organizing and chairing the Haskell Committee, an international group of computer scientists who designed Haskell, a pure functional programming language. He is an editor of the *Journal of Functional Programming*, member of the ACM and IEEE, member of the editorial boards of the International Journal of Parallel Programming and Lisp and Symbolic Computation, and a charter member of IFIP WG2.8 Working Group on Functional Programming. He served as associate editor of *ACM TOPLAS*. He has published more than 100 papers, and has consulted for Los Alamos National Laboratory, IBM T.J. Watson Research Laboratory, and Intermetrics, Inc. He is also a recipient of an IBM Faculty Development Award (1984–1985), and a Presidential Young Investigator Award (1985).

Aidan Humphreys

Aidan Humphreys received his M.S. in information technology from the University of London in 1988. He currently works as a systems integrator based in Frankfurt, Germany. Perl is an essential tool for his work implementing client/server systems for financial institutions across Europe. Aidan owes his fast motorcar to several crucial Perl programs.

Brian W. Kernighan

Brian W. Kernighan holds a B.A.Sc. from the University of Toronto and a Ph.D. from Princeton University. He has been at Bell Laboratories since 1969, first with AT&T, and now with Lucent Technologies. He has a wide range of interests, including typesetting, combinatorics, and tools and little languages. Kernighan was partly responsible for V7 UNIX. He wrote ratfor, ditroff, eqn, and pic. He is the *K* of K&R and of awk, and the co-author of *Software Tools* and *The Unix Programming Environment*.

David Klappholz

David Klappholz earned a B.S. in mathematics and humanities from MIT in 1966, and an M.S.E.E. and a Ph.D. in computer and information science from the University of Pennsylvania in 1972 and 1974. He has taught at Columbia University, at the Polytechnic Institute of New York, and at Stevens Institute of Technology, where he is currently a professor of computer science. Dr. Klappholz was the founding editor of the MIT/Longmans Research Monograph Series on Parallel and Distributed Processing, and is on the editorial boards of a number of journals. He has consulted for such agencies as the Institute for Defense Analysis and Lawrence Livermore National Laboratory. He has lectured on database systems for such firms as AT&T, Lucent, Bellcore, and GEC Marconi, and is currently working on a book on database management systems.

Cameron Laird

Cameron Laird manages a software and publishing consultancy with co-author Kathryn Soraiz from just outside Houston, Texas. Cameron has more than two decades of commercial experience in software, mostly in high-performance systems programming. Nowadays, he concentrates on Web work and process control.

Cameron also contributed chapters to *UNIX Unleashed* and *Red Hat Linux Unleashed*. For other articles and books he's written on Tcl and related subjects, see `http://starbase.neosoft.com/~claird/misc.writing/publications.html`.

Peter S. Langston

Peter S. Langston mixes computers and music; his recent work in algorithmic composition and software tools for composition, arrangement, and performance brings to bear 30 years of experience as a computer researcher and an even longer tenure as a performing musician and composer.

Peter has worked as a programmer (Commercial Union Leasing Co. and the Smithsonian Astrophysical Observatory), systems analyst/UNIX guru (the Harvard Science Center and Davis, Polk & Wardwell, a Wall Street law firm), department founder/designer (LucasArts/Lucasfilm Ltd. and Segue Software), and computer researcher (Bell Communications Research). Peter appears twice in the *Hacker's Dictionary* (aka the Jargon file), once as the creator of a computer game called Empire and once for his system of broadcasting audio over Ethernet connections called Radio Free Ethernet.

Mark Lutz

Mark Lutz is a software engineer and the author of the book *Programming Python* from O'Reilly. His experience includes work with compilers, development tools, scripting language applications, technical writing, and training. Mark has been involved with Python since 1992 when he became one of its first adopters and evangelists. He can be reached by email at `lutz@rmii.com` or on the Web at `http://rmi.net/~lutz`.

Hal Pomeranz

Hal Pomeranz is the founder and technical lead of Deer Run Associates, a firm specializing in system and network connectivity and security solutions. He has been active in the system and network management/security field for more than 10 years, and is a regular speaker and organizer for technical conferences and professional gatherings. Hal is a columnist for the USENIX newsletter and other technical publications and has served on the board of directors for several professional societies.

Prior to founding Deer Run Associates, Hal held network and systems management positions at some of the largest commercial (AT&T Bell Labs, TRW Information Systems), government (NASA Ames Research Center), and educational (University of Pennsylvania) institutions in the United States. Most recently he was director for infrastructure development and information security officer for the Internet Engineering Division of CUC International, where he was responsible for developing the real-time transactional and security systems for CUC's Internet services.

He holds a bachelor of arts in mathematics with a minor in computer science from Swarthmore College.

Arnold Robbins

Arnold Robbins, an Atlanta native, is a professional programmer and technical author. He has been working with UNIX systems since 1980, when he was introduced to a PDP-11 running a version of the 6th Edition of UNIX. He has been a heavy awk user since 1987, when he became involved with gawk, the GNU project's version of awk. As a member of the POSIX 1003.2 ballotting group, he helped shape the POSIX standard for awk. He is currently the maintainer of gawk and its documentation. The documentation is available from the Free Software Foundation and has also been published by SSC as *Effective AWK Programming*.

Kathryn Soraiz

Kathryn Soraiz manages a software and publishing consultancy with co-author Cameron Laird from just outside Houston, Texas. Kathryn has a background in distribution engineering. In recent years, she has focused on document management and publications.

For other articles she has written on Tcl, see `http://starbase.neosoft.com/~claird/misc.writing/publications.html`.

Ed Weiss

Ed Weiss is a professional consultant who has extensive experience working on software development environments, designing and maintaining large computer networks, and integrating new technology. His most recent work has been helping corporations utilize object-oriented technology on very large projects. Ed discovered computers way back in the 1970s, although he won't admit it if you ask him. He maintained and supported Perl throughout AT&T Bell Laboratories for many years. Ed has been teaching computer courses since 1979.

CHAPTER 1

Little Languages[1]

by Jon Bentley

When you say "language," most programmers think of the big ones, such as Fortran or COBOL or Pascal. In fact, a language is any mechanism to express intent, and the input to many programs can be viewed profitably as statements in a language. This chapter is about those "little languages."

Programmers deal with microscopic languages every day. Consider printing a floating-point number in six characters, including a decimal point and two subsequent digits. Rather than write a subroutine for the task, a Fortran programmer specifies the format `F6.2`, and a COBOL programmer defines the picture `999.99`. Each of these descriptions is a statement in a well-defined little language. While the languages are quite different, each is appropriate for its problem domain. Although a Fortran programmer might complain that `999999.99999` is too long when `F12.5` could do the job, the COBOLer can't even express in Fortran such common financial patterns as `$,$$$,$$9.99`. Fortran is aimed at scientific computing; COBOL is designed for business.

In the good old days, real programmers would swagger to a key punch and, standing the whole time, crank out nine cards like:

```
//SUMMARY    JOB    REGION=(100K, 50K)
//           EXEC   PGM=SUMMAR
//SYSIN      DD     DSNAME=REP.8601,DISP=OLD
//                  UNIT=2314,SPACE=(TRK,(1,1,1)),
//                  VOLUME=SER=577632
//SYSOUT     DD     DSNAME=SUM.8601,DISP=(,KEEP),
//                  UNIT=2314,SPACE=(TRK,(1,1,1)),
//                  VOLUME=SER=577632
// SYSABEND DD      SYSOUT=A
```

[1]This chapter is reprinted with the permission of AT&T Bell Laboratories from Bentley, J. 1988. *More Programming Pearls: Confessions of a Coder*. Reading, MA: Addison-Wesley.

Today's young whippersnappers do this simple job by typing

```
summarize<jan.report>jan.summary
```

Modern successors to the old "job control" languages are not only more convenient to use, they are more powerful than their predecessors.

Languages surround programmers, yet many programmers don't exploit linguistic insights. Examining programs under a linguistic light can give you a better understanding of the tools you now use, and can teach you design principles for building elegant interfaces to your future programs. This chapter will show how the user interfaces to half a dozen interesting programs can be viewed as little languages.

This chapter is built around Brian Kernighan's Pic language for making line drawings.[2] Its compiler is implemented on the UNIX system, which is particularly supportive and exploitative of language processing.

The next section introduces Pic and the following section compares it to alternative systems. Subsequent sections discuss some little languages that compile into Pic and the little languages used to build Pic.

1.1. The Pic Language

If you're talking about compilers, you might want to depict their behavior with a picture:

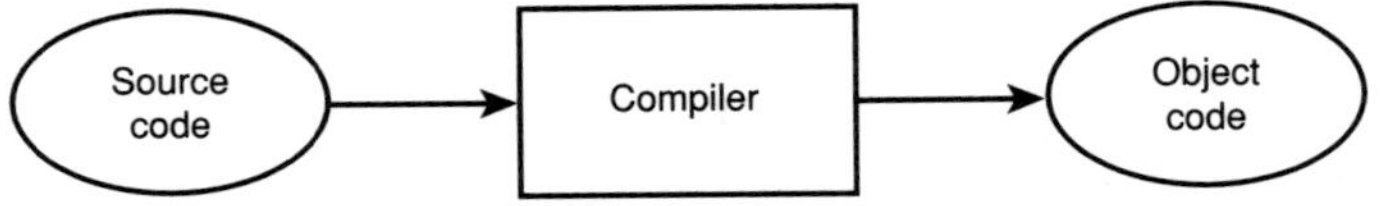

(This diagram is genuine Pic output, as are all pictures in this book; we'll see its input description shortly.) Some contexts may call for a little more detail about the internal structure of the compiler. This picture shows a structure typical of many compilers:

[2]B. W. Kernighan wrote "PIC—A Language for Typesetting Graphics" (*Software—Practice and Experience 12*, pp. 1–21, 1982). Kernighan described an updated version of the language in "PIC—A Graphics Language for Typesetting, Revised User Manual" (Bell Labs Computing Science Technical Report Number 116, December 1984).

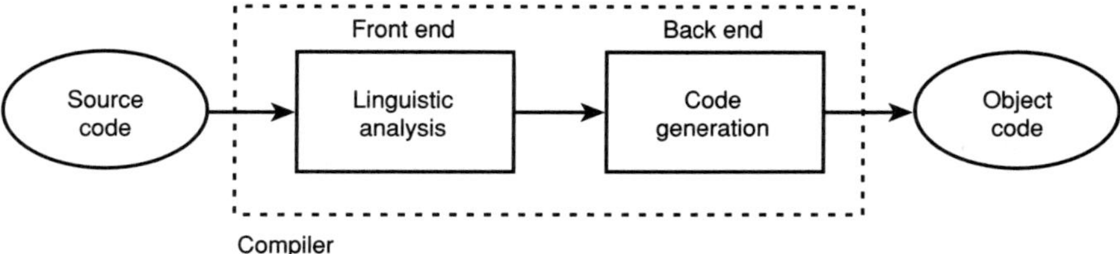

This diagram also describes the two tasks that a program for drawing pictures must perform: A back end draws the picture while a front end interprets user commands to decide what picture to draw.

And just how does a user describe a picture? There are (broadly) three ways to do the job. An interactive program allows the user to draw the program with a hand-controlled device, and a subroutine library adds picture primitives to the constructs in a programming language. We'll return to these approaches in the next section.

The third approach to describing pictures is the topic of this chapter: a little language. In Kernighan' Pic language, for instance, the first figure in this section is described as

```
ellipse "Source" "Code"
arrow
box "Compiler"
arrow
ellipse "Object" "Code"
```

The first input line draws an ellipse of default size and stacks the two strings at its center. The second line draws an arrow in the default direction (moving right), and the third line draws a box with the text at its center. The implicit motion after each object makes it easy to draw the picture and convenient to add new objects to an existing picture.

This nonsense picture illustrates several other devices that Pic supports, including lines, double arrowheads, and dashed boxes:

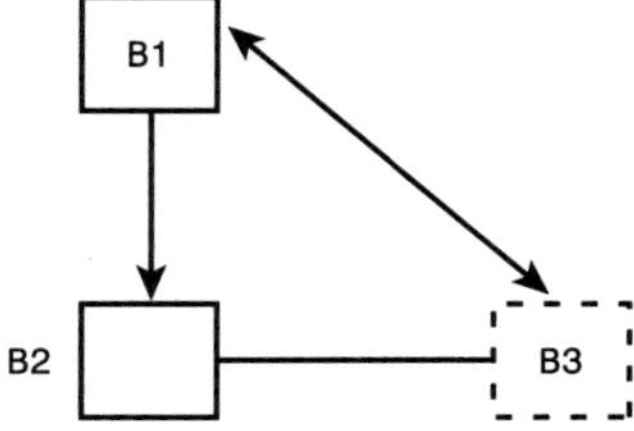

The program that draws it places objects by implicit motions, by explicit motions, and by connecting existing objects:

```
boxht = .4; boxwid = .4
down    # set default direction
B1: box "B1"
arrow
B2: box
"B2 " at B2.w rjust
line right .6 from B2.e
B3: box dashed wid .6 "B3"
line <-> from B3.n to B1.e
```

The `boxht` and `boxwid` variables represent the default height and width of a box in inches. Those values can also be explicitly set in the definition of a particular box. Text following the `#` character is a comment, up to the end of the line. Labels such as `B1`, `B2`, and `B3` name objects; `LongerName` is fine too. The western point of box `B2` is referred to as `B2.w`; one could also refer to `B2.n` or `B2.nw`, for the northwest corner. A line of the form *string* `at` *position* places a text string at a given position; `rjust` right-justifies the string (strings can also be left justified or placed above or below positions).

These devices were used to draw this figure, which gives a yet more detailed view of a compiler:

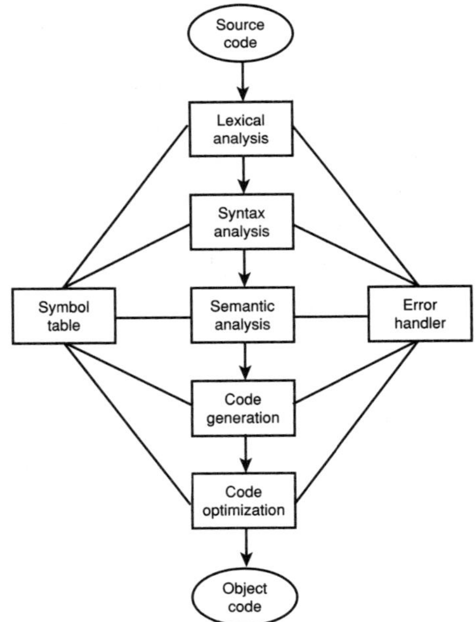

Any particular compiler translates one source language into one object language. How can an organization maintain 5 different languages on 5 different machines? A brute-force approach writes 25 compilers:

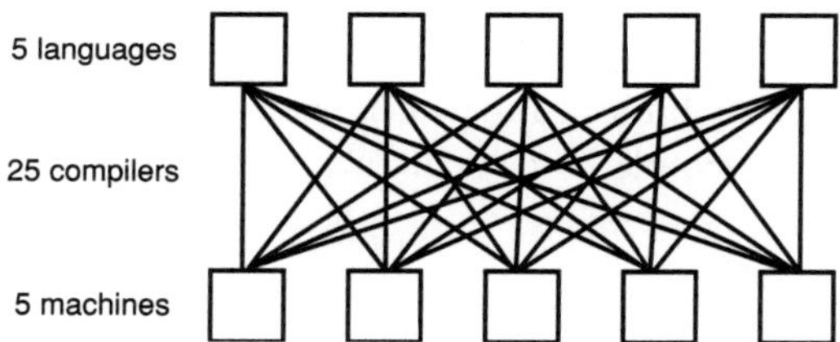

An *intermediate language* circumvents much of this complexity. A new language is installed by writing a front end that translates into the intermediate language, and a new machine is installed by a back end that translates the intermediate language into the machine's output code:

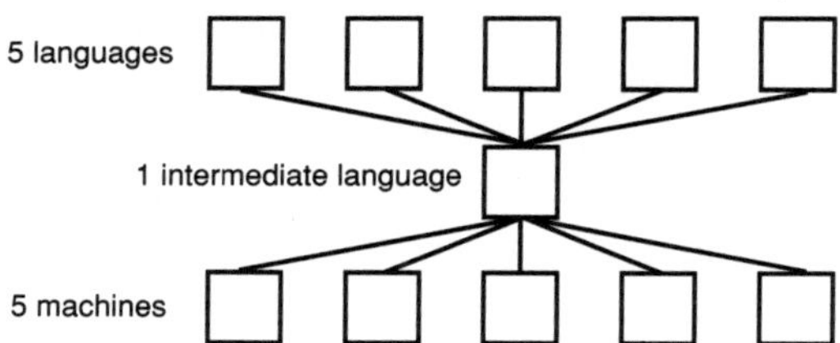

If there are *L* languages on *M* machines, the brute-force approach constructs *L*×*M* distinct compilers, while the intermediate language needs just *L* front ends and *M* back ends. (Pic compiles its output into a picture-drawing subset of the troff typesetting language, which in turn produces an intermediate language suitable for interpretation on a number of output devices, from terminal display programs to laser printers to phototypesetters.)

The last figure uses two Pic programming constructs, variables and loops:

```
n = 5                                       # number of langs & machines
boxht = boxwid = .2
h = .3; w = .35                             # height & width for spacing
I: box at w*(n+1)/2,0                       # intermediate language box
for I = 1 to n do {
        box with .s at i*w, h               # language box
        line from last box.s to I.n
        box with .n at i*w, -h              # machine box
        line from the last box.n to I.s
}
"1 intermediate language " at I.w rjust
"5 languages " at 2nd box .w rjust
"5 machines " at 3nd box .w rjust
```

The picture of the brute-force approach is described by a single loop to draw the boxes, followed by two nested loops to make all pairwise interconnections.

The examples in this section should give you an idea of the structure of Pic, but they only hint at its power. I have not mentioned a number of Pic's facilities, such as built-in functions, `if` statements, macro processing, file inclusion, and a simple block structure.

1.2. Perspective

In this section we'll consider several approaches to picture-drawing programs and compare them to Pic. Although the particulars are for pictures, the general lessons apply to designing user interfaces for many kinds of programs.

An interactive drawing program allows the user to enter a picture with a spatial input device such as a mouse or a drawing pad and displays the picture as it is drawn. Most interactive systems have a menu that includes items such as boxes, ellipses, and lines of various flavors (vertical, horizontal, dotted, etc.). Immediate feedback makes such systems quite comfortable for drawing many simple pictures, but drawing this picture on an interactive system would require a steady hand and the patience of Job:

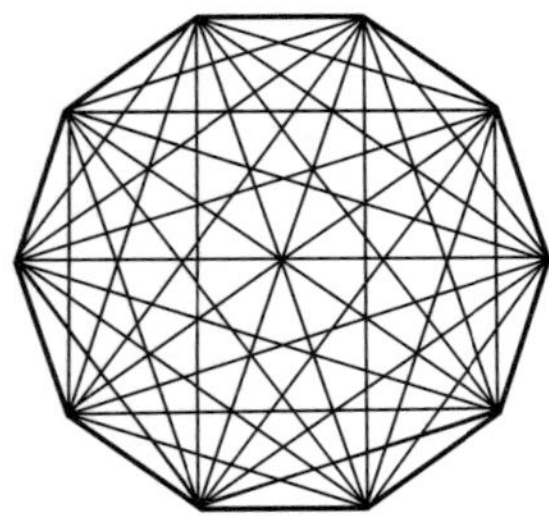

Pic's programming constructs allow the picture to be drawn easily:

```
pi = 3.14159; n = 10; r = .4
s = 2*pi/n
for i = 1 to n-1 do {
  for j = I+1 to n do {
       line from r*cos(s*i), r*sin(s*i)\
             to   r*cos(s*j), r*sin(s*j)
  }
}
```

(The backslash character `\` at the end of a line allows the line to be continued on the next line.)

Handy as such features are, doesn't parsimony dictate that variables and `for` loops properly belong in a full programming language?[3] This concern is addressed by a subroutine library that adds pictures to the primitives supported by a given language. Given a subroutine line `(x1, y1, x2, y2)`, one could easily draw the last picture in Pascal:

```
pi := 3.14159; n := 10; r := 0.4;
s := 2*pi/n;
for i := 1 to n-1 do
   for j := i+1 to n do
      line (r*cos(s*i), r*sin(s*i),
            r*cos(s*j), r*sin(sin(s*j) );
```

Unfortunately, to draw this picture:

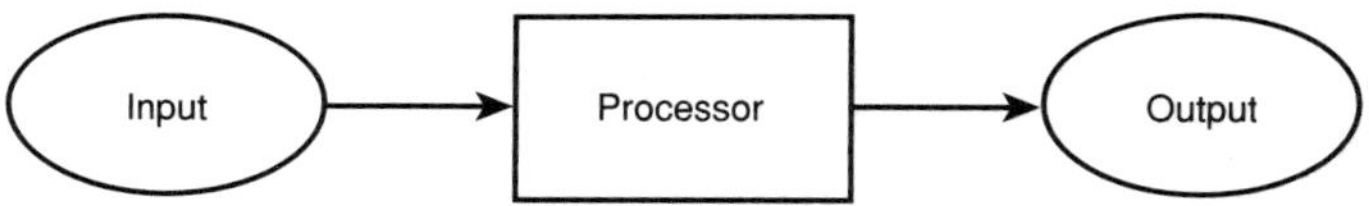

One must write, compile, execute, and debug a program containing subroutine calls like these:

```
ellipse(0.3, 0, 0.6, 0.4)
text(0.3, 0, "Input")
arrow(0.75, 0, 0.3, 0)
box(1.2, 0, 0.6, 0.4)
text(1.2, 0, "Processor")
arrow(1.65, 0, 0.3, 0)
ellipse(2.1, 0, 0.6, 0.4)
text(2.1, 0, "Output")
```

Even such simple code may be too hard for some nonprogrammers who find Pic comfortable, such as technical typists or software managers. The first two arguments to each routine give the x and y coordinates of the center of the object; later arguments give its width and height or a text string. These routines are rather primitive; more clever routines might, for instance, have an implicit motion associated with objects.

So far I've used the term "little language" intuitively. The time has come for a more precise definition. I'll restrict the term *computer language* to textual inputs, and thus ignore the spatial and temporal languages defined by cursor movements and button clicks: A computer language enables a textual description of an object to be processed by a computer program.

[3]Arguments beyond taste suggest that Pic's `for` loops may be inappropriate: Their syntax differs from similar loops elsewhere in the UNIX system, and Pic's `for` loops are orders of magnitude slower than those in other languages. Purists may write loops in other languages to generate Pic output; I am a delighted if compromised user of Pic's `for` loops—the quilts and stereograms in the exercises were easy to generate using that construct.

The object being described might vary widely, from a picture to a program to a tax form. Defining "*little*" is harder: It might imply that a first-time user can use the system in half an hour or master the language in a day, or perhaps that the first implementation took just a few days. In any case, a little language is specialized to a particular problem domain and does not include many features found in conventional languages.

Pic qualifies in my book as a little language, although admittedly a big little language. Its tutorial and user manual is 26 pages long (including over 50 sample pictures); I built my first picture in well under an hour. Kernighan had the first implementation up and stumbling within a week of putting pencil to coding form. The current version is about 4,000 lines of C code and represents several months of effort spread over five years. Although Pic has many features of big languages (variables, `for` statements, and labels), it is missing many other features (declarations, `while` and `case` statements, and facilities for separate compilation). I won't attempt a more precise definition of a little language; if the linguistic analogy gives you insight into a particular program, use it, and if it doesn't, ignore it.

We have considered three different approaches to specifying pictures: interactive systems, subroutine libraries, and little languages. Which one is best? Well, that depends.

- Interactive systems are probably the easiest to use for drawing simple pictures, but a large collection of pictures may be hard to manage. (Given 50 pictures in a long paper, how do you make all ellipses 0.1 inches wider and 0.05 inches shorter?)
- If your pictures are generated by big programs, subroutine libraries can be easy and efficient. Libraries are usually uncomfortable for drawing simple pictures, though.
- Little languages are a natural way to describe many pictures; they can be integrated easily into document production systems to include pictures in larger documents. Pictures can be managed using familiar tools such as file systems and text editors.

I've used picture-drawing programs based on each of the three models: interactive drawers, subroutine libraries, and little languages. Each type of system is handy for drawing some pictures and awkward for others.[4]

[4]In terms of implementation difficulty, all three approaches have a front end for specification and a back end for picture drawing. Subroutine libraries use a language's procedure mechanism as a front end: It may be clumsy, but it's familiar and free. Little languages can use standard compiler technology for their front end; we'll see such tools in section 1.4. Because interactive systems usually involve real-time graphics, they are typically the hardest to implement and the least portable (often with two back ends: an interactive one shows the picture as it is being drawn, and a static one writes the complete picture to a file).

1.3. Pic Preprocessors

One of the greatest advantages of little languages is that one processor's input can be another processor's output. So far we've only thought of Pic as an input language. In this section we'll briefly survey two very small languages for describing specialized classes of pictures; their compilers generate Pic programs as output.

We'll start with Scatter, a Pic preprocessor that makes scatter plots from x,y data. The output of Scatter is fed as input to Pic, which in turn feeds the troff document formatter.

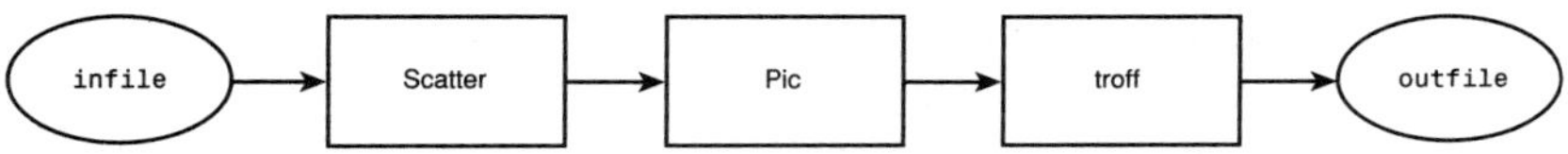

This structure is easy to implement as a UNIX pipeline of processes:

```
scatter infile | pic | troff >outfile
```

(The UNIX Shell that interprets such commands is, of course, another little language. In addition to the | operator for constructing pipelines, the language includes common programming commands such as `if`, `case`, `for`, and `while`.)

Pic is a big little language, Scatter is at the other end of the spectrum. This Scatter input uses all five kinds of commands in the language.

```
size x 1.8
size y 1.2
range x 1870 1990
range y 35 240
label x Year
label y Population
ticks x 1880 1930 1980
ticks y 50 100 150 200
file pop.d
```

The `size` commands give the width (`x`) and height (`y`) of the frame in inches. The `range` commands tell the spread of the dimensions, and labels and ticks are similarly specified. Ranges are mandatory for both dimensions; all other specifications are optional. The description must also specify an input file containing x,y pairs. The first few lines in the file `pop.d` are

```
1880        50.19
1890        62.98
1900        76.21
1910        92.22
1920        106.02
```

The x value is a year and the y value is the United States population in millions in the census of that year. Scatter turns that simple description of a scatter plot into a 23-line Pic program that produces this graph:

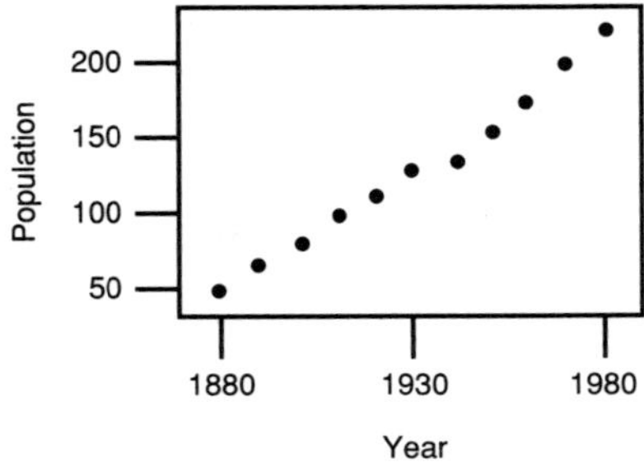

The Scatter language is tiny but useful. Its "compiler" is a 24-line Awk program that I built in just under an hour. (In many environments, Snobol's string-processing facilities would make it the language of choice for quickly implementing a little language; Awk is a more natural choice in my UNIX environment.) A slightly larger little language for drawing graphs is described in Section 6.2 of *The AWK Programming Language...*; it is not a Pic preprocessor, but rather prints the graph as an array of characters.

Chemists often draw chemical structure diagrams like this representation of the antibiotic penicillin G:

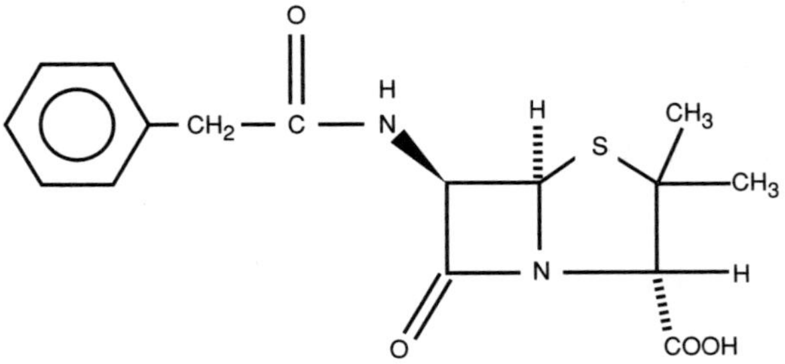

A chemist could draw that picture in Pic, but it is a tedious and time-consuming task. It is more natural for an author with a chemical background to describe the structure in the Chem language, using familiar terms like *benzene rings*, *double bonds*, and *back bonds*:

```
R1:     ring4 pointing 45 put N at 2
        doublebond -135 from R1.V3 ; O
        backbond up from R1.V1 ; H
        frontbond -45 from R1.V4 ; N
```

```
        H above N
        bond left from N ; C
        doublebond up ; O
        bond length .1 left from C ; CH2
        bond length .1 left
        benzene pointing left
R2:     flatring5 put S at 1 put N at 4 with .V5 at R1.V1
        bond 20 from R2.V2 ; CH3
        bond 90 from R2.V2 ; CH3
        bond 90 from R2.V3 ; H
        backbond 170 from R2.V3 ; COOH
```

The history of Chem is typical of many little languages. Late one Monday afternoon, Brian Kernighan and I spent an hour with Lynn Jelinski, a Bell Labs chemist, moaning about the difficulty of writing. She described the hassles of including chemical structures in her documents: the high cost and inordinate delays of dealing with a drafting department. We suspected that her task might be appropriate for a Pic preprocessor, so she lent us a recent monograph rich in chemical diagrams.

That evening Kernighan and I each designed a microscopic language that could describe many of the structures, and implemented them with Awk processors, each about 50 lines long. Our model of the world was way off base—the book was about polymers, so our languages were biased towards linear structures. Nevertheless, the output was impressive enough to convince Jelinski to spend a couple of hours educating us about the real problem. By Wednesday we had built a set of Pic macros with which Jelinski could, with some pain, draw structures of genuine interest to her; that convinced her to spend even more time on the project. Over the next few days we built and threw away several little languages that compiled into those macros. A week after starting the project, the three of us had designed and implemented the rudiments of the current Chem language, whose evolution since then has been guided by real users. The current version is about 500 lines of Awk and uses a library of about 70 lines of Pic macros. Jelinski, Kernighan, and I describe the language and present the complete code in *Computers and Chemistry*, vol. 11, no. 4, pp. 281–297, 1987.

These two brief examples hint at the power of preprocessors for little languages. Pic produces line drawings. Scatter extends it to scatter plots and Chem deals with chemical structures. Each preprocessor was easy to implement by compiling into Pic. It would be more difficult to extend interactive drawing programs to new problem domains such as graphs or chemistry.

1.4. Little Languages for Implementing Pic

In this section we'll turn from using Pic to building it. We'll study three UNIX tools that Kernighan used to construct the Pic language. Each of the tools can be viewed as providing a little language for describing part of the programmer's job. This section briefly sketches the three tools; the Further Reading describes all of them in detail. The purpose of this section is to hint at the breadth of little languages; you may skip to the next section any time you feel overwhelmed by the details.

An earlier figure illustrates the components in a typical compiler; this figure shows that Pic has many, but not all, of those components:

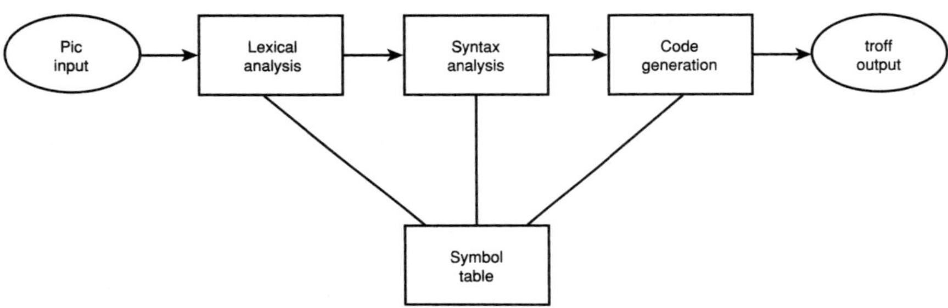

We'll first study the Lex program, which generates Pic's lexical analyzer. Then we'll turn to Yacc, which performs the syntax analysis. Finally we'll look at Make, which manages the 40 source, object, header, testing, and documentation files used by Pic.

A lexical analyzer (or lexer) breaks the input text into units called *tokens*. It is usually implemented as a subroutine; at each call it returns the next token in the input text. For instance, on the Pic input line

```
L: line dashed down .8 left .4 from B1.s
```

a lexer should return the following sequence:

```
SYMBOL: L
LINE
DASHED
DOWN
NUMBER: 0.8
LEFT
NUMBER: 0.4
FROM
SYMBOL: B1
SOUTH
```

Constructing a lexer is straightforward but tedious, and therefore ideal work for a computer. Mike Lesk's Lex language specifies a lexer by a series of pattern-action pairs. The Lex program reads that description and builds a C routine to implement the lexer. When the lexer recognizes the regular expression on the left, it performs the action on the right. Here is a fragment of the Lex description of Pic:

```
">"                     return(GT);
"<"                     return(LT);
">="                    return(GE);
"<="                    return(LE);
"<-"                    return(HEAD1);
"->"                    return(HEAD2);
"<->"                   return(HEAD12);
"."(s|south)            return(SOUTH);
"."(b|bot|bottom)       return(SOUTH);
```

The regular expression (a|b) denotes either a or b. Given a description in this form, the Lex program generates a C function that performs lexical analysis.

Those regular expressions are simple; Pic's definition of a floating point number is more interesting:

```
({D}+("."?){D}*|"."{D}+)((e|E)("+"|-)?{D}+)
```

The string "{D}" denotes the digits 0..9. (In the spirit of this chapter, observe that regular expressions are a microscopic language for describing patterns in text strings.) Constructing a recognizer for that monster is tedious and error-prone work for a human. Lex quickly and accurately constructs a lexer from a description that is easy to prepare.

Yacc is an acronym for "yet another compiler-compiler." Steve Johnson's program is a parser generator; it can be viewed as a little language for describing languages. Its input has roughly the same pattern-action form as Awk and Lex: When a pattern on the left-hand side is recognized, the action on the right is performed. While Lex's patterns are regular expressions, Yacc supports context-free languages. Here is part of Pic's definition of an arithmetic expression:

```
expr:
       NUMBER
     | VARNAME            { $$ = getfval($1): }
     | expr '+' expr      { $$ = $1 + $3; }
     | expr '-' expr      { $$ = $1 - $3; }
     | expr '*' expr      { $$ = $1 * $3; }
     | expr '/' expr      { if ($3 == 0.0) {
                                 error("division by zero");
                                 $3 = 1.0;
                             }
                          { $$ = $1/ $3;}
                          { $$ = $2;}
     | '(' expr ')'
       ...
;
```

Given a description like this, Yacc builds a parser. When the parser finds `expr + expr`, it returns (in `$$`) the sum of the first expression (`$1`) and the second expression (which is the third object, `$3`). The complete definition describes the precedence of operators (`*` binds before `+`), comparison operators (such as `<` and `>`), functions, and several other minor complications.

A Pic program can be viewed as a sequence of primitive geometric objects. A primitive is defined as

```
primitive:
       BOX attrlist           { boxgen($1); }
     | CIRCLE attrlist        { elgen($1); }
     | ELLIPSE attrlist       { elgen($1); }
     | ARC attrlist           { arcgen($1); }
     | LINE attrlist          { linegen($1); }
       ...
;
```

When the parser sees an ellipse statement, it parses the attribute list and then calls the routine `elgen`. It passes to that routine the first component in the phrase, the token `ELLIPSE`. The `elgen` routine uses that token to decide whether to generate a general ellipse or a circle (a special-case ellipse with length equal to width).

All Pic primitives have the same attribute list; some primitives, however, ignore some attributes. An attribute list is either empty or an attribute list followed by an attribute:

```
attrlist:;
       attrlist attr
     | /* empty */
     ;
```

And here is a small part of the definition of an attribute:

```
attr
       DIR                { storefattr($1, !DEF, $2); }
     | DIR                { storefattr($1, DEF, 0.0); }
     | FROM position      {storeoattr($1, $2); }
     | TO position        {storeoattr($1, $2); }
     | AT position        { storeoattr($1, $2); }
       ...
;
```

As each attribute is parsed, the appropriate routine stores its value.

These tools tackle well-studied problems. Lex and Yacc package lexer and parser technology: The programmer defines the lexical and syntactic structure in straightforward little languages, and the programs generate high-quality processors. Not only are the descriptions easy to generate in the first place, they make the language easy to modify.

Stu Feldman's Make program addresses a more mundane problem that is nonetheless difficult and crucial for large programs: keeping up-to-date versions of the files containing header code, source code, object code, documentation, test cases, etc. Here is an abbreviated version of the file that Kernighan uses to describe the files associated with Pic:

```
OFILES = picy.o picl.o main.o print.o \
         misc.o symtab.o blockgen.o \
CFILES = main.c print.c misc.c symtab.c \
         ...
          blockgen.c boxgen.c circgen.c \
SRCFILES = picy.y pic1.1 pic.h $(CFILES)
pic:     $(OFILES)
         cc $(OFILES) -lm
$(OFILES): pic.h y.tab.h
manual:
         pic manual | eqn | troff -ms >manual.out
backup: $(SRCFILES) makefile pictest.a manual
         push safemachine $? /usr/bwk/pic
         touch backup
bundle:
         bundle $(SRCFILES) makefile README
```

The file starts with the definition of three names: `OFILES` are the object files, `CFILES` contain C code, and the sources files `SRCFILES` consist of the C files and the Yacc description `picy.y`, the Lex description `picl.l`, and a header file. The next line states that Pic must have up-to-date versions of object files. (Make's internal tables tell how to make object files from source files.) The next line tells how to combine those into a current version of Pic. The following line states that the object files depend on the two named header files. When Kernighan types `make pic`, Make checks the currency of all object files (`file.o` is current if its modification time is later than `file.c`), recompiles out-of-date modules, and then loads the needed pieces along with the appropriate function libraries.

The next two lines tell what happens when Kernighan types `make manual`: The file containing the user manual is processed by Troff and two preprocessors. The `backup` command saves on `safemachine` all modified files, and the `bundle` command wraps the named files into a package suitable for mailing. Although Make was originally designed specifically with compiling in mind, Feldman's elegant general mechanism gracefully supports all these additional housekeeping functions.

1.5. Principles

Little languages are an important part of the popular Fourth- and Fifth-Generation Languages and Application Generators, but their influence on computing is broader. Little languages often provide an elegant interface for humans to control complex programs or for modules in a large system to communicate with one another. Although most of the examples in this chapter are large "systems programs" on the UNIX system, some ideas have been used in a fairly mundane data processing system implemented in BASIC on a microcomputer.

The principles of language design summarized below are well known among designers of big programming languages. They are just as relevant to the design of little languages.

1.5.1. Design Goals

Before you design a language, carefully study the problem you are trying to solve. Should you instead build a subroutine library or an interactive system? An old rule of thumb states that the first 10 percent of programming effort provides 90 percent of the functionality; can you make do with an Awk or a BASIC or a Snobol implementation that cheaply provides the first 90 percent, or do you have to use more powerful tools like Lex and Yacc and Make to get to 99.9 percent?

1.5.2. Simplicity

Keep your language as simple as possible. A smaller language is easier for its implementers to design, build, document, and maintain and is easier for its users to learn and use.

1.5.3. Fundamental Abstractions

Typical computer languages are built around the world-view of a von Neumann computer: Instructions operate on small chunks of data. The designer of a little language has to be more creative: The primitive objects might be geometric symbols, chemical structures, context-free languages, or the files in the program. Operations on objects vary just as widely, from fusing two benzene rings to recompiling a source file. Identifying these key players is old hat to programmers; the primitive objects are a program's abstract data types, and the operations are the key subroutines.

1.5.4. Linguistic Structure

Once you know the basic objects and operations, there are still many ways of writing down their interactions. The infix arithmetic expression

`2+3*4` might be written in postfix as `234*+` or functionally as `plus (2,times(3,4))`; there is often a tradeoff between naturalness of expression and ease of implementation. But whatever else you may or may not include in your language, be sure to allow indentation and comments.

1.5.5. Yardsticks of Language Design

Rather than preach about tasteful design, I've chosen as examples useful languages that illustrate good taste. Here are some of their desirable properties:

Orthogonality: Keep unrelated features unrelated.

Generality: Use an operation for many purposes.

Parsimony: Delete unneeded operations.

Completeness: Can the language describe all objects of interest?

Similarity: Make the language as suggestive as possible.

Extensibility: Make sure the language can grow.

Openness: Let the user "escape" to use related tools.

1.5.6. The Design Process

Like other great software, great little languages are grown, not built. Start with a solid, simple design, expressed in a notation like Backus-Naur form. Before implementing the language, test your design by describing a wide variety of objects in the proposed language. After the language is up and running, iterate design to add features as dictated by the needs of your customers.

1.5.7. Insights from Compiler Building

When you build the processor for your little language, don't forget lessons from compilers. As much as possible, separate the linguistic analysis in the front end from the processing in the back end; that will make the processor easier to build and easier to port to a new system or new use of the language. And when you need them, use compiler-building tools like Lex, Yacc, and Make.

1.6. Problems

- Most systems provide a package for sorting files; the interface is usually a little language. Evaluate the language provided by your system. The UNIX system `sort`, for instance, is invoked by a command like

```
sort -t: +3n
```

This line says to use the character : as the field separator and to sort the file so that the fourth field (skip the first three fields) occurs in numeric order. Design a less cryptic language and implement it, perhaps as a preprocessor that generates commands for your system sort.

- Lex uses a little language for regular expressions to specify lexical analyzers. What other programs on your system employ regular expressions? How do they differ, and why?
- Study different languages for describing bibliographic references. How do the languages differ in applications such as document retrieval systems and bibliography programs in document production systems? How are little languages used to perform queries in each system?
- Study examples of what might be the littlest languages of them all: assemblers, format descriptions, and stack languages.
- Many people can perceive a three-dimensional image by crossing their eyes and fusing the two halves of stereograms:

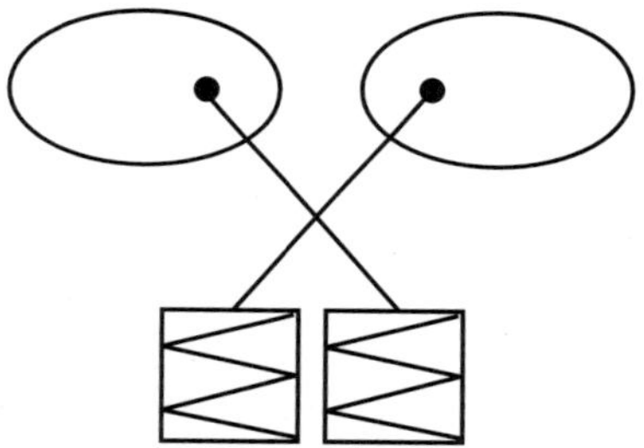

A small survey I conducted suggests that about half the readers of this chapter should be able to perceive these three-dimensional scenes; the other half will get a headache trying:

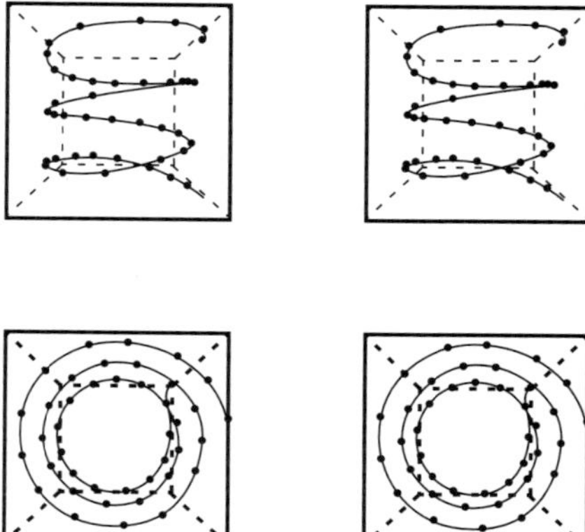

These pictures were drawn by a 40-line Pic program. Design and implement a three-dimensional language for describing stereograms.

- Design and implement little languages. Interesting pictorial domains include electrical diagrams, data structures such as arrays, trees, and graphs (drawing Finite State Machines is especially interesting), and pictorially scored games, such as bowling and baseball. Another interesting domain is describing musical scores. Consider both rendering the score on a sheet of paper and playing it on a music generator.
- Design a little language to deal with common forms in your organization, such as expense reports for trips.
- How can processors of little languages respond to linguistic errors? (Consider the options available to compilers for large languages.) How do particular processors respond to errors?

1.7. Further Reading

You may never have heard of *Compilers: Principles, Techniques, and Tools* by Aho, Sethi, and Ullman, but you'd probably recognize the cover of the "new Dragon Book" (published in 1986 by Addison-Wesley). And you *can* judge this book by its cover: It is an excellent introduction to the field of compilers, with a healthy emphasis on little languages. Furthermore, the book makes extensive use of Pic to tell its story in pictures. (Most of the compiler pictures in this chapter were inspired by pictures in that book.)

Chapter 8 of *The UNIX Programming Environment* by Kernighan and Pike (Prentice-Hall, 1984) is the case history of a little language. They start with a language for evaluating expressions, then add variables and functions, and finally add control constructs and user-defined functions to achieve a fairly expressive programming language. Throughout the process Kernighan and Pike use the UNIX Tools sketched in this chapter to design, develop, and document their language. Chapter 6 of *The AWK Programming Language* describes how Awk can easily process very little languages.

CHAPTER 2

A System for Typesetting Mathematics[1]*: EQN*

by Brian W. Kernighan and Lorinda L. Cherry

2.1. Abstract

This chapter describes the design and implementation of a system for typesetting mathematics. The language has been designed to be easy to learn and to use by people (for example, secretaries and mathematical typists) who know neither mathematics nor typesetting. Experience indicates that the language can be learned in an hour or so, for it has few rules and fewer exceptions. For typical expressions, the size and font changes, positioning, line drawing, and the like necessary to print according to mathematical conventions are all done automatically. For example, the input

```
sum from i=0 to infinity x sub i = pi over 2
```

produces

$$\sum_{i=0}^{\infty} x_i = \frac{\pi}{2}$$

The syntax of the language is specified by a small context-free grammar; a compiler-compiler is used to make a compiler that translates this language into typesetting commands. Output may be produced on either a phototypesetter or on a terminal with forward and reverse half-line motions. The system interfaces directly with text formatting programs, so mixtures of text and mathematics may be handled simply.

This chapter is a revision of a paper originally published in *CACM*, March 1975.

---

[1]This chapter is reprinted with permission from Kernighan, B. W., and L. L. Cherry. 1977. *A System for Typesetting Mathematics*. Computing Science Technical Report No. 17. Murray Hill, NJ: Bell Laboratories. Revision based on the 1975 publication *A System for Typesetting Mathematics*. *CACM* 18(3): 151. New York: ACM Publishers.

2.2. Introduction

Mathematics is known in the trade as *difficult*, or *penalty, copy* because it is slower, more difficult, and more expensive to set in type than any other kind of copy normally occurring in books and journals.

—*A Manual of Style* (University of Chicago Press, 1969)

One difficulty with mathematical text is the multiplicity of characters, sizes, and fonts. An expression such as

$$\lim_{x \to \pi/2} (\tan x)^{\sin 2x} = 1$$

requires an intimate mixture of Roman, italic, and Greek letters, in three sizes, and a special character or two. ("Requires" is perhaps the wrong word, but mathematics has its own typographical conventions that are quite different from those of ordinary text.) Typesetting such an expression by traditional methods is still an essentially manual operation.

A second difficulty is the two dimensional character of mathematics, which the superscript and limits in the preceding example showed in its simplest form. This is carried further by

$$a_0 + \cfrac{b_1}{a_1 + \cfrac{b_2}{a_2 + \cfrac{b_3}{a_3 + \cdots}}}$$

and still further by

$$\int \frac{dx}{ae^{mx} - be^{-mx}} = \left\{ \begin{array}{l} \dfrac{1}{2m\sqrt{ab}} \log \dfrac{\sqrt{a}e^{mx} - \sqrt{b}}{\sqrt{a}e^{mx} + \sqrt{b}} \\ \dfrac{1}{m\sqrt{ab}} \tanh^{-1} \left(\dfrac{\sqrt{a}}{\sqrt{b}} e^{mx} \right) \\ \dfrac{-1}{m\sqrt{ab}} \coth^{-1} \left(\dfrac{\sqrt{a}}{\sqrt{b}} e^{mx} \right) \end{array} \right.$$

These examples also show line-drawing, built-up characters like braces and radicals, and a spectrum of positioning problems. (Section 2.6 shows what a user has to type to produce these on our system.)

2.3. Photocomposition

Photocomposition techniques can be used to solve some of the problems of typesetting mathematics. A phototypesetter is a device that exposes a piece of photographic paper or film, placing characters wherever they are wanted. The Graphic Systems phototypesetter (Graphic Systems) on the UNIX operating system (Ritchie & Thompson, 1974) works by shining light through a character stencil. The character is made the right size by lenses, and the light beam directed by fiber optics to the desired place on a piece of photographic paper. The exposed paper is developed and typically used in some form of photo-offset reproduction.

On UNIX, the phototypesetter is driven by a formatting program called troff (Ossanna, 1977). troff was designed for setting running text. It also provides all of the facilities that one needs for doing mathematics, such as arbitrary horizontal and vertical motions, line-drawing, size changing, but the syntax for describing these special operations is difficult to learn, and difficult even for experienced users to type correctly.

For this reason we decided to use troff as an "assembly language," by designing a language for describing mathematical expressions, and compiling it into troff.

2.4. Language Design

The fundamental principle upon which we based our language design is that the language should be easy to use by people (for example, secretaries) who know neither mathematics nor typesetting.

This principle implies several things. First, "normal" mathematical conventions about operator precedence, parentheses, and the like cannot be used, for to give special meaning to such characters means that the user has to understand what he or she is typing. Thus the language should not assume, for instance, that parentheses are always balanced, for they are not in the half-open interval $(a,b]$. Nor should it assume $\sqrt{a+b}$ can be replaced by $(a+b)^{1/2}$, or that $1/(1-x)$ is better written as $\frac{1}{1-x}$ (or vice versa).

Second, there should be relatively few rules, keywords, special symbols and operators, and the like. This keeps the language easy to learn and remember. Furthermore, there should be few exceptions to the rules that do exist: If something works in one situation, it should work everywhere. If a variable can have a subscript, then a subscript can have a subscript, and so on without limit.

Third, "standard" things should happen automatically. Someone who types `x=y+z+1` should get $x=y+z+1$. Subscripts and superscripts should automatically be printed in an appropriately smaller size, with no special intervention. Fraction bars have to be made the right length and positioned at the right height. And so on. Indeed a mechanism for overriding default actions has to exist, but its application is the exception, not the rule.

We assume that the typist has a reasonable picture (a two-dimensional representation) of the desired final form, as might be handwritten by the author of a paper. We also assume that the input is typed on a computer terminal much like an ordinary typewriter. This implies an input alphabet of perhaps 100 characters, none of them special.

A secondary, but still important, goal in our design was that the system should be easy to implement, since neither of the authors had any desire to make a long-term project of it. Since our design was not firm, it was also necessary that the program be easy to change at any time.

To make the program easy to build and to change, and to guarantee regularity ("it should work everywhere"), the language is defined by a context-free grammar, described in section 2.5. The compiler for the language was built using a compiler-compiler.

A priori, the grammar/compiler-compiler approach seemed the right thing to do. Our subsequent experience leads us to believe that any other course would have been folly. The original language was designed in a few days. Construction of a working system sufficient to try significant examples required perhaps a person-month. Since then, we have spent a modest amount of additional time over several years tuning, adding facilities, and occasionally changing the language as users make criticisms and suggestions.

We also decided quite early that we would let troff do our work for us whenever possible. troff is quite a powerful program, with a macro facility, text and arithmetic variables, numerical computation and testing, and conditional branching. Thus we have been able to avoid writing a lot of mundane but tricky software. For example, we store no text strings, but simply pass them on to troff. Thus we avoid having to write a storage management package. Furthermore, we have been able to isolate ourselves from most details of the particular device and character set currently in use. For example, we let troff compute the widths of all strings of characters; we need know nothing about them.

A third design goal is special to our environment. Since our program is only useful for typesetting mathematics, it is necessary that it interface cleanly with the underlying typesetting language for the benefit of users who want to set intermingled mathematics and text (the usual case). The standard mode of operation is that when a document is typed, mathematical expressions are input as part of the text, but marked by user settable delimiters. The program reads this input and treats as comments those things that are not mathematics, simply passing them through untouched. At the same time it converts the mathematical input into the necessary troff commands. The resulting output is passed directly to troff where the comments and the mathematical parts both become text and/or troff commands.

2.5. The Language

We will not try to describe the language precisely here. Throughout this section, we will write expressions exactly as they are handed to the typesetting program (hereinafter called EQN), except that we won't show the delimiters that the user types to mark the beginning and end of the expression. The interface between EQN and troff is described at the end of this section.

As we said, typing `x=y+z+1` should produce $x=y+z+1$, and indeed it does. Variables are made italic, operators and digits become Roman, and normal spacings between letters and operators are altered slightly to give a more pleasing appearance.

Input is free-form. Spaces and new lines in the input are used by EQN to separate pieces of the input; they are not used to create space in the output. Thus

```
x = y
  +z+1
```

also gives $x=y+z+1$. Free-form input is easier to type initially; subsequent editing is also easier, for an expression may be typed as many short lines.

Extra white space can be forced into the output by several characters of various sizes. A tilde (~) gives a space equal to the normal word spacing in text; a circumflex gives half this much, and a tab character spaces to the next tab stop.

Spaces (or tildes, etc.) also serve to delimit pieces of the input. For example, to get

$$f(t)=2\pi\int\sin(\Omega t)dt$$

we write

```
f(t) = 2 pi int sin ( omega t )dt
```

Here spaces are necessary in the input to indicate that `sin`, `pi`, `int`, and `omega` are special, and potentially worth special treatment. EQN looks up each such string of characters in a table, and if appropriate gives it a translation. In this case, `pi` and `omega` become their Greek equivalents, `int` becomes the integral sign (which must be moved down and enlarged so it looks "right"), and `sin` is made Roman, following conventional mathematical practice. Parentheses, digits, and operators are automatically made Roman wherever found.

Fractions are specified with the keyword `over`:

```
a+b over c+d+e = 1
```

produces

$$\frac{a+b}{c+d+e}=1$$

Similarly, subscripts and superscripts are introduced by the keywords `sub` and `sup`:

$$x^2+y^2=z^2$$

is produced by

```
x sup 2 + y sup 2 = z sup 2
```

The spaces after the 2s are necessary to mark the end of the superscripts; similarly the keyword `sup` has to be marked off by spaces or some equivalent delimiter. The return to the proper baseline is automatic. Multiple levels of subscripts or superscripts are of course allowed: `xsupysupz` is x^{y^z}. The construct *`something`* `sub` *`something`* `sup` *`something`* is recognized as a special case, so `x sub i sup 2` is x_i^2 instead of x_{i^2}.

More complicated expressions can now be formed with these primitives:

$$\frac{\partial^2 f}{\partial x^2} = \frac{x^2}{a^2} + \frac{y^2}{b^2}$$

is produced by

```
{partial sup 2 f} over {partial x sup 2} =
x sup 2 over a sup 2 + y sup 2 over b sup 2
```

Braces ({}) are used to group objects together; in this case they indicate unambiguously what goes over what on the left-hand side of the expression. The language defines the precedence of `sup` to be higher than that of `over`, so no braces are needed to get the correct association on the right side. Braces can always be used when in doubt about precedence.

The braces convention is an example of the power of using a recursive grammar to define the language. It is part of the language that if a construct can appear in some context, then any expression in braces can also occur in that context.

There is a `sqrt` operator for making square roots of the appropriate size: `sqrt a+b` produces $\sqrt{a+b}$ and

```
x = {-b +- sqrt{b sup 2 -4ac}} over 2a
```

is

$$x = \frac{-b \pm \sqrt{b^2 - 4ac}}{2a}$$

Since large radicals look poor on our typesetter, `sqrt` is not useful for tall expressions.

Limits on summations, integrals, and similar constructions are specified with the keywords `from` and `to`. To get

$$\sum_{i=0}^{\infty} x_i \rightarrow 0$$

we need type only

```
sum from i=0 to inf x sub i -> 0
```

Centering and making the Σ big enough and the limits smaller are all automatic. The `from` and `to` parts are both optional, and the central part (e.g., the Σ) can in fact be anything:

```
lim from {x -> pi /2} ( tan~x) = inf
```

is

$$\lim_{x \rightarrow \pi/2} (\tan x) = \infty$$

Again, the braces indicate just what goes into the `from` part.

There is a facility for making braces, brackets, parentheses, and vertical bars of the right height, using the keywords `left` and `right`:

```
left [ x+y over 2a right ]~=~1
```

makes

$$\left[\frac{x+y}{2a} \right] = 1$$

A `left` need not have a corresponding `right`, as we shall see in the next example. Any characters may follow `left` and `right`, but generally only various parentheses and bars are meaningful.

Big brackets, etc., are often used with another facility, called *piles*, which make vertical piles of objects. For example, to get

$$sign\ (x) \equiv \left\{ \begin{array}{c} 1 \text{ if } x>0 \\ 0 \text{ if } x=0 \\ -1 \text{ if } x<0 \end{array} \right.$$

we can type

```
sign (x) ~==~ left {
  rpile {1 above 0 above -1}
  ~~lpile {if above if above if}
  ~~lpile {x>0 above x=0 above x<0}
```

The construction `left {` makes a left brace big enough to enclose the `rpile {...}`, which is a right-justified pile of `above ... above ...`. `lpile` makes a left-justified pile. There are also centered piles. Because of the recursive language definition, a pile can contain any number of elements; any element of a pile can of course contain piles.

Although EQN makes a valiant attempt to use the right sizes and fonts, there are times when the default assumptions are simply not what is wanted. For instance, the italic *sign* in the previous example would conventionally be in Roman. Slides and transparencies often require larger characters than normal text. Thus we also provide size and font changing commands: `size 12 bold {A~x~=~y}` will produce **A x = y**. `size` is followed by a number representing a character size in points. (One point is 1/72 inch; this chapter is set in 10-point type.)

If necessary, an input string can be quoted in `"..."`, which turns off grammatical significance and any font or spacing changes that might otherwise be done on it. Thus we can say

```
lim~ roman "sup" ~x sub n = 0
```

to ensure that the supremum doesn't become a superscript:

$$\lim\ \mathrm{sup}\ x_n = 0$$

Diacritical marks, long a problem in traditional typesetting, are straightforward:

$$\underset{\cdot}{x} + \hat{x} + \tilde{y} + \hat{X} + \ddot{Y} = \overline{z + Z}$$

is made by typing

```
x dot under + x hat + y tilde
+ X hat + Y dotdot = z+Z bar
```

There are also facilities for globally changing default sizes and fonts, for example for making viewgraphs or for setting chemical equations. The language allows for matrices, and for lining up equations at the same horizontal position.

Finally, there is a definition facility, so a user can say

```
define name "..."
```

at any time in the document; henceforth, any occurrence of the token "`name`" in an expression will be expanded into whatever was inside the double quotes in its definition. This lets users tailor the language to their own specifications, for it is quite possible to redefine keywords like `sup` or `over`. Section 2.6 shows an example of definitions.

The EQN preprocessor reads intermixed text and equations, and passes its output to troff. Since troff uses lines beginning with a period as control words (e.g., `.ce` means "center the next output line"), EQN uses the sequence `.EQ` to mark the beginning of an equation and `.EN` to mark the end. The `.EQ` and `.EN` are passed through to troff untouched, so they can also be used by a knowledgeable user to center equations, number them automatically, etc. By default, however, `.EQ` and `.EN` are simply ignored by troff, so by default equations are printed in-line.

`.EQ` and `.EN` can be supplemented by troff commands as desired; for example, a centered display equation can be produced with the input:

```
.ce
.EQ
x sub i = y sub i ...
.EN
```

Since it is tedious to type `.EQ` and `.EN` around very short expressions (single letters, for instance), the user can also define two characters to serve as the left and right delimiters of expressions. These characters are recognized anywhere in subsequent text. For example, if the left and right delimiters have both been set to `#`, the input:

```
Let #x sub i#, #y# and #alpha# be positive
```

produces

Let x_i, y and α be positive

Running a preprocessor is strikingly easy in UNIX. To typeset text stored in file `f`, one issues the command

```
eqn f | troff
```

The vertical bar connects the output of one process (EQN) to the input of another (troff).

2.6. Language Theory

The basic structure of the language is not a particularly original one. Equations are pictured as a set of "boxes," pieced together in various ways. For example, something with a subscript is just a box followed by another box moved downward and shrunk by an appropriate amount. A fraction is just a box centered above another box, at the right altitude, with a line of correct length drawn between them.

The grammar for the language is shown here:

```
eqn     : box | eqn box

box     : text
        | { eqn }
        | box OVER box
        | SQRT box
        | box SUB box | box SUP box
        | [ L | C | R ]PILE { list }
        | LEFT text eqn [ RIGHT text ]
        | box [ FROM box ] [ TO box ]
        | SIZE text box
        | [ROMAN | BOLD | ITALIC] box
        | box [HAT | BAR | DOT | DOTDOT | TILDE]
        | DEFINE text text

list    : eqn | list ABOVE eqn

text    : TEXT
```

For purposes of exposition, we have collapsed some productions. In the original grammar, there are about 70 productions, but many of these are simple ones used only to guarantee that some keyword is recognized early enough in the parsing process. Symbols in capital letters are terminal symbols; lowercase symbols are non-terminals, that is, syntactic categories. The vertical bar (|) indicates an alternative; the brackets ([]) indicate optional material. A TEXT is a string of non-blank characters or any string inside double quotes; the other terminal symbols represent literal occurrences of the corresponding keyword.

The grammar makes it obvious why there are few exceptions. For example, the observation that something can be replaced by a more complicated something in braces is implicit in the productions

```
eqn    : box | eqn box
box    : text | { eqn }
```

Anywhere a single character could be used, *any* legal construction can be used.

Clearly, our grammar is highly ambiguous. What, for instance, do we do with the input

```
a over b over c
```

Is it

```
{a over b} over c
```

or is it

```
a over {b over c}?
```

To answer questions like this, the grammar is supplemented with a small set of rules that describe the precedence and associativity of operators. In particular, we specify (more or less arbitrarily) that `over` associates to the left, so the first alternative is the one chosen. On the other hand, `sub` and `sup` bind to the right because this is closer to standard mathematical practice. That is, we assume x^{a^b} is $x^{(a^b)}$, not $(x^a)^b$.

The precedence rules resolve the ambiguity in a construction like

```
a sup 2 over b
```

We define `sup` to have a higher precedence than `over`, so this construction is parsed as $\frac{a^2}{b}$ instead of $a^{\frac{2}{b}}$.

Naturally, a user can always force a particular parsing by placing braces around expressions.

The ambiguous grammar approach seems to be quite useful. The grammar we use is small enough to be easily understood, for it contains none of the productions that would be normally used for resolving ambiguity. Instead, the supplemental information about precedence and associativity (also small enough to be understood) provides the compiler-compiler with the information it needs to make a fast, deterministic parser for the specific language we want. When the language is supplemented by the disambiguating rules, it is in fact LR(1) and thus easy to parse (Aho & Johnson, 1974).

The output code is generated as the input is scanned. Any time a production of the grammar is recognized, (potentially) some troff commands are output. For example, when the lexical analyzer reports that it has found a TEXT (i.e., a string of contiguous characters), we have recognized the production

```
text    : TEXT
```

The translation of this is simple. We generate a local name for the string, then hand the name and the string to troff, and let troff perform the storage management. All we save is the name of the string, its height, and its baseline.

As another example, the translation associated with the production

```
box : box OVER box
```

is

```
Width of output box =
  slightly more than largest input width
Height of output box =
  slightly more than sum of input heights
Base of output box =
  slightly more than height of bottom input box
String describing output box =
  move down;
  move right enough to center bottom box;
  draw bottom box (i.e., copy string for bottom box);
  move up;
  move left enough to center top box;
  draw top box (i.e., copy string for top box);
  move down and left;
  draw line full width;
  return to proper base line.
```

Most of the other productions have equally simple semantic actions. Picturing the output as a set of properly placed boxes makes the right sequence of positioning commands quite obvious. The main difficulty is in finding the right numbers to use for esthetically pleasing positioning.

With a grammar, it is usually clear how to extend the language. For instance, one of our users suggested a TENSOR operator to make constructions like

$${}^{l}_{m}\mathrm{T}^{kj}_{ni}$$

Grammatically, this is easy: It is sufficient to add a production like

```
box : TENSOR { list }
```

Semantically, we need only juggle the boxes to the right places.

2.7. Experience

There are really three aspects of interest—how well EQN sets mathematics, how well it satisfies its goal of being easy to use, and how easy it was to build.

The first question is easily addressed. One of our users commented that although the output is not as good as the best hand-set material, it is still better than average, and much better than the worst. In any case, who cares? Printed books cannot compete with the birds and flowers of illuminated manuscripts on esthetic grounds, either, but they have some clear economic advantages.

Some of the deficiencies in the output could be cleaned up with more work on our part. For example, we sometimes leave too much space between a Roman letter and an italic one. If we were willing to keep track of the fonts involved, we could do this better more of the time.

Some other weaknesses are inherent in our output device. It is hard, for instance, to draw a line of an arbitrary length without getting a perceptible overstrike at one end.

As to ease of use, at the time of writing, the system has been used by two distinct groups. One user population consists of mathematicians, chemists, physicists, and computer scientists. Their typical reaction has been something like

- It's easy to write, although I make the following mistakes...
- How do I do...?
- It botches the following things.... Why don't you fix them?
- You really need the following features...

The learning time is short. A few minutes gives the general flavor, and typing a page or two of a paper generally uncovers most of the misconceptions about how it works.

The second user group is much larger, the secretaries and mathematical typists who were the original target of the system. They tend to be enthusiastic converts. They find the language easy to learn (most are largely self-taught), and have little trouble producing the output they want. They are of course less critical of the esthetics of their output than users trained in mathematics. After a transition period, most find using a computer more interesting than a regular typewriter.

The main difficulty that users have seems to be remembering that a blank is a delimiter; even experienced users use blanks where they shouldn't and omit them when they are needed. A common instance is typing

```
f(x sub i)
```

which produces

$$f(x_{i)})$$

instead of

$$f(x_i)$$

Since the EQN language knows no mathematics, it cannot deduce that the right parenthesis is not part of the subscript.

The language is somewhat prolix, but this doesn't seem excessive considering how much is being done, and it is certainly more compact than the corresponding troff commands. For example, here is the source for the continued fraction expression in section 2.1 of this chapter:

```
a sub 0 + b sub 1 over
 {a sub 1 + b sub 2 over
  {a sub 2 + b sub 3 over
   {a sub 3 + ... }}}
```

This is the input for the large integral of section 2.1; notice the use of definitions:

```
define emx "{e sup mx}"
define mab "{m sqrt ab}"
define sa "{sqrt a}"
define sb "{sqrt b}"
int dx over {a emx - be sup -mx} ~=~
left { lpile {
     1 over {2 mab} ~log~
          {sa emx - sb} over {sa emx + sb}
  above
   1 over mab ~ tanh sup -1 ( sa over sb emx )
  above
   -1 over mab ~ coth sup -1 ( sa over sb emx )
}
```

As to ease of construction, we have already mentioned that there are really only a few person-months invested. Much of this time has gone into two things—fine-tuning (what is the most esthetically pleasing space to use between the numerator and denominator of a fraction?), and changing things found deficient by our users (shouldn't a tilde be a delimiter?).

The program consists of a number of small, essentially unconnected modules for code generation, a simple lexical analyzer, a canned parser that we did not have to write, and some miscellany associated with input files and the macro facility. The program is now about 1600 lines of C (Kernighan & Ritchie, 1978), a high-level language reminiscent of BCPL. About 20 percent of these lines are print statements, generating the output code.

The semantic routines that generate the actual troff commands can be changed to accommodate other formatting languages and devices. For example, in less than 24 hours, one of us changed the entire semantic package to drive nroff, a variant of troff, for typesetting mathematics on teletypewriter devices capable of reverse line motions. Since many potential users do not have access to a typesetter, but still have to type mathematics, this provides a way to get a typed version of the final output that is close enough for debugging purposes, and sometimes even for ultimate use.

2.8. Conclusions

We think we have shown that it is possible to do acceptably good typesetting of mathematics on a phototypesetter, with an input language that is easy to learn and use and that satisfies many users' demands. Such a package can be implemented in short order, given a compiler-compiler and a decent typesetting program underneath.

Defining a language, and building a compiler for it with a compiler-compiler seems like the only sensible way to do business. Our experience with the use of a grammar and a compiler-compiler has been uniformly favorable. If we had written everything into code directly, we would have been locked into our original design. Furthermore, we would have never been sure where the exceptions and special cases were. But because we have a grammar, we can change our minds readily and still be reasonably sure that if a construction works in one place it will work everywhere.

2.9. Acknowledgments

We are deeply indebted to J. F. Ossanna, the author of troff, for his willingness to modify troff to make our task easier and for his continuous assistance during the development of our program. We are also grateful to A. V. Aho for help with language theory, to S. C. Johnson for aid with the compiler-compiler, and to our early users A. V. Aho, S. I. Feldman, S. C. Johnson, R. W. Hamming, and M. D. McIlroy for their constructive criticisms.

2.10. References

Aho, A. V., and S. C. Johnson. 1974. LR Parsing. *Computing Surveys* 6(2):99–124.

Kernighan, B. W., and D. M. Ritchie. 1978. *The C programming language*. Englewood Cliffs, NJ: Prentice-Hall.

Ossanna, J. F. 1977. *Troff user's manual.* Bell Laboratories Computing Science Technical Report No. 54.

Ritchie, D. M., and K. L. Thompson. 1974. The UNIX Time-Sharing System. *Communications of the ACM* 17(7):365–375.

University of Chicago Press. 1969. *A manual of style* (12th ed.). Chicago: Author, p. 295.

Graphic Systems. *Model C/A/T phototypesetter.* Hudson, NH: Author.

CHAPTER 3

Domain-Specific Languages

by Paul Hudak

3.1. An Introduction to Domain-Specific Languages

When most people think of a programming language, they think of a *general purpose* language: one capable of programming any application with relatively the same degree of expressiveness and efficiency. For many applications, however, there are more natural ways to express the solution to a problem than those afforded by general purpose programming languages. As a result, researchers and practitioners in recent years have developed many different *domain specific* languages, or DSLs, which are tailored to particular application domains. With an appropriate DSL, you can develop complete application programs for a domain more quickly and more effectively than with a general purpose language. Ideally, a well-designed DSL captures precisely the semantics of an application domain, no more and no less.

Table 3.1 is a partial list of domains for which DSLs have been created. As you can see, the list covers quite a lot of ground. For a list of some popular DSLs that you may have heard of, look at Table 3.2.[1]

The first example is a set of tools known as Lex and Yacc, which are used to build lexers and parsers. Thus, ironically, they are good tools for *building* DSLs (more on this later). Note that there are several document preparation languages listed; for example, LaTeX was used to create the original draft of this chapter. Also on the list are examples of scripting

[1]Both of these tables are incomplete; feel free to add your favorite examples to them.

languages, such as Perl, Tcl, and Tk, whose general domain is that of scripting text and file manipulation, GUI widgets, and other software components. When used for scripting, Visual Basic can also be viewed as a DSL, even though it is usually thought of as general purpose. I have included one other general-purpose language, Prolog, because it is excellent for applications specified using predicate calculus.[2]

The tongue-in-cheek comment in Table 3.2 regarding the application domain for the Excel Macro language points out just how powerful—and general purpose—a DSL can be, despite original intentions.

Table 3.1. *Application domains.*

Scheduling
Modeling
Simulation
Graphical user interfaces
Lexing and parsing
Symbolic computing
Attribute grammars
CAD/CAM
Robotics
Hardware description
Silicon layout
Text/pattern matching
Graphics and animation
Computer music
Databases
Distributed/parallel computing
Logic
Security

[2]Other examples of this sort include the general-purpose functional languages Haskell and ML, which are excellent for functional specifications; we will use Haskell later as a vehicle for designing new DSLs.

Table 3.2. *Popular DSLs.*

DSL	*Application*
Lex, Yacc	Program lexing and parsing
Perl	Text/file manipulation/scripting
VHDL	Hardware description
TeX, LaTeX, troff	Document layout
HTML, SGML	Document markup
SQL, LDL, QUEL	Databases
pic, PostScript	2D graphics
Open GL	High-level 3D graphics
Tcl, Tk	GUI scripting
Mathematica, Maple	Symbolic computation
AutoLisp/AutoCAD	Computer-aided design
Csh	OS scripting (UNIX)
IDL	Component technology (COM/CORBA)
Emacs Lisp	Text editing
Prolog	Logic
Visual Basic	Scripting and more
Excel Macro Language	Spreadsheets and many things never intended

It is often said that *abstraction* is the most important factor in writing good software, a point that I firmly believe in. Software designers are trained to use a variety of abstraction mechanisms: abstract data types, (higher-order) functions and procedures, modules, classes, objects, monads, continuations, and so on. An important point about these mechanisms is that they are fairly *general*; for example, most algorithmic strategies and computational structures can be implemented using either functional or object-oriented abstraction techniques. Although generality is good, we might ask what the ideal abstraction for a particular application is. In my opinion it is a DSL: the ultimate abstraction of a problem domain.

3.1.1. Advantages of DSLs

Programs written in DSLs have the following advantages over those written in more conventional languages:

- They are more concise.
- They can be written more quickly.

- They are easier to maintain.
- They are easier to reason about.

These advantages are the same as those claimed for programs written in conventional high-level languages, so perhaps DSLs are just *very* high-level languages? In some sense, this is true. But programs written in a DSL also have one other important characteristic:

- They can often be written by nonprogrammers.

More precisely, they can be written by nonprogrammers who are nevertheless experts in the domain for which the DSL was designed. This helps bridge the gap (often a chasm) between developer and user, a potentially major hidden cost in software development. It also raises an important point about DSL design: A user immersed in a domain *already knows* the domain semantics. All the DSL designer needs to do is provide a notation to express those semantics.

3.1.2. The Payoff of DSLs

DSLs certainly seem to have the potential to improve our programming productivity, but is there some way to quantify this argument? I believe there is, as illustrated in Figure 3.1. Here we see that the initial cost of DSL development may be high compared to the equivalent cost of tooling up for an application under a more traditional software development scenario. The slope of the curve for aggregate software development cost should be considerably lower using a DSL, and thus at some point, the DSL approach should yield significant savings. Of course, if you are using an existing DSL, the initial tooling-up cost will be very low. In any case, if you are contemplating designing your own DSL, this is the chart to show to your boss.

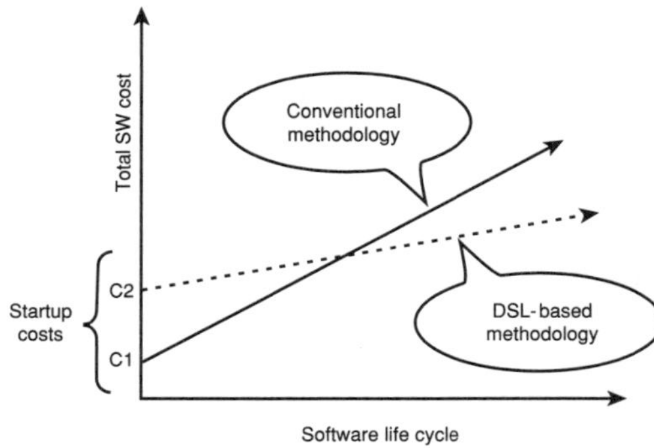

Figure 3.1. *The payoff of DSL technology.*

3.1.3. A Few Examples

Before going further, let's look at a few instances of DSLs to get a feel for their power and simplicity. For starters, Listing 3.1 shows a simplified version of the HTML code used to generate my home page on the WWW. Although some might not think of HTML as a programming language, it is nevertheless a notation for specifying a certain kind of computation: namely, document layout parameters.

Listing 3.1. *An example of HTML code.*

```
<title> Professor Paul Hudak's Home Page </title>
<body background="backgrounds/gray_weave.gif" >

<h1> Professor Paul Hudak </h1>
<hr>
<img src="hudak.gif">
<img align=top src="yale-haskell-logo.gif">
<p>
<b> Computer Science Department, Yale University </b>
<p> <hr> <p>
<h2> Functional Programming </h2>
Here I briefly describe some of my work in functional programming:
<ul>
<li> The best introduction to Haskell is the tutorial
<a href="http://www.haskell.org/tutorial"> A Gentle Introduction to
Haskell </a>.
<li> ...
<li> ...
</ul>
<address>
Paul Hudak,
<a href="mailto:paul.hudak@yale.edu"> paul.hudak@yale.edu </a>
</address>
</body>
```

In HTML, regions of text that are to be treated in a special way begin with a *tag* enclosed in angle brackets and end with the same tag including a slash character. For example, in Listing 3.1, the text `Professor Paul Hudak's Home Page` is enclosed in a pair of `title` tags, giving a title to the document, which is then used by browsers to, for example, label bookmark entries. The next line marks the beginning of the body of the page and specifies what background color to use. Then the first line of actual text appears, rendered in the style `h1`, which is a document *heading*. Following this text are two images (`img`), one a picture of me, one a group logo, both referenced as `.gif` files. The single commands `<p>` and `<hr>` generate new paragraphs and draw horizontal lines. The section that begins with `<ul>` is an unnumbered list, with each entry beginning with the tag `<li>`. The first entry in this list references another WWW page using what is called an *anchor*, whose tag includes the URL. The effect of this tag is that the text `A Gentle Introduction to Haskell` will be highlighted and will take the user to the page referenced by the URL if it is clicked. The other list items are omitted, and the page closes with my address anchored in a different way: If you click on my email address, your mailer will open an outgoing message with my address already loaded in the To: field.

There is quite a lot going on here! But I think that with my explanation, you should now understand it, and that in a day's time, I could teach you enough HTML that you could handle 90% of all WWW applications.

As another example, suppose we are implementing a programming language whose BNF syntax includes the following specification (Ahu, Sethi, & Ullman, 1987):

```
expr = expr + term   | term
term = term * factor  | factor
factor = (expr)   | digit
```

which is the standard way to define simple arithmetic expressions. Using Yacc (Johnson, 1975), this specification can be used almost directly:

```
expr     : expr '+' term
         | term               ;
term     : term '*' factor
         | factor             ;
factor   : '(' expr ')'
         | DIGIT              ;
```

Yacc will take this code and generate a parser for the little language that it represents; Yacc is a program that generates other programs. It also has several other features that allow you to specify actions to be taken for each line in the code. I also believe that, if you are familiar with BNF syntax and basic C programming, I could teach you how to use Yacc expertly within one day's time.

As a final example, let's look at some SQL code. SQL is a language for creating and querying relational databases. We will ignore how SQL is used to set up a database and concentrate on what queries look like. Here is the first example:

```
SELECT  firstName, lastName, address
FROM    employee
WHERE   firstName = 'Cathy' AND birthDate = '07/04/1950'
```

This query is almost self-explanatory: it is SELECTing the first name, last name, and address FROM the employee relation WHERE the first name of the employee is Cathy AND the birthdate is July 4, 1950. SQL queries can be quite complex; for example, they can be nested, as in the following:

```
SELECT firstName, lastName, address
FROM   employee
```

```
WHERE   salary > ALL (SELECT salary
                      FROM employee
                      WHERE firstName = 'Paul')
```

This query selects all employees whose salary is greater than that of any employee whose first name is Paul.

SQL is a powerful language for programming databases (there are other languages that are claimed to be more powerful, such as QUEL). If you are familiar with databases, my feeling is that you could learn quite a bit about SQL within a day's time, although it might take years to become an expert at using this particular DSL in the context of real-world database systems.

In the remainder of this chapter, I discuss the motivation of DSLs, their basic characteristics, how to design and implement them, how to embed them in existing languages, and avenues for further development. I am particularly keen on conveying the idea that you can "roll your own" DSL: You don't have to rely on existing DSLs to take advantage of this useful technology.[3]

3.2. The DSL Software Development Method

The basic DSL software development method can be summarized as follows:

1. Define your domain.
2. Design a DSL that accurately captures the domain semantics.
3. Build software tools to support the DSL.
4. Develop applications (domain instances) using the new DSL infrastructure.

Of course, this is not necessarily a linear process: Revision, refinement, enhancement, and so on are often necessary.

The first two steps are difficult but are the key to successful application of the methodology. If the domain itself is properly identified, the DSL design should go smoothly, especially if you have experience in basic programming language principles to begin with.

There are several ways in which you could implement a DSL. If treated as a conventional language, conventional techniques could be used: Build

[3]In this regard, my message is the same as that given by Jon Bentley in his excellent article on little languages (Bentley, 1986), although DSLs are not necessarily little.

a conventional lexer and parser based on the BNF syntax; perform various high-level analyses, transformations, and optimizations on the abstract syntax generated by the parser; and then generate executable code for some host machine. In the case of a DSL, this standard approach may be modified in a number of ways:

- Use Lex and Yacc (themselves DSLs), or similar tools, to facilitate the construction of the lexer and parser.
- Use a structured editor or other programming environment generator (such as the Synthesizer Generator; Reps, 1984) to create the infrastructure for a more sophisticated programming environment.
- Generate code for an abstract machine (e.g., a byte-code interpreter) rather a real machine, or generate code in another language, such as C.
- Write an interpreter rather than a compiler.

3.3. Domain-Specific Embedded Languages

Despite all the promise, there are potential problems with the DSL methodology. To start, it may be that performance is poor: Very high-level languages are notoriously less efficient than lower-level languages. If performance using conventional languages is already a problem, designing a DSL may not be the best approach. On the other hand, there are certain domains where high-level optimizations are possible on DSL programs, whose results are sufficiently complex that programming them directly in a conventional language is difficult, tedious, and error prone. Query optimizations in the domain of databases is an example of this, and in such cases, a DSL may be justified as a way to *improve* performance. In any case, there are many application domains where performance is not the bottleneck, so this argument is not a show-stopper.

Another concern is the generation of a Tower of Babel through the creation of a new language for every domain. This is certainly a valid concern. On the other hand, if the languages are simple enough, the problem might not be nearly as bad as you might think, and in a later section, we will discuss ways to make new DSLs similar enough in look-and-feel to reduce the overhead of learning many new languages.

A final concern is the potential for unacceptable startup costs: design time, implementation, documentation, and so on. It can be fairly difficult to design and implement a programming language from scratch: a two- to five-year year effort is not uncommon. Moreover, there's a good chance that we won't get it right the first time. The DSL will evolve, and we will experience all the difficulties associated with that evolution. To state this concern in concrete terms, what if the startup costs shown in Figure 3.1 are so high that we never break even? What if we get it all wrong and incur the startup cost several more times during a software system's life cycle?

Dangers lurk in every software design methodology, and there are no silver bullets, of course. We must understand the benefits as well as the limitations of whatever methodology we are using and proceed with caution.

In the case of the DSL methodology, I would like to use the rest of this chapter to discuss several techniques that can greatly alleviate most of the problems addressed above. These techniques rest on two key thoughts:

- We begin with the assumption that we really don't want to build a new programming language from scratch. Better, let's inherit the infrastructure of some other language—tailoring it in special ways to the domain of interest—thus yielding a domain-specific *embedded* language (DSEL).
- Building on this base, we can then concentrate on semantics issues. Sound abstraction principles can be used at this level to build language tools that are themselves easy to understand, highly modular, and straightforward to evolve.

3.3.1. Syntax Versus Semantics

Tools such as Lex (Lesk, 1975) and Yacc (Johnson, 1975), as well as more sophisticated programming environment generators (e.g., Reps, 1984), have been shown to be quite useful in designing new programming languages; they are certainly better than building lexers and parsers from scratch. On the other hand, they are still rather tedious to use, and in any case, syntactic minutiae should arguably be the least of a language designer's worries. This is another twist on the slogan "semantics is more important than syntax" often bellowed in programming language circles. This is not to say that syntax doesn't matter—I believe that it does—but rather places syntax in proper perspective.

However, when you focus on semantics issues, many of the details still don't matter much. Even a deep issue such as the evaluation order of arguments is often something that people can adjust to, as long as they know exactly what it is for the language they are using. The precise behavior of variable-binding constructs, pattern-matching rules, endless details in type systems, major differences in module functionality, and so on are examples of debates that rage in the programming language design community. Other examples of semantics minutiae include names of predefined functions, the lexical order of their arguments, exactly how they behave under all circumstances, and an endless list of similar issues concerning the functionality of the software libraries that are essential to making a programming language practical.

The bottom line is that once a programming language is chosen, people get the job done, and they usually appreciate the high-level language that they are using.

3.3.2. DSELs Inherit Language Features

The point is, instead of designing a programming language from scratch, why not borrow most of the design decisions made for some other language? While we're at it, let's borrow as many as we can of the tools designed for this other language as well. Aside from the obvious advantage of being able to reuse many ideas and artifacts, DSELs have certain advantage over DSLs.

First off, although I pointed out earlier that a DSL should capture precisely the semantics of an application domain, no more and no less, a DSL in fact is not usually used in total isolation. Users of even (or perhaps especially) the most elegant DSLs may find themselves frustrated at not having access to more general programming language features. Of course, these features do not have to be used by those who don't need them.

Secondly, if we design several DSELs for different domains, all derived from the same base language, then programmers in the different domains can share a common core language. Indeed, for a large application, it is quite conceivable to have more than one DSEL. For them all to have a similar look-and-feel is a clear advantage:

- Allows for rapid DSL design; if nothing else, it can be viewed as a way to prototype a DSL.
- Facilitates change, whether for experimentation, fault correction, or design evolution.
- Provides a familiar look and feel, especially for several different DSLs embedded in the same language. In other words, it reduces the size of the Tower of Babel.
- Facilitates reuse of syntax, semantics, implementation code, software tools, documentation, and other related artifacts.

Of course, danger lurks in this approach as well: We may find that our DSL becomes limited by the power and prejudices of the underlying host language. It is important to design the DSL abstractly first and then search for a suitable host.

Implementing a DSEL can be achieved by writing a preprocessor for the host language (and possibly a postprocessor of program output) or by directly modifying the host language implementation. The former is more desirable because it removes dependency on other evolving systems. In many cases, the embedding can be achieved without any preprocessor at all: This is called a *pure* embedding. For this to work, the host language needs to be suitably rich in syntax and semantics (we will see examples of this shortly).

In the remainder of this chapter, I describe the results of using the functional language Haskell (Hudak, Peyton Jones, & Wadler, 1992) to build DSELs. Haskell has several features that make it particularly suitable for this—in particular, higher-order functions, lazy evaluation, and type classes—but other languages could conceivably be used instead. On the other hand, there are features that don't exist in any language (to my knowledge) that would make things even easier; there is much more work to be done.

3.3.3. An Example

It is surprisingly straightforward to design a DSEL for many specific applications. We and others in the Haskell community have done so using Haskell in many domains, including lexer and parser generation, graphics, animation, simulation, concurrency, computer music, GUI construction, scripting, hardware description, VLSI layout, pretty printing, and geometric region analysis. The latter domain—geometric region analysis—came about through an experiment conducted jointly by DARPA, ONR, and the Naval Surface Warfare Center (NSWC). This well-documented experiment (see Carlson, Hudak, & Jones, 1993; Caruso, 1993) demonstrates not only the viability of the DSEL approach, but also its evolvability. Three different versions of the system were developed, each capturing more advanced notions of the target system, with no a priori knowledge of the changes that would be required. The modularity afforded by the DSEL made these nontrivial changes quite easy to incorporate.

The resulting notation is not only easy to design, but it's also easy to use and reason about. Listing 3.2 shows some of the code to give the reader a feel for its simplicity and clarity. Because the domain semantics is captured concisely, it is possible even for nonprogrammers to understand much of the code. In the NSWC experiment, those completely unfamiliar with Haskell were able to grasp the concepts immediately; some even expressed disbelief that the code was actually executable.

(A few notes on Haskell syntax: a type such as `Point -> Bool` is the type of functions that map values of type `Point` to values of type `Bool`. In Listing 3.2, the name `Region` is given to this type. A statement such as `circle :: Radius -> Region` declares that the value `circle` is a function from type `Radius` to type `Region`. Function application in Haskell is written `f x y`; this is the same as `f(x,y)` in many other languages. Also in Haskell, any function can be used in infix position by enclosing it in backquotes. Thus ``p `inRegion` r`` is the same as `inRegion p r`.)

Listing 3.2. *An example of a DSEL for a naval application.*

```
-- Geometric regions are represented as functions:
type Region  =  Point -> Bool

-- So to test a point's membership in a region, we do:
inRegion       :: Point -> Region -> Bool
p 'inRegion' r = r p

-- Given suitable definitions of "circle", "outside", and /\:
circle    :: Radius -> Region
             -- creates a circular region with the given radius
outside   :: Region -> Region
             -- the logical negation of a region
(/\)      :: Region -> Region -> Region
             -- the intersection of two regions
(\/)      :: Region -> Region -> Region
             -- the union of two regions

-- We can then define a function to generate an annulus:
annulus       :: Radius -> Radius -> Region
annulus r1 r2 = outside (circle r1) /\ circle r2
```

Note that operators such as `/\`, `\/` and `outside` take regions as arguments. Regions are themselves represented as functions, so it is not surprising that higher-order functions are the key underlying abstraction needed to create this simple DSL. For example, the definition of `/\` is given by

```
(r1 /\ r2) p = r1 p && r2 p
```

which can be read "The intersection of `r1` and `r2` is a region that, when applied to a point `p`, returns the conjunction of `r1` applied to `p` and `r2` applied to `p`." More abstractly: "A point `p` lies in the intersection of `r1` and `r2` if it lies in both `r1` and `r2`."

Another important advantage of the DSEL approach is that it is highly amenable to formal methods, especially when using a language such as

Haskell with a clean underlying semantics. The key point is that you can reason directly within the domain semantics, rather than within the semantics of the programming language. In the NSWC experiment, several properties of the DSEL were straightforwardly proved that would have been much more difficult to prove in most of the competing designs. For example, to prove associativity of region intersection

```
(r1 /\ r2) /\ r3 = r1 /\ (r2 /\ r3)
```

we can use the definition of `/\` given here to reason equationally

```
   ((r1 /\ r2) /\ r3) p
 = (r1 /\ r2) p && r3 p          (unfolding of /\)
 = (r1 p && r2 p) && r3 p        (unfolding of /\)
 = r1 p && (r2 p && r3 p)        (associativity of &&)
 = r1 p && (r2 /\ r3) p          (folding of /\)
 = (r1 /\ (r2 /\ r3)) p          (folding of /\)
```

The *unfolding* of a function definition means replacing an instance of the left-hand side with the right-hand side, whereas the *folding* of a function definition means replacing an instance of the right with the left.

This simple use of formal methods results in a rich algebra that captures the domain semantics quite nicely.

3.4. Modular Semantics

In section 3.5.1, I describe how an implementation of a DSL can be constructed in a modular way, thus facilitating reuse of software components across possibly many DSL design efforts. The root of that process, however, is a good understanding of the domain semantics itself—one that recognizes layers of abstraction rather than one monolithic structure.

3.4.1. Simple Graphics

To demonstrate the modular design of a DSL, let's look at a simplified version of Fran (Elliott & Hudak, 1997), a DSEL for building functional reactive animations. We begin with some simple operators for manipulating graphical objects, or pictures, as shown in Listing 3.3.[4]

Listing 3.3. *A simple graphics DSEL.*

```
-- Atomic objects:
circle                   -- a unit circle
square                   -- a unit square
import "p.gif"           -- an imported bit-map
```

[4]These are not unlike those for geometric regions given previously but are even more like Henderson's functional graphics (Henderson, 1982).

```
-- Composite objects:
scale      v p          -- scale picture p by vector v
color      c p          -- color picture p with color c
trans      v p          -- translate picture p by vector v
p1 'over'    p2         -- overlay p1 on p2
p1 'above'   p2         -- place p1 above  p2
p1 'beside' p2          -- place p1 beside p2
```

With these operators, a rich algebra of pictures can be established. For example, `scale`, `color`, and `trans` all distribute over `over`, `above`, and `beside`, and the latter three are all associative. With these axioms, many useful properties of graphical objects can then be proven.

3.4.2. Simple Animations

Next, we note that the relationship between pictures and animations is quite simple: An animation is simply a time-varying picture! In Haskell, we could express the type associated with animations by writing

```
type Animation = Time -> Picture
```

In fact, many sorts of things could be time varying. Thus I will adopt a more generic viewpoint by defining the notion of a (polymorphic) *behavior* and then defining animations in terms of it:

```
type Behavior a = Time -> a
type Animation  = Behavior Picture
```

Now for the key step, we can "lift" all our operators on pictures to work on behaviors as well:

```
(b1 'overB'   b2) t = b1 t 'over'   b2 t
(b1 'aboveB'  b2) t = b1 t 'above'  b2 t
(b1 'besideB' b2) t = b1 t 'beside' b2 t
```

We can also lift the other operators, but we note that the vector and color arguments might also be time-varying, so we write

```
(scaleB v b) t    = scale (v t) (b t)
(colorB c b) t    = color (c t) (b t)
(transB v b) t    = trans (v t) (b t)
```

Finally, we define a new function to return the current time:

```
time t = t
```

With this simple transformation, we can now express continuous-time animations. For example, let's first define a couple of simple utility behaviors. The first varies smoothly and cyclically between –1 and +1:

```
wiggle = sin (pi * time)
```

Using `wiggle`, we can then define a function that smoothly varies between its two argument values:

```
wiggleRange lo hi = lo + (hi-lo) * (wiggle+1)/2
```

Now let's create a very simple animation: a red, pulsating ball:

```
ball = colorB red (scaleB (wiggleRange 0.5 1) circle)
```

We can also develop a rich algebra of animations. In fact, the entire algebra of pictures generalizes directly to animations. With time as a first-class value, there are even more opportunities for expressiveness if we add time-specific operators. For example, in Fran, we have an operator for expressing time transformations:

```
anim 'aboveB' (timeTransform (-1) anim)
```

displays animation `anim` with a copy of itself just above itself and delayed by 1 second.

Perhaps more importantly, Fran has an operator for expressing integration over time. To express the behavior of a falling ball, for example, we can write

```
let y = y0 + integral v
    v = v0 + integral g
in translate (x0,y) ball
```

where `(x0,y0)` is the initial position of the ball, `v0` is its initial velocity, and `g` is gravity. These equations can be read literally as the standard equations learned in introductory physics to describe the same phenomenon. Indeed, partial differential equations in general can be written and directly executed in Fran.

As you might guess, we can also develop a useful algebra of time, which includes such basic axioms as

```
timeTransform f (timeTransform g b)
                        = timeTransform (f . g) b
integral k              = k * time
integral time           = 0.5*time**2
integral (sin time)     = cos time
```

where `(f . g)` in Haskell denotes the composition of the functions `f` and `g`.

3.4.3. Reactive Animations

For the third and last layer of our modular semantic structure, we will add *reactivity*. This layer is reminiscent of CSP or similar process algebra and is based on a notion of an *event*. Primitive events include things such as mouse clicks and key presses but additionally include predicate events such as `time > 5`. There are also ways to combine events and filter them. The basic reactive expression then has the form

```
b1 'until' e => b2
```

which can be read "Behave as `b1` until event `e` occurs and then behave as `b2`." For example, here is a circle that changes color every time the left mouse button is pressed:

```
colorB (cycle red green blue) circle
where cycle c1 c2 c3 =
          c1 'until' leftButtonPress => cycle c2 c3 c1
```

Again we find that the previous algebraic semantics still holds in the reactive framework—nothing gets broken—and additionally, there is an algebra of reactivity that is reminiscent of that for other process calculii.

3.5. Advanced Support for DSELs

In this section, I describe some recent research and development efforts that promise to make the DSL/DSEL methodology even more attractive for industrial-strength software development.

3.5.1. Modular Interpreters

A DSEL in Haskell can be thought of as a higher-order algebraic structure, a first-class value that has the look and feel of syntax. In some sense, it is just a notation; its semantics is captured by an *interpreter*. This permits another opportunity for modular design, in turn facilitating evolution of the system because changes in the domain semantics are in many cases inevitable.

The design of truly modular interpreters has been an elusive goal in the programming language community for many years. In particular, we would like to design the interpreter so that different language features can be isolated and given individualized interpretations in a building-block manner. These building blocks can then be assembled to yield languages that have only a few, a majority, or even all of the individual language features. Progress by several researchers (Espinosa, 1995; Liang, 1996; Liang & Hudak, 1996; Liang, Hudak, & Jones, 1995; Moggi, 1989; Steele, 1994) has led to some key principles on which you can base such modular interpreters and compilers. The use of *monads* (Peyton Jones & Wadler, 1993; Wadler, 1990) to structure the design was critical.

This approach means that language features can be added long after the initial design, even if they involve fundamental changes in the interpreter functionality. For example, you can build a series of languages and interpreters that begin with a small calculator language (just numbers), then a simple first-order language with variables, then a higher-order language with several calling conventions, then a language with errors and exceptions, and so on, as suggested in Figure 3.2. At each level, the new language features can be added, along with their semantics, without altering any previous code.

It is also possible with this approach to capture not only domain-specific semantics, but also domain-specific optimizations. These optimizations can be done incrementally and independently from each other and from the core semantics. This idea has been used to implement traditional compiler optimizations (Liang, 1996; Liang & Hudak, 1996), but the same techniques could be used for domain-specific optimizations.

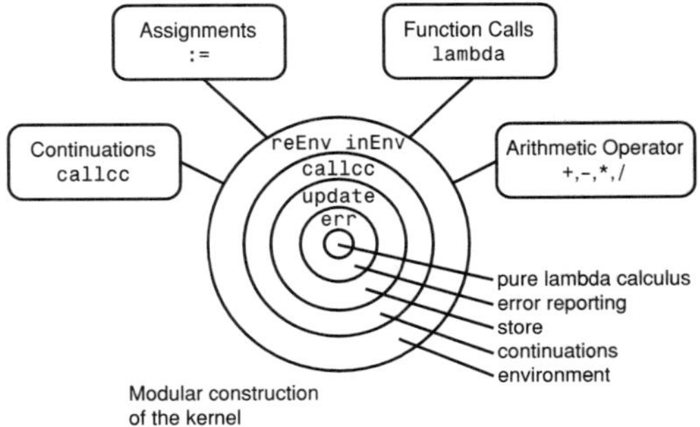

Figure 3.2. *Modular monadic interpreter structure.*

A conventional interpreter maps, say, a term, environment, and store to an answer. In contrast, a modular monadic interpreter maps terms to computations, where the details of the environment, store, and so on are hidden in the computation:

```
interp :: Term -> InterpM Value
```

`InterpM Value` is the interpreter monad of final answers.

What makes the interpreter modular is that all three components—the term type, the value type, and the monad—are configurable. To illustrate, if we initially want to have an interpreter for a small number-expression language, we can fill in the definitions as follows:

```
type Value   = OR Int Bottom
type Term    = TermA
type InterpM = ErrorT Id
```

The first line declares the answer domain to be the union of integers and "bottom" (the undefined value). The second line defines terms as `TermA`, the abstract syntax for arithmetic operations. The final line defines the interpreter monad as a transformation of the identify monad `Id`. The monad transformer `ErrorT` accounts for the possibility of errors—in this case, arithmetic exceptions. At this point, the interpreter behaves like a calculator:

```
Run> ((1+4)*8)
     40
Run> (3/0)
     ERROR: divide by 0
```

Now if we want to add function calls, we can extend the value domain with function types, add the abstract syntax for function calls to the term type, and apply the monad transformer `EnvT Env` to introduce an environment `Env`:

```
type Value   = OR Int (OR Function Bottom)
type Term    = OR TermF TermA
type InterpM = EnvT Env (ErrorT Id)
```

Here is a test run:

```
Run> ((\x.(x+4)) 7)
     11
Run> (x+4)
     ERROR: unbound variable: x
```

We can further add other features such as conditionals, lazy evaluation, `letrec` declarations, nondeterminism, continuations, tracing, profiling, and even references and assignment to our interpreter. Whenever a new value domain (such as Boolean) is needed, we extend the `Value` type; to add a new semantic feature (such as a store or continuation), we apply the corresponding monad transformer.

3.5.2. Language Tools and Instrumentation

Despite the importance in software development of language tools such as debuggers, profilers, tracers, and performance monitors, traditionally they have been treated in rather ad hoc ways. I believe that a more disciplined approach to designing such tools will benefit the software development process. Indeed, it is possible to develop a methodology for tool generation that shares much with previously identified goals: It is highly modular, domain-specific, and evolvable. Under this scheme, tools can be layered onto the system without affecting each other; changes and additions are thus easily accomplished. A tool specified in this framework can be automatically combined with the corresponding standard semantics to yield a composite semantics that incorporates the behaviors of both. Figure 3.3 is a flow diagram for the overall methodology, and Figure 3.4 shows its compositional nature.

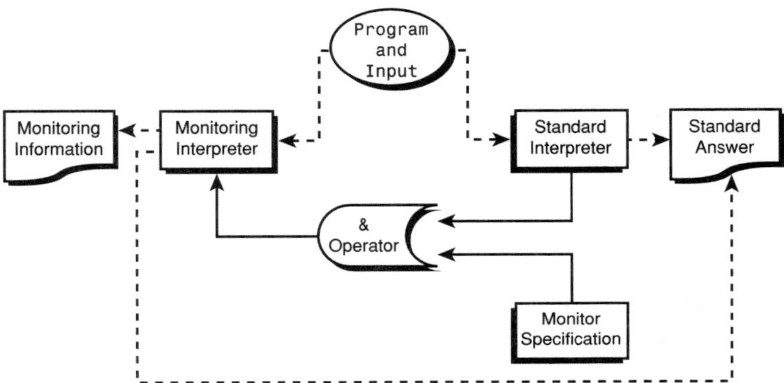

Figure 3.3. *System diagram.*

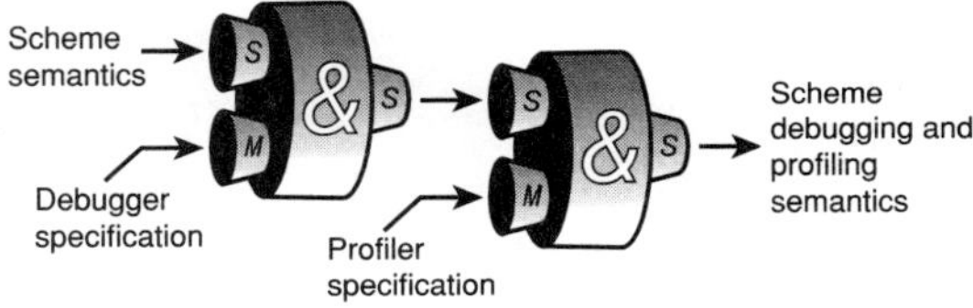

Figure 3.4. *Composing monitors.*

3.5.3. Partial Evaluation

To use DSELs and their corresponding modular interpreters in a practical sense, we can use program transformation and partial evaluation technology to improve performance. For example, we can use partial evaluation to optimize the composed interpreters described previously in two ways: specializing the tool generator with respect to a tool specification automatically yields a concrete tool—that is, an interpreter instrumented with tool actions—and specializing the tool itself (from the previous step) with respect to a source program produces an instrumented program—that is, a program with embedded code to perform the tool actions. Figure 3.5 provides a useful viewpoint of these two levels of optimization.

The current state-of-the-art in partial evaluation technology is unfortunately not robust enough to perform these transformations directly on Haskell programs. The dramatic improvement in performance that can be achieved, however, is providing the impetus to create partial evaluation tools that will satisfy this need.

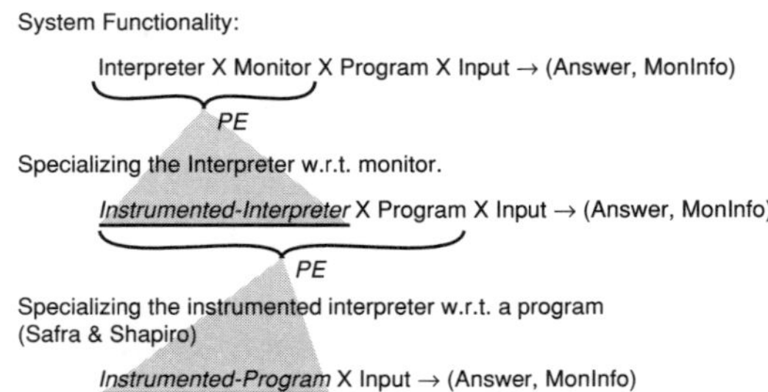
System Functionality:
Interpreter X Monitor X Program X Input → (Answer, MonInfo)
PE
Specializing the Interpreter w.r.t. monitor.
Instrumented-Interpreter X Program X Input → (Answer, MonInfo)
PE
Specializing the instrumented interpreter w.r.t. a program
(Safra & Shapiro)
Instrumented-Program X Input → (Answer, MonInfo)

Figure 3.5. *Partial evaluation optimization levels.*

3.6. Conclusion

I have described a methodology for designing and implementing domain-specific languages. Some of the techniques to do this are well-known, being similar to techniques for implementing conventional programming languages. Others are much newer, yet many of these have been used well enough to give us confidence of their success. The notion of an embedded DSL is especially attractive, due to its simplicity and power.

I urge you to search for opportunities to use DSLs and to create new ones—however small—when the need arises. A well-designed DSL should capture the essence of your application domain, and in that sense, there is no better way to structure your software system. There are no hard-and-fast rules for designing a DSL, but the following guidelines may be useful:

- Use the KISS (keep it simple, stupid) principle.
- "Little languages" are a good thing; read Jon Bentley's article.
- Concentrate on the domain semantics; do not get hung up on syntax.
- Don't let performance dominate the design, and don't let the design dominate performance.
- Prototype your design; refine and iterate.
- Keep the end user in mind; remember that success equals a happy customer.

3.7. References

Aho, A. V., R. Sethi, and J. D. Ullman. 1987. *Compiler principles, techniques and tools*. Reading, MA: Addison-Wesley.

Bentley, J. 1986. Little languages. *CACM* 29(8):711–721.

Carlson, W. E., P. Hudak, and M. P. Jones. 1993. *An experiment using Haskell to prototype "Geometric Region Servers" for Navy Command and Control.* Research Report 1031, Department of Computer Science, Yale University, New Haven, CT.

Caruso, J. 1993. *Prototyping demonstration problem for the Prototech Hiper-d Joint Prototyping Demonstration Project.* CCB Report 0.2, Naval Surface Warfare Center, Dahlgren, Virginia.

Elliott, C., and P. Hudak. 1997. Functional reactive animation. *International Conference on Functional Programming*, pp. 163–173.

Espinosa, D. 1995. *Semantic Lego*. Ph.D. dissertation, Columbia University, New York.

Henderson, P. 1982. Functional geometry. In *Proceedings of the 1982 ACM Symposium on Lisp and Functional Programmming*, pp. 179–187.

Hudak, P., S. Peyton Jones, and P. Wadler (Eds.). 1992. Report on the programming language Haskell, a non-strict purely functional language (Version 1.2). *ACM SIGPLAN Notices* 27(5):R1–R164.

Johnson, S. C. 1975. *Yacc—Yet another compiler compiler*. Technical Report 32. Murray Hill, NJ: Bell Laboratories.

Lesk, M. E. 1975. *Lex—A lexical analyzer generator*. Technical Report 39. Murray Hill, NJ: Bell Laboratories.

Liang, S., and P. Hudak. April 1996. Modular denotational semantics for compiler construction. *European Symposium on Programming.*

Liang, S., P. Hudak, and M. Jones. 1995. Monad transformers and modular interpreters. *Proceedings of the 22nd ACM Symposium on Principles of Programming Languages*, San Francisco, pp. 333–343.

Liang, S. 1996. *Modular monadic semantics and compilation.* Ph.D. dissertation, Yale University, New Haven, CT.

Moggi, E. 1989. Computational lambda-calculus and monads. *Proceedings of the 4th IEEE Symposium on Logic in Computer Science*, Pacific Grove, CA, pp. 14–23.

Peyton Jones, S., and P. Wadler. 1993. Imperative functional programming. *Proceedings of the 20th Symposium on Principles of Programming Languages,* Charleston, SC, pp. 71–84.

Reps, T. W. 1984. *Generating language-based environments*. Cambridge, MA: MIT Press.

Steele, G. L., Jr. 1994. Building interpreters by composing monads. *Conference Record of POPL '94: 21st ACM SIGPLAN-SIGACT Symposium on Principles of Programming Languages,* Portland, Oregon, pp. 472–492

Wadler, P. 1990. Comprehending monads. *Proceedings of the Symposium on Lisp and functional programming*, Nice, France, pp. 61–78.

CHAPTER 4

Essential Features of UNIX Formatting Languages

by Jaap Akkerhuis

In most programming languages, the I/O model, the interface with the environment—author, reader/consumer—is ignored or left as an "implementation detail" to be dealt with by yet another standards committee. However, presenting information *like this*, on paper, screen, or by whatever means *you* are consuming this right now, is in the domain of problems of this chapter. The UNIX-tools take care of the O part of I/O and are a fine example of demonstrating how to deal with the challenge of presenting information, and, by the same token, illustrate why programming languages are conceived, developed, and become obsolete, depending on the problems to be solved.

The central role of the UNIX formatting tools is occupied by the troff text processor. First, I'll sketch the history and the evolution of the program. Then I will devote some time to some of the concepts—or lack thereof—of the core formatter, which will allow me to explain how the various preprocessors make use of these concepts. Further sections will deal with these preprocessors. The languages implemented have often a more traditional feel than the core formatting tools.

The description of the various tools is based on the *Documenter's WorkBench Release 3.4* (AT&T, 1993).

4.1. A Concise History of troff

Like many other formatters, troff traces its ancestry to the formatter RUNOFF, which appeared in the MIT Compatible Time Sharing System around 1964. It follows the same model: text interspersed with commands.

When the prototype of MULTICS was running at Bell Laboratories, a text formatter based on RUNOFF was soon implemented. After the MULTICS project was abandoned and with the development of UNIX, a version known as roff was implemented on the PDP 7 (Ritchie, 1980). The success of this system was actually quite important in the evolution of UNIX. The success of the first UNIX versions led to the procurement of a PDP 11 for use as a base for a typesetting system for the Bell Labs patent department. The PDP 7 version was ported to the PDP 11, and by the end of 1971, this was in daily use. The experience of this use led to the development of nroff (short for *new roff*) by Joe Ossanna in 1974. In 1975, it was adapted to the Wang C/A/T 4 typesetter and became known as n/troff, being essentially the same program. nroff produces output for typewriter-style output devices, like lineprinters, teletypes, and so on, and troff for the typesetter. During the transition from UNIX V6 to V7, troff was rewritten in the C programming language. This placed a heavy demand on the C compiler and a special version was produced, also known as *Typesetter C*, an addition to UNIX V6.2.

The n/troff (Ossanna, 1979) combination—to which I from now on refer to as troff—meant a new direction in the system. The old roff system had built-in knowledge about the page layout. It knew about page elements like headers and footers, whereas troff had much less built-in knowledge about these. Instead, there is an extensive set of commands and some powerful functions like "traps" (software interrupts) and "diversions" (temporary output containers, which can, on demand, be inserted in the output stream). These, combined with a powerful "macro" facility, made troff a more versatile program than its predecessors. Therefore, it is often referred to as the central formatting engine of the UNIX text processing tools. This improved functionality led to the development of macro packages like `-ms`, the manuscript macros. After that time, it underwent slow but steady evolution, mostly to aid in implementing preprocessors like `tbl` for tabular and `eqn` for mathematical material until Ossanna's death in late 1977. In 1979, when Bell Labs bought a new typesetter, troff was modified by Brian Kernighan so that it would produce output for various typesetters (Kernighan, 1982). Since then, the internals have been moderately revised. Also, quite a few different pre- and postprocessors have been developed. The whole set of tools is also known as the Documenter's WorkBench.

There have been various commercial versions sold, like Sqroff by the Canadian company Soft Quad, based on DWB 2.0, and there is also a public domain version called groff, which is completely rewritten from scratch (in C++).

4.2. troff—The Formatting Engine

As I said before, although troff doesn't have any fixed concepts as to how the actual page layout will be, it has some primitive concepts and some necessary capabilities. There is a concept of page length as well as line length. troff also knows how to fill and to adjust spaces in a line. (This process is known in the typesetting trade as justification.) For this process, it knows how to hyphenate words when necessary. The hyphenation algorithm is meant for American English. Instead of using the standard troff, it is also possible to use the TeX algorithm, and if the proper dictionary is loaded, hyphenation in other languages can be achieved.

The input stream consists of text lines interspersed with control lines. Control lines start with a *control character*—normally a `.` (period) or `'` (a single quote)—followed by one or two characters specifying a *request* or user-defined macro to be executed. Some requests or macros force out, or *break*, the current partial-filled output line. The `'` control character suppresses this function and is therefore called the *no-break* control character.

Various special functions are introduced in the input by means of the *escape* character, normally the backslash (`\`). As an example, the Greek character α can be inserted in the input with the control sequence—for example, `\(*a`. Other sequences can refer to user-defined *string* macros, referring values stored in internal *registers* (built-in or user-definable variables), switching of fonts (typefaces), character sizes, and so on. By default, the input lines are collected, newline characters are replaced by spaces, and output is left and right justified.

4.2.1. Macro Definition

To start a new paragraph with some extra line spacing (or leading) and some extra indentation, you would typically insert requests. For the beginning of the current paragraph, you might have

```
. . . definitions
.sp .7
.ti +1m
To start a new paragraph ...
```

This `.sp` request says to break the current output line and start a new one with .7 point extra base line spacing (leading). The `.ti` non-breaking request says that we want a temporary indentation of 1 em wide. It is, of course, tiresome to have to repeat the sequence all the time. Therefore, we can define this sequence into a macro and use it instead:

```
.de PP
.sp .7      \" space .7 em
.ti +1m     \" temporary indent 1 m
.ft R       \" default font is Roman
..
```

The definition of the macro starts with the `.de` request, and it is ended by the two single periods on a line. The `\"` sequence introduces a comment until the end of the input line. The `.ft R` statement is a safeguard just in case the previous paragraph ended using a different font from the one we want to use. It is obvious that the macro should be used as in

```
. . . last line of old paragraph
.PP
First line of new paragraph
```

Our paragraph macros are crude. Unlike the original sequence, we have a safeguard against the fact that we just might have had a font change; quite a few things are in an unknown state. The line length, point size, or justification mode might have changed, among other things. Macro definitions might include other macros, so we can easily define a macro `.RT`, which brings the formatter in a known state and then does whatever is needed for a specific request:

```
.\" Indented paragraph
.de PP
.RT                          \" return to known state
.sp \\n(PDu                  \" extra paragraph baseline spacing
.if !\\n(.$ .ti \\n(PIu      \" if no argument, do temporary indent
..
.\" left aligned paragraph
.de LP
.PP 1
..
.nr PD .7m
.nr PI 1m
```

There are a couple things to notice. Not only do we use the `.RT` macro in `.PP`, but we also get rid of the absolute value for the paragraph distance. By issuing `.sp \\n(PDu`, we specify to use for the extra baseline spacing the value in basic units as set in register `PD`. The double backslash is needed, so the variable is *interpolated* when the macro is *read back* (that is, when it is executed, not when it is defined). This trick allows us to parameterize our macro packet by storing values in registers. The next line, `.if ..`, shows the use of a conditional statement. If we don't have an argument to the macro, do the temporary indentation as specified in the `PI`,

Paragraph Indentation register. The somewhat-contrived definition of `.LP` shows how the `.PP` macro can be reused and its function changed by giving it an arbitrary argument.

4.2.2. Strings

Strings are a special form of macros. They can be interpolated at any moment. By a human user, they are often used as shortcuts. As you may have noticed by now, the word UNIX is typeset in capitals but of smaller type than normal. This can be done by issuing `\s-1UNIX\s0`. The `\s-1` drops the size one point, and `\s0` pops it back to whatever the previous size was. Instead of typing this all the time, you can define a macro more easily as

```
.ds UX \s-1UNIX\s0
```

which can be used by typing `\*(UX` in the input.

Preprocessors frequently define or append strings and macros on-the-fly.

4.2.3. Traps

Although troff doesn't have a built-in model of elements of a page, the macro capabilities and its use can define these, yet they still have to be inserted by the user. This is, of course, impractical when dealing with running headers or footers. You can insert in the source of the document calls to macros to create this, but that is naturally a very cumbersome, if not impossible, process. Although the original roff had a concept about running headers and footers, troff knows only about the current page length, and it introduced the concept of *traps* instead. Basically, traps are a form of software interrupts. Whenever the output reaches a certain position, or "sweeps the trap," a request of macro will be called, just as it would be in the input stream. Such an interrupt is specified (known as "planting the trap") on the output stream with the `.wh` request:

```
.wh N FT
```

When the position *N* is reached, call `FT`. If *N* is negative, the position is relative from the page bottom. This concept is not only good enough to spare the user infinite trial-and-error cycles about where to put a call for running footer and header macros, but it is also general enough that other features, like footnotes, can be implemented as well.

In the most simple application of this device, the running headers and footers don't have any information to display but only give whitespace at the beginning and end of each page, thus defining the page margins.

```
.de HE                    \" define the header
'sp 1i                    \" 1 inch baseline spacing
..
```

```
.de Fo                  \" define the footer
'bp                     \" start new page
..
.wh 0 He                \" header at top of page
.wh -1i Fo              \" footer at 1 inch from bottom of page
.pl 8i                  \" page length
```

The header definition gives one inch of whitespace from the top of the page, and the footer specifies that a new page should be issued. The footer definition, `Fo`, simply generates a new page.

Note the use of the no-break control character `'` to prevent the last line on the page from being sent to the output instantaneously. It effectively delays the execution of the `.Fo` macro, and thus the new page, until the line is completely filled. In the `He` macro, the no-break character performs the same function. It prevents the output of whatever is still hanging around in internal buffers of troff and delays this output until the header macro is executed and thus outputs the whitespace, the top-of-page margin. In troff's own terms, the no-break control character prevents "flushing of the current partial filled output line."

But how do these macros get executed in the first place? They are controlled by the `.wh` requests. The `.wh -1i Fo` statement specifies that whenever the output reaches the area 1 inch from the bottom of the page, the `Fo` macros should be executed. Similarly, the statement `.wh 0 He` means that the first thing on the new page that gets executed is a call to the macro `He`. The page length is the size of the page including the top and bottom margin; it is set to 8 inches. With the macros and the trap settings above, this gives a text page with a length of 6 inches.

4.3. The Footer Revisited

The preceding header and footer definitions are pretty basic. They don't do anything except arrange for some space; but a real-life example does quite a bit more. Normally, you want to have the left-hand page (verso) number on the left and the right-hand page (recto) number on the right. This can be easily arranged with the next definition:

```
.de Fo              \" define the footer
'sp .5i
.if e .tl '%'''     \" if even page
.if o .tl '''%'     \" if odd page
'bp                 \" start new page
..
.wh -1i Fo          \" footer at 1 inch from bottom of page
```

Now, as the trap is sprung and the `Fo` macro is called, we first space a half inch vertically. The next two lines contain conditional statements.

The first stands for "if the page is even, execute request tl," and the other executes this when the page is odd. The tl request itself displays a three-part title, so

```
.tl 'Left'Middle'Right'
```

produces the following output:

Left Middle Right

The % is recognized by the tl and will print the current page number. So, the combination of the if and the tl gives the desired effect.

There are some interesting things to note. The tl request doesn't cause a break, so it is not necessary to use the non-break character ('). Also, we just print the page number "as is," in whatever current font and point size are in use. Because those might change, we really want to specify them as well. In this simple case, we do it directly:

```
.if e .tl '\s8\fH%\fP\s0'''                \" if even page
```

The \s8 says to use the size 8 points. The \fH specifies the use of the Helvetica (sans-serif) font, and \fP specifies to go back to the previous font—to what we were using all along. Similarly, \s0 specifies to go back to the previous point size. The \f.. and \s.. are the *inline* forms of the pt, to set point size, and ft, to set font requests. It is important to note that we can go back to a previous value without the need to know what it was. A lot of these requests maintain such a one-level deep stack, and without this feature, the trap mechanism would be less effective.

4.4. Header Refinement

A more-detailed example of use of the one-level deep stack mechanism for the parameters manipulated by requests will be shown in the next expanded version of the header definition. To give a realistic example, we first consider the function of a running header.

In most books, the running headers are used as aids to the reader to locate a chapter or major section easily. Instead of consulting the table of contents, you often merely flip through the pages, and by looking at the running headers passing by, the desired passage can be found. For our refined header, we want to have this functionality. To show how we gather the information about the chapter and major section title, we introduce two macros. As a side effect, it will show some other features of the troff input language.

4.4.1. Chapter Macro

The chapter macro takes a single argument, the chapter title, and stores it away for later referral by the header macro. Its definition could be as follows:

```
   .de CH
   .if !\\n(.$=1 .tm CH: Illegal number of arguments
3  .ds CT \\$1
   .bp
   .nr CN +1
6  .rs
   .sp 3i
   .ft HB
9  .ps 14p
   Chapter \\n(SN
   .sp 18p
12 \\*(CT
   .ps 10
   .ft R
15 .sp 1i
   .nr SN 0 1
   ..
```

This macro has more function than just storing some information. The first line starts the definition, and the second does some rudimentary syntax checking. If we don't have a single argument when the macro is called, an error message is produced to the error stream, but processing will continue. If this is not what you want, replace the `tm` (terminal message) macro with the `ab` (abort) macro. In that case, troff will exit after printing the message. We store the argument in register `CT` at line 3. Then we generate a page with `bp` because we want the new chapter to start on a fresh page. After that, we raise the current chapter number, stored in register variable `CN`, by one. The `rs` (restore spacing) on line 6 is necessary so that the space request on the next line will work. Normally, you don't want to generate vertical spacing at a new page to prevent extra spacing such as that introduced by section macros and the like. However, we want to have some space for a distinguished chapter opening here.

This uses the font Helvetica Bold and consists of two lines: the chapter announcement with number and title at 18 points below the announcement. The escape sequence `\\*(CT` interpolates the string `CT`, the chapter title that we had defined before and is given as argument to the `CH` macro call. The roman font and standard point size are set, and a 1-inch space is generated. Calling this new macro as

```
.CH "Page boundaries"
.LP
Page boundaries ...
```

results in something like this:

Chapter 1

Page Boundaries

Page boundaries are simulated with lines in this and in further example outputs, when necessary.

The last line of the macro's definition resets the section number register (SN) to zero with an auto-increment of one. Its use will be shown in the next example.

4.4.2. The Section Macro

This macro, SC, follows a similar pattern as the chapter macro. At first, the same minimal syntax checking takes place, and the section title is stored. Then some whitespace is issued, followed by printing of the section header, and so on:

```
.de SC
.if !\\n(.$=1 .tm SC: Illegal number of arguments
.ds ST \\$1
.sp
.ft B
\\n+(SN. \\*(ST
.ft R
.sp 0.5
..
```

The section title is stored in the string ST, an extra line space is added, and after printing of the section number and title, we insert another half line space. The only new thing introduced in this example is the way we print the section number. In the chapter macro, it was defined as `.nr SN value increment`, with a starting value of zero and auto-increment of one. The notation `\\n+(SN` means that the register SN is first incremented with the amount specified before being interpolated.

4.5. The Refined Header

Thanks to our definitions of the chapter and section macros, we now can access the values of the current chapter and section numbers and titles and can use these in our definition for the running header. In the chapter and section definitions, we have made a liberal use of the one-level deep stack for things like the point size and the current font. For the header, we don't want to break that mechanism in any way. Remember, the header gets executed via a software interrupt, the trap, and might easily break a sequence of the following text:

```
... text, to quote:
.ft I
A long \fBquote\fR that might run over several lines \fIbefore
switching back to the roman font and could have \f(BIabsolute
specified\fI font changes as well.
.ft R
```

Normally, this would look like the following:

> ...text, to quote:
> *A long* **quote** that might run over several lines *before switching back to the roman font and could have* ***absolute specified*** *font changes as well.*

But as you see in this example, the input text doesn't care about going back to the previous font. Therefore, in the header definition, we cannot blindly rely on what the current font is. On the other hand, because we don't know where the interrupt takes place, we might actually destroy the one-level stack of fonts the user depends on, if we are not careful. This explains the amount of extra code in our extended header example:

```
.de He
.nr p0 \\n(.s
.ps
.nr p1 \\n(.s
.ps \\n(Hs
.nr f0 \\n(.f
.ft
.nr f1 \\n(.f
'sp .5i
.ft HB
.tl '\s10C\s8HAPTER: \s10\\n(CH''\s10\\n(SN. \\*(ST'
.ps \\n(p1
.ps \\n(p0
.ft \\n(f1
.ft \\n(f0
'sp .5i
..
```

At first, you see that the current point size, stored in the read-only register `.s`, is saved away in the register `p0`. By invoking the `ps` request without an argument, we revert to the previous point size so the `.s` register contains this now. We save this again, in `p1`. We do the same with the font. Now we can safely change fonts and point size at will, because at the end of the macro, we restore the value in the one-level deep stack and current point size. First, we set the size to the value stored in `p1` and then to the value in `p0`. After this, it is unnoticeable that we have changed these values. Of course, instead of writing this out in the header, we could have defined macros in the style of the RT macro above to save and restore these values. They might be useful in other macros as well.

In this version of the header macro, the title request tl picks up the stored values of the chapter number, subsection number, and title and prints them as a running header.

4.6. Environments

There is actually another way you can separate how the header is typeset and how the current page text is treated. troff has the concept of multiple *environments*. Normal processing takes place in environment number 0. In this environment are the usual default values for point size, fonts, baseline spacing, line length, and so on. Issuing requests, one can change these values. However, there are three different environments, each with its own set of default values. They are completely separated, even from the "previous values" when applicable. It's not unlike switching to a completely different state in the formatter. This can simplify the previous header definition in the following way.

First, in the current environment, we set the line length and the title length—which is used by the tl request—to four inches. Then we do the same in environment 1, where we will process the header. Also, there we set the font to be used to Helvetica bold and the point size to 10. In the header definition, we first switch to this environment, do some spacing, print the running header and additional spacing, and switch back to the previous environment. This way, we can do whatever we want in the header without disturbing the state it is in.

This mechanism is elegant, and it is quite tempting to do the same for footers, section headers, and other textual elements:

```
.ll 4i      \" line length
.lt 4i      \" length of title
.ev 1       \" switch to environment 1
.ll 4i
.lt 4i
.ft HB
.ps 10
.ev \" back to environment 0
.de He
.ev 1
'sp .5i
.tl 'C\s8HAPTER:  \s0\\n(CN''\\n(SN.  \\*(ST'
'sp .5i
.ev
..
```

But there are only three of these environments, so care must be taken to use this only when really necessary. In general, the method of preserving the current state—and later restoring it—is the preferred method for headers, footers, and other elements. This concept really shines in how deferred textual elements such as footnotes are implemented. These are done with the aid of another device, the *diversion* macro mechanism.

4.7. Diversions

Normally, after processing its input, troff sends the output to the standard output stream in an intermediate format to be processed by a postprocessor into a language that the final output device understands. For example, this can be PostScript, PCL, or anything else, depending on the actual printer used. However, it is possible to *divert* the output to a macro in troff in a form suitable to be *read back* later by troff by calling this macro in the usual way. Also, it is possible to find out features about such a diversion, among them, how long it is. An example of use of this concept is the way the preceding troff code examples were executed.

4.7.1. Diversions, Environments, and Text Blocks

The examples have not only a clearly different font, but are also kept together as a single block of text. Furthermore, the blocks are never interrupted by a page break. They either fit in the available space or are moved and begun on the new page, directly after the running header. In order to be able to do the latter, we have to know how deep the text block is and decide when to print it. We set up an environment for processing the sample: the "sample environment." The diversion to a macro concept is, of course, used to store the block of text processed in this environment.

Our first macro starts the diversion, but first we set up the sample environment:

```
.ev 1           \" example environment
.ft CW          \" typewriter font
.ps 9           \" needs to be somewhat smaller
.nf             \" don't fill the lines
.ev
.\" Keep Start macro
.de KS
.br             \" break (flush) current output line
.ev 1           \" switch to example env
.di BL          \" divert output to macro BL
..
```

In the sample environment, we set the font we want in a slightly smaller size to make it look more pleasant compared to the surrounding text and also specify that we don't want the automatic adjustment of lines taking place (in lines 1 to 5 of this example). In the definition of KS, the macro that collects the input, we at first break—flush the partial collected output line in the current environment—and then switch to the sample environment (1). With di BL, we divert the output from whatever troff reads from the input stream to BL, the macro where we store the processed input.

Processing of the diverted text block is ended with a call to the macro KE, which is defined here:

```
.de KE
.br              \" break (flush current output line
.di              \" End current diversion
.if \\n(dn>=\\n(.t .bp     \" size bigger than left on page
.nf              \" already processed prepare to read back as-is
.in 1i           \" indent slightly
.sp              \" give some space before example
.BL              \" read back diverted text in macro BL
.in              \" unindent
.sp              \" space after example
.ev              \" return to original environment
..
```

Each environment has its own output buffer, partially filled or not. Therefore, KE starts to flush this with the br request. Then we end the diversion of the output. The dn register contains the vertical height of the just-finished diversion. The .t register gives us the place of the next trap that might interrupt reading back the diverted text. We test with if ... whether this can occur. If so, we first generate a new page with the bp request. The diverted text is read back in the same environment by BL. As an extra, we indent the whole block 1 inch.

The preceding example is somewhat contrived. Using no-fill mode to read the text to be diverted saves us from various complications because it effectively leaves the text unformatted. Also, when we need to generate the new page, it leaves a much shorter one, which is not pleasant aesthetically.

4.7.2. Floating Text Blocks

In the next, more realistic, example, we solve these problems. We allow an arbitrary block to be delayed. This block can contain arbitrary text to be output as a single block. It may or may not be formatted and won't cause an ugly page break. That also means that if the block is delayed to the next page, we want to see the current line continue, as nothing special has happened.

The float starting macros are straightforward, similar to those used earlier:

```
.de KF
.ev 1
.di BL
..
```

We merely divert (switch) to a new environment and start to process the input for which output is collected in the diversion `BL`. A major difference is that we don't break the partially filled output buffer in the current environment when a macro is called. This way, we don't yet interrupt the processing. The macro that ends the current diversion also decides whether we print the diversion and have to break that partial filled line or delay it until later. It first breaks the partial filled output buffer in the environment where we collect the diversion with `br` and then ends the current diversion by issuing a `di` request without argument. Then follows an `if-else` statement. The simple form is

```
.ie condition anything
.el alternative
```

and states that, if the condition is true, *`anything`* will be executed and if not, the *`alternative`*. Because we want to execute more than one statement, the escaped curly brackets such as `\{` define the blocks we want to execute. The condition in the final example questions whether the size of the last finished diversion incremented with two times the vertical baseline spacing is smaller than the distance to the trap. If so, we switch back to the environment we were in before the `KF` macro started and flush that line with `br`, the break statement. The macro `PB` will now print the diverted text block:

```
.de KE
.br
.di
.ie (\\n(dn+2v)<\\n(.t \{\
.    ev
.    br
.   PB \}
.el \{\
.   nr KW 1
.   ev \}
..
.de PB
.ev 1
.nf
.in .2i
.sp
.BL
.sp
.in
.fi
.ev
..
```

At first, we go back to the environment where we collected the diversion. Remember that, unlike a macro, a diversion contains already-processed text; thus, the no-fill request `nf` prevents us from again reformatting the already-processed diversion. Then we indent somewhat and add an empty line before we read back the diversion `BL`. After that, we add a line of spacing, undo the indentation, and restore with `fi` the default fill mode before we leave this environment.

What happens when the macro and the two extra lines of spacing don't fit is taken care of in the else part (`el`) of the conditional in `KE`. Then there is insufficient space, so the only thing we can do is to store in variable `KW` that there is a floating keep diversion waiting to be output and return to the previous environment where we continue as if nothing had happened. The actual printing on the next page is handled by an extension of our well-known friend `HE`, the header definition:

```
.de HE
. . . other header processing code
.if \\n(KW \{\
.rr KW
.PB
.\}
..
```

After its usual chores, it checks whether there is still a diversion floating around, checking the `KW` register. If so, it first throws away this variable and then just prints the diversion `BL` by calling `PB`, which takes care of all the details. It could have set the `KW` register to zero instead of just tossing it, but whatever method is used, it should be done before reading the diversion, just in case it is longer than the current page, to prevent it from being read back more than once—something we don't really want. In case the text block is longer than the current page length, it will act as the normal input and thus hit the footer trap that will start a new page on which the header will be output and the process continues.

4.8. Wandering Traps: An Overview of a Possible Footnote Implementation

Earlier, we learned that delaying text to be output later is relatively easy. For footnotes, however, we need to do something more: We also need to shorten the current text page with the size of the footnote. This is done by dynamically changing the trap position at the beginning of the footer.

The footnote will be printed in the extra space thus created. A footnote will get collected with the start of the macro FS, and it will end by FE:

```
.de FS
.da FN      \" append to diversion FN
.ev 1       \" Footnote environment
.fi         \" fill mode
..
```

With da, we append here to the footnote diversion. There might be more than one on a page, and if we just divert to FN, we would destroy the previously collected footnotes. To end a footnote, the FE macro is used. In its simplest form, it would look like this:

```
.de FE
.br                     \" break last line of footnote
.di                     \" End diversion
.ev                     \" Leave footnote environment
.ch Fo -\\n(dn          \" change trap
```

However, this definition doesn't compensate for the fact that the footnote collected in FN might be bigger than the current available space. In that case, we want to start the footer at the next blank line:

```
.de FE
. . . code as before
.if (\\n(nl+1v)>(\\n(.p-\\n(dn .ch Fo \\n(nlu+1v
..
```

The nl register has the baseline position of the current partial filled output line, 1v is the current baseline spacing, and the .p register is the length of the current page, including the bottom margin. So if that doesn't fit, we move the trap to the next line. The footer itself prints the footnote:

```
de Fo
. . . footer processing
if there is a footnote \{\
.ev 1
.nf                                 \" no fill mode
.FN                                 \" print the footnote
.rm FN                              \" delete footnote diversion
.if '\\n(.z'Fx' .di                 \" end excess diversion if any
.ev\}
. . . other processing
..
```

After the footnote is printed, it is completely removed. To get the excess part of the footnote, we have a second trap installed at the bottom margin. When this one is hit, it will merely divert the excess to the diversion Fx. So, after reading this back, we check whether the footnotes are in a diversion called Fx, and if so, we end this one. The macro collecting the excess is trivial:

```
.de FX
.di Fx
.nr XX 1
..
.     \" trap planting and hiding
.wh \n(.p Fo
.wh -1i FX
.ch Fo -1i
```

The trap normally invoking the footer macro is first placed at the end of the page. Then, at the start of the bottom margin, the footnote excess-collecting macro is set. After that, the footer macro is planted on top of this trap, thus hiding its existence. Normally, when there are no footnotes, only the footer trap is called. But, when there are footnotes, the footer macro is moved away, thus exposing the excess trap. If the footnote, while being read back, is bigger than the available space, the excess trap FX is called and the rest of the footnote is stored away.

In the header, we make sure that the footer trap is planted back into its normal place and also save the excess diversion if necessary:

```
.de He
. . .
.ch Fo -1i
.if \\n(XX>0 .SX
. . .
..
.de SX       \" Save excess
.FS
.nf
.Fx
.FE
.rr XX
..
```

The macro SX saves the excess in the first footnote on the new page. There are more small details to be dealt with, which make the actual code difficult to understand, but a full example can be found in the original tutorial appendix to the manual by Ossanna.

4.9. Macro Packages

The basic input language of troff is quite complex and is also a bit awkward. Some people like to compare it to *line noise*, the garbage you get with a bad modem connection. In most cases, a user does not have to deal with the language because he uses a macro package. Most macro packages define standard macros to create paragraphs, automatically numbered paragraphs, footnotes, and so on.

A well-written macro package does more than just provide an easy-to-use interface or markup language to the user. Not only does it take care of the many details that make a nice-looking document, but often it provides a logical structure for the text. This structure makes it easy to analyze the text or place it in a different format when needed. A macro package is similar to the SGML model of documentation. With SGML (Standard Generalized Markup Language), you have a documentation-type definition that defines the tags for the markup and also defines the structure of the document (Goldfarb, 1990). The tags are not supposed to specify how the document will look; they often merely specify a structure element—a paragraph, footnote, or section title. Most of these tags are actually hinting at how the result should look (for example, the tag `<emphasis>`). What the markup will do to the document depends on the document processing system. The document can be parsed to see whether its syntax violates the defined structure in the document type definition (DTD). In systems capable of handling colors, a tag like `<emphasis>` might come out in red, whereas in other systems, it will set it in **bold** or sans serif type. A footnote in one document style may turn into a footnote on the same page but in another style into an endnote; whereas in an online information retrieval system, it most likely will turn into a hyperlink. A separate standard using DSSSL (the Documentation Semantic Specification Standard Language) has been proposed for defining the semantics of the tags in a uniform way.

Although macros can have some limited sanity control, and footnotes might check whether they are not already in a footnote, the troff language is not suited for implementation of a full parser, but it is reasonably well suited to express the semantics of the markup. Different behavior of the processor—troff—in different cases can be accomplished by carefully parameterizing the macros. With an extra set of tools forcing standard conventions, troff can function in such a generalized markup system (Nelson & L'Hommedieu, 1989).

One of the first well-known macro packages was the `ms`, or manuscript macro package (Lesk, 1979b). It is targeted toward medium-sized reports, technical memoranda, and similar documents, in the house style of the AT&T Bell Laboratories. It provides the usual facilities for paragraphs and sections—with optional automatic numbering, page headers, footnotes, and equations. It is also possible to generate multicolumn formats. By just changing some macros, it is possible to generate different versions of the same document from the same source. An *Internal Memorandum* could turn into a *Released Paper* format with the aid of a couple of macros. All macros have names in uppercase only to make them identifiable from the built-in requests. A lot of the default values like point size and line length are stored in well-known registers. This makes it easy to adapt these things to your own taste. And as a last resort, it is always possible to use requests directly to get the desired effect. The package was often modified to adapt to different styles. There are versions that implement styles of various journals such as *JACM*. These variations can range from simple additional macros that change the default parameters to extensive rewrites with additional facilities, like the one delivered with the 4.2 Berkeley Software Distribution.

The more recent `mm` macros, or memorandum macros, of the Programmer's WorkBench version of UNIX try to implement a more generic document style (Smith & Mashey, 1980). The macros specify more types of the various text elements. The package can accommodate more types of documents—not only memoranda but also various letter styles. As usual, you can use some of the normal requests to tinker with the output, change built-in parameters, and also (with other macros) change some of the semantics of the macros. Like the `ms` macros, the `mm` macros are all uppercase and thus are distinct from the built-in request.

A different approach is taken by the `me` macro package (Allman, 1984). Instead of defining a set of commands on top of the native one, it blends them in with the native requests. This way, it gives the feeling that standard requests have been augmented. The package also redefines some of the standard requests. As an example, the `ll` requests change the line length in not only the current environments but also in the others. Again, a lot of the values are parameterized with registers, and also special hooks are provided in some of the macros where you can add code. By using a rigid naming convention for its internal variables and macros, it is safe for the users to add their own macro definitions. Apart from the default style, there are two other styles implemented: the UC Berkeley thesis style and, again, the *JACM*.

The opposite approach is taken by the *monk* text-formatting program (Murrel & Kowalski, 1990). It is actually not a macro package at all, but a preprocessor. It has its own input language for markup of the document. This markup knows about the usual text elements such as paragraphs, numbered lists, text blocks, and the like. The language is quite different from troff's control character and one- or two-character commands, but it shares one similarity, a control character—in this case, the bar (|):

```
|footnote(This specifies a |italic(footnote) in monk.)
```

The preceding example shows that this control character doesn't need to be at the beginning of the line. The actual semantics belonging to the markup tags are stored in a "typographical database." It is possible to specify various types of documents among, them are letters, technical memoranda, and papers to be included in proceedings of the ACM. Depending on this, the semantics of the markup tags are different, but, in the end, everything is translated into troff requests and macros in a style not dissimilar to the `MM` macros. In monk, troff is used as a virtual formatting engine.

From a computing architectural point of view, troff forms a micro programmable machine. The standard requests form the micro instruction set. A macro package can be compared to the micro program, defining a virtual machine with certain properties, whereas monk defines an even higher level, comparable to an interpreter like BASIC. A big difference is that, in this case, the micro instructions are still visible and usable in the higher levels to do finite tinkering.

Just how easy and successful this tinkering can be depends on the macro machine or language. With the `me` macros, it can be done quite effectively. The `mm` and `ms` macros require some more care, whereas in the *monk* language, you have to be extremely careful not to disturb code generated by the program. Of course, the need to add direct requests is a function of how well the job that needs to be done matches the capabilities of the tools available.

4.10. Eqn—Language for Mathematical Typesetting

Mathematical typesetting is difficult to do correctly in general. You might create a simple equation like $x_1 = y^z$ directly in troff, with something ugly like

```
\fIx\fP\v'0.3'\s-31\s0\v'-.03'\^...,
```

The preceding input means

1. Switch to the italic font.
2. Print the `x`.
3. Go back to the previous font.
4. Go down somewhat.
5. Go three points smaller in size.
6. Print a `1`.

7. Go back to original size.
8. Go back up somewhat.
9. Add a small space.

This takes care of the x_1 part. It isn't only an unpleasant sight, but it is also very tedious and hard to get right. And to get a really nice result, you also need to know about the many rules covering mathematical typesetting. The preprocessor eqn takes care of most of these details (Kernighan & Cherry, 1975). It is designed to make it easy for users to specify the mathematical expression in a free form to accomplish the task at hand: to give the mathematical expression without having to concern themselves with many details like whitespace needed and the typographical conventions. A design goal was that a mathematics language processor should also fit in the already-available text-processing environment.

The language is implemented using a standard parser generator (Johnson, 1975a), which aids in portability. All essential calculations are done by troff. This keeps the preprocessor simple; it doesn't need to know about the sizes of characters.

4.10.1. Some Examples of eqn

The example we used previously is easily generated with

```
x sub 1 ^= ^
      y sup z
```

The `sub` calls for a subscript, similar with `sup`, where a superscript is requested. The `^`s identify some extra space around the equal sign. It is often found that, without it, something like $x_1{=}y^z$ looks too tight. The spaces surrounding `sub` and `sup` are required to mark them as keywords, whereas the space after the `1` demarks the end of the subscript. Extra spaces and newlines, when not needed syntactically, are ignored. They help to keep the input equations readable and easy to edit. Because not many keyboards provide Greek symbols, eqn knows about these and various other mathematical symbols. For example,

```
x=2 pi int sin ( omega t ) dt
```

produces

$$x{=}2\pi \int \sin\,(\omega t)\ dt.$$

The variables are printed in an *italic* font; the Greek characters are called by name, `pi` and `omega`, just as the integral sign is called `int` and the sine function `sin`, but those are printed in a roman font.

Fractions are specified with the keyword `over`:

$$d = \frac{100\sqrt{4\beta^2 + \gamma^2 E_i^2}}{4\alpha + 3\gamma E_i^2} \qquad \text{X,21}$$

Another feature of this example is the use of the braces ({}) to group things as a single unit:

```
.EQ I X,21
d=
        { 100 sqrt { 4 beta sup 2 + gamma sup 2 { E sub i } sup 2 } }
                over
        { 4 alpha + 3 gamma { E sub i } sup 2}
.EN
```

The placement of the label at the right of the formula is not a function of the eqn preprocessor, but of the macro package used. Also, the argument `I` to the macro indents the formula somewhat instead of centering it by default.

The next example consists actually of two different `EQ/EN` pairs, but they are bonded together:

```
.EQ I
Y sub roman av mark = 1 over T int from 0 to T y ^ dt = ...
.EN
.EQ I
lineup = -1 left [ e sup -10 - e sup 0 right ] = ...
.EN
```

The `mark` keyword saves the current place of the `=`, and the following `lineup` aligns the equal signs:

$$Y_{\mathrm{av}} = \frac{1}{T}\int_0^T y\,dt = \cdots$$

$$= -1\left[e^{-10} - e^{0}\right] = \cdots$$

The `roman` keyword specifies that the next element, the subscript, is forced to the Roman font, and the `left [` specifies the left big square bracket. The size of such a bracket is automatically adjusted to whatever comes after it. More commands that deal with general mathematical constructs are described in the user manual (Kernighan & Cherry, 1978).

Another class of commands deals directly with the output. You can not only force font size as shown in the preceding example, but you also can adjust something when really needed, overriding built-in values. Keywords like `down` and `up` replace the awkward standard troff notation. Similarly, you can change things like point size, fonts, and so on. It is possible to have the equations inline. To do so, you define two delimiting characters of such an inline equations with

```
.EQ
delim $$
.EN
```

Now anything between two `$$`s is processed by eqn, so `$zeta sub i$` returns ζ_i. For big things like $\sum_{i=0}^{i=\infty} x^i$ enough room is left so it doesn't interfere with the lines surrounding it. Care has to be taken about the vertical size of inline equations. Although eqn does this compensation automatically, if the space is too big, the end result might not always be nice looking. In those cases, a display will likely produce better results.

eqn has its own macro processor. This allows users to define their own constructs. When a term like $j\omega C_1$ is used a lot, you might be inclined to make a shortcut; therefore, a macro can be defined as in

```
.EQ
define jwC ' j omega C sub 1 '
.EN
```

If just one part like the subscript changes a lot, the macro can be defined to take arguments.

The definition

```
.EQ
define jwC ' j omega C sub { "$1 } '
.EN
```

provides such a mechanism, so `jwC(2)` generates $j\omega C_2$ and `jwc (i j )` results in $j\omega C_{ij}$ (Kernighan & Cherry, 1990).

eqn has been a success: The ease with which the language allows specification of equations has proven to be successful not only with the standard UNIX environment, but also in various popular mathematics-oriented newsgroups on Usenet.

4.11. Tables

troff has primitives to handle tables. There is, of course, the traditional tab stop model. You can place tabs on any position you want, and after you issue a special command usually marked as tab on your keyboard, a movement will take place to this position in one or another form. Because the character normally causes some space, we represent it here as the symbol Ⓣ. Because the movement is from the current position on the input line to the tab stop, it actually only makes sense to use tabs in no-fill mode. Tabs can be set with the `ta` request. Each argument sets a tab at a certain distance and takes an optional alignment specification character. The default alignment is left `L`, which means that the *next string* will be placed aligned with its left on the tab stop. A right-aligned tab `R` will have the right of the *next string* placed on the tab stop, and a centered-aligned tab stop will have the center of the *next string* on the tab stop. The *next string* consists of the input characters following the tab up to the next tab or end of the line. The next input

```
.ta 1i +2iC 5iR
.nf
ⓉLeft alignedⓉCenteredⓉRight aligned
```

will generate

|Left aligned   Cent|ered   Right Aligned|

The vertical lines are added here to show the tab stop placements but are, of course, not part of the normal output. The tab distances can be specified using the various scale indicators possible.

The *field* mechanism is another way in which tabs can be used. A field is contained between a pair of *field delimiter* characters and consists of substrings separated by *padding* indicator characters. The field length is the distance on the input line to the next tab. The difference between the length of the substrings is divided among the padding places indicated. So if the field delimiter is a `#` and the padding indicator is a `@`, the preceding example could also be made with

```
.ta 1i 5i
.fc # @
Ⓣ#Left aligned@Centered@Right aligned#
.fc
```

As usual, we specify the tab stops; the alignment isn't specified because the field mechanism takes care of that. The `fc` request with the arguments `# @` declares `#` as the field delimiter and `@` as the padding indicator. The first tab Ⓣ takes our position to that tab stop, and after that, the `#..@..@..#` takes care of the alignment of the (sub) strings. The last call of `fc` without arguments switches the field mechanism off. This allows us to use the characters `#` and `@` without triggering this mechanism.

The field mechanism can align things around arbitrary spots. If we want a table of numbers, maybe representing money, aligned on the decimal, we can do this with two fields. The first field specifies the part before the dot, and the second field takes care of the period itself and what comes after it. Inside the field, we use the padding indicator extensively. The command `#$@@221#` specifies a field with a substring consisting of dollar sign aligned to the left and a right-aligned substring with the number 221. The `#.0123@#` field specifies the left-aligned substring starting with a period. Note that this takes only one padding indicator, just as was done with the first field on the last line.

```
.nf
.ta 1i 1.5i
.fc # @
#$@@221##.0123@#
#$@@3##.14@#
#$@@217,002,010##.004@#
#@on the dot##.@#
.fc
.fi
```

As usual, dealing with raw troff is not a feast for the eye, but it yields more or less the desired result. Not only is the code hard to read or to type, it is also difficult to get the tab stops right:

```
$           221.0123
$              3.14
$217,002,010.004
    on the dot.
```

In the third row of our table, the columns smash into each other. The distance between the tab stops above is of course dependent on the length of the strings in the rows of this table.

The preprocessor tbl takes care of these two problems (Lesk, 1979a). The input to this tool consists of two parts: a small specification that declares how the table should be built and a data part. From this last part, it first sends the data to troff with a bunch of requests to allow troff to determine things like tab stops and other details. After that, it dumps the data again—this time with the necessary requests to use the tabs and field position in the first phase. As an example, consider this table[1]:

Condition Name	True if
o	Current page number is odd
e	Current page number is even
t	Formatter is troff
n	Formatter is nroff

[1]The table shows the built-in conditions of the `if` request.

There are quite a few things to notice. The table itself is centered on the page and consists of two columns and a couple of rows. In the first column, the first entry is bigger than the entries following, whereas in the second column, the situation is reversed. These are things an author doesn't really want to specify. There is also a clear demarcation in the table. Above the horizontal line, the entries are like the header of a table, and below that the entries look like "regular" data. If we look at the input for this table, we can clearly recognize these elements:

```
   .TS
   center;
3  c c
   c ^
   _ _
6  cB l.
   ConditionⓉTrue if
   NameⓉ^
9  oⓉCurrent page number is odd
   eⓉCurrent page number is even
   tⓉFormatter is troff
12 nⓉFormatter is nroff
   .TE
```

Just as with eqn, the tbl preprocessor processes only some part of the input—the part delimited with the TS/TE macros. In this specific example, the whole tbl input consists of four parts: an optional part that deals with the table as a whole, a second for the header of the table, and the last part that specifies the data. After that, the data follows. For this example, the optional part `center;`[2] specifies that the whole table should be centered. The form of the table is specified in lines 3 to 6. The period on the sixth line ends this type of specification; after that, the data for the table starts. Of this data, the first two entries, lines 7 and 8, are treated according to lines 3 and 4 of the specification. Then the horizontal line is printed as specified in line 5, and the rest of the data is treated according to the last line (6) of the table specification part. The specification itself dictates the following: On the first row, the two columns should be centered (line 3); on the second row, the first column should be centered (line 4); the second column won't contain data, but the available vertical space will be used to spread out the data or "staggered" over the rows in these columns. After that, we draw a horizontal line (line 5). The rest of the table consists of rows with the first column centered and printed in **boldface**, and the second column is left-aligned.

[2]A request from individuals who speak British English has resulted in modern versions of tbl allowing "centre" as an alternative spelling.

Although this is a very common way to specify a table, it is also possible to make it yet clearer by using the table continue (`.T&`) command:

```
.TS
center;
c c
c ^.
ConditionⓉTrue if
Name
_
.T&
cB l.
oⓉCurrent page number is odd
eⓉCurrent page number is even
tⓉFormatter is troff
nⓉFormatter is nroff
.TE
```

The beginning of the code is the same, but now we have the header with the data to come, and then the table continues specifying the new format to use. It is not possible to change certain things like the number of columns of global options. The `.T&` is not recognized after the first two hundred lines of a table. This is the number of lines that the algorithm generated by tbl looks ahead.[3]

Tables can be more than one page long. For such a table, we want a repeated header so that we can still see the column headers. How it looks depends on the macro package used:

Formatting State Vector	
Component	Meaning
Left Margin	The amount of space between the left edge of the paper and the left edge of content in the body area
Right Margin	The amount of space between the right edge of the paper and the right edge of content in the body area
Top Margin	The amount of space from the top edge of the topmost edge of the text area (this is the same as available Page Header Area)
Bottom Margin	The amount of space from the top edge to the bottommost edge of the footnote area

[3]In DWB3.4, this number can be changed with the option `maxlines(n)`.

Formatting State Vector	
Component	Meaning
Line spacing	The amount of space from one baseline of text to the next
Baseline Offset	The amount of space from the baseline to vertical placement of content, such as subscripting
Paragraph Spread Above	The minimum amount of space between the current paragraph and the preceding
Paragraph Spread Below	The minimum amount of space between the current paragraph and the following
Paragraph Indentation	The amount of space that the first line of the paragraph should be indented
. . .	. . .
Text	Content targeted for the main body-area

The header of this table is repeated, and every entry has a box around it. Another interesting thing is that some of the entries have a lot of text, which are independently formatted. The input from this example looks like

```
.TS H
allbox center;
cb s
c c.
Formatting State Vector
ComponentⓉMeaning
.TH
.T&
l l.
Left MarginⓉT{
The amount of space between left edge of paper and left
edge of content in body area
T}
Right MarginⓉT{
The amount of ...
T}
...
\&. . .Ⓣ. . .
.sp .5
TextⓉT{
Content targeted for the main body area
T}
```

The option H to the macro TS marks the start of a table with a repeated heading, and the TH denotes the end of this repeated heading and the start of the body of the table. After the options declaration, the first line of the specification demands that this should be typeset using a bold font cb s and centered over the whole table. The next line, c c., specifies two centered column headers; the period in this line ends this specification part, and the next two lines consist of the data to be used. All material between the table start macro (TS) and the table header ending macro, TH, is considered to be the repeating table header. This table header may be placed on top of the pages where the table continues. The way this is implemented depends, again, on the macro package used. The basic assumption is that, with the H option, the TS macro will *divert* all the input into a macro, until a TH macro is called. Whenever necessary, this diversion can be read back and be output. In case of a table crossing more than one page, a page header macro, such as previously defined, takes care of this. The MM macros implement not only the H option but also N. With this option, the MM macros allows us to use the header on a page, even if the table doesn't continue, after a TE macro is issued. This is used in situations in which the user wants to change the format of a table and in which T& cannot be used. How .TS H/.TH will eventually be implemented, used, or abused, for the *tbl* processor this doesn't matter. It just dutifully copies whatever argument is provided with TS and passes on the line starting with .TH (including arguments) after the troff code it produced to generate what might be used as a table header. It is up to the macro definition and thus to troff itself to decide what to do with this information.

A text block is specified between T{ and T}. Note that the T} must be at the beginning of a line; additional columns may follow after a tab on the same line. The field mechanism cannot be used by tbl for these text blocks because they run over more than one line. Instead, tbl takes care of remembering the current vertical position, then indents to the horizontal position to where the block should start, returns to the vertical position and changes the horizontal position again, puts down the block, and so on. To determine the size of these blocks, tbl first stores the text as-is into macros. After the table is ended or after the maxlines of entries, whatever comes first, the width of the blocks is calculated. If there is no width specified in the text block itself or in the table format specification, the default is to use $LxC/(N+1)$ where L is the current line length, C is the number of table columns spanned by the text, and N is the total number of columns in the table. When it is known what the width of the text blocks needs to be, the macros are reread by troff with the desired line length, and the resulting output is put into diversions. As a final step, the positioning takes place, and the diversions are read back in no-fill mode.

Just as with eqn, it is possible to insert troff requests directly. In the last example, we used `sp` to make some extra space around the dots. Interpreting of the dots by troff is prevented by placing the troff non-printing character `\&` in front. And, of course, it is also possible to use *eqn* in the tables. In the next example, we have a table with two formulas:

```
.EQ
delim $$
.EN
.TS
doublebox, center;
cBp+1 cBp+1
l l.
.sp 2p
NameⓉDefinition

GammaⓉ$GAMMA (z) = int sub 0 sup inf t sup (z-1) e sup -t dt$
ErrorⓉT{
$roman erf (x) = 2 over sqrt pi int sub 0 sup z
e sup {-t sup 2} dt$
T}
.sp 2p
.TE
```

The double lines are specified with `doublebox`; the headers of the columns are again set in a boldface (`B`) and in a slightly bigger size (`p+1`). The entries `.ps +2p` tweak the space between the table and the lines surrounding it. Extra vertical space could have been specified similarly, but the empty line works just as well:

Name	Definition
Gamma	$\Gamma(z) = \int_0^\infty t^{(z-1)}\, e^{-t} dt$
Error	$\mathrm{erf}(x) = \frac{2}{\sqrt{\pi}} \int_0^z e^{-t^2} dt$

Care should be taken that tbl and eqn are run in the proper order and that the eqn delimiter is not used in the code generated by the first; otherwise, the output is scrambled beyond recognition. Dollar signs, as used above, are fine.

The way tables can be specified with tbl comes quite naturally to the user. The right set of table-formatting options and the ways the data can be specified provide the proper elements and enable the user to create tables in various styles. tbl seems to offer the right approach. Not only has a book been published (McGilton & McNabb, 1989) showing off what can be done with these primitives, but the mere fact that these haven't changed in over nearly 20 years confirms their success.

4.12. Preprocessors

The concept of *preprocessing* exploits one of the fundamental concepts of the UNIX operating system: the possibility that the output of one program can be used as input into the next one as if they are connected to each other by a pipe. A pipeline using tbl, eqn, and troff would be specified in the command language by

```
tbl files | eqn | troff -ms | dpost | lpr
```

takes the input files and processes the parts it needs. After tbl, the output goes into eqn and later troff—using the ms macros. The troff output is converted into PostScript and sent to the print spooler:

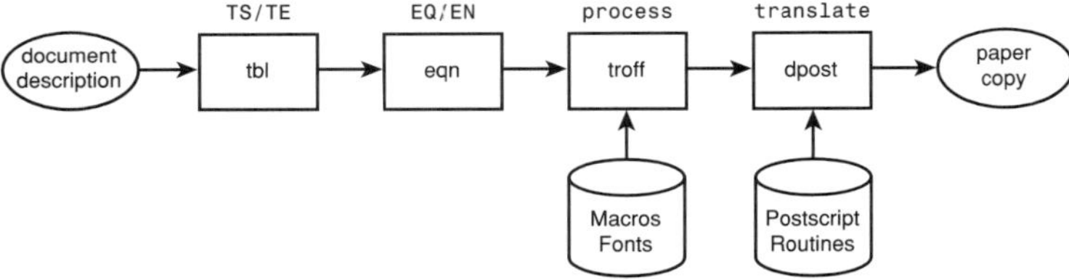

The data flows from left to right, and each preprocessor processes its part. troff adds the macro definitions from the disks. These definitions can also be part of the input, but that hardly makes sense. Every document then would have a copy of these definitions. troff first reads and interprets the macros before the first character is processed. Output devices used to have different ways they could be controlled; therefore, after troff, there always comes a translator to that control language. Nowadays, most devices speak PostScript. dpost is one of the programs that translates troff output into PostScript.

This model is a mixed blessing. The preprocessing programs don't have any knowledge about things like the width of the characters, the current line length, and other values they might want to use. That keeps the programs quite simple and small. On the other hand, it forces them to generate code so troff can figure that all out. The code should also be robust enough so that other preprocessors can add their code without breaking the original algorithm. In the earlier example of a formula inside a table, eqn must provide additional code to get the right space around the formula to the code tbl normally generates.

4.13. Graphics

An old proverb says "a picture paints a thousand words." On the other hand, a single textual description of an image most likely results in very dissimilar pictures when interpreted. For poets, form and content are natural, but other authors don't always think about the printing process; it is the message that they care about. When the message gets printed, often it comes as a shock that there are other dimensions to reckon with. At one time, I made eqn and troff—with the necessary postprocessors—available for the local mathematicians. That way, they could write their own reports without having to queue up for the next slot in the typing pool. I immediately got a complaint that it didn't fly because a variable—let's call it x—was typeset in an *italic* font. Pleading that this is the traditional way mathematics is printed wasn't convincing, until I pulled out a random book from the bookshelf and showed that this variable—what the person who complained obviously must have read at one time—indeed was printed according to this tradition. Whether you are typing a message on a Smith-Corona typewriter or on the next-generation automatic keyboard, what you do create on paper or screen is quite a picture.

In the original troff, there are functions to do simple line drawings by repeating suitable characters. The `\l'Nc'` and `\L'...'` *requests* generate horizontally (`\l`) or vertically (`\L`) repeated sequences, from character `c` over the distance `N`. These functions are used—and needed—by the table preprocessor to draw boxes around the table cells and eqn to extend the line after the √ symbol properly $\sqrt{\text{like this}}$. It is, of course, also possible to draw with just a period, but that would not only generate a lot of data to send to the typesetter; it would also take a lot of time as well—because originally typesetting was slow. When more modern machines arrived around 1979, troff got a facility added to draw simple graphical objects. At the same time, it was decided that troff would not directly generate the commands for the C/A/T/4 typesetter but some easy-to-understand intermediate language. This meant that whatever drawing primitive was available on the typesetter at hand could be used. These commands are

`\D'l dh dv'`	Draw line from current position by `dh dv`.
`\D'c d1'`	Draw circle of diameter `d1` with left side at current position.
`\D'e d1 d2'`	Draw ellipse of diameters `d1 d2`.

`\D'a dh1 dv1 dh2 dv2'`	Draw arc from current position to `dh1+dh2 dv1+dv2`, with center at `dh1 dv1` from current position.
`\D'~ dh1 dv1 dh2 dv2 ...'`	Draw B-spline from current position by `dh1 dv1`, then by `dh2 dv2`, and so on.

As usual, using these commands directly is hard, but they are meant to be generated. Here the "divide and concur" strategy found in the UNIX style of computing shines again. The final code is generated by a program—the preprocessor—while the context is provided by another program—in this case troff—and the actual user interface is provided by another program that deals with the problems at hand.

One of the better known graphic preprocessors is PIC (Kernighan, 1982b). Just using simple terms like

```
.PS
ellipse "ellipse" ; move; box dashed "box" ; line .75i "a" "line"
circle "circle"; arrow "arrow" above ljust
.PE
```

generates the following line-drawing diagram:

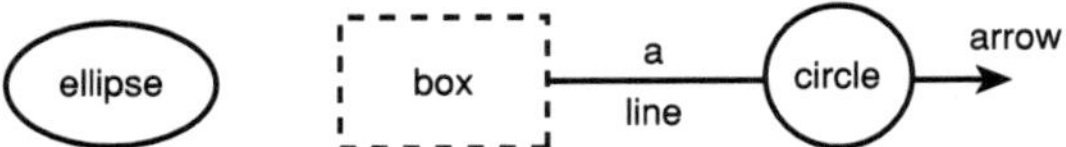

Optional text arguments between double quotes are placed on top of the objects; if the object is a line, and you have more than one, they are centered above and below. Optional arguments such as `above` and `ljust` can change this behavior; in this example, it places the strings above and left adjusted from the center of the arrow. The way objects are drawn and the size can be influenced by more optional arguments; here `dashed` to the box, the `.75i` to the line are demonstrated. The `PS`/`PE` macro pair brackets the part of the input that pic should process. They are also passed through, so they can be used in a macro package that provides the context. In this case, I use the `ms` macro because it centers the picture. The actual code generated for just a single

```
.PS
ellipse
.PE
```

statement, which produced this output:

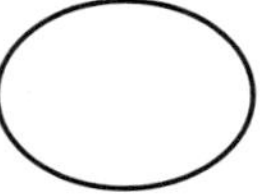

looks essentially like this:

```
        .nr 00 \n(.u
        .nf
3       .PS 0.500i 0.750i
        \v'0.250i'\D'e 0.750i 0.500i'
        .sp -1
6       .sp 1+0.500i
        .PE
        .if \n(00 .fi
```

At first, the current line-filling mode is preserved, and then it is changed to no-fill. The picture start macro is augmented with arguments giving the size of the picture. The first argument is the vertical size, and the second is the horizontal. The first `\v'...'` command in the fourth line spaces .25 inch and then `\D'e...` draws the actual ellipse. Because we are in no-fill mode, every line of input actually generates an extra output line. We compensate after each line-drawing command with negative spacing of one line. For the final part, we space the complete size of the picture downward plus one baseline spacing. Saving and restoring the fill mode could, of course, have been done within the PS/PE macros. Having pic provide the code has the advantage that it works even if the macro package doesn't have these macros defined.

Instead of describing all capabilities of pic, I'll merely explain the ones we have used in the earlier pipeline picture. For all the details, refer to the manual (Kernighan, 1984, 1990). The standard boxes and ellipses are used, of course, for the bulk of the picture. Objects automatically have names attached to them by labeling them, and they have *corners* named by compass points:

```
B: box "B.c" height 1 wid 1.5
      " B.e" at B.e ljust
      " B.ne" at B.ne ljust
      " B.se" at B.se ljust
      "B.s" at B.s below
      "B.n" at B.n above
      "b.sw " at B.sw rjust
      "B.w " at B.w rjust
      "B.nw " at B.nw rjust
```

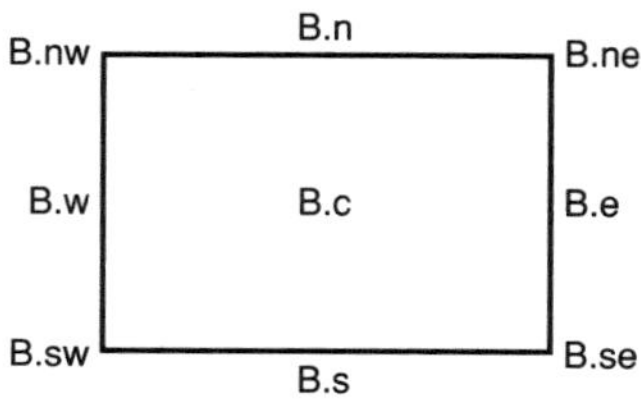

It is also possible to refer to an earlier-drawn anonymous object. The prototypical drum is defined as a macro and uses this last method:

```
define drum {
     ellipse ht.15;
     line down from last ellipse.w
     line down from last ellipse.e
     arc from end of 2nd last line \
        to end of last line radius 1
}
```

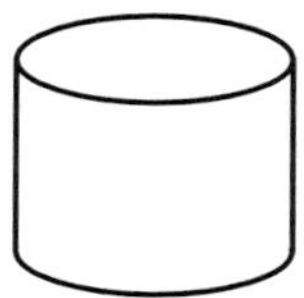

We draw an ellipse with a height of .15 inch. From the west and east corners, we draw two straight lines over the default length downward and then draw an arc with a radius of 1 inch between the endpoints of these last two lines. This last value was determined experimentally. From these two examples, you can correctly conclude that `ht` is short for `height`. More of these short forms are possible, such as `rad` and `wid` instead of `radius` and `width`. We now have about everything in place to draw the pipeline picture:

```
       ellipse "document" "description" ; arrow
       box "tbl" ; arrow ; box "eqn" ; arrow
Troff: box "troff" ; arrow
Dpost: box "dpost" ; arrow
       ellipse "paper" "copy"
```

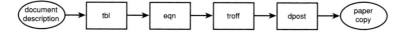

document description → tbl → eqn → troff → dpost → paper copy

Here we draw the basic pipeline. The labels `Troff:` and `Dpost:` mark the points we can later reference to connect the "drums." Note the square brackets `[ ]`. From the drum, they make a single object, a *block*, with its compass points. That way, we can place it with its northern point at the point by the vector `0, .25` below `Troff.s`. We can then place the text strings on top of this last block. Because we have labeled this with `D1:`, an arrow can be drawn to connect the drum to the troff box:

```
D1:   [ drum ] with .n at Troff.s - 0,.25
      "Macros" "Fonts" at last []
      arrow from D1.n to Troff.s

D2:   [ drum ] with .n at Dpost.s - 0,.25
      box invis at D2 "Postscript" "Routines"
      arrow from D2.n to Dpost.s
```

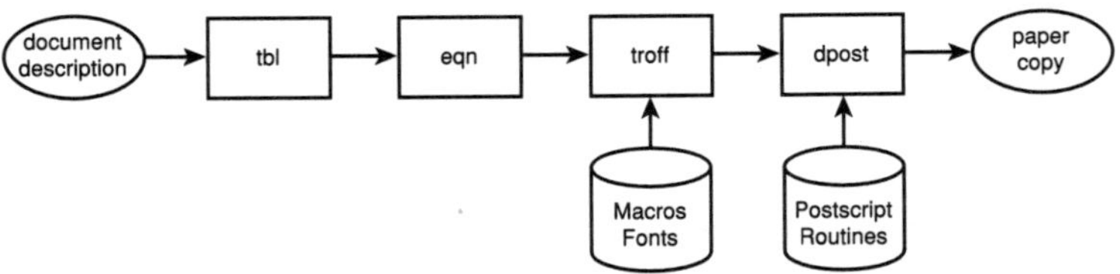

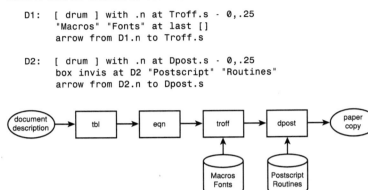

For the PostScript routine database, we use another common method. We place the drum box as before, but now, instead of directly referring to it, we refer to the place it is located, `D2`, and at this position draw an invisible box with text strings placed on it. Using invisible boxes to place text strings is a common method. The next macro uses it to place the final labels on the drawing:

```
define process {
     box invis "\f(CW\s-1$1\s0\fP"
}
```

The `$1` is the argument given, when a macro is called as `macro ( argument )`. If there is no argument, just an invisible box is drawn and the string is basically a no-op. At the calling of the macro, the parenthesis should be given; otherwise, the `$1` is interpreted to be just a string:

```
process(argument); line; process() ; line; process
```

argument — [ ] — $1   *# invis boxes are here outlined with dots*

The `\f(CW\s-1` and `\s0\fP` are raw troff commands. At first, the font is changed to the typewriter font, and its size is knocked down a bit. After the argument is printed, the size and font are restored. There are multiple ways to decorate the final labeling of our drawing with this function. We can just move around to the right place using the historic information of their placement

```
move to 1st box.n; up ; process (TS/TE)
move to 2nd box.n; up ; process (EQ/EN)
```

or declare them to be a block with the `[ .. ]` idiom to anchor them to the desired position

```
[ process(process) ] with .s at 3rd box.n
[process(translate)] with .s at Dpost.n
```

Whatever method is used, it won't matter for the resulting pipeline picture, of which a miniature is shown here. There is no preferred way to use the various constructs in the pic language; it solely depends on the complexity of the final result and the way the user seems able to reach that.

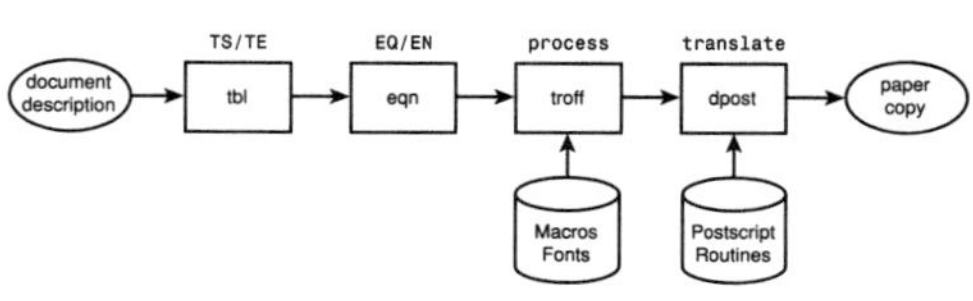

The pic language is implemented as a compiler would be. There is a proper parser and a lexical scanner, using the UNIX compiler tools yacc (Johnson, 1975) and lex (Lesk, 1975). The resulting language helps the user to use all the placing commands in a reliable way. These tools make it easy to throw in some more traditional language constructs such as the usual `for` loops and `if ... then` statements. Familiar standard libraries can be included just as easily; therefore, drawing a clipped sinusoidal waveform is just as easy:

```
.PS 2i 1.5i
pi = atan2 (0,-1)
for i = 0 to 3 * pi by 0.1 do {
        "-" at i/2, 0
        s = 2 * sin(i)
        if s > 1.8  then {s = 1.8 }
        if s < -1.8 then {s = -1.8}
        "\s-4x\s0" at i/2, s/2
}
.PE
```

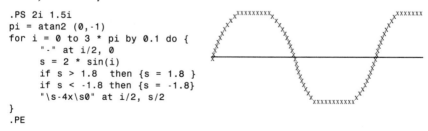

pic was conceived at a time when there were hardly any decent input devices around, just standard (glass) teletypes. That made a linear representation of a figure nearly the only possibility. Much of the primitives—corners and the like—make it easy to position and line them relative to each other. And, of course, having pic integrated with the rest of the standard UNIX documentation software is a big win.

4.13.1. cip

Inspired by the success of the pic language, many preprocessors were created. Each of them was tuned to execute specific tasks in the graphical domain. Some were implemented as real compilers just like pic. One of the first was grap (Bentley & Kernighan, 1986, 1990), a language for typesetting graphs. Others, such as chem, allow the creation of chemical formulae.

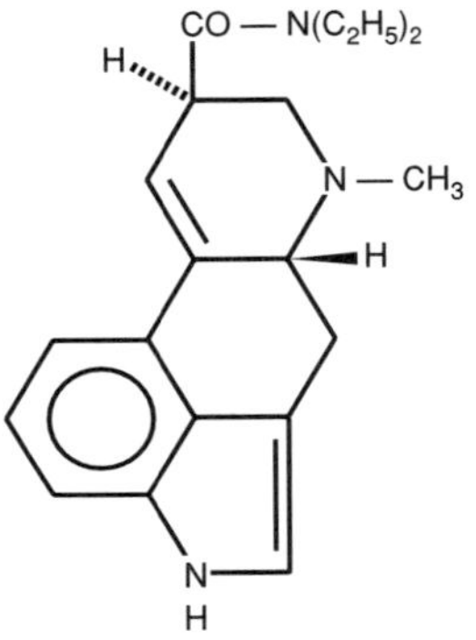

Programs like chem lead to the concept of "little languages," small ad-hoc languages for specific problems (Bentley, 1989). Often they use a tool like awk (Aho, Kernighan, & Weinberger, 1988) for the implementation. But whatever implementation method is used, they all share the same concept: The (graphics) material is described as linear text. Although a description language like pic is powerful, you can still spend hours describing in words a hand-drawn sketch that took five minutes to create. With the advance of bitmapped devices combined with a pointer interface like a mouse, such as the blit terminal (Locanti & Pike, 1982), interactive interfaces became easily available.

The cip drawing system (Browning, 1990) was created as a graphical front end for pic. With the mouse, you can sketch a picture on the display. Its output is in the pic language; therefore, the name is obvious. The cip system not only generates but also reads a picture description in pic. This is necessary not only to enable the user to draw the picture in more than one interactive session, but it also allows the user to refine an existing picture interactively. Sometimes it is really easier to describe things in a textual language than to describe them graphically. cip enables the user to manipulate and define complex objects consisting of basic primitives. These are pic macros. It is also possible to break an instance of such an object, the execution result of a defined macro, into its parts and manipulate these individually.

The interactive system is not as sophisticated as current drawing programs. Going back and forth between the interactive drawing and editing the output with an arbitrary text editor, however, is relatively easy after getting used to it. A big win is that this drawing system seamlessly interfaces with the existing text processing system.

cip is not just a single program; it is really a system in the traditional UNIX way of computing: having small programs solve subproblems well and connecting them together to accomplish the entire task. It consists of two parts. The user interface runs inside the bitmap terminal, which is connected to the host computer by a serial line. The host part of pic provides the file system interface and parses the pic input files. Even over slow data links[4], that makes the interaction pleasant for the user.

4.13.2. picasso

Modern technology such as the microcomputer made high-resolution pixel-addressed input and output devices possible and economical. Bitmapped displays and mice opened new methods for input. Raster output devices, electrostatic plotters like the Versatec or the Canon laser printers, revolutionized the control of final representation. In particular, this started to erode troff's up-to-now successful model of the physical output. troff's world consisted of simple character cells based on the centuries-old tradition of typesetting technology. Traditional and more modern typesetters could be addressed that way. They also often gave way to simple graphical capabilities exploited by pic. A change from this model was introduced by the Apple LaserWriter. Although based on the Canon laser printer hardware, it hides all the difficulties of the pixel-addressing capabilities behind the PostScript (Adobe Systems, 1985) language. Not only the borders between character cells and line drawing disappeared, but textures, colors, and other graphical models were also integrated.

The LaserWriter—and thus PostScript—became widely available for quite reasonable prices and started to replace the expensive traditional typesetters as output devices for troff. Of course, the added capabilities of PostScript were also made available to the user. One way came in the form of yet another preprocessor, psfig (Batchelder & Darrell, 1987). This method relied on the Adobe PostScript back end for troff. The postprocessor developed at the Bell Labs provided another method (Dreschler & Wilks, 1988), and using this method, it was possible to extend pic to use some features of the PostScript model. Although the fill operator

[4]At that time, a 2400 baud modem was considered fast.

works in the next example, the argument `0.9` demands from the user some knowledge of the PostScript language and semantics:

```
.PS
box fill 0.9
box ht boxht/2 wid boxwid/2 "filled" at last box
.PE
```

The syntax for `fill` is clumsy but could be repaired. The real problem is that semantics collide. Normally, an invisible box in pic doesn't show the outline but is used only to place its attributes. However, the extensions to pic for PostScript's features require knowledge of the PostScript language on the part of the user; otherwise, there may be unpleasant surprises:

```
.PS
box ht boxht/2 wid boxwid/2 "filled"
box fill 0.9 at last box
.PE
```

The picasso drawing program is designed for the PostScript language (Nelson, 1988). picasso's input language was inspired by pic, and the program acts as a true preprocessor to the traditional troff pipelined formatting process. Some new attributes take advantage of the PostScript imaging model, but the output is PostScript and not meant to be processed by troff. The only things it asks of troff is that enough space be reserved on a page so that it can fill that space with the described picture:

```
.PS 1i 1i
d = 0.5
[ box ht d wid 3.5 weight d/20
      box ht d wid d/2 filled 0.5 noedge
      spline weight 0.2 edge .75 right d \
      then up d then right d then up d
]
linecolor = red; lineweight = 0.375
circle rad 3 at last block
line from last circle .4th to last circle .8th
.PE
```

It is the task of the PostScript postprocessor, dpost, to include the PostScript routines into the PostScript it generates from troff's output.

The real power of picasso lies in its interactive mode. Using the OpenLook (Sun Microsystems, 1988) graphics widgets, it forms a drawing system with all the features you expect.

4.14. troff Output Language

As I have said before, troff has a simple-minded view of the final output. It assumes only that it can place simple character cells on the final output device. Details of how to control the output devices, especially things such as the drawing functions, are left for the postprocessor. troff's output language reflects this simple view:

Command	*Description*
s*n*	Set point size to *n*
f*n*	Set font to *n*
c*c*	Print ASCII character *c*
C*xx*	Print character *xx*; terminate *xx* by whitespace
N*n*	Print character *b* on current font
H*n*	Go to absolute horizontal position *n* (*n*≥0)
V*n*	Go to absolute vertical position *n* (*n*≥0, down is positive)
h*n*	Go *n* horizontally; *n* < 0 is to the left
v*n*	Go *n* vertically; *n* < 0 is up
nnc	Move right *nn*, the print ASCII character *c*; *nn* must be exactly 2 digits
p*n*	New page *n* begins; set vertical position to 0
n*b a*	End of line (information only—no action required); *b* = space before line, *a* after paddable word space information only—no action required)

`w`	Paddable word space (information only—no action required)
`Dc ... \n`	Graphics function `c`; see below
`x ... \n`	Device control function; see below
`# ... \n`	Comment

The language itself is independent of any specific output device and consists of simple commands. The *xx* for the C command is the character in a special character escape sequence. Sequences that end in digits must be followed by a nondigit. Unless mandatory for certain constructs, blanks, tabs and newlines may be used as separators. All positioning parameters have been computed into the basic units in the resolution of the output device. The device and graphics command forms actually are in an open-ended style. They can be expanded if needed.

The graphics commands are similar to the `\D` escape sequence explained in the discussion about pic. An escape sequence like `\D'l dh dv'` maps directly into the output command `Dl dh dv`. This leads to the next similar table:

Drawing Function	*Description*
`Dl` *dh dv*	Draw line from current position by *dh dv*
`Dc` *d*	Draw circle of diameter *d* with left side at current position
`De` dh_1 dv_2	Draw ellipse of diameters dh_1 dv_2
`Da` dh_1 dv_1 dh_2 dv_2	Draw arc from current position to dh_1+dh_2, dv_1+dv_2, center at dh_1, dv_1 from current position
`D~` dh_1 dv_1 dh_2 $dvsub_2$ ...	Draw B-spline from current position by dh_1, dv_1, then by dh_2, dv_2, and so on

The device-specific commands begin with the `x`, and then the real command, and the possible other arguments to the command. We show only the more important ones:

Device Command	*Description*
`x T` *s*	Name of typesetter is *s*
`x r` *n h v*	Resolution in *n* inch; *h* = minimum horizontal motion, *v* = minimal vertical

`x i`	Initialize
`x f n n s`	Mount font `s` in position *n*
`x s`	Stop—done forever
`x t`	Generate trailer information if needed
`x X any`	Generated by the `\x` function

Some subcommands like `i` are spelled out as `init`. The commands `x T`, `x r` ..., and `x i` should come first, and of course, the `xs` comes last.

The following is the output of troff for a typical PostScript printer. The document is a single page with the traditional "`Hello world.`" program presented here in two columns:

```
X T post          x font 8 HB
x res 720 1 1     x font 9 S1
x init            x font 10 S
V0                s10
p1                f1
x font 1 R        H720
x font 2 I        V120
x font 3 B        cH
x font 4 BI       72e44l28l28ow75w72o50r33l28d50.n120 0
x font 5 CW       x trailer
x font 6 H        V7920
x font 7 HI       x stop
```

The output is pretty straightforward. One of the features not shown here is that each page is self-contained. This allows reordering of pages by the postprocessor.

4.14.1. Font and Device Descriptions

Normally, troff and the postprocessor read the same font and device description. The last one contains the capabilities of the typesetter, such as the resolution, the character set used, point size possible, and various other details. The font file lists from every character in a font its width, whether the character is an ascender and/or descender, and more of these details. The files are as simple and effective as the output language described previously. For our discussion, it is not necessary to go into the details.

4.14.2. Using the troff Output Language

Because the output language is easy to parse, it is relatively easy to write a driver for a specific output device. All the values of the positioning commands are in the resolution of the output device. Writing such a driver is a relatively easy job, but other uses can be made of the simple structure.

High-quality output devices such as typesetters are often expensive to run, and experimenting when each page costs $3 is hardly economical. Therefore, to simulate such a typesetter, you can easily write a small program that takes the input for such a device and scales the values to the resolution of another, cheaper, device. This method is often used for proofreading the final output. For a primitive version, which only scales the values, the result isn't all that great because width values of the *glyphs* of those devices are generally different. And not all of the font families supported might be the same, so they also might be substituted. But still, after getting used to the anomalies in the simulation, a user can have some idea how the output might look.

I have actually built a couple of programs that form such a proofreading system. The target device was a Harris 7500 typesetter, and it could be simulated on a simple Versatec electrostatic printer, the blit bitmapped terminal, and non–PostScript-based laser printers—especially after I managed to get details of the Harris font generation machine out of this device and could scale and simulate these as well. That was the hard part; dealing with the troff output language has never been a problem.

4.15. Extending troff's Capabilities by Manipulating the Output Language

The regular troff output language is not only easy to process for final printing, it is also used as a vehicle to extend the troff systems into areas it was never designed to handle. Most often this is handled by specialized macros that work in concert with a special postprocessor module(s). These are added into the troff pipeline before the device driver.

4.15.1. Fine-Tuning the Output

Although the troff macro packages perform an adequate job for certain layout tasks, they do not create orphan lines, a section header is never isolated at the bottom of a page, and they are poor on other tasks. They don't prevent the creation of widow lines (last partial lines of a paragraph at the top of a page before the new paragraph starts) or perform vertical justification, thus leaving the lines on a page spread unbalanced.

The goal of the `-mpm` macro package is to produce better page makeup than the `-ms` does. It includes most of the functionality of the latter, and it does vertical justification and automatic figure placement while avoiding widows (Kernighan & Van Wyk, 1990). Apart from the usual functions of the macros, it doesn't instruct troff to do special calculations for the page makeup. Instead, using the `\X'....'` mechanism, it inserts commands to the special page makeup preprocessor, `pm` (Kernighan & Van Wyk, 1989), in the troff output. The `pm` macros separate the input to `pm`—thus the output of troff—into *slugs*. There are two basic types of slugs: the `vbox`, which contains printable material, and `sp` slugs, which represent a paddable (vertical) space. These basic slugs belong to groups of four different types:

- *Breakable stream*—The slug can be split, but the order of the parts cannot be changed.
- *Breakable float*—The slugs can be split, but the order of the parts doesn't need to be preserved; they can *float* through the document.
- *Unbreakable float*—The order of the slugs can be changed, but the slugs cannot be split.
- *Unbreakable stream*—No splitting or reordering is allowed.

The "command language" also defines parameters such as the minimal size allowed for a `vbox` slug, or maximum shrinkage or stretch that might apply to a `sp` slug. Together with the built-in default rules, these parameters enable the `pm` postprocessor to do vertical adjustments of page spreads or multiple-column material to prevent widows—a `vbox` slug must have at least *n* lines—and orphans.

The whole page makeup system works quite well and has produced a number of interesting books, mentioned in the original paper. One problem is that because reordering from the output can take place, it is sometimes surprising to the user where the actual output might appear. Footnotes, for instance, might not fall on the same page where they are called out.

4.15.2. Support for Non-European Writing Systems

Though troff was originally developed in a primarily English-speaking environment, in principle it can be used with any language written from left to right. Originally, there was no support for languages written right to left, such as Farsi, Hebrew, Arabic, and so on. If you have the proper fonts, you can simply type the word `desrever`, but things are breaking rapidly. What can we do when we have more than a single word? In that case, not only the characters in a word should be reversed, but also the order of the words in the output.

USER'S MANUAL FOR
`ditroff/ffortid`™ 1
An Adaptation of the UNIX™2 `ditroff`
for Formatting Bi-Directional Text

by

Cary Buchman[3]
Daniel M. Berry

סדריד לשסוש של
`ditroff/ffortid`
חתאסח של `ditroff` של UNIX
לצריכת טמסט דו-ביווני

טאת

ארי כוכמו
רויאל ברי

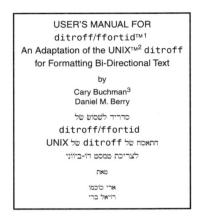

Just as in the page makeup programs mentioned previously, it is possible to reverse the order with a handful of specialized macros and a troff output language processor—in this case, ffortid (Buchman, Berry, & Gonczarowski, 1985). We have printed here part of the title page from the User Manual, showing some of its capabilities. The input, also for the left-to-right portions, comes in *time order*. It is the order in which the text is thought of as it is being written. It is the order in which the properly formatted text is read out loud. Therefore, it is not necessary to input the text `reversed`. When the writing order should be reversed, a special macro is called to insert some special tokens in the output stream. From the standard `w` token, which is normally not used in the troff output language the postprocessor can find individual words and revert the characters in a word. Furthermore, the `n` tokens denote the end of a troff output line. With this information, the postprocessor can reverse the words in a line as well.

Inspired by the success of this method, a system for dealing with top-to-bottom written languages was created and combined with a system capable of formatting tridirectional text (Becker & Berry, 1989).

4.15.3. Index Creation: Data Gathering from the Output Language

The user can send messages to the error output with the `tm` request. A line of the form

```
.tm ix: A Word @ Page: \n%
```

produces

```
is: A Word @ Page: 30
```

When these messages are collected in a file, you can manipulate them and turn them into troff input that can be processed to generate a subject index (Bentley & Kernighan, 1989). Inspired by these tools, for the 4.3 Release of the Documenter's WorkBench, we created a complete index package that can generate two-level indexes (Akkerhuis, 1994).

An idea often proposed is to generate the index terms automatically by scanning documents to create a list of subjects and collecting each subject entry. In general, these methods do not produce great indexes, and they tend to generate more subjects than would be useful in a good index. As in writing a good document, creating a useful subject index requires careful thought and consideration. Selecting index terms—the topic and subtopic entries—requires knowledge of the material and the target audience. Often, an index term represents a concept covered in some discussion, even though the actual words in the index entry may never be used in the text. The `mkindex` indexing tools merely help the indexer to manage and generate the index. For example, an index might look like this:

```
Absolute styles, 30
Abstract syntax notation (ASN.1), 74,
        497-498
    attributes description, 440
    difficulties using, 198 230-233
...
ASN.1, See Abstract Syntax Notation

...
Deleting
    constituents, 366
    construction expressions, 483
    of documents, 358-359
...
```

For the user, the interface is quite simple, although in the next explanation, we ignore some of the details. To identify an index term, you issue a special macro:

```
.IX "Absolute styles"
```

And for a subtopic, you provide a second argument to this macro:

```
.IX "Abstract syntax Notation (ASN.1)" "attributes description"
```

When terms are treated on multiple pages, the numbers are collected, and if they are on consecutive pages, ranges are constructed instead of the individual page numbers. You can also force these ranges with a variation of the index macro

```
.Ir "Deleting" "iterators"
```

It starts such a range, and

```
.Ie "Deleting" "iterators"
```

ends it. Cross references such as *See* can be constructed with the special `I%` macro. For example,

```
.I% "ASN.1" %see "Abstract Syntax Notation"
```

produces the desired effect. The final output produced by the package is again troff input. It is just a list of terms interspersed with macros:

```
.YY a A
.ds Is \&Absolute styles
.XX
\&Absolute styles, 30
.ds Is \&Abstract syntax notation \&ASN.1.XX
\&Abstract syntax notation \&ASN.1.ZZ
\&attributes description, 440
.ZZ
\&difficulties using, 198, 230\&en233
.ZZ
\&type identifiers, 304
...
.YY d D
.ds Is \&Deleting
.XX
```

There are default definitions of the macro body, but the user is, of course, completely free to adapt it as necessary. The `YY` macro is used to create the usual big header consisting of a single letter; the `XX` denotes that the next line contains the main subject part; and `ZZ`, the subtopic part. The main subject is also remembered in the string `Is`. It could be used by the index printing macros package as a running header on the page or as *continued* main subject heading in case of a page break.

The actual implementation is done in a *shell* script, calling a dozen or so awk scripts and a hefty use of the `sort` program. The major part of the code is actually devoted to sanity checking. For example, the use should be warned when a *See Also* reference is made to a nonexisting term or if a chain of references becomes circular.

4.16. Automatic Inclusion of References

In the UNIX system, many utilities exist to search through files for text, but most of them are based on a linear scan through an entire file. Using inverted indexes, it is possible to search more quickly through larger databases. As a side effect of a study of such systems, the refer preprocessor was born (Lesk, 1978). From a possible imprecise citation, it searches in a bibliographic citation database to find a single paper. If the paper cannot be found or if there are too many, a message is printed. The database can be a systemwide default, traditionally found in `\usr\dict\papers`, but can also be one specified by the user.

For example, the reference to the troff manual was specified as

```
...
The
n/troff
.[
Ossanna
.]
combination to which ...
```

This chapter was, of course, originally printed using refer, and by default the citation[5] would have been printed as a numbered footnote. For this paper, we have accumulated all the references at the end.

4.16.1. The Reference Specification

A reference file is a set of bibliographical references that is used by refer. The references specification uses a special format that consists of lines starting with a `%` sign followed by a key letter. Each reference is separated by a blank line. The meaning of a key letter is assigned with the macro package used. Most times, at least the standard set as defined in the original paper, which uses the `ms` macros, is available. These key letters are

Key	*Information Specified*
A	Author's name
B	Book containing item
C	City of publication
D	Date of publication
E	Editor of book containing item
G	Government order number
I	Issuer (publisher)
J	Journal name containing item
K	Keywords (for searching)
L	Label field used by `-k` option of refer
M	Bell Labs Memorandum Label (undefined)
N	Number within volume

[5]J. F. Ossanna, "NROFF/TROFF User's Manual," in UNIX Programmer's Manual, ed. M. D. McIlroy and B. W. Kernighan, AT&T Bell Laboratories, Murray Hill, New Jersey (January 1979). Includes tutorial.

O	Other commentary, printed at the end of item
P	Page number(s)
R	Technical report reference
S	Series title
T	Title of item
V	Volume number
X	Abstract—used by `roffbib`, not by refer
Y,Z	Ignored by refer

Not all keys are always printed; it depends on the type of reference. A journal might start as a technical report or a memorandum, so these labels are not printed. The `K` is used only for searching and is never printed. The nonprinting labels like `X` are often used by a different program such as roffbib (Tuthill, 1984), a Berkeley addition to the refer tools.

Our example reference could have been specified as

```
%A J. F. Ossanna
%T NROFF/TROFF User's Manual
%B UNIX Programmer's Manual
%V 2
%E M.D. McIlroy and B.W. Kernighan
%I AT&T Bell Laboratories
%C Murray Hill, New Jersey
%D January 1979
%M Memorandum Label
%O Includes tutorial
%Z Terse, but complete documentation of troff
```

The order of the labels is not important. If there are multiple keys present, only the last one is used—except for the `%A`. In that case, the authors are shown in the order given. Sometimes it is useful to be able to override the labels to change the date, the journal, or other things from the default:

```
.[
imprecise quotation
%R Override report name
.]
```

4.16.2. Output of refer

Just as other classical troff preprocessors, refer doesn't format the references itself but leaves that to troff. Its output consists of macros and string definitions that are used by the macro package. For our example, we get something like

```
... n/troff\*([.1\*(.]
.]-
.ds [A J. F. Ossanna
.ds [T NTROFF/TROFF User's Manual
.ds [B UNIX Programmer's Manual
.ds [V 2
...
.][ 3 article-in-book
```

The `]-` macro can be used for initialization, and the final `][` should print strings collected at that time in a suitable format. The argument tells this macro which type of reference is called for. refer also adds strings such as `\*([.1\*(.]` in the text to label the references. Again, these can be used to print the label in various ways. There are similar string definitions that deal with punctuation marks around the labels.

Normally, refer and a standard macro package print the references in footnotes. However, when you use the `-e` option to refer, all references are delayed until the sequence

```
.[
$LIST$
.]
```

is encountered. Extra macros are added to the list, such as `.]<` and `.]>`, to aid in formatting the list. Also, the list is sorted and the sorting order can be influenced by the `-s` option of refer. The default is to sort on author order and then on date (`-sAD`), whereas `-sA+T` sorts on all authors and then title. To sort on two authors, the journal title is specified with `-sA2J`. The specification of the sort flags is a tiny language itself!

Other options regulate the labels used in the collected list. Normally, it is just a number, but the `-1` option creates tags consisting of the senior author's last name, the data, and a disambiguating letter. For example, `-13,2` produces `Ben89a` for the "little languages" paper. Several possibilities enable a wide range of styles. Most of these variations are accomplished by inserting calls to macros and strings to be defined by the macro package.

4.17. References

Most references here are to the original publications. The Bell Laboratories Computer Science reports are often in one or another form in documentation delivered with UNIX-based systems. The Programmer's Manual for the seventh edition is also published separately by Holt, Rinehart, and Winston (New York) and contains these reports. The same manual is also available electronically at `http://netlib.bell-labs.com/7thEdMan`. Copies of other Computer Science Research Reports can be found there as well. And, of course, the DWB3.4 Documentation set contains user manuals for all of the tools.

Adobe Systems Inc. 1985. *PostScript language reference manual.* Reading, MA: Addison-Wesley.

Aho, A. V., B. W. Kernighan, and P. J. Weinberger. 1988. *The Awk programming language*. Reading, MA: Addison-Wesley.

Akkerhuis, J. April 1994. *mkindex—Indexing tools for DWB*. Technical memorandum. Murray Hill, NJ: Bell Laboratories.

Allman, E. P. 1984. Writing papers with NROFF using -me. *UNIX programmers manual, 4.2 Berkeley Software Distribution.*

AT&T Bell Laboratories, *Documenter's WorkBench Release 3.4*. This Release was prepared by Jaap Akkerhuis, Richard L. Dreschler, Carmela L'Hommedieu, Don B. Knudsen, Carl Mee, Nils-Peter Nelson, and Manijeh Shayegan. Murray Hill, NJ: Bell Laboratories. This document contains all the preprocessors and an optional add-on package for X Window systems. As an extra, it also contains some of the more popular authoring utilities.

Batchelder, N., and T. Darrell. 1987. Psfig—A DITROFF preprocessor for PostScript figures (pp. 31–42). *USENIX Conference Proceedings,* Phoenix, AZ.

Becker, Z., and D. Berry. 1989. triroff, an adaptation of the device-independent troff for formatting tri-directional text. *Electronic Publishing—Origination, Dissemination and Design* New York: Wiley.

Bentley, J. L. 1989. Little languages for pictures in awk. *AT&T Technical Journal* 68(4):21–32.

Bentley, J. L., and B. W. Kernighan. 1986. Grap—A language for typesetting graphs. *Communications of the ACM* 29(8):782–792.

Bentley, J. L., and B. W. Kernighan. 1989. Tools for printing indexes. *Electronic publishing—Origination, dissemination and design* New York: Wiley.

Bentley, J. L., and B. W. Kernighan. 1990. Grap—A language for typesetting graphs tutorial and user manual. A. G. Hume and M. D. McIlroy (Eds.), *Unix research system—Tenth edition*. Murray Hill, NJ: Bell Laboratories.

Browning, S. A. 1990. Cip user's manual: One picture is worth a thousand words. A. G. Hume and M. D. McIlroy (Eds.), *Unix research system—Tenth edition*. Murray Hill, NJ: Bell Laboratories.

Buchman, C., D. M. Berry, and J. Gonczarowski. 1985. DITROFF/FFORTID, an adaptation of the UNIX DITROFF for formatting bi-directional text. *ACM Transactions on Office Information Systems* 3(4):380–397.

Dreschler, R. L., and A. R. Wilks. 1988. PostScript pictures in troff documents. Technical memorandum. Murray Hill, NJ: Bell Laboratories.

Goldfarb, C. F. 1990. *The SGML handbook*. Oxford, England: Oxford University Press.

S. C. Johnson. 1975 Yacc—Yet another compiler-compiler. Computer Science Technical Report No. 32. Murray Hill, NJ: Bell Laboratories.

Kernighan, B. W. 1982a. A typesetter independent TROFF. *Computer Science Technical Report* 97. Murray Hill, NJ: Bell Laboratories.

Kernighan, B. W. 1982b. PIC—A language for typesetting graphics. *Software Practice & Experience*. 12:1–20.

Kernighan, B. W. 1984. PIC—A graphic language for typesetting (revised user manual). Computer Science Technical Report No. 116. Murray Hill, NJ: Bell Laboratories.

Kernighan, B. W. 1990. PIC—A graphics language for typesetting user manual. A. G. Hume and M. D. McIlroy (Eds.), *Unix research system—Tenth edition*. Murray Hill, NJ: Bell Laboratories.

Kernighan, B. W., and L. L. Cherry. 1975. A system for typesetting mathematics. *Communications of the ACM* 18(3):151–157.

Kernighan, B. W., and L. L. Cherry. 1978. *Typesetting mathematics—User's guide* (2nd ed.). Bell Laboratories, Murray Hill, NJ.

Kernighan, B. W., and L. L. Cherry. 1990. Typesetting mathematics—User's guide. A. G. Hume and M. D. McIlroy (Eds.), *Unix research system—Tenth edition*. Murray Hill, NJ: Bell Laboratories.

Kernighan, B. W., and C. J. Van Wyk. 1989. Page makeup by postprocessing text formatter output. *Computing Systems* 2(2):103–132.

Kernighan, B. W., and C. J. Van Wyk. 1989. The -mpm macro package. A. G. Hume and M. D. McIlroy (Eds.), *Unix research system—Tenth edition*. Murray Hill, NJ: Bell Laboratories.

Lesk, M. E. 1975. Lex—A lexical analyzer generator. Computer Science Technical Report No. 39. Murray Hill, NJ: Bell Laboratories.

Lesk, M. E. 1978. Some applications of inverted indexes on the UNIX system. *UNIX programmer's manual.* Murray Hill, NJ: Bell Laboratories.

Lesk, M. E. 1979a. TBL—A program to format tables. *UNIX programmer's manual.* Murray Hill, NJ: Bell Laboratories.

Lesk, M. E. 1979b. Typing documents on the UNIX system: Using the -ms macros with troff and nroff. *UNIX programmer's manual*, Murray Hill, NJ: Bell Laboratories.

Locanti, B. N., and R. Pike. 1982. The Blit. *Software Practice & Experience* 8.

McGilton, H., and M. McNabb. 1989. *Typesetting tables on the UNIX system.* Los Altos, CA: Thriliton Press.

Murrel, S. L., and T. J. Kowalski. 1990. Typing documents on the UNIX system: Using Monk 0.6. A. G. Hume and M. D. McIlroy (Eds.), *Unix research system—Tenth edition.* Murray Hill, NJ: Bell Laboratories.

Nelson, N.-P. 1988. *Picasso 1.0—An OPEN LOOK drawing program.* Technical memorandum. Murray Hill, NJ: Bell Laboratories.

Nelson, N.-P., and C. L'Hommedieu. 1989. An open architecture corporate publishing platform. *AT&T Technical Journal.* 68(4):100–110.

Ossanna, J. F. 1979. NROFF/TROFF user's manual. M. C. McIlroy and B. W. Kernighan (Eds.), *UNIX programmer's manual.* Murray Hill, NJ: Bell Laboratories.

Ritchie, D. M. 1980. The evolution of the Unix time-sharing system. *AT&T Bell Laboratories Technical Journal* 63(6, Part 2):1577–1593. This paper was first presented at the Language Design and Programming Methodology conference at Sydney, Australia, 1979.

Smith, D. W., and J. R. Mashey. 1980. *MM—Memorandum macros.* Murray Hill, NJ: Bell Laboratories.

Sun Microsystems Inc. 1988. *OPEN LOOK graphical user interface, functional specification.* Palo Alto, CA.

Tuthill, B. 1984. Refer—A bibliography system. *UNIX Programmers Manual, 4.2 Berkeley Software Distribution, Supplementary Documents.*

CHAPTER 5

awk[1]

by Arnold Robbins

Arnold Robbins, an Atlanta native now living in Israel, is a professional programmer and technical author. He has been working with UNIX systems since 1980, when he was introduced to a PDP-11 running a version of the sixth edition of UNIX. He has been a heavy awk user since 1987, when he became involved with gawk, the GNU project's version of awk. As a member of the POSIX 1003.2 balloting group, he helped shape the POSIX standard for awk. He is currently the maintainer of gawk and its documentation. The documentation is available from the Free Software Foundation and has also been published by SSC as *Effective awk Programming*.

5.1. Introduction

This chapter teaches you about the awk language and how you can use it effectively. You should already be familiar with basic system commands, such as cat and ls,[2] and basic shell facilities, such as input/output (I/O) redirection and pipes.

Implementations of the awk language are available for many different computing environments. This chapter, while describing the awk language in general, also describes a particular implementation of awk called gawk

[1]This chapter is derived from Robbins, A. *Effective awk Programming*, published by SSC (Seattle, WA) and the Free Software Foundation (Boston, MA). Copyright © by the Free Software Foundation (FSF). The FSF is a nonprofit organization dedicated to the production and distribution of freely distributable software. The text of this chapter and the original gawk documentation on which is it based are freely copiable.

[2]These commands are available on POSIX-compliant systems, as well as on traditional UNIX-based systems. If you are using another operating system, you still need to be familiar with the ideas of I/O redirections and pipes.

(which stands for "GNU awk"). gawk runs on a broad range of UNIX systems, ranging from 80386 PC-based computers, up through large-scale systems, such as Crays. gawk has also been ported to MS-DOS and OS/2 PCs, Atari and Amiga micro-computers, and VMS.

5.1.1. History of awk and gawk

The name awk comes from the initials of its designers: Alfred V. Aho, Peter J. Weinberger, and Brian W. Kernighan. The original version of awk was written in 1977 at AT&T Bell Laboratories. In 1985, a new version made the programming language more powerful, introducing user-defined functions, multiple input streams, and computed regular expressions. This new version became generally available with UNIX System V Release 3.1. The version in System V Release 4 added some new features and also cleaned up the behavior in some of the "dark corners" of the language. The specification for awk in the POSIX Command Language and Utilities standard further clarified the language based on feedback from both the gawk designers and the original Bell Labs awk designers.

The GNU implementation, gawk, was written in 1986 by Paul Rubin and Jay Fenlason, with advice from Richard Stallman. John Woods contributed parts of the code as well. In 1988 and 1989, David Trueman, with help from Arnold Robbins, thoroughly reworked gawk for compatibility with the newer awk. Current development focuses on bug fixes, performance improvements, standards compliance, and occasionally, new features.

5.2. Getting Started with awk

The basic function of awk is to search files for lines (or other units of text) that contain certain patterns. When a line matches one of the patterns, awk performs specified actions on that line. awk keeps processing input lines in this way until the end of each input file is reached.

Programs in awk are different from programs in most other languages because awk programs are data-driven; that is, you describe the data you want to work with and then what to do when you find it. Most other languages are procedural; you have to describe, in great detail, every step the program is to take. When working with procedural languages, it is usually much harder to clearly describe the data your program will process. For this reason, awk programs are often refreshingly easy to both write and read.

When you run awk, you specify an awk program that tells awk what to do. The program consists of a series of rules. It may also contain function definitions, an advanced feature that we will ignore for now. Each rule specifies one pattern to search for and one action to perform when that pattern is found.

Syntactically, a rule consists of a pattern followed by an action. The action is enclosed in curly braces to separate it from the pattern. Rules are usually separated by newlines. Therefore, an awk program looks like this:

```
pattern { action }
pattern { action }
...
```

5.2.1. A Rose by Any Other Name

The awk language has evolved over the years. The language described in this chapter is often referred to as "new awk."

Because of this, many systems have multiple versions of awk. Some systems have an awk utility that implements the original version of the awk language and a nawk utility for the new version. Others have an oawk for the "old awk" language and plain awk for the new one. Still others only have one version, usually the new one.[3]

All in all, this makes it difficult for you to know which version of awk you should run when writing your programs. The best advice we can give here is to check your local documentation. Look for awk, oawk, and nawk, as well as for gawk. It is most likely that you have some version of new awk on your system, and that is what you should use when running your programs.

Throughout this chapter, whenever we refer to a language feature that should be available in any complete implementation of POSIX awk, we simply use the term awk. When referring to a feature that is specific to the GNU implementation, we use the term gawk.

5.2.2. How to Run awk Programs

There are several ways to run an awk program. If the program is short, it is easiest to include it in the command that runs awk, like this:

```
awk 'program' input-file1 input-file2 ...
```

where *program* consists of a series of patterns and actions, as described earlier. (The reason for the single quotes is described in section 5.2.2.1.)

[3]Often, these systems use gawk for their awk implementation!

When the program is long, it is usually more convenient to put it in a file and run it with a command like this:

```
awk -f program-file input-file1 input-file2 ...
```

5.2.2.1. One-Shot Throw-Away `awk` Programs

Once you are familiar with `awk`, you will often type in simple programs the moment you want to use them. Then you can write the program as the first argument of the `awk` command, like this:

```
awk 'program' input-file1 input-file2 ...
```

where *`program`* consists of a series of patterns and actions, as described earlier.

This command format instructs the shell, or command interpreter, to start `awk` and use the *`program`* to process records in the input files. There are single quotes around *`program`* so that the shell doesn't interpret any `awk` characters as special shell characters. They also cause the shell to treat all of *`program`* as a single argument for `awk` and allow *`program`* to be more than one line long.

This format is also useful for running short or medium-sized `awk` programs from shell scripts because it avoids the need for a separate file for the `awk` program. A self-contained shell script is more reliable because there are no other files to misplace.

As an interesting side point, the command

```
awk '/foo/' files ...
```

is essentially the same as

```
egrep foo files ...
```

5.2.2.2. Running `awk` Without Input Files

You can also run `awk` without any input files. If you type the command line

```
awk 'program'
```

then `awk` applies the *`program`* to the standard input, which usually means whatever you type on the terminal. This continues until you indicate end-of-file by typing Ctrl+D. (On other operating systems, the end-of-file character may be different. For example, on OS/2 and MS-DOS, it is Ctrl+Z.)

For example, the following program prints a friendly piece of advice (from Douglas Adams's *The Hitchhiker's Guide to the Galaxy*), to keep you from worrying about the complexities of computer programming (`BEGIN` is a feature we haven't discussed yet):

```
$ awk "BEGIN" { print \"Don't Panic!\" }"
Don't Panic!
```

This program does not read any input. The `\` before each of the inner double quotes is necessary because of the shell's quoting rules, in particular because it mixes both single quotes and double quotes.

This next simple `awk` program emulates the `cat` utility; it copies whatever you type at the keyboard to its standard output. (Why this works is explained shortly.)

```
$ awk '{ print }'
Now is the time for all good men
  Now is the time for all good men
to come to the aid of their country.
  to come to the aid of their country.
Four score and seven years ago, ...
  Four score and seven years ago, ...
What, me worry?
  What, me worry?
Ctrl+D
```

5.2.2.3. Running Long Programs

Sometimes your `awk` programs can be very long. In this case, it is more convenient to put the program into a separate file. To tell `awk` to use that file for its program, you type

```
awk -f source-file input-file1 input-file2 ...
```

The `-f` instructs the `awk` utility to get the `awk` program from the file *`source-file`*. Any file name can be used for *`source-file`*. For example, you could put the program

```
BEGIN { print "Don't Panic!" }
```

into the file `advice`. Then this command

```
awk -f advice
```

does the same thing as this one:

```
awk "BEGIN { print \"Don't Panic!\" }"
```

which was explained earlier, in section 5.2.2.2. Note that you don't usually need single quotes around the file name that you specify with `-f` because most file names don't contain any of the shell's special characters. Notice that in `advice`, the `awk` program did not have single quotes around it. The quotes are only needed for programs that are provided on the `awk` command line.

If you want to identify your awk program files clearly as such, you can add the extension .awk to the file name. This doesn't affect the execution of the awk program, but it does make housekeeping easier.

5.2.2.4. Executable awk Programs

Once you have learned awk, you may want to write self-contained awk scripts, using the #! script mechanism. You can do this on many UNIX systems[4] (and someday on the GNU system).

For example, you could update the file advice to look like this:

```
#! /bin/awk -f

BEGIN    { print "Don't Panic!" }
```

After making this file executable (with the chmod utility), you can simply type advice at the shell, and the system will arrange to run awk[5] as if you had typed awk -f advice.

```
$ advice
  Don't Panic!
```

Self-contained awk scripts are useful when you want to write a program that users can invoke without their having to know that the program is written in awk.

Some older systems do not support the #! mechanism. You can get a similar effect using a regular shell script. It would look something like this:

```
: The colon ensures execution by the standard shell.
awk 'program' "$@"
```

Using this technique, it is *vital* to enclose the *program* in single quotes to protect it from interpretation by the shell. If you omit the quotes, only a shell wizard can predict the results.

The "$@" causes the shell to forward all the command-line arguments to the awk program, without interpretation. The first line, which starts with a colon, is used so that this shell script will work even if invoked by a user who uses the C shell. (Not all older systems obey this convention, but many do.)

---

[4]The #! mechanism works on Linux systems, UNIX systems derived from Berkeley UNIX, System V Release 4, and some System V Release 3 systems.

[5]The line beginning with #! lists the full file name of an interpreter to be run and an optional initial command-line argument to pass to that interpreter. The operating system then runs the interpreter with the given argument and the full argument list of the executed program. The first argument in the list is the full file name of the awk program. The rest of the argument list will either be options to awk, or data files, or both.

5.2.2.5. Comments in awk Programs

A comment is some text that is included in a program for the sake of human readers; it is not really part of the program. Comments can explain what the program does and how it works. Nearly all programming languages have provisions for comments because programs are typically hard to understand without their extra help.

In the `awk` language, a comment starts with the sharp sign character (`#`) and continues to the end of the line. The `#` does not have to be the first character on the line. The `awk` language ignores the rest of a line following a sharp sign. For example, we could have put the following into `advice`:

```
# This program prints a nice friendly message. It helps
# keep novice users from being afraid of the computer.
BEGIN    { print "Don't Panic!" }
```

You can put comment lines into keyboard-composed throw-away `awk` programs also, but this usually isn't very useful; the purpose of a comment is to help you or another person understand the program at a later time.

5.2.3. A Very Simple Example

The following command runs a simple `awk` program that searches the input file `BBS-list` for the string of characters `foo`. (A string of characters is usually called a string. The term string is perhaps based on similar usage in English, such as “a string of pearls” or “a string of cars in a train.”)

```
awk '/foo/ { print $0 }' BBS-list
```

When lines containing `foo` are found, they are printed because `print $0` means print the current line. (Just `print` by itself means the same thing, so we could have written that instead.)

You will notice that slashes, `/`, surround the string `foo` in the `awk` program. The slashes indicate that `foo` is a pattern to search for. This type of pattern is called a regular expression and is covered in more detail later. The pattern is allowed to match parts of words. There are single quotes around the `awk` program so that the shell won't interpret any of it as special shell characters.

Here is what this program prints:

```
$ awk '/foo/ { print $0 }' BBS-list
  fooey        555-1234       2400/1200/300    B
  foot         555-6699       1200/300         B
  macfoo       555-6480       1200/300         A
  sabafoo      555-2127       120/300          C
```

In an awk rule, either the pattern or the action can be omitted, but not both. If the pattern is omitted, then the action is performed for *every* input line. If the action is omitted, the default action is to print all lines that match the pattern.

Thus, we could leave out the action (the print statement and the curly braces) in the example, and the result would be the same: All lines matching the pattern 'foo' would be printed. By comparison, omitting the print statement but retaining the curly braces makes an empty action that does nothing; then no lines would be printed.

5.2.4. An Example with Two Rules

The awk utility reads the input files one line at a time. For each line, awk tries the patterns of each of the rules. If several patterns match, then several actions are run, in the order in which they appear in the awk program. If no patterns match, then no actions are run.

After processing all the rules (perhaps none) that match the line, awk reads the next line. This continues until the end of the file is reached.

For example, the awk program

```
/12/ { print $0 }
/21/ { print $0 }
```

contains two rules. The first rule has the string 12 as the pattern and print $0 as the action. The second rule has the string 21 as the pattern and also has print $0 as the action. Each rule's action is enclosed in its own pair of braces.

This awk program prints every line that contains the string 12 or the string 21. If a line contains both strings, it is printed twice, once by each rule.

This is what happens if we run this program on our two sample data files, BBS-list and inventory-shipped, as shown here:

```
$ awk '/12/ { print $0 }
   > /21/ { print $0 }' BBS-list inventory-shipped
  aardvark     555-5553        1200/300         B
  alpo-net     555-3412        2400/1200/300    A
  barfly       555-7685        1200/300         A
  bites        555-1675        2400/1200/300    A
  core         555-2912        1200/300         C
  fooey        555-1234        2400/1200/300    B
  foot         555-6699        1200/300         B
  macfoo       555-6480        1200/300         A
  sdace        555-3430        2400/1200/300    A
  sabafoo      555-2127        1200/300         C
  sabafoo      555-2127        1200/300         C
  Jan   21   36   64 620
  Apr   21   70   74 514
```

Note how the line in BBS-list beginning with sabafoo was printed twice, once for each rule.

5.2.5. A More Complex Example

Here is an example to give you an idea of what typical awk programs do. This example shows how awk can be used to summarize, select, and rearrange the output of another utility. It uses features that haven't been covered yet, so don't worry if you don't understand all the details.

```
ls -lg | awk '$6 == "Nov" { sum += $5 }
              END { print sum }'
```

This command prints the total number of bytes in all the files in the current directory that were last modified in November (of any year). (In the C shell, you would need to type a semicolon and then a backslash at the end of the first line; in a POSIX-compliant shell, such as the Bourne shell or Bash, the GNU Bourne Again shell, you can type the example as shown.)

The ls -lg part of this example is a system command that gives you a listing of the files in a directory, including file size and the date the file was last modified. Its output looks like this:

```
-rw-r--r--  1 arnold   user    1933 Nov  7 13:05 Makefile
-rw-r--r--  1 arnold   user   10809 Nov  7 13:03 gawk.h
-rw-r--r--  1 arnold   user     983 Apr 13 12:14 gawk.tab.h
-rw-r--r--  1 arnold   user   31869 Jun 15 12:20 gawk.y
-rw-r--r--  1 arnold   user   22414 Nov  7 13:03 gawk1.c
-rw-r--r--  1 arnold   user   37455 Nov  7 13:03 gawk2.c
-rw-r--r--  1 arnold   user   27511 Dec  9 13:07 gawk3.c
-rw-r--r--  1 arnold   user    7989 Nov  7 13:03 gawk4.c
```

The first field contains read-write permissions, the second field contains the number of links to the file, and the third field identifies the owner of the file. The fourth field identifies the group of the file. The fifth field contains the size of the file in bytes. The sixth, seventh, and eighth fields contain the month, day, and time that the file was last modified. Finally, the ninth field contains the name of the file.

The $6 == "Nov" in our awk program is an expression that tests whether the sixth field of the output from ls -lg matches the string "Nov". Each time a line has the string "Nov" for its sixth field, the action sum += 5 is performed. This adds the fifth field (the file size) to the variable sum. As a result, when awk has finished reading all the input lines, sum is the sum of the sizes of files whose lines matched the pattern. (This works because awk variables are automatically initialized to zero.)

After the last line of output from `ls` has been processed, the `END` rule is executed, and the value of `sum` is printed. In this example, the value of `sum` would be `80600`.

Before you can move on to more advanced `awk` programming, you have to know how `awk` interprets your input and displays your output. By manipulating fields and using `print` statements, you can produce some very useful and impressive looking reports.

5.2.6. awk Statements Versus Lines

Most often, each line in an `awk` program is a separate statement or separate rule, like this:

```
awk '/12/  { print $0 }
     /21/  { print $0 }' BBS-list inventory-shipped
```

However, `gawk` will ignore newlines after any of the following:

```
,    {    ?    :    ||    &&    do    else
```

A newline at any other point is considered the end of the statement. (Splitting lines after `?` and `:` is a minor `gawk` extension. The `?` and `:` referred to here is a three-operand conditional expression.)

If you would like to split a single statement into two lines at a point where a newline would terminate it, you can *continue* it by ending the first line with a backslash character, `\`. The backslash must be the final character on the line to be recognized as a continuation character. This is allowed absolutely anywhere in the statement, even in the middle of a string or regular expression:

```
awk '/This regular expression is too long, so continue it\
 on the next line/ { print $1 }'
```

We have generally not used backslash continuation in the sample programs in this book. Because in `gawk` there is no limit on the length of a line, it is never strictly necessary; it just makes programs more readable. For this same reason, as well as for clarity, we have kept most statements short in the sample programs presented throughout the book. Backslash continuation is most useful when your `awk` program is in a separate source file, instead of typed on the command line. You should also note that many `awk` implementations are more particular about where you may use backslash continuation. For example, they may not allow you to split a string constant using backslash continuation. Thus, for maximal portability of your `awk` programs, it is best not to split your lines in the middle of a regular expression or a string.

Note that backslash continuation does not work as described with the C shell. Continuation with backslash works for awk programs in files and also for one-shot programs, provided you are using a POSIX-compliant shell, such as the Bourne shell or Bash, the GNU Bourne-Again shell. But the C shell (csh) behaves differently! There, you must use two backslashes in a row, followed by a newline. Note also that when using the C shell, every newline in your awk program must be escaped with a backslash:

```
% awk 'BEGIN {\
?   print \\
?        "hello, world" \
? }'
   hello, world
```

Here, the % and ? are the C shell's primary and secondary prompts, analogous to the standard shell's $ and >.

awk is a line-oriented language. Each rule's action has to begin on the same line as the pattern. To have the pattern and action on separate lines, you *must* use backslash continuation; there is no other way.

Note that backslash continuation and comments do not mix. As soon as awk sees the # that starts a comment, it ignores *everything* on the rest of the line:

```
$ gawk 'BEGIN { print "dont panic" # a friendly'\
>                                      BEGIN rule
> }'
        gawk: cmd. line:2:                BEGIN rule
        gawk: cmd. line:2:                ^parse error
```

Here, it looks like the backslash would continue the comment onto the next line. However, the backslash-newline combination is never even noticed because it is hidden inside the comment. Thus, the BEGIN is noted as a syntax error.

When awk statements within one rule are short, you might want to put more than one of them on a line. You do this by separating the statements with a semicolon, ;.

This also applies to the rules themselves. Thus, the previous program could have been written:

```
/12/ { print $0 } ; /21/ { print $0 }
```

> ***Note:*** The requirement that rules on the same line must be separated with a semicolon was not in the original awk language; it was added for consistency with the treatment of statements within an action.

5.2.7. Other Features of awk

The awk language provides a number of predefined, or built-in variables, which your programs can use to get information from awk. There are other variables your program can set to control how awk processes your data.

In addition, awk provides a number of built-in functions for doing common computational and string-related operations.

5.2.8. When to Use awk

You might wonder how awk might be useful for you. Using utility programs, advanced patterns, field separators, arithmetic statements, and other selection criteria, you can produce much more complex output. The awk language is very useful for producing reports from large amounts of raw data, such as summarizing information from the output of other utility programs like ls. (See section 5.2.5.)

Programs written with awk are usually much smaller than they would be in other languages. This makes awk programs easy to compose and use. Often, awk programs can be quickly composed at your terminal, used once, and thrown away. Because awk programs are interpreted, you can avoid the (usually lengthy) compilation part of the typical edit-compile-test-debug cycle of software development.

Complex programs have been written in awk, including a complete retargetable assembler for eight-bit microprocessors and a microcode assembler for a special purpose Prolog computer. However, awk's capabilities are strained by tasks of such complexity.

If you find yourself writing awk scripts of more than, say, a few hundred lines, you might consider using a different programming language. Emacs Lisp is a good choice if you need sophisticated string or pattern-matching capabilities. The shell is also good at string and pattern matching; in addition, it allows powerful use of the system utilities. More conventional languages, such as C, C++, and Lisp, offer better facilities for system programming and for managing the complexity of large programs. Programs in these languages may require more lines of source code than the equivalent awk programs, but they are easier to maintain and usually run more efficiently.

5.3. Useful One-Line Programs

Many useful awk programs are short, just a line or two. Here is a collection of useful, short programs to get you started. Some of these programs contain constructs that haven't been covered yet. The description of the program will give you a good idea of what is going on.

Most of the examples use a data file named data. This is just a placeholder; if you were to use these programs yourself, you would substitute your own file names for data.

This program prints the length of the longest input line:

```
awk '{ if (length ($0) > max) max = length($0) }
     END { print max }' data
```

This program prints every line that is longer than 80 characters:

```
awk 'length ($0) > 80' data
```

The sole rule has a relational expression as its pattern and has no action (so the default action, printing the record, is used).

This program prints the length of the longest line in data:

```
expand data | awk '{ if (x < length()) x = length() }
                  END { print "maximum line length is " x }'
```

The input is processed by the expand program to change tabs into spaces, so the widths compared are actually the right-margin columns.

This program prints every line that has at least one field:

```
awk 'NF > 0' data
```

This is an easy way to delete blank lines from a file (or rather, to create a new file similar to the old file but from which the blank lines have been deleted).

This program prints seven random numbers from zero to 100, inclusive:

```
awk 'BEGIN { for (i = 1; i <= 7; i++)
               print int(101 * rand()) }'
```

This program prints the total number of bytes used by *files*:

```
ls -lg files | awk '{ x += 5 } ; END { print "total bytes: " x }'
```

This program prints the total number of kilobytes used by *files*:

```
ls -lg files | awk '{ x+=$5 }
                    END { print "total K-bytes: " (x + 1023)/1024 }'
```

This program prints a sorted list of the login names of all users:

```
awk -F: '{ print $1 }' /etc/passwd | sort
```

This program counts lines in a file:

```
awk 'END { print NR }; data
```

This program prints the even-numbered lines in the data file. If you were to use the expression `NR %2 == 1` instead, it would print the odd-numbered lines:

```
awk 'NR % 2 == 0' data
```

5.4. Regular Expressions

A regular expression, or regexp, is a way of describing a set of strings. Because regular expressions are such a fundamental part of `awk` programming, their format and use deserve a separate section.

A regular expression enclosed in slashes (`/`) is an `awk` pattern that matches every input record whose text belongs to that set.

The simplest regular expression is a sequence of letters, numbers, or both. Such a regexp matches any string that contains that sequence. Thus, the regexp `foo` matches any string containing `foo`. Therefore, the pattern `/foo/` matches any input record containing the three characters `foo`, anywhere in the record. Other kinds of regexps let you specify more complicated classes of strings.

Initially, the examples will be simple. As we explain more about how regular expressions work, we will present more complicated examples.

5.4.1. How to Use Regular Expressions

A regular expression can be used as a pattern by enclosing it in slashes. Then the regular expression is tested against the entire text of each record. (Normally, it only needs to match some part of the text in order to succeed.) For example, this prints the second field of each record that contains the three characters `foo` anywhere in it:

```
$ awk '/foo/ { print $2 }' BBS-list
  555-1234
  555-6699
  555-6480
  555-2127
```

Regular expressions can also be used in matching expressions. These expressions allow you to specify the string to match against; it need not be the entire current input record. The two operators `~` and `!~` perform regular expression comparisons. Expressions using these operators can be used as patterns or in `if`, `while`, `for`, and `do` statements:

- *`exp ~ /regexp/`*—This is true if the expression *`exp`* (taken as a string) is matched by *`regexp`*. The following example matches, or selects, all input records with the uppercase letter `J` somewhere in the first field:

  ```
  $ awk '$1 ~ /J/' inventory-shipped
    Jan 13 25 15 115
    Jun 31 42 75 492
    Jul 24 34 67 436
    Jan 21 36 64 620
  ```

  So does this:

  ```
  awk '{ if ($1 ~ /J/) print }' inventory-shipped
  ```

- *`exp !~ /regexp/`*—This is true if the expression *`exp`* (taken as a character string) is not matched by *`regexp`*. The following example matches, or selects, all input records whose first field does not contain the uppercase letter `J`:

  ```
  $ awk '{ $1 !~  /J/' inventory-shipped
    Feb  15  32  24 226
    Mar  15  24  34 228
    Apr  31  52  63 420
    May  16  34  29 208
  ...
  ```

When a regexp is written enclosed in slashes, like `/foo/`, we call it a regexp constant, much like `5.27` is a numeric constant and `"foo"` is a string constant.

5.4.2. Escape Sequences

Some characters cannot be included literally in string constants (`"foo"`) or regexp constants (`/foo/`). You represent them instead with *escape* sequences, which are character sequences beginning with a backslash (`\`).

One use of an escape sequence is to include a double-quote character in a string constant. Because a plain double quote would end the string, you must use `\"` to represent an actual double-quote character as a part of the string:

```
$ awk 'BEGIN { print "He said \"hi!\" to her." }'
    He said "hi!" to her.
```

The backslash character itself is another character that cannot be included normally; you write `\\` to put one backslash in the string or regexp. Thus, the string whose contents are the two characters `"` and `\` must be written `"\"\\"`.

Another use of backslash is to represent unprintable characters such as tab or newline. Although there is nothing to stop you from entering most unprintable characters directly in a string constant or regexp constant, they may look ugly.

Here is a list of all the escape sequences used in `awk` and what they represent. Unless noted otherwise, all of these escape sequences apply to both string constants and regexp constants:

`\\`	A literal backslash, `\`.
`\a`	The "alert" character, Ctrl+G, ASCII code 7 (BEL).
`\b`	Backspace, Ctrl+H, ASCII code 8 (BS).
`\f`	Formfeed, Ctrl+L, ASCII code 12 (FF).
`\n`	Newline, Ctrl+J, ASCII code 10 (LF).
`\r`	Carriage return, Ctrl+M, ASCII code 13 (CR).
`\t`	Horizontal tab, Ctrl+I, ASCII code 9 (HT).
`\v`	Vertical tab, Ctrl+K, ASCII code 11 (VT).
`\`*nnn*	The octal value *nnn*, where *nnn* is one to three digits between `0` and `7`. For example, the code for the ASCII ESC (escape) character is `033`.
`\x`*hh*...	The hexadecimal value *hh*, where *hh* is hexadecimal digits (`0` through `9` and either `A` through `F` or `a` through `f`). Like the same construct in ANSI C, the escape sequence continues until the first nonhexadecimal digit is seen. However, using more than two hexadecimal digits produces undefined results. (The `\x` escape sequence is not allowed in POSIX `awk`.)
`\/`	A literal slash (necessary for regexp constants only). You use this when you want to write a regexp constant that contains a slash. Because the regexp is delimited by slashes, you need to escape the slash that is part of the pattern, in order to tell awk to keep processing the rest of the regexp.

`\"` A literal double quote (necessary for string constants only). You use this when you want to write a string constant that contains a double quote. Because the string is delimited by double quotes, you need to escape the quote that is part of the string, in order to tell `awk` to keep processing the rest of the string.

In `gawk`, two additional character sequences that begin with backslash have special meaning in regexps. See section 5.4.4 gawk.

In a string constant, what happens if you place a backslash before something that is not one of the characters in the list? POSIX `awk` purposely leaves this case undefined. There are two choices:

- Strip the backslash out. This is what UNIX `awk` and `gawk` both do. For example, `a\qc` is the same as `aqc`.
- Leave the backslash alone. Some other `awk` implementations do this. In such implementations, `a\qc` is the same as if you had typed `a\\qc`.

In a regexp, a backslash before any character that is not in the list, and not listed in section 5.4.4, means that the next character should be taken literally, even if it would normally be a regexp operator. For example, `/a\+b/` matches the three characters `a+b`.

For complete portability, do not use a backslash before any character not listed.

Another interesting question arises. Suppose you use an octal or hexadecimal escape to represent a regexp metacharacter (see section 5.4.3). Does `awk` treat the character as a literal character or as a regexp operator?

It turns out that historically, such characters were taken literally. However, the POSIX standard indicates that they should be treated as real metacharacters, and this is what `gawk` does. However, in compatibility mode, `gawk` treats the characters represented by octal and hexadecimal escape sequences literally when used in regexp constants. Thus, `/a\52b/` is equivalent to `/a\*b/`.

To summarize:

- The escape sequences in the list are always processed first for both string constants and regexp constants. This happens very early, as soon as `awk` reads your program.

- gawk processes both regexp constants and dynamic regexps (see sections 5.4.7 and 5.4.4).
- A backslash before any other character means to treat that character literally.

5.4.3. Regular Expression Operators

You can combine regular expressions with the following characters, called regular expression operators, or metacharacters, to increase the power and versatility of regular expressions.

The escape sequences described in section 5.4.2 are valid inside a regexp. They are introduced by a \. They are recognized and converted into the corresponding real characters as the very first step in processing regexps.

Here is a list of metacharacters. All characters that are not escape sequences and that are not listed stand for themselves:

- \—This is used to suppress the special meaning of a character when matching. For example, \$ matches the character $.
- ^—This matches the beginning of a string. For example, ^@chapter matches the '^@chapter' at the beginning of a string and can be used to identify chapter beginnings in Texinfo source files. The ^ is known as an anchor because it anchors the pattern to match only at the beginning of the string.

  It is important to realize that ^ does not match the beginning of a line embedded in a string. In this example, the condition is not true:

  ```
  if ("line1\nLINE 2"   /^L/) ...
  ```

- $—This is similar to ^, but it matches only at the end of a string. For example, p$ matches a record that ends with a p. The $ is also an anchor and also does not match the end of a line embedded in a string. In this example, the condition is not true:

  ```
  if ("line1\nLINE 2" ~ /1$/) ...
  ```

- .—The period, or dot, matches any single character, including the newline character. For example, .P matches any single character followed by a P in a string. Using concatenation, we can make a regular expression like U.A, which matches any three-character sequence that begins with U and ends with A.

In strict POSIX mode, . does not match the NUL character, which is a character. Other versions of awk may not be able to match the NUL character.

- [...]—This is called a *character list*. It matches any one of the characters that are enclosed in the square brackets. For example, [MVX] matches any one of the characters M, V, or X in a string.

  Ranges of characters are indicated by using a hyphen between the beginning and ending characters and enclosing the whole thing in brackets. For example, [0-9] matches any digit. Multiple ranges are allowed. For example, the list [A-Za-z0-9] is a common way to express the idea of "all alphanumeric characters."

  To include one of the characters \,], -, or ^ in a character list, put a \ in front of it. For example, [d\]] matches either d or].

  This treatment of \ in character lists is compatible with other awk implementations and is also mandated by POSIX. The regular expressions in awk are a superset of the POSIX specification for Extended Regular Expressions (EREs). POSIX EREs are based on the regular expressions accepted by the traditional egrep utility.

  Character classes are a new feature introduced in the POSIX standard. A character class is a special notation for describing lists of characters that have a specific attribute, but where the actual characters themselves can vary from country to country or from character set to character set. For example, the notion of what is an alphabetic character differs in the USA and in France.

  A character class is only valid in a regexp inside the brackets of a character list. Character classes consist of [:, a keyword denoting the class, and :]. Here are the character classes defined by the POSIX standard:

[:alnum:]	Alphanumeric characters.
[:alpha:]	Alphabetic characters.
[:blank:]	Space and tab characters.
[:cntrl:]	Control characters.
[:digit:]	Numeric characters.
[:graph:]	Characters that are printable and are also visible. (A space is printable but not visible, whereas an a is both.)
[:lower:]	Lowercase alphabetic characters.

`[:print:]`	Printable characters (characters that are not control characters).
`[:punct:]`	Punctuation characters (characters that are not letter, digits, control characters, or space characters).
`[:space:]`	Space characters (such as space, tab, and formfeed, to name a few).
`[:upper:]`	Uppercase alphabetic characters.
`[:xdigit:]`	Characters that are hexadecimal digits.

For example, before the POSIX standard, to match alphanumeric characters, you had to write `/[A-Za-z0-9]/`. If your character set had other alphabetic characters in it, this would not match them. With the POSIX character classes, you can write `/[[:alnum:]]/`, and this will match all the alphabetic and numeric characters in your character set.

Two additional special sequences can appear in character lists. These apply to non-ASCII character sets, which can have single symbols (called *collating elements*) that are represented with more than one character, as well as several characters that are equivalent for collating, or sorting, purposes. (For example, in French, a plain "e" and a grave-accented "è" are equivalent.)

Collating symbols	A collating symbol is a multicharacter collating element enclosed in `[.` and `.]`. For example, if `ch` is a collating element, then `[[.ch.]]` is a regexp that matches this collating element, whereas `[ch]` is a regexp that matches either `c` or `h`.
Equivalence classes	An equivalence class is a locale-specific name for a list of characters that are equivalent. The name is enclosed in `[=` and `=]`. For example, the name `e` might be used to represent all of `e`, `è`, and `è`. In this case, `[[=e]]` is a regexp that matches any of `e`, `è`, or `è`.

These features are very valuable in non-English speaking locales.

Caution: The library functions that `gawk` uses for regular expression matching currently only recognize POSIX character classes; they do not recognize collating symbols or equivalence classes.

- [^ ...]—This is a complemented character list. The first character after the [must be a ^. It matches any characters except those in the square brackets. For example, [^0-9] matches any character that is not a digit.

- |—This is the alternation operator, and it is used to specify alternatives. For example, ^P|[0-9] matches any string that matches either ^P or [0-9]. This means it matches any string that starts with P or contains a digit.

  The alternation applies to the largest possible regexps on either side. In other words, | has the lowest precedence of all the regular expression operators.

- (...)—Parentheses are used for grouping in regular expressions as in arithmetic. They can be used to concatenate regular expressions containing the alternation operator, |. For example, @(samp|code)\{[^}]+\} matches both @code{foo} and @samp{bar}. (These are Texinfo formatting control sequences.)

- *—This symbol means that the preceding regular expression is to be repeated as many times as necessary to find a match. For example, ph* applies the * symbol to the preceding h and looks for matches of one p followed by any number of hs. This will also match just p if no hs are present.

  The * repeats the smallest possible preceding expression. (Use parentheses if you want to repeat a larger expression.) It finds as many repetitions as possible:

  ```
  awk '/\(c[ad][ad]*r x\)/ { print }' sample
  ```

  prints every record in sample containing a string of the form (car x), (cdr x), (cadr x), and so on. Notice the escaping of the parentheses by preceding them with backslashes.

- +—This symbol is similar to *, but the preceding expression must be matched at least once. This means that wh+y would match why and whhy but not wy, whereas wh*y would match all three of these strings. This is a simpler way of writing the last * example:

  ```
  awk '/\(c[ad]+r x\)/ { print }' sample
  ```

- ?—This symbol is similar to *, but the preceding expression can be matched either once or not at all. For example, fe?d will match fed and fd, but nothing else.

- `{n}`, `{n,}`, and `{n,m}`—One or two numbers inside braces denote an *interval expression*. If there is one number in the braces, the preceding regexp is repeated `n` times. If there are two numbers separated by a comma, the preceding regexp is repeated `n` to `m` times. If there is one number followed by a comma, then the preceding regexp is repeated at least `n` times:

`wh{3}y`	Matches `whhhy` but not `why` or `whhhhy`.
`wh{3,5}y`	Matches `whhhy` or `whhhhy` or `whhhhhy`, only.
`wh{2,}y`	Matches `whhy` or `whhhy`, and so on.

  Interval expressions were not traditionally available in `awk`. As part of the POSIX standard, they were added to make `awk` and egrep consistent with each other.

  However, because old programs may use `{` and `}` in regexp constants, by default `gawk` does not match interval expressions in regexps. If either `--posix` or `--re-interval` are specified, then interval expressions are allowed in regexps.

In regular expressions, the `*`, `+`, and `?` operators, as well as the braces `{` and `}`, have the highest precedence, followed by concatenation and finally by `|`. As in arithmetic, parentheses can change how operators are grouped.

If `gawk` is in compatibility mode, character classes and interval expressions are not available in regular expressions.

The next section discusses the GNU-specific regexp operators and provides more detail concerning how command-line options affect the way `gawk` interprets the characters in regular expressions.

5.4.4. Additional Regexp Operators Only in gawk

GNU software that deals with regular expressions provides a number of additional regexp operators. These operators are described in this section and are specific to `gawk`; they are not available in other `awk` implementations.

Most of the additional operators are for dealing with word matching. For our purposes, a word is a sequence of one or more letters, digits, or underscores (_):

- `\w`—This operator matches any word-constituent character—that is, any letter, digit, or underscore. Think of it as a shorthand for `[[:alnum:]_]`.

- \W—This operator matches any character that is not word-constituent. Think of it as a shorthand for [^[:alnum:]_].
- \<—This operator matches the empty string at the beginning of a word. For example, /\<away/ matches away but not stowaway.
- \>—This operator matches the empty string at the end of a word. For example, /stow\>/ matches stow but not stowaway.
- \y—This operator matches the empty string at either the beginning or the end of a word (the word boundary). For example, \yballs?\y matches either ball or balls as a separate word.
- \B—This operator matches the empty string within a word. In other words, \B matches the empty string that occurs between two word-constituent characters. For example, /\Brat\B/ matches crate, but it does not match dirty rat. \B is essentially the opposite of \y.

There are two other operators that work on buffers. In Emacs, a buffer is, naturally, an Emacs buffer. For other programs, the regexp library routines that gawk uses consider the entire string to be matched as the buffer.

For awk, because ^ and $ always work in terms of the beginning and end of strings, these operators don't add any new capabilities. They are provided for compatibility with other GNU software:

- \`—This operator matches the empty string at the beginning of the buffer.
- \'—This operator matches the empty string at the end of the buffer.

In other GNU software, the word boundary operator is \b. However, that conflicts with the awk language's definition of \b as backspace, so gawk uses a different letter.

An alternative method would have been to require two backslashes in the GNU operators, but this was deemed to be too confusing, and the current method of using \y for the GNU \b appears to be the lesser of two evils.

The various command-line options control how gawk interprets characters in regexps:

- No options—In the default case, gawk provide all the facilities of POSIX regexps and the GNU regexp operators described previously. However, interval expressions are not supported.

- `--posix`—Only POSIX regexps are supported, the GNU operators are not special (e.g., `\w` matches a literal `w`). Interval expressions are allowed.
- `--traditional`—Traditional UNIX `awk` regexps are matched. The GNU operators are not special, interval expressions are not available—and neither are the POSIX character classes (`[[:alnum:]]` and so on). Characters described by octal and hexadecimal escape sequences are treated literally, even if they represent regexp metacharacters.
- `--re-interval`—Allow interval expressions in regexps, even if `--traditional` has been provided.

5.4.5. Case Sensitivity in Matching

Case is normally significant in regular expressions, both when matching ordinary characters (i.e., not metacharacters) and inside character sets. Thus a `w` in a regular expression matches only a lowercase `w` and not an uppercase `W`.

The simplest way to do a case-independent match is to use a character list: `[Ww]`. However, this can be cumbersome if you need to use it often, and it can make the regular expressions harder to read. There are two alternatives that you might prefer.

One way to do a case-insensitive match at a particular point in the program is to convert the data to a single case, using the `tolower` or `toupper` built-in string functions (which we haven't discussed yet):

```
tolower($1) ~ /foo/ { ... }
```

converts the first field to lowercase before matching against it. This will work in any POSIX-compliant implementation of `awk`.

Another method, specific to `gawk`, is to set the variable `IGNORECASE` to a non-zero value. When `IGNORECASE` is not zero, all regexp and string operations ignore case. Changing the value of `IGNORECASE` dynamically controls the case sensitivity of your program as it runs. Case is significant by default because `IGNORECASE` (like most variables) is initialized to zero:

```
x = "aB"
if (x ~ /ab/) ...   # this test will fail

IGNORECASE = 1
if (x ~ /ab/) ...   # now it will succeed
```

In general, you cannot use IGNORECASE to make certain rules case insensitive and other rules case sensitive because there is no way to set IGNORECASE just for the pattern of a particular rule.

To do this, you must use character lists or tolower. However, one thing you can do only with IGNORECASE is turn case sensitivity on or off dynamically for all the rules at once.

IGNORECASE can be set on the command line or in a BEGIN rule. Setting IGNORECASE from the command line is a way to make a program case insensitive without having to edit it.

Prior to Version 3.0 of gawk, the value of IGNORECASE only affected regexp operations. It did not affect string comparison with ==, !=, and so on. Beginning with Version 3.0, both regexp and string comparison operations are affected by IGNORECASE.

Beginning with Version 3.0 of gawk, the equivalences between uppercase and lowercase characters are based on the ISO-8859-1 (ISO Latin-1) character set. This character set is a superset of the traditional 128 ASCII characters, which also provides a number of characters suitable for use with European languages.

The value of IGNORECASE has no effect if gawk is in compatibility mode. Case is always significant in compatibility mode.

5.4.6. How Much Text Matches?

Consider the following example:

```
echo aaaabcd | awk '{ sub(/a+/, "<A>"); print }'
```

This example uses the sub function to make a change to the input record. Here, the regexp /a+/ indicates "one or more a characters," and the replacement text is <A>.

The input contains four a characters. What will the output be? In other words, how many is "one or more"; will awk match two, three, or all four a characters?

The answer is, awk (and POSIX) regular expressions always match the leftmost, longest sequence of input characters that can match. Thus, in this example, all four a characters are replaced with <A>:

```
$ echo aaaabcd | awk '{ sub(/a+/, "<A>"); print }'
    <A>bcd
```

For simple match/no-match tests, this is not so important. But when doing regexp-based field and record splitting, and text matching and substitutions with the `match`, `sub`, `gsub`, and `gensub` functions, it is very important. Understanding this principle is also important for regexp-based record and field splitting.

5.4.7. Using Dynamic Regexps

The right-hand side of a `~` or `!~` operator need not be a regexp constant (i.e., a string of characters between slashes). It may be any expression. The expression is evaluated and converted if necessary to a string; the contents of the string are used as the regexp. A regexp that is computed in this way is called a *dynamic regexp*:

```
BEGIN { identifier_regexp = "[A-Za-z_][A-Za-z_0-9]+" }
$0 ~ identifier_regexp    { print }
```

sets `identifier_regexp` to a regexp that describes `awk` variable names and tests if the input record matches this regexp.

> ***Note:*** When using the `~` and `!` operators, there is a difference between a regexp constant enclosed in slashes and a string constant enclosed in double quotes. If you are going to use a string constant, you have to understand that the string is in essence scanned twice: the first time when `awk` reads your program and the second time when it goes to match the string on the left-hand side of the operator with the pattern on the right. This is true of any string-valued expression (such as `identifier_regexp`), not just string constants.

What difference does it make if the string is scanned twice? The answer has to do with escape sequences and particularly with backslashes. To get a backslash into a regular expression inside a string, you have to type two backslashes.

For example, `/\*/` is a regexp constant for a literal `*`. Only one backslash is needed. To do the same thing with a string, you would have to type `"\\*"`. The first backslash escapes the second one so that the string actually contains the two characters `\` and `*`.

Given that you can use both regexp and string constants to describe regular expressions, which should you use? The answer is "regexp constants" for several reasons:

- String constants are more complicated to write and more difficult to read. Using regexp constants makes your programs less error-prone. Not understanding the difference between the two kinds of constants is a common source of errors.

- It is also more efficient to use regexp constants: awk can note that you have supplied a regexp and store it internally in a form that makes pattern matching more efficient. When using a string constant, awk must first convert the string into this internal form and then perform the pattern matching.
- Using regexp constants is better style; it shows clearly that you intend a regexp match.

5.5. gawk Summary

This section provides a brief summary of the gawk command line and the awk language. It is designed to serve as quick reference. It is therefore terse but complete.

5.5.1. Command-Line Options Summary

The command line consists of options to gawk itself, the awk program text (if not supplied via the -f option), and values to be made available in the ARGC and ARGV predefined awk variables:

```
gawk [POSIX or GNU style options] -f source-file [--] file ...
gawk [POSIX or GNU style options] [--] 'program' file ...
```

The options that gawk accepts are

`-F fs`
`--field-separator fs`
: Use *fs* for the input field separator (the value of the FS predefined variable).

`-f program-file`
`--file program-file`
: Read the awk program source from the file *program-file*, instead of from the first command-line argument.

`-mf NNN`
`-mr NNN`
: The f flag sets the maximum number of fields, and the r flag sets the maximum record size. These options are ignored by gawk because gawk has no predefined limits; they are only for compatibility with the Bell Labs research version of UNIX awk.

`-v var=val`
`--assign var=val`
: Assign the variable *var* the value *val* before program execution begins.

`-W traditional`

`-W compat`

`--traditional`

`--compat` Use compatibility mode, in which `gawk` extensions are turned off.

`-W copyleft`

`-W copyright`

`--copyleft`

`--copyright` Print the short version of the General Public License on the standard output and exit. This option may disappear in a future version of `gawk`.

`-W help`

`-W usage`

`--help`

`--usage` Print a relatively short summary of the available options on the standard output and exit.

`-W lint`

`--lint` Give warnings about dubious or non-portable `awk` constructs.

`-W lint-old`

`--lint-old` Warn about constructs that are not available in the original Version 7 UNIX version of `awk`.

`-W posix`

`--posix` Use POSIX compatibility mode, in which `gawk` extensions are turned off and additional restrictions apply.

`-W re-interval`

`--re-interval` Allow interval expressions (see section 5.4.3), in regexps.

`-W source=`*`program-text`*

`--source` *`program-text`* Use *`program-text`* as `awk` program source code. This option allows mixing command-line source code with source code from files and is particularly useful for mixing command-line programs with library functions.

`-W version`

`--version` Print version information for this particular copy of `gawk` on the error output.

`--` Signal the end of options. This is useful to allow further arguments to the `awk` program itself to start with a `-`. This is mainly for consistency with POSIX argument-parsing conventions.

Any other options are flagged as invalid but are otherwise ignored.

5.5.2. Language Summary

An `awk` program consists of a sequence of zero or more pattern-action statements and optional function definitions. One or the other of the pattern and action may be omitted.

```
pattern     { action statements }
pattern
            { action statements }

function name(parameter list)      { action statements }
```

`gawk` first reads the program source from the *`program-file(s)`*, if specified, or from the first non-option argument on the command line. The `-f` option may be used multiple times on the command line. `gawk` reads the program text from all the *`program-file`* files, effectively concatenating them in the order they are specified. This is useful for building libraries of `awk` functions, without having to include them in each new `awk` program that uses them. To use a library function in a file from a program typed in on the command line, specify `--source 'program'`, and type your program in between the single quotes.

The environment variable `AWKPATH` specifies a search path to use when finding source files named with the `-f` option. The default path, which is `.:/usr/local/share/awk`,[6] is used if `AWKPATH` is not set. If a file name given to the `-f` option contains a `/` character, no path search is performed.

`gawk` compiles the program into an internal form and then proceeds to read each file named in the `ARGV` array. The initial values of `ARGV` come from the command-line arguments. If there are no files named on the command line, `gawk` reads the standard input.

[6]The path may use a directory other than `/usr/local/share/awk`, depending upon how `gawk` was built and installed.

If a file named on the command line has the form `var=val`, it is treated as a variable assignment: The variable `var` is assigned the value `val`. If any of the files have a value that is the null string, that element in the list is skipped.

For each record in the input, `gawk` tests to see if it matches any `pattern` in the `awk` program. For each pattern that the record matches, the associated `action` is executed.

5.5.3. Variables and Fields

`awk` variables are not declared; they come into existence when they are first used. Their values are either floating-point numbers or strings. `awk` also has one-dimensional arrays; multiple-dimensional arrays may be simulated. There are several predefined variables that `awk` sets as a program runs; these are summarized in the following sections.

5.5.3.1. Fields

As each input line is read, `gawk` splits the line into fields, using the value of the `FS` variable as the field separator. If `FS` is a single character, fields are separated by that character. Otherwise, `FS` is expected to be a full regular expression. In the special case that `FS` is a single space, fields are separated by runs of spaces, tabs, or newlines.[7] If `FS` is the null string (`""`), then each individual character in the record becomes a separate field. Note that the value of `IGNORECASE` (see section 5.4.5) also affects how fields are split when `FS` is a regular expression.

Each field in the input line may be referenced by its position, `$1`, `$2`, and so on. `$0` is the whole line. The value of a field may be assigned to as well. Field numbers need not be constants:

```
n=5
print $n
```

prints the fifth field in the input line. The variable `NF` is set to the total number of fields in the input line.

References to non-existent fields (i.e., fields after `$NF`) return the null string. However, assigning to a non-existent field (e.g., `$(NF+2) = 5`) increases the value of `NF`, creates any intervening fields with the null string as their value, and causes the value of `$0` to be recomputed, with the fields being separated by the value of `OFS`. Decrementing `NF` causes the

[7]In POSIX `awk`, newline does not separate fields.

values of fields past the new value to be lost and the value of `$0` to be recomputed, with the fields being separated by the value of `OFS`.

5.5.3.2. Built-in Variables

`gawk`'s built-in variables are

`ARGC`	The number of elements in `ARGV`. See `ARGV` later in this table for what is actually included in `ARGV`.
`ARGIND`	The index in `ARGV` of the current file being processed. When `gawk` is processing the input data files, it is always true that `'FILENAME == ARGV[ARGIND]'`.
`ARGV`	The array of command-line arguments. The array is indexed from zero to `ARGC - 1`. Dynamically changing `ARGC` and the contents of `ARGV` can control the files used for data. A null-valued element in `ARGV` is ignored. `ARGV` does not include the options to `awk` or the text of the `awk` program itself.
`CONVFMT`	The conversion format to use when converting numbers to strings.
`FIELDWIDTHS`	A space-separated list of numbers describing the fixed-width input data.
`ENVIRON`	An array of environment variable values. The array is indexed by variable name, each element being the value of that variable. Thus, the environment variable `HOME` is `ENVIRON["HOME"]`. One possible value might be `/home/arnold`. Changing this array does not affect the environment seen by programs that `gawk` spawns via redirection or the `system` function. (This may change in a future version of `gawk`.) Some operating systems do not have environment variables. The `ENVIRON` array is empty when running on these systems.
`ERRNO`	The system error message when an error occurs using `getline` or `close`.
`FILENAME`	The name of the current input file. If no files are specified on the command line, the value of `FILENAME` is the null string.
`FNR`	The input record number in the current input file.
`FS`	The input field separator, a space by default.

`IGNORECASE`	The case-sensitivity flag for string comparisons and regular expression operations. If `IGNORECASE` has a nonzero value, then pattern matching in rules, record separating with `RS`, field splitting with `FS`, regular expression matching with `'~'` and `!~`, and the `gensub`, `gsub`, `index`, `match`, `split`, and `sub` built-in functions all ignore case when doing regular expression operations, and all string comparisons are done ignoring case. The value of `IGNORECASE` does not affect array subscripting.
`NF`	The number of fields in the current input record.
`NR`	The total number of input records seen so far.
`OFMT`	The output format for numbers for the `print` statement, `"%.6g"` by default.
`OFS`	The output field separator, a space by default.
`ORS`	The output record separator, by default a newline.
`RS`	The input record separator, by default a newline. If `RS` is set to the null string, then records are separated by blank lines. When `RS` is set to the null string, then the newline character always acts as a field separator, in addition to whatever value `FS` may have. If `RS` is set to a multicharacter string, it denotes a regexp; input text matching the regexp separates records.
`RT`	The input text that matched the text denoted by `RS`, the record separator.
`RSTART`	The index of the first character last matched by `match`; zero if no match.
`RLENGTH`	The length of the string last matched by `match`; `-1` if no match.
`SUBSEP`	The string used to separate multiple subscripts in array elements, by default `"\034"`.

5.5.3.3. Arrays

Arrays are subscripted with an expression between square brackets (`[` and `]`). Array subscripts are always strings; numbers are converted to strings as necessary, following the standard conversion rules.

If you use multiple expressions separated by commas inside the square brackets, then the array subscript is a string consisting of the concatenation of the individual subscript values, converted to strings, separated by the subscript separator (the value of `SUBSEP`).

The special operator `in` may be used in a conditional context to see if an array has an index consisting of a particular value:

```
if (val in array)
        print array[val]
```

If the array has multiple subscripts, use `(i, j, ...) in array` to test for existence of an element.

The `in` construct may also be used in a `for` loop to iterate over all the elements of an array.

You can remove an element from an array using the `delete` statement.

You can clear an entire array using `delete` *`array`*.

5.5.3.4. Data Types

The value of an `awk` expression is always either a number or a string.

Some contexts (such as arithmetic operators) require numeric values. They convert strings to numbers by interpreting the text of the string as a number. If the string does not look like a number, it converts to zero.

Other contexts (such as concatenation) require string values. They convert numbers to strings by effectively printing them with `sprintf`.

To force conversion of a string value to a number, simply add zero to it. If the value you start with is already a number, this does not change it.

To force conversion of a numeric value to a string, concatenate it with the null string.

Comparisons are done numerically if both operands are numeric or if one is numeric and the other is a numeric string. Otherwise one or both operands are converted to strings and a string comparison is performed. Fields, `getline` input, `FILENAME`, `ARGV` elements, `ENVIRON` elements, and the elements of an array created by `split` are the only items that can be numeric strings. String constants such as `"3.1415927"` are not numeric strings; they are string constants.

Uninitialized variables have the string value `""` (the null, or empty, string). In contexts where a number is required, this is equivalent to zero.

5.5.4. Patterns

An `awk` program is mostly composed of rules, each consisting of a pattern followed by an action. The action is enclosed in `{` and `}`. Either the pattern may be missing, or the action may be missing, but not both. If the pattern is missing, the action is executed for every input record. A missing action is equivalent to `{ print }`, which prints the entire line.

Comments begin with the `#` character and continue until the end of the line. Blank lines may be used to separate statements. Statements normally end with a newline; however, this is not the case for lines ending in a `,`, `{`, `?`, `:`, `&&`, or `||`. Lines ending in `do` or `else` also have their statements automatically continued on the following line. In other cases, a line can be continued by ending it with a `\`, in which case the newline is ignored.

Multiple statements may be put on one line by separating each one with a `;`. This applies to both the statements within the action part of a rule (the usual case) and to the rule statements.

See section 5.2.2.5 for information on awk's commenting convention; see section 5.2.6 for a description of the line-continuation mechanism in awk.

5.5.4.1. Pattern Summary

awk patterns may be one of the following:

```
/regular expression/
relational expression
pattern && pattern
pattern || pattern
pattern ? pattern : pattern
(pattern)
! pattern
pattern1, pattern2
BEGIN
END
```

`BEGIN` and `END` are two special kinds of patterns that are not tested against the input. The action parts of all `BEGIN` rules are concatenated as if all the statements had been written in a single `BEGIN` rule. They are executed before any of the input is read. Similarly, all the `END` rules are concatenated and executed when all the input is exhausted (or when an `exit` statement is executed). `BEGIN` and `END` patterns cannot be combined with other patterns in pattern expressions. `BEGIN` and `END` rules cannot have missing action parts.

For */regular-expression/* patterns, the associated statement is executed for each input record that matches the regular expression. Regular expressions are summarized later in this section.

A *relational* expression may use any of the operators defined later in the section on actions. These generally test whether certain fields match certain regular expressions.

The `&&`, `||`, and `!` operators are logical "and," logical "or," and logical "not," respectively, as in C. They do short-circuit evaluation, also as in C, and are used for combining more primitive pattern expressions. As in most languages, parentheses may be used to change the order of evaluation.

The `?:` operator is like the same operator in C. If the first pattern matches, then the second pattern is matched against the input record; otherwise, the third is matched. Only one of the second and third patterns is matched.

The *`pattern1`*`,` *`pattern2`* form of a pattern is called a range pattern. It matches all input lines starting with a line that matches *`pattern1`* and continuing until a line that matches *`pattern2`*, inclusive. A range pattern cannot be used as an operand of any of the pattern operators.

5.5.4.2. Regular Expressions

Regular expressions are based on POSIX EREs (extended regular expressions). The escape sequences allowed in string constants are also valid in regular expressions (see section 5.4.2). Regexps are composed of characters as follows:

`c`	Matches the character *`c`* (assuming *`c`* is none of the characters in this list).
`\`*`c`*	Matches the literal character *`c`*.
`.`	Matches any character, *including* newline. In strict POSIX mode, . does not match the `NUL` character, which is a character with all bits equal to zero.
`^`	Matches the beginning of a string.
`$`	Matches the end of a string.
`[`*`abc...`*`]`	Matches any of the characters *`abc...`* (character list).
`[[:`*`class`*`:]]`	Matches any character in the character class. Allowable classes are `alnum`, `alpha`, `blank`, `cntrl`, `digit`, `graph`, `lower`, `print`, `punct`, `space`, `upper`, and `xdigit`.
`[[.`*`symbol`*`.]]`	Matches the multicharacter collating symbol *`symbol`*. `gawk` does not currently support collating symbols.
`[[=`*`classname`*`=]]`	Matches any of the equivalent characters in the current locale named by the equivalence class *`classname`*. `gawk` does not currently support equivalence classes.

`[^abc...]`	Matches any character except `abc...` (negated character list).
`r1|r2`	Matches either `r1` or `r2` (alternation).
`r1r2`	Matches `r1` and then `r2` (concatenation).
`r+`	Matches one or more `r`s.
`r*`	Matches zero or more `r`s.
`r?`	Matches zero or one `r`s.
`(r)`	Matches `r` (grouping).
`r{n}`, `r{n,}`, `r{n,m}`	Matches at least `n`, `n` to any number, or `n` to `m` occurrences of `r` (interval expressions).
`\y`	Matches the empty string at either the beginning or the end of a word.
`\B`	Matches the empty string within a word.
`\<`	Matches the empty string at the beginning of a word.
`\>`	Matches the empty string at the end of a word.
`\w`	Matches any word-constituent character (alphanumeric characters and the underscore).
`\W`	Matches any character that is not word-constituent.
``\` ``	Matches the empty string at the beginning of a buffer (same as a string in `gawk`).
`\'`	Matches the empty string at the end of a buffer.

The various command-line options control how `gawk` interprets characters in regexps:

No options	In the default case, `gawk` provides all the facilities of POSIX regexps and the GNU regexp operators described earlier. However, interval expressions are not supported.
`--posix`	Only POSIX regexps are supported; the GNU operators are not special (e.g., `\w` matches a literal `w`). Interval expressions are allowed.
`--traditional`	Traditional UNIX `awk` regexps are matched. The GNU operators are not special, interval expressions are not available, and neither are the POSIX character classes (`[[:alnum:]]` and so on). Characters described by octal and hexadecimal escape sequences are treated literally, even if they represent regexp metacharacters.

`--re-interval`	Allow interval expressions in regexps, even if `--traditional` has been provided.

5.5.5. Actions

Action statements are enclosed in braces, `{` and `}`. A missing action statement is equivalent to `{ print }`.

Action statements consist of the usual assignment, conditional, and looping statements found in most languages. The operators, control statements, and input/output statements available are similar to those in C.

Comments begin with the `#` character and continue until the end of the line. Blank lines may be used to separate statements. Statements normally end with a newline; however, this is not the case for lines ending in a `,`, `{`, `?`, `:`, `&&`, or `||`. Lines ending in `do` or `else` also have their statements automatically continued on the following line. In other cases, a line can be continued by ending it with a `\`, in which case the newline is ignored.

Multiple statements may be put on one line by separating each one with a `;`. This applies to both the statements within the action part of a rule (the usual case) and to the rule statements.

See section 5.2.2.5 for information on `awk`'s commenting convention; see section 5.2.6 for a description of the line-continuation mechanism in `awk`.

5.5.5.1. Operators

The operators in `awk`, in order of decreasing precedence, are

`(...)`	Grouping.
`$`	Field reference.
`++ --`	Increment and decrement, both prefix and postfix.
`^`	Exponentiation (`**` may also be used, and `**=` for the assignment operator, but they are not specified in the POSIX standard).
`+ - !`	Unary plus, unary minus, and logical negation.
`* / %`	Multiplication, division, and modulus.
`+ -`	Addition and subtraction.
space	String concatenation.
`< <= > >= != ==`	The usual relational operators.

`~ !~`	Regular expression match, negated match.
`in`	Array membership.
`&&`	Logical and.
`||`	Logical or.
`?:`	A conditional expression. This has the form *expr1 ? expr2 : expr3*. If *expr1* is true, the value of the expression is *expr2*; otherwise, it is *expr3*. Only one of *expr2* and *expr3* is evaluated.
`= += -= *= /= %= ^=`	Assignment. Both absolute assignment (*var=value*) and operator assignment (the other forms) are supported.

5.5.5.2. Control Statements

The control statements are as follows:

```
if (condition) statement [ else statement ]
while (condition) statement
do statement while (condition)
for (expr1; expr2; expr3) statement
for (var in array) statement
break
continue
delete array[index]
delete array
exit [ expression ]
{ statements }
```

5.5.5.3. I/O Statements

The input/output statements are as follows:

`getline`	Set `$0` from next input record; set `NF`, `NR`, `FNR`.
`getline < file`	Set `$0` from next record of *file*; set `NF`.
`getline var`	Set *var* from next input record; set `NR`, `FNR`.
`getline var < file`	Set *var* from next record of *file*.
command `| getline`	Run *command*, piping its output into `getline`; sets `$0`, `NF`, `NR`.
command `| getline var`	Run *command*, piping its output into `getline`; sets *var*.

`next`	Stop processing the current input record. The next input record is read, and processing starts over with the first pattern in the `awk` program. If the end of the input data is reached, the `END` rules, if any, are executed.
`nextfile`	Stop processing the current input file. The next input record read comes from the next input file. `FILENAME` is updated, `FNR` is set to one, `ARGIND` is incremented, and processing starts over with the first pattern in the `awk` program. If the end of the input data is reached, the `END` rules, if any, are executed. Earlier versions of `gawk` used `next file`; this usage is still supported but is considered to be deprecated.
`print`	Prints the current record.
`print` *`expr-list`*	Prints expressions.
`print` *`expr-list`* `>` *`file`*	Prints expressions to *`file`*. If *`file`* does not exist, it is created. If it does exist, its contents are deleted the first time the `print` is executed.
`print` *`expr-list`* `>>` *`file`*	Prints expressions to *`file`*. The previous contents of *`file`* are retained, and the output of `print` is appended to the file.
`print` *`expr-list`* `|` *`command`*	Prints expressions, sending the output down a pipe to *`command`*. The pipeline to the command stays open until the `close` function is called.
`printf` *`fmt, expr-list`*	Format and print.
`printf` *`fmt, expr-list`* `> file`	Format and print to *`file`*. If file does not exist, it is created. If it does exist, its contents are deleted the first time the `printf` is executed.

`printf fmt, exprt-list >> file`	Format and print to `file`. The previous contents of `file` are retained, and the output of `printf` is appended to the file.
`printf fmt, expr-list | command`	Format and print, sending the output down a pipe to `command`. The pipeline to the command stays open until the `close` function is called.

`getline` returns `0` on end of file and `-1` on an error. In the event of an error, `getline` will set `ERRNO` to the value of a system-dependent string that describes the error.

5.5.5.4. `printf` Summary

Conversion specifications have the form `%[flag][width][.prec]format`. Items in brackets are optional.

The `awk` `printf` statement and `sprintf` function accept the following conversion specification formats:

`%c`	An ACSII character. If the argument used for `%c` is numeric, it is treated as a character and printed. Otherwise, the argument is assumed to be a string, and only the first character of that string is printed.
`%d`, `%i`	A decimal number (the integer part).
`%e`, `%E`	A floating-point number of the form `[-]d.dddddde[+-]dd`. The `%E` format uses `E` instead of `e`.
`%f`	A floating-point number of the form `[-]ddd.dddddd`.
`%g`, `%G`	Use either the `%e` or `%f` formats, whichever produces a shorter string, with nonsignificant zeros suppressed. `%G` will use `%E` instead of `%e`.
`%o`	An unsigned octal number (again, an integer).
`%s`	A character string.
`%x`, `%X`	An unsigned hexadecimal number (an integer). The `%X` format uses `A` through `F` instead of `a` through `f` for decimal 10 through 15.
`%%`	A single `%` character; no argument is converted.

Optional, additional parameters may lie between the `%` and the control letter:

`-`	The expression should be left-justified within its field.

- space — For numeric conversions, prefix positive values with a space and negative values with a minus sign.
- `+` — The plus sign, used before the width modifier (later in this list), says to always supply a sign for numeric conversions, even if the data to be formatted is positive. The `+` overrides the space modifier.
- `#` — Use an "alternate form" for certain control letters. For `o`, supply a leading zero. For `x`, and `X`, supply a leading `0x` or `0X` for a nonzero result. For `e`, `E`, and `f`, the result will always contain a decimal point. For `g`, and `G`, trailing zeros are not removed from the result.
- `0` — A leading `0` (zero) acts as a flag that indicates output should be padded with zeros instead of spaces. This applies even to non-numeric output formats. This flag only has an effect when the field width is wider than the value to be printed.
- *`width`* — The field should be padded to this width. The field is normally padded with spaces. If the `0` flag has been used, it is padded with zeros.
- *`.prec`* — A number that specifies the precision to use when printing. For the `e`, `E`, and `f` formats, this specifies the maximum number of significant digits. For the `d`, `o`, `i`, `u`, `x`, and `X` formats, it specifies the minimum number of digits to print. For the `s` format, it specifies the maximum number of characters from the string that should be printed.

Either or both of the *`width`* and *`prec`* values may be specified as `*`. In that case, the particular value is taken from the argument list.

5.5.5.5. Special File Names

When doing I/O redirection from either `print` or `printf` into a file, or via `getline` from a file, `gawk` recognizes certain special file names internally, These file names allow access to open file descriptors inherited from `gawk`'s parent process (usually the shell). The file names are

- `/dev/stdin` — The standard input.
- `/dev/stdout` — The standard output.
- `/dev/stderr` — The standard error output.
- `/dev/fd/`*`n`* — The file denoted by the open file descriptor *`n`*.

In addition, reading the following files provides process-related information about the running `gawk` program. All returned records are terminated with a newline.

`/dev/pid`	Returns the process ID of the current process.
`/dev/ppid`	Returns the parent process ID of the current process.
`/dev/pgrpid`	Returns the process group ID of the current process.
`/dev/user`	At least four space-separated fields, containing the return values of the `getuid`, `geteuid`, `getgid`, and `getegid` system calls. If there are any additional fields, they are the group IDs returned by `getgroups` system call. (Multiple groups may not be supported on all systems.)

These file names may also be used on the command line to name data files. These file names are only recognized internally if you do not actually have files with these names on your system.

These file names will become deprecated in version 3.1 of `gawk`; a new, more extensible method will be provided for obtaining the same information.

5.5.5.6. Built-in Functions

`awk` provides a number of built-in functions for performing numeric operations, string-related operations, and I/O-related operations.

The built-in arithmetic functions are

`atan2(`*`y,x`*`)`	The arctangent of *`y/x`* in radians.
`cos(`*`expr`*`)`	The cosine of *`expr`*, which is in radians.
`exp(`*`expr`*`)`	The exponential function (`e ^` *`expr`*).
`int(`*`expr`*`)`	Truncates to integer.
`log(`*`expr`*`)`	The natural logarithm of *`expr`*.
`rand()`	A random number between zero and one.
`sin(`*`expr`*`)`	The sine of *`expr`*, which is in radians.
`sqrt(`*`expr`*`)`	The square root function.
`srand([`*`expr`*`])`	Use *`expr`* as a new seed for the random number generator. If no *`expr`* is provided, the time of day is used. The return value is the previous seed for the random number generator.

`awk` has the following built-in string functions:

`gensub(`*regex*`,` *subst*`,` *how* `[,` *target*`])`	If *how* is a string beginning with `g` or `G`, then replace each match of *regex* in *target* with *subst*. Otherwise, replace the *how*th occurrence. If `target` is not supplied, use `$0`. The return value is the changed string; the original *target* is not modified. Within *subst*, `\n`, where *n* is a digit from one to nine, can be used to indicate the text that matched the *n*th parenthesized subexpression. This function is `gawk`-specific.
`gsub(`*regex*`,` *subst* `[,`*target*`])`	For each substring matching the regular expression *regex* in the string *target*, substitute the string *subst*, and return the number of substitutions. If *target* is not supplied, use `$0`.
`index(`*str*`,` *search*`)`	Returns the index of the string *search* in the string *str* or `0` if search is not present.
`length([`*str*`])`	Returns the length of the string *str*. The length of `$0` is returned if no argument is supplied.
`match(`*str*`,` *regex*`)`	Returns the position in *str* where the regular expression *regex* occurs, or zero if *regex* is not present, and sets the values of `RSTART` and `RLENGTH`.
`split(`*str*`,` *arr* `[,` *regex*`])`	Splits the string *str* into the array *arr* on the regular expression *regex*, and returns the number of elements. If *regex* is omitted, `FS` is used instead. *regex* can be the null string, causing each character to be placed into its own array element. The array *arr* is cleared first.

`sprintf(fmt, expr-list)`	Prints `expr-list` according to `fmt`, and returns the resulting string.
`sub(regex, substr[, target])`	Just like `gsub`, but only the first matching substring is replaced.
`substr(str, index [, len])`	Returns the `len`-character substring of `str` starting at `index`. If `len` is omitted, the rest of `str` is used.
`tolower(str)`	Returns a copy of the string `str`, with all the uppercase characters in `str` translated to their corresponding lowercase counterparts. Nonalphabetic characters are left unchanged.
`toupper(str)`	Returns a copy of the string `str`, with all the lowercase characters in `str` translated to their corresponding uppercase counterparts. Nonalphabetic characters are left unchanged.

The I/O-related functions are

`close(expr)`	Close the open file or pipe denoted by `expr`.
`fflush([expr])`	Flush any buffered output for the output file or pipe denoted by `expr`. If `expr` is omitted, standard output is flushed. If `expr` is the null string (`""`), all output buffers are flushed.
`system(cmd-line)`	Execute the command `cmd-line`, and return the exit status. If your operating system does not support `system`, calling it will generate a fatal error. `system("")` can be used to force `awk` to flush any pending output. This is more portable, but less obvious, than calling `fflush`.

5.5.5.7. Time Functions

The following two functions are available for getting the current time of day and for formatting time stamps. They are specific to `gawk`:

`systime()`	Returns the current time of day as the number of seconds since a particular epoch (midnight, January 1, 1970 UTC, on POSIX systems).
`strftime([`*`format`*`[, `*`timestamp`*`]])`	Formats *`timestamp`* according to the specification in *`format`*. The current time of day is used if no *`timestamp`* is supplied. A default format equivalent to the output of the date utility is used if no *`format`* is supplied.

5.5.5.8. String Constants

String constants in `awk` are sequences of characters enclosed in double quotes (`"`). Within strings, certain escape sequences are recognized, as in C. These are

`\\`	A literal backslash.
`\a`	The alert character; usually the ASCII BEL character.
`\b`	Backspace.
`\f`	Formfeed.
`\n`	Newline.
`\r`	Carriage return.
`\t`	Horizontal tab.
`\v`	Vertical tab.
`\x`*`hex digits`*	The character represented by the string of hexadecimal digits following the `\x`. As in ANSI C, all following hexadecimal digits are considered part of the escape sequence. For example, `"\x1B"` is a string containing the ASCII ESC (escape) character. (The `\x` escape sequence is not in POSIX `awk`.)

`\ddd`	The character represented by the one-, two-, or three-digit sequence of octal digits. Thus, `"\033"` is also a string containing the ASCII ESC (escape) character.
`\c`	The literal character `c`, if `c` is not one of the items in this list.

The escape sequences may also be used inside constant regular expressions (e.g., the regexp `/[ \t\f\n\r\v]/` matches whitespace characters).

See section 5.4.2 for more information.

5.5.6. User-Defined Functions

Functions in `awk` are defined as follows:

```
function name(parameter-list) { statements }
```

Actual parameters supplied in the function call are used to instantiate the formal parameters declared in the function. Arrays are passed by reference; other variables are passed by value.

If there are fewer arguments passed than there are names in *`parameter-list`*, the extra names are given the null string as their value. Extra names have the effect of local variables.

The open parenthesis in a function call of a user-defined function must immediately follow the function name, without any intervening whitespace. This is to avoid a syntactic ambiguity with the concatenation operator.

The word `func` may be used in place of `function` (but not in POSIX `awk`).

Use the `return` statement to return a value from a function.

5.5.7. Historical Features

There are two features of historical `awk` implementations that `gawk` supports.

First, it is possible to call the `length` built-in function not only with no arguments, but even without parentheses!

```
a = length
```

is the same as either of

```
a = length()
a = length($0)
```

Here's an example:

```
$ echo abcdef ¦ awk '{ print length }'
6
```

This feature is marked as deprecated in the POSIX standard, and `gawk` will issue a warning about its use if `--lint` is specified on the command line. (The ability to use `length` this way was actually an accident of the original UNIX `awk` implementation. If any built-in function used `$0` as its default argument, it was possible to call that function without the parentheses. In particular, it was common practice to use the `length` function in this fashion, and this usage was documented in the `awk` manual page.)

The other historical feature is the use of either the `break` statement or the `continue` statement outside the body of a `while`, `for`, or `do` loop. Traditional `awk` implementations have treated such usage as equivalent to the `next` statement. More recent versions of UNIX `awk` do not allow it. `gawk` supports this usage if `--traditional` has been specified.

5.6. Installing gawk

This section provides instructions for installing `gawk` on the various platforms that are supported by the developers. The primary developers support UNIX (and one day, GNU), whereas the other ports were contributed. The file ACKNOWLEDGMENT in the `gawk` distribution lists the electronic mail addresses of the people who did the respective ports.

5.6.1. The gawk Distribution

This section first describes how to get the `gawk` distributions, how to extract it, and then what is in the various files and subdirectories.

5.6.1.1. Getting the gawk Distribution

There are three ways you can get GNU software:

- You can copy it from someone else who already has it.
- You can order `gawk` directly from the Free Software Foundation. Software distributions are available for UNIX, MS-DOS, and VMS, on tape and CD-ROM. The address is

  Free Software Foundation
  59 Temple Place, Suite 330
  Boston, MA 02111-1307 USA
  Phone: +1-617-542-5942
  Fax (including Japan): +1-617-542-2652
  Email: `gnu@gnu.org`

  Ordering from the FSF directly contributes to the support of the foundation and to the production of more free software.

- You can get `gawk` by using anonymous `ftp` to the Internet host `ftp.gnu.org`, in the directory `/pub/gnu`.

  Here is a list of alternate `ftp` sites from which you can obtain GNU software. When a site is listed as *`site:directory`*, the *`directory`* indicates the directory where GNU software is kept. You should use a site that is geographically close to you.

  Asia:

  ```
  cair-archive.kaist.ac.kr:/pub/gnu
  ftp.cs.titech.ac.jp
  ftp.nectec.or.th:/pub/mirrors/gnu
  utsun.s.u-tokyo.ac.jp:/ftpsync/prep
  ```

  Australia:

  `archie.au:/gnu`
  (`archie.oz` or `archie.oz.au` for ACSnet)

  Africa:

  ```
  ftp.sun.ac.za:/pub/gnu
  ```

  Middle East:

  ```
  ftp.technion.ac.il:/pub/unsupported/gnu
  ```

  Europe:

  ```
  archive.eu.net
  ftp.denet.dk
  ftp.eunet.ch
  ftp.funet.fi:/pub/gnu
  ftp.ieunet.ie:pub/gnu
  ftp.informatik.rwth-aachen.de:/pub/gnu
  ftp.informatik.tu-muenchen.de
  ftp.luth.se:/pub/unix/gnu
  ftp.mcc.ac.uk
  ftp.stacken.kth.se
  ftp.sunet.se:/pub/gnu
  ftp.univ-lyon1.fr:pub/gnu
  ftp.win.tue.nl:/pub/gnu
  irisa.irisa.ft:/pub/gnu
  ```

isy.liu.se

nic,switch,ch:/mirror/gnu

src.doc.ic.ac.uk:/gnu

unix.hensa.ac.uk:/pub/uunet/systems/gnu

South America:

ftp.inf.utfsm.cl:/pub/gnu

ftp.unicamp.br:/pun/gnu

Western Canada:

ftp.cs.ubc.ca:/mirror2/gnu

USA:

col.hp.com:/mirrors/gnu

f.ms.uky.edu:/pub3/gnu

ftp.cc.gatech.edu:/pub/gnu

ftp.cs.columbia.edu:/archives/gnu/prep

ftp.digex.net:/pub/gnu

ftp.hawaii.edu:/mirrors/gnu

ftp.kpc.com:/pub/mirror/gnu

ftp.uu.net:/systems/gnu

gatekeeper.dec.com:/pub/GNU

jaguar.utah.edu:/gnustuff

labrea.stanford.edu

mrcnext.sco.uiuc.edu: /pub/gnu

vixen.cso.uiuc.edu:/gnu

wuarchive.wustl.edu:/systems/gnu

5.6.1.2. Extracting the Distribution

gawk is distributed as a tar file compressed with the GNU Zip program, gzip.

Once you have the distribution (for example, gawk-3.0.3.tar.gz), first use gzip to expand the file, and then use tar to extract it. You can use the following pipeline to produce the gawk distribution:

```
# Under System V, add '0' to the tar flags
gzip -d -c gawk-3.0.3.tar.gz | tar -xvpf -
```

This will create a directory named gawk-3.0.3 in the current directory.

The distribution file name is of the form `gawk-V.R.n.tar.gz`. The *V* represents the major version of `gawk`, the *R* represents the current release of version *V*, and the *n* represents a *patch level*, meaning that minor bugs have been fixed in the release. The current patch level is 3, but when retrieving distributions, you should get the version with the highest version, release, and patch level. (Note that release levels greater than or equal to 90 denote beta, or non-production software; you might not want to retrieve such a version unless you don't mind experimenting.)

If you are not on a UNIX system, you will need to make other arrangements for getting and extracting the `gawk` distribution. You should consult a local expert.

5.6.1.3. Contents of the `gawk` Distribution

The `gawk` distribution has a number of C source files, documentation files, subdirectories, and files related to the configuration process (see section 5.6.2) and several subdirectories related to different, non-UNIX, operating systems.

Various `.c`, `.y`, and `.h` files	These files are the actual `gawk` source code.
`README`, `README_d/README.*`	Descriptive files: `README` for `gawk` under UNIX and the rest for the various hardware and software combinations.
`INSTALL`	A file providing an overview of the configuration and installation process.
`PORTS`	A list of systems to which `gawk` has been ported and which have successfully run the test suite.
`ACKNOWLEDGMENT`	A list of the people who contributed major parts of the code or documentation.
`ChangeLog`	A detailed list of source code changes as bugs are fixed or improvements made.

`NEWS`	A list of changes to `gawk` since the last release or patch.
`COPYING`	The GNU General Public License.
`FUTURES`	A brief list of features or changes being contemplated for future releases, with some indication of the time frame for the feature, based on its difficulty.
`LIMITATIONS`	A list of those factors that limit `gawk`'s performance. Most of these depend on the hardware or operating system software and are not limits in `gawk` itself.
`POSIX.STD`	A description of one area where the POSIX standard for `awk` is incorrect and how `gawk` handles the problem.
`PROBLEMS`	A file describing known problems with the current release.
`doc/awkforai.txt`	A short article describing why `gawk` is a good language for AI (artificial intelligence) programming.

`doc/README.card`
`doc/ad.block`
`doc/awkcard.in`
`doc/cardfonts`
`doc/colors`
`doc/macros`
`doc/no.colors`
`doc/setter.outline`
	The troff source for a five-color `awk` reference card. A modern version of troff such as GNU troff (groff) is needed to produce the color version. See the file `README.card` for instructions if you have an older troff.

`doc/gawk.1`	The troff source for a manual page describing `gawk`. This is distributed for the convenience of UNIX users.

`doc/gawk.texi`	The Texinfo source file for the `gawk` documentation. It should be processed with TeX to produce a printed document and with `makeinfo` to produce an Info file.
`doc/gawk.info`	The generated Info file for the `gawk` documentation.
`doc/igawk.1`	The troff source for a manual page describing the `igawk` program.
`doc/Makefile.in`	The input file used during the configuration process to generate the actual `Makefile` for creating the documentation.

`Makefile.in`
`acconfig.h`
`aclocal.m4`
`configh.in`
`configure`
`custom.h`
`missing/*`
	These files and subdirectory are used when configuring `gawk` for various UNIX systems. They are explained in detail in section 5.6.2.

`awklib/extract.awk`, `awklib/Makefile.in`	The `awklib` directory contains a copy of `extract.awk`, which can be used to extract the sample programs from the Texinfo source file for the `gawk` documentation and a `Makefile.in` file, which `configure` uses to generate a `Makefile`. As part of the process of building `gawk`, the library functions and the `igawk` program are extracted into ready-to-use files. They are installed as part of the installation process.
`atari/*`	Files needed for building `gawk` on an Atari ST.

`pc/*`	Files needed for building `gawk` under MS-DOS and OS/2.
`vms/*`	Files needed for building `gawk` under VMS.
`test/*`	A test suite for `gawk`. You can use `make check` from the top-level `gawk` directory to run your version of `gawk` against the test suite. If `gawk` successfully passes `make check`, then you can be confident of a successful port.

5.6.2. Compiling and Installing gawk on UNIX

Usually, you can compile and install `gawk` by typing only two commands. However, if you do use an unusual system, you may need to configure `gawk` for your system yourself.

5.6.2.1. Compiling gawk for UNIX

After you have extracted the `gawk` distribution, `cd` to `gawk-3.0.3`. Like most GNU software, `gawk` is configured automatically for your UNIX system by running the `configure` program. This program is a Bourne shell script that was generated automatically using GNU `autoconf`. (The `autoconf` software is described fully in *Autoconf-Generating Automatic Configuration Scripts*, which is available from the Free Software Foundation.)

To configure `gawk`, simply run `configure`:

```
sh ./configure
```

This produces a `Makefile` and `config.h` tailored to your system. The `config.h` file describes various facts about your system. You might want to edit the `Makefile` to change the `CFLAGS` variable, which controls the command-line options that are passed to the `C` compiler (such as optimization levels or compiling for debugging).

Alternatively, you can add your own values for most `make` variables, such as `CC` and `CFLAGS`, on the command line when running `configure`:

```
CC=cc CFLAGS=-g sh ./configure
```

See the file `INSTALL` in the `gawk` distribution for all the details.

After you have run `configure` and possibly edited the `Makefile`, type

```
make
```

and shortly thereafter, you should have an executable version of `gawk`. That's all there is to it! (If these steps do not work, please send in a bug report.)

CHAPTER 6

sed[1]

by Dale Dougherty and Arnold Robbins

Dale Dougherty is president and CEO of Songline Studios, an affiliate of O'Reilly & Associates specializing in the development of online content. The founding editor or the Nutshell series, Dale has written *sed & awk*, *DOS Meets UNIX* (with Tim O'Reilly), *Using UUCP & Usenet* (with Grace Tudino), and *Guide to the Pick System* (all published by O'Reilly).

Arnold Robbins, an Atlanta native, is a professional programmer and technical author. He has been working with UNIX systems since 1980, when he was introduced to a PDP-11 running a version of the sixth edition of UNIX. He has been a heavy awk user since 1987, when he became involved with gawk, the GNU project's version of awk. As a member of the POSIX 1003.2 balloting group, he helped shape the POSIX standard for awk. He is currently the maintainer of gawk and its documentation. The documentation is available from the Free Software Foundation and has also been published by SSC as *Effective Awk Programming.*

6.1. Understanding Basic Operations

If you are starting out to learn sed and awk, you can benefit from looking at how much they have in common.

- They are invoked using similar syntax.
- They are both stream-oriented, reading input from text files one line at a time and directing the result to standard output.
- They use regular expressions for pattern matching.
- They allow the user to specify instructions in a script.

---

[1]This chapter is reprinted with permission from Dougherty, D., and Robbins, A. 1997. *sed & awk*. Cambridge, MA: O'Reilly.

One reason they have so much in common is that their origins can be found in the same line editor, ed. In this chapter, we begin by taking a brief look at ed and show how sed and awk were logical steps towards the creation of a programmable editor.

Where sed and awk differ is in the kind of instructions that control the work they do. Make no mistake; this is a major difference, and it affects the kinds of tasks that can best be performed with these programs.

This section looks at the command-line syntax of sed and awk and the basic structure of scripts. It also offers a tutorial, using a mailing list, that will give you a taste of script writing. It is valuable to see sed and awk scripts side-by-side before you concentrate on either one of them.

6.1.1. awk, by sed and grep, out of ed

You can trace the lineage of awk to sed and grep, and through those two programs to ed, the original UNIX line editor.

Have you ever used a line editor? If so, it will be much easier for you to understand the line orientation of sed and awk. If you have used vi, a full-screen editor, then you are familiar with a number of commands that are derived from its underlying line editor, ex (which in turn is a superset of the features in ed).

Let's look at some basic operations using the line editor ed. Don't worry; this is an exercise intended to help you learn sed and awk, not an attempt to convince you of the wonders of line editors. The ed commands that are shown in this exercise are identical to the sed commands you'll learn later on. Feel free to experiment with ed on your own to get a sense of how it works. (If you're already familiar with ed, feel free to skip to the next section.)

To use a line editor, you work on one line at a time. It is important to know what line you are positioned at in the file. When you open a file using ed, it displays the number of characters in the file and positions you at the last line.

```
$ ed test
339
```

There is no prompt. If you enter a command that ed does not understand, it prints a question mark as an error message. You can enter the print command, p, to display the current line.

```
p
label on the first box.
```

By default, a command affects only the current line. To make an edit, you move to the line that you want to edit and then apply the command. To move to a line, you specify its *address*. An address might consist of a line number, a symbol indicating a specific position in the file, or a regular expression. You can go to the first line by entering the line number 1. Then you can enter the delete command to remove that line.

```
1
You might think of a regular expression
d
```

Entering `1` makes the first line the current line, displaying it on the screen. The delete command in ed is `d` and here it deletes the current line. Rather than moving to a line and then editing it, you can prefix an editing command with an address that indicates which line or range of lines is the object of the command. If you enter `1d`, the first line would be deleted.

You can also specify a regular expression as an address. To delete a line containing the word `regular`, you could issue this command:

```
/regular/d
```

where slashes delimit the regular expression and `regular` is the string you want to match. This command deletes the first line containing `regular` and makes the line following it the current line.

> ***Note:*** Make sure you understand that the delete command deletes the whole line. It does not just delete the word `regular` on the line.

To delete *all* the lines that contain the regular expression, you'd prefix the command with the letter `g` for global.

```
g/regular/d
```

The global command makes all lines that match the regular expression the object of the specified command.

Deleting text can take you only so far. Substituting text (replacing one bit of text with another) is much more interesting. The substitution command, `s`, in ed is:

```
[address]s/pattern/replacement/flag
```

`pattern` is a regular expression that matches a string in the current line to be replaced by *`replacement`*. For example, the following command replaces the first occurrence of `regular` with `complex` on the current line.

```
s/regular/complex/
```

No address is specified, so it affects only the first occurrence on the current line. It is an error if `regular` is not found on the current line. To look for multiple occurrences on the *same* line, you must specify `g` as a flag:

```
s/regular/complex/g
```

This command changes all occurrences on the current line. An address must be specified to direct this command to act upon more than the current line. The following substitution command specifies an address:

```
/regular/s/regular/complex/g
```

This command affects the first line that matches the address in the file. Remember, the first `regular` is an address and the second is a pattern to match for the substitution command. To make it apply to all lines, use the global command, putting `g` before the address.

```
g/regular/s/regular/complex/g
```

Now the substitution is made everywhere—all occurrences on all lines.

> *Note:* Note the different meanings of `g`. The `g` at the beginning is the global command that means make the changes on all lines matched by the address. The `g` at the end is a flag that means change each occurrence on a line, not just the first.

The address and the pattern need not be the same.

```
g/regular expression/s/regular/complex/g
```

On any line that contains the string `regular expression`, replace `regular` with `complex`. If the address and the pattern are the same, you can tell ed by specifying two consecutive delimiters (`//`).

```
g/regular/s//complex/g
```

In this example, `regular` is specified as the address and the pattern to be matched for substitution is the same. If it seems that we've covered these commands quickly and that there is a lot to absorb, don't worry. We will be covering these commands again later on.

The familiar UNIX utility grep is derived from the following global command in ed:

```
g/re/p
```

which stands for "global regular expression print." grep is a line-editing command that has been extracted from ed and made available as an external program. It is hard-wired to perform one editing command. It takes the regular expression as an argument on the command line and uses it as the address of lines to print. Here's an example, looking for lines matching `box`:

```
$ grep 'box' test
You are given a series of boxes, the first one labeled "A",
label on the first box.
```

It prints all lines matching the regular expression.

One more interesting feature of ed is the ability to *script* your edits, placing them in a separate file and directing them as input to the line editor. For instance, if a series of commands were put in a file named `ed-script`, the following command executes the script:

```
ed test < ed-script
```

This feature makes ed a programmable editor; that is, you can script any action that you might perform manually.

sed was created as a special-purpose editor that was meant to execute scripts exclusively; unlike ed, it cannot be used interactively. sed differs from ed primarily in that it is stream-oriented. By default, all of the input to sed passes through and goes to standard output. The input file itself is not changed. If you actually do want to alter the input file, you typically use the shell mechanism for output redirection, and when you are satisfied with the edits you've made, replace the original file with the modified version.

ed is not stream-oriented and changes are made to the file itself. An ed script must contain commands to save the file and quit the editor. It produces no output to the screen, except what may be generated by a specific command.

The stream orientation of sed has a major impact on how addressing is applied. In ed, a command without an address affects only the current line. sed goes through the file, a line at a time, such that each line becomes the current line, and the commands are applied to it. The result is that sed applies a command without an address to *every* line in the file.

Look at the following substitution command:

```
s/regular/complex/
```

If you entered this command interactively in ed, you'd substitute `complex` for the first occurrence of `regular` on the current line. In an ed script, if this was the first command in the script, it would be applied only to the last line of the file (ed's default current line). However, in a sed script, the same command applies to all lines. That is, sed commands are implicitly global. In sed, the previous example has the same result as the following global command in ed:

```
g/regular/s//complex/
```

Note: Understanding the difference between current-line addressing in ed and global-line addressing in sed is very important. In ed you use addressing to *expand* the number of lines that are the object of a command; in sed, you use addressing to *restrict* the number of lines affected by a command.

sed also was designed with a number of additional commands that support script writing. . . .

awk was developed as a programmable editor that, like sed, is stream-oriented and interprets a script of editing commands. Where awk departs from sed is in discarding the line-editor command set. It offers in its place a programming language modeled on the C language. The `print` statement replaces the `p` command, for example. The concept of addressing is carried over, such that:

```
/regular/ { print }
```

prints those lines matching `regular`. The braces (`{}`) surround a series of one or more statements that are applied to the same address.

The advantage of using a programming language in scripts is that it offers many more ways to control what the programmable editor can do. awk offers expressions, conditional statements, loops, and other programming constructs.

One of the most distinctive features of awk is that it *parses*, or breaks up, each input line and makes individual words available for processing with a script. (An editor such as vi also recognizes words, allowing you to move word by word, or make a word the object of an action, but these features can only be used interactively.)

Although awk was designed as a programmable editor, users found that awk scripts could do a wide range of other tasks as well. The authors of awk never imagined it would be used to write large programs. But, recognizing that awk was being used in this way, the authors revised the language, creating nawk to offer more support for writing larger programs and tackling general-purpose programming problems. This new version, with minor improvements, is now codified by the POSIX standard.

6.1.2. Command-Line Syntax

You invoke sed and awk in much the same way. The command-line syntax is:

```
command [options] script filename
```

Like almost all UNIX programs, sed and awk can take input from standard input and send the output to standard output. If a `filename` is specified, input is taken from that file. The output contains the processed information. Standard output is the display screen, and typically the output from these programs is directed there. It can also be sent to a file, using I/O redirection in the shell, but it must not go to the same file that supplies input to the program.

The `options` for each command are different. We will demonstrate many of these options in upcoming sections. . . .

The `script` specifies what instructions to perform. If specified on the command line, the script must be surrounded in single quotes if it contains a space or any characters that might be interpreted by the shell (`$` and `*`, for instance).

One option common to both sed and awk is the `-f` option that allows you to specify the name of a script file. As a script grows in size, it is convenient to place it in a file. Thus, you might invoke sed as follows:

```
sed -f scriptfile inputfile
```

Figure 6.1 shows the basic operation of sed and awk. Each program reads one input line at a time from the input file, makes a copy of the input line, and executes the instructions specified in the script on that copy. Thus, changes made to the input line do not affect the actual input file.

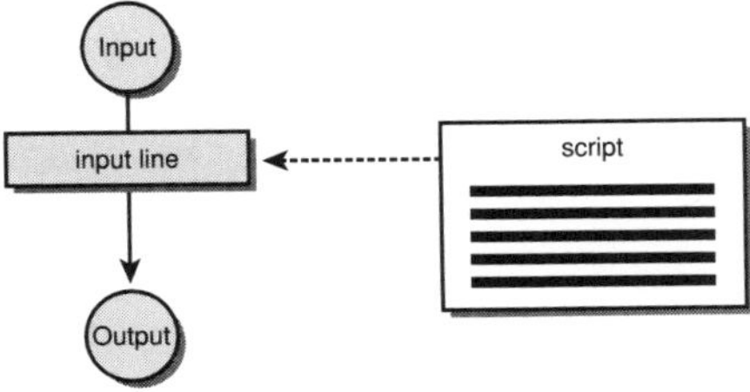

FIGURE 6.1. *How sed and awk work.*

6.1.2.1. Scripting

A script is where you tell the program what to do. At least one line of instruction is required. Short scripts can be specified on the command line; longer scripts are usually placed in a file where they can easily be revised and tested. In writing a script, keep in mind the sequence in which instructions will be executed and how each instruction changes the input line.

In sed and awk, each instruction has two parts: a *pattern* and a *procedure*. The pattern is a regular expression delimited with slashes (`/`). A procedure specifies one or more actions to be performed.

As each line of input is read, the program reads the first instruction in the script and checks the *pattern* against the current line. If there is no match, the *procedure* is ignored and the next instruction is read. If there is a match, then the action or actions specified in the *procedure* are followed. All of the instructions are read, not just the first instruction that matches the input line.

When all the applicable instructions have been interpreted and applied for a single line, sed outputs the line and repeats the cycle for each input line. Awk, on the other hand, does not *automatically* output the line; the instructions in your script control what is finally done with it.

The contents of a procedure are very different in sed and awk. In sed, the procedure consists of editing commands like those used in the line editor. Most commands consist of a single letter.

In awk, the procedure consists of programming statements and functions. A procedure must be surrounded by braces.

In the sections that follow, we'll look at a few scripts that process a sample mailing list.

6.1.2.2. Sample Mailing List

In the upcoming sections, the examples use a sample file, named `list`. It contains a list of names and addresses:

```
$ cat list
John Daggett, 341 King Road, Plymouth MA
Alice Ford, 22 East Broadway, Richmond VA
Orville Thomas, 11345 Oak Bridge Road, Tulsa OK
Terry Kalkas, 402 Lans Road, Beaver Falls PA
Eric Adams, 20 Post Road, Sudbury MA
Hubert Sims, 328A Brook Road, Roanoke VA
Amy Wilde, 334 Bayshore Pkwy, Mountain View CA
Sal Carpenter, 73 6th Street, Boston MA
```

If you like, create this file on your system or use a similar one of your own making. Because many of the examples in this section are short and interactive, you can enter them at your keyboard and verify the results.

6.1.3. Using sed

There are two ways to invoke sed: Either you specify your editing instructions on the command line or you put them in a file and supply the name of the file.

6.1.3.1. Specifying Simple Instructions

You can specify simple editing commands on the command line.

```
sed [-e] 'instruction' file
```

The `-e` option is necessary only when you supply more than one instruction on the command line. It tells sed to interpret the next argument as an instruction. When there is a single instruction, sed is able to make that determination on its own. Let's look at some examples.

Using the sample input file, `list`, the following example uses the `s` command for substitution to replace `MA` with `Massachusetts`.

```
$ sed 's/MA/Massachusetts/' list
John Daggett, 341 King Road, Plymouth Massachusetts
Alice Ford, 22 East Broadway, Richmond VA
Orville Thomas, 11345 Oak Bridge Road, Tulsa OK
Terry Kalkas, 402 Lans Road, Beaver Falls PA
Eric Adams, 20 Post Road, Sudbury Massachusetts
Hubert Sims, 328A Brook Road, Roanoke VA
Amy Wilde, 334 Bayshore Pkwy, Mountain View CA
Sal Carpenter, 73 6th Street, Boston Massachusetts
```

Three lines are affected by the instruction but all lines are displayed.

Enclosing the instruction in single quotes is not required in all cases, but you should get in the habit of always doing it. The enclosing single quotes prevent the shell from interpreting special characters or spaces found in the editing instruction. (The shell uses spaces to determine individual arguments submitted to a program; characters that are special to the shell are expanded before the command is invoked.)

For instance, the first example could have been entered without them, but in the next example, they are required, since the substitution command contains spaces:

```
$ sed 's/ MA/, Massachusetts/' list
John Daggett, 341 King Road, Plymouth, Massachusetts
Alice Ford, 22 East Broadway, Richmond VA
Orville Thomas, 11345 Oak Bridge Road, Tulsa OK
Terry Kalkas, 402 Lans Road, Beaver Falls PA
```

```
Eric Adams, 20 Post Road, Sudbury, Massachusetts
Hubert Sims, 328A Brook Road, Roanoke VA
Amy Wilde, 334 Bayshore Pkwy, Mountain View CA
Sal Carpenter, 73 6th Street, Boston, Massachusetts
```

In order to place a comma between the city and state, the instruction replaced the space before the two-letter abbreviation with a comma and a space.

There are three ways to specify multiple instructions on the command line:

1. Separate instructions with a semicolon.

   ```
   sed 's/ MA/, Massachusetts/; s/ PA/, Pennsylvania/' list
   ```
2. Precede each instruction by `-e`.

   ```
   sed -e 's/ MA/, Massachusetts/' -e 's/ PA/, Pennsylvania/' list
   ```

3. Use the multiline entry capability of the Bourne shell.[2]

   Press RETURN after entering a single quote and a secondary prompt (`>`) will be displayed for multiline input.

   ```
   $ sed '
   > s/ MA/, Massachusetts/
   > s/ PA/, Pennsylvania/
   > s/ CA/, California/' list
   John Daggett, 341 King Road, Plymouth, Massachusetts
   Alice Ford, 22 East Broadway, Richmond VA
   Orville Thomas, 11345 Oak Bridge Road, Tulsa OK
   Terry Kalkas, 402 Lans Road, Beaver Falls, Pennsylvania
   Eric Adams, 20 Post Road, Sudbury, Massachusetts
   Hubert Sims, 328A Brook Road, Roanoke VA
   Amy Wilde, 334 Bayshore Pkwy, Mountain View, California
   Sal Carpenter, 73 6th Street, Boston, Massachusetts
   ```

   This technique will not work in the C shell. Instead, use semicolons at the end of each instruction, and you can enter commands over multiple lines by ending each line with a backslash. (Or you could temporarily go into the Bourne shell by entering `sh` and then type the command.)

In the example above, changes were made to five lines and, of course, all lines were displayed. Remember that nothing has changed in the input file.

[2]These days there are many shells that are compatible with the Bourne shell and work as described here: ksh, bash, pdksh, and zsh, to name a few.

Command Garbled

The syntax of a sed command can be detailed, and it's easy to make a mistake or omit a required element. Notice what happens when incomplete syntax is entered:

```
$ sed -e 's/MA/Massachusetts' list
sed: command garbled: s/MA/Massachusetts
```

sed will usually display any line that it cannot execute, but it does not tell you what is wrong with the command.[3] In this instance, a slash, which marks the search and replacement portions of the command, is missing at the end of the substitute command.

GNU sed is more helpful:

```
$ gsed -e 's/MA/Massachusetts' list
gsed: Unterminated `s' command
```

6.1.3.2. Script Files

It is not practical to enter longer editing scripts on the command line. That is why it is usually best to create a script file that contains the editing instructions. The editing script is simply a list of sed commands that are executed in the order in which they appear. This form, using the `-f` option, requires that you specify the name of the script file on the command line.

```
sed -f scriptfile file
```

All the editing commands that we want executed are placed in a file. We follow a convention of creating temporary script files named `sedscr`.

```
$ cat sedscr
s/ MA/, Massachusetts/
s/ PA/, Pennsylvania/
s/ CA/, California/
s/ VA/, Virginia/
s/ OK/, Oklahoma/
```

The following command reads all of the substitution commands in `sedscr` and applies them to each line in the input file `list`:

```
$ sed -f sedscr list
John Daggett, 341 King Road, Plymouth, Massachusetts
Alice Ford, 22 East Broadway, Richmond, Virginia
Orville Thomas, 11345 Oak Bridge Road, Tulsa, Oklahoma
Terry Kalkas, 402 Lans Road, Beaver Falls, Pennsylvania
Eric Adams, 20 Post Road, Sudbury, Massachusetts
```

[3]Some vendors seem to have improved things. For instance, on SunOS 4.1.x, sed reports "sed: Ending delimiter missing on substitution: `s/MA/Massachusetts`".

```
Hubert Sims, 328A Brook Road, Roanoke, Virginia
Amy Wilde, 334 Bayshore Pkwy, Mountain View, California
Sal Carpenter, 73 6th Street, Boston, Massachusetts
```

Once again, the result is ephemeral, displayed on the screen. No change is made to the input file.

If a sed script can be used again, you should rename the script and save it. Scripts of proven value can be maintained in a personal or system-wide library.

Saving Output

Unless you are redirecting the output of sed to another program, you will want to capture the output in a file. This is done by specifying one of the shell's I/O redirection symbols followed by the name of a file:

```
$ sed -f sedscr list > newlist
```

Do not redirect the output to the file you are editing or you will clobber it. (The `>` redirection operator truncates the file before the shell does anything else.) If you want the output file to replace the input file, you can do that as a separate step, using the `mv` command. But first make very sure your editing script has worked properly! . . .

Suppressing Automatic Display of Input Lines

The default operation of sed is to output every input line. The `-n` option suppresses the automatic output. When specifying this option, each instruction intended to produce output must contain a print command, `p`. Look at the following example.

```
$ sed -n -e 's/MA/Massachusetts/p'
list John Daggett, 341 King Road, Plymouth Massachusetts
Eric Adams, 20 Post Road, Sudbury Massachusetts
Sal Carpenter, 73 6th Street, Boston Massachusetts
```

Compare this output to the first example in this section. Here, only the lines that were affected by the command were printed.

Mixing Options (POSIX)

You can build up a script by combining both the `-e` and `-f` options on the command line. The script is the combination of all the commands in the order given. This appears to be supported in UNIX versions of sed, but this feature is not clearly documented in the manpage. The POSIX standard explicitly mandates this behavior.

Summary of Options

Table 6.1 summarizes the sed command-line options.

TABLE 6.1. *Command-line options for sed.*

Option	*Description*
`-e`	Editing instruction follows.
`-f`	Filename of script follows.
`-n`	Suppress automatic output of input lines.

6.1.4. Using awk

Like sed, awk executes a set of instructions for each line of input. You can specify instructions on the command line or create a script file.

6.1.4.1. Running awk

For command lines, the syntax is:

```
awk 'instructions' files
```

Input is read a line at a time from one or more *files* or from standard input. The *instructions* must be enclosed in single quotes to protect them from the shell. (Instructions almost always contain curly braces and/or dollar signs, which are interpreted as special characters by the shell.) Multiple command lines can be entered in the same way as shown for sed: separating commands with semicolons or using the multiline input capability of the Bourne shell.

awk programs are usually placed in a file where they can be tested and modified. The syntax for invoking awk with a script file is:

```
awk -f script files
```

The `-f` option works the same way as it does with sed.

While awk instructions have the same structure as sed, consisting of *pattern* and *procedure* sections, the procedures themselves are quite different. Here is where awk looks less like an editor and more like a programming language. There are statements and functions instead of one- or two-character command sequences. For instance, you use the `print` statement to print the value of an expression or to print the contents of the current input line.

awk, in the usual case, interprets each input line as a record and each word on that line, delimited by spaces or tabs, as a field. (These defaults can be changed.) One or more consecutive spaces or tabs count as a single delimiter. awk allows you to reference these fields, in either patterns or procedures. `$0` represents the entire input line. `$1`, `$2`, . . . refer to the individual fields on the input line. awk splits the input record before the script is applied. Let's look at a few examples, using the sample input file `list`.

The first example contains a single instruction that prints the first field of each line in the input file.

```
$ awk '{ print $1 }' list
John
Alice
Orville
Terry
Eric
Hubert
Amy
Sal
```

`$1` refers to the value of the first field on each input line. Because there is no pattern specified, the print statement is applied to all lines. In the next example, a pattern `/MA/` is specified but there is no procedure. The default action is to print each line that matches the pattern.

```
$ awk '/MA/' list
John Daggett, 341 King Road, Plymouth MA
Eric Adams, 20 Post Road, Sudbury MA
Sal Carpenter, 73 6th Street, Boston MA
```

Three lines are printed. . . . An awk program can be used more like a query language, extracting useful information from a file. We might say that the pattern placed a condition on the selection of records to be included in a report, namely that they must contain the string `MA`. Now we can also specify what portion of a record to include in the report. The next example uses a `print` statement to limit the output to the first field of each record.

```
$ awk '/MA/ { print $1 }' list
John
Eric
Sal
```

It helps to understand the above instruction if we try to read it aloud: *Print the first word of each line containing the string* `MA`. We can say "word" because by default awk separates the input into fields using either spaces or tabs as the field separator.

In the next example, we use the `-F` option to change the field separator to a comma. This allows us to retrieve any of three fields: the full name, the street address, and the city and state.

```
$ awk -F, '/MA/ { print $1 }' list
John Daggett
Eric Adams
Sal Carpenter
```

Do not confuse the `-F` option to change the field separator with the `-f` option to specify the name of a script file.

In the next example, we print each field on its own line. Multiple commands are separated by semicolons.

```
$ awk -F, '{ print $1; print $2; print $3 }' list
John Daggett
 341 King Road
 Plymouth MA
Alice Ford
 22 East Broadway
 Richmond VA
Orville Thomas
 11345 Oak Bridge Road
 Tulsa OK
Terry Kalkas
 402 Lans Road
 Beaver Falls PA
Eric Adams
 20 Post Road
 Sudbury MA
Hubert Sims
 328A Brook Road
 Roanoke VA
Amy Wilde
 334 Bayshore Pkwy
 Mountain View CA
Sal Carpenter
 73 6th Street
 Boston MA
```

Our examples using sed changed the content of incoming data. Our examples using awk rearrange the data. In the preceding awk example, note how the leading blank is now considered part of the second and third fields.

6.1.4.2. Error Messages

Each implementation of awk gives you different error messages when it encounters problems in your program. Thus, we won't quote a particular version's messages here; it'll be obvious when there's a problem. Messages can be caused by any of the following:

- Not enclosing a procedure within braces (`{}`)
- Not surrounding the instructions within single quotes (`''`)
- Not enclosing regular expressions within slashes (`//`)

6.1.4.3. Summary of Options

Table 6.2 summarizes the awk command-line options.

TABLE 6.2. *Command-line options for awk.*

Option	*Description*
`-f`	Filename of script follows.
`-F`	Change field separator.
`-v`	`var=value` follows. . . .

6.1.5. Using sed and awk Together

In UNIX, pipes can be used to pass the output from one program as input to the next program. Let's look at a few examples that combine sed and awk to produce a report. The sed script that replaced the postal abbreviation of a state with its full name is general enough that it might be used again as a script file named `nameState`:

```
$ cat nameState
s/ CA/, California/
s/ MA/, Massachusetts/
s/ OK/, Oklahoma/
s/ PA/, Pennsylvania/
s/ VA/, Virginia/
```

Of course, you'd want to handle all states, not just five, and if you were running it on documents other than mailing lists, you should make sure that it does not make unwanted replacements.

The output for this program, using the input file `list`, is the same as we have already seen. In the next example, the output produced by `nameState` is piped to an awk program that extracts the name of the state from each record.

```
$ sed -f nameState list ¦ awk -F, '{ print $4 }'
 Massachusetts
 Virginia
 Oklahoma
 Pennsylvania
 Massachusetts
 Virginia
 California
 Massachusetts
```

The awk program is processing the output produced by the sed script. Remember that the sed script replaces the abbreviation with a comma and the full name of the state. In effect, it splits the third field containing the city and state into two fields. `$4` references the fourth field.

What we are doing here could be done completely in sed, but probably with more difficulty and less generality. Also, since awk allows you to replace the string you match, you could achieve this result entirely with an awk script.

While the result of this program is not very useful, it could be passed to `sort ¦ uniq -c`, which would sort the states into an alphabetical list with a count of the number of occurrences of each state.

Now we are going to do something more interesting. We want to produce a report that sorts the names by state and lists the name of the state followed by the name of each person residing in that state. The following example shows the `byState` program.

```
#! /bin/sh
awk -F, '{
     print $4 ", " $0
     }' $* ¦
sort ¦
awk -F, '
$1 != LastState {
     LastState = $1
     print $1
     print "\t" $2
}
$1 == LastState {
     print "\t" $2
}'
```

This shell script has three parts. The program invokes awk to produce input for the `sort` program and then invokes awk again to test the sorted input and determine if the name of the state in the current record is the same as in the previous record. Let's see the script in action:

```
$ sed -f nameState list ¦ byState
 California
      Amy Wilde
 Massachusetts
      Eric Adams
      John Daggett
      Sal Carpenter
 Oklahoma
      Orville Thomas
 Pennsylvania
      Terry Kalkas
 Virginia
      Alice Ford
      Hubert Sims
```

The names are sorted by state. This is a typical example of using awk to generate a report from structured data.

To examine how the `byState` program works, let's look at each part separately. It's designed to read input from the `nameState` program and expects `$4` to be the name of the state. Look at the output produced by the first line of the program:

```
$ sed -f nameState list ¦ awk -F, '{ print $4 ", " $0 }'
 Massachusetts, John Daggett, 341 King Road, Plymouth, Massachusetts
 Virginia, Alice Ford, 22 East Broadway, Richmond, Virginia
 Oklahoma, Orville Thomas, 11345 Oak Bridge Road, Tulsa, Oklahoma
 Pennsylvania, Terry Kalkas, 402 Lans Road, Beaver Falls, Pennsylvania
 Massachusetts, Eric Adams, 20 Post Road, Sudbury, Massachusetts
 Virginia, Hubert Sims, 328A Brook Road, Roanoke, Virginia
 California, Amy Wilde, 334 Bayshore Pkwy, Mountain View, California
 Massachusetts, Sal Carpenter, 73 6th Street, Boston, Massachusetts
```

The `sort` program, by default, sorts lines in alphabetical order, looking at characters from left to right. In order to sort records by state, and not names, we insert the state as a sort key at the beginning of the record. Now the `sort` program can do its work for us. (Notice that using the `sort` utility saves us from having to write sort routines inside awk.)

The second time awk is invoked we perform a programming task. The script looks at the first field of each record (the state) to determine if it is the same as in the previous record. If it is not the same, the name of the state is printed followed by the person's name. If it is the same, then only the person's name is printed.

```
$1 != LastState {
     LastState = $1
     print $1
     print "\t" $2
}
$1 == LastState {
     print "\t" $2
}'
```

There are a few significant things here, including assigning a variable, testing the first field of each input line to see if it contains a variable string, and printing a tab to align the output data. Note that we don't have to assign to a variable before using it (because awk variables are initialized to the empty string). . . . For now, don't worry too much about understanding what each statement is doing. Our point here is to give you an overview of what sed and awk can do.

In this section, we have covered the basic operations of sed and awk. We have looked at important command-line options and introduced you to scripting. . . .

6.2. Writing sed Scripts

To use sed, you write a script that contains a series of editing actions and then you run the script on an input file. sed allows you to take what would be a *hands-on* procedure in an editor such as vi and transform it into a *look-no-hands* procedure that is executed from a script.

When performing edits manually, you come to trust the cause-and-effect relationship of entering an editing command and seeing the immediate result. There is usually an "undo" command that allows you to reverse the effect of a command and return the text file to its previous state. Once you learn an interactive text editor, you experience the feeling of making changes in a safe and controlled manner, one step at a time.

Most people new to sed will feel there is greater risk in writing a script to perform a series of edits than in making those changes manually. The fear is that by automating the task, something will happen that cannot be reversed. The object of learning sed is to understand it well enough to see that your results are predictable. In other words, you come to understand the cause-and-effect relationship between your editing script and the output that you get.

This requires using sed in a controlled, methodical way. In writing a script, you should follow these steps:

1. Think through what you want to do before you do it.
2. Describe, unambiguously, a procedure to do it.
3. Test the procedure repeatedly before committing to any final changes.

These steps . . . describe a methodology for writing programs of any kind. The best way to see if your script works is to run tests on different input samples and observe the results.

With practice, you can come to rely upon your sed scripts working just as you want them to. (There is something analogous in the management of one's own time, learning to trust that certain tasks can be delegated to others. You begin testing people on small tasks, and if they succeed, you give them larger tasks.)

This section, then, is about making you comfortable writing scripts that do your editing work for you. This involves understanding three basic principles of how sed works:

- All editing commands in a script are applied in order to each line of input.
- Commands are applied to all lines (globally) unless line addressing restricts the lines affected by editing commands.
- The original input file is unchanged; the editing commands modify a copy of original input line and the copy is sent to standard output.

After covering these basic principles, we'll look at four types of scripts that demonstrate different sed applications. These scripts provide the basic models for the scripts that you will write. Although there are a number of commands available for use in sed, the scripts in this section purposely use only a few commands. Nonetheless, you may be surprised at how much you can do with so few. . . . The idea is to concentrate from the outset on understanding how a script works and how to use a script before exploring all the commands that can be used in scripts.

6.2.1. Applying Commands in a Script

Combining a series of edits in a script can have unexpected results. You might not think of the consequences one edit can have on another. New users typically think that sed applies an individual editing command to all lines of input before applying the next editing command. But the opposite is true. sed applies the entire script to the first input line before reading the second input line and applying the editing script to it. Because sed is always working with the latest version of the original line, any edit that is made changes the line for subsequent commands. sed doesn't retain the original. This means that a pattern that might have matched the original input line may no longer match the line after an edit has been made.

Let's look at an example that uses the substitute command. Suppose someone quickly wrote the following script to change `pig` to `cow` and `cow` to `horse`:

```
s/pig/cow/
s/cow/horse/
```

What do you think happened? Try it on a sample file. We'll discuss what happened later, after we look at how sed works.

6.2.1.1. The Pattern Space

sed maintains a *pattern space*, a workspace or temporary buffer where a single line of input is held while the editing commands are applied.[4]

The transformation of the pattern space by a two-line script is shown in Figure 6.2. It changes "The Unix System" to "The UNIX Operating System."

Initially, the pattern space contains a copy of a single input line. In Figure 6.2, that line is "The Unix System." The normal flow through the script is to execute each command on that line until the end of the script is reached. The first command in the script is applied to that line, changing "Unix" to "UNIX." Then the second command is applied, changing "UNIX System" to "UNIX Operating System."[5]

Note that the pattern for the second substitute command does not match the original input line; it matches the current line as it has changed in the pattern space.

When all the instructions have been applied, the current line is output and the next line of input is read into the pattern space. Then all the commands in the script are applied to that line.

As a consequence, any sed command might change the contents of the pattern space for the next command. The contents of the pattern space are dynamic and do not always match the original input line. That was the problem with the sample script at the beginning of this section. The first command would change `pig` to `cow` as expected. However, when the second command changed `cow` to `horse` on the same line, it also changed the `cow` that had been a `pig`. So, where the input file contained pigs and cows, the output file has only horses!

This mistake is simply a problem of the order of the commands in the script. Reversing the order of the commands—changing `cow` into `horse` before changing `pig` into `cow`—does the trick.

```
s/cow/horse/
s/pig/cow/
```

[4]One advantage of the one-line-at-a-time design is that sed can read very large files without any problems. Screen editors that have to read the entire file into memory, or some large portion of it, can run out of memory or be extremely slow to use in dealing with large files.

[5]Yes, we could have changed "Unix System" to "UNIX Operating System" in one step. However, the input file might have instances of "UNIX System" as well as "Unix System." So by changing "Unix" to "UNIX," we make both instances consistent before changing them to "UNIX Operating System."

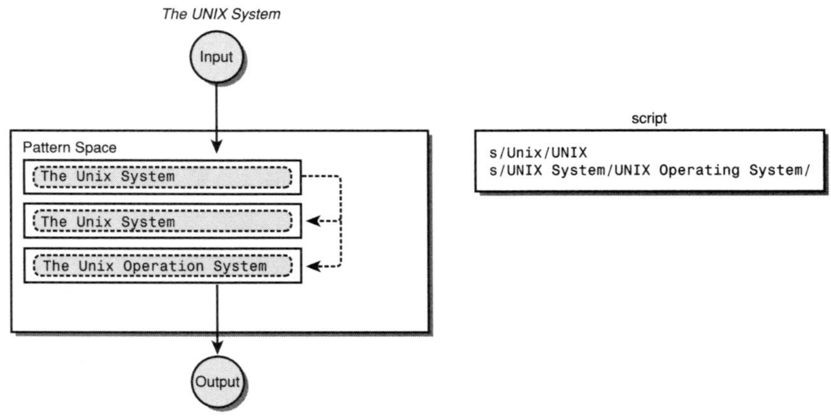

FIGURE 6.2. *The commands in the script change the contents of the pattern space.*

Some sed commands change the flow through the script . . . .For example, the `N` command reads another line into the pattern space without removing the current line, so you can test for patterns across multiple lines. Other commands tell sed to exit before reaching the bottom of the script or to go to a labeled command. sed also maintains a second temporary buffer called the *hold space*. You can copy the contents of the pattern space to the hold space and retrieve them later. . . .

6.2.2. A Global Perspective on Addressing

One of the first things you'll notice about sed commands is that sed will apply them to every input line. Sed is implicitly global, unlike ed, ex, or vi. The following substitute command will change every `CA` into `California`.

```
s/CA/California/g
```

If the same command were entered from the ex command prompt in vi, it would make the replacement for all occurrences on the current line only. In sed, it is as though each line has a turn at becoming the current line and so the command is applied to every line. Line addresses are used to supply context for, or *restrict*, an operation. (In short: Nothing gets done in vi unless you tell it which lines to work on, while sed will work on every line unless you tell it not to.) For instance, by supplying the address

Sebastopol to the previous substitute command, we can limit the replacement of CA by California to just lines containing Sebastopol.

```
/Sebastopol/s/CA/California/g
```

An input line consisting of Sebastopol, CA would match the address and the substitute command would be applied, changing it to Sebastopol, California. A line consisting of San Francisco, CA would not be matched and the substitution would not be applied.

A sed command can specify zero, one, or two addresses. An address can be a regular expression describing a pattern, a line number, or a line addressing symbol.

- If no address is specified, then the command is applied to each line.
- If there is only one address, the command is applied to any line matching the address.
- If two comma-separated addresses are specified, the command is performed on the first line matching the first address and all succeeding lines up to and including a line matching the second address.
- If an address is followed by an exclamation mark (!), the command is applied to all lines that do *not* match the address.

To illustrate how addressing works, let's look at examples using the delete command, d. A script consisting of simply the d command and no address produces no output since it deletes *all* lines:

```
d
```

When a line number is supplied as an address, the command affects only that line. For instance, the following example deletes only the first line:

```
1d
```

The line number refers to an internal line count maintained by sed. This counter is not reset for multiple input files. Thus, no matter how many files were specified as input, there is only one line 1 in the input stream.

Similarly, the input stream has only one last line. It can be specified using the addressing symbol $. The following example deletes the last line of input:

```
$d
```

The `$` symbol should not be confused with the `$` used in regular expressions, which means the end of the line.

When a regular expression is supplied as an address, the command affects only the lines matching that pattern. The regular expression must be enclosed by slashes (`/`). The following delete command

```
/^$/d
```

deletes only blank lines. All other lines are passed through untouched.

If you supply two addresses, then you specify a range of lines over which the command is executed. The following example shows how to delete all lines blocked by a pair of macros, in this case, `.TS` and `.TE`, that mark `tbl` input.

```
/^\.TS/,/^\.TE/d
```

It deletes all lines beginning with the line matched by the first pattern and up to and including the line matched by the second pattern. Lines outside this range are not affected. The following command deletes from line 50 to the last line in the file:

```
50,$d
```

You can mix a line address and a pattern address:

```
1,/^$/d
```

This example deletes from the first line up to the first blank line, which, for instance, will delete a mailer header from an Internet mail message that you have saved in a file.

You can think of the first address as enabling the action and the second address as disabling it. Sed has no way of looking ahead to determine if the second match will be made. The action will be applied to lines once the first match is made. The command will be applied to *all* subsequent lines until the second match is made. In the previous example, if the file did not contain a blank line, then all lines would be deleted.

An exclamation mark (`!`) following an address reverses the sense of the match. For instance, the following script deletes all lines *except* those inside `tbl` input:

```
/^\.TS/,/^\.TE/!d
```

This script, in effect, extracts `tbl` input from a source file.

6.2.2.1. Grouping Commands

Braces (`{}`) are used in sed to nest one address inside another or to apply multiple commands at the same address. You can nest addresses if you want to specify a range of lines and then, within that range, specify another address. For example, to delete blank lines only inside blocks of `tbl` input, use the following command:

```
/^\.TS/,/^\.TE/{
        /^$/d
}
```

The opening curly brace must end a line and the closing curly brace must be on a line by itself. Be sure there are no spaces after the braces.

You can apply multiple commands to the same range of lines by enclosing the editing commands within braces, as shown below:

```
/^\.TS/,/^\.TE/{
     /^$/d
     s/^\.ps 10/.ps 8/
     s/^\.vs 12/.vs 10/
}
```

This example not only deletes blank lines in `tbl` input, but it also uses the substitute command, `s`, to change several `troff` requests. These commands are applied only to lines within the `.TS/.TE` block.

6.2.3. Testing and Saving Output

In our previous discussion of the pattern space, you saw that sed:

1. Makes a copy of the input line.
2. Modifies that copy in the pattern space.
3. Outputs the copy to standard output.

What this means is that sed has a built-in safeguard so that you don't make changes to the original file. Thus, the following command line:

```
$ sed -f sedscr testfile
```

does not make the change in `testfile`. It sends all lines to standard output (typically the screen)—the lines that were modified as well as the lines that are unchanged. You have to capture this output in a new file if you want to save it.

```
$ sed -f sedscr testfile > newfile
```

The redirection symbol (`>`) directs the output from sed to the file `newfile`. Don't redirect the output from the command back to the input file or you will overwrite the input file. This will happen *before* sed even gets a chance to process the file, effectively destroying your data.

One important reason to redirect the output to a file is to verify your results. You can examine the contents of `newfile` and compare it to `testfile`. If you want to be very methodical about checking your results (and you should be), use the `diff` program to point out the differences between the two files.

```
$ diff testfile newfile
```

This command will display lines that are unique to `testfile` preceded by a `<` and lines unique to `newfile` preceded by a `>`. When you have verified your results, make a backup copy of the original input file and then use the `mv` command to overwrite the original with the new version. Be sure that the editing script is working properly before abandoning the original version.

Because these steps are repeated so frequently, you will find it helpful to put them into a shell script. While we can't go into much depth about the workings of shell scripts, these scripts are fairly simple to understand and use. Writing a shell script involves using a text editor to enter one or more command lines in a file, saving the file and then using the `chmod` command to make the file executable. The name of the file is the name of the command, and it can be entered at the system prompt. If you are unfamiliar with shell scripts, follow the shell scripts presented in this book as recipes in which you make your own substitutions.

The following two shell scripts are useful for testing sed scripts and then making the changes permanently in a file. They are particularly useful when the same script needs to be run on multiple files.

6.2.3.1. `testsed`

The shell script `testsed` automates the process of saving the output of sed in a temporary file. It expects to find the script file, `sedscr`, in the current directory and applies these instructions to the input file named on the command line. The output is placed in a temporary file.

```
for x
do
     sed -f sedscr $x > tmp.$x
done
```

The name of a file must be specified on the command line. As a result, this shell script saves the output in a temporary file with the prefix `tmp.`. You can examine the temporary file to determine if your edits were made correctly. If you approve of the results, you can use `mv` to overwrite the original file with the temporary file.

You might also incorporate the `diff` command into the shell script. (Add `diff $x tmp.$x` after the `sed` command.)

If you find that your script did not produce the results you expected, remember that the easiest "fix" is usually to perfect the editing script and run it again on the original input file. Don't write a new script to "undo" or improve upon changes made in the temporary file.

6.2.3.2. runsed

The shell script `runsed` was developed to make changes to an input file permanently. In other words, it is used in cases when you would want the input file and the output file to be the same. Like `testsed`, it creates a temporary file, but then it takes the next step: copying the file over the original.

```
#! /bin/sh

for x
do
     echo "editing $x: \c"
     if test "$x" = sedscr; then
         echo "not editing sedscript!"
      elif test -s $x; then
          sed -f sedscr $x > /tmp/$x$$
         if test -s /tmp/$x$$
         then
              if cmp -s $x /tmp/$x$$
             then
                 echo "file not changed: \c"
             else
                 mv $x $x.bak  # save original, just in case
                 cp /tmp/$x$$ $x
             fi
             echo "done"
         else
              echo "Sed produced an empty file\c"
             echo " - check your sedscript."
         Fi
         rm -f /tmp/$x$$
     else
         echo "original file is empty."
     Fi
 done
 echo "all done"
```

To use `runsed`, create a sed script named `sedscr` in the directory where you want to make the edits. Supply the name or names of the files to edit on the command line. Shell metacharacters can be used to specify a set of files.

```
$ runsed ch0?
```

`runsed` simply invokes `sed -f sedscr` on the named files, one at a time, and redirects the output to a temporary file. `runsed` then tests this temporary file to make sure that output was produced before copying it over the original.

The muscle of this shell script (line 9) is essentially the same as `testsed`. The additional lines are intended to test for unsuccessful runs—for instance, when no output is produced. It compares the two files to see if changes were actually made or to see if an empty output file was produced before overwriting the original.

However, `runsed` does not protect you from imperfect editing scripts. You should use `testsed` first to verify your changes before actually making them permanent with `runsed`.

6.2.4. Four Types of sed Scripts

In this section, we are going to look at four types of scripts, each one illustrating a typical sed application.

6.2.4.1. Multiple Edits to the Same File

The first type of sed script demonstrates making a series of edits in a file. The example we use is a script that converts a file created by a word processing program into a file coded for troff.

One of the authors once did a writing project for a computer company, here referred to as BigOne Computer. The document had to include a product bulletin for Horsefeathers Software. The company promised that the product bulletin was online and that they would send it. Unfortunately, when the file arrived, it contained the formatted output for a line printer, the only way they could provide it. A portion of that file (saved for testing in a file named `horsefeathers`) follows.

```
                    HORSEFEATHERS SOFTWARE PRODUCT BULLETIN

  DESCRIPTION
+ ___________

  BigOne Computer  offers three  software packages from the  suite
     of Horsefeathers  software products  --  Horsefeathers  Business
   BASIC, BASIC  Librarian,  and LIDO.  These software products can
   fill  your    requirements    for    powerful,    sophisticated,
   general-purpose business  software providing you with a base for
   software customization or development.
```

```
Horsefeathers  BASIC is  BASIC optimized for use on  the  BigOne
   machine with UNIX  or MS-DOS operating systems.  BASIC Librarian
 is a full screen program editor, which also provides the ability
```

Note that the text has been justified with spaces added between words. There are also spaces added to create a left margin.

We find that when we begin to tackle a problem using sed, we do best if we make a mental list of all the things we want to do. When we begin coding, we write a script containing a single command that does one thing. We test that it works, then we add another command, repeating this cycle until we've done all that's obvious to do. ("All that's obvious" because the list is not always complete, and the cycle of implement-and-test often adds other items to the list.)

It may seem to be a rather tedious process to work this way and indeed there are a number of scripts where it's fine to take a crack at writing the whole script in one pass and then begin testing it. However, the one-step-at-a-time technique is highly recommended for beginners because you isolate each command and get to easily see what is working and what is not. When you try to do several commands at once, you might find that when problems arise you end up recreating the recommended process in reverse; that is, removing commands one by one until you locate the problem.

Here is a list of the obvious edits that need to be made to the Horsefeathers Software bulletin:

1. Replace all blank lines with a paragraph macro (`.LP`).
2. Remove all leading spaces from each line.
3. Remove the printer underscore line, the one that begins with a `+`.
4. Remove multiple blank spaces that were added between words.

The first edit requires that we match blank lines. However, in looking at the input file, it wasn't obvious whether the blank lines had leading spaces or not. As it turns out, they do not, so blank lines can be matched using the pattern `^$`. (If there were spaces on the line, the pattern could be written `^□*$`.) Thus, the first edit is fairly straightforward to accomplish:

```
s/^$/.LP/
```

It replaces each blank line with `.LP`. Note that you do not escape the literal period in the replacement section of the substitute command. We can put this command in a file named `sedscr` and test the command as follows:

```
$ sed -f sedscr horsefeathers
                         HORSEFEATHERS SOFTWARE PRODUCT BULLETIN
 .LP
   DESCRIPTION
 +    __________
 .LP
   BigOne Computer  offers three  software packages from the  suite
   of Horsefeathers  software products  --  Horsefeathers  Business
   BASIC, BASIC  Librarian,  and LIDO.  These software products can
   fill  your    requirements    for    powerful,     sophisticated,
   general-purpose business  software providing you with a base for
   software customization or development.
 .LP
   Horsefeathers  BASIC is  BASIC optimized for use on  the  BigOne
   machine with UNIX  or MS-DOS operating systems.  BASIC Librarian
   is a full screen program editor, which also provides the ability
```

It is pretty obvious which lines have changed. (It is frequently helpful to cut out a portion of a file to use for testing. It works best if the portion is small enough to fit on the screen yet is large enough to include different examples of what you want to change. After all edits have been applied successfully to the test file, a second level of testing occurs when you apply them to the complete, original file.)

The next edit that we make is to remove the line that begins with a `+` and contains a line-printer underscore. We can simply delete this line using the delete command, `d`. In writing a pattern to match this line, we have a number of choices. Each of the following would match that line:

```
/^+/
/^+□/
/^+□□*/
/^+□□*__*/
```

As you can see, each successive regular expression matches a greater number of characters. Only through testing can you determine how complex the expression needs to be to match a specific line and not others. The longer the pattern that you define in a regular expression, the more comfort you have in knowing that it won't produce unwanted matches. For this script, we'll choose the third expression:

```
/^+□□*/d
```

This command will delete any line that begins with a plus sign and is followed by at least one space. The pattern specifies two spaces, but the second is modified by `*`, which means that the second space might or might not be there.

This command was added to the sed script and tested, but since it only affects one line, we'll omit showing the results and move on. The next edit needs to remove the spaces that pad the beginning of a line. The pattern for matching that sequence is very similar to the address for the previous command.

```
s/^□□*//
```

This command removes any sequence of spaces found at the beginning of a line. The replacement portion of the substitute command is empty, meaning that the matched string is removed.

We can add this command to the script and test it.

```
$ sed -f sedscr horsefeathers
HORSEFEATHERS SOFTWARE PRODUCT BULLETIN
.LP
DESCRIPTION
.LP
BigOne Computer  offers three  software packages from the  suite
of Horsefeathers  software products  --  Horsefeathers  Business
BASIC, BASIC  Librarian,  and LIDO.  These software products can
fill  your   requirements   for   powerful,   sophisticated,
general-purpose business  software providing you with a base for
software customization or development.
.LP
Horsefeathers  BASIC is  BASIC optimized for use on  the  BigOne
machine with UNIX  or MS-DOS operating systems.  BASIC Librarian
is a full screen program editor, which also provides the ability
```

The next edit attempts to deal with the extra spaces added to justify each line. We can write a substitute command to match any string of consecutive spaces and replace it with a single space.

```
s/□□*/□/g
```

We add the global flag at the end of the command so that all occurrences, not just the first, are replaced. Note that, like previous regular expressions, we are not specifying how many spaces are there, just that one or more be found. There might be two, three, or four consecutive spaces. No matter how many, we want to reduce them to one.[6]

Let's test the new script:

```
$ sed -f sedscr horsefeathers
HORSEFEATHERS SOFTWARE PRODUCT BULLETIN
.LP
DESCRIPTION
.LP
```

[6]This command will also match just a single space. But since the replacement is also a single space, such a case is effectively a no-op.

```
BigOne Computer offers three software packages from the suite
of Horsefeathers software products -- Horsefeathers Business
BASIC, BASIC Librarian, and LIDO. These software products can
fill your requirements for powerful, sophisticated,
general-purpose business software providing you with a base for
software customization or development.
.LP
Horsefeathers BASIC is BASIC optimized for use on the BigOne
machine with UNIX or MS-DOS operating systems. BASIC Librarian
is a full screen program editor, which also provides the ability
```

It works as advertised, reducing two or more spaces to one. On closer inspection, though, you might notice that the script removes a sequence of two spaces following a period, a place where they might belong.

We could perfect our substitute command such that it does not make the replacement for spaces following a period. The problem is that there are cases when three spaces follow a period and we'd like to reduce that to two. The best way seems to be to write a separate command that deals with the special case of a period followed by spaces.

```
s/\.□□*/.□□/g
```

This command replaces a period followed by any number of spaces with a period followed by two spaces. It should be noted that the previous command reduces multiple spaces to one, so that only one space will be found following a period.[7]

Nonetheless, this pattern works regardless of how many spaces follow the period, as long as there is at least one. (It would not, for instance, affect a filename of the form `test.ext` if it appeared in the document.) This command is placed at the end of the script and tested:

```
$ sed -f sedscr horsefeathers
HORSEFEATHERS SOFTWARE PRODUCT BULLETIN
.LP
DESCRIPTION
.LP BigOne Computer offers three software packages from the suite
of Horsefeathers software products -- Horsefeathers Business
BASIC, BASIC Librarian, and LIDO.  These software products can
fill your requirements for powerful, sophisticated,
general-purpose business software providing you with a base for
software customization or development.
.LP
Horsefeathers BASIC is BASIC optimized for use on the BigOne
machine with UNIX or MS-DOS operating systems.  BASIC Librarian
is a full screen program editor, which also provides the ability
```

[7]The command could therefore be simplified to `s/\.□/.□□/g`.

It works. Here's the completed script:

```
s/^$/.LP/
/^+□□*/d
s/^□□*//
s/□□*/□/g
s/\.□□*/.□□/g
```

As we said earlier, the next stage would be to test the script on the complete file (`hf.product.bulletin`), using `testsed`, and examine the results thoroughly. When we are satisfied with the results, we can use `runsed` to make the changes permanent:

```
$ runsed hf.product.bulletin
done
```

By executing `runsed`, we have overwritten the original file.

Before leaving this script, it is instructive to point out that although the script was written to process a specific file, each of the commands in the script is one that you might expect to use again, even if you don't use the entire script again. In other words, you may well write other scripts that delete blank lines or check for two spaces following a period. Recognizing how commands can be reused in other situations reduces the time it takes to develop and test new scripts. It's like a singer learning a song and adding it to his or her repertoire.

6.2.4.2. Making Changes Across a Set of Files

The most common use of sed is in making a set of search-and-replacement edits across a set of files. Many times these scripts aren't very unusual or interesting, just a list of substitute commands that change one word or phrase to another. Of course, such scripts don't need to be interesting as long as they are useful and save doing the work manually.

The example we look at in this section is a conversion script, designed to modify various "machine-specific" terms in a UNIX documentation set. One person went through the documentation set and made a list of things that needed to be changed. Another person worked from the list to create the following list of substitutions.

```
s/ON switch/START switch/g
s/ON button/START switch/g
s/STANDBY switch/STOP switch/g
s/STANDBY button/STOP switch/g
s/STANDBY/STOP/g
s/[cC]abinet [Ll]ight/control panel light/g
s/core system diskettes/core system tape/g
s/TERM=542[05] /TERM=PT200 /g
s/Teletype 542[05]/BigOne PT200/g
s/542[05] terminal/PT200 terminal/g
```

```
s/Documentation Road Map/Documentation Directory/g
s/Owner\/Operator Guide/Installation and Operation Guide/g
s/AT&T 3B20 [cC]omputer/BigOne XL Computer/g
s/AT&T 3B2 [cC]omputer/BigOne XL Computer/g
s/3B2 [cC]omputer/BigOne XL Computer/g
s/3B2/BigOne XL Computer/g
```

The script is straightforward. The beauty is not in the script itself but in sed's ability to apply this script to the hundreds of files comprising the documentation set. Once this script is tested, it can be executed using `runsed` to process as many files as there are at once.

Such a script can be a tremendous time-saver, but it can also be an opportunity to make big-time mistakes. What sometimes happens is that a person writes the script, tests it on one or two out of the hundreds of files and concludes from that test that the script works fine. While it may not be practical to test each file, it is important that the test files you do choose be both representative and exceptional. Remember that text is extremely variable and you cannot typically trust that what is true for a particular occurrence is true for all occurrences.

Using grep to examine large amounts of input can be very helpful. For instance, if you wanted to determine how `core system diskettes` appears in the documents, you could grep for it everywhere and pore over the listing. To be thorough, you should also grep for `core`, `core system`, `system diskettes`, and `diskettes` to look for occurrences split over multiple lines. (You could also use the `phrase` script . . . to look for occurrences of multiple words over consecutive lines.) Examining the input is the best way to know what your script must do.

In some ways, writing a script is like devising a hypothesis, given a certain set of facts. You try to prove the validity of the hypothesis by increasing the amount of data that you test it against. If you are going to be running a script on multiple files, use `testsed` to run the script on several dozen files after you've tested it on a smaller sample. Then compare the temporary files to the originals to see if your assumptions were correct. The script might be off slightly and you can revise it. The more time you spend testing, which is actually rather interesting work, the less chance you will spend your time unraveling problems caused by a botched script.

6.2.4.3. Extracting Contents of a File

One type of sed application is used for extracting relevant material from a file. In this way, sed functions like grep, with the additional advantage that the input can be modified prior to output. This type of script is a good candidate for a shell script.

Here are two examples: extracting a macro definition from a macro package and displaying the outline of a document.

Extracting a Macro Definition

troff macros are defined in a macro package, often a single file that's located in a directory such as `/usr/lib/macros`. A troff macro definition always begins with the string `.de`, followed by an optional space and the one- or two-letter name of the macro. The definition ends with a line beginning with two dots (..). The script we show in this section extracts a particular macro definition from a macro package. (It saves you from having to locate and open the file with an editor and search for the lines that you want to examine.)

The first step in designing this script is to write one that extracts a specific macro, in this case, the `BL` (Bulleted List) macro in the `-mm` package.[8]

```
$ sed -n  "/^\.deBL/,/^\.\.$/p" /usr/lib/macros/mmt
.deBL
.if\\n(.$<1 .)L \\n(Pin 0 1n 0 \\*(BU
.if\\n(.$=1 .LB 0\\$1 0 1 0 \\*(BU
.if\\n(.$>1 \{.ie !\w^G\\$1^G .)L \\n(Pin 0 1n 0 \\*(BU 0 1
.el.LB 0\\$1 0 1 0 \\*(BU 0 1 \} ..
```

sed is invoked with the `-n` option to keep it from printing out the entire file. With this option, sed will print only the lines it is explicitly told to print via the print command. The sed script contains two addresses: The first matches the start of the macro definition `.deBL` and the second matches its termination, .. on a line by itself. Note that dots appear literally in the two patterns and are escaped using the backslash.

The two addresses specify a range of lines for the print command, `p`. It is this capability that distinguishes this kind of search script from grep, which cannot match a range of lines.

We can take this command line and make it more general by placing it in a shell script. One obvious advantage of creating a shell script is that it saves typing. Another advantage is that a shell script can be designed for more general usage. For instance, we can allow the user to supply information from the command line. In this case, rather than hard-code the name of the macro in the sed script, we can use a command-line argument to supply it. You can refer to each argument on the command line

[8]We happen to know that the `-mm` macros don't have a space after the `.de` command.

in a shell script by positional notation: The first argument is `$1`, the second is `$2`, and so on. Here's the `getmac` script:

```
#! /bin/sh
# getmac -- print mm macro definition for $1
sed -n "/^\.de$1/,/^\.\.$/p" /usr/lib/macros/mmt
```

The first line of the shell script forces interpretation of the script by the Bourne shell, using the `#!` executable interpreter mechanism available on all modern UNIX systems. The second line is a comment that describes the name and purpose of the script. The sed command, on the third line, is identical to the previous example, except that `BL` is replaced by `$1`, a variable representing the first command-line argument. Note that the double quotes surrounding the sed script are necessary. Single quotes would not allow interpretation of `$1` by the shell.

This script, `getmac`, can be executed as follows:

```
$ getmac BL
```

where `BL` is the first command-line argument. It produces the same output as the previous example.

This script can be adapted to work with any of several macro packages. The following version of `getmac` allows the user to specify the name of a macro package as the second command-line argument.

```
#! /bin/sh
# getmac - read macro definition for $1 from package $2
file=/usr/lib/macros/mmt
mac="$1"
case $2 in
  -ms) file="/work/macros/current/tmac.s";;
  -mm) file="/usr/lib/macros/mmt";;
  -man) file="/usr/lib/macros/an";;
esac
sed -n "/^\.de *$mac/,/^\.\.$/p" $file
```

What is new here is a `case` statement that tests the value of `$2` and then assigns a value to the variable `file`. Notice that we assign a default value to file so if the user does not designate a macro package, the `-mm` macro package is searched. Also, for clarity and readability, the value of `$1` is assigned to the variable `mac`.

In creating this script, we discovered a difference among macro packages in the first line of the macro definition. The `-ms` macros include a space between `.de` and the name of the macro, while `-mm` and `-man` do not. Fortunately, we are able to modify the pattern to accommodate both cases.

```
/^\.de *$mac/
```

Following `.de`, we specify a space followed by an asterisk, which means the space is optional.

The script prints the result on standard output, but it can easily be redirected into a file, where it can become the basis for the redefinition of a macro.

Generating an Outline

Our next example not only extracts information; it modifies it to make it easier to read. We create a shell script named `do.outline` that uses sed to give an outline view of a document. It processes lines containing coded section headings, such as the following:

```
.Ah "Shell Programming"
```

The macro package we use has a chapter heading macro named `Se` and hierarchical headings named `Ah`, `Bh`, and `Ch`. In the `-mm` macro package, these macros might be `H`, `H1`, `H2`, `H3`, etc. You can adapt the script to whatever macros or tags identify the structure of a document. The purpose of the `do.outline` script is to make the structure more apparent by printing the headings in an indented outline format.

The result of `do.outline` is shown below:

```
$ do.outline ch13/sect1
CHAPTER  13 Let the Computer Do the Dirty Work
      A.  Shell Programming
            B.  Stored Commands
            B.  Passing Arguments to Shell Scripts
            B.  Conditional Execution
            B.  Discarding Used Arguments
            B.  Repetitive Execution
            B.  Setting Default Values
            B.  What We've Accomplished
```

It prints the result to standard output (without, of course, making any changes within the files themselves).

Let's look at how to put together this script. The script needs to match lines that begin with the macros for:

- Chapter title (`.Se`)
- Section heading (`.Ah`)
- Subsection heading (`.Bh`)

We need to make substitutions on those lines, replacing macros with a text marker (A, B, for instance) and adding the appropriate amount of spacing (using tabs) to indent each heading. (Remember, the • denotes a tab character.)

Here's the basic script:

```
sed -n '
s/^\.Se /Chapter /p
s/^\.Ah /·A. /p
s/^\.Bh /··B.  /p' $*
```

`do.outline` operates on all files specified on the command line (`$*`). The `-n` option suppresses the default output of the program. The sed script contains three substitute commands that replace the codes with the letters and indent each line. Each substitute command is modified by the `p` flag that indicates the line should be printed.

When we test this script, the following results are produced:

```
CHAPTER   "13" "Let the Computer Do the Dirty Work"
     A.   "Shell Programming"
           B.   "Stored Commands"
           B.   "Passing Arguments to Shell Scripts"
```

The quotation marks that surround the arguments to a macro are passed through. We can write a substitute command to remove the quotation marks.

```
s/"//g
```

It is necessary to specify the global flag, `g`, to catch all occurrences on a single line. However, the key decision is where to put this command in the script. If we put it at the end of the script, it will remove the quotation marks after the line has already been output. We have to put it at the top of the script and perform this edit for all lines, regardless of whether or not they are output later in the script.

```
sed -n '
s/"//g
s/^\.Se /Chapter /p
s/^\.Ah /·A. /p
s/^\.Bh /··B.  /p' $*
```

This script now produces the results that were shown earlier.

You can modify this script to search for almost any kind of coded format. For instance, here's a rough version for a TeX file:

```
sed -n '
s/[{}]//g
s/\\section/·A. /p
s/\\subsection/··B.  /p' $*
```

6.2.4.4. Edits to Go

Let's consider an application that shows sed in its role as a true stream editor, making edits in a pipeline—edits that are never written back into a file.

On a typewriter-like device (including a CRT), an em dash is typed as a pair of hyphens (`--`). In typesetting, it is printed as a single, long dash (—). troff provides a special character name for the em dash, but it is inconvenient to type `\(em`.

The following command changes two consecutive dashes into an em dash.

```
s/--/\\(em/g
```

We double the backslashes in the replacement string for `\(em` since the backslash has a special meaning to sed.

Perhaps there are cases in which we don't want this substitute command to be applied. What if someone is using hyphens to draw a horizontal line? We can refine this command to exclude lines containing three or more consecutive hyphens. To do this, we use the `!` address modifier:

```
/---/!s/--/\\(em/g
```

It may take a moment to penetrate this syntax. What's different is that we use a pattern address to restrict the lines that are affected by the substitute command, and we use `!` to reverse the sense of the pattern match. It says, simply, "If you find a line containing three consecutive hyphens, don't apply the edit." On all other lines, the substitute command will be applied.

We can use this command in a script that automatically inserts em dashes for us. To do that, we will use sed as a preprocessor for a troff file. The file will be processed by sed and then piped to troff.

```
sed '/---/!s/--/\\(em/g' file ¦ troff
```

In other words, sed changes the input file and passes the output directly to troff, without creating an intermediate file. The edits are made on-the-go and do not affect the input file. You might wonder why not just make the changes permanently in the original file? One reason is simply that it's not necessary; the input remains consistent with what the user typed, but troff still produces what looks best for typeset-quality output. Furthermore, because it is embedded in a larger shell script, the transformation of hyphens to em dashes is invisible to the user and not an additional step in the formatting process.

We use a shell script named `format` that uses sed for this purpose. Here's what the shell script looks like:

```
#! /bin/sh
eqn=  pic=  col=
files=  options=  roff="ditroff -Tps"
sed="¦ sed '/---/!s/--/\\(em/g'"
while [ $# -gt 0 ]
do
     case $1 in
       -E) eqn="¦ eqn";;
       -P) pic="¦ pic";;
       -N) roff="nroff"  col="¦ col"  sed= ;;
       -*) options="$options $1";;

       *) if [ -f $1 ]
            then files="$files $1"
            else echo "format: $1: file not found"; exit 1
            fi;;
     esac
     shift
 done
 eval "cat $files $sed ¦ tbl $eqn $pic ¦ $roff $options $col ¦ lp"
```

This script assigns and evaluates a number of variables (prefixed by a dollar sign) that construct the command line that is submitted to format and print a document. (Notice that we've set up the `-N` option for nroff so that it sets the sed variable to the empty string since we only want to make this change if we are using troff. Even though nroff understands the `\(em` special character, making this change would have no actual effect on the output.)

Changing hyphens to em dashes is not the only "prettying up" edit we might want to make when typesetting a document. For example, most keyboards do not allow you to type open and close quotation marks (“and” as opposed to "and"). In `troff`, you can indicate a open quotation mark by typing two consecutive grave accents, or backquotes (``), and a close quotation mark by typing two consecutive single quotes (''). We can use sed to change each doublequote character to a pair of single open quotes or close quotes (depending on context), which, when typeset, will produce the appearance of a proper “double quote.”

This is a considerably more difficult edit to make because there are many separate cases involving punctuation marks, space, and tabs. Our script might look like this:

```
s/^"/``/
s/"$/''/
s/"?□/''?□/g
```

```
s/"?$/''?/g
s/□"/□``/g
s/"□/''□/g
s/·"/·``/g
s/"·/''·/g
s/")/'')/g
s/"]/'']/g
s/("/(``/g
s/\["/\[``/g
s/";/'';/g
s/":/'':/g
s/,"/,''/g
s/",/'',/g
s/\."/.\\\&''/g
s/"\./''.\\\&/g
s/\\(em\\^"/\\(em``/g
s/"\\(em/''\\(em/g
s/\\(em"/\\(em``/g
s/@DQ@/"/g
```

The first substitute command looks for a quotation mark at the beginning of a line and changes it to an open quote. The second command looks for a quotation mark at the end of a line and changes it to a close quote. The remaining commands look for the quotation mark in different contexts, before or after a punctuation mark, a space, a tab, or an em dash. The last command allows us to get a real doublequote (") into the troff input if we need it. We put these commands in a "cleanup" script, along with the command changing hyphens to dashes, and invoke it in the pipeline that formats and prints documents using troff.

6.2.5. Getting to the PromiSed Land

You have now seen four different types of sed scripts, as well as how they are embedded inside shell scripts to create easy-to-use applications. More and more, as you work with sed, you will develop methods for creating and testing sed scripts. You will come to rely upon these methods and gain confidence that you know what your script is doing and why.

Here are a few tips:

1. *Know thy input!* Carefully examine your input file, using grep, before designing your script.

2. *Sample before buying.* Start with a small sample of occurrences in a test file. Run your script on the sample and make sure the script is working. Remember, it's just as important to make sure the script *doesn't* work where you *don't* want it to. Then increase the size of the sample. Try to increase the complexity of the input.

3. *Think before doing.* Work carefully, testing each command that you add to a script. Compare the output against the input file to see what has changed. Prove to yourself that your script is complete. Your script may work perfectly, based on your assumptions of what is in the input file, but your assumptions may be wrong.
4. *Be pragmatic!* Try to accomplish what you can with your sed script, but it doesn't have to do 100 percent of the job. If you encounter difficult situations, check and see how frequently they occur. Sometimes it's better to do a few remaining edits manually.

As you gain experience, add your own "scripting tips" to this list. You will also find that these tips apply equally well when working with awk.

6.3. Basic sed Commands

The sed command set consists of 25 commands. In this section, we introduce four new editing commands: `d` (delete), `a` (append), `i` (insert), and `c` (change). We also look at ways to change the flow control (i.e., determine which command is executed next) within a script.

6.3.1. About the Syntax of sed Commands

Before looking at individual commands, there are a couple of points to review about the syntax of all sed commands. . . .

A line address is optional with any command. It can be a pattern described as a regular expression surrounded by slashes, a line number, or a line-addressing symbol. Most sed commands can accept two comma-separated addresses that indicate a range of lines. For these commands, our convention is to specify:

```
[address]command
```

A few commands accept only a single line address. They cannot be applied to a range of lines. The convention for them is:

```
[line-address]command
```

Remember also that commands can be grouped at the same address by surrounding the list of commands in braces:

```
address {
        command1
        command2
        command3
}
```

The first command can be placed on the same line with the opening brace but the closing brace must appear on its own line. Each command can have its own address and multiple levels of grouping are permitted. Also, as you can see from the indentation of the commands inside the braces, spaces and tabs at the beginning of lines are permitted.

When sed is unable to understand a command, it prints the message "Command garbled." One subtle syntax error is adding a space after a command. This is not allowed; the end of a command must be at the end of the line.

Proof of this restriction is offered by an "undocumented" feature: Multiple sed commands can be placed on the same line if each one is separated by a semicolon.[9]

The following example is syntactically correct:

```
n;d
```

However, putting a space after the `n` command causes a syntax error. Putting a space *before* the `d` command is okay.

Placing multiple commands on the same line is highly discouraged because sed scripts are difficult enough to read even when each command is written on its own line. (Note that the change, insert, and append commands must be specified over multiple lines and cannot be specified on the same line.)

6.3.2. Comment

You can use a comment to document a script by describing its purpose. In this section, our full script examples begin with a comment line. A comment line can appear as the first line of a script. In System V's version of sed, a comment is permitted only on the first line. In some versions, including sed running under SunOS 4.1.x and with GNU sed, you can place comments anywhere in the script, even on a line following a command. The examples in this book will follow the more restrictive case of System V sed, limiting comments to the first line of the script. However, the ability to use comments to document your script is valuable and you should make use of it if your version of sed permits it.

[9]Surprisingly, the use of semicolons to separate commands is not documented in the POSIX standard.

An octothorpe (#) must be the first character on the line. The syntax of a comment line is:

```
#[n]
```

The following example shows the first line of a script:

```
# wstar.sed: convert WordStar files
```

If necessary, the comment can be continued on multiple lines by ending the preceding line with a backslash.[10]

For consistency, you might begin the continuation line with # so that the line's purpose is obvious.

If the next character following `#` is `n`, the script will not automatically produce output. It is equivalent to specifying the command-line option `-n`. The rest of the line following the `n` is treated as a comment. Under the POSIX standard, `#n` used this way must be the first two characters in the file.

6.3.3. Substitution

We have already demonstrated many uses of the substitute command. Let's look carefully at its syntax:

```
[address]s/pattern/replacement/flags
```

where the *flags* that modify the substitution are:

- `n` — A number (1 to 512) indicating that a replacement should be made for only the nth occurrence of the *pattern*.
- `g` — Make changes globally on all occurrences in the pattern space. Normally only the first occurrence is replaced.
- `p` — Print the contents of the pattern space.
- `w file` — Write the contents of the pattern space to *file*.

The substitute command is applied to the lines matching the *address*. If no address is specified, it is applied to all lines that match the *pattern*, a regular expression. If a regular expression is supplied as an address, and no *pattern* is specified, the substitute command matches what is matched by the address. This can be useful when the substitute command is one of multiple commands applied at the same address. For an example, see the section "Checking Out Reference Pages" later in this chapter.

[10]This does not work with GNU sed (Version 2.05) though.

Unlike addresses, which require a slash (`/`) as a delimiter, the regular expression can be delimited by any character except a blank or a newline. Thus, if the pattern contained slashes, you could choose another character, such as an exclamation mark, as the delimiter.

```
s!/usr/mail!/usr2/mail!
```

Note that the delimiter appears three times and is required after the *`replacement`*. Regardless of which delimiter you use, if it does appear in the regular expression, or in the replacement text, use a backslash (`\`) to escape it.

Once upon a time, computers stored text in fixed-length records. A line ended after so many characters (typically 80), and then the next line started. There was no explicit character in the data to mark the end of one line and the beginning of the next; every line had the same (fixed) number of characters. Modern systems are more flexible; they use a special character (referred to as *newline*) to mark the end of the line. This allows lines to be of arbitrary[11] length.

Since newline is just another character when stored internally, a regular expression can use `\n` to match an *embedded* newline. This occurs . . . in the special case when another line is appended to the current line in the pattern space. . . .

The *`replacement`* is a string of characters that will replace what is matched by the regular expression. . . . In the *`replacement`* section, only the following characters have special meaning:

`&`	Replaced by the string matched by the regular expression.
`\n`	Matches the `n`th substring (`n` is a single digit) previously specified in the *`pattern`* using `\(` and `\)`.
`\`	Used to escape the ampersand (`&`), the backslash (`\`), and the substitution command's delimiter when they are used literally in the replacement section. In addition, it can be used to escape the newline and create a multiline *`replacement`* string.

Thus, besides metacharacters in regular expressions, sed also has metacharacters in the replacement. See the next section, "Replacement Metacharacters," for examples of using them.

[11]Well, more or less. Many UNIX programs have internal limits on the length of the lines that they will process. Most GNU programs, though, do not have such limits.

flags can be used in combination where it makes sense. For instance, gp makes the substitution globally on the line and prints the line. The global flag is by far the most commonly used. Without it, the replacement is made only for the first occurrence on the line. The print flag and the write flag both provide the same functionality as the print and write commands (which are discussed later in this chapter) with one important difference. These actions are contingent upon a successful substitution occurring. In other words, if the replacement is made, the line is printed or written to file. Because the default action is to pass through all lines, regardless of whether any action is taken, the print and write flags are typically used when the default output is suppressed (the -n option). In addition, if a script contains multiple substitute commands that match the same line, multiple copies of that line will be printed or written to file.

The numeric flag can be used in the rare instances where the regular expression repeats itself on a line and the replacement must be made for only one of those occurrences by position. For instance, a line, perhaps containing tbl input, might contain multiple tabs. Let's say that there are three tabs per line, and you'd like to replace the second tab with >. The following substitute command would do it:

```
s/·/>/2
```

· represents an actual tab character, which is otherwise invisible on the screen. If the input is a one-line file such as the following:

```
Column1·Column2·Column3·Column4
```

the output produced by running the script on this file will be:

```
Column1·Column2>Column3·Column4
```

Note that without the numeric flag, the substitute command would replace only the first tab. (Therefore, 1 can be considered the default numeric flag.)

6.3.3.1. Replacement Metacharacters

The replacement metacharacters are backslash (\), ampersand (&), and \n. The backslash is generally used to escape the other metacharacters, but it is also used to include a newline in a replacement string.

We can do a variation on the previous example to replace the second tab on each line with a newline.

```
s/·/\
/2
```

Note that no spaces are permitted after the backslash. This script produces the following result:

```
Column1·Column2
Column3·Column4
```

Another example comes from the conversion of a file for troff to an ASCII input format for Ventura Publisher. It converts the following line for troff:

```
.Ah "Major Heading"
```

to a similar line for Ventura Publisher:

```
@A HEAD = Major Heading
```

The twist in this problem is that the line needs to be preceded and followed by a blank line. It is an example of writing a multiline replacement string.

```
/^.Ah/{
s/.Ah */\
\
@A HEAD = /
s/""//g
s/$/\
/
      }
```

The first substitute command replaces `.Ah` with two newlines and `@A HEAD =`. A backslash at the end of the line is necessary to escape the newline. The second substitution removes the quotation marks. The last command matches the end of line in the pattern space (not the embedded newlines) and adds a newline after it.

In the next example, the backslash is used to escape the ampersand, which appears literally in the replacement section.

```
s/ORA/O'Reilly \& Associates, Inc./g
```

It's easy to forget about the ampersand appearing literally in the replacement string. If we had not escaped it in this example, the output would have been "O'Reilly ORA Associates, Inc."

As a metacharacter, the ampersand (`&`) represents the extent of the pattern match, not the line that was matched. You might use the ampersand to match a word and surround it by troff requests. The following example surrounds a word with point-size requests:

```
s/UNIX/\\s-2&\\s0/g
```

Because backslashes are also replacement metacharacters, two backslashes are necessary to output a single backslash. The `&` in the replacement string refers to `UNIX`. If the input line is:

```
on the UNIX Operating System.
```

then the substitute command produces:

```
on the \s-2UNIX\s0 Operating System.
```

The ampersand is particularly useful when the regular expression matches variations of a word. It allows you to specify a variable replacement string that corresponds to what was actually matched. For instance, let's say that you wanted to surround with parentheses any cross reference to a numbered section in a document. In other words, any reference such as `See Section 1.4` or `See Section 12.9` should appear in parentheses, as `(See Section 12.9)`. A regular expression can match the different combination of numbers, so we use `&` in the replacement string and surround whatever was matched.

```
s/See Section [1-9][0-9]*\.[1-9][0-9]*/(&)/
```

The ampersand makes it possible to reference the entire match in the replacement string.

Now let's look at the metacharacters that allow us to select any individual portion of a string that is matched and recall it in the replacement string. A pair of escaped parentheses are used in sed to enclose any part of a regular expression and save it for recall. Up to nine "saves" are permitted for a single line. `\n` is used to recall the portion of the match that was saved, where `n` is a number from 1 to 9 referencing a particular "saved" string in order of use.

For example, to put the section numbers in boldface when they appeared as a cross reference, we could write the following substitution:

```
s/\(See Section \)\([1-9][0-9]*\.[1-9][0-9]*\)/\1\\fB\2\\fP/
```

Two pairs of escaped parentheses are specified. The first captures `See Section□` (because this is a fixed string, it could have been simply retyped in the replacement string). The second captures the section number. The replacement string recalls the first saved substring as `\1` and the second as `\2`, which is surrounded by bold-font requests.

We can use a similar technique to match parts of a line and swap them. For instance, let's say there are two parts of a line separated by a colon. We can match each part, putting them within escaped parentheses and swapping them in the replacement.

```
$ cat test1
first:second
one:two
$ sed  's/\(.*\):\(.*\)/\2:\1/' test1
second:first
two:one
```

The larger point is that you can recall a saved substring in any order and multiple times, as you'll see in the next example.

Correcting Index Entries

. . . The first step in creating an index is to place index codes in the document files. We use an index macro named .XX, which takes a single argument, the index entry. A sample index entry might be:

```
.XX "sed, substitution command"
```

Each index entry appears on a line by itself. When you run an index, you get a collection of index entries with page numbers that are then sorted and merged in a list. An editor poring over that list will typically find errors and inconsistencies that need to be corrected. It is, in short, a pain to have to track down the file where an index entry resides and then make the correction, particularly when there are dozens of entries to be corrected.

sed can be a great help in making these edits across a group of files. One can simply create a list of edits in a sed script and then run it on all the files. A key point is that the substitute command needs an address that limits it to lines beginning .XX. Your script should not make changes in the text itself.

Let's say that we wanted to change the index entry above to `sed, substitute command`. The following command would do it:

```
/^\.XX/ /s/sed, substitution command/sed, substitute command/
```

The address matches all lines that begin with .XX and only on those lines does it attempt to make the replacement. You might wonder, why not specify a shorter regular expression? For example:

```
/^\.XX/ /s/substitution/substitute/
```

The answer is simply that there could be other entries that use the word "substitution" correctly and that we would not want to change.

We can go a step further and provide a shell script that creates a list of index entries prepared for editing as a series of sed substitute commands.

```
#! /bin/sh
# index.edit -- compile list of index entries for editing.
grep "^\.XX" $* ¦ sort -u ¦
sed '
s/^\.XX \(.*\)$/\/^\\.XX \/s\/\1\/\1\//'
```

The `index.edit` shell script uses grep to extract all lines containing index entries from any number of files specified on the command line. It passes this list through `sort` which, with the `-u` option, sorts and removes duplicate entries. The list is then piped to sed, and the one-line sed script builds a substitution command.

Let's look at it more closely. Here's just the regular expression:

```
^\.XX \(.*\)$
```

It matches the entire line, saving the index entry for recall. Here's just the replacement string:

```
\/^\\.XX \/s\/\1\/\1\/
```

It generates a substitute command beginning with an address: a slash, followed by two backslashes—to output one backslash to protect the dot in the `.XX` that follows—then comes a space, then another slash to complete the address. Next we output an `s` followed by a slash, and then recall the saved portion to be used as a regular expression. That is followed by another slash and again we recall the saved substring as the replacement string. A slash finally ends the command.

When the `index.edit` script is run on a file, it creates a listing similar to this:

```
$ index.edit ch05
/^\.XX /s/"append command(a)"/"append command(a)"/
/^\.XX /s/"change command"/"change command"/
/^\.XX /s/"change command(c)"/"change command(c)"/
/^\.XX /s/"commands:sed, summary of"/"commands:sed, summary of"/
/^\.XX /s/"delete command(d)"/"delete command(d)"/
/^\.XX /s/"insert command(i)"/"insert command(i)"/
/^\.XX /s/"line numbers:printing"/"line numbers:printing"/
/^\.XX /s/"list command(l)"/"list command(l)"/
```

This output could be captured in a file. Then you can delete the entries that don't need to change and you can make changes by editing the replacement string. At that point, you can use this file as a sed script to correct the index entries in all document files.

When doing a large book with lots of entries, you might use grep again to extract particular entries from the output of `index.edit` and direct them into their own file for editing. This saves you from having to wade through numerous entries.

There is one small failing in this program. It should look for metacharacters that might appear literally in index entries and protect them in regular expressions. For instance, if an index entry contains an asterisk, it will not be interpreted as such, but as a metacharacter. To make that change effectively requires the use of several advanced commands. . . .

6.3.4. Delete

We previously showed examples of the delete command (`d`). It takes an address and deletes the contents of the pattern space if the line matches the address.

The delete command is also a command that can change the flow of control in a script. That is because once it is executed, no further commands are executed on the "empty" pattern space.[12]

The delete command causes a new line of input to be read and a new pass on the editing script to begin from the top. (In this behavior, it is the same as the `next` command, which you'll encounter later in this chapter.)

The important thing to remember is that if the line matches the address, the entire line is deleted, not just the portion of the line that is matched. (To delete a portion of a line, use the substitute command and specify an empty replacement.) In the previous section, we showed a command to delete blank lines:

```
/^$/d
```

Another use of the delete command could be to strip out certain troff requests, such as those that add spacing, break the page, and turn fill mode off and on:

```
/^\.sp/d
/^\.bp/d
/^\.nf/d
/^\.fi/d
```

These commands delete an entire line. For instance, the first command will delete the line `.sp 1` or `.sp .03v`.

The delete command can be used to delete a range of lines. In the previous section, there is an example of deleting all tables from a file by deleting the lines between the `.TS` and `.TE` macros. There is also a delete command (`D`) used to delete a portion of a multiline pattern space. . . .

[12] UNIX documentation reads "no further commands are attempted on the corpse of a deleted line." R.I.P.

6.3.5. Append, Insert, and Change

The append (`a`), insert (`i`), and change (`c`) commands provide editing functions that are commonly performed with an interactive editor, such as vi. You may find it strange to use these same commands to "enter" text using a noninteractive editor. The syntax of these commands is unusual for sed because they must be specified over multiple lines. The syntax follows:

```
append     [line-address]a\
     text
insert     [line-address]i\
     text
change     [address]c\
     text
```

The insert command places the supplied text before the current line in the pattern space. The append command places it after the current line. The change command replaces the contents of the pattern space with the supplied text.

Each of these commands requires a backslash following it to escape the first end-of-line. The *text* must begin on the next line. To input multiple lines of text, each successive line must end with a backslash, with the exception of the very last line. For example, the following insert command inserts two lines of text at a line matching `<Larry's Address>`:

```
/<Larry's Address>/i\
4700 Cross Court\
French Lick, IN
```

Also, if the text contains a literal backslash, add an extra backslash to escape it.[13]

The append and insert commands can be applied only to a single line address, not a range of lines. The change command, however, can address a range of lines. In this case, it replaces *all* addressed lines with a single copy of the text. In other words, it deletes each line in the range but the supplied text is output only once. For example, the following script, when run on a file containing a mail message:

```
/^From /,/^$/c\
<Mail Header Removed>
```

[13]UNIX documentation says that any leading tabs or spaces in the supplied text will disappear on output. This appears to work on System V and GNU sed, but not older versions, such as SunOS 4.1.x. If they disappear on your system, the solution is to put a backslash at the beginning of the line, preceding the first tab or space. The backslash is not output.

removes the entire mail-message header and replaces it with the line `<Mail Header Removed>`. Note that you will see the opposite behavior when the change command is one of a group of commands, enclosed in braces, that act on a range of lines. For instance, the following script:

```
/^From /,/^$/{
     s/^From //p
     c\
<Mail Header Removed>
}
```

will output `<Mail Header Removed>` for each line in the range. So, while the former example outputs the text once, this example will output it 10 times if there are 10 lines in the range.

The change command clears the pattern space, having the same effect on the pattern space as the delete command. No command following the change command in the script is applied.

The insert and append commands do not affect the contents of the pattern space. The supplied text will not match any address in subsequent commands in the script, nor can those commands affect the text. No matter what changes occur to alter the pattern space, the supplied text will still be output appropriately. This is also true when the default output is suppressed; the supplied text will be output even if the pattern space is not. Also, the supplied text does not affect sed's internal line counter.

Let's look at an example of the insert command. Suppose we wanted to source a local file of macros in all the files of a particular document. In addition, we'd like to define a page header string that identifies the document as a draft. The following script inserts two new lines of text before the first line of a file:

```
1i\
.so macros\
.ds CH First Draft
```

After sed executes this command, the pattern space remains unchanged. The new text is output before the current line. A subsequent command could not successfully match `macros` or `First Draft`.

A variation of the previous example shows the append command adding a line to the end of a file:

```
$a\
End of file
```

The `$` is a line-addressing symbol that matches the last line of a file. The supplied text will be output after the current line, so it becomes the last line in the output. Note that even though only one line is output, the supplied text must start on a line by itself and cannot be on the same line as the append command.

The next example shows the insert and append commands used in the same script. The task here is to add a few troff requests before the macro that initializes a list and several after the macro that closes the list.

```
/^\.Ls/i\
.in 5n\
.sp .3
/^\.Le/a\
.in 0\
.sp .3
```

The insert command puts two lines before the `.Ls` macro and the append command puts two lines after the `.Le` macro.

The insert command can be used to put a blank line before the current line, or the append command to put one after, by leaving the line following it blank.

The change command replaces the contents of the pattern space with the text you provide. In effect, it deletes the current line and puts the supplied text in its place. It can be used when you want to match a line and replace it entirely. Let's say for instance that a file contains a lot of explicit troff spacing requests with different amounts of spacing. Look at the following series:

```
.sp 1.5
.sp
.sp 1
.sp 1.5v
.sp .3v
.sp 3
```

If you wanted to change all the arguments to `.5`, it is probably easier to use the change command than try to match all the individual arguments and make the proper substitution.

```
/^\.sp/c\
.sp .5
```

This command allows us to ignore the arguments and replace them regardless of what they are.

6.3.6. List

The list command (`l`) displays the contents of the pattern space, showing nonprinting characters as two-digit ASCII codes. It is similar in function to the list (`:l`) command in vi. You can use this command to detect "invisible" characters in the input.[14]

```
$ cat test/spchar
Here is a string of special characters: ^A  ^B
^M ^G

$ sed -n -e "l" test/spchar
Here is a string of special characters: \01 \02
\15 \07

$ # test with GNU sed too
$ gsed -n -e "l" test/spchar
Here is a string of special characters: \01  \02
\r \a
```

Because the list command causes immediate output, we suppress the default output or we would get duplicate copies of the lines.

You cannot match a character by ASCII value (nor can you match octal values) in sed.[15]

Instead, you have to find a key combination in vi to produce it. Use Ctrl+V to quote the character. For instance, you can match an Esc character (`^[`). Look at the following script:

```
# list line and replace ^[ with "Escape"
l
s/^[/Escape/
```

Here's a one-line test file:

```
The Great ^[ is a movie starring Steve McQueen.
```

Running the script produces the following output:

```
The Great \33 is a movie starring Steve McQueen.
The Great Escape is a movie starring Steve McQueen.
```

GNU sed produces this:

```
The Great \1b is a movie starring Steve McQueen.
The Great Escape is a movie starring Steve McQueen.
```

[14]GNU sed displays certain characters, such as carriage return, using the ANSI C escape sequences, instead of straight octal. Presumably, this is easier to comprehend for those who are familiar with C (or awk . . .).

[15]You can do this in awk, however.

The `^[` character was made in vi by entering Ctrl+V, then pressing the Esc key.

6.3.6.1. Stripping Out Nonprintable Characters from nroff Files

The UNIX formatter nroff produces output for line printers and CRT displays. To achieve such special effects as bolding, it outputs the character followed by a backspace and then outputs the same character again. A sample of it viewed with a text editor might look like:

```
N^HN^HN^HNA^HA^HA^HAM^HM^HM^HME^HE^HE^HE
```

which bolds the word NAME. There are three overstrikes for each character output. Similarly, underlining is achieved by outputting an underscore, a backspace and then the character to be underlined. The following example is the word `file` surrounded by a sequence for underscoring it.

```
_^Hf_^Hi_^Hl_^He
```

It might be necessary at times to strip these printing "special effects," perhaps if you are given this type of output as a source file. The following line removes the sequences for emboldening and underscoring:

```
s/.^H//g
```

It removes any character preceding the backspace along with the backspace itself. In the case of underlining, . matches the underscore; for emboldening, it matches the overstrike character. Because it is applied repeatedly, multiple occurrences of the overstrike character are removed, leaving a single character for each sequence. Note that `^H` is entered in vi by pressing Ctrl+V followed by Ctrl+H.

A sample application is "de-formatting" an nroff-produced man page found on an older System V UNIX system.[16]

If you should want to access the formatted pages with a text editor, you'd want to get a clean version. (In many ways, this is a similar problem to one we solved in converting a word processing file in the previous section.) A formatted man page captured in a file looks like this:

```
^[9      who(1)                                                   who(1)
^[9 N^HN^HN^HNA^HA^HA^HAM^HM^HM^HME^HE^HE^HE
        who - who is on the system?
S^HS^HS^HSY^HY^HY^HYN^HN^HN^HNO^HO^HO^HOP^HP^HP^HPS^HS^HS^HSI^HI
        who [-a] [-b] [-d] [-H] [-l] [-p] [-q] [-r] [-s] [-t] [-T]
```

[16]For a while, many System V UNIX vendors only provided preformatted manpages. This allowed the `man` command to show information quickly, instead of having to format it, but the lack of troff source to the manpages made it difficult to fix documentation errors. Fortunately, most vendors of modern UNIX systems supply source for their manuals.

```
        [-u] [_^Hf_^Hi_^Hl_^He]
            who am I
            who am I
  D^HD^HD^HDE^HE^HE^HES^HS^HS^HSC^HC^HC^HCR^HR^HR^HRI^HI^HI^HIP^HP
        who can list the user's name, terminal line, login time,
        elapsed time since activity occurred on the line, and the
  ...
```

In addition to stripping out the bolding and underlining sequences, there are strange escape sequences that produce form feeds or various other printer functions. You can see the sequence `^[9` at the top of the formatted manpage. This escape sequence can simply be removed:

```
s/^[9//g
```

Once again, the Esc character is entered in vi by typing Ctrl+V followed by pressing the Esc key. The number 9 is literal. There are also what look to be leading spaces that supply the left margin and indentation. On further examination, it turns out that leading spaces precede the heading such as NAME, but a single tab precedes each line of text. Also, there are tabs that unexpectedly appear in the text, which have to do with how nroff optimizes for display on a CRT screen.

To eliminate the left margin and the unwanted tabs, we add two commands to our previous two:

```
# sedman -- deformat nroff-formatted manpage
s/.^H//g
s/^[9//g
s/^[□·]*//g
s/·/ /g
```

The third command looks for any number of tabs or spaces at the beginning of a line. (A tab is represented by · and a space by □.) The last command looks for a tab and replaces it with a single space. Running this script on our sample manpage output produces a file that looks like this:

```
who(1)                                                     who(1)
NAME
who - who is on the system?
SYNOPSIS
who [-a] [-b] [-d] [-H] [-l] [-p] [-q] [-r] [-s] [-t] [-T]
[-u] [file]
who am I
who am I
DESCRIPTION
who can list the user's name, terminal line, login time,
elapsed time since activity occurred on the line, and the
...
```

This script does not eliminate the unnecessary blank lines caused by paging. . . .

6.3.7. Transform

The transform command is peculiar, not only because it is the least mnemonic of all sed commands. This command transforms each character by position in string abc to its equivalent in string xyz.[17]

Its syntax follows:

```
[address]y/abc/xyz/
```

The replacement is made by character position. Therefore, it has no idea of a "word." Thus, a is replaced by x anywhere on the line, regardless of whether or not it is followed by a b. One possible use of this command is to replace lowercase letters with their uppercase counterparts.

```
y/abcdefghijklmnopqrstuvwxyz/ABCDEFGHIJKLMNOPQRSTUVWXYZ/
```

This command affects the entire contents of the pattern space. If you want to convert a single word on the input line, you could do it by using the hold space. . . . (The process is not trivial: you output the line up to the word you want to change, delete that portion of the line, copy the line after the word to the hold space, transform the word, and then append the contents of the hold space back to the pattern space.)

6.3.8. Print

The print command (p) causes the contents of the pattern space to be output. It does not clear the pattern space nor does it change the flow of control in the script. However, it is frequently used before commands (d, N, b) that do change flow control. Unless the default output is suppressed (-n), the print command will cause duplicate copies of a line to be output. It can be used when default output is suppressed or when the flow control through the program avoids reaching the bottom of the script.

Let's look at a script that shows how the print command might be used for debugging purposes. It is used to show what the line looked like before you made any changes.

```
#n Print line before and after changes.
/^\.Ah/{
p
s/"//g
s/^\.Ah //p
}
```

[17]This command is patterned after the UNIX tr command, which translates characters. This is a useful command in its own right; see your local documentation for details. Undoubtedly sed's y command would have been named t, if t had not already been taken . . . .

Note that the print flag is supplied to the substitute command. The substitute command's print flag differs from the print command in that it is conditional upon a successful substitution.

Here's a sample run of the above script:

```
$ sed -f sed.debug ch05
.Ah "Comment"
Comment
.Ah "Substitution"
Substitution
.Ah "Delete"
Delete
.Ah "Append, Insert and Change"
Append, Insert and Change
.Ah "List"
List
```

Each affected line is printed twice. . . .

6.3.9. Print Line Number

An equal sign (=) following an address prints the line number of the matched line. Unless you suppress the automatic output of lines, both the line number and the line itself will be printed. Its syntax is:

```
[line-address]=
```

This command cannot operate on a range of lines.

A programmer might use this to print certain lines in a source file. For instance, the following script prints the line number followed by the line itself for each line containing a tab followed by the string `if`. Here's the script:

```
#n print line number and line with if statement
/	if/{
=
p
}
```

Note that `#n` suppresses the default output of lines. Now let's see how it works on a sample program, `random.c`:

```
$ sed -f sedscr.= random.c
192
	if( rand_type == TYPE_0 ) {
234
	if( rand_type == TYPE_0 ) state[ -1 ] = rand_type;
236
	if( n < BREAK_1 ) {
252
		if( n < BREAK_3 ) {
274
	if( rand_type == TYPE_0 ) state[ -1 ] = rand_type;
303
	if( rand_type == TYPE_0 ) state[ -1 ] = rand_type;
```

The line numbers might be useful in finding problems reported by the compiler, which typically lists the line number.

6.3.10. Next

The next command (`n`) outputs the contents of the pattern space and then reads the next line of input *without* returning to the top of the script. Its syntax is:

```
[address]n
```

The next command changes the normal flow control, which doesn't output the contents of the pattern space until the bottom of the script is reached and which always begins at the top of the script after reading in a new line. In effect, the next command causes the next line of input to replace the current line in the pattern space. Subsequent commands in the script are applied to the replacement line, not the current line. If the default output has not been suppressed, the current line is printed before the replacement takes place.

Let's look at an example of the next command in which we delete a blank line only when it follows a pattern matched on the previous line. In this case, a writer has inserted a blank line after a section heading macro (`.H1`). We want to remove that blank line without removing all blank lines in the file. Here's the sample file:

```
.H1 "On Egypt"

Napoleon, pointing to the Pyramids, said to his troops:
  "Soldiers, forty centuries have their eyes upon you."
```

The following script removes that blank line:

```
/^\.H1/{
n
/^$/d
}
```

You can read this script as follows: "Match any line beginning with the string `.H1`, then print that line and read in the next line. If that line is blank, delete it." The braces are used to apply multiple commands at the same address.

In a longer script, you must remember that commands occurring before the next command will not be applied to the new input line, nor will commands occurring after it be applied to the old input line. . . .

6.3.11. Reading and Writing Files

The read (r) and write (w) commands allow you to work directly with files. Both take a single argument, the name of a file. The syntax follows:

```
[line-address]r file
[address]w file
```

The read command reads the contents of *file* into the pattern space after the addressed line. It cannot operate on a range of lines. The write command writes the contents of the pattern space to the *file*.

You must have a single space between the command and the filename. (Everything after that space and up to the newline is taken to be the filename. Thus, leading or embedded spaces will become part of the filename.) The read command will not complain if the file does not exist. The write command will create a file if it does not exist; if the file already exists, the write command will overwrite it each time the script is invoked. If there are multiple instructions writing to the same file in one script, then each write command appends to the file. Also, be aware that you can only open up to 10 files per script.

The read command can be useful for inserting the contents of one file at a particular place in another file. For instance, let's say that there is a set of files and each file should close with the same one- or two-paragraph statement. A sed script would allow you to maintain the closing separately while inserting it as needed, for instance, when sending the file to the printer.

```
sed '$r closing' $* ¦ pr ¦ lp
```

The $ is an addressing symbol specifying the last line of the file. The contents of the file named closing are placed after the contents of pattern space and output with it. This example does not specify a pathname, assuming the file to be in the same directory as the command. A more general-purpose command should use the full pathname.

You may want to test out a few quirks of the read command. Let's look at the following command:

```
/^<Company-list>/r company.list
```

That is, when sed matches a line beginning with the string <Company-list>, it is going to append the contents of the file company.list to the end of the matched line. No subsequent command will affect the lines read from the file. For instance, you can't make any changes to the list of companies that you've read into the file. However, commands that address the original line will work. The previous command could be followed by a second command:

```
/^<Company-list>/d
```

to delete the original line. So that if the input file was as follows:

```
For service, contact any of the following companies:
<Company-list>
Thank you.
```

running the two-line script would produce:

```
For service, contact any of the following companies:
     Allied
     Mayflower
     United
Thank you.
```

Suppressing the automatic output, using the `-n` option or `#n` script syntax, prevents the original line in the pattern space from being output, but the result of a read command still goes to standard output.

Now let's look at examples of the write command. One use is to extract information from one file and place it in its own file. For instance, imagine that we had a file listing the names of salespeople alphabetically. For each person, the listing designates which of four regions the person is assigned to. Here's a sample:

```
Adams, Henrietta          Northeast
Banks, Freda              South
Dennis, Jim               Midwest
Garvey, Bill              Northeast
Jeffries, Jane            West
Madison, Sylvia           Midwest
Sommes, Tom               South
```

Writing a script for a seven-line file, of course, is ridiculous. Yet such a script can potentially handle as many names as you can put together and is reusable.

If all we wanted was to extract the names for a particular region, we could easily use grep to do it. The advantage with sed is that we can break up the file into four separate files in a single step. The following four-line script does it:

```
/Northeast$/w region.northeast
/South$/w region.south
/Midwest$/w region.midwest
/West$/w region.west
```

All of the names of salespeople that are assigned to the Northeast region will be placed in a file named `region.northeast`.

The write command writes out the contents of the pattern space when the command is invoked, not when end of the script is reached. In the previous example, we might want to remove the name of the region before writing it to file. For each case, we could handle it as we show for the Northeast region:

```
/Northeast$/{
     s///
     w region.northeast
     }
```

The substitute command matches the same pattern as the address and removes it. There are many different uses for the write command; for example, you could use it in a script to generate several customized versions of the same source file.

6.3.11.1. Checking Out Reference Pages

Like many programs, a sed script often starts out small and is simple to write and simple to read. In testing the script, you may discover specific cases for which the general rules do not apply. To account for these, you add lines to your script, making it longer, more complex, and more complete. While the amount of time you spend refining your script may cancel out the time saved by not doing the editing manually, at least during that time your mind has been engaged by your own seeming sleight-of-hand: "See! The computer did it."

We encountered one such problem in preparing a formatted copy of command pages that the writer had typed as a text file without any formatting information. Although the files had no formatting codes, headings were used consistently to identify the format of the command pages. A sample file is shown below.

```
*******************************************************************

NAME:     DBclose - closes a database

SYNTAX:
     void     DBclose(fdesc)
          DBFILE *fdesc;

USAGE:
     fdesc     - pointer to database file descriptor

DESC:  DBclose() closes a file when given its database
file descriptor. Your pending writes to that file will be
completed before the file is closed.  All of your update
locks are removed.
*fdesc becomes invalid.

Other users are not affected when you call DBclose().
Their update locks and pending writes are not changed.
```

```
Note that there is no default file as there is in BASIC.
*fdesc must specify an open file.

DBclose() is analogous to the CLOSE statement in BASIC.

RETURNS:
    There is no return value

*****************************************************************
```

The task was to format this document for the laser printer, using the reference header macros we had developed. Because there were perhaps 40 of these command pages, it would have been utter drudgery to go through and add codes by hand. However, because there were that many, and even though the writer was generally consistent in entering them, there would be enough differences from command to command to have required several passes.

We'll examine the process of building this sed script. In a sense, this is a process of looking carefully at each line of a sample input file and determining whether or not an edit must be made on that line. Then we look at the rest of the file for similar occurrences. We try to find specific patterns that mark the lines or range of lines that need editing.

For instance, by looking at the first line, we know we need to eliminate the row of asterisks separating each command. We specify an address for any line beginning and ending with an asterisk and look for zero or more asterisks in between. The regular expression uses an asterisk as a literal and as a metacharacter:

```
/^\*\**\*$/d
```

This command deletes entire lines of asterisks anywhere they occur in the file. We saw that blank lines were used to separate paragraphs, but replacing every blank line with a paragraph macro would cause other problems. In many cases, the blank lines can be removed because spacing has been provided in the macro. This is a case where we put off deleting or replacing blank lines on a global basis until we have dealt with specific cases. For instance, some blank lines separate labeled sections, and we can use them to define the end of a range of lines. The script, then, is designed to delete unwanted blank lines as the last operation.

Tabs were a similar problem. Tabs were used to indent syntax lines and in some cases after the colon following a label, such as NAME. Our first thought was to remove all tabs by replacing them with eight spaces, but there were tabs we wanted to keep, such as those inside the syntax line.

So we removed only specific cases, tabs at the beginning of lines and tabs following a colon.

```
/^·/s///
/:·/s//:/
```

The next line we come across has the name of the command and a description.

```
NAME:     DBclose - closes a database
```

We need to replace it with the macro `.Rh 0`. Its syntax is:

```
.Rh 0 "command" "description"
```

We insert the macro at the beginning of the line, remove the hyphen, and surround the arguments with quotation marks.

```
/NAME:/ {
     s//.Rh 0 "/
     s/ - /" "/
     s/$/"/
     }
```

We can jump ahead of ourselves a bit here and look at what this portion of our script does to the sample line:

```
.Rh 0 "DBclose" "Closes a database file"
```

The next part that we examine begins with SYNTAX. What we need to do here is put in the `.Rh` macro, plus some additional troff requests for indentation, a font change, and no-fill and no-adjust. (The indentation is required because we stripped the tabs at the beginning of the line.) These requests must go in before and after the syntax lines, turning the capabilities on and off. To do this, we define an address that specifies the range of lines between two patterns, the label and a blank line. Then, using the change command, we replace the label and the blank line with a series of formatting requests.

```
/SYNTAX:/,/^$/ {
     /SYNTAX:/c\
.Rh Syntax\
.in +5n\
.ft B\
.nf\
.na
     /^$/c\
.in -5n\
.ft R\
.fi\
.ad b
     }
```

Following the change command, each line of input ends with a backslash except the last line. As a side effect of the change command, the current line is deleted from the pattern space.

The USAGE portion is next, consisting of one or more descriptions of variable items. Here we want to format each item as an indented paragraph with a hanging italicized label. First, we output the .Rh macro; then we search for lines having two parts separated by a tab and a hyphen. Each part is saved, using backslash-parentheses, and recalled during the substitution.

```
/USAGE:/,/^$/ {
     /USAGE:/c\
.Rh Usage
     /\(.*\)·- \(.*\)/s//.IP "\\fI\1\\fR" 15n\
\2./
     }
```

This is a good example of the power of regular expressions. Let's look ahead, once again, and preview the output for the sample.

```
.Rh Usage
.IP "\fIfdesc\fR" 15n
pointer to database file descriptor.
```

The next part we come across is the description. We notice that blank lines are used in this portion to separate paragraphs. In specifying the address for this portion, we use the next label, RETURNS.

```
/DESC:/,/RETURNS/ {
     /DESC:/i\
.LP
     s/DESC: *$/.Rh Description/
     s/^$/.LP/
}
```

The first thing we do is insert a paragraph macro because the preceding USAGE section consisted of indented paragraphs. (We could have used the variable-list macros from the -mm package in the USAGE section; if so, we would insert the .LE at this point.) This is done only once, which is why it is keyed to the DESC label. Then we substitute the label DESC with the .Rh macro and replace all blank lines in this section with a paragraph macro.

When we tested this portion of the sed script on our sample file, it didn't work because there was a single space following the DESC label. We changed the regular expression to look for zero or more spaces following the label. Although this worked for the sample file, there were other problems when we used a larger sample. The writer was inconsistent in his use of the DESC label. Mostly, it occurred on a line by itself; sometimes, though, it was included at the start of the second paragraph. So we had to add another pattern to deal with this case. It searches for the label followed by a space and one or more characters.

```
s/DESC: *$/.Rh Description/
s/DESC: \(.*\)/.Rh Description\
\\1/
```

In the second case, the reference header macro is output followed by a newline.

The next section, labeled `RETURNS`, is handled in the same way as the `SYNTAX` section.

We do make minor content changes, replacing the label `RETURNS` with `Return Value` and consequently adding this substitution:

```
s/There is no return value\.*/None./
```

The very last thing we do is delete remaining blank lines.

```
/^$/d
```

Our script is put in a file named `refsed`. Here it is in full:

```
# refsed -- add formatting codes to reference pages
/^\*\**\*$/d
/^·/s///
/:·/s//:/
/NAME:/ {
     s//.Rh 0 "/
     s/ - /" "/
     s/$/"/
}
/SYNTAX:/,/^$/ {
     /SYNTAX:/c\
.Rh Syntax\
.in +5n\
.ft B\
.nf\
.na
     /^$/c\
.in -5n\
.ft R\
.fi\
.ad b
}
/USAGE:/,/^$/ {
     /USAGE:/c\ .Rh Usage
     /\(.*\)·- \(.*\)/s//.IP "\\fI\1\\fR" 15n\
\2./
}
/DESC:/,/RETURNS/ {
     /DESC:/i\
```

```
.LP
    s/DESC: *$/.Rh Description/
    s/DESC: \(.*\)/.Rh Description\
\1/
    s/^$/.LP/
}
/RETURNS:/,/^$/ {
    /RETURNS:/c\
.Rh "Return Value"
    s/There is no return value\.*/None./
}
/^$/d
```

As we have remarked, you should not have sed overwrite the original. It is best to redirect the output of sed to another file or let it go to the screen. If the sed script does not work properly, you will find that it is generally easier to change the script and rerun it on the original file than to write a new script to correct the problems caused by a previous run.

```
$ sed -f refsed refpage
.Rh 0 "DBclose" "closes a database"
.Rh Syntax
.in +5n
.ft B
.nf
.na
void    DBclose(fdesc)
    DBFILE *fdesc;
.in -5n
.ft R
.fi
.ad b
.Rh Usage
.IP "\fIfdesc\fR" 15n
pointer to database file descriptor.
.LP
.Rh Description
DBclose() closes a file when given its database file descriptor.
Your pending writes to that file will be completed before the
file is closed.  All of your update locks are removed.
*fdesc becomes invalid.
.LP
Other users are not effected when you call DBclose().  Their update
locks and pending writes are not changed.
.LP
Note that there is no default file as there is in BASIC.
*fdesc must specify an open file.
.LP
DBclose() is analogous to the CLOSE statement in BASIC.
.LP
.Rh "Return Value"
None.
```

6.3.12. Quit

The quit command (q) causes sed to stop reading new input lines (and stop sending them to the output). Its syntax is:

```
[line-address]q
```

It can take only a single-line address. Once the line matching *address* is reached, the script will be terminated.[18]

For instance, the following one-liner uses the quit command to print the first 100 lines from a file:

```
$ sed '100q' test
...
```

It prints each line until it gets to line 100 and quits. In this regard, this command functions similarly to the UNIX head command.

Another possible use of quit is to quit the script after you've extracted what you want from a file. For instance, in an application like getmac . . . , there is some inefficiency in continuing to scan through a large file after sed has found what it is looking for.

So, for example, we could revise the sed script in the getmac shell script as follows:

```
sed -n "
/^\.de *$mac/,/^\.\./{
p
/^\.\./q
}" $file
```

The grouping of commands keeps the line:

```
/^\.\./q
```

from being executed until sed reaches the end of the macro we're looking for. (This line by itself would terminate the script at the conclusion of the first macro definition.) The sed program quits on the spot and doesn't continue through the rest of the file looking for other possible matches.

Because the macro definition files are not that long, and the script itself not that complex, the actual time saved from this version of the script is negligible. However, with a very large file, or a complex, multiline script

[18]You need to be very careful not to use q in any program that writes its edits back to the original file. After q is executed, no further output is produced. It should not be used in any case where you want to edit the front of the file and pass the remainder through unchanged. Using q in this case is a very dangerous beginner's mistake.

that needs to be applied to only a small part of the file, this version of the script could be a significant timesaver.

If you compare the following two shell scripts, you should find that the first one performs better than the second. The following simple shell program prints out the top 10 lines of a file and then quits:

```
for file
do
     sed 10q $file
done
```

The next example also prints the first 10 lines using the print command and suppressing default output:

```
for file
do
     sed -n 1,10p $file
done
```

CHAPTER 7

SQL

by David Klappholz

SQL is the most widely used query language for relational databases; it has gone through two standardizations, with a third in progress, and exists in numerous implementations and dialects that go well beyond the standards. Because of the proliferation of SQL's dialects, I concentrate here on the basics common to all or most versions of the language rather than on a review of the numerous implementations. My approach is more tutorial than exhaustive. I elaborate on those aspects of the language that are the most powerful, and, therefore, the most interesting, and simply mention some aspects of the language that, although they may be critically necessary in practice, are fundamentally simple, easy to learn, and not particularly interesting.

Because SQL is closely tailored to the relational approach to database management, an understanding of SQL requires at least an elementary understanding of that approach and of its historical motivation. The two major approaches that prevailed before the invention of the relational approach, the *hierarchical* approach and the *network* approach, are both relatively cumbersome; both render the writing of query code relatively difficult because they require the programmer to deal directly with the complex data structures used to store the contents of a database. The relational approach to data storage and retrieval was proposed by E. F. Codd in 1970 to alleviate precisely this problem. The success of the relational approach, which currently dominates the market for database software, is due, at least in part, to the development of SQL and to the development of techniques for the optimization of SQL code.

Codd's genius, as it is now viewed, was in proposing that data be stored in simple data structures (*relations*), in showing how relations can be conceptually linked to one another in simple ways (*foreign key references*), and, finally, in proposing a simple yet powerful language for retrieving data (*relational algebra*). I begin the discussion of the relational approach, in section 7.1, by considering the details of Codd's first major contribution, the notions of

- A relation scheme
- A relational database scheme
- A relational database
- A candidate key for a relation scheme
- A foreign key reference from one relation scheme to another

Because SQL is directly derivative of Codd's second major contribution, relational algebra, I devote a significant part of this introductory section to a detailed consideration of that language, of its expressive power, and of the limits to its expressive power, which constituted the motivation for the development of SQL (section 7.2).

7.1. Relational Database Fundamentals

Codd proposed that data be stored as relations: sets of ordered tuples of values, with values of positionally identical components in different tuples of the same relation all coming from the same *domain*. For reasons that I need not go into here, Codd soon adopted the convention that domains be sets of *atomic* values; that is, neither were complex values with subparts of different types to be allowed as components of tuples, nor were sets with members of a single type.

As it turns out, it is simpler to view Codd's relations as *tables* with named columns—column names referred to as *attributes*—than to think of them as relations, and it is simpler to think of tuples as *rows* of such tables. In this view, the predominant one among practitioners, a domain is simply an elementary datatype such as *integer*, *floating point*, *character*, *string*, and so on. For the duration of the discussion of Codd's contributions, I assume, with Codd, that a table (relation) is a *set* of rows (tuples)—that is, that no table has two or more identical rows.

7.1.1. Database and Table Schemes and Instances

Because concrete examples are already called for, and become increasingly necessary as you proceed through further discussion of the relational approach, I point you to Figure 7.1, which shows the relational database scheme (type declaration) for a database designed to hold information about American manufacturing companies. (Because the relational scheme of a real database is typically quite large, the example shown in Figure 7.1 is that of a toy version of a manufacturing-industry database; the example has, however, been designed to illustrate all the ideas that are relevant to the subsequent discussion.)

A relational database scheme consists of individual relation schemes (type declarations), *table schemes* in the terminology that I use here; in the case of Figure 7.1, the schemes are for tables named company, division, site, product, person, works_for, and skill.

```
company(co_name, govt_id, ceo_ssn, hq_loc)
division(co_id, div_name, subdiv_of, dir_ssn, div_hq)
site(co_id, div_name, loc)
product(prod_id, manuf_co, manuf_div, loc, prod_descr)
person(ssn, name, address)
works_for(ssn, co_id, div_name, salary, emp_id, sup_ssn)
skill(ssn, prod_id, manuf_co)
```

FIGURE 7.1.

These schemes specify that instances of the tables hold information (attribute values) of the following sorts:

- Each row of the company table holds

  co_name: The name of a company.

  govt_id: The tax identification number assigned to the company by the federal government.

  ceo_ssn: The Social Security number of the company's chief executive officer.

  hq_loc: The name of the city in which the company's headquarters are located.

- Each row of the division table holds

  co_id: The tax identification number assigned to a company by the federal government.

  div_name: The name of a division of the company.

  subdiv_of: The name of that division of the company of which this division is a direct subdivision. The value of subdiv_of is null if the division is a first-level subdivision—that is, not a subdivision of any division. Note that the single `co_id` attribute serves as the company identifier for both the division (`div_name`) and the superdivision (`subdiv_of`), a fact that implies that a division of one company cannot be a subdivision of a division of a different company.

`dir_ssn`: The Social Security number of the division's director.

`div_hq`: The city in which the division's headquarters are located.

- Each row of the `site` table holds

  `co_id`: The tax identification number assigned to a company by the federal government.

  `div_name`: The name of a division of the company.

  `loc`: The name of a city in which a site (installation) of the division of the company is located. (If you want to distinguish among different installations located in the same city, then you add, say, an *address* attribute.)

- Each row of the `product` table holds

  `manuf_co`: The tax identification number assigned to a company by the federal government.

  `prod_id`: The company-assigned identifier of a product that the company manufactures.

  `manuf_div`: The division of the company by which the product is manufactured.

  `loc`: The location (site) of the division of the company at which the product is manufactured.

  `prod_descr`: The company-assigned description of the product.

- Each row of the `person` table holds

  `ssn`: A Social Security number.

  `name`: The name of the person with that Social Security number.

  `address`: The address of the person with that Social Security number.

- Each row of the `works_for` table holds

  `ssn`: A Social Security number.

  `co_id`: The tax identification number assigned, by the federal government, to a company that employs the person with that Social Security number.

div_name: The name of the division of the company to which the person is assigned.

salary: The person's yearly salary from the company.

emp_id: The identification number assigned to the person by the company.

sup_ssn: The Social Security number of the person's direct supervisor in the company.

- Each row of the skill table holds

manuf_co: The tax identification number assigned to a company by the federal government.

prod_id: The identifier of a product manufactured by the company.

ssn: The Social Security number of a person trained in the manufacture of the product for the company.

A relational database is an instance of a relational database scheme, which, in turn, is a collection of instances of the database scheme's table schemes—one of each. A sample (partial) instance of the manufacturing company database scheme is shown in Figures 7.2A–7.2G.

co_name	govt_id	ceo_ssn	hq_loc
New York Tire	111-22-3333	999-00-0001	New York
New Jersey Tire	222-33-4444	999-00-0002	Trenton
Southern Axle	333-44-5555	999-00-0001	Atlanta
Atlanta Axle	444-55-6666	999-00-0003	Atlanta
Maryland Brake	555-66-7777	999-00-0004	Columbia
Georgia Brake	666-77-8888	999-00-0005	Atlanta
Florida Brake	777-88-9999	999-00-0006	Pensacola
Ohio Windshield	888-99-0000	999-00-0007	Toledo
. . .	. . .	. . .	. . .

FIGURE 7.2A. *The company table.*

co_id	div_name	subdiv_of	dir_ssn	div_hq
666-77-8888	innovation	null	888-00-0001	Valdosta
666-77-8888	research	innovation	888-00-0001	Boston
666-77-8888	development	innovation	888-00-0002	Nashville
333-44-5555	personnel	null	888-00-0003	New York
333-44-5555	manufacturing	null	888-00-0005	Boston
333-44-5555	axle	manufacturing	888-00-0006	Cambridge
333-44-5555	front axle	axle	888-00-0007	Mattapan
333-44-5555	rear axle	axle	888-00-0008	Roxbury
444-55-6666	communications	null	888-00-0010	West Chester
444-55-6666	purchasing	null	888-00-0011	Bensalem
.	.	.	.	.
.	.	.	.	.
.	.	.	.	.

FIGURE 7.2B. *The* `division` *table.*

co_id	div_name	loc
333-44-5555	front axle	Atlanta
333-44-5555	front axle	Valdosta
333-44-5555	front axle	Memphis
333-44-5555	manufacturing	Cleveland
333-44-5555	manufacturing	Nashville
333-44-5555	manufacturing	New Orleans
888-99-0000	purchasing	Toledo
888-99-0000	communications	Columbus
888-99-0000	communications	Dayton
.	.	.
.	.	.
.	.	.

FIGURE 7.2C. *The* `site` *table.*

product_id	manuf_co	manuf_div	loc	prod_descr
FA-S/1	333-44-5555	front axle	Valdosta	small light-weight front axle
FA-S/2	333-44-5555	front axle	Valdosta	small heavy-weight front axle
FA-L/1	333-44-5555	front axle	Atlanta	large light-weight rust-proof front axle
FA-L/2	333-44-5555	front axle	Atlanta	large light-weight plain front axle
FA-L/3	333-44-5555	front axle	Atlanta	large medium-weight rust-proof front axle
. . .	. . .	. . .	. . .	. . .

FIGURE 7.2D. *The* `product` *table.*

ssn	name	address
999-00-0001	Joseph Jones	76 Main Street, Atlanta, GA
999-00-0002	Daniel Smith	42 Main Street, Atlanta, GA
999-00-0003	Donald Smith	76 Main Street, Atlanta, GA
999-00-0004	Denis Smith	90 Main Street, Atlanta, GA
777-00-0001	Jehosaphat Jones	32 Main Street, Atlanta, GA
777-00-0002	Jennifer Jones	29 Main Street, Atlanta, GA
777-00-0003	Janet Jones	87 Main Street, Atlanta, GA
777-00-0004	Janice Jones	63 Main Street, Atlanta, GA
777-00-0005	Joline Jones	29 Main Street, Atlanta, GA
777-00-0006	Jud Jones	29 Main Street, Atlanta, GA
777-00-0007	Jerusha Jones	29 Main Street, Atlanta, GA
. . .	. . .	. . .

FIGURE 7.2E. *The* `person` *table.*

ssn	co_id	div_name	salary	emp_id	sup_ssn
777-00-0001	333-44-5555	front axle	51000	EMP/FA-1	888-00-0004
777-00-0002	333-44-5555	front axle	52000	EMP/FA-2	888-00-0004
777-00-0003	333-44-5555	front axle	53000	EMP/FA-3	888-00-0004
777-00-0004	333-44-5555	front axle	54000	EMP/FA-4	888-00-0004
777-00-0005	333-44-5555	null	600000	EMP/1	null
777-00-0006	333-44-5555	front axle	56000	EMP/FA-6	888-00-0004
. . .	. . .	. . .	. . .	. . .	. . .

FIGURE 7.2F. *The* `works_for` *table*

ssn	prod_id	manuf_co
777-00-0005	FA-S/1	333-44-5555
777-00-0005	FA-S/2	333-44-5555
777-00-0005	FA-L/1	333-44-5555
777-00-0005	FA-L/2	333-44-5555
777-00-0006	FA-L/1	333-44-5555
777-00-0006	FA-L/2	333-44-5555
777-00-0006	FA-L/3	333-44-5555
. . .	. . .	. . .

FIGURE 7.2G. *The* `skill` *table.*

Although I have indicated that a relational database's scheme may be thought of as its type declaration and that the individual schemes for the database's tables may be thought of as the type declarations for those tables, I must note one proviso: A relational database consists of exactly *one* instance of each of its relation schemes, whereas in the context of general purpose programming languages, *multiple* instances of a user-declared type are always allowed.

7.1.2. Keys and Their Implications

In the listings of the attributes of the various tables of the manufacturing-company database, I have used the articles *a*, *an*, and *the* in such way as to indicate that certain items must be unique and that others need not be; for example, in indicating that attribute `co_name` of `company` will hold *the* name of *a* company, I have implied that a company cannot have more than one name.

Although this particular detail may be obvious, both it and others, some of them anything but obvious, must be formally specified as part of a database's or a table's scheme. Details of this sort are specified by the database designer through the choice of *candidate keys*—often referred to simply as keys—and foreign key references. A key is specified in a database scheme through the use of underlining as in Figure 7.1; thus, for example, the fact that `govt_id` is underlined in the scheme for `company` records the database designer's designation of `govt_id` as the key for `company`. Note that a key may consist of more than one attribute, such as `{co_id, div_name}` of `division`; a key may even consist of all the attributes of a scheme, such as `{ssn, prod_id, manuf_co}` of `skill`. Finally, a table scheme may have more than one key, in which case the database designer often chooses one as the *primary key*. (In the notation for database schemes used in Figure 7.1, if a table has multiple keys, it is possible to indicate only the primary key.)

The designation, by a database designer, of a set of attributes as a key for a table constitutes the imposition, by the designer, of the constraint that an instance of the table is not deemed *legal* if any two rows of the instance agree on the values of these attributes. Thus, for example, the designation of `govt_id` as the key for `company` represents the imposition of the constraint that an instance of `company` is not legal if two rows have the same `govt_id` value. The fact that `co_name` was not designated as part of the key represents the lack of any such constraint on that attribute; that is, the designer has decided that different companies are allowed to have the same name. The designation of `{co_id, div_name}` for `division` represents the imposition of the constraint that an instance of `division` is not legal if two rows agree on the values of both the `co_id` attribute and the `div_name` attribute. (There would be no problem, however, if two rows agreed on one of the two attributes but not the other—that is, if a company had two or more differently named divisions or if different companies had divisions with the same name.)

An alternative way of interpreting the key constraint on `company` is that a company is uniquely identified by its `govt_id`, but note that the phrase "is uniquely identified by" suggests an assertion about the real world. However, the designation of a key represents only the database designer's assertion of a constraint on instances of tables—an aspect of the designer's decision as to how the database is to *model* the real world.

The implications, both obvious and non-obvious, of the choices of keys for the manufacturing-industry database are as follows:

- In the case of `company(co_name, govt_id, ceo_ssn, hq_loc)`

  A company cannot have more than one name.

  Different companies can have the same name.

  A company cannot have more than one tax identification number.

  Different companies cannot have the same tax identification number.

  A company cannot have more than one chief executive officer.

  Different companies can have the same person as chief executive officer.

  A company cannot have more than one headquarters location.

  Different companies can have the same headquarters location.

- In the case of `division(co_id, div_name, subdiv_of, dir_ssn, div_hq)`

  A company cannot have different divisions with the same name.

  Different companies can have divisions with identical names.

  A division of a company cannot be a subdivision of a division of a different company.

  A division can be a subdivision of itself. (If you want to rule this out, you must do so in some fashion other than the designation of key constraints.)

  A division of a company cannot be a (direct) subdivision of more than one division.

  Different divisions of a company can be (direct) subdivisions of the same division.

  A person can be the director of more than one division of a company.

A person can be the director of divisions of different companies.

A division of a company cannot have more than one division headquarters city.

Different divisions of a company can have the same division headquarters city.

Divisions of different companies can have the same division headquarters city.

- In the case of `site(co_id, div_name, loc)`

  Different divisions of a company can have sites in the same city.

  Divisions of different companies can have sites in the same city.

- In the case of `product(prod_id, manuf_co, manuf_div, loc, prod_descr)`

  Different companies can manufacture products with the same product identifier.

  If different companies manufacture products with the same product identifier, those products can be manufactured by divisions with the same name.

  If different companies manufacture products with the same product identifier, those products can be manufactured by divisions with different names.

  If different companies manufacture products with the same product identifier, those products can have identical descriptions.

  If different companies manufacture products with the same product identifier, those products can have different descriptions.

  If a product is manufactured by a division of a company at a specific site of that division of the company, then it cannot be manufactured at any other of the division's sites.

- In the case of `person(ssn, name, address)`

  Different people cannot have the same Social Security number.

  Different people can have the same name.

  Different people can have the same address.

- In the case of `works_for(ssn, co_id, div_name, salary, emp_id, sup_ssn)`

A person can work for more than one company. (If you want to rule out this possibility, you do so by designating just `ssn` as the key of `works_for`.)

A company can have more than one person working for it.

A person cannot work for more than one division of a company.

A person cannot have more than one salary from a company.

A person can have the same salary from different companies.

A person can have different salaries from different companies.

A person cannot have more than one employee identifier from a company.

A person can have the same employee identifier from different companies.

A person can have different employee identifiers from different companies.

A person cannot have more than one supervisor in a company. (Note that the choice of key for `works_for` does not imply that an employee's supervisor need work for the same division of the company, nor that the supervisor even work for the company; nor can such a restriction be imposed on the scheme of Figure 7.1 through the use of foreign key references. If such a restriction is desired, then it must be imposed in some other fashion.)

A person can have the same supervisor in different companies.

A person can have different supervisors in different companies.

- In the case of `skill(ssn, prod_id, manuf_co)`

  A person can be trained in the manufacture of different products for the same company.

  A person can be trained in the manufacture of products with the same product identifiers for different companies.

  A person can be trained in the manufacture of products with different product identifiers for different companies.

  Different people can be trained in the manufacture of a product for a company.

7.1.3. Foreign Key References and Their Implications

As indicated at the beginning of this chapter, Codd proposed the notion of a foreign key reference to enable the database designer to specify conceptual connections between tables. By way of introducing the notion of a foreign key reference, I point you to the `govt_id` attribute of `company` and the `co_id` attribute of `division`. You recall that the `govt_id` attribute of `company` is intended to hold a company's government-assigned tax identification number, a company's unique identification insofar as the manufacturing-industry database is concerned. The database designer has also specified that `co_id` in `division` hold the identifier of a company; that is, `division`'s `co_id` attribute will hold government-assigned tax identification numbers.

The database designer must, of course, communicate to the direct users of the database the fact that an attribute of one table is the same as a, possibly same-named, possibly differently named, attribute of a different table.[1] Without such information, the application programmer is unable to write code for queries that require references to tables which are related in this way.[2]

Codd's terminology for the sameness of two sets of attributes is that one is a foreign key reference to the other; in the case of the example, `co_id` of `division` is a foreign key reference to `govt_id` of `company`, rather than the other way around, because `govt_id` of `company` is its table's key and `co_id` of `division` is not its table's key. The direction of a foreign key reference is always to a key because of the implication, discussed in the immediately following paragraph, of a foreign key reference as a constraint on legal instances of database tables.

Just as the database designer's choice of a key for a table scheme amounts to the imposition of a constraint on what constitutes a legal instance of that table, the choice of two sets of attributes from two different tables and the assertion of a foreign key reference from one of the sets of attributes to the other constitutes the designer's imposition of a constraint on the legality of table instances. In the example, the constraint is that a `division` table instance is not deemed to be legal if it contains a row with a `co_id` value that is not also the `govt_id` value of some row in the `company`

[1]You can also have a differently named attribute of the same table.

[2]An example of such a query is "Find every company that has its headquarters in Atlanta and has a division with divisional headquarters in Boston," a query that requires reference to the `company` and `division` tables and that requires awareness of the sameness of `govt_id` in the former and `co_id` in the latter.

table; a `division` table may not contain information about a division of a company about which the database has no `company` table information.

The foreign key references for the manufacturing-industry database scheme are shown in Figure 7.3, in which the directions of the arrows indicate the directions of the references. (One foreign key reference, a reference that is a bit difficult to represent in the notation of Figure 7.3, has been omitted but is, nevertheless, intended to hold; that reference is from `{co_id, subdiv_of}` of `division` to `{co_id, div_name}` of `division`; the database is not allowed to hold information about one division's being a superdivision of another, unless the superdivision is recorded in the database as a division of the same company as the subdivision.) Note that just as a key need not be a single attribute, a foreign key reference may be from a non-singleton set of attributes to another set of attributes of the same cardinality.

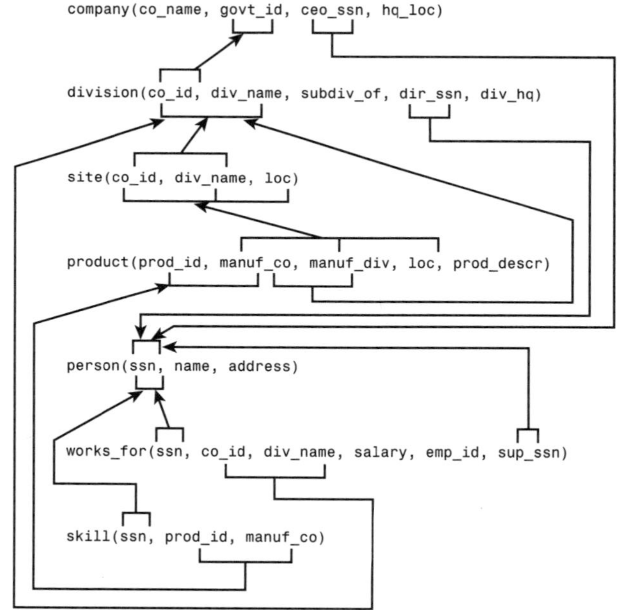

FIGURE 7.3.

Having discussed Codd's first major contribution, the invention of the notion of a relational database and the definition of its basic components, it is time to proceed to a discussion of Codd's second major contribution, relational algebra. Before doing so, I consider the more general subject of querying a relational database.

7.2. Querying a Relational Database

Given that a relational database consists of multiple tables, it should come as no surprise that the retrieval of information from such a database sometimes requires reference to a single table and sometimes requires reference to multiple tables. (In what follows, I use the word *table*, rather than the phrase *table scheme* or the phrase *table instance* when no confusion is expected to result; in the present case, of course, I have in mind *table instance*; schemes cannot be queried.) Consider as examples the queries of Figures 7.4A–7.4G. The first query requires reference to only `company`; the second requires reference to `company` and `division`; each of the subsequent queries requires reference to one more table than does the previous one so that the seventh requires reference to all seven tables.

Find every company with a headquarters in Atlanta.

FIGURE 7.4A.

Find every company with headquarters in Atlanta that has a division whose divisional headquarters is in Boston.

FIGURE 7.4B.

Find every company with headquarters in Atlanta that has a division whose divisional headquarters is in Boston and whose division has a site in Cleveland.

FIGURE 7.4C.

Find every company with headquarters in Atlanta that has a division whose divisional headquarters is in Boston, whose division has a site in Cleveland, and whose division manufactures a product with the ID `FA-S/2`.

FIGURE 7.4D.

> Find every company with headquarters in Atlanta whose chief executive officer is named Joline Jones, and that has a division whose divisional headquarters is in Boston and whose division has a site in Cleveland, and whose division manufactures a product with the ID `FA-S/2`.

FIGURE 7.4E.

> Find every company with headquarters in Atlanta whose chief executive officer, Joline Jones, earns more than $500,000 per year for her work for the company, and that has a division whose divisional headquarters is in Boston and whose division has a site in Cleveland, and whose division manufactures a product with the ID `FA-S/2`.

FIGURE 7.4F.

> Find every company with headquarters in Atlanta whose chief executive officer, Joline Jones, earns more than $500,000 per year for her work with the company, and that has a division whose divisional headquarters is in Boston and whose division has a site in Cleveland, and whose division manufactures a product with the ID `FA-S/2` in whose manufacture the chief executive officer happens to be trained.

FIGURE 7.4G.

7.2.1. Nested-Loop Queries

Single-table queries can usually be implemented as single-level loops, and multiple-table queries can often be implemented as nested loops, the level of nesting often being identical to the number of tables involved.

The pseudo-code loop nests of Figures 7.5A–7.5G are potential implementations of the queries of Figures 7.4A–7.4G. Note that in Figures 7.5B–7.5G, each simple condition in the `if` statement tests for an attribute value's being equal to a scalar value mentioned in the English query, for two rows' being related by a foreign key reference, or for two rows' being related by an indirect foreign key reference.

```
for i = 1 to no_rows(company) do
  if company[i][hq_loc] = "Atlanta"
  then output(company[i][govt_id])
```

FIGURE 7.5A.

```
for i = 1 to no_rows(company) do
      for j = 1 to no_rows(division) do
        if (company[i][hq_loc] = "Atlanta")
           and (division[j][div_hq] = "Boston")
           and (division[j][co_id] = company[i][govt_id])
        then output(company[i][govt_id])
```

FIGURE 7.5B.

```
for i = 1 to no_rows(company) do
  for j = 1 to no_rows(division) do
    for k = 1 to no_rows(site) do
      if (company[i][hq_loc] = "Atlanta")
        and (division[j][div_hq] = "Boston")
        and (division[j][co_id] = company[i][govt_id])
        and (site[k][loc] = "Cleveland")
        and (site[k][co_id] = division[j][co_id])
        and (site[k][div_name] = division[j][div_name])
      then output(company[i][govt_id])
```

FIGURE 7.5C.

```
for i = 1 to no_rows(company) do
  for j = 1 to no_rows(division) do
    for k = 1 to no_rows(site) do
      for m = 1 to no_rows(product) do
        if (company[i][hq_loc] = "Atlanta")
           and (division[j][div_hq] = "Boston")
           and (division[j][co_id] = company[i][govt_id])
           and (site[k][loc] = "Cleveland")
           and (site[k][co_id] = division[j][co_id])
           and (site[k][div_name] = division[j][div_name])
           and (product[m][prod_id] = "FA-S/2")
           and (product[m][manuf_co] = site[k][co_id])
           and (product[m][manuf_div] = site[k][div_name])
        then output(company[i][govt_id])
```

FIGURE 7.5D.

```
for i = 1 to no_rows(company) do
  for j = 1 to no_rows(division) do
    for k = 1 to no_rows(site) do
      for m = 1 to no_rows(product) do
        for n = 1 to no_rows(person) do
          if (company[i][hq_loc] = "Atlanta")
             and (division[j][div_hq] = "Boston")
             and (division[j][co_id] = company[i][govt_id])
             and (site[k][loc] = "Cleveland")
             and (site[k][co_id] = division[j][co_id])
             and (site[k][div_name] = division[j][div_name])
             and (product[m][prod_id] = "FA-S/2")
             and (product[m][manuf_co] = site[k][co_id])
             and (product[m][manuf_div] = site[k][div_name])
             and (person[n][name] = "Joline Jones")
             and (person[n][ssn] = company[i][ceo_ssn])
          then output(company[i][govt_id])
```

FIGURE 7.5E.

```
for i = 1 to no_rows(company) do
  for j = 1 to no_rows(division) do
    for k = 1 to no_rows(site) do
      for m = 1 to no_rows(product) do
        for n = 1 to no_rows(person) do
          for p = 1 to no_rows(works_for) do
            if (company[i][hq_loc] = "Atlanta")
               and (division[j][div_hq] = "Boston")
               and (division[j][co_id] = company[i][govt_id])
               and (site[k][loc] = "Cleveland")
               and (site[k][co_id] = division[j][co_id])
               and (site[k][div_name] = division[j][div_name])
               and (product[m][prod_id] = "FA-S/2")
               and (product[m][manuf_co] = site[k][co_id])
               and (product[m][manuf_div] = site[k][div_name])
               and (person[n][name] = "Joline Jones")
               and (person[n][ssn] = company[i][ceo_ssn])
               and (works_for[p][salary] > 500000)
               and (works_for[p][ssn]  = person[n][ssn])
               and (works_for[p][co_id]  = company[i][govt_id])
            then output(company[i][govt_id])
```

FIGURE 7.5F.

```
for i = 1 to no_rows(company) do
  for j = 1 to no_rows(division) do
    for k = 1 to no_rows(site) do
      for m = 1 to no_rows(product) do
        for n = 1 to no_rows(person) do
          for p = 1 to no_rows(works_for) do
            for q = 1 to no_rows(skill) do
              if (company[i][hq_loc] = "Atlanta")
                 and (division[j][div_hq] = "Boston")
                 and (division[j][co_id] = company[i][govt_id])
                 and (site[k][loc] = "Cleveland")
                 and (site[k][co_id] = division[j][co_id])
                 and (site[k][div_name] = division[j][div_name])
                 and (product[m][prod_id] = "FA-S/2")
                 and (product[m][manuf_co] = site[k][co_id])
                 and (product[m][manuf_div] = site[k][div_name])
                 and (person[n][name] = "Joline Jones")
                 and (person[n][ssn] = company[i][ceo_ssn])
                 and (works_for[p][salary] > 500000)
                 and (works_for[p][ssn]   = person[n][ssn])
                 and (works_for[p][co_id]   = company[i][govt_id])
                 and (skill[q][prod_id] = "FA-S/2")
                 and (skill[q][ssn] = person[n][ssn])
                 and (skill[q][manuf_co] = company[i][govt_id])
              then output(company[i][govt_id])
```

FIGURE 7.5G.

In all the sample queries, it was rows of different tables that were compared to one another. In cases in which rows of the same table must be compared with one another, the depth of loop nesting required is usually incremented by one for each additional row that must be examined. For example, the query of Figure 7.6A requires that pairs of rows of skill be examined, a fact that is reflected in the two-level loop nest in its potential implementation in Figure 7.6B.

> Find every person who is trained in the manufacture of at least two different products for the company whose government ID is 111-22-3333.

FIGURE 7.6A.

```
for i = 1 to no_rows(skill) do
  if (skill[i][co_id] = "111-22-3333") then
     for j = 1 to no_rows(skill) do
       if (skill[j][co_id] = "111-22-3333")
         and (skill[i][ssn] = skill[j][ssn])
         and (skill[i][prod_id] <> skill[j][prod_id])
       then output(skill[i][ssn])
```

FIGURE 7.6B.

Codd, realizing that the expression of queries in a highly stylized algebraic language would be far more likely to lead to the development of methods for query optimization than their expression in a general-purpose programming language, invented just such a language, *relational algebra*.

7.2.2. The Basics of Relational Algebra

Although relational algebra is, indeed, a query language, it has never been standardized and is not directly available to the user of any serious commercial database software product. Justification for its consideration here is two-fold: First, from a pedagogical point of view, an understanding of the fundamentals of relational algebra renders SQL much easier to learn; second, many commercial database products translate SQL into (proprietarily modified and extended) relational algebra as a first step in the query optimization process, making an understanding of relational algebra critical to an understanding of that process.

Relational algebra is a system of expressions, all of whose operators take tables as operands and produce tables as results (values). The basic operators of relational algebra are

- `select`, denoted σ, a unary operator that takes the place of the `if` in the nested-loop query implementations of Figures 7.5A–7.5G.
- `project`, denoted π, a unary operator that, roughly speaking, takes the place of `output()` in the nested-loop query implementations of Figures 7.5A–7.5G.
- `cartesian product`, denoted $\times$, a binary operator, familiar from set theory, which takes the place of loop nesting in the nested-loop query implementations of Figures 7.5B–7.5G.
- `rename`, denoted ρ, a unary operator that renames a table, a technical necessity in relational algebra, which doesn't have a parallel in the nested-loop query implementations of Figures 7.5A–7.5G.

- The binary set operators ∪, ∩, and - (set union, set intersection, and set difference).

7.2.2.1. The `select` Operator

The `select` operator returns the table that results from deleting from its operand all rows that do not satisfy the subscripted condition (see Figure 7.7, which shows the use of the `select` operator in expressing the query of Figure 7.4A.)

$$\sigma_{\text{hq\_loc} = \text{"Atlanta"}}(\texttt{company})$$

FIGURE 7.7.

The relational algebra expression of Figure 7.7 has as its value (i.e., it returns) a table with four columns, the columns of `company`. It contains all and only those rows of the instance of `company` shown in Figure 7.2A that have the value `Atlanta` in their `hq_loc` attributes as shown in Figure 7.8.

co_name	govt_id	ceo_ssn	hq_loc
Southern Axle	333-44-5555	999-00-0001	Atlanta
Atlanta Axle	444-55-6666	999-00-0003	Atlanta
Georgia Brake	666-77-8888	999-00-0005	Atlanta
.	.	.	.
.	.	.	.
.	.	.	.

FIGURE 7.8.

7.2.2.2. The `project` Operator

If, on the other hand, the result desired is a single-column table of `govt_ids` (of companies headquartered in Atlanta), then you apply the `project` operator to the result of the `select` operator. The `project` operator returns the result of deleting from its operand all columns except those listed in the subscripted attribute list. The relational algebra expression of Figure 7.9 produces precisely the desired result; the part of the result that can be gleaned from the tables of Figures 7.2A–7.2G is shown in Figure 7.10.

$\pi_{\texttt{govt\_id}}(\sigma_{\texttt{hq\_loc = "Atlanta"}}(\texttt{company}))$

FIGURE 7.9.

govt_id
333-44-5555
444-55-6666
666-77-8888
. . .

FIGURE 7.10.

7.2.2.3. The Cartesian Product Operator

When a query requires reference to more than one table, the *cartesian product* operator is used. The cartesian product operator takes two tables, T1 and T2, and produces a table, each of whose rows consists of a row of T1 concatenated with a row of T2; cartesian product produces all possible such rows. Cartesian product can be used to write relational algebra versions of the queries of Figures 7.4B–7.4G as you will see presently. The query of Figure 7.4B requires a two-way cartesian product; that of Figure 7.4C, a three-way cartesian product; . . . and that of Figure 7.4G, a seven-way cartesian product. Even the two-way example results in a table containing 80 rows, making it too bulky to show in its entirety; the seven-way example results in a table with the following number of rows:

```
no_rows(company)*no_rows(division)*no_rows(site)*no_rows(product)
                        *no_rows(person)*no_rows(works_for)*no_rows(skill)

                  = 8*10*9*5*11*6*7 = 1,663,200
```

Although this large a table can easily be managed by database software, it is implausibly large to be shown here. I therefore illustrate the results of cartesian product—that is, the entire table produced by a cartesian product—through the use of a small free-standing example. Consider, therefore, the tables of Figures 7.11 and 7.12; the result of computing their cartesian product is the table of Figure 7.13.

ssn	name
000-00-0000	John Smith
000-00-0001	Jane Smith
000-00-0002	Jodie Smith

FIGURE 7.11.

author	isbn	title
000-00-0000	67543	"Stuff"
000-00-0000	98763	"Things"
000-00-0001	84213456	"Things & Stuff"
000-00-0001	983215	"Stuff & Things"

FIGURE 7.12.

ssn	name	author	isbn	title
000-00-0000	John Smith	000-00-0000	67543	"Stuff"
000-00-0000	John Smith	000-00-0000	98763	"Things"
000-00-0000	John Smith	000-00-0001	84213456	"Things & Stuff"
000-00-0000	John Smith	000-00-0001	983215	"Stuff & Things"
000-00-0001	Jane Smith	000-00-0000	67543	"Stuff"
000-00-0001	Jane Smith	000-00-0000	98763	"Things"
000-00-0001	Jane Smith	000-00-0001	84213456	"Things & Stuff"
000-00-0001	Jane Smith	000-00-0001	983215	"Stuff & Things"
000-00-0002	Jodie Smith	000-00-0000	67543	"Stuff"
000-00-0002	Jodie Smith	000-00-0000	98763	"Things"
000-00-0002	Jodie Smith	000-00-0001	84213456	"Things & Stuff"
000-00-0002	Jodie Smith	000-00-0001	983215	"Stuff & Things"

FIGURE 7.13.

As an example of the use of cartesian product in writing relational algebra queries, consider Figure 7.14, which shows its use in expressing the query of Figure 7.4B.

```
πcompany.govt_id(σ  [company × division])
                 (company.govt_id = division.co_id)
                  and(company.hq_loc = "Atlanta")
                  and(division.div_hq = "Boston")
```

FIGURE 7.14.

In the relational algebra expression of Figure 7.14, I used conventional record-field *dot* notation to indicate which table an attribute is associated with; although doing so is not actually required unless two relations that occur in an expression have same-named attributes, I persist in the use of this notation to render relational algebra expressions easier to read. Figures 7.15–7.19 show relational algebra expressions for the queries of Figures 7.4C–7.4G.

```
πcompany.govt_id(σ  [company × division × site])
                 (company.govt_id = division.co_id)
                  and(company.hq_loc = "Atlanta")
                  and(division.div_hq = "Boston")
                  and(site.co_id = company.govt_id)
                  and(site.div_name = division.div_name)
                  and(site.loc = "Cleveland")
```

FIGURE 7.15.

```
πcompany.govt_id(σ  [company × division × site × product])
                 (company.govt_id = division.co_id)
                  and(company.hq_loc = "Atlanta")
                  and(division.div_hq = "Boston")
                  and(site.co_id = company.govt_id)
                  and(site.div_name = division.div_name)
                  and(site.loc = "Cleveland")
                  and(product.manuf_co = company.govt_id)
                  and(product.manuf.div = site.div_name)
                  and(product.prod_id = FA-S/2)
```

FIGURE 7.16.

```
πcompany.govt_id(σ  [company × division × site × product ×  person])
                 (company.govt_id = division.co_id)
                  and(company.hq_loc = "Atlanta")
                  and(division.div_hq = "Boston")
                  and(site.co_id = company.govt_id)
                  and(site.div_name = division.div_name)
                  and(site.loc = "Cleveland")
                  and(product.manuf_co = company.govt_id)
                  and(product.manuf.div = site.div_name)
                  and(product.prod_id = FA-S/2)
                  and(person.ssn = company.ceo_ssn)
                  and(person.name = "Joline Jones")
```

FIGURE 7.17.

```
πcompany.govt_id(σ   [company × division × site × product ×
                      person × works_for])
                 (company.govt_id = division.co_id)
                      and(company.hq_loc = "Atlanta")
                      and(division.div_hq = "Boston")
                      and(site.co_id = company.govt_id)
                      and(site.div_name = division.div_name)
                      and(site.loc = "Cleveland")
                      and(product.manuf_co = company.govt_id)
                      and(product.manuf.div = site.div_name)
                      and(product.prod_id = FA-S/2)
                      and(person.ssn = company.ceo_ssn)
                      and(person.name = "Joline Jones")
                      and(works_for.ssn = person.ssn)
                      and(works_for,co_id = company.govt_id)
                      and(works_for.salary > 500000)
```

FIGURE 7.18.

```
πcompany.govt_id(σ   [company × division × site × product ×
                      person × works_for × skill])
                    (company.govt_id = division.co_id)
                     and(company.hq_loc = "Atlanta")
                     and(division.div_hq = "Boston")
                     and(site.co_id = company.govt_id)
                     and(site.div_name = division.div_name)
                     and(site.loc = "Cleveland")
                     and(product.manuf_co = company.govt_id)
                     and(product.manuf_div = site.div_name)
                     and(product.prod_id = FA-S/2)
                     and(person.ssn = company.ceo_ssn)
                     and(person.name = "Joline Jones")
                     and(works_for.ssn = person.ssn)
                     and(works_for,co_id = company.govt_id)
                     and(works_for.salary > 500000)
                     and(skill.ssn = person.ssn)
                     and(skill.prod_id = product.prod_id)
                     and(skill.manuf_co = company.govt_id)
```

FIGURE 7.19.

Note that because the relational algebra expressions of Figures 7.14–7.19 are relational algebra expressions for the queries of Figures 7.4A–7.4G, and because the nested-loop programs of Figures 7.5A–7.5G are potential implementations of the same queries, the nested-loop programs may be used to evaluate the relational algebra expressions of Figures 7.14–7.19; that is, cartesian products need not be computed. Note, however, that the number of iterations of each of the nested-loop programs is exactly the same as the number of rows of the corresponding cartesian product so that although the nested-loop implementations save storage, the amount of time they require is still proportional to the product of the numbers of rows of all the tables involved.

7.2.2.4. The `rename` Operator

Cartesian product is also used, but with the aid of the `rename` operator, when different rows of the same table must be compared. What is actually done in such cases is not literally the comparison of two different rows of the same table, but, rather, the comparison of rows from two renamed copies of the table. The `rename` operator assigns the name found in its subscript to its single operand. For example, the relational algebra expression of Figure 7.20 is an implementation of the query of Figure 7.6A. Figure 7.21 shows the cartesian product of the two renamed tables.

$\pi_{skill1.ssn}(\sigma\ [\rho_{skill1}(skill) \times \rho_{skill2}(skill)])$

```
(skill1.co_id = 111-22-3333)
  and(skill2.co_id = skill1.co_id)
  and(skill1.ssn = skill2.ssn)
  and(skill1.prod_id <> skill2.prod_id)
```

FIGURE 7.20.

skill1.ssn	skill1. prod_id	skill1. manuf_co	skill2.ssn	skill2. prod_id	skill2. manuf_co
777-00-0005	FA-S/1	333-44-5555	777-00-0005	FA-S/1	333-44-5555
777-00-0005	FA-S/1	333-44-5555	777-00-0005	FA-S/2	333-44-5555
777-00-0005	FA-S/1	333-44-5555	777-00-0005	FA-L/1	333-44-5555
777-00-0005	FA-S/1	333-44-5555	777-00-0005	FA-L/2	333-44-5555
777-00-0005	FA-S/1	333-44-5555	777-00-0006	FA-L/1	333-44-5555
777-00-0005	FA-S/1	333-44-5555	777-00-0006	FA-L/2	333-44-5555
777-00-0005	FA-S/1	333-44-5555	777-00-0006	FA-L/3	333-44-5555
777-00-0005	FA-S/2	333-44-5555	777-00-0005	FA-S/1	333-44-5555
777-00-0005	FA-S/2	333-44-5555	777-00-0005	FA-S/2	333-44-5555
777-00-0005	FA-S/2	333-44-5555	777-00-0005	FA-L/1	333-44-5555
777-00-0005	FA-S/2	333-44-5555	777-00-0005	FA-L/2	333-44-5555
. . .	. . .	. . .	. . .	. . .	. . .

FIGURE 7.21.

7.2.2.5. The `Set` Operators

The relational algebra expressions that you have seen thus far have involved the operators σ, π, ×, and ρ; none have utilized set union, intersection, or difference. Examples of queries that can be written in relational algebra using the binary set operators are shown in Figures 7.22A–7.22C, with corresponding relational algebra expressions in Figures 7.23A–7.23C.

Find all companies that do not have a division named `research`.

FIGURE 7.22A.

Find all companies that have neither a division named `research` nor a division named `development`.

FIGURE 7.22B.

Find all companies that are either lacking a division named `research` or lacking a division named `development`.

FIGURE 7.22C.

$$\pi_{\texttt{company.govt\_id}}[\texttt{company}] \; - \; \pi_{\texttt{co\_id}}(\sigma_{\texttt{division.div\_name = "research"}}[\texttt{division}])$$

FIGURE 7.23A.

$$[\pi_{\texttt{company.govt\_id}}(\texttt{company}) \; - \; \pi_{\texttt{co\_id}}(\sigma_{\texttt{division.div\_name = "research"}}(\texttt{division}))]$$

$$\cap \; [\pi_{\texttt{company.govt\_id}}(\texttt{company}) \; - \; \pi_{\texttt{co\_id}}(\sigma_{\texttt{division.div\_name ="development"}}(\texttt{division}))]$$

FIGURE 7.23B.

$$[\pi_{\text{company.govt\_id}}(\text{company}) \;-\; \pi_{\text{co\_id}}(\sigma_{\text{division.div\_name = "research"}}(\text{division}))]$$

$$\cup \;\; [\pi_{\text{company.govt\_id}}(\text{company}) \;-\; \pi_{\text{co\_id}}(\sigma_{\text{division.div\_name = "development"}}(\text{division}))]$$

FIGURE 7.23C.

7.2.3. Reprise of Relational Algebra Operators

Additional details regarding the relational algebra operators are as follows:

- $\sigma_{\text{<condition>}}\text{<expression>}$

  <condition> must not refer to any attributes other than those in the value of <expression>.

  <condition> may be a simple condition—that is, a comparison of two values, either of which may be the value of a named attribute or a literal value.

  The comparison operators are <, <=, =, <>, >=, and >.

  <condition> may also be a compound condition—that is, a boolean expression involving simple conditions combined using ands, ors, and nots.

- $\pi_{\text{<attribute list>}}\text{<expression>}$

  <attribute list> must not contain any attributes other than those in the value of <expression>.

  If the deletion from the value of <expression> of all columns in <attribute list> results in two or more rows' being identical, then the final result contains only one instance of that row.

- <expression1> × <expression2>

  If the value of <expression1> has n columns and r1 rows and the value of <expression2> has m columns and r2 rows, then the result is an (n+m)-column table with r1*r2 rows.

  For each row in the value of <expression1> and for each row in the value of <expression2>, the result contains a row whose first n attributes' values are those of the row of <expression1> and whose remaining m attributes' values are those of the row of <expression2>—and no other rows.

- ρ<new name>(<attribute list>)<expression>

  The number of attributes in <attribute list> must be the same as the number of attributes in the value of <expression>.

  The parenthesized <attribute list> is optional; if it is present, then the final result is a table identical to the value of <expression> except that its name is <new name> and the names of its attributes are those of <attribute list>.

  If the parenthesized <attribute list> is missing, then the result is exactly the same as in the preceding item except that the names of the attributes of the final result are those of the value of <expression>.

- <expression1> ∪ <expression2>, <expression1> ∩ <expression2>, <expression1> - <expression2>

  The value of <expression1> must have the same number of columns as the value of <expression2>.

  The types of the attributes of the value of <expression1> must be the same as the types of the attributes of the value of <expression2>.

  If the application of ∪ results in two or more rows' being identical, then the final result contains only one instance of that row.

Before I leave the discussion of the expressive power of relational algebra and proceed to consider the type of query that can't be expressed, I revisit the question of the use of the dot (path-expression-style) notation to indicate which table an attribute comes from. Recall, in this regard, that up to this point I have prefixed every attribute name with a table name. In general, however, a table name need not be appended unless there is ambiguity as to which table a particular occurrence of an attribute name belongs to. Thus, for example, the query of Figure 7.19 could be written as in Figure 7.24 with no change in its meaning.

```
πgovt_id(σ [company × division × site × product × person × works_for × skill])
           (govt_id = division.co_id)
           and(hq_loc = "Atlanta")
           and(div_hq = "Boston")
           and(site.co_id = govt_id)
           and(site.div_name = division.div_name)
           and(site.loc = "Cleveland")
           and(product.manuf_co = govt_id)
           and(manuf_div = site.div_name)
           and(product.prod_id = "FA-S/2")
           and(person.ssn = ceo_ssn)
           and(name = "Joline Jones")
           and(works_for.ssn = person.ssn)
           and(works_for,co_id = govt_id)
           and(salary > 500000)
           and(skill.ssn = person.ssn)
           and(skill.prod_id = product.prod_id)
           and(skill.manuf_co = company.govt_id)
```

FIGURE 7.24.

7.2.3.1. Limitations on the Expressive Power of Relational Algebra

The most basic SQL statement has essentially the same conceptual form and meaning as the skeletal relational algebra expression shown in Figure 7.25, albeit with considerably different syntax.

```
π<attribute list>(σ<condition>[<table1> × <table2> × ... × <tablen>])
```

FIGURE 7.25.

In addition, SQL statements of this basic form may be combined using set union, set intersection, and set difference. What, then, is missing from relational algebra that is required in a commercial query language? The most obvious limitation of relational algebra is that selection conditions can involve only attribute names and literal constants. The query of Figure 7.26A, for example, cannot be formulated in relational algebra but could easily be formulated if relational algebra were extended to allow arithmetic expressions in selection conditions as in Figure 7.26B.

Find every employee of the company with `govt_id` 333-44-5555 who earns twice as much working for that company as does the supervisor of the division of the company to which the employee is assigned.

FIGURE 7.26A.

$\pi_{emp.ssn}(\sigma\ [\rho_{emp}(\texttt{works\_for}) \times \rho_{sup}(\texttt{works\_for})])$

```
        (emp.co_id = 333-44-5555)
          and(sup.co_id = emp.co_id)
          and(emp.sup_ssn = sup.ssn)
          and(emp.salary = 2*sup.salary)
```

FIGURE 7.26B.

The `select` operator in relational algebra is limited in more ways than just this one. Even if relational algebra were extended to allow arithmetic expressions in selection conditions, there would appear to be no way, in relational algebra, to decide whether a row should be included in the value of an expression on the basis of summary statistics of an entire table. For example, it would appear to be impossible to write the queries of Figures 7.27A–7.27F in relational algebra.

Find every company that has exactly three divisions.

FIGURE 7.27A.

Find every company that has more divisions with headquarters in Baltimore than divisions with headquarters in St. Louis.

FIGURE 7.27B.

Find every division whose total salary budget exceeds $3,000,000 per year.

FIGURE 7.27C.

Find every division whose average salary exceeds $50,000 per year.

FIGURE 7.27D.

Find the person(s) who is (are) paid the highest salary by the company whose `govt_id` is 666-77-8888.

FIGURE 7.27E.

Find the person(s) who is (are) paid the lowest salary by the company whose `govt_id` is 666-77-8888.

FIGURE 7.27F.

The summary-statistics functions that appear to be necessary for the expression of the queries of Figures 7.27A–7.27F are:

- COUNT the number of rows in a table.
- SUM the values of an attribute.
- AVERAGE the values of an attribute.
- Find the MINIMUM value of an attribute.
- Find the MAXIMUM value of an attribute.

The reader who is already acquainted with SQL will recognize COUNT, SUM, AVERAGE, MAXIMUM, and MINIMUM as the so-called aggregate functions of SQL. The COUNT query of Figure 7.27B, the SUM query of Figure 7.27C, and the AVERAGE query of Figure 7.27D cannot be written in relational algebra; the COUNT query of Figure 7.27A can, however, be written in relational algebra as, somewhat surprisingly[3], can the `MAXIMUM` and `MINIMUM` queries of Figures 7.27E and 7.27F (see Figures 7.28A–7.28C). To understand how it is that the relational algebra expression of Figure 7.28A implements the query of Figure 7.27A, note that

- The first major subexpression of Figure 7.28A—the one before the difference operator—finds the `co_ids` of companies that have three or more divisions.
- The second major subexpression of Figure 7.28A—the one after the difference operator—finds the `co_ids` of companies that have four or more divisions.

The relational algebra expression of Figure 7.28B is best understood by noting that

- The first major subexpression of Figure 7.28B—the one before the difference operator—finds the `ssns` of all people who work for the company in question.
- The second major subexpression of Figure 7.28B—the one after the difference operator—finds the `ssns` of people who work for the company in question and for whom there is someone working for the company who is paid more.
- The entire expression therefore finds the `ssns` of people who work for the company and for whom there is no one working for the company who is paid more.

The relational algebra expression of Figure 7.28C is best understood by noting that

- The first major subexpression of Figure 7.28C—the one before the difference operator—finds the `ssns` of all people who work for the company in question.
- The second major subexpression of Figure 7.28C—the one after the difference operator—finds the `ssns` of people who work for the company in question and for whom there is someone working for the company who is paid less.
- The entire expression therefore finds the `ssns` of people who work for the company and for whom there is no one working for the company who is paid less.

---

[3]The authors of at least one popular textbook indicate that queries of this sort cannot be written in relational algebra.

Note, however, that even if a query can be expressed in relational algebra, its expression may be extremely verbose. Consider as an example, the length of the relational algebra expression that would be required if the query of Figure 7.27A were changed to request companies with exactly 30 divisions.

$$\pi_{\text{div1.co\_id}}(\sigma_{\substack{\text{(div1.co\_id = div2.co\_id)} \\ \text{and(div2.co\_id = div3.co\_id)} \\ \text{and(div1.div\_name <> div2.div\_name)} \\ \text{and(div1.div\_name <> div3.div\_name)} \\ \text{and(div2.div\_name <> div3.div\_name)}}} [\rho_{\text{div1}}(\text{division}) \times \rho_{\text{div2}}(\text{division}) \times \rho_{\text{div3}}(\text{division})])$$

$$- \pi_{\text{div1.co\_id}}(\sigma_{\substack{\text{(div1.co\_id = div2.co\_id)} \\ \text{and(div2.co\_id = div3.co\_id)} \\ \text{and(div3.co\_id = div4.co\_id)} \\ \text{and(div1.div\_name <> div2.div\_name)} \\ \text{and(div1.div\_name <> div3.div\_name)} \\ \text{and(div1.div\_name <> div4.div\_name)} \\ \text{and(div2.div\_name <> div3.div\_name)} \\ \text{and(div2.div\_name <> div4.div\_name)} \\ \text{and(div3.div\_name <> div4.div\_name)}}} [\rho_{\text{div1}}(\text{division}) \times \rho_{\text{div2}}(\text{division}) \times \rho_{\text{div3}}(\text{division}) \times \rho_{\text{div4}}(\text{division})])$$

FIGURE 7.28A.

$$\pi_{\text{ssn}}(\sigma_{\text{co\_id = 555-55-5555}} [\text{works\_for}]) - \pi_{\text{wf\_1.ssn}}(\sigma_{\substack{\text{(w\_f1.co\_id = 555-55-5555)} \\ \text{and(w\_f1.co\_id = w\_f2.co\_id)} \\ \text{and(w\_f1.salary < w\_f2.salary)}}} [\rho_{\text{w\_f1}}(\text{works for}) \times \rho_{\text{w\_f2}}(\text{works for})])$$

FIGURE 7.28B.

$$\pi_{\text{ssn}}(\sigma_{\text{co\_id = 555-55-5555}} [\text{works \_for}]) - \pi_{\text{wf\_1.ssn}}(\sigma_{\substack{\text{(w\_f1.co\_id = 555-55-5555)} \\ \text{and(w\_f1.co\_id = w\_f2.co\_id)} \\ \text{and(w\_f1.salary > w\_f2.salary)}}} [\rho_{\text{w\_f1}}(\text{works\_for}) \times \rho_{\text{w\_f2}}(\text{works for})])$$

FIGURE 7.28C.

Each of COUNT, AVG, SUM, MIN, and MAX takes a table as its operand and produces a scalar value as its result—or, if you care to look at it that way, a table with a single row and a single column. If you were to add these functions to relational algebra, an appropriate place to add them would be the subscripted list of a project operator. (It is, of course, in SQL's analog of the project operator that these functions are permitted to occur in SQL.)

If you did so, then the query of Figure 7.29A might be written as in Figure 7.29B. Note, however, that the wording of the queries in Figures 7.27A–7.27F suggests that the results of these functions are to be used in selection conditions, that is, in places where relational algebra allows only attribute names and literal constants. The logical extension of the addition of the six aggregate functions to a query language would therefore be to allow single-value-producing expressions to appear in (be embedded in) select conditions. If you took this logical next step in the case of relational algebra, then you could write the queries of Figures 7.27A–7.27F as in Figures 7.30A–7.30F, in which the original English queries have been repeated for the sake of convenience. Naturally, SQL handles this construct in an analogous fashion.

Find the number of employees of the company whose govt_id is 333-44-5555, the average of the salaries paid by the company to its employees, the company's total salary budget, and the minimum and maximum salaries paid by the company to its employees.

FIGURE 7.29A.

$$\pi_{\text{COUNT(ssn), AVG(salary), SUM(salary), MIN(salary), MAX(salary)}}(\sigma_{\text{co\_id = "333-44-5555"}}(\text{works\_for})$$

FIGURE 7.29B.

Find every company that has exactly three divisions.

$$\pi_{company.govt\_id}(\sigma_{(\pi_{COUNT(division.div\_name)}(\sigma_{company.govt\_id=division.co\_id}(division)))=3}\ (company))$$

FIGURE 7.30A.

Find every company that has more divisions with headquarters in Baltimore than divisions with headquarters in St. Louis.

$$\pi_{company.govt\_id}(\sigma_{(\pi_{COUNT(division.div\_name)}(\sigma_{(company.govt\_id\ =\ division.co\_id)\ and\ (division.div\_hq\ =\ \text{"Baltimore"})}(division)))\ >\ (\pi_{COUNT(division.div\_name)}(\sigma_{(company.govt\_id\ =\ division.co\_id)\ and\ (division.div\_hq\ =\ \text{"Saint Louis"})}(division)))}\ (company))$$

FIGURE 7.30B.

Find every division whose total salary budget exceeds $3,000,000 per year.

$$\pi_{division.co\ id,\ division.div\ name}(\sigma_{\pi_{SUM(works\_for.salary)}(\sigma_{(works\_for.co\_id\ =\ division.co\_id)\ and\ (works\_for.div\_name=division.div\_name)}(works\_for)))\ >\ 3000000}\ (division))$$

FIGURE 7.30C.

Find every division whose average salary exceeds $50,000 per year.

```
πdivision.co_id, division.div_name(σ (division))
                 πAVG(works_for.salary)(σ(works_for))  > 50000
                                 (works for.co id = division.co id)
                                  and(works for.div_name =
                                      division.div_name)
```

FIGURE 7.30D.

Find the person(s) who is (are) paid the highest salary by the company whose `govt_id` is 666-77-8888.

```
πssn(σ  (ρw_f1(works_for)))
     (w_f1.govt_id = "666-77-8888")
       and πMAX(w_f2.salary)(σ(ρw_f2(works_for))) = w_f1.salary
```

FIGURE 7.30E.

Find the person(s) who is (are) paid the lowest salary by the com-pany whose `govt_id` is 666-77-8888.

```
πssn( σ  (ρw_f1(works_for)))
        (w_f1.govt_id = "666-77-8888")
          and πMIN(w_f2.salary)(σ(ρw_f2(works_for))) = w_f1.salary
```

FIGURE 7.30F.

Suppose, then, that you have added the functions COUNT, AVG, SUM, MIN, and MAX to relational algebra. One final type of query that was of interest to the designers of SQL would still be inexpressible in relational algebra—the type of query that requires a table to be partitioned into subtables and summary statistics to be computed for each of the subtables. An example of such a query is shown in Figure 7.31, in which the `works_for` table must be partitioned into subtables, each of which contains rows relating to exactly one company, rows that all agree on their values of co_id; the average of the salary fields must then be computed and output for each of the subtables.

For each company (that is, for each company with a listing in the company table), find the average salary paid by the company to its employees.

FIGURE 7.31.

Finally, but not exhaustively, it is impossible to express *transitive closure* queries in relational algebra, queries such as that of Figure 7.32; this is also, by the way, a limitation of SQL, one that is being addressed in current standardization discussions.

Find all ancestor divisions of the research division of the company whose co_id is 111-11-2222, that is, the division of which the research division is a subdivision (the company's *immediate* ancestor), the division of which the research division's immediate ancestor is a subdivision, and so on.

FIGURE 7.32.

If your curiosity has been whetted sufficiently to be desirous of developing a clearer, more formal, view of the sorts of queries that can be written in relational algebra and those that can't, you might want to consult one of the many relational database textbooks that discuss the other of Codd's two proposed query languages, *relational calculus*, a language based upon first-order predicate calculus and equivalent in expressive power to relational algebra. Relational calculus is not, however, recommended for those with a purely practical interest in relational database programming; nor is it recommended as part of an introductory course in relational database systems as its non-procedural, that is, non-computational, nature is extremely confusing to most students, even those with strong programming backgrounds.

7.3. SQL Basics

The presentation of a programming language typically proceeds through discussions of the following topics:

- The system of built-in data types
- The system of type constructors
- The type declaration statement
- The variable declaration statement
- The system of built-in operations on variables
- The system of expressions
- The scope rules
- The assignment statement
- The control-flow statements

SQL is a very-high-level special-purpose language so that not all of these categories are directly applicable; it is, nevertheless, instructive to compare SQL's constructs to those of a lower-level, general-purpose programming language.

Each of the SQL standards specifies a list of built-in data types that include types for character strings, of both fixed and varying lengths (`CHAR` and `VARCHAR`); bit strings, of both fixed and varying lengths (`BIT` and `BIT VARYING`); integers, of both standard length and short (`INT` and `SMALLINT`); fixed-point numbers with user-declarable numbers of digits and numbers of digits after the decimal point (`DECIMAL`); reals and double-precision reals (`FLOAT`, `REAL`, and `DOUBLE PRECISION`); and dates (`DATE`), times (`TIME`), and time intervals (`INTERVAL`).

Each standard also specifies a number of built-in functions on built-in types—functions that compute the lengths of variable-length character (`CHAR_LENGTH`) and bit strings (`BIT_LENGTH`); functions that cast values of one type to another type (`CAST`); functions that return the current time (`CURRENT_TIME`) and date (`CURRENT_DATE`), and so on. Most commercial database products add their own built-in types and built-in operations on these types—in some cases, extremely long lists of both. In line with my expressed intention to discuss the most powerful and interesting aspects of SQL, rather than to be exhaustive, I omit any further discussion of built-in types and operations on built-in types, except to note that SQL enables the user to declare and name restricted versions of built-in types using the **CREATE DOMAIN** statement[4]. There are also **ALTER DOMAIN** and **DROP DOMAIN** statements with obvious meanings.

SQL's only type constructor is `table of <list of built-in types>`, with a type declaration statement whose introductory keywords are, not surprisingly, **CREATE TABLE**; the **CREATE TABLE** statements necessary to declare the table schemes of Figure 7.1, together with their keys and foreign key references, are shown in Figures 7.33A–7.33G. (Note that for every table scheme, I have indicated that none of the attributes in the scheme's key may be NULL, a fairly common practice.) As indicated in the discussion of relational algebra, only a single instance of each user-declared type is permitted, so **CREATE TABLE** is simultaneously SQL's type declaration statement and its variable declaration statement.

```
CREATE TABLE company
   (  co_name        VARCHAR(30),
      govt_id        CHAR(11)      NOT NULL,
      ceo_ssn        CHAR(11),
      hq_loc         VARCHAR(30),
      PRIMARY KEY(govt_id),
      FOREIGN KEY(ceo_ssn) REFERENCES person(ssn))
```

FIGURE 7.33A.

```
CREATE TABLE division
   (  co_id          CHAR(11),        NOT NULL,
      divname        VARCHAR(30)      NOT NULL,
      subdiv_of      VARCHAR(30),
      dir_ssn        CHAR(11),
      div_hq         VARCHAR(30),
      PRIMARY KEY(co_id, div_name),
      FOREIGN KEY(co_id) REFERENCES company(govt_id),
      FOREIGN KEY(dir_ssn) REFERENCES person(ssn))
```

FIGURE 7.33B.

[4]For example, **CREATE DOMAIN** foobar **AS VARCHAR**(30) declares foobar as a name of the type VARCHAR(30). VARCHAR(30) is the designation of the built-in type "variable-length character string with maximum length of 30 characters." **CREATE DOMAIN** foobar AS **VARCHAR**(30) declares foobar as a name of the type VARCHAR(30) because it is perfectly legal to declare additional domains with specifications of VARCHAR(30).

```
CREATE TABLE site
  (  co_id         CHAR(11),        NOT NULL,
     divname       VARCHAR(30)      NOT NULL,
     loc           VARCHAR(30)      NOT NULL,¦
     PRIMARY KEY(co_id, div_name, loc),
     FOREIGN KEY(co_id, div_name)   REFERENCES division(co_id, div_name),
     FOREIGN KEY(dir_ssn)           REFERENCES person(ssn))
```

FIGURE 7.33C.

```
CREATE TABLE product
  (  prod_id       VARCHAR(10       NOT NULL,
     manuf_co      CHAR(11)         NOT NULL,
     manuf_div     VARCHAR(30),
     loc           VARCHAR(30),
     prod_descr    VARCHAR(50),
     PRIMARY KEY(prod_id, manuf_co),
     FOREIGN KEY(manuf_co, manuf_div, loc)
                                    REFERENCES site(co_id,manuf_div, loc)),
     FOREIGN KEY(manuf_co, manuf_div)
                                    REFERENCES division(co_id, div_name))
```

FIGURE 7.33D.

```
CREATE TABLE person
 (  ssn           CHAR(11)         NOT NULL,
    name          VARCHAR(30),
    address       VARCHAR(50),
    PRIMARY KEY(ssn))
```

FIGURE 7.33E.

```
CREATE TABLE works_for
  ( ssn          CHAR(11)          NOT NULL,
    co_id        CHAR(11)          NOT NULL,
    div_name     VARCHAR(30),
    salary       DECIMAL(9,2),
    emp_id       VARCHAR(15),
    sup_ssn      CHAR(11),
    PRIMARY KEY(ssn, co_id),
    FOREIGN KEY(ssn)               REFERENCES person(ssn),
    FOREIGN KEY(co_id, div_name) REFERENCES division(co_id, div_name),
    FOREIGN KEY(sup_ssn)           REFERENCES person(ssn))
```

FIGURE 7.33F.

```
CREATE TABLE skill
( ssn               CHAR(11)     NOT NULL,
prod_id             VARCHAR(10)  NOT NULL,
manuf_co            VARCHAR(30)  NOT NULL,
PRIMARY KEY(ssn, prod_id, manuf_co),
FOREIGN KEY(ssn)                   REFERENCES person(ssn),
FOREIGN KEY(prod_id, manuf_co)     REFERENCES product(prod_id, manuf_co))
```

FIGURE 7.33G.

Because SQL is a language intended to deal with *persistent* values—values whose existence persists beyond the execution of a single program, possibly over a large period of time—SQL also has a type redeclaration statement (**ALTER TABLE**) and a type deletion statement (**DELETE TABLE**). Naturally, there are statements for populating a table with rows (**INSERT**), for deleting rows (**DELETE**), and for modifying rows (**UPDATE**).

The notion of an expression in SQL, or, at least, the closest thing to an expression in SQL, is based on SQL's most interesting statement, the **SELECT-FROM-WHERE** statement, or SFW for short. For the purposes of this discussion, I define an SQL expression as follows:[5]

```
<exp> = SFW | <exp> EXCEPT <exp> | <exp> UNION <exp> | <exp> INTERSECT
<exp>
```

An SFW is similar to a project-select-cartesian product in relational algebra, rendering SQL expressions similar to those of relational algebra. You should note, however, that, in contradistinction to the assumption that I

[5]**EXCEPT** is SQL's notation for set difference.

made when I discussed relational algebra, in the realm of SQL, tables may have duplicate rows.

Finally, those control-flow constructs that SQL has are buried in the SFW statement; the notion of *scope* in SQL is meaningful only in the context of (nested) SFW statements, and the closest thing that SQL has to an assignment statement, unless one considers the **INSERT** and **UPDATE** statements to be assignments, is the **CREATE VIEW** (section 7.4.7), a statement that takes an entire SQL expression as a substatement. I therefore proceed to a discussion of the SQL expression.

7.4. SQL Expressions

The most interesting aspect of the SQL expression is the SFW, so I devote the bulk of the discussion to a detailed discussion of it. In its most general form, the SFW consists of six clauses as in Figure 7.34; the last four clauses are, however, optional, in fact independently optional except for the interdependence of the **GROUP BY** and **HAVING** clauses: The **HAVING** clause may be present only if the **GROUP BY** clause is present.

```
SELECT <output list>
FROM <table list>
WHERE <condition>
GROUP BY <attribute list>
HAVING <condition>
ORDER BY <attribute list>
```

FIGURE 7.34.

The first point that should be noted for the reader familiar with relational algebra is that **SELECT** in the SFW corresponds to `project` (π) in relational algebra and that **WHERE** is the SFW's version of `select` (σ). The second point to be noted is that the order of execution of the clauses of an SFW statement is not precisely as might be expected but is, rather, as follows:

- **FROM**
- **WHERE**
- **GROUP BY**
- **HAVING**
- **ORDER BY**
- **SELECT**

(Because **SELECT** serves the function of `project` in relational algebra, and because `project` is, effectively, the operator that outputs the results of a query, it should not come as a surprise that **SELECT** is executed last—although the reader might justifiably wonder why it takes first position syntactically.) In an SFW statement that is missing one or more optional clauses, each missing clause may be thought of as being replaced by a no-op, with the order of execution remaining as outlined.

The quickest way to understand the SFW statement is to note that the relational algebra expression of Figure 7.35A can be translated into SQL as the SFW statement of Figure 7.35B. More concretely, the queries of Figures 7.4A–7.4G may be translated into SQL as shown in Figures 7.36A–7.36G.

$$\pi_{\texttt{<attribute list>}}(\sigma_{\texttt{<condition>}}[\texttt{<table}_1\texttt{>} \times \texttt{<table}_2\texttt{>} \times \texttt{...} \times \texttt{<table}_n\texttt{>}])$$

FIGURE 7.35A.

```
SELECT <attribute list>
FROM <table1>, <table2>, ... , <tablen>
WHERE <condition>
```

FIGURE 7.35B.

```
SELECT company.govt_id
FROM company
WHERE hq_loc = "Atlanta"
```

FIGURE 7.36A.

```
SELECT company.govt_id
FROM company, division
WHERE (company.govt_id = division.co_id)
      AND (company.hq_loc = "Atlanta")
      AND (division.div_hq = "Boston")
```

FIGURE 7.36B.

```
SELECT company.govt_id
FROM company, division, site
WHERE (company.govt_id = division.co_id)
      AND (company.hq_loc = "Atlanta")
      AND (division.div_hq = "Boston")
      AND (site.co_id = company.govt_id)
      AND (site.div_name = division.div_name)
      AND (site.loc = "Cleveland")
```

FIGURE 7.36C.

```
SELECT company.govt_id
FROM company, division, site, product
WHERE (company.govt_id = division.co_id)
      AND (company.hq_loc = "Atlanta")
      AND (division.div_hq = "Boston")
      AND (site.co_id = company.govt_id)
      AND (site.div_name = division.div_name)
      AND (site.loc = "Cleveland")
      AND (product.manuf_co = company.govt_id)
      AND (product.manuf.div = site.div_name)
      AND (product.prod_id = FA-S/2)
```

FIGURE 7.36D.

```
SELECT company.govt_id
FROM company, division, site, product, person
WHERE (company.govt_id = division.co_id)
      AND (company.hq_loc = "Atlanta")
      AND (division.div_hq = "Boston")
      AND (site.co_id = company.govt_id)
      AND (site.div_name = division.div_name)
      AND (site.loc = "Cleveland")
      AND (product.manuf_co = company.govt_id)
      AND (product.manuf.div = site.div_name)
      AND (product.prod_id = FA-S/2)
      AND (person.ssn = company.ceo_ssn)
      AND (person.name = "Joline Jones")
```

FIGURE 7.36E.

```
SELECT company.govt_id
FROM company, division, site, product, person, works_for
WHERE (company.govt_id = division.co_id)
      AND (company.hq_loc = "Atlanta")
      AND (division.div_hq = "Boston")
      AND (site.co_id = company.govt_id)
      AND (site.div_name = division.div_name)
      AND (site.loc = "Cleveland")
      AND (product.manuf_co = company.govt_id)
      AND (product.manuf.div = site.div_name)
      AND (product.prod_id = FA-S/2)
      AND (person.ssn = company.ceo_ssn)
      AND (person.name = "Joline Jones")
      AND (works_for.ssn = person.ssn)
      AND (works_for,co_id = company.govt_id)
      AND (works_for.salary > 500000)
```

FIGURE 7.36F.

```
SELECT company.govt_id
FROM company, division, site, product, person, works_for, skill
WHERE (company.govt_id = division.co_id)
      AND (company.hq_loc = "Atlanta")
      AND (division.div_hq = "Boston")
      AND (site.co_id = company.govt_id)
      AND (site.div_name = division.div_name)
      AND (site.loc = "Cleveland")
      AND (product.manuf_co = company.govt_id)
      AND (product.manuf.div = site.div_name)
      AND (product.prod_id = FA-S/2)
      AND (person.ssn = company.ceo_ssn)
      AND (person.name = "Joline Jones")
      AND (works_for.ssn = person.ssn)
      AND (works_for,co_id = company.govt_id)
      AND (works_for.salary > 500000)
      AND (skill.ssn = person.ssn)
      AND (skill.prod_id = product.prod_id)
      AND (skill.manuf_co = company.govt_id)
```

FIGURE 7.36G.

7.4.1. The SELECT Clause

If all the attributes in the table produced by the **FROM** clause are desired in the output, they need not all be listed; rather, the form **SELECT** * may be used with the meaning *select all attributes*. Thus, the SFW of Figure 7.37A has precisely the same meaning as that of Figure 7.37B.

```
SELECT*
FROM company
```

FIGURE 7.37A.

```
SELECT co_name, govt_id, ceo_ssn, hq_loc
FROM company
```

FIGURE 7.37B.

If the projection specified by the attribute list of a SELECT clause (potentially) results in a table with repeated rows, you can ask for repeated rows to be deleted by appending the keyword DISTINCT after the word SELECT and before the list of attributes. (The opposite of DISTINCT is ALL, but as it is the default, it is rarely used.)

Thus, the SFW of Figure 7.38A, without the keyword DISTINCT would, if applied to the tables of Figures 7.2A–7.2G, produce the table of Figure 7.38B; the SFW of Figure 7.39A, with the keyword DISTINCT would produce the table of Figure 7.39B.

```
SELECT hq_loc
FROM company
```

FIGURE 7.38A.

hq_loc
New York
Trenton
Atlanta
Atlanta
Columbia
Atlanta
Pensacola
Toledo
. . .

FIGURE 7.38B.

```
SELECT DISTINCT hq_loc
FROM company
```

FIGURE 7.39A.

hq_loc
New York
Trenton
Atlanta
Columbia
Pensacola
Toledo
. . .

FIGURE 7.39B.

The arithmetic operators that may be used in the **SELECT** and **WHERE** clauses include +, -, *, and /. Parentheses are allowed. Because a computed value in a **SELECT** clause has no attribute name, SQL allows the user to specify a name through the use of the keyword **AS**. Thus, assuming a tax rate of 28%, the query of Figure 7.40A can be written as shown in Figure 7.40B, where the legend `tax` is printed as the name of the second column of the result table.

> Find the tax that must be paid by each person who works for the company whose `govt_id` is 111-22-3333.

FIGURE 7.40A.

```
SELECT works_for.ssn, .28*works_for.salary AS tax
FROM works_for
WHERE works_for.co_id = "111-22-3333"
```

FIGURE 7.40B.

In fact, any attribute in a **SELECT** clause can be renamed for output; thus, if you want the legends on the two columns of the output of Figure 7.40A to be `employee` and `tax`, you can write the query as in Figure 7.41.

```
SELECT works_for.ssn AS employee, .28*works_for.salary AS tax
FROM works_for
WHERE works_for.co_id = "111-22-3333"
```

FIGURE 7.41.

The query in Figure 7.29A, the first example of a query requiring the use of aggregate functions, is easily translated from the extended relational algebra of Figure 7.15B into the SQL of Figure 7.42.

```
SELECT COUNT(ssn), AVG(salary), SUM(salary), MIN(salary), MAX(salary)
FROM works_for
WHERE co_id = "333-44-5555"
```

FIGURE 7.42.

COUNT(ssn) counts the number of occurrences of ssn values in the table produced by the **FROM** and **WHERE** clauses. Because the number of occurrences of ssn values is, like the number of occurrences of any attribute, the same as the number of rows in the table produced by the **FROM** and **WHERE** clauses, you could have used **COUNT**(*), read *count all*, to return the number of rows in the table produced by the **FROM** and **WHERE** clauses.

When you want the number of distinct values that occur as values of an attribute, you add the keyword **DISTINCT** before the name of the attribute as in **COUNT**(**DISTINCT** ssn). In the case of the query of Figure 7.42, ssn and co_id together constitute a key for works_for, and because the **WHERE** clause fixes the value of co_id to a single value, the table produced by the **FROM** and **WHERE** clauses contains no repeated ssn values, thereby causing the number of rows in that table to be precisely the number of people working for the company of interest, so the keyword **DISTINCT** would effect no change in the final result.

In the general case,

```
COUNT(DISTINCT <attribute1> <attribute2> ... <attributen>)
```

returns the number of distinct n-tuples of values in the indicated columns of the table produced by the **FROM** and **WHERE** clauses.

Thus, for example, if the company table were temporarily changed to that of Figure 7.43A, the query of Figure 7.43B would produce a result of 3 (three), whereas the query of Figure 7.43C would produce a result of 1 (one).

co_name	govt_id	ceo_ssn	hq_loc
New York Tire	111-22-3333	999-00-0001	New York
New Jersey Tire	222-33-4444	999-00-0002	Trenton
Atlanta Axle	333-44-5555	999-00-0001	Atlanta
Atlanta Axle	444-55-6666	999-00-0003	Atlanta
Maryland Brake	555-66-7777	999-00-0004	Columbia
Atlanta Axle	666-77-8888	999-00-0005	Atlanta
Florida Brake	777-88-9999	999-00-0006	Pensacola
Ohio Windshield	888-99-0000	999-00-0007	Toledo
.	.	.	.
.	.	.	.
.	.	.	.

FIGURE 7.43A.

```
SELECT COUNT(co_name, hq_loc)
FROM company
```

FIGURE 7.43B.

```
SELECT COUNT(DISTINCT co_name, hq_loc)
FROM company
```

FIGURE 7.43C.

Only the **SELECT** clause and the **HAVING** clause of an SFW may contain an application of an aggregate function; a query such as that shown in Figure 7.44 is, therefore, illegal—on semantic and, as a consequence, syntactic grounds—although the beginning student of SQL is often tempted to write statements of this form.

```
SELECT co_id
FROM works_for
WHERE COUNT(ssn) > 100
```

FIGURE 7.44.

If the incorrectness of the placement of the **COUNT** in the **WHERE** clause of Figure 7.44 is not obvious to you, keep in mind that the condition in a **WHERE** clause, like that in a relational algebra `select`, is applied to each row of the table produced by the **FROM** clause—the table to which the `select` is applied, frequently a simple cartesian product in the case of relational algebra. In the case under consideration, this would mean testing each row of `works_for` for a number of `ssn`s greater than 100.

I delay the discussion of the use of aggregate function in the **SELECT** clauses of embedded SFWs until I have discussed the subject of embedding—in the discussion of the **WHERE** clause.

7.4.2. The WHERE Clause

Being the SFW's version of relational algebra's `select` operator, the **WHERE** clause performs condition testing, on a row-by-row basis, upon the table produced by the **FROM** clause. I begin by considering simple condition tests (section 7.4.2.1) and then proceed to a discussion of tests involving embedded expressions (section 7.4.2.2).

7.4.2.1. Simple Conditions

The SFW's basic comparison operators include <, <=, =, <>, >=, and >. For string comparisons, SQL provides pattern-matching operators named **LIKE** and **NOT LIKE**, where % represents any sequence of one or more characters and _ represents any single character so that the queries of Figures 7.45A–7.45D can be written in SQL as in Figures 7.45E–7.45H.

Find all CEOs whose names start with a *K*.

FIGURE 7.45A.

Find all CEOs whose names don't start with a *K*.

FIGURE 7.45B.

Find all CEOs whose names are five letters long.

FIGURE 7.45C.

Find all CEOs whose names aren't five letters long.

FIGURE 7.45D.

```
SELECT company.ceo_ssn
FROM company, person
WHERE  (company.ceo_ssn = person.ssn)
       AND (person.name LIKE 'K%'
```

FIGURE 7.45E.

```
SELECT company.ceo_ssn
FROM company, person
WHERE  (company.ceo_ssn = person.ssn)
       AND (person.name NOT LIKE 'K%'
```

FIGURE 7.45F.

```
SELECT company.ceo_ssn
FROM company, person
WHERE  (company.ceo_ssn = person.ssn)
       AND (person.name LIKE '_ _ _ _ _'
```

FIGURE 7.45G.

```
SELECT company.ceo_ssn
FROM company, person
WHERE  (company.ceo_ssn = person.ssn)
        AND (person.name NOT LIKE '_ _ _ _ _'
```

FIGURE 7.45H.

Attribute values may be **NULL**, but the **NULL** state of a value cannot be tested through the use of a condition of the form `<attribute name> = NULL`; rather, the proper syntax is `<attribute name> IS NULL`; similarly, a non-**NULL** state is tested as `<attribute name> IS NOT NULL`.

Although the value of an attribute may be tested for being between two specified values through the use of two simple comparisons **AND**ed together, as in

```
(<value 1> <= <attribute value>)
AND (<attribute value> <= <value 2>
```

the two (inclusive) comparisons can also be written as

```
<attribute name> BETWEEN <value 1> AND <value 2>
```

Expressions of the form

```
<attribute name> NOT BETWEEN <value 1> AND <value 2>
```

can also be used—with the obvious meaning.

As I have already hinted, **WHERE** clause conditions can be combined using the logical operators **AND**, **OR**, and **NOT**. As is probably also expected, parentheses may be used in **WHERE** clause conditions.

7.4.2.2. Conditions Involving Embedded Expressions

The queries that I used to introduce the notion of aggregate functions in embedded relational algebra subexpressions, queries in Figures 7.27A–7.27F, can be written in SQL through the use of aggregate functions in the **SELECT** clauses of embedded subexpressions as in Figures 7.46A–7.46F (English queries repeated).

Find every company that has exactly three divisions.

```
SELECT division.co_id
FROM division div1
WHERE  (  SELECT COUNT(div_name)
          FROM division div2
          WHERE div2.co_id = div1.co_id) = 3
```

FIGURE 7.46A.

Find every company that has more divisions with headquarters in Baltimore than divisions with headquarters in St. Louis.

```
SELECT company.govt_id
FROM company
WHERE  (  SELECT COUNT(division.div_name)
          FROM division
          WHERE  company.govt_id = division.co_id)
                 AND (division.div_hq = "Baltimore")

                 >

       (  SELECT COUNT(division.div_name)
          FROM division
          WHERE  (company.govt_id = division.co_id)
                 AND (division.div_hq = "Saint Louis")
```

FIGURE 7.46B.

Find every division whose total salary budget exceeds $3,000,000 per year.

```
SELECT division.co_id, division.div_name
FROM division
WHERE ( SELECT SUM(works_for.salary)
        FROM works_for
        WHERE (works_for.co_id = division.co_id)
             AND (works_for.div_name = division.div_name)) > 3000000
```

FIGURE 7.46C.

Find every division whose average salary exceeds $50,000 per year.

```
SELECT division.co_id, division.div_name
FROM division
WHERE  (   SELECT AVG(works_for.salary)
           FROM works_for
           WHERE (works_for.co_id = division.co_id)
                  AND (works_for.div_name = division.div_name)) > 50000
```

FIGURE 7.46D.

Find the person(s) who is (are) paid the highest salary by the company whose `govt_id` is 666-77-8888.

```
SELECT ssn
FROM works_for wf1
WHERE   w_f1.co_id = "666-77-8888" = ( SELECT MAX(w_f2..salary)
                                      FROM works_for w_f2) = w_f1.salary)
```

FIGURE 7.46E.

Find the person(s) who is (are) paid the lowest salary by the company whose `govt_id` is 666-77-8888.

```
SELECT ssn
FROM works_for w_f1
WHERE   w_f1.co_id = "666-77-8888" = ( SELECT MIN(w_f2.salary)
                                       FROM works for w_f2) = w_f1.salary)
```

FIGURE 7.46F.

In addition to the simple comparison operators, there are also a few non-comparison operators, which can be used to introduce embedded subexpressions:

- **IN** and **NOT IN**
- **EMPTY** and **NOT EMPTY**

- For each `<comparison op>` in `{<, <=, =, <>, >, >=}`:
    - `<comparison op>`**`ALL`**
    - `<comparison op>`**`SOME`**
    - `<comparison op>`**`ANY`**

The uses of these operators and their meanings are as follows: The embedding expression `<value>` **`IN`** `<SFW>`

- Returns `true` if `<SFW>` returns a table with a single column and `<value>` equals the value in one of the rows of the table.
- Returns `false` if `<SFW>` returns a table with a single column and `<value>` does not equal the value in any of the rows of the table.
- Is a syntax error otherwise.

Thus, the query of Figure 7.47A can be written as in Figure 7.47B.

> Find the company headquarters location of every company that has a division headquartered in Atlanta.

FIGURE 7.47A.

```
SELECT company.hq_loc
FROM company
WHERE company.govt_id IN ( SELECT division.co_id
                           FROM division
                           WHERE division.div_hq = "Atlanta")
```

FIGURE 7.47B.

Note, of course, that this is not the only way to write the query of Figure 7.47A; rather, it can be written, without an embedded SFW, as in Figure 7.47C.

```
SELECT company.hq_loc
FROM company, division
WHERE  (company.govt_id = division.co_id)
         AND (division.div_hq = "Atlanta")
```

FIGURE 7.47C.

In fact, SQL has been severely criticized by some because it often allows an English query to be written in numerous different ways.

The embedding expression `<value> NOT IN <SFW>`

- Returns `false` if `<SFW>` returns a table with a single column and `<value>` equals the value in one of the rows of the table.
- Returns `true` if `<SFW>` returns a table with a single column and `<value>` does not equal the value in any of the rows of the table.
- Is a syntax error otherwise.

Thus, the query of Figure 7.48A can be written as in Figure 7.48B.

> Find the company headquarters location of every company that does not have a division headquartered in Atlanta.

FIGURE 7.48A.

```
SELECT company.hq_loc
FROM company
WHERE company.govt_id NOT IN ( SELECT division.co_id
                               FROM division
                               WHERE division.div_hq = "Atlanta")
```

FIGURE 7.48B.

Note that this query can be written in at least one alternative way, but not quite as easily as that of Figure 7.47A; one alternative version, that of Figure 7.48C, uses the operator `set difference`, denoted **EXCEPT** in SQL.

```
SELECT company.hq_loc
FROM company
WHERE company.govt_id IN (( SELECT division.co_id
                            FROM division)
                        EXCEPT
                            (  SELECT division.co_id
                               FROM division
                               WHERE division.div_hq = "Atlanta"))
```

FIGURE 7.48C.

The embedding expression (<value$_1$>, <value$_2$>, ... , <value$_n$>) **IN** <SFW>

- Returns `true` if <SFW> returns a table with `n` columns, and one of the rows of that table has column values of <value$_1$>, <value$_2$>, ... and <value$_n$> in that order.
- Returns `false` if <SFW> returns a table with `n` columns, and none of the rows of that table has column values of <value$_1$>, <value$_2$>, ... and <value$_n$> in that order.
- Is a syntax error otherwise.

Thus, the query of Figure 7.49A can be written as in Figure 7.49B.

Find the division headquarters location of every division (of any company) that has a site in Atlanta.

FIGURE 7.49A.

```
SELECT division.div_hq
FROM division
WHERE (division.co_id, division.div_name) IN ( SELECT site.co_id, site.div_name)
                                               FROM site
                                               WHERE site.loc = "Atlanta")
```

FIGURE 7.49B.

The embedding expression (<value$_1$>, <value$_2$>, ... , <value$_n$>) **NOT IN** <SFW>

- Returns false if <SFW> returns a table with n columns, and one of the rows of that table has column values of <value$_1$>, <value$_2$>, . . . and <value$_n$> in that order.
- Returns true if <SFW> returns a table with n columns, and none of the rows of that table has column values of <value$_1$>, <value$_2$>, . . . and <value$_n$> in that order.
- Is a syntax error otherwise.

Thus, the query of Figure 7.50A can be written as in Figure 7.50B.

> Find the division headquarters location of every division (of any company) that has no site in Atlanta.

FIGURE 7.50A.

```
SELECT division.div_hq
FROM division
WHERE (division.co id, division.div name) NOT IN ( SELECT site.co id, site.div name)
                                                   FROM site
                                                   WHERE site.loc = "Atlanta")
```

FIGURE 7.50B.

The embedding expression **EMPTY** <SFW>

- Returns true if <SFW> returns an empty table, a table with zero rows.
- Returns false otherwise.

Using **EMPTY** <SFW>, you can write the query of Figure 7.50A in yet another way. To understand how, take a short digression into the subject of name scopes in nested expressions.

Once you allow an SFW statement to be embedded in another SFW statement, the question of name scopes arises. In the few cases that you have already seen, the answers were quite obvious; in the query whose **EMPTY**

<SFW> version led to this digression, the answer is considerably less obvious. I therefore introduce the question of scopes with examples that use simple comparison operators to introduce embedding.

For example, suppose that you wrote the query of Figure 7.27F as in Figure 7.51 (English query repeated); the following questions would arise:

- To which copy of `works_for` does `works_for.co_id` refer in the first line of the **WHERE** clause?
- To which copy of `works_for` does `works_for.salary` refer in the embedded **SELECT** clause?
- To which copy of `works_for` does `works_for.co_id` refer in the embedded **WHERE** clause?
- To which copy of `works_for` does `works_for.salary` refer just after the end of the embedded query?

Find the person(s) who is (are) paid the lowest salary by the company whose `govt_id` is 666-77-8888.

```
SELECT ssn
FROM works_for
WHERE   works_for.co_id = "666-77-8888"
        AND ( SELECT MIN(works_for.salary)
              FROM works_for
              WHERE works_for.co_id = "666-77-8888") =works_for.salary
```

FIGURE 7.51.

The answers to all three question are simple once you consider the SFW statement's scope rules:

- Each SFW statement constitutes a name scope (block) that begins at the beginning of its **SELECT** clause and ends at the end of its last clause, which could be a **FROM**, **WHERE**, **GROUP BY**, **HAVING**, or **ORDER BY** clause.
- An SFW's **FROM** clause is the name declaration statement for the scope defined by the SFW statement.
- The scope of a declaration of a name—in a **FROM** clause—runs from the beginning to the end of the **FROM** clause's SFW statement, with breaks for the scopes of embedded declarations of the same name.

The scopes of the two declarations of the name works_for are as shown in Figure 7.52, so that

```
SELECT
        ssn
FROM   works_for
WHERE  works_for.co_id = "666-77-8888"
       AND
         ( SELECT
                         MIN(works_for.salary)
           FROM works_for
           WHERE works_for.co_id = "666-77-8888")
                                              = works_for.salary
```

FIGURE 7.52.

- The occurrence of works_for.co_id in the first line of the **WHERE** clause refers to the declaration of works_for in the outer SFW.
- The occurrence of works_for in the embedded **SELECT** clause refers to the declaration of works_for in the embedded SFW.
- The occurrence of works_for in the embedded **WHERE** clause refers to the declaration of works_for in the embedded SFW.
- The occurrence of works_for just after the end of the embedded query refers to the declaration of works_for in the outer SFW.

Note that the query of Figure 7.51 had no references from the inner scope to names declared in the outer scope; the embedded SFW statement in Figure 7.51 is, therefore, termed an *uncorrelated* subquery. Being uncorrelated, it need be evaluated only once, rather than once per row of the table produced by the outer **WHERE** clause.

An example of a correlated subquery—in fact, examples of two correlated subqueries—may be found in Figure 7.46B. In this case, the two subqueries nested in the outer **WHERE** clause must be evaluated, and the comparison of their values done, once for each row of the company table, the table produced by the outer **FROM** clause.

Note, however, that, even though the number of Baltimore-headquartered divisions and the number of Saint-Louis–headquartered divisions are computed for each company, these numbers cannot be passed from the inner SFW to the outer SFW as would be desired if you were interested in the results of the related query of Figure 7.53A. Rather, a subquery occurs in a comparison, and all that can be passed to the outer query is the boolean result of the comparison. In the simplest SQL version of the query of Figure 7.53A, tables are renamed; I therefore take a small digression to discuss the subject of table renaming.

Find every company that has more divisions with headquarters in Baltimore than divisions with headquarters in St. Louis, and for each such company, find the number of Baltimore-headquartered divisions and the number of St. Louis–headquartered divisions.

FIGURE 7.53A.

Renaming is done in the SFW statement by appending the desired new name, termed, appropriately, an *alias*, to the name of a table in the **FROM** clause. Thus, for example, the relational algebra query of Figure 7.20 (English query in Figure 7.6A) can be written in SQL as in Figure 7.53B.

```
SELECT skill1.ssn
FROM skill skill1, skill skill2
WHERE (skill1.co_id = 111-22-3333)
      AND (skill2.co_id = skill1.co_id)
      AND (skill1.ssn = skill2.ssn)
      AND (skill1.prod_id <> skill2.prod_id)
```

FIGURE 7.53B.

If you want to produce the results requested by the query of Figure 7.53A, you have to write an SFW statement like that of Figure 7.53C—that is, one in which a good deal of unnecessary additional work is done. (For starters, a potentially vastly larger cartesian product must be computed.)

```
SELECT company.govt_id, COUNT(DISTINCT div1.div_name),
            COUNT(DISTINCT div2,div_name)
FROM company, division div1, division div2
WHERE (  SELECT COUNT(division.div_name
         FROM division
         WHERE  (company.govt_id = division.co_id)
                  AND (division.div_name = div1.divname)
                  AND (div_hq = "Baltimore"))

                  >

      (  SELECT COUNT(division.div_name
         FROM division
         WHERE  (company.govt_id = division.co_id)
                  AND (division.div_name = div2.div_name)
                  AND (div_hq = "Saint Louis"))
```

FIGURE 7.53C.

I now return from the large digression, in which I have discussed the topics of scope and table renaming, and I resume the discussion of the embedding operator **EMPTY** <SFW>. Using the newly acquired understanding of name scoping in SQL, you can write the query of Figure 7.50A as in Figure 7.54.

```
SELECT division.div_hq
FROM division
WHERE    EMPTY (  SELECT site.loc
                  FROM site
                  WHERE   (site.loc = "Atlanta")
                            AND (site.co_id = division.co_id)
                            AND (site.div_name = division.div_name))
```

FIGURE 7.54.

The embedding expression **NOT EMPTY** <SFW>

- Returns `false` if <SFW> returns an empty table, a table with zero rows.
- Returns `true` otherwise.

Thus, the query of Figure 7.50A can be written, in yet another way, as in Figure 7.55.

```
SELECT division.div_hq
FROM division
WHERE    NOT EMPTY (  SELECT site.loc
                      FROM site
                      WHERE   (site.loc = "Atlanta")
                              AND (site.co_id = division.co_id)
                              AND (site.div_name = division.div_name))
```

FIGURE 7.55.

The embedding expression `<value> <comparison op>` **`ALL`** `<SFW>`

- Returns `true` if `<SFW>` returns a table with a single column and `<value>` bears the relation `<comparison op>` to the value in every row of that table.
- Returns `false` if `<SFW>` returns a table with a single column and `<value>` does not bear the relation `<comparison op>` to the value in every row of that table—that is, if there is at least one row to whose value `<value>` does not bear the relation `<comparison op>`.
- Is a syntax error otherwise.

Thus, the query of Figure 7.56A can be written as in Figure 7.56B.

> Find every employee (of any company) who earns more than the highest-earning employee of the company with `govt_id` of 111-22-3333.

FIGURE 7.56A.

```
SELECT works_for.ssn
FROM works_for
WHERE    works_for.salary >ALL (  SELECT works_for.salary
                                  FROM works_for
                                  WHERE works_for.co_id = "111-22-3333)
```

FIGURE 7.56B.

This query can, of course, also be written as in Figure 7.56C.

```
SELECT works_for.ssn
FROM works_for
WHERE   works_for.salary > (  SELECT MAX(works_for.salary)
                               FROM works_for
                               WHERE works_for.co_id = "111-22-3333)
```

FIGURE 7.56C.

The embedding expression `<value> <comparison op> SOME <SFW>`

- Returns `true` if `<SFW>` returns a table with a single column and `<value>` bears the relation `<comparison op>` to the value in at least one row of that table.
- Returns `false` if `<SFW>` returns a table with a single column and `<value>` does not bear the relation `<comparison op>` to the value in any row of that table.
- Is a syntax error otherwise.

Thus, the query of Figure 7.57A can be written as in Figure 7.57B.

> Find every employee (of any company) who earns more than at least one employee of the company with the `govt_id` 111-22-3333.

FIGURE 7.57A.

```
SELECT works_for.ssn
FROM works_for
WHERE   works_for.salary >SOME (  SELECT works_for.salary
                                  FROM works_for
                                  WHERE works_for.co_id = "111-22-3333)
```

FIGURE 7.57B.

This query can, of course, also be written as in Figure 7.57C.

```
SELECT works_for.ssn
FROM works_for
WHERE   works_for.salary > (  SELECT MIN(works_for.salary)
                              FROM works_for
                              WHERE works_for.co_id = "111-22-3333)
```

FIGURE 7.57C.

The embedding expression <value> <comparison op> **ANY** <SFW> is identical to <value> <comparison op> SOME <SFW>.

7.4.3. The FROM Clause

At this point,, having seen only the form of the **FROM** clause shown in Figure 7.58, you have possibly come to the conclusion that it is the least complex of the first three clauses of the SFW.

```
FROM <table_1>, <table_2>, ... , <table_n>
```

FIGURE 7.58.

Although this may actually be the case, I have not, by any means, finished the discussion of the **FROM** clause; for starters, exactly the same effect as is obtained by the **FROM** clause of Figure 7.58 is obtained by the **FROM** clause of Figure 7.59.

```
FROM <table_1> CROSS JOIN <table_2> ... CROSS JOIN <table_n>
```

FIGURE 7.59.

If you are puzzled about why the cartesian product operator should have an alternative appellation as peculiar as **CROSS JOIN**, note that join, denoted $\bowtie_{<condition>}$, or simply $\bowtie$, is the name of an auxiliary relational algebra operator—a combination of cartesian product and selects. Before I return to the question of the **CROSS JOIN** nomenclature, I consider the various versions of the **JOIN** operation that are available in SQL.

In the most general case, $\bowtie_{\text{<condition>}}$, is termed *theta-join*; if `<condition>` is a conjunction of simple equality tests, then $\bowtie_{\text{<condition>}}$, is termed *equijoin*; without a subscripted condition, the operator $\bowtie$ is called *natural join*. The relational algebra expression of Figure 7.60A means exactly the same as that of Figure 7.60B.

$$\text{<table}_1\text{>} \bowtie_{\text{<condition>}} \text{<table}_2\text{>}$$

FIGURE 7.60A.

$$\sigma_{\text{<condition>}}(\text{<table}_1\text{>} \bowtie \text{<table}_2\text{>})$$

FIGURE 7.60B.

The expression of Figure 7.61, however, is quite something else.

$$\text{<table}_1\text{>} \bowtie \text{<table}_2\text{>}$$

FIGURE 7.61.

Suppose that the manufacturing-industry database's scheme had been declared as in Figure 7.62, rather than as in Figure 7.1—with similar attributes always having the same name rather than sometimes having different names (for example, with `govt_id` of `company` changed to `co_id` for uniformity with the other table schemes that have a `co_id` attribute).

```
company(co_name, co_id, ceo_ssn, hq_loc)
division(co_id, div_name, subdiv_of, dir_ssn, div_hq)
site(co_id, div_name, loc)
product(prod_id, co_id, div_name, loc, prod_descr)
person(ssn, name, address)
works_for(ssn, co_id, div_name, salary, emp_id, sup_ssn)
skill(ssn, prod_id, co_id)
```

FIGURE 7.62.

If a relational algebra query based upon the revised database scheme of Figure 7.62 began with, say, the three-way cartesian product of Figure 7.63A, it would likely, but not necessarily, continue with a `select` of the form shown in Figure 7.63B.

```
company × division × site
```

FIGURE 7.63A.

```
σ
  (company.co_id = division.co_id)
   and(division.co_id = site.co_id)
   and(division.div_name = site.div_name)
```

FIGURE 7.63B.

Natural join is a combination of cartesian product with a `select` whose condition specifies that all same-named attributes have equal values. The relational algebra expression that combines the cartesian product of Figure 7.63A with the `select` of Figure 7.63B could, thus, be written succinctly as in Figure 7.64.

```
company ⋈ division ⋈ site
```

FIGURE 7.64.

Note, however, that, given the database scheme of Figure 7.1, the relational algebra expression of, for example, Figure 7.19, repeated here as Figure 7.65, would benefit little from the use of the natural join—the reason that I didn't introduce the operator earlier.

```
πcompany.govt_id(σ   [company × division × site ×product ×person×works for × skill])
                (company.govt_id = division.co_id)
                 and(company.hq_loc = "Atlanta")
                 and(division.div_hq = "Boston")
                 and(site.co_id = company.govt_id)
                 and(site.div_name = division.div_name)
                 and(site.loc = "Cleveland")
                 and(product.manuf_co = company.govt_id)
                 and(product.manuf_div = site.div_name)
                 and(product.prod_id = FA-S/2)
                 and(person.ssn = company.ceo_ssn)
                 and(person.name = "Joline Jones")
                 and(works_for.ssn = person.ssn)
                 and(works_for,co_id = company.govt_id)
                 and(works_for.salary > 500000)
                 and(skill.ssn = person.ssn)
                 and(skill.prod_id = product.prod_id)
                 and(skill.manuf_co = company.govt_id)
```

FIGURE 7.65.

Thus far I have discussed only the relational algebra versions of equijoin and natural join. In SQL, equijoin can be written in the syntax of Figure 7.66A, in which case it has exactly the same meaning as the simpler **FROM-WHERE** of Figure 7.66B.

```
FROM <table1> <alias1> JOIN <table2> <alias2>
                        ON <alias1>.<attribute> = <alias2>.<attribute>
```

FIGURE 7.66A.

```
FROM <table1> <alias1>, <table2> <alias2>
WHERE alias1>.<attribute> = <alias2>.<attribute>
```

FIGURE 7.66B.

The equijoin operator can also be written in the syntax of Figure 7.67A, in which case it has exactly the same meaning as the simpler **FROM-WHERE** of Figure 7.67B.

```
FROM <table1> JOIN <table2> USING <attribute>
```

FIGURE 7.67A.

```
FROM <table1> <alias1>, <table2> <alias2>
WHERE alias1>.<attribute> = <alias2>.<attribute>
```

FIGURE 7.67B.

A natural join can be written in the syntax of Figure 7.68A, in which case it has exactly the same meaning as the **FROM-WHERE** of Figure 7.68B, except that the resulting table contains only one column for `<attribute>` rather than two identical columns—on the assumption that <attribute$_1$>, <attribute$_2$>, . . . <attribute$_n$> are precisely those attributes that <table$_1$> and <table$_2$> have in common.

```
FROM <table1> NATURAL JOIN <table2>
```

FIGURE 7.68A.

```
FROM <table1> <alias1>, <table2> <alias2>
WHERE  <(alias1>.<attribute1> = <alias2>.<attribute1>)
        AND (<alias1>.<attribute2> = <alias2>.<attribute2>
                        .
                        .
                        .
        AND (alias1>.<attributen> = <alias2>.<attributen>
```

FIGURE 7.68B.

As you may have guessed by this point, the **CROSS JOIN** nomenclature was invented to distinguish a simple cartesian product (**CROSS JOIN**) from **JOIN ...ON**, **JOIN...USING**, and **NATURAL JOIN**.

The variants of cartesian product with `select` that I have considered thus far aren't variants on the operations themselves, but, rather, variant notations for expressing what is already expressible using simple **FROM** and **WHERE** clauses. There are, however, three variant operations: **LEFT JOIN**, **RIGHT JOIN**, and **FULL JOIN**.

If the cartesian product of two tables is specified in a **FROM** clause, and those rows are selected, in the **WHERE** clause, for equality of an attribute in the first table with an attribute in the second table, then all information contained in rows of the first table that don't match any row of the second table is lost, as is all information contained in rows of the second table that don't match any row of the first table. When that information must be preserved, you use the **LEFT JOIN** to preserve information from first-table rows that don't match, **RIGHT JOIN** to preserve information from second-table rows that don't match, and **FULL JOIN** to preserve information from both first-table rows that don't match and second table rows that don't match.

Consider the shortened and changed `company` and `division` tables of Figures 7.69A–7.69B.

co_name	govt_id	ceo_ssn	hq_loc
New York Tire	111-22-3333	999-00-0001	New York
New Jersey Tire	222-33-4444	777-00-0007	Trenton
Southern Axle	333-44-5555	999-00-0001	Atlanta
Atlanta Axle	444-55-6666	777-00-0007	Atlanta
Maryland Brake	555-66-7777	999-00-0004	Columbia

FIGURE 7.69A.

co_id	div_name	subdiv_of	dir_ssn	div_hq
333-44-5555	axle	manufacturing	888-00-0006	Cambridge
333-44-5555	front axle	axle	777-00-0007	Mattapan
333-44-5555	rear axle	axle	777-00-0007	Roxbury
444-55-6666	communications	null	888-00-0010	West Chester
444-55-6666	purchasing	null	888-00-0011	Bensalem

FIGURE 7.69B.

If you perform an equijoin of the two tables on `ceo_ssn` of `company` and `dir_ssn` of `division`, the result is the table of Figure 7.70. All information is lost about the company whose CEO has Social Security number 999-00-0001 and the company whose CEO has Social Security number 999-00-0004. All information is also lost about the divisions whose directors have Social Security numbers 888-00-0006, 888-00-0010, and 888-00-0011.

co_name	govt_id	ceo_ssn	hq_loc	co_id	div_name	subdiv_of	dir_ssn	div_hq
New Jersey Tire	222-33-4444	777-00-0007	Trenton	333-44-5555	front axle	axle	777-00-0007	Mattapan
New Jersey Tire	222-33-4444	777-00-0007	Trenton	333-44-5555	rear axle	axle	777-00-0007	Roxbury
Atlanta Axle	444-55-6666	777-00-0007	Atlanta	333-44-5555	front axle	axle	777-00-0007	Mattapan
Atlanta Axle	444-55-6666	777-00-0007	Atlanta	333-44-5555	rear axle	axle	777-00-0007	Roxbury

FIGURE 7.70.

The left outer join of the two tables, in the order `company`, `division`, contains all the information in—all the rows of—the result of the equijoin plus all company information for companies whose `ceo_ssn` wasn't equal to the `dir_ssn` of any division—with result-table rows for these companies *right-padded* with NULLs. The SFW for the left outer join is shown in Figure 7.71A with its result in Figure 7.71B.

```
SELECT*
FROM company LEFT JOIN division ON company.ceo_ssn = division.dir_ssn
```

FIGURE 7.71A.

co_name	govt_id	ceo_ssn	hq_loc	co_id	div_name	subdiv_of	dir_ssn	div_hq
New Jersey Tire	222-33-4444	777-00-0007	Trenton	333-44-5555	front axle	axle	777-00-0007	Mattapan
New Jersey Tire	222-33-4444	777-00-0007	Trenton	333-44-5555	rear axle	axle	777-00-0007	Roxbury
Atlanta Axle	444-55-6666	777-00-0007	Atlanta	333-44-5555	front axle	axle	777-00-0007	Mattapan
Atlanta Axle	444-55-6666	777-00-0007	Atlanta	333-44-5555	rear axle	axle	777-00-0007	Roxbury
New York Tire	111-22-3333	999-00-0001	New York	NULL	NULL	NULL	NULL	NULL
Southern Axle	333-44-5555	999-00-0001	Atlanta	NULL	NULL	NULL	NULL	NULL
Maryland Brake	555-66-7777	999-00-0004	Columbia	NULL	NULL	NULL	NULL	NULL

FIGURE 7.71B.

The right outer join of the two tables, in the order company, division, contains all the information in—all the rows of—the result of the equijoin plus all division information for companies whose ceo_ssn wasn't equal to the dir_ssn of any division—with result-table rows for these companies *left-padded* with NULLs. The SFW for the right outer join is shown in Figure 7.72A with its result in Figure 7.72B.

```
SELECT*
FROM company RIGHT JOIN division ON company.ceo_ssn = division.dir_ssn
```

FIGURE 7.72A.

co_name	govt_id	ceo_ssn	hq_loc	co_id	div_name	subdiv_of	dir_ssn	div_hq
New Jersey Tire	222-33-4444	777-00-0007	Trenton	333-44-5555	front axle	axle	777-00-0007	Mattapan
New Jersey Tire	222-33-4444	777-00-0007	Trenton	333-44-5555	rear axle	axle	777-00-0007	Roxbury
Atlanta Axle	444-55-6666	777-00-0007	Atlanta	333-44-5555	front axle	axle	777-00-0007	Mattapan
Atlanta Axle	444-55-6666	777-00-0007	Atlanta	333-44-5555	rear axle	axle	777-00-0007	Roxbury
NULL	NULL	NULL	NULL	333-44-5555	axle	manufacturing	888-00-0006	Cambridge
NULL	NULL	NULL	NULL	444-55-6666	communications	null	888-00-0010	West Chester
NULL	NULL	NULL	NULL	444-55-6666	purchasing	null	888-00-0011	Bensalem

FIGURE 7.72B.

The full outer join of the two tables, in the order company, division, contains all the information in—all the rows of—the result of the equijoin plus all company information for companies whose ceo_ssn wasn't equal to the dir_ssn of any division, plus all division information for companies whose ceo_ssn wasn't equal to the dir_ssn of any division—with result-table rows for the additional rows padded with NULLs to either the right or left as appropriate. The SFW for the full outer join is shown in Figure 7.73A with its result in Figure 7.73B.

```
SELECT*
FROM company FULL JOIN division ON company.ceo_ssn = division.dir_ssn
```

FIGURE 7.73A.

co_name	govt_id	ceo_ssn	hq_loc	co_id	div_name	subdiv_of	dir_ssn	div_hq
New Jersey Tire	222-33-4444	777-00-0007	Trenton	333-44-5555	front axle	axle	777-00-0007	Mattapan
New Jersey Tire	222-33-4444	777-00-0007	Trenton	333-44-5555	rear axle	axle	777-00-0007	Roxbury
Atlanta Axle	444-55-6666	777-00-0007	Atlanta	333-44-5555	front axle	axle	777-00-0007	Mattapan
Atlanta Axle	444-55-6666	777-00-0007	Atlanta	333-44-5555	rear axle	axle	777-00-0007	Roxbury
New York Tire	111-22-3333	999-00-0001	New York	NULL	NULL	NULL	NULL	NULL
Southern Axle	333-44-5555	999-00-0001	Atlanta	NULL	NULL	NULL	NULL	NULL
Maryland Brake	555-66-7777	999-00-0004	Columbia	NULL	NULL	NULL	NULL	NULL
NULL	NULL	NULL	NULL	333-44-5555	axle	manufacturing	888-00-0006	Cambridge
NULL	NULL	NULL	NULL	444-55-6666	communications	null	888-00-0010	West Chester
NULL	NULL	NULL	NULL	444-55-6666	purchasing	null	888-00-0011	Bensalem

FIGURE 7.73B.

7.4.4. The GROUP BY Clause

Up to this point, I have had the luxury of relating SFW queries to queries in the extended version of relational algebra; because I didn't extend relational algebra with analogs to SQL's **GROUP BY** and **HAVING**, this is no longer the case. I therefore begin their discussion by considering their intended use: The **GROUP BY** clause, and, optionally, the **HAVING** clause, are used when the values of aggregate functions are required, but their values on multiple, non-overlapping, subtables of the table produced by the **FROM** clause rather than their values on the entire table produced by the **FROM** clause.

The **GROUP BY** clause partitions the table produced by the **FROM** and **WHERE** clauses; its presence in an SFW statement also changes the meaning of the **SELECT** clause. Whereas the **SELECT** clause of an SFW statement that doesn't have a **GROUP BY** clause produces exactly one line (row) of output, the **SELECT** clause of an SFW statement with a **GROUP BY** clause produces one line (row) per subtable in the partition. In an SFW statement that doesn't have a **GROUP BY** clause, every aggregate function in the **SELECT** clause is applied to the entire table produced by the **FROM** and **WHERE** clauses. When a **GROUP BY** is present, every aggregate function in the **SELECT** clause is applied to each of the subtables in the partition of the table produced by the **FROM** and **WHERE** clauses.

The type of partitioning that can be effected by the **GROUP BY** clause, on the table produced by **FROM** and **WHERE** clauses, is partitioning of that table into subtables, all of whose rows have the same values for some specified subset of the table's attributes. As an example, the SFW statement of Figure 7.74 would partition the company table of Figure 7.2A into the six subtables of Figures 7.75A–7.75F—assuming that the only rows of the tables are those rows explicitly shown in Figure 7.2A. These six tables would not, however, be the final result of the SFW statement; the final result would be the two-column table of Figure 7.76—one row for each of Figures 7.75A–7.75F.

```
SELECT hq_loc, COUNT(hq_loc)
FROM company
GROUP BY hq_loc
```

FIGURE 7.74.

co_name	govt_id	ceo_ssn	hq_loc
New York Tire	111-22-3333	999-00-0001	New York

FIGURE 7.75A.

co_name	govt_id	ceo_ssn	hq_loc
New Jersey Tire	222-33-4444	999-00-0002	Trenton

FIGURE 7.75B.

co_name	govt_id	ceo_ssn	hq_loc
Southern Axle	333-44-5555	999-00-0001	Atlanta
Atlanta Axle	444-55-6666	999-00-0003	Atlanta
Georgia Brake	666-77-8888	999-00-0005	Atlanta

FIGURE 7.75C.

co_name	govt_id	ceo_ssn	hq_loc
Maryland Brake	555-66-7777	999-00-0004	Columbia

FIGURE 7.75D.

co_name	govt_id	ceo_ssn	hq_loc
Florida Brake	777-88-9999	999-00-0006	Pensacola

FIGURE 7.75E.

co_name	govt_id	ceo_ssn	hq_loc
Ohio Windshield	888-99-0000	999-00-0007	Toledo

FIGURE 7.75F.

hq_loc	
New York	1
Trenton	1
Atlanta	3
Columbia	1
Pensacola	1
Toledo	1

FIGURE 7.76.

In the **SELECT** clause of the SFW statement of Figure 7.74, the aggregate function **COUNT** is applied to attribute hq_loc, whose name happens to be the only unaggregated attribute name in the **SELECT** clause. In general, aggregate functions can be applied to one set of attributes while another set occurs unaggregated in the **SELECT** clause. Thus, for example, the query of Figure 7.77A can be written in SQL as shown in Figure 7.77B.

For each company, find the average salary paid by the company to its employees.

FIGURE 7.77A.

```
SELECT co_id, AVG(works_for.salary)
FROM works_for
GROUP BY co_id
```

FIGURE 7.77B.

Although you can put an unaggregated attribute into the **SELECT** list of an SFW with a **GROUP BY**, it makes no sense for that unaggregated attribute not to be one of those on the **GROUP BY**'s list, that is, one of the partitioning attributes. The reason is that the **SELECT** is intended to produce one line of output for each subtable in the partition, but there does not necessarily exist a single value, within any subtable, for any attribute that is not on the **GROUP BY**'s list of partitioning attributes. Consider, as an example, the (illegal) query of Figure 7.78. Exactly what value should be output as ceo_ssn for the subtable whose hq_loc is Atlanta?

```
SELECT hq_loc, COUNT(hq_loc), ceo_ssn
FROM company
GROUP BY hq_loc
```

FIGURE 7.78.

Notice that what I've said is that an unaggregated non-partitioning attribute may not appear on the **SELECT** list of an SFW that has a **GROUP BY** clause. I have not said that every partitioning attribute must appear on the **SELECT** list—and there would be no good reason for such a constraint, although the beginning students of SQL often mistakenly feel there is. For example, the query of Figure 7.79 is perfectly legal—although its output would probably be less than maximally useful because a division is identified by its `co_id` together with its `div_name`.

```
SELECT div_name, COUNT(subdiv_of)
FROM division
GROUP BY co_id, div_name
```

FIGURE 7.79.

The query of Figure 7.79 would, by the way, partition the `division` table of Figure 7.2B into the subtables of Figures 7.80A–7.80J.

co_id	div_name	subdiv_of	dir_ssn	div_hq
666-77-8888	innovation	null	888-00-0001	Valdosta

FIGURE 7.80A.

co_id	div_name	subdiv_of	dir_ssn	div_hq
666-77-8888	research	innovation	888-00-0001	Boston

FIGURE 7.80B.

co_id	div_name	subdiv_of	dir_ssn	div_hq
666-77-8888	development	innovation	888-00-0002	Nashville

FIGURE 7.80C.

co_id	div_name	subdiv_of	dir_ssn	div_hq
111-22-3333	personnel	null	888-00-0003	New York

FIGURE 7.80D.

co_id	div_name	subdiv_of	dir_ssn	div_hq
333-44-5555	manufacturing	null	888-00-0005	Boston

FIGURE 7.80E.

co_id	div_name	subdiv_of	dir_ssn	div_hq
333-44-5555	manufacturing	null	888-00-0005	Cambridge

FIGURE 7.80F.

co_id	div_name	subdiv_of	dir_ssn	div_hq
333-44-5555	front axle	axle	888-00-0007	Mattapan

FIGURE 7.80G.

co_id	div_name	subdiv_of	dir_ssn	div_hq
333-44-5555	rear axle	axle	888-00-0008	Roxbury

FIGURE 7.80H.

co_id	div_name	subdiv_of	dir_ssn	div_hq
444-55-6666	communications	null	888-00-0010	West Chester

FIGURE 7.80I.

co_id	div_name	subdiv_of	dir_ssn	div_hq
444-55-6666	purchasing	null	888-00-0011	Bensalem

FIGURE 7.80J.

7.4.5. The HAVING Clause

When the values of aggregate functions are required for some but not all subtables produced by a **GROUP BY**, the desired subtables can be specified through the use of a **HAVING** clause. Recall that the **WHERE** clause in an SFW statement contains a condition that specifies which rows of a table are desired. In similar fashion, the **HAVING** clause contains a condition that specifies which subtables of a partition are desired. Just as the condition in a **WHERE** clause must be appropriate for application to a row, the condition in a **HAVING** clause must be appropriate for application to a (sub)table. It thus makes sense for a **HAVING** clause condition to involve the application of aggregate functions to a subtable; it doesn't, on the other hand, make sense for such a condition to refer to the unaggregated value of an attribute unless that attribute has the same value for all rows of the subtable—that is, unless it is one of the partitioning attributes in the **GROUP BY** clause.

As a simple example of the use of the **HAVING** clause, consider the query of Figure 7.81A, and the corresponding SFW of Figure 7.81B, which applied to the database instance of Figures 7.2A–7.2F, produces the result shown in Figure 7.81C.

> Find every city in which three or more companies have their headquarters.

FIGURE 7.81A.

```
SELECT company.hq_loc
FROM company
GROUP BY company.hq_loc
HAVING COUNT(company.hq_loc) >= 2
```

FIGURE 7.81B.

hq_loc
Atlanta

FIGURE 7.81C.

A more complex example of the use of the **HAVING** clause may be found in Figure 7.82A–7.82B, with its result in Figure 7.82C.

> Find the name and Social Security number of the CEO of every company that has two or more first-level subdivisions, that is, two or more subdivisions with `subdiv_of` values of `null`.

FIGURE 7.82A.

```
SELECT DISTINCT person.name, company.ceo_ssn
FROM company, division, person
WHERE  (company.govt_id = division.co_id)
       AND (company.ceo_ssn = person.ssn)
       AND (division.subdiv_of IS NULL)
GROUP BY company.govt_id, company.ceo_ssn, person.name
HAVING COUNT(division.subdiv_of) >= 2
```

FIGURE 7.82B.

person.name	company.ceo_ssn
Joseph Jones	999-00-0001
Donald Smith	999-00-0003

FIGURE 7.82C.

Before I complete the discussion of the **HAVING** clause with an explanation of the type of condition that is inappropriate there, note that the **HAVING** clause is not, strictly speaking, necessary to maintain the expressive power of the SFW; rather, for any SFW with a **HAVING** clause, there is an equivalent SFW without one. For example, the SFW of Figure 7.82D is equivalent to that of Figure 7.82B.

```
SELECT DISTINCT person.name, company.ceo_ssn
FROM company, division div1, person
WHERE  (company.govt_id = div1.co_id)
       AND (company.ceo_ssn = person.ssn)
       AND (div1.subdiv_of IS NULL)
       AND ( SELECT COUNT(div2.subdiv_of)
             FROM division div2
             WHERE  (div2.co_id = div1.co_id)
                    AND (div2.subdiv_of IS NULL))  = 2
GROUP BY company.govt_id, company.ceo_ssn, person.name
```

FIGURE 7.82D.

As an example of an SFW statement whose **HAVING** clause makes no sense, consider that of Figure 7.83.

```
SELECT company.hq_loc
FROM company
GROUP BY company.hq_loc
HAVING    COUNT(division.subdiv_of) >= 2
          AND (ceo_ssn = "999-00-0006")
```

FIGURE 7.83.

The problem is, of course, that, in general, a subtable produced by the **GROUP BY** clause will have rows with different values for `ceo_ssn` so that `ceo_ssn = "999-00-0006"` is not a condition of the appropriate type to apply to an entire subtable.

Recall that, as indicated previously, a **HAVING** clause condition may refer to an unaggregated attribute as long as that attribute is one of the partitioning attributes listed in the **GROUP BY** clause. Consider, as an example, the SFW statement of Figure 7.84A, which arises from the query of Figure 7.84B.

```
SELECT DISTINCT person.name, company.ceo_ssn
FROM company, division, person
WHERE  (company.govt_id = division.co_id)
       AND (company.ceo_ssn = person.ssn)
       AND (division.subdiv_of = NULL)
GROUP BY company.govtid, company.ceo_ssn, person.name
HAVING      COUNT(division.subdiv_of) >= 2
            AND (person.name LIKE 'K%')
```

FIGURE 7.84A.

Find the name and Social Security number of the CEO of every company that has two or more first-level subdivisions—that is, two or more subdivisions with `subdiv_of` values of `null`—and whose name starts with a *K*.

FIGURE 7.84B.

Finally, a **HAVING** clause may in fact contain references to only unaggregated attributes; that is, it may contain no applications of aggregate functions whatsoever, as in Figure 7.85A, which arises from the query of Figure 7.85B. If it does, however, it can always be written as a cheaper-to-evaluate SFW statement without **GROUP BY** and **HAVING** clauses, as in Figure 7.85C.

```
SELECT person.name, company.ceo_ssn
FROM company, person
WHERE company.ceo_ssn = person.ssn
GROUP BY company.hq_loc, company.ceo_ssn, person.name
HAVING company.hq_loc = "Atlanta"
```

FIGURE 7.85A.

Find the name and Social Security number of the CEO of every company whose headquarters are located in Atlanta.

FIGURE 7.85B.

```
SELECT person.name, company.ceo_ssn
FROM company, person
WHERE (company.ceo_ssn = person.ssn)
        AND (company.hq_loc = "Atlanta")
```

FIGURE 7.85C.

7.4.6. The ORDER BY Clause

The final clause in the SELECT-FROM-WHERE statement, the ORDER BY clause performs the function of ordering, or sorting, the rows of the table produced by the FROM, WHERE (if present), GROUP BY (if present), HAVING (if present), and SELECT clauses as desired. Ordering is, of course, by the values of one or more attributes and may be by ascending or descending value, ascending being the default.

Consider, as an example, the company table of Figure 7.2A, repeated here as Figure 7.86. If you want a version of the table with the values of co_name in ascending (alphabetical) order, as shown in Figure 7.87, you can do so by executing the SFW statement of Figure 7.88. The same table, but with values of co_name in descending order, as shown in Figure 7.89, can be achieved by executing the SFW statement of Figure 7.90.

co_name	govt_id	ceo_ssn	hq_loc
New York Tire	111-22-3333	999-00-0001	New York
New Jersey Tire	222-33-4444	999-00-0002	Trenton
Southern Axle	333-44-5555	999-00-0001	Atlanta
Atlanta Axle	444-55-6666	999-00-0003	Atlanta
Maryland Brake	555-66-7777	999-00-0004	Columbia
Georgia Brake	666-77-8888	999-00-0005	Atlanta
Florida Brake	777-88-9999	999-00-0006	Pensacola
Ohio Windshield	888-99-0000	999-00-0007	Toledo

FIGURE 7.86.

co_name	govt_id	ceo_ssn	hq_loc
Atlanta Axle	444-55-6666	999-00-0003	Atlanta
Florida Brake	777-88-9999	999-00-0006	Pensacola
Georgia Brake	666-77-8888	999-00-0005	Atlanta
Maryland Brake	555-66-7777	999-00-0004	Columbia
New Jersey Tire	222-33-4444	999-00-0002	Trenton
New York Tire	111-22-3333	999-00-0001	New York
Ohio Windshield	888-99-0000	999-00-0007	Toledo
Southern Axle	333-44-5555	999-00-0001	Atlanta

FIGURE 7.87.

```
SELECT*
FROM company
ORDER BY co_name
```

FIGURE 7.88.

co_name	govt_id	ceo_ssn	hq_loc
Southern Axle	333-44-5555	999-00-0001	Atlanta
Ohio Windshield	888-99-0000	999-00-0007	Toledo
New York Tire	111-22-3333	999-00-0001	New York
New Jersey Tire	222-33-4444	999-00-0002	Trenton
Maryland Brake	555-66-7777	999-00-0004	Columbia
Georgia Brake	666-77-8888	999-00-0005	Atlanta
Florida Brake	777-88-9999	999-00-0006	Pensacola
Atlanta Axle	444-55-6666	999-00-0003	Atlanta

FIGURE 7.89.

```
SELECT*
FROM company
ORDER BY co_name DESC
```

FIGURE 7.90.

Finally, if the original company table had entries for different companies with the same name, as does the modified company table of Figure 7.91, then you might want a version ordered by co_name and secondarily ordered by hq_loc, the version pictured in Figure 7.92. This is readily accomplished through the execution of the SFW statement of Figure 7.93.

co_name	govt_id	ceo_ssn	hq_loc
New Jersey Tire	222-77-7777	999-88-7777	Newark
Southern Axle	555-98-7654	999-33-0004	Apalachicola
Southern Axle	333-12-3456	999-11-0007	Nashville
Southern Axle	333-44-5555	999-00-0001	Atlanta
Ohio Windshield	888-99-0000	999-00-0007	Toledo
New York Tire	111-22-3333	999-00-0001	New York
New Jersey Tire	222-33-4444	999-00-0002	Trenton
Maryland Brake	555-66-7777	999-00-0004	Columbia
Georgia Brake	666-77-8888	999-00-0005	Atlanta
Florida Brake	777-88-9999	999-00-0006	Pensacola
Atlanta Axle	444-55-6666	999-00-0003	Atlanta

FIGURE 7.91.

co_name	govt_id	ceo_ssn	hq_loc
Atlanta Axle	444-55-6666	999-00-0003	Atlanta
Florida Brake	777-88-9999	999-00-0006	Pensacola
Georgia Brake	666-77-8888	999-00-0005	Atlanta
Maryland Brake	555-66-7777	999-00-0004	Columbia
New Jersey Tire	222-77-7777	999-88-7777	Newark
New Jersey Tire	222-33-4444	999-00-0002	Trenton
New York Tire	111-22-3333	999-00-0001	New York
Ohio Windshield	888-99-0000	999-00-0007	Toledo
Southern Axle	555-98-7654	999-33-0004	Apalachicola
Southern Axle	333-44-5555	999-00-0001	Atlanta
Southern Axle	333-12-3456	999-11-0007	Nashville

FIGURE 7.92.

```
SELECT*
FROM company
ORDER BY co_name, hq_loc
```

FIGURE 7.93.

7.4.7. The CREATE VIEW Statement

As indicated previously, the **CREATE VIEW** statement, which allows the user to store and name the value of an SQL expression, with attributes renamed, if desired, is probably SQL's closest construct to an assignment statement. As an example of its use, suppose that you want a table of people's skills together with their names and addresses and the sites of the companies that manufacture the products in whose manufacture they are skilled (trained). The **CREATE VIEW** statement of Figure 7.94 produces just such a table, a table named skills_and_locations. The new table can, of course, be queried through the use of SFW statements via the table name skills_and_locations. The question of updating a view—a table created through the use of a **CREATE VIEW** statement—is a complex one. The only comment appropriate here, because I have not paid much attention to updating base tables—tables created through the use of **CREATE TABLE** statements—is that permissible updates to views are extremely tightly restricted, as you might expect, because of their potentially ambiguous effects on the base tables from which they arise.

```
CREATE VIEW skills_and_locations
AS SELECT person.ssn, person.name, person.address, works_for.co_name,
        product.prod_id, product.loc
FROM skill, person, works_for, product
WHERE  (skill.ssn = person.ssn)
         AND (person.ssn = works_for.ssn)
         AND (skill.manuf_co = product.manuf_co)
```

FIGURE 7.94.

7.5. References

7.5.1. Standards Documents

International Standards Organization. 1987. *Database language SQL.* ISO 9075:1987(E).

International Standards Organization. 1989. *Database language SQL.* ISO 9075:1989(E).

International Standards Organization 1992. *Database language SQL.* ISO 9075:1992(E). (Also available as ANSI X3.135-1992.)

7.5.2. Textbooks (on Relational Database Systems)

Elmasri, R., & S. B. Navathe. 1994 *Fundamentals of database systems* (2nd ed.). Menlo Park, CA: The Benjamin/Cummings Publishing Company. This text, written for the average student of computer science, has a short but adequate introductory chapter on SQL.

Silberschatz, A., H. F. Korth, & S. Sudarshan. 1997. *Database system concepts* (3rd ed.). McGraw-Hill. This text, written for the average student of computer science, has a short but adequate introductory chapter on SQL.

Ullman, J. D. 1988. *Principles of database and knowledge-base system: Volume I: Classical Database Systems; Volume II: The New Technologies.* Computer Science Press. Volume I, written for more formally oriented students of computer science, has a short but adequate introductory chapter on SQL.

Ullman, J. D., and J. Widom. 1997. *A first course in database systems*. Englewood Cliffs, NJ: Prentice Hall. This text, written for the average student of computer science, but also readable by students in management or business programs, has an extensive introduction to SQL.

Vossen, G. 1991. *Database models, database languages, and database management systems*. Reading, MA: Addison-Wesley. This text, written for more formally oriented students of computer science, has a better-than-average chapter on SQL.

Connolly, T., C. Begg, & A. Strachan. 1995. *Database systems, a practical approach to design, implementation, and management*. Reading, MA: Addison Wesley. This text, written for the more practically oriented student of computer science, information science, management, or business, has an extensive introduction to SQL.

7.5.3. SQL-Specific Books for Practitioners

Date, C. J., & H. Darwen. 1993. *A guide to the SQL standard* (3rd ed.). Reading, MA: Addison Wesley.

Cannan, S., & G. Otten. 1992. *SQL—The standard handbook*. McGraw-Hill.

Celko, J. 1995. *SQL for smarties: Advanced SQL programming*. Morgan Kauffman Publishing.

Gruber, M., & J. Celko. 1993. *SQL instant reference*. Berkeley, CA: SYBEX.

Melton, J., & A. R. Simon. 1992. *Understanding the new SQL: A complete guide*. Morgan Kauffman.

CHAPTER 8

Tcl and Tk

by Cameron Laird and Kathryn Soraiz

8.1. Introduction

This chapter introduces Tcl (Tool Command Language) and its companion user interface extension (toolkit), Tk. It answers the questions

- What problems do Tcl and Tk solve?
- What is scripting?
- How does Tcl perform the basic operations of input/output, string processing, data structuring, network programming, and graphical user interface (GUI) interaction?
- How does Tcl compare to other scripting languages?
- Where can one go to find out more?

8.1.1. Why Haven't I Ever Heard of It?

Tcl has been a quiet part of your life for years, and you never knew it.

Tcl has a unique role in software development. No other tool combines its convenience, platform independence, ease of learning, extensibility, power, graphical ability, network awareness, and engineering maturity.

Even with no prior experience, you can download, install, compose, and run your first program in under an hour. It's that simple. Don't be fooled by the ease with which you learn Tcl. This is no toy language. It has a myriad of uses and is a key part of several thousand commercial products and mission critical operations. (See `http://starbase.neosoft.com/~claird/comp.lang.tcl/commercial-tcl.html` for a partial list.)

Tcl manages operations on drilling platforms in the Gulf of Mexico, railroads in South America, merchant ships in the North Sea, submarines at classified locations, and exploration vehicles in space. It's at the heart of telecommunications management for the newest and largest networks, and several pharmaceutical and medical manufacturers makers use it in products in those tightly regulated industries. Many of the most prominent Web sites rely on Tcl applications to deliver their content reliably.

Tcl is easier to use for the jobs in its domain than C, Assembler, or Java. Even so, ease doesn't come at the expense of quality. In fact, many organizations find their quality metrics *improve* as they adopt Tcl in preference to C or C++. Tcl's expressiveness permits coders to focus on the essentials of a problem rather than maintain bloated and fragile "boilerplate" code. And its automatic garbage collection and platform independence eliminate entire categories of errors that plague C-based development.

Even in high-performance scientific and engineering computing, where other languages are clearly superior for processor-intensive operations, Tcl has proven itself an excellent "glue" to prototype experimental configurations, manage distribution of calculations, and provide a convenient user interface.

Fulfilling your needs is simplified when you learn Tcl. Expand Tcl's presence in your world; you'll be glad you did.

8.1.2. How to Read This Chapter

Tcl is a unique programming tool. Because Tcl—the language—is very easy to learn and use, there is far less coding than you would imagine in this chapter. There are plenty of examples to study and practice; they simply don't take a lot of space to showcase or require much time to learn.

8.1.2.1. If You're Already Familiar with Tcl

This chapter and its introduction have a lot to offer you. In section 8.1.4, we give you resources to help you answer questions you may have along the way. Refer to it as needed.

Although you will be better served by reading the chapter in sequence, you can skip directly to section 8.5 for details on the commands that make up Tcl applications.

8.1.2.2. More Than a Language

Tcl is more than a language. John Ousterhout designed and built Tcl and Tk while a professor at the University of California at Berkeley in 1988.

He wanted a simple interpreted language for embedding into other tools—largely those of computer-assisted engineering (CAE). His aim was to give users runtime programmatic control over CAE applications.

He achieved this goal with a simple interpreter and runtime support coded in portable C. The emphasis was to make Tcl easy to embed into applications and to expose the functionality of those applications as Tcl commands. Users scripted application functionality as a sequence of Tcl commands.

As good as this is, the language is only part of the framework John Ousterhout created. This chapter teaches you to appreciate the entire framework and how you can create your own solutions more quickly and accurately with it.

8.1.2.3. Jump on In

Tcl's syntax is extremely simple. There's very little to learn. As with Forth and Lisp, Tcl programs are most often built up from a "little language" specific to a particular project. Although it's helpful to know the capabilities of different commands, don't defer writing your first Tcl programs while you memorize lists of commands and their options. Almost all newcomers to Tcl find it far more effective to cycle between programming a little, studying a little, and programming a little more.

Lastly, following the recommendations mentioned in section 8.1.4 will significantly reduce your learning curve as you write your first Tcl programs. It contains many helpful pointers and references.

8.1.3. Platform Considerations

Tcl operates uniformly across different platforms. You'll have little need to worry about aspects of Tcl that are specific to a particular operating system. The few topics that do vary between platforms are noted explicitly. In each case, we describe the unique behavior or situation for MacOS, UNIX, and Windows. (See Table 8.1.)

TABLE 8.1. *How Tcl operates across the leading operating systems.*

Platform	*Behavioral Response*
Windows	Tcl behaves similarly across Windows 3.1, Windows 95, and Windows NT with few exceptions.
MacOS	Tcl is consistent across all MacOSs.
UNIX	Tcl hides the differences between various flavors of UNIX.

8.1.4. How to Smooth the Curve

The most effective channels for learning Tcl are different from those for C, Awk, or even Perl. You'll make the quickest progress by taking advantage of the resources listed here. They are listed by the order in which they provide the most help to you:

- *Read this chapter.* The book's detailed index serves as a reference for times when you need to look up just one question or idea.
- *Experiment with Tcl itself.* This is more profound advice than experience with other languages would have you expect. The qualitative difference is so great that "experimentation" deserves its place as the second method in this list. Section 8.6.2 hints at the ways you can interrogate Tcl itself to learn its capabilities.
- *Learn to read the documentation distributed with Tcl.* This is a critical skill. Those references contain a wealth of information. See section 8.4.2 for more on this.
- *Browse the World Wide Web.* Tcl is particularly well-endowed with resources available online there. *Thousands* of pages of tutorials, references, introductions, and analyses are freely available. You'll like knowing about three starting points in particular:
    - `http://starbase.neosoft.com/~claird/comp.lang.tcl/tcl_programming.html` collects updates and amplifications specifically relevant to this chapter.
    - `http://www.teraform.com/%7Elvirden/tcl-faq/` is the `comp.lang.tcl` FAQ launcher maintained by Larry Virden. Larry is the author of the official Tcl FAQ documents.
    - `http://www.sunscript.com/` is the home page for the SunScript business group at Sun Microsystems, Inc., responsible for the development of the Tcl core.

  A few readers still do not have practical access to the World Wide Web. We invite them to email us at `claird@NeoSoft.com` with a description of their circumstances. In many cases, the same information is available through email, Usenet updates, or even fax.
- *Read other books.* Books written about Tcl number an order of magnitude fewer than those written for C or Java. With few exceptions, the books written about Tcl are of high quality: accurate, thoughtful, and lucid. (See `http:// www.tcltk.com/consortium/resources/books.html` for a current bibliography of Tcl publications.)

One book, John Ousterhout's *Tcl and the Tk Toolkit*, deserves special mention. The capabilities of Tcl have expanded enormously since its 1994 publication. However, the philosophy Tcl's creator expresses remains fresh and consistent with the latest Tcl release. Although it is severely out of date in its details, this book is still the best-selling Tcl work at the close of 1997.

- *Join* `comp.lang.tcl` and `comp.lang.tcl.announce`. These Usenet newsgroups are active and responsive. Many questions are answered within hours and the collective precision of the `comp.lang.tcl` community is high. This suggestion is especially apt. To program efficiently, it is crucial to re-use what others have already written.
- *Study source code.* This applies in two ways: the processor source code for Tcl and the Contributed Sources Archive. The source code, written in C, that makes up the Tcl processor has an exceptional reputation. More than almost any other freeware project, Tcl has—from its inception—been regarded as unusually readable code. There's a long tradition of Tcl developers who expect to learn about new language facilities by reading the comments in the source code. Tclers consider this no hardship.

  The Official Tcl/Tk Contributed Sources Archive (see `http://www.neosoft.com/tcl/default.html`) includes many examples of successful applications written in Tcl. It is also a rich source of ideas.

There are two more suggestions for you to consider. We set them apart because they have little direct application to Tcl, the language. They are, however, very useful for learning concepts that apply to Tcl.

Tcl is more than a language; it is an entire toolkit. One of Tcl's strengths is its ability to glue other programs—even if written in different languages—into a finished product. The more you expose yourself to other languages and see what kinds of programs are already available for you to use, the more efficient a programmer you become. With Tcl, you reuse the wheel, not reinvent it.

- *Read magazines.* Unlike Perl or C++, Tcl has neither a special-purpose magazine devoted to it, nor even any columns that regularly cover Tcl topics. Magazines such as *Byte*, *Dr. Dobbs,* and *PC Computing* profile Tcl perhaps once a year. Although this pace seems to be accelerating, it's still hard to know where and when you'll find Tcl articles in magazines. Magazine tutorials on other subjects are valuable, however, because Tcl is flexible enough to accommodate good ideas from anywhere.

- *Read other chapters in these volumes.* Tcl shares many of its key concepts with such languages as Perl, Python, Forth, Scheme, and C. You will find that the peculiarities of a specific operating system or communication facility that are documented for other languages often apply to Tcl as well.

8.1.5. Frequently Made Mistakes

A final feature of this chapter deserves comment. Common mistakes or misconceptions are explained at several points, labeled "Frequently Made Mistakes." The aim is to minimize confusion and help readers stay on course. Don't practice the mistakes. Think of them as counter-examples that help sharpen your understanding regarding the limits of definitions and behavior.

Frequently Made Mistakes are a particular value to readers experienced in other languages. The culture or attitude of Tcl is different from those of other leading languages. Just as it's useful for someone moving from Nebraska to New York City to pick up a few tips on the local culture ("lock your car doors"), there is advice ("# is a comment command, not a comment character") that helps simplify acculturation in Tcl immeasurably.

> ***Frequently Made Mistake:*** Common mistakes or misconceptions are explained in several places. Don't practice the mistakes! Think of them as boundary markers for the limits of correct Tcl.

8.2. Introduction: Thinking About Tcl

There are three fundamental lessons to learn about Tcl:

- Tcl is more than just a programming language.
- Where to go to learn more about Tcl.
- How Tcl works as a programming language.

Most of this chapter concentrates on the details of the Tcl programming language. Learning the details of syntax and function will accelerate as you understand how experienced programmers think about Tcl.

8.2.1. The Many Modes of "Hello, World"

Think of "Hello, World" in most programming languages and you think of two "deliverable" aspects: the source code and the executable. When discussing Tcl, there's a lot more to the story than the source-executable pair. Remember, Tcl—the language—is only part of the framework John Ousterhout created in 1988 to promote rapid development of the CAD systems he was researching. You want to exploit the whole framework to create your own solutions quickly and accurately.

Section 8.5.6.1 demonstrates that, with Tcl, the simplest "Hello, World" program can be manifested as all of the following:

- An interactive command
- An executable program that relies on a Tcl interpreter
- A script for interactive submission to a Tcl interpreter
- A standalone executable

At the same time, a Tcl interpreter might appear as

- The standard distribution tclsh interpreter.
- An extension to tclsh—an interpreter with extra capabilities built-in. Tk, Tcl's user interface toolkit, is an example of this. Tk is a copy of Tcl that recognizes commands related to GUIs.
- An interpreter embedded within another program.
- A mobile "agent" that communicates through Tcl's easy network programming interface.
- The plug-in that permits "tclets" to be distributed to WWW clients.
- An HTTP server that supplies scripting capabilities on the server side of Web operations.

Tcl is a powerful tool. Its technology framework makes it simple to try new ideas in Tcl interactively and then migrate the code that embodies them into full-blown applications. As configuration requirements change—and they always do—Tcl lets you reuse the same program in a client-server environment, in an embedded processor, or across an intranet.

This chapter will return to the many manifestations of Tcl. Be on the lookout for ways to ease your work with this flexibility.

8.2.2. What Is Scripting?

There's a final preliminary element to explain before you start to work with Tcl. What are scripts? A script is the end product—a program—created by using a scripting language. That sounds pretty circular. What's a scripting language? A scripting language is a programming language that differs from traditional compiled system languages in four unique ways:

- It processes its scripts with an interpreter.
- Its scripts can report on themselves.
- Pieces can be glued to form a new application.
- The typing of its variables is simple.

8.2.2.1. Interpretation

A Tcl program is commonly referred to as a script. To run a program in a system language, you pass all your work through its compiler. If you want to find out specific information—line count, for example—you step out of where you are and go into that specific utility, rerun the program, and get the results. That's not the case in scripting languages.

Here, programs are "interpreted"—run—in the interpreter. The difference? With Tcl, you see what is going on in your program interactively—as it happens—without having to leave your shell (desktop). We discuss the Tcl interpreter at length in section 8.5.3.

Do scripting languages have a compiler? Many do. Tcl is among these. However, the Tcl compiler is meant for experienced users who perform specialized tasks with performance or security requirements. The Tcl compiler is out of the scope of this work. Do know it's available if you require it. (See `http://starbase.neosoft.com/~claird/comp.lang.tcl/tcl_compilers.html` for more information on Tcl's compilers.)

8.2.2.2. Self-Monitoring

Scripting languages are introspective (see section 8.6.2). This is a qualitative distinction. All languages can report on themselves to one extent or another. The question is how many utilities and subroutines do you want to go through to get your information? With some, such as Fortran, it's not only a matter of taking multiple steps to achieve your end, but also you accomplish your task only after a great deal of difficultly.

Why is this issue of introspective reporting important? During development, Tcl's ability to monitor its own behavior and state largely obviates any need for a debugger. It's easiest simply to have a program report on itself. Even more powerfully, an installed application is able to base decisions on what is going on within the program. The application responds not only to the user, and to other devices, but also to its own condition.

You might use this as a security measure, for example. Suppose your application monitors a nuclear power plant. Various tasks are performed both by the computer and the humans monitoring the plant and the computer system. The computer and the humans respond to alerts generated by the monitoring program.

It's wise to design a fail-safe mode in such a system to protect the computer from responding to too many signals at a time—an overflow rate of, perhaps, over 20 signals per second. How does it work? Well, let's say the program detects it is past its overflow rate. It drops the system back down to fail-safe mode. Why? Couldn't the computer have kept up? Probably so. Neither the plant nor the personnel is endangered at that point; it was simply the computer protecting itself from entering an untested regime. By the time the computer reaches its overflow rate, something physical is probably occurring that needs to be examined and corrected.

Scripting languages' introspective capabilities give particularly powerful ways to express this sort of self-monitoring. This makes for better reporting than is found in compiled languages. Among scripting languages, Tcl's introspection is particularly comprehensive.

8.2.2.3. Gluing

Since it first appeared, Tcl has developed into a rich, stand-alone, cross-platform programming language. Even with these changes, its architecture is best understood as a script—or glue—for external components. Tcl uses programs or pieces of programs that have already been written as "building blocks" and binds them together.

You build using little blocks that are then put together into bigger and bigger pieces. The advantage: You don't construct a big piece and wait until it's complete to evaluate it as to whether it suits your needs. If you had to build an entire wing of the Taj Mahal first, to test its strength to hold the top floor, you'd likely be tearing it down and rebuilding it repeatedly. It's far better to create building blocks that you trust and then assemble them into a final shape.

The best solutions in programming put together pieces that combine the best qualities of different paradigms—fast, compiled languages for segments that strain the processor, highly dynamic methods for responding to user commands, and so on. Gluing together such heterogeneous architectures is what Tcl does superbly.

Okay, so you're not building the Taj Mahal. What does this mean to you? It means you can keep that steam table or audio playback program you spent forever writing when word comes down it was really needed on another system. It used to be you'd start from scratch. Not any more. The result of using Tcl as a scripting language is efficient, effective programming. We've seen many cases of Tcl applications in network management surviving multiple rehostings and rewrites.

As 1998 begins, Dr. Ousterhout continues to lead Tcl's development and also to forcefully advocate his vision of scripting as a mainstay for contemporary software projects. He titles one of his articles on the subject, "Scripting: Higher Level Programming for the 21st Century."

His writing, and that of others (see `http://starbase.neosoft.com/~claird/comp.lang.misc/ portable_scripting.html#scripting` for pointers to them), argues that it is efficient to partition an application into compiled components written in such systems programming languages as C, C++, or Java. Small, simple scripts then configure and assemble the components—often from different languages—into a final application.

This architecture promotes a division of labor that is technically robust and organizationally manageable. Although the subject of building scriptable components is an interesting one, even topical, this chapter touches on it very lightly.

If you learn only one aspect of Tcl, let it be gluing. Folding Tcl into your applications pays big dividends.

8.2.2.4. Typing

No, we are not referring to what you do at a keyboard. The typing we speak of has to do with the characteristics a variable exhibits. Traditional languages expect you to tell the computer whether you're talking about an integer or float. Every variable must be defined explicitly. In scripting languages, the interpreter doesn't require a declaration be made. In this case, the program/script figures out how to treat each numeric value it encounters.

The results:

- Typeless scripting requires less time and is easier to write than system languages because you don't worry about declaring a variable incorrectly.
- Surrendering responsibility for typing to the computer frees you as a programmer to fuss less with details. You're operating on a higher level.

Listing 8.1 shows a minimal Motif program used to create a button. Notice all the lines of header inclusions and declarations it requires.

LISTING 8.1. *A minimal Motif program to create a button.*

```
#include <Xm/Xm.h>
#include <Xm/Form.h>
#include <Xm/PushB.h>


void bye(Widget w, XtPointer clientdata, XtPointer calldata);


int main(int argc, char **argv)
{
    Arg args[5];
    Widget aButton, top;
    XtAppContext app;

        /* Initialize an X application. */
    top = XtAppInitialize(&app, "demo", NULL, 0,
            (Cardinal *) &argc, argv, NULL, args, 0);

        /* Create a single button. */
    aButton = XtVaCreateManagedWidget("Push me",
            xmPushButtonWidgetClass, top, XmNheight, 40,
            XmNwidth, 100, NULL);

        /* Associate a callback to the button. */
    XtAddCallback(aButton, XmNactivateCallback, bye,
            (XtPointer) NULL);

        /* Realize the application, that is, form
            and display all its graphical elements. */
    XtRealizeWidget(top);
        /* Begin listening for all X events of
            interest to this application. */
    XtAppMainLoop(app);
    return(0);
}


void bye(Widget w, XtPointer clientdata, XtPointer calldata)
{
    puts("All done.");
    exit(0);
}
```

Contrast that with its Tk counterpart (see Listing 8.2). The Tk script leaves much of the same information implicit. Tk is content to supply reasonable default values and types when they are not explicitly declared.

LISTING 8.2. *The Tk version of a program to create a button.*

```
button .aButton -text "Push me" -
        command {puts "All done."; exit 0}
pack .aButton
```

You'll spend more time focused on solving your problem and less time coding the solution. This is what makes Tk a more concise and higher-level language.

Line for line, a traditional language such as Fortran is faster to run than a scripting language. This is because of all the interpreting occurring in a scripting language. Part of the reason Fortran runs fast is because all its variables are declared and there is no need for the program to wonder how a variable is to be used. It executes quickly. The tradeoff is that it is slow to develop.

On the other hand, a scripting program such as Tcl is quick and easy to put together. Line for line, it runs slower than Fortran. Keep in mind, however, because we're talking about a Tcl, much less code is involved. The scripted program will probably perform its task faster than the Fortran program.

Also, because a variable's type can mutate during its lifetime, Tcl becomes a much more dynamic language. It binds late. Tcl determines implicitly at runtime what other languages require be declared explicitly at analysis time.

What's best to use? A combination of the two where Tcl fashions pieces of existing programs together into a working application.

8.3. Exclusions

Tcl is too large to capture in a single chapter. Although this one introduces Tcl technology carefully, it deliberately excludes a number of advanced topics:

- Writing extensions (external commands)
- Embedding Tcl
- Use of `text` and `canvas`

- Geometry
- Security
- Name spaces
- Object orientation
- Web interpreters

The following sections describe what you should know about these capabilities.

8.3.1. Writing External Commands

Tcl's original audience was specifically programmers who glued together extensions. Although writing these external commands has become even easier since then, describing all the possibilities has become more difficult. Extensions can now be written

- In C or Java
- For any operating system that supports Tcl, including MacOS, OpenVMS, and UNIX, as well as Windows 3.1, 95, and NT
- Either by hand or with several special-purpose utilities maintained outside SunScript

For current directions on writing extensions in C, refer to `http://starbase.neosoft.com/~claird/comp.lang.tcl/HowToC.html`. `http://starbase.neosoft.com/~claird/comp.lang.tcl/tcl_compilers.html` describes tools that support extension writing.

8.3.2. Embedding Tcl

Tcl is without peer for the ease with which it can be embedded. That is, it is quite easy to put a copy of the Tcl interpreter inside an application otherwise coded in C or another traditional language, to give the application all the facilities of Tcl. This is the logical complement of building an extension, where C-coded facilities are added to Tcl. Many of the same principles apply, so the URLs in the preceding section are where you should start reading.

8.3.3. `text` and `canvas`

Tk is Tcl's powerful GUI extension. Its craftsmanship is so effective that several other languages, including Perl, Python, and Scheme, have adopted Tk as their standard for constructing point-and-click applications. Along with Tk's general assets of ease of use, flexibility, and reliability, it has two particular widgets, or GUI building blocks, that are particular powerhouses. `text` encapsulates a complete small text editor in a single command. `canvas` provides a drawing surface for figures and diagrams. These provide the power evident in the commercial applications of Tk in geographic information systems (GIS), computer-assisted design (CAD), and similar demanding domains. One important point to understand about these two is their inherent dynamism, in comparison to more conventional tools such as Visual Basic. VB is well-suited to rather static form-based interfaces. This is the model for many office automation or commercial programs. Tcl's `canvas`, on the other hand, supports a great deal of flexibility at runtime. This helps write applications that respond in a lively and "intelligent" way to users and is valuable especially in the high-end engineering and scientific displays where Tk is often used.

8.3.4. Geometry

Tk includes three geometry managers: `pack`, `grid`, and `place`. A geometry manager controls placement of graphical elements within a frame and especially how they align or stretch as the frame or other elements move. Tk's geometry managers have a good reputation among graphical programmers for their convenience and power. There is widespread agreement that they are more polished and elegant than, for example, Java's geometry managers. This chapter uses `pack` exclusively, for it applies to the widest range of problems.

8.3.5. Security

Tcl includes several features to support "safe programming"—that is, to give users abilities to control some computing capabilities while restricting them from others. The monitor server described in section 8.6., for example, is a simple script that gives a remote user a lot of flexibility to examine and modify the computer on which it's running. This power can be dangerous, of course. In many situations, it's prudent to enhance such a program so that it prevents actions a user might otherwise command.

Tcl's security model is different from that of Java. Java has a protected "sandbox." The decision of whether an operation is safe or unsafe—whether it's inside the sandbox—is part of the specification of Java. The individual developer has no control over this, only how to use it.

Tcl's security facilities are more like those of operating systems. A programmer has complete control, through the `interp` command, over the operations provided to users. This approach was a deliberate decision by

Tcl designers. It gives greater flexibility to Tcl programmers, compared to their Java counterparts, and correspondingly greater responsibility. It also enjoys the benefit of several decades of industry experience in correct engineering of operating systems. Most of the pitfalls of this security model should already have been worked out.

8.3.6. Name Spaces

Tcl is a prototyping and glue language. It's designed to be quick and easy to use.

Writing large monolithic programs is not Tcl's strength. Tcl certainly serves as the glue in large programs, and Tcl makes short work out of what would be a major project in other languages. A task that requires writing many thousands of lines of Tcl, however, presents specific scale problems. Although it's certainly possible—several commercial applications are known to be in the range of a hundred thousand to a million lines of Tcl source code—Tcl's simplicity falters at large scale. Contrast this with Ada, for example. Ada is hard; it takes a lot of study and writing to create a first Ada program (in general). However, Ada includes excellent facilities for managing large programs.

Key to large-scale programming are ways to isolate different pieces of code from each other, so that, for example, different programmers can work on them without interfering with each other. With Version 8.0, Tcl provides its name-space mechanism to help encapsulate logical units of work. This chapter does not present information on name spaces.

8.3.7. Object Orientation

Tcl has a mixed relation to object-oriented and object-based techniques. Ousterhout deprecates the utility of object orientation for a scripting language in Tcl's niche in his article `http:// www.sunlabs.com/~ouster/scripting.html`. On the other hand, the Tk graphical extension he wrote early in Tcl's history embodies an object-oriented idiom, as his book explains. The proper relation between Tcl and object orientation hasn't yet been settled.

8.3.8. Web Interpreters

Tcl is supple enough to have insinuated itself into Web programming, also. It's very useful for Common Gateway Interface (CGI) programming, although Perl remains far more popular. At least five Hypertext Transfer Protocol (HTTP) servers are known to expose Tcl as a programming interface. For more on both CGI and embedded server-side Tcl programming, see `http://starbase.neosoft.com/~claird/comp.lang.tcl/server_side_tcl.html`.

The client side also is well represented. Along with its Tcl and Tk products, Sunscript makes freely available its plug-in, `http://sunscript.sun.com/plugin/`, to allow for Tcl programming on browser-enabled client machines.

8.4. Starting Off Right

Your Tcl career is destined for success. Even if you start from scratch, you can install it yourself and have your first program running in well under an hour. That's a small investment, and your newfound knowledge will only become more valuable as you use Tcl in future projects. In this section, you'll learn exactly how easy it is to begin.

8.4.1. Installing Tcl

Many readers already have Tcl or Tk installed on their machines. If this is your luck, skip to section 8.4.2.

A minimal Tcl installation usually involves two or three steps:

1. Download a distribution onto your local computer.
2. Depending on your system and requirements, you might need to generate executables or libraries.
3. Complete the installation.

8.4.1.1. Downloading Executables

Distribution bundles for Tcl are relatively small, only a megabyte or two. It's most common in the Tcl world simply to download distributions as needed, either from the authoritative SunScript site `http://sunscript.sun.com/TclTkCore/` or one of its mirrors, among which NeoSoft's `ftp://mirror.neosoft.com/pub/tcl/mirror/ftp.smli.com` is most prominent.

Although several vendors (including Silicon Graphics and Red Hat) have published CD-ROMs that include Tcl distributions, these invariably subordinate Tcl to other requirements and fall out of currency. The newly founded Tcl/Tk Consortium, `http:// www.tcltk.com/consortium`, is considering a long-term commitment to publish an up-to-date Tcl CD-ROM.

8.4.1.2. Generating Executables

Macintosh and Windows releases generally arrive as binaries ready for installation. Even in the instances where this generalization doesn't hold, changes are straightforward.

Distributions for UNIX normally must be generated on your local machine after they've been downloaded. Under UNIX, for example, the sequence in Listing 8.3 usually completes without incident. `$VERSION` in the sequence is a placeholder for such values as `8.0`, `8.1b1`, and so on.

LISTING 8.3. *Generating UNIX executables prior to installation.*

```
ftp ... [retrieve tcl$VERSION.tar.Z]
uncompress tcl$VERSION.tar
tar xf tcl$VERSION.tar
cd tcl$VERSION/unix
configure
make
```

8.4.1.3. Installing Executables

Once any necessary generations are completed, you're ready to install the executables. (See Table 8.2.)

TABLE 8.2. *Installing Tcl on Windows, MacOS, and UNIX.*

Platform	*Installation Procedure*
Windows	Distributions are a standard, self-installing, clickable executable with a name such as `tcl$VERSION`.
MacOS	Distributions are a standard, self-installing, clickable executable with a name such as `tcl$Version`.

UNIX	Launch the standard installation from the command line:
	`cd tcl$VERSION/unix`
	`make install.`

Tcl and Tk are bundled separately. To install Tk, repeat the preceding directions, substituting `tk` for `tcl`. The Tk distribution expects to be unpacked in the same root directory as the Tcl one. The default file structure, therefore, will start with two files (`tcl$VERSION.tar` and `tk$VERSION.tar`) and two directories (`tcl$VERSION` and `tk$VERSION`) in the root directory. It's a mistake for beginners to separate these. Configuring them in different directories is more trouble than it's worth and best left to Tcl experts.

If configuring Tcl and Tk in different directories causes them to not work properly, why are you able to do so in the first place? Why doesn't Tcl look out for you? The answer is it does. When you download Tcl, you have the option of downloading Tk as well. Not everyone chooses Tk. If you download Tcl today and three weeks later decide to install Tk, you might well have forgotten what directory you put Tcl into. Worse, you would have probably forgotten that copying them into the same directory was important at all. Remember: You can install Tcl without Tk; you cannot install Tk without first installing Tcl.

Is there ever a time when you might want to have your resources in different directories? Yes. Let's say you're working on a customized version of Tk and feel you need to keep a standard version of Tk around. Your original version of Tcl and Tk would still be in the same directory. The copy of Tk that you create to customize is what would be put in a different directory.

Releases of Tcl and Tk are also available for MS-DOS, OpenVMS, OS/2, and many other specialty operating systems. Installation of these is not as well standardized as for MacOS, UNIX, and Windows. Each includes specific directions. Read them carefully before you install.

> ***Frequently Made Mistake:*** The Tk distribution expects to be unpacked in the same root directory as the Tcl distribution. The default file structure, therefore, will start with two files (`tcl$VERSION.tar` and `tk$VERSION.tar`) and two directories (`tcl$VERSION` and `tk$VERSION`) in the root directory.

8.4.2. Using Manual Pages

A key benefit of installing Tcl correctly is the subsequent availability of help information. They are often called man pages because they were originally distributed in UNIX "man(ual)" format. They've retained this name even though they're now available on all operating systems.

Table 8.3 explains how to access man pages. One would expect UNIX to have a command-line approach when accessing Tcl Help; however, a couple of GUI interfaces are available for manual pages. It's a sign of Tcl's power and convenience that the most popular of these interfaces, TkMan, was written in Tk.

TkMan is a manual page browser with hypertext links to other man pages and section headers within the same document. It also has clever searching features, "highlighted" personal hot lists, and more. (See `ftp://ftp.cs.berkeley.edu/ucb/people/ phelps/tcltk` for details.)

TABLE 8.3. *Using manual help pages.*

Platform	*Manual Pages*
Windows	Windows installation of Tcl makes several icons available from the Start button, including one labeled Tcl Help. This launches a well-behaved Windows Help session.
MacOS	Within the installed `Tcl/Tk` folder there is a subfolder, `HTML Docs`. In this are several dozen individual `.html` documents that explain Tcl and Tk commands.
UNIX	UNIX users generally access help pages from the command line. To read about the `string` command, for example, type `man string`. Depending on the particular flavor of UNIX, it might be necessary to set the environment variable `MANPATH=/usr/local/man` or another installation dependent value. Contact your system administrator for help in this area.

A final point about the installation of help files: The Tk distribution bundles more than 20 demonstration scripts in its `demo` subdirectory or folder. This, too, goes a long way in teaching the effective use of Tcl/Tk commands.

8.4.3. Running Scripts

To begin exercising your installation, you'll create a minimal GUI application. Your application is built up of small—scripted—pieces. Each step in the construction is simple to guarantee its success and your understanding.

The first step is to launch a `wish` interpreter. The name abbreviates windowing shell, as it was known in its infancy. Nowadays it's called the Tk interpreter. Remember: An interpreter's job is to receive instructions and report the results. In the case of a `wish` interpreter, some of the commands it responds to result in the creation of graphical windows. Tk is an acronym for tool kit. The T in Tk doesn't stand for Tcl.

You begin by launching the wish application. (See Table 8.4 for details.) Two frames (`Console` and `wish$VERSION`) appear on your screen. `Console` interprets Tk commands interactively, whereas `wish$VERSION` is the top level—working area—for your GUI.

TABLE 8.4. *Instructions for launching a wish interpreter.*

Platform	*Instructions*
Windows	To launch the wish application, follow the path Windows Start button | Programs | Tcl | wish.
MacOS	Double-click on the `Wish$VERSION` icon.
UNIX	Invoke `wish` from the command line. If you're using UNIX but are not at the host console, you'll need to adjust your `DISPLAY`. The details of how to do this are not specific to Tcl and are beyond the scope of this chapter. See your system administrator for help.

Your next task is to build a button. At the `Console`'s `%` prompt, type `button .my_button` and then `pack .my_button`. A button appears in the working frame and depresses when clicked—as expected.

To put a label on the button, type

```
my_button configure -text "Push me."
```

Create an action the button can control:

```
.my_button configure -command \
{puts [clock format [clock seconds]]}
```

Now, click on the button (see Table 8.5 for details on how to run your button). Notice what happens. Congratulations; you've successfully installed Tk and your first application is running correctly.

Create a file `my_button.tcl` (see Listing 8.4) on your system and put all the pieces together.

LISTING 8.4. *The contents of the* `my_button.tcl` *file.*

```
# This three-line script creates a small, complete
#    GUI application.
# '#' is the comment command.  See the index
#    for more on how this differs from a comment
#    character.
# '\' at the end of a line serves to continue
#    a command string.
button .my_button -text "Push me." -command \
{.my_label configure -text [clock format [clock seconds]]}
label .my_label
pack .my_button .my_label
```

TABLE 8.5. *How to run your GUI clock application.*

Platform	*How to Operate Button*
Windows	A Tk icon within Windows Explorer should associate with `my_button.tcl`. You can click on it from Windows Explorer.
MacOS	Drag a copy of `my_button.tcl` to the icon labeled Drag & Drop Tclets within the `Tcl/Tk` folder. This creates a clickable form of `my_button.tcl`.
UNIX	Invoke wish my_button.tcl.

8.4.4. Installation Summary

At this point, you have

- Installed Tcl and Tk
- Learned how to access online documentation for Tcl commands
- Launched the Tk interpreter and interactively commanded it to create a small application
- Created an executable (clickable) form of the application

You'll exercise the three latter skills over and over as you progress through this chapter. If you have any problems with the previous exercise, solve them now before proceeding.

8.5. Elements of Tcl Programming

Now you're ready for the heart of this chapter—how to write in Tcl. Again, if you have any unanswered questions about what you've learned so far, refer to section 8.1.4 and section 8.4.1 before moving on. Take your time and get things right. You'll soon be up to speed.

8.5.1. Syntax

Those new to Tcl sometimes complain about its complicated syntax. This highlights a common confusion. Tcl is a command language with a radically simple syntax. What beginners are referring to is Tcl's non-orthogonal command structure. Arguments are command-specific and must be learned as such. Just as gender agreement in a foreign language has you learn the specific gender of each noun, Tcl requires specific arguments be used for each command. This need not slow you down. What's important is that you are aware Tcl behaves this way and that you know how to find the specific command arguments in the documentation when needed.

To write your first program in other languages, you must learn a complicated syntax and a collection of keywords. With Tcl, the syntax is minimal, and you begin programming immediately, even if you only know a single command. As your needs change, you look up a new command or two and grow your expertise incrementally. This approach makes Tcl far more accessible and inviting than other languages. Remember: When you need a different command, look it up; you have the resources (manual pages).

Tcl is a bit like Perl in that it supports abbreviated forms of the most common commands. The more involved and explicit expressions in Tcl are reserved for less frequent operations. This chapter profiles the most popular commands and their arguments. For more specialized commands, we refer students to other sources (see section 8.1.4) for details.

This approach also preserves the accuracy of this chapter. Tcl has gone through approximately one major revision each year. Although SunScript, the development team responsible for Tcl's core, is careful to maintain compatibility between releases, newer versions of Tcl often include new functionality for existing commands. The aim of this chapter, therefore, is to communicate the spirit of Tcl and the invariant center of its commands. Specifics that vary from release to release are best learned by the alternate approaches (refer to section 8.1.4).

With a clean installation of Tcl (see section 8.4.1) and knowledge of where to go for answers (see section 8.1.4), you've launched your Tcl career with the key pieces for success in place. Learn a couple of commands, use them, and learn a couple more, as needed. It's easy.

8.5.2. Tcl Interpreter

When you develop solutions with traditional languages (C, Fortran, Pascal), the deliverables that have your attention are the source and the executable produced from that source. All your work passes through the compiler before it can run. If you're in a C debugging session and need a timing result, you must leave the debugger, recompile for your current conditions, and rerun with a timing utility. To change a library you've linked in, again you exit, recompile, and rerun. Whatever you're after, it's certain to make you leave where you are, cycle through the compiler, and restart your executable. That's not the case with scripting languages, however, and especially not Tcl.

Tcl programmers do the majority of their work in the interpreter. Devotees of scripting languages regard this difference as an important advantage. Why? Because the interpreter is what makes Tcl a flexible language. An interpreter's job is to receive instructions and report the results. That doesn't sound new and it doesn't sound like much.

Okay, here's what is exciting. Tcl and other scripting languages differ from traditional languages because they use an interpreter. So? Interpreters are more versatile than compilers. In a traditional program, to watch a source in action, you must create a different source, compile it, and run it. It's more like surrogate testing. An interpreter lets you see your work "live."

In Tcl, you needn't create an explicit executable to run your script. The interpreter acts as the executable. You can also "batch" your work into a distinct executable. Limiting yourself to using the interpreter in this way, however, is a bit like restricting your Ferrari to the confines of your local subdivision.

Working within the interpreter allows you to look at your script interactively. Again, you do not need a separate executable, the interpreter fills in. For some programmers, the ability to work interactively, access whatever information they wish regarding their scripts, and never have to exit into another shell or desktop is a dream come true.

Tcl's interpreter is made up of two parts: the interpreter's core and Tcl commands. The core does only three things—always in the same order and one command string at a time:

1. Group arguments
2. Substitute results
3. Invoke commands

Let's be clear: Tcl's interpreter can evaluate several command strings—up to an entire script—at a time. However, the interpreter's core only evaluates one command string at a time. The other portion of the interpreter is the commands that came bundled with it—along with any commands you've modified or created.

Tcl's flexibility sometimes throws new users. There are a lot of decisions to make early on. Will you work within the interpreter or not? Do you want to execute interactively from a file on the disk or from what you type directly into the interpreter? Then there is the whole question of what you are doing with Tcl. Will you be gluing or creating GUIs, or do you just want an easy way to speed program development?

8.5.3. Command String Basics

Other languages use programs and subprograms to solve problems. Tcl is different. A Tcl solution is script. A script is a sequence of command strings—sometimes called command lines.

Scripts contain zero or more command strings. How can a script have no command strings? When a file is created, it exists only as a name and contains no explicit instructions. It does, however, contain an empty command string—an implicit no-op (no-operation, or null) command—which acts as a placeholder. The default for many actions in Tcl is the empty script.

Each Tcl command string performs a definite operation (assigns a variable, opens a file, or configures a button). A Tcl command string consists of two parts (command and argument). Some Tcl terms you will be expected to use have multiple meanings. Table 8.6 educates you on basic Tcl definitions and how we use each term.

Both newlines—what the computer sees at the end of the line—and semicolons terminate a command string. The command always appears first and is separated from its arguments by whitespace—either blank characters or tabs.

TABLE 8.6. *Fundamental definitions.*

Term	*Tcl Definition*
script	Textbook: A single statement or individual line of instruction. Also a sequence of statements or lines of instruction. An empty script acts as placeholder and is a valuable tool. Synonyms: Single-line script: command string, command line, command (slang). Multiple-line scripts: command strings, command lines, a Tcl program. Note that when we speak of a script, we refer to the collection of command strings that make up an entire Tcl program.

Term	*Tcl Definition*
`command string`	Textbook: The fundamental unit of Tcl operation. A single line of instruction/code/script. Command strings are made up of two parts: command and arguments. A command string performs a definite action (assigns a value, opens a file, and so on) and is terminated either by a newline or a semicolon. Synonyms: Line of instruction, line of code, script, command line, command statement, command (slang). Note that in this chapter, "command string" refers to a single line of instruction in a Tcl program.
`command`	Popular usage: Refers to a single line of instruction in Tcl. Textbook: Commands are used in statements to generate results. It is always the first word in a statement. Tcl commands are followed by arguments that appear and are passed in a specific order. A Tcl command can be named anything, including any alphanumeric character or symbol in any order. Commands can be modified: • You can change the name and keep its same functionality (see Listing 8.15). • Lets you change its functionality and keep the original name (see Listing 8.14). • Allows you to alter both its functionality and the name, by combining the previous two sequences. • Can be deleted, but only through a C-coded extension, which is outside the scope of this chapter. Synonyms: Instruction, command string (slang), line of code (slang). Note that to avoid confusion, we will use the textbook definition of "command." A single line of instruction in a Tcl program is referred to as a "command string."

continues

TABLE 8.6. *Continued.*

Term	*Tcl Definition*
`argument`	A value/parameter/input passed to the command portion of a statement. Arguments are separated from commands by white space (blank characters or tabs). Tcl requires the arguments for each command appear in a specific order. Note that in Tcl, there is no conceptual difference between a number, letter, alphanumeric combination, or special symbol. Unlike other programming languages, everything is a string; no typing occurs.

8.5.4. Commands

In Tcl, commands are always the first item in a command string. Zero or more arguments follow it (see Listing 8.5). It is the responsibility of the command to recognize what operation is to be performed on the arguments that follow it.

The following command string shows a command (`set`) with two arguments (`x` and `5`):

```
set x 5
```

The `set` command expects the first argument (`x`) to name a variable, and the second argument (`5`) in the command string gives a value to that variable.

The first word in a command string is always a command as shown in Listing 8.5. A command is followed by zero or more arguments.

LISTING 8.5. *Commands (*`set`*,* `open`*, and* `.b1`*) are always the first term in a command string.*

```
set x 5

open $filename

.b1 configure -text hello -command {puts "Hello, World!"}
```

A command string can have multiple commands within it. Each of the statements shown in Listing 8.6 offers a valid syntax. Notice the use of double quotes to group arguments.

LISTING 8.6. *Valid Tcl syntax.*

```
set a "Most command strings occupy a single line."

my_command first second third \
    fourth "Sometimes a command string spans more than one line." \
    sixth

# Multiple commands can appear on a line.
init_driver $other; reset counter; notify "Switching now."
```

At a high level, this is the entire Tcl syntax. There is no special pattern or keyword for assignment, control structures, or any of the other constructs normally used by computer language. Everything is handled as a command. Even the process used to create a new command is controlled by a command (section 8.6.1).

8.5.4.1. Grouping and Substitution

The Tcl interpreter evaluates each command string individually; it does not consider the script as a whole. Remember: The interpreter's job is to receive instructions and to report the results. The core of the Tcl interpreter does only three things—*always* in the same order and one command string at a time:

1. Group arguments.
2. Substitute results.
3. Invoke commands.

Grouping occurs first. Tcl uses curly braces, (`{}`), and double quotes, (`" "`), to group words and white space into a single argument. The difference between these forms is that double quotes allow substitution to occur; substitutions manage variable values and command results. Curly braces only group; therefore, substitution cannot take place:

```
print_line This is a line.
```

is a command string with four arguments (`This`, `is`, `a`, `line.`). Whereas

```
puts "This is a line."
```

and

```
puts {This is a line.}
```

are two commands that share an identical `argument (This is a line.)`. Remember: Double quotes and braces group the argument; they are not part of the argument.

Let's take a look at how grouping and value substitution play out. Both of the following command strings have one argument:

```
puts {This $line.}
```

and

```
puts "This $line."
```

In the first case, the argument is a string of characters (`This $line.`). You use this grouping when you work with a command (`button`, `bind`, `proc`) that has its own substitution rules.

In the second case, the interpreter sees `$line` as a reference to a variable. The value is substituted within the grouping immediately after `This` (with the space following `This` preserved).

The second kind of substitution Tcl supports is the return of command results. Here, brackets—rather than curly braces or double quotes—delimit the argument. This causes an operation to be performed within the argument and then passed back to the command in the command string. Note the following example:

```
puts [clock seconds]
```

Tcl first evaluates the bracketed string (`clock seconds`) as a command string. The resultant value is passed back to the original command (`puts`). The consequence of the entire command string (`put [clock seconds]`) is to print the current time in seconds. Section 8.7.1 shows how to format this result more conventionally.

That's the syntax of Tcl. Remember:

- Tcl's syntax is simple to a fault; it surprises those familiar with other programming languages who expect complexity.
- The Tcl interpreter groups, substitutes, and invokes commands.

That's all it does.

- Grouping with `""` and `{}` differ only in regard to substitution.
- Everything—including control structures—gets done as a command.

8.5.5. Input/Output

Tcl has only three I/O commands (`puts`, `read`, `gets`). They are simple to learn.

Tcl takes simple pieces and combines them flexibly. This achieves a great deal of power.

8.5.5.1. puts

The `puts` command prints its single argument. Combine that simplicity with Tcl's uniform yet flexible syntax rules and you get suprisingly powerful results.

> ***Frequently Made Mistake:*** We know your urge is to skip over this section because of the elementary nature of "Hello, World". After all, you've seen it in C, Pascal, or BASIC. What more could there be to it? Plenty.
>
> We use "Hello, World" extensively in this chapter because it is familiar. It's also as simple as things get. And there's value in introducing fundamental pieces in such a readily understood program.

To prove our point, we again visit the lowly "Hello, World" program. A "Hello, World" program is generally a rather unpromising and even dreary beginning. In this case, it's a quick and easy way to showcase Tcl's versatility, simple structure, and ease of use.

A minimal "Hello, World" is written as

```
puts "Hello, World"
```

As section 8.2.1 promised, Tcl can execute source code in several different ways. This flexibility gives a great advantage to Tcl developers.

More traditional languages struggle to integrate the source and executable aspects of a program in a debugger. With Tcl, all the possibilities and resources are available immediately, from the interpreter:

- "Hello, World" executed as an interactive command.

  Launch an interactive interpreter, either `tclsh` or `wish` (many organizations install these as `tclsh$VERSION` and `wish$VERSION`). At the prompt, type

  ```
  puts "Hello, World"
  ```

  This returns `"Hello, World"`. It also leaves you sitting in the interpreter. You can leave the interpreter at any time with the command

  ```
  exit
  ```

- "Hello, World" written as an executable program.

  Create a file `simplest.tcl` with contents

  ```
  puts "HELLO, World"
  ```

  and invoke

  ```
  tclsh simplest.tcl
  ```

  When launched this way, the interpreter executes your script (`simplest.tcl`) then exits you to the desktop you were in before you launched the interpreter.

  In this case, the script includes a single line. This isn't always so. Applications with tens of thousands of command strings are often invoked this way.

  Remember: The contents of `simplest.tcl` must be a Tcl script. Section 8.8 explains how to go beyond this.

- "Hello, World" written as a script for interactive submission to a Tcl interpreter.

  Start an interpreter and then type

  ```
  source simplest.tcl
  ```

  Again, "Hello, World" comes to your screen. This time, the interpreter stays active, waiting for your next command. This method combines the other two methods.

  Think of source as a kind of shortcut. It's a single command that performs the entire task the script in its argument specifies. There's a natural work flow to the development of Tcl scripts: Experiment with individual command strings within the interpreter, then combine them into a single file to define a logical script, and finally test the script interactively with source.

  Remember: to leave the interpreter, type

  ```
  exit
  ```

The last way mentioned in section 8.2.1 is to write it as a stand-alone executable. This is a single executable file into which has been bundled your Tcl script and the Tcl interpreter. This is an advanced topic and we'll only give the highlights. (See `http://starbase.neosoft.com/~claird/comp.lang.tcl/tcl_compilers.html` for more information on what a stand-alone executable is and how to create one.)

Why would you want to create such a thing? When you want to hand over a solution and don't want to give the recipient a copy of Tcl. It's a free language with no licensing restrictions; why not give it to them? There are two principal reasons: It's easier to install and it keeps the customer from peeking in your code to see how you did it.

When you hand a customer a solution as a stand-alone executable, they don't need to install Tcl and then install the solution. Your customer saves a step. Is this important? It can be. We've all had at least one customer for whom performing a single task was a stretch.

The other reason we mentioned for creating a stand-alone executable—to hide your work from the customer—deserves thought. You limit the customers' access to your code. They can't go in to tweak it—and possibly break it.

Another reason you probably won't want to advertise your code is because of Tcl's ease of use and your bottom line. What do we mean? Well, let's say you charge a customer $6,000 to solve his problem. Do you really want him to know the solution was a five-line script? I don't think so, Tim.

With Tcl, it's quick and easy to create applications. Were we serious about our five-line script? Absolutely. :-)

The `puts` command manages both one- and two-argument invocations. This is because the same `puts` command can also provide an interface to file- and network-oriented output. To create a time stamp (see Listing 8.7), for example, takes only three lines.

LISTING 8.7. *Creating a time stamp.*

```
set file_descriptor [open myfile w]

puts $file_descriptor \
        "The time of this event is [clock format [clock seconds]]."

close $file_descriptor
```

Look at what just happened. When `puts` is invoked with two arguments, it treats the first argument (`$file_descriptor`) as a file handle—a shorthand reference to a file. In the Tcl world, a file handle is also called a channel, file descriptor, or—more rarely—a stream. The `puts` command sends the characters of the second argument (`The time of this event is [clock format [clock seconds]`) to the file handle. The result, in this case, is that the characters of the second argument appear in the file (`myfile w`).

A different variation of the puts command prints the quoted text, without appending the customary newline afterward.

```
puts -nonewline "There's no newline after the
period here."
```

Remember: The syntax of Tcl is simple. The commands of Tcl, however, have idiosyncratic and often relatively complex rules for interpretation. This reality underscores the importance of man pages. They authoritatively document the order in which arguments appear to the "core" Tcl and Tk commands.

Compounding this confusion is the way in which different commands cooperate. The syntactic relationship between commands is simple: There is none. Commands take arguments and return values. Semantically, however, several of them might need to work together.

The puts command is adequate for a large portion of all output operations that commonly arise. In certain circumstances, however, the output channel to which it sends data might be modified by such other commands as close, dup, fconfigure, open, or server. The data themselves are often conditioned just before output by binary, format, or scan. These interactions are difficult to memorize accurately on a first reading, so it's valuable for students of Tcl to return to the manual pages and re-read the details of the core commands from time to time.

8.5.5.2. read, gets

Most other languages have several forms of input and output (print, write, putchar, and so on). This is not the case with Tcl. All output is done with a single command (puts), whereas input uses only two commands (gets and read). The gets command is line oriented, and read is character oriented.

8.5.6. String Processing

Tcl has three major families (see Table 8.7) of commands for manipulating character sequences (format, scan, string, and regular expressions).

8.5.6.1. format, scan

The format and scan commands are in the same family because of how they perform. The scan command undoes the format command. Likewise, the format command undoes a scan command. The format and scan commands generalize the sprintf and sscanf of the C runtime library. The format command builds up character sequences that follow patterns. For instance, we could put raw data into columnar form (see Listing 8.8).

LISTING 8.8. *Script using* `format` *command to create a table.*

```
puts [format %10s%10s $first_column $second_column].
```

TABLE 8.7. *The three major families of commands in string processing.*

Family	*Function/Operation*
`format, scan`	Generalize the `printf` and the `sscanf` of the C runtime library.
`string`	Parses command strings.
Regular expression	A particular way to express parsing rules. It includes `regexp` and `regstr`.

Another use for the `format` command is to enter credit card expiration dates:

```
format %02/%02 $month $year
```

Frequently Made Mistake: Be careful when formatting numbers with leading zeros in Tcl. A "feature" of Tcl since its inception assumes that a number with a leading zero is written in octal.

What does this mean? It means that when August comes around and everyone is off on vacation, programs start crashing for no apparent reason. Although "08" is frequently used as a code for August, it doesn't exist as an octal numeral.

The solution is to trim leading zeros from numeric values (or to not let people take vacation in August).

Note that there is no inherent problem with leading zeroes as long as you don't try to do arithmetic with them.

The `format` command creates sequences and the `scan` command takes them apart. If we applied a `scan` command to Listing 8.8, we would wind up with our original data in its original order because `scan` inverts the `format` command.

Why would you want to take apart a line of ordered data? If you were the Post Office and wanted your optical reader to determine where the mail was headed, you might find the `scan` command helpful indeed. The following script shows you what's involved in separating the necessary information:

```
scan $line "%s %s" city state
```

8.5.6.2. `string`

The `string` command is the only member of this family; however, it has many subcommands (`length`, `range`, and so on) that are used to evaluate the character string itself. The subcommands are very useful and act to change case, tell how long a string is, find a particular character in a string, and more.

The `string` command parses—cuts, chops, or breaks up—character strings. A couple of uses are shown in Listing 8.9.

LISTING 8.9. *Scripts featuring* `string` *subcommands (*`length` *and* `range`*).*

```
string length $my_string

string range $telephone 0 2
```

Listing 8.9 returns the length of the argument (`$my_string`). The second example takes in a telephone number and returns the area code. It's important to know that most of Tcl's indexing is zero-based.

8.5.7. Regular Expressions

The third family of string processor (regular expressions) includes the `regexp` and `regstr` commands. The former of these searches for regular expressions, and the latter searches and replaces. What are regular expressions? It's a large subject. Regular expressions are a particular language to express parsing rules.

What does one look like? It's a bit like looking at the newspaper comics and seeing a balloon full of character strings signifying expletive language.

Listing 8.10 uses `regsub` to translate Houston-area telephone numbers after an area-code split.

LISTING 8.10. *Using* `regsub` *to translate telephone numbers after an area-code split.*

```
proc updated original {
     regsub ^713(-(482¦992¦996¦987)-.*) \
                                              $original {281\1} updated
        return $updated
}
```

The effect of this procedure is this: If a telephone number matches the pattern `713-xxx-dddd`, where `xxx` appears on a list of affected exchanges, then change the `713` to `281`. Otherwise, return the original number unchanged. The actual list of affected exchanges was much longer than the four listed here. Regular expressions easily handle even more complicated patterns than this.

Regular expressions are arcane. One of the benefits of working with regular expressions, however, is the precision of which they're capable. For instance, in Listing 8.10, we can be certain we don't accidently change a telephone number just because numbers matching one of the exchanges were found in the last four digits of the phone number.

8.6. Arithmetic

Tcl's arithmetic is neither speedy in execution nor familiar in appearance. Printing the sum of a pair of numbers is a bit cumbersome:

```
puts "The sum of $addend1 and $addend2 is [expr
$addend1 + $addend2]."
```

This is a reflection of the extreme uniformity of Tcl's processing. Arithmetic is not special in any way. It is just the result of another command string. The command (`expr`) knows about special operators, such as `+`, `*`, `/`, and so on.

The advantage of arithmetic's lack of privilege, of course, is that it's completely integrated with all other Tcl facilities. It's easy to extend arithmetic to process complex numbers, or extended precision numbers, or rationals, or even more sophisticated number systems. Volunteers have already written several such extensions. Although interpreted arithmetic is slower than what's possible in a compiled language, it makes it possible to write a simple calculator in only 12 lines (see Listing 8.11):

LISTING 8.11. *Tcl script to create a calculator.*

```
entry .entry -textvariable expression
label .label
button .button -text Submit -command evaluate

proc evaluate {} {
    global expression

    .label configure -text [eval expr $expression]
}

bind . <Return> evaluate
pack .entry .label .button
```

These few lines create a handy calculator, which is shown in Figure 8.1.

FIGURE 8.1.

8.6.1. proc

There are two kinds of commands in Tcl (external commands and procedures). In use, they are indistinguishable. The `proc` command creates and replaces procedure commands in Tcl.

To create a new external command you need to be outside Tcl, in another language. This is an advanced subject (see section 8.3.1). Any command you create while in Tcl is a procedure command. There is no difference in the way procedure commands and external commands operate, nor in the way they're used.

Why would you want to create a command? To give structure to your work or to reuse a sequence of command strings. Listing 8.12 shows the `proc` time-stamp program. We created this time-stamp program earlier. By reusing the same script, we can create a `timestamp` command with little effort.

LISTING 8.12. *Creating a* `timestamp` *command.*

```
proc timestamp myfile {

     set file_descriptor [open myfile w]

     puts $file_descriptor \
          "The time of this event is [clock format [clock seconds]]."

     close $file_descriptor

}
```

Tcl also permits recursion. Listing 8.13 defines a recursive Fibonacci sequence.

LISTING 8.13. *An example of recursion using a Tcl script.*

```
proc fibonacci n {
    if {$n <= 1} {
        return $n
    }
    return [expr [fibonacci[expr $n - 1]] + fibonacci [expr $n - 2]]]
}
```

8.6.2. Introspection

Introspection labels a process that reports on, and even modifies, itself. Introspection is one of Tcl's strengths.

8.6.2.1. Managing Tcl's Commands

A recurring theme of this chapter is that Tcl is a powerful combination of simple elements. One way to think about Tcl, for example, is in terms of the two fundamentals of syntax parsing and commands.

The kernel of Tcl is a small, simple parser that processes commands. This is the essence of Tcl. Bundled with this kernel are a collection of commands. Notice, however, that while the kernel is essential to Tcl, the particular commands it processes are completely under your control. If you don't like the commands supplied with Tcl, you can create new ones and delete or modify old ones.

You create new commands either with `proc`, as shown in section 8.6.1 or by compiling an "extension" with C, Java, or a similar language.

You can relabel existing commands with `rename`. Several newcomers to Tcl have set up personal copies of the interpreter, which they initialize with

```
rename puts print
rename cd chdir
```

and so on, simply to put a more familiar face on Tcl. Once Tcl executes these, `print` and `chdir` replace `puts` and `cd`, respectively, in every regard. This allows these programmers to write

```
chdir $my_directory
print "This is the string I want to print."
```

in place of

```
cd $my_directory
puts "This is the string I want to print."
```

A more interesting use of `rename` is to modify existing behavior (see Listing 8.14). Suppose you're satisfied with the behavior of `puts`, except that you'd like it to recognize one more flag. You want `-flush` to signal to `puts` that it should do an immediate flush after printing its argument. That's simple.

LISTING 8.14. *A sample sequence that gives new functionality to the existing* `puts` *command.*

```
rename puts puts.old
proc shift list {
     upvar $list local_name
     set local_name [lreplace $local_name 0 0]
}
proc puts args {
     if {{-flush} != [lindex $args 0]} {
          eval puts.old $args
          return
     }
     shift args
     eval puts.old $args
     set channel stdout
     if {{-nonewline} == [lindex $args 0]} {
          shift args
     }
     if {2 == [llength $args]} {
          set channel [lindex $args 0]
     }
     flush $channel
}
```

This sequence first saves the original `puts` under a new name, `puts.old`. Then it defines a small convenience function, `shift`, which replaces a list with a truncated version of itself. Finally, it gives a new "public" face for `puts`, one that relies on `puts.old` to do most of the work.

Note that `shift` doesn't give us much in this instance; defining it is more trouble than simply inlining its effect in the two places it's used. However, it is a convenient command more generally, for there are many other situations where one wants to step successively through the elements of a list. Also, it provides a good example of `upvar`'s ability to give Tcl call-by-reference. Tcl parameter passing is, in general, by value. When you write `command $variable`, `command` knows nothing about `variable`. It only knows that it receives a particular value, the value of `$variable`. `upvar` is a special command that allows a procedure to act on the variables of other procedures, or, more precisely, on variables in other contexts.

Finally, it's easy to duplicate a Tcl procedure, as shown in Listing 8.15.

LISTING 8.15. *Duplicating a Tcl procedure.*

```
proc duplicate {original_command new_command} {
        proc $new_command [info args
$original_command] [info body $original_command]
}
```

Notice the use here of `info`. `info` collects a variety of useful information about a Tcl process, including complete descriptions of all procedures. Here, we duplicate a procedure by creating a new one with both the argument list and procedural body of the original.

For the most part, of course, if there's need for a synonym for a particular command, it's enough to refer to it, as in this example:

```
# This creates a procedure, print, which
# acts identically to puts.
proc print args {
                                        eval puts $args
}
```

The point of the duplicate is that `$new_command` will retain its functionality even if `$original_command` is modified or deleted. That's the difference between a synonym and a duplicate.

8.6.2.2. `info`

Suppose you've written a program that will be used at many different sites. Some of them have installed the latest Tcl interpreter, and some are still using Version 7.5, from a few years ago. Tcl is compatible enough across releases so your program still runs. However, you're missing out on performance improvements you could exploit with Version 8.0. What do you do?

For C programmers, this is often a hard problem. Compiler vendors have released successive versions of their products that differ in syntax and semantics yet give no clean way to detect those differences either at compile time or runtime. This can be a considerable nuisance in practical situations.

Tcl has a one-line solution. The `info` command provides most of Tcl's introspective capabilities. Its `tclversion` subcommand makes it easy to write a program that corrects for any incompatibility between versions.

LISTING 8.16. *A code fragment for accommodating version incompatibilities.*

```
switch [info tclversion] {
    7.5 do_whatever_is_best_for_7.5
    7.6 do_something_else_for_7.6
    8.0 -
    8.1 do_the_same_for_8.0_and_above
    default {
        error \
        I don't know about your version."
    }
}
```

The `info` command also reports on the particular host on which it's running (see Listing 8.17).

LISTING 8.17. *A code fragment that detects the machine on which it's executed.*

```
if {$mymachine == [info hostname]} {
    do_one_thing
} else {
    do_another
}
```

`info` has several other specialized subcommands. Some of them are handy to use interactively. If, for example, you can't remember whether the version of Tcl you're working with provides a particular command ("Was that in 7.5, or did it appear only in 7.6?"), it's often easiest to type

```
info commands
```

and have Tcl itself tell you what commands it knows. The result of such an operation is dynamic, of course. Although the value of `info commands` might start during a particular session as

```
tell socket subst open eof pwd tclMacPkgSearch glob list exec pid
time unknown eval lrange fblocked lsearch gets case lappend proc
break llength auto_execok return pkg_mkIndex unsupported0 linsert
error catch clock info split array if auto_mkindex fconfigure concat
join lreplace source global switch auto_reset update tclPkgUnknown
close cd for auto_load file append format read package set scan
trace seek while flush after vwait continue uplevel foreach rename
fileevent regexp tclPkgSetup upvar expr unset load regsub exit
history interp puts incr lindex lsort string
```

it will change as you add, remove, or modify your own command definitions.

8.6.3. Network Programming

Network programming has the reputation of being difficult and error-prone. An entire industry category ("middleware") has emerged due to the perceived deficiencies in socket-level programming. Socket-level programming is a type of network programming that is as low level as you can get without introducing hardware specifics. Socket refers to a particular type of TCP/IP network connection. Tcl's `socket` command provides an inviting wrapper for this area. Many programmers have built their first successful network applications with Tcl. So can you.

8.6.3.1. Programming on the Server Side

In traditional network programming, the server side is harder to program and easier to mess up. There are three main considerations: synchronization, data verification, and error handling.

Synchronization problems actually take place on both the server and client sides. The volume of their occurrence and the potential for mishap is magnified on the server side. What we mean by synchronization is the way the server orders the communication sessions with its clients. For instance, the server must remember to let the client finish its request before answering, how will lag times be handled, and what to do if the client won't let the server finish giving its information before passing more.

The next pitfall is that the server must multitask several simultaneous requests from multiple clients. The server needs to ensure it is returning the proper information to the correct client.

The last stumbling block is making sure the error handling is correct. This is difficult when you're dealing with multiple clients who behave differently:

- What do you do if you lose one of your connections?
- What should you do if you haven't lost the connection—you just haven't heard from the client for a while?

What does it take to create a server in Tcl? Listing 8.18 is a simple server process that's a model for many useful applications.

LISTING 8.18. *Creating a reporter—a simple server process.*

```
set s [socket -server accept 2828]

proc accept {s a port} {
     fileevent $s readable [list process $s]
     fconfigure $s -translation lf -buffering line
}

proc process {s} {
     global x

          # Trim the terminal newline.
     set l [string trimright [gets $s]]
     if [eof $s] {
          close $s
          set x done
     } else {
          set result [uplevel $l]
          puts $s "The result of evaluating '$l' is '$result'."
          puts "The request was for '$l'."
     }
}

puts Ready.
vwait x; vwait x; vwait x; close $s
```

To exercise this script, start it on a host enabled for TCP/IP networking. Once it says `Ready.`, connect to it with any handy `Telnet`-like client on port 2828. (From a command line, you might request `telnet localhost 2828` or `telnet mymachine.domain.com 2828`.) To ask the reporter about itself, type

```
info hostname
```

then

```
pwd
```

then

```
pid
```

within the Telnet session. Notice that the reporter returns to you information about its host name, its active directory, and its process number. You can ask it what handle it's using for its socket connection:

```
set s
```

You can do almost anything on the remote machine that Tcl lets you do on the machine at which you're typing. You can even connect to it with several different Telnet sessions and use `reporter` to communicate between them. If one session sends the command string

```
set mymessage "This is my message."
```

another `session` can retrieve it with

```
set mymessage
```

This is a remarkably powerful fragment of code. It's handy to embed a little task such as this in any long-running application. A factory monitor, a Web server, a security watchdog, and the user interface for a kiosk accessible to the public are all good candidates. By including this small bit of code in such applications, we immediately gain a powerful and unobtrusive "viewport" on the operation of the server. Consider, for example, a monitor that observes and controls the lighting and ventilation for a factory. It should operate hands-off, on its own, so there might be no provision for a display. With our reporter server running, however, we can send arbitrary command strings to interrogate the monitor about its current status. We can

- Ask the reporter how many commands it has processed.
- Examine the state of the Tcl interpreter.
- Create a trigger that will send back an alarm when a particular condition is reached.

We can even download new procedures to repair a damaged process while it continues to run. This is a basis for a range of exciting technologies—agents, autonomous vehicles, genetic algorithms, fault-tolerant software, and more—that goes far beyond the scope of this chapter.

It's best, of course, to engineer servers so carefully that they run flawlessly through their lifetimes and never require intervention. Even if you don't need a reporter in your application when you deliver it, it can be valuable during development. It gives you the ability to intervene creatively during test sessions, to shorten the cycle between setting up test conditions and observing their results. Incidentally, Tk has another mechanism to do the same: the `send` command controls one Tk instance from another. Notice, however, that any Telnet-like client can control a reporter, but `send` is confined to UNIX instances of Tk as of Version 8.0.

Before installing a reporter in your application, please do understand that this example includes no security provisions. As it's written, it gives such complete control to its clients that it's easy for them to be destructive. Look in the help page for Tcl's `interp` command for an explanation of how you can make reporter safe.

8.6.3.2. Programming on the Client Side

Tcl handles the client side of `socket` sessions equally well. There are still synchronization issues on this end, such as

- How to establish a connection.
- What do you do when you've asked for information and it doesn't come? Do you continue to wait? Do you put something up on the monitor so it can be found out and corrected?

Still, the client side of the fence is much easier to program. As part of a cross-platform configuration management project we did, it was convenient for us to write a program (`smtp_send.tcl`, see Listing 8.19) that relays an email message through an SMTP host.

Read over the `smtp_send.tcl` program again. Notice how easy it is to write a platform-independent scriptable interface to the Simple Mail Transfer Protocol (SMTP). There are many fine mailing agents for end users and no standard way to automate their operation.

LISTING 8.19. *The* `smtp_send.tcl` *program for cross-platform configuration management.*

```
proc drain channel {
        # Get a response, and discard it.
    gets $channel
}

proc puts_now {channel text} {
    puts $channel $text
    flush $channel
}

# RFC 821 governs SMTP.
proc send_SMTP_mail {SMTP_host recipients from subject text} {
    set standard_SMTP_socket 25
    set socket [socket $SMTP_host $standard_SMTP_socket]
    puts_now $socket "MAIL From:<$from>"
    drain $socket
    foreach recipient $recipients {
        puts_now $socket "RCPT To:<$recipients>"
    }
    drain $socket
    puts_now $socket DATA
    drain $socket
    puts $socket "From:  <$from>"
    puts $socket "To:  <$recipients>"
    puts $socket "Subject:  $subject\n"
        # Uniformize newlines.
    foreach line [split $text \n] {
        puts $socket [join $line]
    }
```

```
    puts $socket .\nQUIT
    drain $socket
    close $socket
}
```

Test the mail program for yourself (see Listing 8.20) using your Tcl interpreter. Within a few milliseconds, you'll have a new piece of email in your mailbox.

LISTING 8.20. *Test the mail program.*

```
% source smtp.tcl
% send_SMTP_mail  $MY_SMTP_HOST $ME $FROM Test {
This is the body
of the message.
}
```

Although no one would want to compose email this way, embedding `send_SMTP_mail` within a larger program can be extremely valuable. We have used it to generate automatic reports on system resources and operational upsets from several long-running processes, including factory monitors and Web servers.

More important than this particular application is what it illustrates: Tcl's socket programming is easy to do. Tcl's socket input and output look like conventional Tcl I/O (`puts` and `gets`). In fact, it's often valuable to write an application that can transact either through `sockets`, `console`, or file I/O. This simplifies development and validation because you are able to test it interactively. You thereby factor out networking issues—so things are simpler and easier to create.

Going in the other direction, this uniformity across different I/O channels facilitates enhancement of an existing Tcl line-oriented interface to a socket connection. This is valuable for all the times a locally hosted program needs to "grow up"—get bigger, add functionality—in a network where its processing is to be distributed.

Think, for example, of a program that reads licensing and other security information from a local file. With minimal rewrite, you can use the same routines to read the same information through a socket rather than a file descriptor. Of course, this requires the creation of a server to deliver the security information. However, creating a server could be easier to write and maintain than keeping multiple local copies of a license file current.

Tcl's commands provide a uniform and convenient interface, even in areas where network programming diverges from other I/O. For instance, network applications are more likely to accomodate latencies and interruptions in service than their corresponding file-based programs. Tcl registers asynchronous operations with the same `fileevent` mechanism for both.

8.6.3.3. Network Programming Summary

With Tcl's `socket` command, it takes only a few lines to write a TCP/IP server (see Listing 8.18) or client. Moreover, Tcl's interactive interpreter makes it easy to experiment or debug socket connections that are live.

Network programming is a large subject. This section only touches on Tcl's capabilities. Tcl—or its extensions—also support UDP, NNTP, RPC, SNMP, HTTP, PVM, Linda, and mobile code. If you have a job that deserves to be spread over more than one computer, Tcl will ease your work.

8.7. Miscellaneous Commands

8.7.1. `clock`

The `clock` command has already appeared a couple of times in this chapter. At its simplest

```
clock format $number_of_seconds
```

returns a human-readable date and time. What format are we using? Although it's documented in the man pages, it's so easy to use the Tcl interpreter that working Tcl programmers invariably type an example of the desired format to answer the question of what format to use, such as

```
clock format $example_value
```

Programmers aren't stuck with that default format, however. `clock` supports a small `%`-tagged language that recognizes

```
clock format $number-of-seconds -format "%B %Y"
```

for instance, as a request for conversion to a month name and year.

8.7.2. `comment`

Most Tcl references document its comment feature in a confusing way. It's better to think of `#` as a comment command, not a comment character. Although it doesn't appear in the list `[info commands]` reports, its syntax is that of a command. This is different from the treatment of comments in more traditional compiled language and frequently perplexes beginners. Writing

```
# proc original_procedure argument {
proc my_procedure argument {
}
```

for example, gives an error. See `http://starbase.neosoft.com/~claird/comp.lang.tcl/fmm.html#comments` for a fuller explanation.

8.8. Gluing Tcl with Other Programs

How do you connect Tcl to other programs? How does Tcl glue together building blocks that have already been written?

Other programs are unlikely to be as platform-independent as Tcl. Successive examples of this section apply first to Windows and then to UNIX. Gluing with Tcl under Macintosh is sufficiently different that we touch on it only lightly.

8.8.1. `exec` Is the Easiest Way to Start

In Listing 8.30, we show how to use Tcl to manage the Windows Registry. Suppose you don't need those capabilities. Perhaps you're at a point in your Tcl script where you just need to give your user access to the built- in Windows Registry editor. That's exactly what the `exec regedt32` command does. It pauses Tcl's execution and invokes `regedt32`. After the user exits `regedt32`, control returns to your script.

With Tcl, it's easy to control other programs.

Incidentally, you don't have to wait for the other program to finish. If you instead command

```
exec regedt32 &
```

the Registry editor begins, and your script simultaneously returns to its normal program flow. The `exec` command recognizes `&` as a special character with the meaning, "do this process in the background, and don't wait for it to end before resuming the original program."

Some command-line programs take arguments. Under UNIX, for example, you might

```
exec mail -s "This is a warning." \
$some_user < $warning_message_file
```

The first argument (mail) to exec names a command-line program in the local (UNIX) environment. The exec command passes on its other arguments (-s, "This is a warning," etc.) directly to mail with a few exceptions we cover later. Upon doing that, mail delivers its warning to $some_user.

Many command-line programs print results. For example, under Windows, you might script a memory availablitiy report (see Listing 8.21).

LISTING 8.21. *Windows memory availability report.*

```
set result [split [exec mem] \n]
puts \
     "The mem command tells us that '[lindex $result 2]'"
puts \
     "and also '[lindex $result 8]' are on this machine."
```

You'll then see a result like

```
The mem command tells us that ' 655360 bytes total
     conventional memory'
and also ' 931840 bytes available XMS memory' are on this machine."
```

By writing [exec mem], you're asking exec to return to you as a single value all the output of the mem program. It's most convenient to split this output up into lines and then access particular lines with lindex. In a real program, of course, you might use Tcl's parsing commands, such as scan and regsub, to pick out exactly the data you want from mem's report.

The exec command's simplicity makes it very inviting to combine the capabilities of more than one program. For example, if you're a UNIX system administrator, you can quickly build a point-and-click interface (see Listing 8.22) for your users' common operations with a tiny Tk script.

LISTING 8.22. *Script for a UNIX utility control panel.*

```
button .b1 -text "Go to lunch." \
     -command {exec gotolunch $env(USER)}
button .b2 -text "Back up all work." \
     -command {exec start_backup $env(HOME)}
button .b3 -text "Print weekly report." \
     -command {exec report [exec date]}
pack .b1 .b2 .b3
```

Notice in Listing 8.22 the use of the env global array. This is how Tcl accesses environment variables on all platforms. This script makes a small control panel (see Figure 8.2) and gives users the ability to click on buttons with readable labels, rather than remember arcane program names. Not only that, the control panel takes responsibility for passing the correct arguments to those programs. If `report`, for example, expects to be given a report label as its single argument, the script in Listing 8.22 reliably passes a formatted date such as `Fri Jan  9 10:29:35 CST 1998` as the result of each `[exec date]` operation.

FIGURE 8.2.

`exec` processes a number of characters—`&`, `|`, `>`, `<`, and so on—in special ways. We've already seen that `&` puts a program in the background and `<` directs input from a file into a program. As much as possible, `exec` treats them in ways that will be intuitive for those accustomed to MS-DOS or UNIX shell programming. See `exec`'s help entry for full details.

> ***Frequently Made Mistake:*** Programmers with experience in shell programming repeat a few characteristic errors with `exec`. Although the special characters generally have the meanings they do in shell, `exec` does not use the shell. Remember that it uses its first argument as the name of a program and passes the other arguments to that program. Confusion arises, for example, when someone writes `exec ls "-l -t"`. In this case, `ls` complains that it doesn't recognize the single argument `"-l -t"`. It works correctly, though, with `exec ls -l -t`.

8.8.2. `exec` Connects to the Operating System

Here's an example of how Tcl can wrap operating system differences. When asked for a small application that reports on recent `comp.lang.tcl*` postings on a particular subject, we wrote a script (see Listing 8.23) for this little control panel (see Figure 8.3).

FIGURE 8.3.

Launch this program as a Wish8.0 application under MacOS, UNIX, or Windows. Enter a search term, such as `threading` or `socket`, and the application launches an instance of Netscape that interrogates the Alta Vista database for recent articles on that topic. Notice that only one procedure (`launch_browser`) has any content that is specific to a particular operating machine. The rest of the script is pure Tcl.

LISTING 8.23. *Script to locate* `comp.lang.tcl` *article.*

```
proc create_control_panel {} {
    label .label -text "Enter keywords here:    "
    entry .entry -textvariable keyword_list
    button .button -text Submit -command \ search_for_keywords
    bind . <Return> search_for_keywords
    pack .label .entry .button -side left
}
proc format_URL args {
    set site http://www.altavista.digital.com/cgi-bin/query?
    set query_string pg=q&text=yes&act=search&what=news&kl=XX
    set search_string &q=%2B%22comp.lang.tcl%22
    foreach keyword $args {
        set search_string $search_string+%2B$keyword
    }
    set URL "$site$query_string$search_string"
}
proc launch_browser URL {
    global tcl_platform
    switch $tcl_platform(platform) {
        macintosh {
            package require Tclapplescript
            Applescript execute "
                tell application \"Netscape 1.1N\"
                    open(file \"$URL\")
                    Activate -1
                end tell
            "
        }
        unix {
            exec netscape $URL &
        }
        windows {
            set executable \
            {/Program Files/Netscape/Communicator/Program/netscape}
            exec $executable $URL &
        }
        default {
            puts "What is '$tcl_platform(platform)'?"
        }
```

```
    }
}
proc search_for_keywords {} {
    global keyword_list
    if {{} == [string trim $keyword_list]} return
    launch_browser [eval format_URL $keyword_list]
}
create_control_panel
```

8.8.3. Pure Tcl

Tcl programmers use *pure Tcl* in a couple of different senses. The idea is that a script includes nothing that depends on a particular extension or operating system and thus should work reliably on any machine. Often *pure Tcl* is said when *pure Tk* would be more precise.

In any case, pure Tcl is a description, not a prescription. There's nothing inherently wrong with impure Tcl. The most important quality of an application is that it meets its users needs. For example, in UNIX both

```
set line [exec head -1 $file]
```

and

```
set fp [open $file w]
gets $fp line
close $fp
```

put the first line of the file (`$file`) into the variable `line`. The first approach is quicker to type and probably easier to maintain for those comfortable with UNIX. The second runs faster and is portable across operating systems. Each is appropriate in specific situations.

One habit that will ease any cross-platform work you do is to abstract and isolate dependencies on a particular operating system. That's why `tcl_search.tcl` is pure with the exception of one procedure. If it requires enhancement some day, it will be easy to identify where changes need to be made.

One of Tcl's introspection facilities—its ability to report on itself—is the `tcl_platform` global array. It's a convenient way to determine the operating system, version, and hardware type on which an interpreter is currently running.

This `tcl_search.tcl` might be refined quite a bit. With a bit more work, it could cope intelligently with a failure to find a correctly installed Netscape. It might log statistical reports. It could handle more complicated queries. Remember, however, why we use Tcl: to solve problems efficiently and reliably. As it stands, `tcl_search.tcl` meets its requirements, so adding to it just distracts resources from more important tasks. Cultivate your own sense of simplicity to help you make best use of Tcl.

8.8.4. `open` Gives Finer Control

Although `exec` is easy to use, Tcl provides other glues that take a bit more programming and yield commensurately greater control over the blocks.

Listing 8.24 is an example of such, written under Windows.

LISTING 8.24. *A scripted* `chkdsk` *program.*

```
set fd [open "|chkdsk"]
while {1} {
     gets $fd line
     puts $line
     if [eof $fd] break
}
close $fd
```

This starts a `chkdsk` process in an MS-DOS shell that examines the disk and looks for errors. It reads successive lines of its output. Doing this, rather than, say, `puts [exec chkdsk]`, has the advantage of giving immediate access to intermediate results. If there's some reason to stop and take other action after completing a certain amount, we can do so by modifying the script to examine the value of `$line`. We can, for example, stop precisely when `chkdsk` reports

```
10 percent completed.
```

`open` also has options to provide both for read/write access and for asynchronous processing. See the manual page for details.

8.8.5. Other Possibilities

There are several other ways, beyond the scope of this chapter, that Tcl acts as glue. If external components are bundled as an application programming interface (API), Tcl can be extended to include them. If the components communicate through a common networking protocol—including TCP/IP, DCOM, RMI, and so on—either Tcl or an existing extension probably can make a direct interface. For more information on these topics, it's best to browse the `comp.lang.tcl.announce` newsgroup.

8.9. Putting It All Together: A Web Survey Example

Brent Welch, Tcl evangelist for SunScript and author of *Practical Programming in Tcl and Tk*, kindly contributed an extensive example that illustrates the concepts you've just learned. This section analyzes Brent's Web survey in detail.

8.9.1. Requirements

8.9.1.1. Background

The SunScript business group periodically surveys the community of Tcl programmers. Survey results help determine how and when they schedule a release of new or enhanced features.

These surveys are a long-standing tradition in the Tcl world. At first, their informality and crude quantification contributed to their charm. As the survey population increased, tallying the results became cumbersome.

Brent realized he could save himself time and improve the quality of the surveys by using Tcl to structure the job more efficiently.

8.9.1.2. Requirements Analysis

Brent works with a marketing specialist to prepare and analyze the survey. From this perspective, a survey is a collection of questions and possible answers—multiple choice, yes/no, and fill-in-the-blank. Communication with respondents is through the Web. Results need to be reported in terms of such statistics as total answers, averages, percentages, and so on.

Notice that the same abstract data is showing up in multiple places. Marketers compose questions and mark them up on paper. Respondents access the questions as Hypertext Markup Language (HTML) forms that their Web browsers display. This requires a data store to correlate answers and questions. Finally, written reports are forwarded to the management group responsible for setting Tcl's development course.

8.9.1.3. Solution

Key Idea: Conveniently Structured Data

Brent wanted a way to express surveys that simplified all the transformations they need to undergo. Authoring HTML, in particular, had been a time-consuming part of previous surveys. As he tells it, "This time, I decided to let Tcl do the work. I sketched out a set of commands that my colleague would use to specify the questions. There was a different command for each kind of question, such as multiple choice, yes/no, or fill in the blank. It took me about one minute to explain the necessary syntax to the person designing the survey. For example, the different kinds of questions looked as shown in Listing 8.25.

LISTING 8.25. *Sample survey specification.*

```
Multiple age "What is your age?" {
        "under 20" "20-29" "30-39" "40-49" "50 and over"
}
Checkbox  proglang "What programming languages do you know?" {
        Tcl Perl Basic C C++ Java JavaScript Pascal Lisp Cobol
        Fortran Smalltalk  Other
}
YesNo student "Are you a full time student?"
Fillin name 1 "Your Name"
Fillin comment 5 "Additional comments"
Scale chocolate "How much do you like chocolate?"
Message "This is just some text to go into the survey"
```

Brent continued,

> *The numeric argument to* `Fillin` *is how many lines to use for the response area. The* `Multiple` *and* `Checkbox` *questions take a list of possible answers. The difference is that* `Multiple` *only allows one answer, but* `Checkbox` *allows more than one possible answer. The* `Scale` *question lets the user specify his answer on a scale from 1 to 10. This was quite natural for the survey designer to use and the syntax didn't seem to be a problem. To her, it was a survey specification. To me, it was a Tcl program!*

Brent's right: These examples aren't just easy for humans to read. Tcl can easily process them as specifications of different actions it performs. Let's see how that happens.

Generating a Web Form

The first part of the solution is a small Tcl script that reads a survey specification and emits to `stdout` the HTML source for a survey. This output might be directed into a file served up to the Web or embedded in a standard CGI applicaton, further marked up by hand, or imported into an HTML editor. The Tcl script's responsibility is just to transform the specification into HTML.

This is how it does so: First, it defines procedures for handling each of the several kinds of questions. Then it `source`s the specification.

The specification is a collection of data `source` takes as its argument in a script. What's going on?

This idiom is emblematic of Tcl. Toggling between looking at a particular thing both as data and as program, or as specification and action, is so common that it almost defines Tcl. Only Lisp and Forth, among other prominent languages, exploit this duality so often.

In fact, Harrison and McLennan, in their book *Effective Tcl/Tk Programming* devote an entire section to this theme:

> *Tcl is not just a command language: It is also a data language. Whenever you find yourself inventing a text-based file format, think about saving the information as a series of Tcl commands. You can load the data by executing it in a Tcl interpreter where the commands are defined. In fact, this same idea has revolutionized the output format for most printers. Today, almost all documents are formatted as a series of commands in the PostScript language. (p. 176)*

What's the advantage? Tcl already can parse commands, act on them, and report errors in them. The syntax for commands is already documented. Tcl already is flexible about processing commands; they can be `source`d, interpreted interactively, wrapped up into an executable, distributed to a remote agent, and so on. Think how much it will simplify to have all those advantages available also to your data files!

Listing 8.26 shows what it takes to begin executing a survey specification.

LISTING 8.26. `survey.tcl`, *which prepares HTML forms.*

```
proc YesNo {key question} {
Map $key $question
puts "$question<ul> No <input type=radio name=$key value=0>"
puts " Yes <input type=radio name=$key value=1></ul><hr>"
}

proc Map {key question} {
global Map
if {[info exists Map($key)]} {
puts stderr "$key duplicated with:\n$Map($key)\n$question"
     append Map($key) \n$question
     } else {
     set Map($key) $question
     }
     }

     proc Fillin {key lines question} {
     Map $key $question
     if {$lines == 1} {
     puts "$question<ul><input type=text name=$key size=40></ul>"
```

```
} else {
puts "$question<ul><textarea name=$key"
puts "rows=$lines cols=40></textarea></ul"
}
puts "<hr>"
}

proc Multiple {key question answers} {
Map $key $question
puts "$question<ul><select name=$key multiple>"
foreach a $answers {
puts "<option>$a"
}
puts "</select></ul><hr>"
}
proc CheckBox {key question answers} {
Map $key $question
puts "<p>$question<ul>"
foreach a $answers {
puts "<li><input type=checkbox name=$key value=\"$a\"> $a"
}
puts "</ul><hr>"
}
proc Checkbox [info args CheckBox] [info body CheckBox]

proc Scale {key question} {
global scale
Map $key $question
if {[info exists scale(table)]} {
puts "<tr><td><select name=$key>"
} else {
puts "<p>$question<ul><select name=$key>"
}
foreach a {noanswer 1 2 3 4 5 6 7 8 9 10} {
global scale
Map $key $question
if {[info exists scale(table)]} {
puts "<tr><td><select name=$key>"
} else {
puts "<p>$question<ul><select name=$key>"
}
foreach a {noanswer 1 2 3 4 5 6 7 8 9 10} {
puts "<option>$a"
}
puts "</select>"
if {![info exists scale(table)]} {
puts "</ul>"
} else {
puts "<td>$question</td></tr>"
}
}
proc Message {string} {
puts "<p>$string"
}
```

Brent explains these:

> *The* `YesNo` *question is formed with two HTML radio buttons and some text for the question. The radio buttons share the form variable, which is the key to the question. The* `<ul>` *tags indent the Yes and No choices, and the cryptic* ` ` *is used to force a space.*
>
> *The* `Map` *procedure keeps the association between the question and its identifying key in a Tcl array. This map will be used later when processing the form data. You can also put the question right into the form with a hidden field, but that clutters the data returned when the user submits the form. Instead, the program will save the map to a file after it generates the form.*
>
> *The* `Fillin` *procedure takes an argument that defines how many lines are available for user input. HTML has a one-line form item and a multiline text area. In this example, we just hardwire the width to 40 characters.*
>
> *The* `Multiple` *question has a list of answers. An HTML* `<select>` *form item is used, which is displayed as a listbox by browsers. Each item in the listbox is defined with an* `<option>` *tag.*

If you apply Listing 8.26 to the specifications shown in Listing 8.25, the result you'll see is shown in Listing 8.27.

LISTING 8.27. *An example of generated HTML output.*

```
What is your age?<ul><select name=age multiple>
<option>under 20
<option>20-29
<option>30-39
<option>40-49
<option>50 and over
</select></ul><hr>
<p>What programming languages do you know?<ul>
<li><input type=checkbox name=proglang value="Tcl"> Tcl
<li><input type=checkbox name=proglang value="Perl"> Perl
<li><input type=checkbox name=proglang value="Basic"> Basic
<li><input type=checkbox name=proglang value="C"> C
<li><input type=checkbox name=proglang value="C++"> C++
<li><input type=checkbox name=proglang value="Java"> Java
<li><input type=checkbox name=proglang
    value="JavaScript"> JavaScript
<li><input type=checkbox name=proglang value="Pascal"> Pascal
<li><input type=checkbox name=proglang value="Lisp"> Lisp
<li><input type=checkbox name=proglang value="Cobol"> Cobol
<li><input type=checkbox name=proglang value="Fortran"> Fortran
<li><input type=checkbox name=proglang value="Smalltalk"> Smalltalk
<li><input type=checkbox name=proglang value="Other"> Other
</ul><hr>
```

```
Are you a full time student?<ul> No
    <input type=radio name=student value=0>
 Yes <input type=radio name=student value=1></ul><hr>
Your Name<ul><textarea name=name rows=1 cols=40></textarea></
ul>
<hr>
Additional comments<ul><textarea
    name=comment rows=5 cols=40></ textarea></
ul>
<hr>
<p>How much do you like chocolate?<ul><select name=chocolate>
<option>noanswer
<option>1
<option>2
<option>3
<option>4
<option>5
<option>6
<option>7
<option>8
<option>9
<option>10
</select>
</ul>
<p>This is just some text to go into the survey
```

A Web browser then interprets this into the screen display, the beginning of which is shown in Listing 8.28.

LISTING 8.28. *Partial on-screen display of a Tcl survey.*

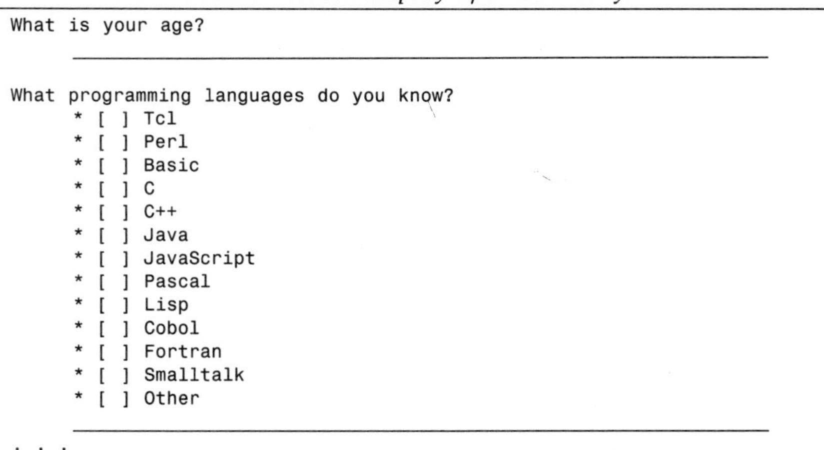

```
What is your age?
     ____________________________________________________

What programming languages do you know?
     * [ ] Tcl
     * [ ] Perl
     * [ ] Basic
     * [ ] C
     * [ ] C++
     * [ ] Java
     * [ ] JavaScript
     * [ ] Pascal
     * [ ] Lisp
     * [ ] Cobol
     * [ ] Fortran
     * [ ] Smalltalk
     * [ ] Other
     ____________________________________________________
. . .
```

How to Run a Survey

Now we have a sample specification file and a script for turning it into a Web form. We can reuse the specification to create from it a Tk application. This might be useful on a local machine in a public area that is not connected to the Web.

Although this script defines the same procedures—`YesNo`, `Map`, and so on—their actions are quite different. Instead of emitting HTML descriptions, the following Tk script defines visual widgets for a Tk application.

LISTING 8.29. `questions.tcl`, *which runs a GUI local to a desktop.*

```
option add *Hr.background blue
option add *Message.aspect 1000
option add *Entry.width 50

proc Driver {survey} {
     set in [open $survey]
     set X [read $in]
     close $in
     Survey_Init .survey
     eval $X
     Survey_Close
}

proc Survey_Init {parent} {
     global survey
     if ![winfo exists $parent] {
          toplevel $parent -class Survey
     }
     eval destroy [winfo children $parent]
     catch {unset survey}
     set survey(uid) 0
     set survey(qnum) 0
     set survey(parent) $parent
     set survey(frame) [Scrolled_Frame $parent]
}
proc Survey_Close {} {
     global survey
     Hr
     Message "Thank you for your time."
     set f [frame [NextWidget]]
     button $f.submit -text "Submit" -command SurveySubmit
     button $f.cancel -text "Cancel" -command SurveyCancel
     pack $f.submit $f.cancel -padx 10 -side left
     pack $f -side top -anchor w
}
proc SurveySubmit {} {
     global survey
     set out stdout
     foreach key $survey(keys) {
          set w $survey($key,widget)
          switch [winfo class $w] {
               Entry {
                    set answer [$w get]
               }
               Text {
                    set answer [$w get 1.0 end]
               }
               Listbox {
                    set i [$w curselection]
```

```
                    if {[string length $i] == 0} {
                        set answer {}
                    } else {
                        set answer [$w get [$w curselection]]
                    }
                }
                Scale -
                Yesno {
                    set answer $survey($key,response)
                }
            }
            puts $out [list Data $key $answer]
        }
        if {$out != "stdout"} {
            close $out
        }
    }
proc SurveyCancel {} {
    global survey
    destroy $survey(parent)
}

proc NextWidget {} {
    global survey
    return $survey(frame).[incr survey(uid)]
}

proc Scrolled_Frame {parent} {
    set c [canvas $parent.can -yscrollcommand "$parent.yscroll set"]
    scrollbar $parent.yscroll -command "$c yview" -orient vertical
    grid $parent.can $parent.yscroll -sticky news
    grid columnconfigure $parent 0 -weight 1
    grid rowconfigure $parent 0 -weight 1

    set f [frame $parent.can.f]
    $c create window 0 0 -anchor nw -window $f
    bind $f <configure> [list ScrolledFrameSize $c $f]
    return $f
}
proc ScrolledFrameSize {can f} {
    set w [winfo reqwidth $f]
    set h [winfo reqheight $f]
    $can configure -scrollregion "0 0 $w $h"
}

proc Hr {} {
    set hr [frame [NextWidget] -width 1 -height 3 -class Hr]
    pack $hr -side top -fill x
}

proc Message {string} {
    set msg [message [NextWidget] -text $string -justify left]
    pack $msg -side top -anchor w
}

proc Ask {key question {answers {}}} {
    global survey
    lappend survey(keys) $key
    set survey($key,question) $question
```

```
    set survey($key,answers) $answers
    Hr
    Message "[incr survey(qnum)] $question"
}
proc Map {key widget} {
    global survey
    set survey($key,widget) $widget
}
proc SetMax {varname value} {
    upvar 1 $varname var
    if {![info exists var] ¦¦ ($value > $var)} {
        set var $value
    }
    return $var
}

proc Fillin {key lines question} {
    Ask $key $question
    set w [NextWidget]
    if {$lines == 1} {
        entry $w -textvariable survey($key,response)
    } else {
        text $w -height $lines

    Map $key $w
    pack $w -fill x -padx 10
}

proc Multiple {key question answers} {
    Ask $key $question
    set l [listbox [NextWidget] -height [llength $answers] \
        -exportselection false]
    set max 0
    foreach a $answers {
        SetMax max [string length $a]
        $l insert end $a
    }
    $l config -width $max
    Map $key $l
    pack $l -padx 10 -anchor w
}

proc YesNo {key question} {
Ask $key $question
            set f [frame [NextWidget] -borderwidth 4 -class Yesno]
            radiobutton $f.yes -text Yes \
            -variable survey($key,response) -value yes
            radiobutton $f.no -text No \
            -variable survey($key,response) -value no
            pack $f.yes $f.no -padx 10 -side left
            pack $f -side top -anchor w
            Map $key $f
}
proc Checkbox {key question answers} {
            Ask $key $question
            set f [frame [NextWidget] -class Checkbox]
            set x 0
            foreach a $answers {
                    checkbutton $f.$x -text $a \
```

```
                        -variable survey($key,response,$a)
                        pack $f.$x -side top -anchor w
                        incr x
                        }
                Map $key $f
                pack $f -padx 10 -anchor w
}
proc Scale {key question {low 1} {high 10}} {
      Ask $key $question
     set s [scale [NextWidget] -from $low -to $high -showvalue true \
         -variable survey($key,response) -orient horizontal]
     pack $s -side top -anchor w -padx 10
     Map $key $s
}
```

Try this script by launching a `wish` interpreter and then typing

```
source survey.tcl
Driver data.tcl
```

The result you see will be a scrollable frame, as shown in Figure 8.4.

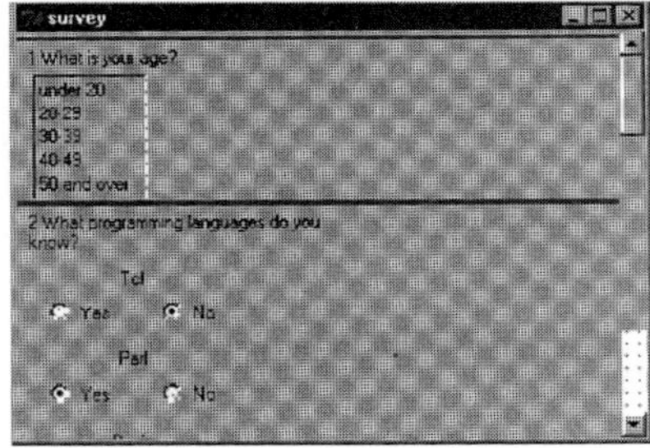

FIGURE 8.4.

Brent describes this script:

> *A scrolled frame is created inside the top level. The* `Scrolled_Frame` *procedure is described later.* `Survey_Init` *sets several elements of the survey array. It is clean and convenient to use a global array for related information. Another option is to use a* `namespace` *variable. For testing purposes, the top level is deleted and the global array is unset in case we build the survey form another time.*
>
> *The survey [is] implemented as a stack of widgets within the mainframe. The global counter* `survey(uid)` *is used to generate names for each widget in the stack. Many of the widgets are frames that contain other widgets, but this is not always the case. The* `NextWidget` *procedure hides the global variable and returns the name of the next widget in the stack. It uses the* `incr` *command to increment the* `survey(uid)` *variable.*
>
> *Each question is separated from the next question by a horizontal line. One way to get the line is to have a thin frame with a blue background. The* `Hr` *procedure implements the horizontal line. The frame is packed with fill set in the X direction so it spans the containing frame. In this case, the width of the frame is ignored. The frame is given the* `Hr` *class so its color and other attributes can be set with the* `option` *command and the resource database.*
>
> *As with the HTML implementation, the* `YesNo` *question is implemented as a pair of radio buttons. A radio button is associated with a Tcl variable, and each button stores a different value into the button. In this case, a member of the survey global array is used as the variable. The two radio buttons are grouped together in their own frame. This frame is given the* `YesNo` *class, which will be used later to identify the type of the question.*
>
> *The* `Ask` *procedure keeps a list of question keys, the question, and the possible answers. It also displays the question. The* `Map` *procedure remembers which widget is used for each question. This will be used when the user is done with the survey.*
>
> *The* `Fillin` *question uses an* `entry` *widget for a one-line answer and a* `text` *widget for a multiline answer. The* `entry` *widget has a very convenient feature; its* `-textvariable` *attribute associates a Tcl variable with the contents of the widget.*
>
> *The multiple-choice question is naturally implemented by a Tk* `listbox` *widget. The* `listbox` *supports four different selection modes, and the browse mode restricts the user to selecting a single item. When a Tk widget is created, a Tcl command is also created with the same name. This command is used to operate on the widget. In* `Multiple`*, the* `$1` *variable holds this name and it is used as a command.*

The only fine point to the `Multiple` *procedure is to find out how wide the longest answer is and set the width of the* `listbox` *to that value. The* `SetMax` *procedure sets a variable to a new value if that value is greater than its current value. It takes a variable name as an argument and uses the* `upvar` *command to bring that variable into the scope of the procedure. This is how you pass variables by reference in Tcl. The* `"info exists"` *command is used to test if the variable exists. It is important to do this before you test its value!*

The `Checkbox` *question is similar to the* `Multiple` *question except that it allows multiple answers to the question. These are implemented as a set of check buttons, one for each possible answer. The check button is associated with a Tcl variable, which is an element of the survey array.*

Getting the answers back for the `Checkbox` *question requires a bit of work. First we use the ability of "array names" to return array indices that match a pattern in order to select the right elements of the survey array. Then we use* `regsub` *to get the answer out of the array index. Finally, if the variable is set, then we add the answer to the list of all answers to the question. The* `CheckboxAnswer` *procedure will be used later in the* `SurveySubmit` *procedure.*

The last question type is the scale, which is naturally implemented by the Tk `scale` *widget. The* `scale` *widget can be associated with a Tcl variable, just like the* `entry`*,* `checkbutton`*, and* `radiobutton` *widgets. The* `Scale` *procedure has two parameters with default values, low and high. If these are not passed as arguments, then those parameters get the default values from the* `proc` *declaration.*

The survey could be too big to fit onto the screen, which is a common problem. We solve this problem by creating a frame inside a canvas so we can use the canvas's ability to scroll. You can use the `Scrolled_Frame` *procedure for many applications.*

The `scrollbar` *is an independent widget that you can hook to several other Tk widgets. The protocol between the* `scrollbar` *and the other widget uses Tcl commands. When the user manipulates the* `scrollbar`*, it uses its* `-command` *attribute to signal the other widget it is time to scroll. When the scrolled widget changes its contents or its view, it signals the* `scrollbar` *with its* `-yscroll` *command and* `-xscroll` *command attributes. You can register your own procedures for special effects such as scrolling more than one widget with a single* `scrollbar`*. In this case, we just use the built-in operations (e.g.,* `set`*,* `yview`*, and* `xview`*) that are designed to support scrollbars.*

The grid geometry manager is used to position the scrollbars and the canvas. The first grid command puts the canvas and the vertical scrollbar on row zero. The second grid command puts the horizontal scrollbar on row 1, and it will be just as wide as the canvas. The next grid commands configure the grid to let row zero and column zero change size by setting their weight equal to 1. This means the canvas will expand automatically when the user changes the size of the window. The `-sticky` *settings cause the widget to stick to the north, south, east, or west sides of the grid cell occupied by the widget.*

The canvas supports many different graphic objects, and it also lets you put Tk widgets on its surface. Here we just put a single Tk frame on the canvas. It is positioned at 0, 0, which is the upper-left corner of the canvas. The `-anchor` *setting is* `nw` *for northwest, which puts the upper-left corner of the frame at the specified position. The main trick to a scrolled frame is to reconfigure the canvas's scroll region when the frame changes size, which it will do when widgets are packed inside it. The* `ScrolledFrameSize` *procedure is bound to the* `<Configure>` *event on the frame, which occurs when it changes size.*

Finally we have to deal with the results of the survey! First we put a standard closing on the survey, which has a thank-you note, a cancel button, and a submit button.

The `SurveySubmit` *command collects the answers. It runs through the list of keys, and for each key, it queries the widget that is registered for that question. The class of the widget is used to indicate what kind of question it is and that determines how to get the information. The widgets that are associated with Tcl variables make this easy. Others require more work.*

This example just prints the data to standard output. You could use a different file. Note that the output is formatted as a Tcl list, and in fact, it is a Tcl command named `Data` *that takes two arguments (question key, answers). The survey questions start out as Tcl commands and the answers end up as Tcl commands, too. Having the questions as Tcl commands makes it easy to implement the survey in different ways, and having the results in Tcl command form makes it very easy to write a program to process the results.*

8.9.2. Principles

This example illustrates a number of themes that are common in Tcl projects:

- The easiest way to solve a fairly small, simple requirement (correspondence between survey specification and survey form) is with a general-purpose solution.
- The same text appears as both code and data.

- The solution is portable. In this case, the Tcl code can be used across three platforms (MacOS, UNIX, and Windows) and has a Web manifestation.
- A good solution eliminates redundancy. It reuses the same data, automating its transformation between related forms.

This is typical of Tcl development work. For a small investment of time and care to construct the right abstraction, we receive a solution that solves our problem with surprising generality.

8.10. Software Engineering with Tcl

Beginners with Tcl seem to ask at least as many questions about Tcl's commercial or engineering status (What license governs its use? Who supports it? What tools are there for testing Tk?) as about details of the language itself. This section answers the most common engineering concerns Tcl raises.

8.10.1. Commercial Application

"Is Tcl safe for real programs? Isn't it just a toy language?"

Someone in every organization asks these questions. The simple answers are: yes; no. (See `http://starbase.neosoft.com/~claird/comp.lang.tcl/commercial-tcl.html` for a partial list of projects and applications that make use of Tcl's versatile abilities.)

This chapter reflects Tcl's capacity to meet the needs of diverse projects and programming styles of practitioners. As of this printing, companies such as Oracle, Digital Equipment, and Cray rely on Tcl as the development language for their high-end Enterprise Manager, AltaVista Forum, and Cray Visualization products. DUX Software used Tk to create Multi Player SimCity. Several companies in electronic design automation, including Cadence, Mentor Graphics, and National Semiconductor, rely on Tk to build their schematics.

A plurality of Tcl programmers use it to build GUIs. However, many other Tcl programmers never program GUIs. Some even target systems that don't support bitmapped graphics. Telebit uses an embedded Tcl in its NetBlazer to give customers easy programmability of its router. The Voyager probe to Mars relies on Tcl to glue certain system components together.

For many users, Tcl's cross-platform portability is paramount. Others are indifferent to any capabilities beyond those for a particular operating system.

Many wrap up their applications and don't want customers to know their dependence on Tcl, whereas others expose Tcl—the language—and provide end users access to control an application.

8.10.2. Licenses

The copyright that governs Tcl's use is a simple one. The few lines in the `license.terms` file that accompanies every distribution make clear that anyone may freely use part of all of a Tcl distribution for any purpose. The aim of the license is simply to prevent anyone else from taking the Tcl intellectual property and restricting its use.

Sun Microsystems has been the principal patron of Tcl development since 1994. Its support has been so respectful of the independence of Tcl that even rival hardware manufacturers Santa Cruz Operation, Silicon Graphics, Digital Equipment, and Linux use Tcl in their products. Even Sun's competitors recognize that Tcl will remain a free and well-constructed product well into the future.

8.10.3. Support

Tcl is different from Visual Basic or Delphi in that the development team does not offer support contracts for its product. Although this might be unfamiliar with some organizations, it offers advantages. Several vendors outside Sun offer training and technical support. Linux and FreeBSD have demonstrated that freeware operating systems have their place in corporate computing. In similar fashion, existing Tcl vendors and consultants provide an infrastructure entirely comparable to that of more proprietary tools. It's safe to choose Tcl, and the FAQ gives contact information for the providers who make it so.

8.10.4. Portability

How portable is Tcl? Will it continue to support different platforms?

Although it's possible to write host-dependent applications in Tcl, there's little need. The surprise most newcomers report when first working with Tcl across platforms is a happy one: It's as portable as advertised and more.

SunScript has repeated several times its commitment to maintain the health and compatibility of Tcl and Tk across UNIX, Windows, and MacOS. In fact, John Ousterhout told the 1997 annual Tcl Workshop that even Windows 3.1 would be supported at least for all patches to Version 8.0. (See `http://starbase.neosoft.com/~claird/comp.lang.tcl/workship.html`.)

8.10.5. Style and Utilities

SunScript now maintains a well-received *Style Guide* at `ftp://ftp.sunlabs.com/pub/tcl/docs/styleGuide.tar.gz`. The FAQ lists several tools that ease development of Tcl programs, including language-oriented editors, an enhanced console, syntax validators, and more.

8.10.6. Architecture

Although it's possible to assemble everything in a systems programming language, the edit-compile-debug cycle just takes too long when you are fine-tuning an application. If there is a Tcl interpreter linked into the application, it is easy to reload scripts into your running application to test changes and fix bugs.

Speed is also important during initial development; early customer feedback can have large effects on the overall design of an application. Scripts make it easy to quickly assemble components into prototype applications.

The division between components and scripts—or bricks and glue—has a deep effect on the architecture of applications. Components are designed for reuse. They have well defined methods—behavior and properties. Flexibility in components is achieved by calling out to the script level. For example, the action associated with a user interface button can simply be a script that is evaluated when the button is clicked. As another example, the Tk canvas widget associates scripts with user actions on graphic items such as lines, boxes, text, and images. The hard work of managing the display of thousands of graphic objects is handled by the canvas widget, and the behavior of those objects is specified with simple scripts. The use of two programming models, scripting and system programming, leads to a clean separation between the details of the components and the overall application contstruction.

8.10.6.1. Moving Boundaries

The details of coding interfaces between Tcl and other languages, such as C and Java, are beyond the scope of this introduction. These interfaces are easy in themselves. However, the full range of possibilities, including different compilers and different operating systems, is too broad for this chapter and too dependent on the specific requirements of a particular project.

There are several principles every Tcl programmer should know, however:

- It's easy to write an interface between C and Tcl. See `http://starbase.neosoft.com/~claird/ comp.lang.tcl/HowToC.html` for details.
- With the 1998 official release of Jacl and Tcl Blend, SunScript supports a fully featured interface between Tcl and Java.(See `http://www.developer.com/news/ techfocus/010598_jacl.html`.)
- Several independent engineers support tools that automate aspects of the C-Tcl (and also C++ to Tcl, Fortran to Tcl, and so on) interface. See `http://starbase.neosoft.com/~claird/comp.lang.tcl/tcl_compilers.html`.
- Because the C-Tcl interface is so well-engineered, "moving the boundary" is an accepted and desirable aspect of many Tcl development projects.

The meaning of the latter point is this: A team can do a prototype of an application in pure Tcl or some other standard package (pure ExpectTk and so on). If it turns out that the prototype happens to meet all requirements for the finished deliverable, so much the better. If not, and if the deficiencies have to do with performance or platform-specific functions not directly available in Tcl, the next step is a natural one. The team (re)writes a small piece or two in C or Java. Incremental development continues in this fashion until the project is complete.

The possibility of "moving the boundary" between the responsibilities of Tcl and C should be settled before a project starts. Organizations that religiously observe the prescription that prototypes should be discarded are not candidates for this approach.

Others, however, are more comfortable with iterative experimentation and should know ahead of time how well Tcl lends itself to this approach.

Stricter methodologies of partnering Tcl with C are also possible. Some engineers, for example, use Tcl only for testing. They build a "scaffold" in Tcl, which they use to buttress and frame deliverables coded in a traditional compiled language. When the final product is ready, they discard all the scaffolding.

Tcl offers a wealth of possibilities for adding value to development processes. This is an advanced topic for which interested readers should consult current literature (start with the bibliography available at `http://starbase.neosoft.com/~claird/ comp.lang.tcl/tcl-references.html`).

8.10.7. Deployment

Tcl's flexibility makes delivery of finished solutions more interesting than is the case with more traditional tools. Most conventional is to install Tcl (or Tk) interpreters on each target machine and distribute an application simply as the script that implements it. However, this chapter has already demonstrated a number of different ways to package a single algorithm or utility: as a stand-alone executable, plug-enabled Web application, and so forth. The choice between these alternatives depends on organizational factors beyond the scope of this chapter.

What's important for newcomers to Tcl is to understand how crucial it is that each project clearly define its goal in terms of specific deliverables. These deliverables need to be compatible with organizational standards for configuration management, quality assurance, and security. If an application will be installed as a script, there needs to be a mechanism for distributing the script securely and for ensuring that its hosts are properly equipped with Tcl interpreters of a compatible version. If binaries are distributed, attention needs to go to the tasks of automating their generation and synchronizing their versions.

8.10.8. Summary of Software Engineering Issues

The traditional lessons of software engineering—careful, explicit plans; maximal coherence with minimal connectivity; and so on—apply to Tcl. Tcl's free availability and strength at rapid gluing of external components present differences from conventional programming. Particular organizations need to decide for themselves whether to see those differences as pitfalls or opportunities.

8.11. Extensions to Tcl

One key to the success of working Tcl programmers is their knowledge of available extensions. An efficient developer's instinct is always to look for a reusable solutions. This applies with special force for Tcl. Although only a few extensions (most prominently Tk and Tcl Blend) are officially supported, there's no stigma and few liabilities to using any of the others. 1997 saw the publication of *Tcl/Tk Tools*, a book devoted exclusively to unofficially unsupported extensions.

The most popular extensions include

- `Expect`, for automating interaction with command-line applications
- `BLT`, `Tix`, and others that enhance graphics capabilities
- `Scotty`, which has powerful commands for monitoring network operations
- `TclX`, with UNIX facilities and abstractions for Tcl running under UNIX or Windows
- `OraTcl`, `SybTcl`, `Libpgtcl`, and so on, which interface conveniently to relational database managers
- `[incr Tcl]` and other object-oriented extensions
- `Tcl-DP` and `tkpvm`, which enable distributed applications

For current pointers to each of these, see the FAQ `http:// www.teraform.com/%7Elvirden/tcl-faq/part5.html`.

8.12. Tcl's Future

Version 8.1a1 appeared at the beginning of 1998. This update enhances Version 8.0 in the areas of

- Unicode
- Platform-specific functionality
- Threading
- Modularity

8.12.1. Unicode

The implementation of data structures in Tcl has always been simple and consistent. "Everything is a string" and strings have been represented as the null-terminated character arrays familiar to C programmers.

This approach worked well for the first eight years of Tcl's history. It has a couple of major discomforts, however:

- It makes no provision for those working with binary data (i.e., multimedia encodings, computer internal formats, etc.).

- It provides no help to those working outside the ASCII character set, or, worse, to those involved in multibyte characters.
- Volunteers had written more-or-less well-supported extensions to Tcl to address one or the other of these challenges.

The 8.1 release is designed to settle the issues for good. It represents data internally in UTF-8 (a standard known under several names, including the UCS-2 encoding of ISO 10646). This solves all known language-specific problems both with writing Japanese, Korean, Russian, and other human languages, as well as transmission and reception of binary computer data.

8.12.2. Platform-Specific Functionality

Version 8.x of Tcl strengthens its suitability for the applications platforms of the late '90s. With the move from 4.2 to 8.0, Tk switched from a uniformly Motif-like appearance to native look-and-feel. This means that UNIX and OpenVMS releases retain classic Tk styling, and the MacOS and Windows ones are built to look like native applications of those interfaces.

Along with these changes in appearance, the internals of Tcl are acquiring more intimate ties with operating system facilities.

8.12.2.1. Windows Registry, DCOM, and More

Windows Tcl has a very convenient interface to the Registry. Listing 8.30 shows its use. Executing the code on one machine gave over 100 pages of the sort shown in Listing 8.31.

LISTING 8.30. *Code to print selected Registry data.*

```
package require registry 1.0
proc action {} {
     set rootnames_list {HKEY_CURRENT_CONFIG HKEY_USERS}
     foreach rootname $rootnames_list {
          set key_list [find_all_keys $rootname]
          foreach key [protect $key_list] {
               report_on $key
          }
     }
}
proc find_all_keys keypath {
          # Ignore security restrictions.
     if [catch {registry keys $keypath} list] return ""
     if {"" == $list} {
          return $keypath
     }
     set return_value ""
     foreach subkey $list {
```

```
        set return_value [concat $return_value \
            [find_all_keys "$keypath\\$subkey"]]
    }
    return $return_value
}
proc protect list_with_back_slashes {
    regsub -all {\\} $list_with_back_slashes {\\\\} protected
    return $protected
}
proc report_on key {
        # Ignore security restrictions.
    if [catch {registry values $key} value_list] {
        return
    }
    foreach value $value_list {
            # Ignore security restrictions.
        if {![catch {registry get $key $value} datum]} {
            puts "$key:\n\t$value:\n\t\t$datum"
        }
    }
}
action
```

LISTING 8.31. *A sample of data printed from the Registry program.*

```
HKEY_CURRENT_CONFIG\System\CurrentControlSet\Services
    \VgaSave\Device0:
    DefaultSettings.BitsPerPel:
        4
            .
            .
            .
HKEY_USERS\.DEFAULT\AppEvents\EventLabels\Close:
    :
        Close program
HKEY_USERS\.DEFAULT\AppEvents\EventLabels\EmptyRecycleBin:
    :
        Empty Recycle Bin
            .
            .
            .
HKEY_USERS\.DEFAULT\Console:
    HistoryBufferSize:
        50
HKEY_USERS\.DEFAULT\Console:
    ScreenBufferSize:
        1638480
            .
            .
            .
HKEY_USERS\S-1-5-21-555250877-973698154-378935785-500\Software
    \Microsoft\Telnet:
    Rows:
        25
HKEY_USERS\S-1-5-21-555250877-973698154-378935785-500\Software
    \Microsoft\Telnet:
    Columns:
        80
```

```
HKEY_USERS\S-1-5-21-555250877-973698154-378935785-500\Software
     \Microsoft\Telnet:
     Machine1:
          starbase.neosoft.com
               .
               .
               .
```

The Registry command—available only for the Windows 95 and Windows NT releases of Tcl—can also add, delete, and update keys and values. Listing 8.32 illustrates Tcl's ability to create a new key.

LISTING 8.32. *Restrict remote access to the Registry.*

```
% set remote {HKEY_LOCAL_MACHINE\System\CurrentControlSet\Control\
SecurePipeServers\winreg}
HKEY_LOCAL_MACHINE\System\CurrentControlSet\Control\SecurePipeServers\
winreg
% registry key $remote
unable to open key:  The system cannot find the file specified.
% registry set $remote
% registry key $remote
% set value Description
Description
% registry set $remote $value "Registry Server" sz
% registry value $remote $value
Description
% registry get $remote $value
Registry Server
```

This is the first step in configuring an NT machine to restrict remote access to the Registry. Most system administrators use Microsoft's `regedt32` when performing such tasks. It is a powerful and convenient Registry editor. What Tcl offers is the ability to script, or automate, such interactions with complete programmatic control. This is an enormous boon to anyone responsible for more than, say, two machines.

Windows Tcl also is gaining ability with ActiveX and DCOM. ActiveX capabilities, for example, will move into official Tcl releases for Windows in 1998.

8.12.2.2. Tcl and Java as Partners

Perhaps most dramatically, SunScript adopted in 1997 a strong initiative to make Tcl "the scripting language of the Internet," as SunScript employment advertisements have promoted it. The most visible outcome of this is a newly streamlined interface with Java. Two freeware products, Jacl and Tcl Blend, appeared first near the end of 1997. Jacl is an implementation of Tcl and Tk written in Java, rather than C. Tcl Blend is an extension to Tcl that has robust abilities to load, examine, execute, and update Java classes. This technology opens several possibilities:

- Existing Tcl applications can immediately run on JavaStations and other unusual JVMs.
- Tcl developers can leverage their efforts with Java components.
- Java programmers will find the convenience of the Tcl shell for interactive development of Java classes.
- Application teams can make new and more efficient partitions of projects by coding bricks in Java and gluing them together with Tcl.

It seems likely that Tcl will have a third major (concurrent) career. Developed originally as an embeddable extension language, it acquired the strength during the '90s to be regarded as an independent, capable programming language. Now, it seems poised for another expansion—into the domain of rapid development of commercial applications with an emphasis on its strengths in Internet client/server programming and Java compatibility.

8.12.3. Threading

One remnant of Tcl's origin as a tiny embeddable library is that it doesn't respect contemporary threading models. The situation with Tcl 8.0 is this: Although it is possible to embed distinct independent instances of a Tcl interpreter in multiple threads, it is not safe for multiple threads to access a single interpreter. The present interpreter expects to have its process to itself. Multiple threads confuse it and cause inconsistent values to be returned.

It seems likely that an 8.x release will render Tcl thread-safe.

8.12.4. Modularity

Tcl faces a number of technical challenges. Improvements in Tcl's modularity will be one way to ease reliable maintenance across platforms, issues of deployment in special environments (unsupported operating systems and supported operating systems with physical or security limitations) and commercial requirements.

It appears that Tcl will move in the direction of appearing as a tiny kernel, with many of its current capabilities bundled into loadable packages. Among the candidates for such a partition are networking functions (`socket`), GUI (everything specific to Tk), an expanded regular-expression command, and even the parser. To promote such changes, the `package` mechanism itself, along with its indexing, is also a candidate for upgrade during 1998–1999.

8.13. Summary

You know how to program in Tcl. You know what problems are good candidates for Tcl solutions and the "scripted components" architecture behind Tcl's origin. You've written GUI applications, read from and written to external files, parsed user input, and glued together external components. You know how to comment your scripts and the difference between `""` and `{}` quoting. You know what to do when you have a question about a Tcl feature. You're ready to exploit the features of the latest Tcl release. You have a feel for the platform-independence and operating system access of Tcl and Tk. You know the names of the leading extensions to Tcl. You're thinking like a Tcl programmer!

8.14. References

The most important references are two online ones: `http://starbase.neosoft.com/~claird/comp.lang.tcl/tcl-references.html` and `URL:http://www.tclconsortium.org/`. These two Web sites list and comment on both books and articles concerning Tcl.

The following are the leading books on Tcl:

Foster-Johnson, E. 1997. *Graphical applications with Tcl and Tk* (2nd edition). New York: M&T Books.

Harrison, M., and M. McLennan. 1998. *Effective Tcl/Tk programming.* Reading, MA: Addison-Wesley.

Ousterhout, J. K. 1994. *Tcl and the Tk toolkit.* Reading, MA: Addison-Wesley.

Welch, B. 1997. *Practical programming in Tcl/Tk.* Upper Saddle River, NJ: Prentice Hall.

CHAPTER 9

Perl Basics[1]

by Mike Glover, Aidan Humphreys, and Ed Weiss

Perl's popularity can be attributed to many things, one of which is the ease with which programs can be built. Unlike C or any other compiled language, Perl is interpreted, which greatly reduces development time. This allows the programmer to build larger and more complex programs in less time. Unfortunately, this reduction in time has a negative side effect: Some programmers do not give themselves enough time to get to know the language. This speedy development process can lead to inferior and inefficient code. The more complex the programs become, the more important it is to understand the syntax and semantics of the language.

This chapter will introduce the syntax and semantics of the Perl programming language so programmers new to Perl can get a good foundation for building effective Perl programs. Anyone familiar with Perl 4 should look through this chapter; this is an introduction to Perl 5, not just to Perl.

Throughout this book, the phrases *scalar context* and *array context* are used. Scalar context means that a function is being called and the return value of the function is a scalar value. The following example demonstrates calling a function named `scalarContextFunction` in a scalar context:

```
$returnValue = scalarContextFunction();
```

The result of the call to `scalarContextFunction` is stored in the scalar variable named `$returnValue`. A scalar is Perl's most basic data type.

[1]This chapter is reprinted with permission from Glover, M., A. Humphreys, and E. Weiss. 1996. *Perl 5 How-To*. Corte-Madera, CA: Waite Group Press.

When a function is called in an array context, the function returns a list. The following example demonstrates calling a function in an array context:

```
@returnValue = arrayContextFunction();
```

The variable `@returnValue` is the array that contains the information returned from the call to the function `arrayContextFunction`.

Some functions, such as the `values` and `keys` functions, can be used in both a scalar context and an array context. This means these functions have multiple personalities. For example, when the `keys` function is used in a scalar context, it returns the number of elements of the given associative array. When `keys` is called in an array context, it returns a list of all the keys of the given associative array.

9.1. Scalar Data Types

The *scalar data type* is the most basic form of a data container Perl has. A *scalar variable* can reference a string value or an integer value. In fact, Perl has three contexts in which it will interpret a scalar variable: string context, numeric context, and miscellaneous context. The latter of the three contexts is discussed in section 9.4.

Perl treats strings and integers with almost the same regard—almost, but not completely. There is a visible difference. To define or assign a scalar variable in a Perl script, you need to create a scalar variable and assign it a value. For example, the following three lines:

```
$name="Gizmo";
$age=3;
$height=4.5;
```

define three scalar variables. One scalar variable, `$name`, contains a string data value; `$age` contains a double data value; `$height` contains a float value. When a scalar variable is assigned, the syntax of the assignment assists the Perl interpreter in deciding the variable type. If the value of the variable is surrounded in single or double quotes, then Perl treats the variable as a string. If there are no quotes, then Perl has to decide if the value is a string or a numeric value. This is demonstrated in the following Perl script:

```
#!/usr/local/bin/perl -w
$firstName=Gizmo;
$lastName="Senegal";
$age="3";
```

If you were to run this script, you would get a warning about an unquoted string. Here is the output:

```
Unquoted string "Gizmo" may clash with future reserved word at
bareword.pl line 3
```

The warning is telling you that the bare word `Gizmo` may be a future reserved word like a function name, which may change the context of the assignment if a function named `Gizmo` is added to Perl. Take notice of the assignment of the variable `$age`. The assignment of `$age` uses quotes, which means that Perl will initially treat this scalar value as a string instead of a numeric value. Although this is acceptable, this should be considered poor style and should be avoided.

9.2. Arrays

Perl has a data structure that is strictly known as an array of scalars; this structure is more commonly known as an array or a list. Perl's arrays can be used as a simple list, a stack, or even the skeleton of a complex data structure. This section outlines Perl's arrays so you can gain an understanding of how to use arrays in various ways.

Perl's array of scalars can be declared by any number of methods. One common method is to define an array to be empty, as in the following example:

```
@myList = ();
```

Keep in mind that Perl does not always require variables, including arrays, to be defined before use. The above example is provided merely as an example of how to define an empty array or how to empty an existing array. The above example defines an empty array of scalars named `@myList`.

9.2.1. Using Arrays as an Indexed List

The most common method of using an array as an indexed list is to directly assign the array all of its values at once, if possible. The following example sets the array variable `@months` to the months of the year:

```
@months = qw (JUNK Jan Feb March April May June July Aug Sept Oct Nov
Dec);
```

There are two items to mention regarding the above example: the space holder `JUNK` and the keyword `qw`. Because arrays start at index `0`, `JUNK` is used as a space holder. The list entry of `$months[0]` is filled with `JUNK` so `Jan` can be referenced at `$months[1]`, `June` at `$months[6]`, and `Dec` at

`$months[12]`. The `qw` keyword was introduced with Perl 5. The two following lines of Perl code assign the same values to the list `@array`:

```
@array = qw (a b c d e);
@array = (™a™, ™b™, ™c™, ™d™, ™e™);
```

The `qw` keyword is a shortened form used to extract individual words from a string. In the above case, the individual words are the names of the months, and the result of running `qw` on them is stored in the array `@months`. If the array cannot be assigned all at once, you can set the individual array elements on an individual basis. For example, you could have set the `@months` array in the following fashion:

```
$months[0] = "JUNK";
$months[1] = "Jan";
$months[2] = "Feb";
...
$months[12] = "Dec";
```

The ellipses are included for brevity; the rest of the `@months` array would have to be assigned in the same fashion. The above piece of code sets the value of `$months[0]` to the string value of `"JUNK"`, `$months[1]` to `"Jan"`, `$months[2]` to `"Feb"`, etc. Notice when you assign the array elements directly, you use the `$` character, not the `@` character. The `$` character at the beginning of an array tells Perl that one individual element of the array, not the complete array, is to be assigned. You can extract the information from an array in multiple ways. One of the most common is to index the array elements directly. The following script demonstrates directly indexing an array's contents:

```
#!/usr/local/bin/perl -w

my @months = qw (JUNK Jan Feb March April May June July Aug Sept Oct Nov
Dec);

for ($x=0; $x <= $#months; $x++)
{
   print "Index[$x] = $months[$x]\n";
}
```

The word `$#months` is actually a Perl convention that tells you the value of the largest subscript of an array. If `$#months` returns `-1`, the array is empty.

Here is the output of this script:

```
Index[0] = JUNK
Index[1] = Jan
Index[2] = Feb
Index[3] = March
Index[4] = April
Index[5] = May
Index[6] = June
Index[7] = July
```

```
Index[8] = Aug
Index[9] = Sept
Index[10] = Oct
Index[11] = Nov
Index[12] = Dec
```

9.2.2. Using Arrays as Stacks

You can store information in an array using several methods. One method is to use the `push` function to push information onto the top of the array, treating the array as a stack:

```
push (@myList, "Hello");
push (@myList, "World!");
```

The above example pushes two strings, `"Hello"` and `"World!"`, onto the array variable `@myList`. Because you used the `push` function, the variable `@myList` is being used as a last in first off (LIFO) stack. A LIFO stack works much like a dish stack in a cafeteria. Dishes are pushed onto the top of the stack and all the other dishes are pushed down. When dishes are removed from the stack, they are removed from the top and all the other dishes move toward the top of the stack. Figure 9.1 represents a LIFO stack using the dish stack analogy.

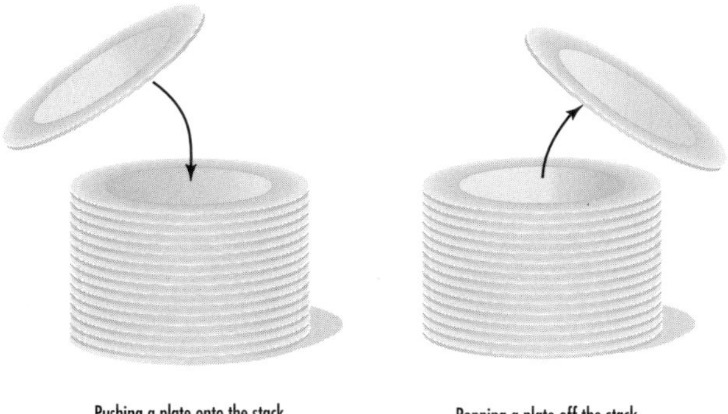

FIGURE 9.1. *LIFO stack diagram.*

To get information off the top of the stack, use the `pop` function. Using the example above, if you were to call `pop` on the array `@myList`, the value `"World!"` would be returned because it was the last element pushed on the stack. The following script demonstrates how to use an array as a stack:

```
#!/usr/local/bin/perl -w

push (@myList, "Hello");
push (@myList, "World!");
push (@myList, "How");
```

```
push (@myList, "Are");
push (@myList, "You?");

while ( $index = pop(@myList) )
{
   print "Popping off stack: $index\n";
}
```

Here's the output of this script:

```
Popping off stack: You?
Popping off stack: Are
Popping off stack: How
Popping off stack: World!
Popping off stack: Hello
```

Notice that elements are popped off in reverse order. This is the effect of the LIFO stack. When an element is popped off, the item is actually removed; once all the elements have been popped, the stack is empty.

9.3. Associative Arrays

Associative arrays are arrays that are indexed by string value instead of by integer index value. Figure 9.2 outlines the component elements of a standard list. Figure 9.3 outlines what an associative array could look like. To make things a little clearer, we will compare a regular array against an associative array. If you have an array named `@scalarArray` and you want to print out the first element of the array, you would use the following syntax:

```
print $scalarArray[0];
```

Indexes	Record Values
0	
1	
2	
3	
4	
5	
6	

FIGURE 9.2. *Component elements of a standard list.*

Key
Records
Gizmo
Parrot
Elmo
Budgie
Timmy
Cat
Fegus
Dog

FIGURE 9.3. *Outline of an associative array.*

Associative arrays, unlike scalar arrays, do not have a sense of order; there is no true first addressable element. This is because the indexes of the associative array are strings and the information is not stored in a predictable order. To retrieve a value from an associative array, you must know the key. If you know a key of the associative array `%associativeArray` and you want to print out the value, you would use the following syntax:

```
print $associativeArray{'mike'};
```

This example prints out the value of a key named `mike` in the associative array named `%associativeArray`.

Many programming languages, including C, do not have native associative array capabilities. Perl is an exception to this rule. This section demonstrates how to propagate and investigate Perl's associative array of scalars.

Perl's associative array of scalars can be declared using any number of methods. A common one is to declare an empty associative array, as in the following example:

```
%cities = ();
```

9.3.1. Populating an Associative Array

Keep in mind that Perl does not require variables, including associative arrays, to be defined before use. The above example is provided as an example of how to define an empty associative array or how to empty an existing array. It creates an empty associative array of scalars named `%cities`, which maintains a list of cities and their respective locations in Canada. Note the differences between the definition of a normal array of scalars and an associative array of scalars. The normal array is distinguished by the `@` character, whereas the associative array is distinguished by the `%` character.

Much like the normal array, an associative array can have all its values assigned at once. The following piece of Perl code assigns three records to the associative array `%cities`:

```
%cities = ("Toronto" => "East", "Calgary" => "Central", "Vancouver" =>
'West');
```

The operator `=>` is equivalent to a comma; its main purpose is to create a visual association between pairs. Thus, the following two lines are equivalent:

```
%cities = ("Toronto" => "East", "Calgary" => "Central", "Vancouver" =>
'West');
%cities = ("Toronto", "East", "Calgary", "Central", "Vancouver",
'West');
```

Like the standard array, the associative array can be populated by individual elements as well. For example, the following lines of Perl code populate the associative array `%cities` with the same values listed above:

```
$cities{'Toronto'} = "East";
$cities{'Vancouver'} = "West";
$cities{'Calgary'} = "Central";
```

9.3.2. Extracting Information from an Associative Array

You can list the contents of an associative array using one of three functions: `keys`, `values`, or `each`. The `keys` function returns a list of the keys of the given associative array when used in a list context and the number of keys when used in a scalar one. The keys returned from the `keys` function are merely indexes into the associative array. The `keys` function is the most common function used to extract information from an associative array. When used in a list context, the `keys` function returns a list of all the keys of the given associative array. The following Perl script lists the contents of an associative array:

```
#!/usr/local/bin/perl -w

my %cities = ("Toronto" => "East", "Calgary" => "Central", "Vancouver"
=> 'West');

for $key (keys %cities)
{
   print "Key: $key Value: $cities{$key} \n";
}
```

Here's the output of this script:

```
Key: Toronto Value: East
Key: Calgary Value: Central
Key: Vancouver Value: West
```

If you are interested only in the values of the associative array, then you could use the `values` function instead. The following script lists the contents of an associative array using the `values` function:

```
#!/usr/local/bin/perl -w

my %cities = ("Toronto" => "East", "Calgary" => "Central", "Vancouver"
=> 'West');

for $value (values %cities)
{
   print "Value: $value \n";
}
```

Here's the output of this script:

```
Value: East
Value: Central
Value: West
```

The obvious advantage of using the `keys` function over the `values` function is that with the `keys` function you can also get the values of the associative array. The third method you can use to list the contents of an associative array is to use the `each` function. This function returns a key-value pair from the associative array. The following script demonstrates the `each` function:

```
#!/usr/local/bin/perl -w

my %cities = ("Toronto" => "East", "Calgary" => "Central", "Vancouver"
=> 'West');

while ( ($key, $value) = each %cities )
{
   print "Key: $key Value: $value \n";
}
```

Here's the output of this script:

```
Key: Toronto Value: East
Key: Calgary Value: Central
Key: Vancouver Value: West
```

9.4. References

References are a data type introduced with Perl 5. Calling a reference a data type is a very loose use of the term data type. A reference is more a generic entity that can point to any given data type, native or generated. For the C programmers reading this, a reference is nothing more than a pointer.

One of the biggest complaints about Perl 4 was that creating a complex data type was almost impossible. Even creating a simple matrix was something the gurus did because they knew what potions to brew. With references, potions need not be brewed, incantations need not be uttered, and little bags of tricks can be used for marbles. References fill the void in Perl 4.

9.4.1. Creating a Reference

When a reference is created, a new instance of the reference is created and stored in the receiving scalar. This is done so that if the original reference disappears, the scalar reference will still have a copy of the original. The following script demonstrates the creation of a reference:

```
#!/usr/local/bin/perl -w

# Set up the data types.
my $scalarVar = "Gizmo was here.";

# Create the reference to $scalarVar
my $scalarRef = \$scalarVar;
```

This example creates a reference named `$scalarRef` to a scalar variable named `$scalarVar`. There are several different types of references; they are outlined below.

9.4.2. Dereferencing a Reference

Perl's references do not automatically dereference themselves when used. References are scalars; if you were to print out a reference without trying to dereference it, then the scalar would print out information about itself. For example, say you type in the following script:

```
#!/usr/local/bin/perl -w

# Set up the data types.
my $scalarVar = "Gizmo was here.";
my @arrayVar = qw (Sunday Monday Tuesday Wednesday Thursday Friday
Saturday);
my %hashVar = ("Toronto" => "East", "Calgary" => "Central", "Vancouver"
=> 'West');

# Create the references
my $scalarRef = \$scalarVar;
my $arrayRef = \@arrayVar;
my $hashRef = \%hashVar;

# Print out the references.
print "$scalarRef \n";
print "$arrayRef \n";
print "$hashRef \n";
```

The script would print out something like the following:

```
SCALAR(0xaddc4)
ARRAY(0xadec0)
HASH(0xade30)
```

The next seven sections demonstrate how to create and dereference scalar references, array references, hash references, code references, anonymous array references, anonymous hash references, and anonymous subroutine references.

9.4.3. Scalar References

A scalar reference is created by using the backslash operator on an existing scalar variable. The following example creates a reference to the variable `$scalarVariable`:

```
$scalarRef = \$scalarVariable;
```

To dereference the scalar reference, add a `$` to the beginning of the reference. This means the variable will have two `$` signs before the variable name when you are printing out the contents of the scalar reference. If the reference variable is called `$scalarRef`, use the following syntax to print out the contents of the reference:

```
print $$scalarRef;
```

The following code segment creates a reference to a scalar, then prints out the contents of the reference:

```
#!/usr/local/bin/perl -w

# Create the scalar variable
my $scalarVariable = "Gizmo was here.";

# Create the scalar reference
my $scalarRef = \$scalarVariable;

# Print out the contents of the scalar variable
print "Var: $scalarVariable\n";

# Print out the contents of the scalar reference.
# Note the double $$
print "Ref: " . $$scalarRef . "\n";
```

Here's the output of this script:

```
Var: Gizmo was here.
Ref: Gizmo was here.
```

9.4.4. Array References

One way to create an array reference is to use the backslash operator on an existing array variable. The following script creates a reference to an array variable named `@months`, then prints out the contents of the array reference:

```
#!/usr/local/bin/perl -w

# Create the array
my @months = qw (Jan Feb March April May June July Aug Sept Oct Nov
Dec);

# Create the array reference.
My $arrayRef = \@months;
```

```
# Print out the contents of the array reference.
for $month (@$arrayRef)
{
   print "Month: $month \n";
}
```

Here's the output of this script:

```
Month: Jan
Month: Feb
Month: March
Month: April
Month: May
Month: June
Month: July
Month: Aug
Month: Sept
Month: Oct
Month: Nov
Month: Dec
```

9.4.5. Hash References

One way to create a hash reference is to use the backslash operator on an existing hash variable. The following script creates a reference to a hash variable named `%who` and then prints out the contents of the hash reference:

```
#!/usr/local/bin/perl -w

# Create the associative array
my %who = ('Name' => 'Gizmo', 'Age' => 3, 'Height' => '10 cm', 'Weight'
=> '10 gm');

# Create the hash reference
my $hashRef = \%who;
 # Print out the contents of the associative array.
for $key (sort keys %$hashRef)
{
   $value = $hashRef->{$key};
   printf "Key: %10s Value: %-40s\n", $key, $value;
}
```

Here's the output of this script:

```
Key:        Age Value: 3
Key:     Height Value: 10 cm
Key:       Name Value: Gizmo
Key:     Weight Value: 10 gm
```

9.4.6. Code References

A code reference is a reference to a subroutine. Code references are mainly used for callback functions. One way to create a code reference is to use the backslash operator on a function name. The following script creates a reference to a subroutine named `callBack` and then dereferences the reference to call the subroutine:

```
#!/usr/local/bin/perl -w

# Define the callback function.
sub callBack
{
   my ($mesg) = @_;

   print "$mesg\n";
}

# Create the code reference
my $codeRef = \&callBack;

# Call the callback function with different parameters.
&$codeRef ("Hi Mike!");
&$codeRef ("How Are You?");
```

Here's the output of this script:

```
Hi Mike!
How Are You?
```

9.4.7. Anonymous Array References

An anonymous array is an array without a name. This means the array has been defined and stored into a reference instead of an array. Anonymous arrays are one of the best additions, in our opinion, to Perl 5. There will be times when you may want to create a temporary array but don't feel like creating a new array name. When you use an anonymous array, Perl creates the namespace for the array. This means Perl picks the name of the array instead of the programmer; this appeals to most people's lazy side. According to Larry Wall, the author of Perl, the three great virtues of a programmer are "laziness, impatience, and hubris." (*Programming Perl*, p. xiv)

To create an anonymous array, use square brackets around a list. The following script creates an anonymous array and prints out some of the contents:

```
#!/usr/local/bin/perl -w

# Create the anonymous array reference.
My $arrayRef = [[1,2,3,4], 'a', 'b', 'c', 'd', 'e', 'f'];

# Print out some of the array
print $arrayRef->[0][0] . "\n";
print $arrayRef->[0][1] . "\n";
print $arrayRef->[1] . "\n";
```

Here's the output of this script:

```
1
2
a
```

Notice that the above example creates an anonymous array inside an anonymous array. This is a way to create a matrix in Perl 5.

9.4.8. Anonymous Hash References

Anonymous hash references are created the same way anonymous array references are created. The hash is created and the reference is stored directly into the reference. Anonymous hash references have the same appeal as anonymous array references: The programmer does not need to create a name for the array. The following script makes a hash reference and prints out some of the contents:

```
#!/usr/local/bin/perl -w

my $hashRef = {'Name' => 'Gizmo', 'Age' => 3, 'Height' => '10 cm'};

print $hashRef->{'Name'} . "\n";
print $hashRef->{'Age'} . "\n";
print $hashRef->{'Height'} . "\n";
```

Here's the output of this script:

```
Gizmo
3
10 cm
```

9.4.9. Anonymous Subroutine References

An anonymous subroutine is a subroutine that has been defined without a name. The following script creates a reference to an anonymous function:

```
#!/usr/local/bin/perl -w

my $codeRef = sub { my $mesg = shift; print "$mesg\n"; };

&$codeRef ("Hi Mike");
&$codeRef ("How Are You?");
```

Here's the output of this script:

```
Hi Mike
How Are You?
```

9.5. Regular Expressions

Regular expressions are used to search for patterns. The stronger the pattern-matching abilities, the more valuable the programming language becomes. Compared to other programming languages, compiled and interpreted, Perl has one of the most powerful pattern-matching capabilities. This section outlines the syntax of Perl's regular expressions and demonstrates Perl's powerful pattern-matching capabilities. This section is broken into two subsections: "Regular Expression Syntax" and "Pattern-Matching Operators." The "Regular Expression Syntax" section outlines the syntax of Perl's regular expressions; the "Pattern-Matching Operators" section takes the rules defined in the "Regular Expressions" section and applies them to basic examples.

9.5.1. Regular Expression Syntax

Perl's regular expressions are so vast that a complete book could be dedicated to them. Because we don't have that luxury, this section outlines some of the more commonly used expressions and expression syntaxes.

The most common operator used when using regular expressions on strings is what Perl calls a *pattern-binding operator*. The pattern-binding operator looks like `=~` or `!~`. The syntax of the pattern-binding operator is

```
$string =~ /regular expression/expression modifier
```

The regular expression can be anything from a basic scalar value to a complex regular expression looking for a complex pattern. The expression modifier is an optional element to the regular expression. If you were to look for a pattern of `Hello` in a scalar named `$sentence`, the syntax would look like the following:

```
$sentence =~ /Hello/;
```

If `$sentence` contains the value of `Hello`, then the above statement would return `True`. To take full advantage of Perl's regular expressions, you need to understand the syntax of the expressions. This subsection outlines everything from expression modifiers to expression quantifiers to predefined character patterns.

9.5.2. Modifiers

An expression modifier can be added to most regular expressions to modify the behavior of the expression. Table 9.1 lists the expression modifiers and what they do.

TABLE 9.1. *Regular expression modifiers.*

Modifier Name	*Purpose*
`i`	Makes the search case-insensitive.
`m`	If the string has newline characters embedded within it, the metacharacters `^` and `$` will not work correctly. This modifier tells Perl to treat this line as a multiple line.
`s`	The character `.` matches any character except a new line. This modifier treats this line as a single line, which allows `.` to match a newline character.
`x`	Allows whitespace in the expression.

For example, if you were to perform a basic case-insensitive search, you would use the `I` modifier. The following example demonstrates how to use a modifier on a regular expression:

```
#!/usr/local/bin/perl -w

# Create a basic string.
my $string = "Hello World!";

if ($string =~ /"Hello World!"/)
{
   print "Case Match!\n";
}

if ($string =~ /"hello WORLD!"/i)
{
   print "Case insensitive Match!\n";
}
```

Here's the output of this script:

```
Case Match!
Case insensitive Match!
```

9.5.3. Metacharacters

A *metacharacter* is a character that carries a special meaning. Metacharacters are used to make searches more specific so very complicated search patterns can be constructed. Table 9.2 outlines Perl's regular expression metacharacters and their meanings.

TABLE 9.2. *Regular expression metacharacters.*

Metacharacter	*Purpose*
`\`	Tells Perl to accept the following character as a regular character; this removes special meanings from any metacharacter.
`^`	Matches the beginning of the string, unless `/m` is used.
`.`	Matches any character except a newline character, unless `/s` is used.
`$`	Matches the end of the string, unless `/m` is used.
`¦`	Expresses alternation. This means the expressions will search for multiple patterns in the same string.
`()`	Groups expressions to assist in alternation and back referencing.
`[]`	Looks for a set of characters.

The following example performs a very specific spell check on a text file. It looks for misspelled instances of the words "language" and "expression":

```
#!/usr/local/bin/perl -w

while (<STDIN>)
{
   # Look for incorrect spelling of 'language' and 'expression'.
   print if ( /(L¦l)angau[gG]e¦(E¦e)xprestion/ );
}
```

Use the following text file as input for the script. The misspelled words are highlighted:

```
Perl is an interpreted langauge optimized for scanning arbitrary
text files, extracting information from those text files, and
printing reports based on that information.  It's also a good
langauGe for many system management tasks.  The langauge is
intended to be practical (easy to use, efficient, complete) rather
than beautiful (tiny, elegant, minimal).  It combines (in the author's
opinion, anyway) some of the best features of C,
sed, awk, and sh, so people familiar with those langauges should
have little difficulty with it. (Langauge historians will also note
some vestiges of csh, Pascal, and even BASIC-PLUS.)  Exprestion
syntax corresponds quite closely to C exprestion syntax.
```

Here's the output of this script:

```
Perl is an interpreted langauge optimized for scanning arbitrary
langauGe for many system management tasks.  The langauge is
sed, awk, and sh, so people familiar with those langauges should
have little difficulty with it. (Langauge historians will also note
some vestiges of csh, Pascal, and even BASIC-PLUS.)  Exprestion
syntax corresponds quite closely to C exprestion syntax.
```

9.5.4. Pattern Quantifiers

A *pattern quantifier* allows the programmer to write dynamic regular expressions without having to write out each possible instance of the pattern explicitly. Table 9.3 outlines each quantifier and its purpose.

TABLE 9.3. *Regular expression pattern quantifiers.*

Quantifier	*Purpose*
`*`	Matches 0 or more times.
`+`	Matches 1 or more times.
`?`	Matches 0 or 1 times.
`{n}`	Matches exactly `n` times.
`{n,}`	Matches at least `n` times.
`{n,m}`	Matches at least `n` times but no more than `m` times.

The following example scans an array of numbers looking for a number that starts with 870 and is followed by three 2s in a row:

```
#!/usr/local/bin/perl -w

my @numbers = qw (870226980 870222428 870222315 870641520 870222318);

for (@numbers)
{
   if ( /^8702{3)/)
   {
      print $_ . "\n";
   }
}
```

Here's the output of this script:

```
870222428
870222315
870222318
```

9.5.5. Character Patterns

Perl uses a number of character patterns to look for special instances of patterns. Table 9.4 lists sequences of special characters and their purpose.

TABLE 9.4. *Regular expression character patterns.*

Sequence	*Purpose*
`\w`	Matches an alphanumeric character. Alphanumeric also includes _.
`\W`	Matches a nonalphanumeric character.
`\s`	Matches a whitespace character. This includes space and tab.
`\S`	Matches a nonwhitespace character.
`\d`	Matches a digit.
`\D`	Matches a nondigit character.
`\b`	Matches a word boundary.
`\B`	Matches a nonword boundary.
`\A`	Matches only at beginning of string.
`\Z`	Matches only at end of string.
`\G`	Matches only where previous `m//g` left off.

The following example gets the current date in the UNIX date format and looks for the hours, minutes, and seconds:

```
#!/usr/local/bin/perl -w

# Get the date in the standard date format. (ex: Tue Oct 24 19:03:03
1995 )
my $date = localtime();

# Search through the date looking for the hour, minute, and second.
if ($date =~ /(\d\d):(\d\d):(\d\d)/)
{
   # Save the information.
   my $hours = $1;
   my $minutes = $2;
   my $seconds = $3;

   print "Hours  : $hours \n";
   print "Minutes: $minutes \n";
   print "Seconds: $seconds \n";
}
```

Here's the output of this script:

```
Hours  : 19
Minutes: 08
Seconds: 04
```

9.5.6. Pattern-Matching Operators

Pattern-matching operators are the keywords in Perl that perform pattern matches. The difference between regular expression syntax and pattern-matching operators is that regular expressions allow the programmer to build complex expressions, whereas pattern-matching operators allow the programmer to perform the searches. This subsection outlines Perl's pattern-matching operators and how to use them.

The syntax used to perform a pattern match on a string is

```
$string =~ /regular expression/expression modifier (optional)
```

The operator `=~` performs a search looking for the regular expression within the given string. For example, the following Perl script scans text looking for the word *the*:

```
#!/usr/local/bin/perl -w

while (<STDIN>)
{
   print if ($_ =~ /the/);
}
```

Here's the output of this script:

```
intended to be practical (easy to use, efficient, complete) rather
(in the author's opinion, anyway) some of the best features of C,
```

Notice that the word *rather* was selected as well. Because the search looks for the pattern *the*, any word that contains the pattern will be selected.

9.6. Operators: Numeric and String

Perl, like other programming languages, has a number of operators for both strings and numeric values. The operators can be broken down into four distinct groups: string operators, numeric operators, assignment operators, and equivalence operators. The next two subsections, "String Operators" and "Numeric Operators," outline all the string and numeric operators and what should be expected when the operators are used.

9.6.1. String Operators

Perl has a number of string operators that do everything from basic string concatenation to case conversion. Perl can even increment string values. The most often used string operators are assignment operators and equivalence checks. Unfortunately, the most common mistake is made when trying to perform an equivalence check on a string value; many programmers use numeric operators instead. The following two statements demonstrate the right and wrong ways to perform an equivalence check on a string:

```
# Wrong!!!
if ($string == "Hello")
{
   # Do something...
}

# Right!
if ($string eq "Hello")
{
   # Do something...
}
```

The following script demonstrates the correct use of three of the operators listed in Table 9.5—`eq`, `lt`, and `gt`:

```
#!/usr/local/bin/perl -w

# Do this forever.
for (;;)
{
   # Get the information from the user.
   print "Enter a word: ";
   my $word1 = <STDIN>; chomp $word1;
   print "Enter another word: ";
   my $word2 = <STDIN>; chomp $word2;

   # Perform some basic string operations
   if ($word1 eq $word2)
   {
      print "The two phrases are equivalent.\n";
   }
   elsif ($word1 lt $word2)
   {
      print "<$word1> is alphabetically less than <$word2>\n";
   }
   elsif ($word1 gt $word2)
   {
      print "<$word1> is alphabetically greater than <$word2>\n";
   }
}
```

Here's the output of this script:

```
Enter a word: Hello
Enter another word: There
<Hello> is alphabetically less than <There>
Enter a word: Xenophobia
Enter another word: Hiccup
<Xenophobia> is alphabetically greater than <Hiccup>
Enter a word: This is the end.
Enter another word: This is the end.
The two phrases are equivalent.
```

Table 9.5 outlines Perl's string operators and the purpose of each.

TABLE 9.5. *String operators.*

Operator	*Purpose*
`x`	Returns a string consisting of the string on the left of the operand, repeated the number of times of the right operand.
`.`	Concatenates the two strings on both sides of the operator.
`eq`	Returns `True` if the two operands are equivalent, `False` otherwise.
`ne`	Returns `True` if the two operands are not equal, `False` otherwise.
`le`	Returns `True` if the operand on the left is stringwise less than the operand on the right of the operator. Returns `False` otherwise.
`lt`	Returns `True` if the operand on the left is stringwise less than or equal to the operand on the right of the operator. Returns `False` otherwise.
`ge`	Returns `True` if the operand on the left is stringwise greater than or equal to the operand on the right of the operator. Returns `False` otherwise.
`gt`	Returns `True` if the operand on the left is stringwise greater than the operand on the right of the operator. Returns `False` otherwise.
`cmp`	Returns `-1`, `0`, or `1` if the left operand is stringwise less than, equal to, or greater than the right operand.
`,`	Evaluates the left operand, then evaluates the right operand. It returns the result of the right operand.
`++`	Increments the string by one alphabetic value.

9.6.2. Numeric Operators

Perl has the standard set of numeric operators plus a few extras. The following example demonstrates some of the more basic operators. Note that the equivalence operations performed on the values parallel those of the string equivalence example:

```
#!/usr/local/bin/perl -w

# Do this forever.
for (;;)
{
   # Get the information from the user.
   print "Enter a number: ";
   my $num1 = <STDIN>; chomp $num1;
   print "Enter another number: ";
   my $num2 = <STDIN>; chomp $num2;

   # Perform some basic numeric operations
   my $sum = $num1 + $num2;
   my $diff = $num1 - $num2;

   print "The sum of $num1 and $num2 is $sum\n";
   print "The difference of $num1 and $num2 is $diff\n";

   if ($num1 == $num2)
   {
      print "Both numbers are equal.\n";
   }
   elsif ($num1 < $num2)
   {
      print "$num1 is numerically less than $num2\n";
   }
   elsif ($num1 > $num2)
   {
      print "$num1 is numerically greater than $num2\n";
   }
}
```

Here's the output of this script:

```
Enter a number: 1
Enter another number: 2
The sum of 1 and 2 is 3
The difference of 1 and 2 is -1
1 is numerically less than 2
Enter a number: 42
Enter another number: 5
The sum of 42 and 5 is 47
The difference of 42 and 5 is 37
42 is numerically greater than 5
Enter a number: 68
Enter another number: 68
The sum of 68 and 68 is 136
The difference of 68 and 68 is 0
Both numbers are equal.
```

Table 9.6 lists Perl's numeric operators and their purpose.

TABLE 9.6. *Numeric operators.*

Operator	*Purpose*
+	Computes the additive value of the two operands.
-	Computes the difference between the two operands.
*	Computes the multiplication of the two operands.
/	Computes the division between the two operands.
%	Computes the modulus (remainder) of the two operands.
==	Returns True if the two operands are equivalent, False otherwise.
!=	Returns True if the two operands are not equal, False otherwise.
<=	Returns True if the operand on the left is numerically less than or equal to the operand on the right of the operator. Returns False otherwise.
<	Returns True if the operand on the left is numerically less than the operand on the right of the operator. Returns False otherwise.
=>	Returns True if the operand on the left is numerically greater than or equal to the operand on the right of the operator. Returns False otherwise.
>	Returns True if the operand on the left is numerically greater than the operand on the right of the operator. Returns False otherwise.
<=>	Returns -1 if the left operand is less than the right, +1 if is it greater than, and 0 (False) otherwise.
&&	Performs a logical AND operation. If the left operand is False, the right operand is not evaluated.
¦¦	Performs a logical OR operation. If the left operand is True, then the right operator is not evaluated.
&	Returns the value of the two operators bitwise ANDed.
¦	Returns the value of the two operators bitwise ORed.
^	Returns the value of the two operators bitwise XORed.
++	Increment operator. Increments the variable's value by 1.
--	Decrement operator. Decrements the variable's value by 1.
**	Computes the power of the left-hand value to the power of the right-hand value.
+=	Adds the value of the right-hand operand to the value of the left-hand operand.

Operator	Purpose
-=	Subtracts the value of the right-hand operand from the value of the left-hand operand.
*=	Multiplies the value of the left-hand operand with the value of the right-hand operand.
>>	Shifts the left operand right by the number of bits that is specified by the right operand.
<<	Shifts the left operand left by the number of bits that is specified by the right operand.
~	Performs a 1s complement of the operator. This is a unary operator.

When using arithmetic operators, precedence plays a large role. A general rule of thumb is to use parentheses wherever possible to force precedence. Using parentheses also helps the reader fully understand what you intend. The following example demonstrates the dangers of not using parentheses around operations:

```
#!/usr/local/bin/perl -w

# Get the values from the user.
print "Enter the first number : ";
my $num1 = <STDIN>; chomp $num1;
print "Enter the second number: ";
my $num2 = <STDIN>; chomp $num2;
print "Enter the third number : ";
my $num3 = <STDIN>; chomp $num3;

# Calculate:  A*B-C
my $answer = $num1 * $num2 - $num3;
print "$num1 * $num2 - $num3 = $answer \n";

# Calculate:  (A*B)-C
$answer = ($num1 * $num2) - $num3;
print "($num1 * $num2) - $num3 = $answer \n";

# Calculate:  A*(B-C)
$answer = $num1 * ($num2 - $num3);
print "$num1 * ($num2 - $num3) = $answer \n";
```

Here's the output of this script:

```
Enter the first number : 2
Enter the second number: 3
Enter the third number : 4
2 * 3 - 4 = 2
(2 * 3) - 4 = 2
2 * (3 - 4) = -2
```

Notice that Perl follows standard arithmetic precedence; it multiplies before it adds or subtracts. This is fine if that is what you intended. If not, you will end up with a drastically different answer. The first of the three operations performs an operation using standard precedence. As a result, the calculation performed is `(A * B) - C`, which is exactly the same calculation as the second operation. The third operation performs `A * (B-C)`, which reveals a completely different answer.

9.7. Control Statements

When talking about flow control with respect to programming languages, we are talking about the control the programmer has over the way the program behaves. Without flow control, a program will not loop, cycle, or iterate to perform repetitive tasks. This section outlines Perl's flow control statements and shows how to use them effectively. This section is broken into three subsections: conditional control statements, loop control statements, and labels.

9.7.1. Conditional Control Statements

There are two conditional control statements in Perl: the `if` statement and the `unless` statement. The `if` statement performs a task if the expression given to it is `True`. The syntax of an `if` statement is

```
if (Expression) {Code Segment}
if (Expression) {Code Segment} else {Code Segment}
if (Expression) {Code Segment} elsif {Code Segment} ... else {Code
Segment}
```

The code segment can be anything from a simple line of Perl code to several hundreds of lines (yuck!). When either the `else` or `elsif` statement is used, it means if the expression given to the `if` is not `True`, then the respective code segment will be run. The following Perl script demonstrates the use of the `if` statement, using both the `elsif` and `else` statements:

```
#!/usr/local/bin/perl -w

while (<STDIN>)
{
   chomp;

   if ($_ < 10)
   {
      print "$_ is less than 10.\n";
   }
   elsif ($_ < 20)
   {
      print "$_ is between the values of 10 and 19.\n";
   }
   else
```

```
        {
            print "$_ is greater than or equal to 20.\n";
        }
    }
```

Here's the output of this script:

```
10
10 is between the values of 10 and 19.
9
9 is less than 10.
11
11 is between the values of 10 and 19.
19
19 is between the values of 10 and 19.
20
20 is greater than or equal to 20.
22
22 is greater than or equal to 20.
```

The `unless` statement works the opposite of the `if` statement. The `unless` statement will only perform a task if the resultant operation is `False`. This is a little backwards sometimes, which is why we avoid the `unless` statement. Using the `unless` statement can make the code hard to understand. The following example outlines the use of the `unless` statement:

```
#!/usr/local/bin/perl -w

while (<STDIN>)
{
    chop;
    print "I have found what I'm looking for: <$_>\n" unless $_ ne
"Gizmo";
}
```

The script is looking for the string `"Gizmo"`; when it finds it, it prints out a message. The whole of the intelligence is on the line

```
print "I have found what I'm looking for: <$_>\n" unless $_ ne "Gizmo";
```

The `unless` statement twists the logic so that the operation on the left side of the `unless` statement will be evaluated only if the operation on the right side evaluates to `False`. In the above example, the message is printed only if the variable `$_` is equal to `"Gizmo"`. Because the right side has to evaluate to `False` for the print statement to run, you need to check if the value is not equal to `"Gizmo"`. When it is equal to `"Gizmo"`, the string check evaluates to `False`, and the message is printed out. (Confused yet?) This is why we avoid the `unless` statement unless it lends itself to the situation, which it can.

Here's the output of this script:

```
Hi There
Good morning.
Gizmo
I have found what I'm looking for: <Gizmo>
```

9.7.2. Loop Control Statements

Loop control statements allow you to create loops within the flow of the program. One of the most often used statements is the `for` loop. The `for` loop allows you to create a loop that will loop for a predetermined number of times. This could be anything from counting from 1 to 10 to cycling through an array and printing out the contents. An example of a `for` loop is the following script, which prints out the numbers from 1 to 10:

```
#!/usr/local/bin/perl -w

for ($x=1; $x <= 10; $x++)
{
   print $x . ", ";
}
print "\n";
```

This example can be rewritten to list the numeric values explicitly. Modify the above script and change the lines

```
for ($x=1; $x <= 10; $x++)
{
   print $x . ", ";
}
```

to

```
for (1..10)
{
   print $_ . ", ";
}
```

The `for` loop is also used to create infinite loops. To create an infinite loop using a `for` loop, remove the loop conditions from the statement. The following example demonstrates how to create an infinite loop using a `for` loop:

```
#!/usr/local/bin/perl -w

for (;;)
{
   print "This is the loop that never ends, it goes on and on my
friends...\n";
}
```

The `foreach` statement is very much like the `for` loop except it iterates through list values. The following is an example of a `foreach` loop:

```
#!/usr/local/bin/perl

# Create a list of the days of the week.
@days = qw (Monday Tuesday Wednesday Thursday Friday Saturday Sunday);

# Cycle through the loop, and print out the contents.
foreach $day (@days)
{
   print "$day\n";
}
```

Here's the output of this script:

```
Monday
Tuesday
Wednesday
Thursday
Friday
Saturday
Sunday
```

In the above example, the variable `$day` is created locally to the `foreach` loop. If the variable `$day` is not specified, then `$_` will be used.

The other popular control statement is the `while` loop. The `while` loop is a little different than the `for` loop in that it evaluates a conditional statement before entering the loop. The `while` loop is mainly used to create a loop that ends on a conditional statement. The following script counts from 1 to 10 using a `while` loop:

```
#!/usr/local/bin/perl

# Set the value of x
$x=1;

while ($x <= 10)
{
   print $x++ . ", ";
}
print "\n";
```

Here's the output of this script:

```
1, 2, 3, 4, 5, 6, 7, 8, 9, 10
```

9.7.3. Labels

Labels are used when you want to jump to a specific location within the code. This type of action is normally shunned by experienced programmers because using it can make it difficult to follow the flow of the program and it can also raise the heated discussion of the `goto` statement.

Be that as it may, Perl has this ability, and it should be discussed. So far, we have not been totally honest about the true syntax of the `for`, `foreach`, and `while` statements. An optional label can be appended to these statements so jumps to their specific location can be made. Following is the true syntax of the `for`, `foreach`, and `while` statements:

```
Label while (Conditional Expression) Code Block
Label while (Conditional Expression) Code Block Continue Code Block
Label for (Expression; Expression; Expression) Code Block
Label foreach Variable (Array or List) Code Block
Label Code Block Continue
```

When a label is defined, a block has to be defined. This means that if a label is defined, then a pair of braces needs to be used to encapsulate the associated code segment. The best purpose for labels is if the program has to break out of several blocks at one time. The following example uses the `last` keyword to break out of nested `for` loops:

```
#!/usr/local/bin/perl -w

# Define the label name.
EXIT:
{
    # Create an infinite loop to demonstrate how last will
    # break out of multiple code blocks.
    for (;;)
    {
         my $x = 0;
        for (;;$x++)
        {
            print "$x, \n";
            last EXIT if $x >= 5;
        }
    }
}
print "Out of for loops.\n";
```

Here's the output of this script:

```
1, 2, 3, 4, 5,
Out of for loops.
```

9.8. Subroutines, Packages, and Modules

Subroutines, packages, and modules give programmers the ability to write modular code. A *subroutine* is a block of code that performs a specific task that can be referenced by name. *Packages* and *modules* are blocks of code that, in most cases, perform a specific task. They allow programmers to create variables under different namespaces. A namespace is, effectively, where variables reside. As a default, any variables defined globally are put into the `main` namespace. A variable in a package named `"Foo"` would reside under the `"Foo"` namespace.

9.8.1. Subroutines

A subroutine is defined by the `sub` keyword and the block of code that follows. A block of code is contained with the `{}` characters. The syntactical definition of a Perl subroutine is

```
sub NAME { CODE }
```

where `NAME` is the name of the subroutine and `CODE` is the block of code. The following example demonstrates a subroutine declaration and calling the subroutine:

```
#!/usr/local/bin/perl -w

# Declare the subroutine named usage
sub usage
{
    my ($program, $exitCode) = @_;

    print "Usage: $program [-v] [-h]\n";
    exit $exitCode;
}

usage ($0, 1);
```

Here's the output of this script:

```
Usage: chap_01/howto08/sub.pl [-v] [-h]
```

When a subroutine is called with parameters, the parameters follow the subroutine name in list format. The example above calls the subroutine with the program name, `$0`, and an integer value that represents the exit value of the script. When a subroutine is called with parameters, the subroutine must somehow get the options being sent to it. This is done by using the special array `@_`. The line

```
my ($program, $exitCode) = @_;
```

creates two local variables, `$program` and `$exitCode`, from the global array `@_`. In Perl 4, to call a subroutine, an ampersand must proceed the subroutine name. In Perl 5, this is no longer necessary. Don't worry; this is still supported for backward compatibility.

9.8.2. Packages

A package is nothing more than a separate namespace for variables to reside in. The package provides a place for the programmer to hide, but not protect, private data. When a subroutine or variable is defined outside of a package, it is actually placed in the `main` package. To declare a package, use the `package` keyword. To define a package, use the syntax

```
package NAME;
```

where NAME is the name of the package. The scope of the package declaration is from the declaration to the end of the enclosing block. This means if a package is declared at the top of a script, then everything in the script is considered to be part of the package. The following example is a package named `Nothing` and a subroutine within the package named `doNothing`:

```
package Nothing;

sub doNothing
{
   print "This package does nothing!\n";
}

1;
```

The `1;` is needed so that the `require` or `use` statements do not report an error when they try to include this package. If the `1;` is omitted, the `require` statement returns a zero value, which is `False`, which also happens to be an error. To avoid this, force the package to return a nonzero value through the use of `1;`. To include this package in a Perl script, use the `require` keyword. The following example requires the package created above and calls the subroutine declared within it:

```
#!/usr/local/bin/perl -w

# Use the package nothing.
require "Nothing.pl";

# Call the subroutine doNothing inside the package Nothing.
Nothing::doNothing();
```

Here's the output of this script:

```
This package does nothing!
```

As it stands, packages are being degraded by modules.

9.8.3. Modules

Modules are nothing more than packages with some extra frills. Modules behave the same way packages do; they hide data and subroutines and allow programmers to create portable code. Why use a module? Modules and packages do not pollute namespaces: The only time a variable gets quashed is because you, not the module, stepped on it. A module is equivalent to a constructor when you use the `begin` keyword and is equivalent to a destructor when you use the `end` keyword. Perl also has a concept of classes, which allows programmers to create objects. With the addition of classes comes methods, which means that objects can be created and methods can be defined for those objects. All in all, C++ programmers should be pleased.

Like packages, a module is defined by the package keyword; the scope of the module declaration is from the package keyword to the end of the block. The following example is a module that reads the password file and stores the account information in an object:

```
package Acctinfo;

# Set up internal variables.
sub new
{
    my $self = {};
    my ($loginId, $passwd, $uid, $gid, $quota);
    my ($comment, $gcos, $home, $shell);
    my $login = getlogin();

    # Get information from the passwd file.
    ($loginId, $passwd, $uid, $gid, $quota, $comment, $gcos, $home,
    $shell) = getpwnam($login);

    # Store information in the object.
    $self->{'login'} = $login;
    $self->{'uid'} = $uid;
    $self->{'gid'} = $gid;
    $self->{'home'} = $home;
    $self->{'shell'} = $shell;

    # Bless this object...
    return bless $self;
}

# Return the user's login id.
sub getloginid
{
    my $self = shift;
    return $self->{'login');
}

# Return the user's uid
sub getuid
{
    my $self = shift;
    return $self->{'uid'};
}

# Return the user's gid
sub getgid
{
    my $self = shift;
    return $self->{'gid'};
}
# Return the user's home
sub gethome
{
    my $self = shift;
    return $self->{'home'};
}
```

```
# Return the user's shell
sub getshell
{
    my $self = shift;
    return $self->{'shell'};
}

1;
```

As a convention, modules are given the extension `.pm`. The following example uses the module defined above and calls one of the methods defined:

```
#!/usr/local/bin/perl -w

# Use the account information module.
use Acctinfo;

# Call the new method.
my $passwordObject = new Acctinfo();

# Get the uid.
my $uid = $passwordObject->getuid();

# Print out the results.
print "UID: $uid \n";
```

Here's the output of this script:

```
UID: 501
```

To include a Perl 5 module, use the keyword `use`. Notice that the `.pm` extension is not needed when using the `use` keyword.

9.9. Variable Localization

To be able to create complex programs, you must be able to control variables and specify where and how long they survive. This ability is called *variable localization.*

When a variable is defined in Perl, the variable is created in the global variable namespace by default. In actuality, variables are placed in the namespace of the package in which they are defined. Because the default package is called `main`, all variables that are not specifically defined in a named package or subroutine are defined in the `main` package. To demonstrate this, the following example creates a global variable `$myvar` and prints out the global instance of the variable and the package-specific variable:

```
#!/usr/local/bin/perl -w

# Define a variable.
$myvar = "Hello";
```

```
# Print out the global variable.
print "Global   : $myvar \n";

# Print out the package specific variable.
print "Specific: $main::myvar \n";
```

Here's the output of this script:

```
Global   : Hello
Specific: Hello
```

There are two keywords to localize a variable in Perl: LOCAL and MY. The local keyword is Perl 4's method of localizing a variable. Perl 5 can use both local and a new keyword, MY. The local keyword makes the variable local to the enclosed block, whereas MY totally hides the variable from the outside world. In any case, the use of MY is strongly encouraged. To demonstrate how to use MY, the following function creates a global variable named $xxx and prints out the value. A function is called that defines a variable with the same name. If Perl had no concept of variable localization, then this new definition would clobber the existing value of $xxx. The last print statement verifies that the global value of $xxx has not been changed:

```
#!/usr/local/bin/perl -w

# Define a basic subroutine.
sub myFunction
{
   # Define $xxx locally within this function.
   my $xxx = 5;

   # Print out the local value of $xxx
   print "Inside the function \$xxx = $xxx \n";
}

# Set the variable $xxx
my $xxx = 1;

# Print out the global value of the variable
print "Before function \$xxx = $xxx \n";
# Call the function.
myFunction();

# Print out the global value of the variable
print "After function \$xxx = $xxx \n";
```

Here's the output of this script:

```
Before function $xxx = 1
Inside the function $xxx = 5
After function $xxx = 1
```

There are some restrictions on which variables can and cannot be localized. Trying to localize the global variable $_ will not work.

9.10. Special Variables

Perl has over 50 predefined variables that are set or can be set when a Perl script is running. These variables can affect everything from the starting index in an array to the output field separator. The only problem with having so many predefined variables is that most of them are a mystery. This section outlines Perl's predefined variables. Table 9.7 provides details on the default value of the variables and a short description of what each variable does. The names of the predefined variables are cryptic; the `English.pm` module was created to help remove this cryptic element. The following example demonstrates how to use the `English.pm` module:

```
#!/usr/local/bin/perl -w

use English;

# Print out the process id using the standard variable.
print "PID          : Standard: $$ ";

# Print out the process id using the English value assigned.
print "English: $PROCESS_ID\n";

# Print out the real user ID using the standard variable.
print "Real User ID: Standard: $< ";

# Print out the real user id using the English value assigned.
print "English: $REAL_USER_ID\n";

# Print out the Perl version using the standard variable.
print "Perl Version: Standard: $] ";

# Print out the Perl version using the English value assigned.
print "English: $PERL_VERSION\n";
```

Run this script, and here's the output:

```
PID              : Standard: 238 English: 238
Real User ID     : Standard: 501 English: 501
Perl Version     : Standard: 5.001 English: 5.001
```

Table 9.7 lists Perl's special variables and what they do.

TABLE 9.7. *Perl's special variables.*

Variable	*Default Value*	*Description*
`$_`	N/A	The default input and pattern-searching space.
`$digit`	N/A	Contains the subpattern from a successful parentheses pattern match.
`$&`	N/A	The string from the last successful pattern match.

Variable	*Default Value*	*Description*
`` $` ``	N/A	The preceding string to the last successful pattern match.
`$'`	N/A	The string following the last successful pattern match.
`$+`	N/A	The last bracket matched from the last search pattern.
`$*`	0	Controls internal string multiline pattern matching.
`$.`	N/A	The current input line number of last filehandle read.
`$/`	\n	The input record separator.
`$¦`	0	If set to nonzero, forces a flush of the currently selected stream after every write.
`$,`	N/A	The output field separator for the print command.
`$"`	Space	The separator that joins elements of arrays interpolated in strings.
`$\`	N/A	The output record separator for the `print` command.
`$;`	`\034`	The subscript separator for multi-dimensional array emulation. This special variable should be superseded by correct array emulation in Perl 5.
`$#`	N/A	The output format for printed numbers.
`$%`	N/A	The page number of the currently selected output stream.
`$=`	60	The page length of the currently selected output stream.
`$-`	N/A	The number of lines left on the current page.
`$~`	`filehandle`	The name of the current report format for the currently selected output stream.
`$^`	`filehandle`	The name of the current top of page format for the currently selected output stream.
`$:`	`\n-`	The characters used to fill a continuation field.
`$^L`	`\f`	The default form feed character.

TABLE 9.7. *Continued.*

Variable	*Default Value*	*Description*
`$?`	N/A	The status value returned from the last system, pipe close, or backtick command.
`$!`	N/A	Contains the current value of `errno`.
`$@`	N/A	The Perl syntax error from the last `eval` statement.
`$$`	N/A	The process ID (PID) of the current running Perl script.
`$<`	N/A	The real user ID (UID) of the current running process.
`$>`	N/A	The effective UID of the current running process.
`$(`	N/A	The real group ID (GID) of the current running process.
`$)`	N/A	The effective GID of the current running process.
`$0`	N/A	The name of the file of the Perl script.
`$[`	0	The index of the first element of an array. This is very dangerous to change. Only use it if absolutely necessary.
`$]`	N/A	The string printed out when Perl is run with the `-v` command line option.
`$^A`	N/A	The accumulator for form line and write operations.
`$^D`	N/A	The current value of the debugging flags.
`$^F`	2	The maximum number of system file descriptors.
`$^I`	N/A	Contains the current value of the in-place editing flag (i.e., `-i`).
`$^P`	N/A	Internal debugging flag.
`$^T`	N/A	The time in which the script began running. The time is in seconds since January 1, 1970.
`$^W`	N/A	The current value of the warning switch.
`$^X`	N/A	The name of the Perl binary that was executed.
`$ARGV`	N/A	The name of the current file when reading from `<>`.

Table 9.8 lists all of Perl's special arrays and what they do.

TABLE 9.8. *Perl's special arrays.*

Array	*Description*
`@ARGV`	The command line arguments issued when the script was started.
`@EXPORT`	The list of methods the package will export by default.
`@EXPORT_OK`	The list of methods the package will export by request.
`@INC`	The include path of directories to search looking for libraries or Perl scripts that are to be evaluated by the `do` command.
`@ISA`	The list of base classes of the package.
`@_`	The parameter array for subroutines.
`%ENV`	This associative array contains your current environment.
`%INC`	This associative array contains a record for each entry that has been required using `do` or `require`.
`%OVERLOAD`	Used to overload operators in a package.
`%SIG`	This associative array contains signal handlers for various signals. This is set by the programmer, so initially there are no signals trapped unless the programmer has explicitly stated them in the script.

CHAPTER 10

Perl Tips and Tricks

by Hal Pomeranz

10.1. Context

10.1.1. Scalar Versus List Context

Perl programmers often talk about the *context* of a given statement or expression. This means simply the type of data that the statement is expecting to operate on. The two major contexts are *list context* and *scalar context*. Consider the following examples:

```
$x     = 'one';         # scalar assignment
$y     = 'two';         # ditto
@list  = ($x, $y);      # list assignment
$count = @list;         # scalar assignment!
```

This last line is noteworthy in two respects. First, assignment to a scalar on the left-hand side (LHS) forces the list variable on the right-hand side (RHS) into a scalar context. Second and more interestingly, the list variable has a useful meaning in a scalar context; the value of `$count` is now equal to the number of elements in `@list`, or the integer `2`. It is important to note that this is not a type coercion; rather, Perl just happens to assign meaning to list variables in a scalar context.[1]

Every operation in Perl is evaluated in terms of scalar or list context, and many operators and functions are overloaded, returning very different information in scalar and list contexts. Here's an example:

```
$_ = 'Thursday, May 12, 1997';
if (/(\w+), (\w+) (\d+), (\d+)/) {
     ($wday, $mon, $day, $year) =
          /(\w+), (\w+) (\d+), (\d+)/;
}
```

---

[1]The reason for this is in no way mysterious. It is convenient to say

```
while (@list) { # peel off values and do work }
```

In a scalar context (such as conditional expressions in an `if` block) the pattern-match operator returns a literal that evaluates to `true` (to be precise, pattern match returns the integer `1`) or `false` (a null string). However, in a list context (such as assignment to a list of scalars), pattern match returns a list of the subexpressions in the pattern. This latter behavior makes pattern match a flexible mechanism for parsing strings.

Context becomes more mysterious in compound expressions and when side effects enter the picture. For example, the preceding fragment could instead be written:

```
$_ = 'Thursday, May 12, 1997';
if (($wday, $mon, $day, $year) = /(\w+), (\w+) (\d+), (\d+)/) {
    # do something else here
}
```

Taking the assignment statement by itself for a moment, the pattern match is evaluated in a list context and returns a list of its subexpressions. However, the value of the assignment statement must then be evaluated in a scalar context forced by being in a condition of an `if` block. Perl defines the value of an assignment statement to be the result of evaluating the RHS—in this case, the list of subexpressions returned from the pattern match in its list context. This list is now evaluated in a scalar context, giving the number of subexpressions returned by the pattern match—which is zero if the pattern match fails and non-zero (`4`, in fact) if it succeeds—and the "right thing" happens (that is, the `if` block is only evaluated if the pattern match succeeds).

However, scalar or list context can sometimes manifest themselves in unexpected ways, as in the following:

```
my($line) = <INPUT>;
```

The `my()` function actually forces a list context. This causes the input file to be read in completely. The first line of the file is assigned to `$line`, but the rest of the file contents are discarded. Perhaps the greatest challenge to Perl programming is knowing whether or not a given expression is in a scalar or list context.

10.1.2. Types of Scalar Context

Perl also keeps track of what type of scalar is needed: boolean, numeric, or string. In the vast majority of cases, Perl silently transforms variables from one type of scalar to another:

```
$string = '123';
$value = $string + 1;     # $value is 124
```

Similarly, the pattern-match example in section 10.1.1 demonstrates conversion from a numeric scalar (the number of subexpressions returned by the pattern match) to a boolean value to evaluate the conditional expression in the `if` statement.

In extremely rare cases, the programmer must force a scalar from one type to another:

```
@octets  = split(/\./, '192.168.132.214');
@mask    = split(/\./, '255.255.255.192');
$network = $octets[3] & $mask[3];                # DOESN'T WORK!
```

The bitwise `and` operator does not automatically coerce strings to numbers, and consequently the preceding code does not provide the numeric network portion of the last octet as might be expected. The last line must be written

```
$network = ($octets[3] + 0) & ($mask[3] + 0);    # CORRECT
```

to achieve the expected behavior. Perl has no notion of type casts, so conversion between different types of scalars must be done by using the scalar in a numeric (as shown previously) or string context.

It is worth mentioning that, in a boolean sense, all the following variables evaluate to `false`:

```
$number = 0;            # numerically 0
$str1   = '';           # null string
$str2   = '0';          # string which evaluates to 0
$scalar = undef;        # undefined value
```

Perl provides a `length()` function that can be used to distinguish between a null string and a string that is numerically `0`. It is also sometimes useful to distinguish between a scalar that is defined but evaluates to `false` (`$number`, `$str1`, and `$str2` in the preceding examples) and a variable whose value is undefined (`$scalar`). Perl supplies a `defined()` function for this purpose. Be aware, however, that undefined scalars often become defined as a side effect of being evaluated in some expression; it is best to check whether a scalar is defined as soon as possible after that scalar may have been assigned the undefined value.

10.2. References

A relatively recent addition to Perl is the ability to created nested data structures (lists of lists, hashes of lists, etc.). This new functionality came wrapped up with a new abstract data type: the *reference*. A reference is a scalar that can be thought of as containing the address of some other data. A compound object, such as a list of lists, then is simply a list whose elements are all references to other lists. Unlike other languages, however, it is not necessary to preallocate storage for the referenced data structures; as with simple lists and hashes, Perl automatically handles memory allocation at runtime.

10.2.1. Creating Simple References

Perl references can be created in one of three ways: allocation as a side effect of usage, explicit creation with the `\` operator, or static declaration. Most commonly, programmers simply depend on Perl automatically instantiating data structures as the reference is introduced and used. Dereferencing and using references are covered in the following sections.

Perl does provide the `\` operator, which can be used to create a reference to an existing named data structure:

```
$scalar_ref = \$some_scalar;
$list_ref   = \@a_list;
$hash_ref   = \%another_hash;
```

C programmers will notice the similarity to the `&` operator in that language. In practice, the `\` operator is not widely used in Perl programs.

Perl provides the ability to `statically` compose references to anonymous data structures in the following fashion:

```
$list_ref = ['a', 'b', 'c'];
$list_ref = ['a', [1, 2, 3], 'c'];

$hash_ref = { 'carrots'  =>  'orange',
              'apples'   =>  'red',
              'eggplant' =>  'purple', };

$hash_ref = { 'carrots'  =>  'orange',
              'apples'   =>  ['red', 'golden'],
              'eggplant' =>  'purple', };
```

Square brackets are used to construct anonymous list references, and curly braces for hash references. In other words, use the same braces that are used when normally indexing the appropriate data type. The second and fourth examples above demonstrate how to compose nested data structures. Nesting can be arbitrarily deep, but in practice, more than three levels of nesting becomes difficult to type correctly, to say nothing of reading and understanding the code at a later date.

10.2.2. Dereferencing

Given a normal list in Perl, obtaining the second element is straightforward:

```
@a_list = ('a', 'b', 'c');

$second_elt = $a_list[1];
```

Suppose instead you want to obtain the second element via a reference to this same list. There are three semantically equivalent methods for dereferencing in Perl:

```
$list_ref = \@a_list;

$second_elt = $list_ref->[1];          # follow pointer

$second_elt = $$list_ref[1];           # use reference, not "a_list"
$second_elt = ${$list_ref}[1];         # use block
```

The first syntax should again look somewhat familiar to C programmers—the `->[1]` means get the second element from the list pointed to by `$list_ref`—but is not commonly used by Perl programmers given that there is a more concise syntax available. In the second (more preferred) syntax, the list name `@a_list` is simply replaced by the reference.

It is also always permissible to replace a variable name or reference with a block whose value is a reference, as shown in the third sample syntax. While the block syntax is clearly not necessary in this simple example, it is necessary to resolve precedence problems when dereferencing nested data structures. In the example below, the value of `$time{'greenwich'}` becomes a reference to the list of values returned by `gmtime()`. In the second line of the example, the seconds value is extracted into a scalar variable:

```
@{ $time{'greenwich'} } = gmtime();

$seconds = shift @{$time{'greenwich'}};
```

10.2.3. Manipulating Nested Structures

The previous example demonstrates how to manipulate an entire list that is referenced by an element of some other data structure (a hash in this case). The `$seconds` value could be obtained without using `shift()` with this:

```
$seconds = $time{'greenwich'}->[0];
```

It turns out that the `->` is optional in this case so that the following is equivalent:

```
$seconds = $time{'greenwich'}[0];
```

This is the way such dereferences are generally written.

It is always important to remember, however, that such nested data structures are not truly multidimensional. The following code fragment does not give meaningful output:

```
@list = ([1, 2, 3], [5], [6, 7, 8]);

print @list, "\n";
```

Instead use this:

```
foreach $ref (@list) {
    print "[ @$ref ], \t";
}
print "\n";
```

Another point of caution is to be careful when using references to nested data structures. Given the reference

```
$hash_ref = { 'primes' => [2, 3, 5, 7],
              'vowels' => ['a', 'e', 'i', 'o', 'u'], };
```

one syntax for getting at the `'i'` value in the vowels list is this:

```
$char = $hash_ref->{'vowels'}->[2];    # $char is 'i'
```

Recall that the `->` between the subscripts is optional:

```
$char = $hash_ref->{'vowels'}[2];    # still 'i'
```

The following is also equivalent:

```
$char = $$hash_ref{'vowels'}[2];        # note extra '$'!
```

because `$foo->{'bar'}` is equivalent to `$$foo{'bar'}`. Dropping the second `$` is an extremely common mistake, and the programmer ends up manipulating a completely different, and probably undefined, data structure. Since Perl creates new data structures silently, the programmer may have significant trouble tracking down the error.

10.2.4. Encoding for Arbitrary Data Structures

When dealing with nested data structures in Perl, it is often useful to be able to encode those structures in a portable format that can be written to secondary storage for later use by the same or some other application. For example, shopping cart contents for CGI-based Web commerce applications could be stored between CGI invocations in such a fashion, or long running programs could write out intermediate results and be shut down to resume later from a given checkpoint.

Previous examples demonstrate how to statically compose nested data structures such as

```
$ref = [['a', 'b', 'c'], ['1', '2', '3']];
```

If it were possible to take `$ref` and somehow generate the corresponding string

```
"[['a', 'b', 'c'], ['1', '2', '3']]"
```

then this string could later be used to create another reference with the help of Perl's `eval()` operator:

```
$new_ref = eval("[['a', 'b', 'c'], ['1', '2', '3']]");
```

`$ref` and `$new_ref` would point to copies of the same data structure.

There is a straightforward recursive mechanism for doing precisely this encoding:

```
sub encode_ref {
    my($ref) = @_;
    my($string, $type, $elt, $key, $safe_key);

    $string = undef;
    $type = ref($ref);

    if ($type eq 'ARRAY') {
        $string = '[';
        foreach $elt (@$ref) {
            $string .= encode_ref($elt);
            $string .= ',';
        }
        $string .= ']';
    }
    elsif ($type eq 'HASH') {
        $string = '{';
        foreach $key (keys(%$ref)) {
            ($safe_key = $key) =~ s/(\W)/\\$1/g;
            $string .= '"' . $safe_key . '"=>';
            $string .= encode_ref($$ref{$key});
            $string .= ',';
        }
        $string .= '}';
    }
    elsif (!$type) {        # it's a plain scalar
        $ref =~ s/(\W)/\\$1/g;
        $string = '"' . $ref . '"';
    }
    else { die "Can't encode object of type $type\n"; }

    return($string);
}
```

Note the use of the built-in `ref()` operator, which gives the type of the object pointed to by a given reference or returns `null` if `$ref` is in fact just a scalar.

Note also the careful treatment of all scalars (including hash keys) to avoid problems when encoding strings like this:

```
this" is a problem
so is this\
and $this one
```

Rather than list all the possible dangerous characters, the function simply puts a backslash in front of every non-alphanumeric character.

10.3. Data Structures and Databases

Perl provides a mechanism for linking associative arrays to the typical hashed-file databases provided with UNIX and UNIX-like systems—DBM, NDBM, and even the Free Software Foundation's GDBM and the Berkeley DB file formats. For non-UNIX systems, Perl provides its own portable (albeit fairly slow) SDBM file format. Usage for any of these file types is essentially equivalent; examples in this section use NDBM files. See the Perl language documentation for specific information about other file types.

10.3.1. Manipulating NDBM Files

To manipulate the elements of an NDBM file through a Perl hash, it is first necessary to set up the linkage between the two:

```
use Fcntl;
use NDBM_File;

tie(%some_hash, NDBM_File, 'myNDBMfile', O_RDWR|O_CREAT, 0644) ||
        die "Unable to open NDBM file: $!\n";
```

The first two lines cause Perl to load library modules that support the arguments used in the `tie()` function. The `Fcntl` module contains the `O_RDWR` and `O_CREAT` constants, as well as other useful objects. The `NDBM_File` module contains constants and methods used to operate on the NDBM file itself.

The `tie()` function binds a variable to an object class—in this case, `%some_hash` to an NDBM file (and, yes, Perl has full-blown object-oriented semantics that are not discussed here). The remaining arguments to `tie()` are object specific. The first of these arguments is the root name of the NDBM file; `myNDBMfile.dir` and `myNDBMfile.pag` are actually created on disk. The next argument specifies that the database should be opened for reading and writing (as opposed to `O_RDONLY`) and the database files should be created if they don't already exist. The last argument is the mode, or access-rights, the files should be created with, if applicable.

`%some_hash` may now be manipulated as if it were any other associative array, with the exception that modifying, adding, or removing elements from `%some_hash` has the effect of modifying the NDBM file on disk:

```
$some_hash{'foo'}  = 'bar';     # create new NDBM element
$some_hash{'foo'} .= 'baz';     # NDBM file entry now 'barbaz'
delete($some_hash{'foo'});      # remove NDBM file entry
```

Note that when deleting elements from a hash tied to an NDBM or other database file, the deleted element is not returned as when dealing with normal hashes. Use `defined()` to check for success after `delete()`:

```
if (defined($some_hash{'foo'})) {
    die "delete() failed!\n";
}
```

Note that only simple scalars (not references) may be stored in UNIX file databases. Use the `encode_ref()` function presented in section 10.2.4 to store complex data structures in these databases.

It is almost never a good idea to do the following:

```
foreach $elt (keys(%some_hash)) {     # DANGER!
    ...
}
```

The size of the NDBM file is unknown and `keys()` may return an unacceptably large list. Better instead to use this:

```
while (($key, $value) = each(%some_hash)) {
    ...
}
```

The programmer must be careful *never* to add values to an associative array while iterating over it with `each()` or the program may terminate unexpectedly or produce erroneous output.

Finally, break the connection between a hash and an underlying NDBM file, which closes the NDBM file as a side effect:

```
untie(%some_hash);
```

10.3.2. Locking

Clearly any useful database application must consider a locking protocol. Unfortunately, for UNIX hashed-file databases, locking is only available at a per-file level, as opposed to per-record locks. Perl does not provide a built-in locking mechanism, but the following functions can be used as a simplified interface to `fcntl()`-style file locking:

```
use Fcntl;
use NDBM_File;

sub lock_file {
   my($file, $type) = @_;
   my($struct);

   open($file, ">> $file") || return(undef);
   $struct = pack("ssx32", $type, 0);
   return(fcntl($file, F_SETLKW, $struct));
}
```

```
sub unlock_file {
   my($file) = @_;
   my($struct, $status);

   $struct = pack("ssx32", F_UNLCK, 0);
   $status = fcntl($file, F_SETLKW, $struct);
   close($file);
   return($status);
}

lock_file('myNDBMfile', F_WRLCK) || die "Can't lock file: $!\n";
tie(%some_hash, NDBM_File, 'myNDBMfile', O_RDWR|O_CREAT, 0644) ||
        die "Unable to open NDBM file: $!\n";

# ... code here ...

untie(%some_hash);
unlock_file("myNDBMfile") || die "unlock failed: $!";
```

Note that `lock_file()` is actually creating and locking a file called `myNDBMfile`, rather than the actual `.dir` and `.pag` files that make up the NDBM database. By using a lock on a different file, the program avoids a race condition with two processes opening the same NDBM file and then attempting to modify the contents.

10.4. Transforming and Sorting Data

10.4.1. Data Transformations

It is often useful to invert a list into an associative array:

```
for (@list) {
    $hash{$_} += 1;
}
```

for this allows the programmer to quickly check whether an element is a member of a given list:

```
if ($hash{'something'}) {
    print "something's in there!\n";
}
else { print "we've got nothing\n"; }
```

Perl provides the `keys()` operator to extract the keys of an associative array into a list. One side effect of converting a list into a hash and then back again is that the new list contains the unique list of elements from the old list, albeit most likely in a different order:

```
for (@list) {
    $hash{$_} += 1;
}
@unique_elts = keys(%hash);
```

10.4.2. Sorting

Order is, of course, important. Perl provides a `sort()` function that returns a list in alphabetically sorted order:

```
@sorted_list = sort(@list);
foreach $key (sort(keys(%hash))) { ...
```

Alphabetical sorting is not always desired, so Perl allows the programmer to specify an arbitrary function for sorting the data:

```
sub numeric { $a <=> $b }
@sorted_list = sort numeric @list;
```

To improve performance, the normal argument-passing mechanism is suspended, so the programmer-defined function merely compares the variables `$a` and `$b` and must return less than zero, `0`, or greater than zero to indicate the relative order of these two elements. As the sort proceeds, various elements of the list are assigned and reassigned to `$a` and `$b`, which are passed by reference to the comparison subroutine; modifying either of these variables in the course of comparison has highly deleterious effects.

Note that the subroutine name may be replaced by a block, so the preceding example could be written more tersely as follows:

```
@sorted_list = sort { $a <=> $b } @list;
```

By the way, the preceding example is an ascending numeric ordering. Descending order can be achieved with this:

```
@sorted_list = sort { $b <=> $a } @list;
```

but don't forget this:

```
@sorted_list = reverse(sort { $a <=> $b } @list);
```

"There's more than one way to do it!" is the motto for Perl programmers, although it makes theoretical computer scientists throw up their hands in disgust.

Aside from concessions to the special nature of `$a` and `$b`, the code in the sort function may be as complex as desired. For example, the idiom for sorting the keys of a hash by the numeric value associated with each key is

```
foreach $key (sort { $hash{$b} <=> $hash{$a} } keys(%hash)) { ...
```

Perhaps the sort should be performed on the numeric value associated with the key and then alphabetically on the key itself as a secondary criterion:

```
foreach $key (sort { $hash{$b} <=> $hash{$a} ||
                     $a cmp $b               } keys(%hash) { ...
```

The || operator is a short-circuit operator in Perl as in many other languages, and its value is the value of the first comparison that evaluates to true. Thus, `$a` and `$b` are compared if and only if the values `$hash{$a}` and `$hash{$b}` are equal.

It is often worthwhile to preprocess data for complicated sorts. For example, a list of IP addresses could be sorted as follows:

```
sub IPsort {
    @a_octs = split(/\./, $a);
    @b_octs = split(/\./, $b);
    $a_octs[0] <=> $b_octs[0] || $a_octs[1] <=> $b_octs[1] ||
        $a_octs[2] <=> $b_octs[2] || $a_octs[3] <=> $b_octs[3];
}

@sorted = sort IPsort @iaddrs;
```

Because each element of `@iaddrs` may be passed to the sort routine several times (and therefore `split()` several times, etc.), it is easier to split all the elements first and convert the octets to a format that can be more readily compared:

```
for (@iaddrs) {
    $string{$_} = sprintf("%d%03d%03d%03d", split(/\./));
}

@sorted = sort { $string{$a} cmp $string{$b} } @iaddrs;
```

This latter version runs several times faster than the first.

10.5. Regular Expressions

Aside from coercion and manipulation of various types of data, one of Perl's other strengths is its powerful and flexible regular expression engine. Perl's regular expression syntax uses the syntax of the UNIX `egrep(1)` and `awk(1)` utilities as a basis and then extends these concepts with several powerful and subtle additional features.

10.5.1. Backreferences

As mentioned in section 10.1.1, Perl's pattern-match operator, in a list context, returns a list of all the subexpressions in a given regular expression:

```
$_ = 'Mon Dec  1 17:43:13 PST 1997';
($hour, $min, $sec) = /(\d+):(\d+):(\d+)/;
```

Note that nested subexpressions are returned in order by leftmost parenthesis, as shown in the following example:

```
$_ = 'Mon Dec  1 17:43:13 PST 1997';
($time, $hour, $min, $sec) = /((\d+):(\d+):(\d+))/;
```

At the end of the preceding example, the value of `$time` is `17:43:13`.

Subexpressions are available within a pattern match as well. Perl instantiates the special variables `\1`, `\2`, and so on with whatever was matched by a given subexpression. For example, the following matches a single or double quote followed by zero or more characters followed by another quote, which is the same as the quote matched in the first subexpression:

```
/(["']).*\1/          # beware greedy pattern match!
```

It turns out that Perl's greedy pattern-matching behavior (discussed in section 10.5.2) makes the preceding pattern match incorrect for most uses.

Outside of a pattern match, subexpressions are available in the special variables `$1`, `$2`, and so on. The initial example in this section could have been written

```
$_ = 'Mon Dec  1 17:43:13 PST 1997';
if (/(\d+):(\d+):(\d+)/) {
     $hour = $1;
     $min = $2;
     $sec = $3;
}
```

In the `encode_ref()` function from section 10.2.4, these special variables are used in the context of the substitution operator:

```
$ref =~ s/(\W)/\\$1/g;
```

Note that `$1`, `$2`, and so on are automatically locally scoped to exist only to the end of the enclosing block or the next pattern match. Obtain the values from these variables as quickly as possible after the pattern match occurs, or simply assign the results of the pattern match to a list as done earlier—or run the risk of these values becoming lost.

It is sometimes useful to be able to use parentheses as a grouping operator without creating backreferences. Placing `?:` immediately following the opening parenthesis prevents backreferencing:

```
($quote, $text, $unquote) = /(["'])((?:\\.|[^\\])*)(\1)/;
```

This code is simply a more complicated version of a regular expression seen earlier:

```
/(["']).*\1/
```

This newer, more complicated version handles strings containing backslash-escaped quotes, such as

```
"here is \" such a string"
```

The text that should be captured between the matching quotes is zero or more occurrences of either any backslashed character or any character that isn't a backslash on its own. The inner parentheses are needed to group around the `or` construct and for the `*` operator, but producing backreferences is not desired.

10.5.2. Greedy and Minimal Matching

As mentioned previously, Perl uses a greedy pattern-matching algorithm; that is, Perl's regular expression engine attempts to match as much of the string as possible. This is often useful:

```
$_ = '/usr/local/bin/perl';
($dir, $prog) = /^(.*)/(.*)$/;        # $dir is /usr/local/bin
```

Sometimes, however, this behavior yields unexpected results:

```
$_ = "hello, world" "hello, mom";
($quote, $text) = /(["'])(.*)\1/;     # $text is 'hello...mom'
```

In the first example, Perl matches the `/` character as far right in the string as possible. Because `$prog` should be the last component of the path and `$dir` the rest, this is exactly what is desired. In the second example, however, what is probably desired is to match only the first quoted expression, `"hello, world"`. However, Perl is constrained to match only a leading quote and a matching trailing quote with anything in between and therefore grabs as much of `$_` as possible, or `'hello, world" "hello, mom'`, and returns it into `$text`.

One common idiom for thwarting greedy matching is

```
($quote, $text) = /(["'])([^\1]*)\1/;
```

In other words, match a quote followed by zero or more occurrences of any character except that quote and then the matching quote.

However, this idiom doesn't work when the closing delimiter is longer than a single character. A recent addition to the Perl regular expression syntax is the `?` modifier to the `*` and `+` operators, which specifies minimal matching behavior instead of maximal matching behavior. The previous example could be rewritten as

```
($quote, $text) = /(["'])(.*?)\1/;     # same as previous
```

10.5.3. Other Regular Expression Tricks

A previous example demonstrated the special `?:` operator, which causes parentheses used for grouping not to produce backreferences. Perl provides several other special operators that may be embedded in regular expressions in a similar fashion.

Perl provides zero-width positive (`?=...`) and negative (`?!...`) look-ahead markers. Here is an example:

```
($word) = /(\w+(?=\s+))/;
```

matches one or more alphanumeric characters that are followed by whitespace, without making the whitespace part of `$word`. The canonical example of negative look-ahead assertions is

```
/\Z(?!\n)/
```

The `\Z` and `$` operators match the end of line mark but match before any trailing `\n`. The preceding expression causes `\Z` to match only at the true end of string after any trailing newlines have been exhausted.

Pattern-match modifiers that normally appear after the trailing `/`, as in

```
if (/case insensitive/i) { ...
```

may be embedded in regular expressions as

```
if (/(?i)case insensitive/) { ...
```

This is particularly useful in cases such as

```
$pattern = '(?i)case insensitive';

# ... some code here ...

if (/$pattern/) { ...
```

All these complex operators tend to make it possible to write complex regular expressions that are difficult for the human reader to parse and understand. Even the fairly simple quoted string example

```
($quote, $text, $unquote) = /(["'])((?:\\.|[^\1\\])*)(\1)/;
```

tends to become visual noise to the experienced Perl programmer. Perl provides the `x` modifier for the pattern match, which causes the Perl parser to ignore whitespace and comments embedded in a regular expression. Therefore, the preceding example may instead be written

```
($quote, $text, $unquote) = / (["'])              # a quote
                              ((?:\\.|[^\1\\])*)  # (backslash
                                                  # anything or
                                                  # not quote)*
                              \1                  # the matching quote
                              /x;                 # extended format
```

which, if not more readable, is at least self-documenting.

Finally, Perl provides the special `e` modifier for the substitution operator, `s///`. This causes the RHS of the substitution to be evaluated as executable Perl code, similar to being run by `eval()`. For example, the following code is used by millions of CGI programs every day:

```
$val =~ s/\+/ /g;
$val =~ s/%(\w\w)/sprintf("%c", hex($1))/eg;
```

This decodes data from form submissions from gibberish that looks like the following:

```
%22e+%3d+mc**2%22%2c+he+said.
```

The result is readable strings such as

```
"e = mc**2", he said.
```

Reversing this process to achieve the original gibberish is left to you as an exercise.

10.6. Network Programming

One area in which Perl surpasses other scripting languages is in its surprisingly rich and remarkably straightforward interprocess communications facilities, particularly in the area of Internet domain socket communication. Syntax is borrowed heavily from the UNIX/C Berkeley socket code but optimized for brevity and comprehensibility as shown in the following sections.

10.6.1. TCP Clients

Following is a simple function to get a page from a remote Web server and return the lines of the page in a list:

```
use Socket;

sub get_url {
    my($url) = @_;
    my($hostname, $path, $port, $proto, $addr, $saddr, @lines);

    ($hostname, $port, $path) =
        $url =~ /^http:\/\/([^\/:]+):?(\d*)(.*)$/;
    $port = $port || 80;

    $proto = getprotobyname('tcp') or die "getprotobyname(): $!\n";
    $addr  = gethostbyname($hostname)
                                    or die "gethostbyname(): $!\n";
    $saddr = sockaddr_in($port, $addr);
```

```
        socket(SOCK, PF_INET, SOCK_STREAM, $proto)
                                    or die "socket(): $!\n";
        connect(SOCK, $saddr)       or die "connect(): $!\n";
        select(SOCK); $| = 1; select(STDOUT);    # nonblocking

        print SOCK "GET $path\n";
        @lines = <SOCK>;
        close(SOCK);
        return(@lines);
    }
```

It's worth noting here why this code segment is so much more terse and readily readable than the corresponding C version. Obviously, Perl's postfix conditionals help immensely here, along with the special `$!` variable (which C programmers know as `perror(3)`). Note also how simple it is to make a socket nonblocking in Perl: Simply select the socket to be the current output file handle and set the special variable `$|`.

Of particular interest in this example is the behavior of the `getprotobyname()` and `gethostbyname()` calls. In list context, these functions return a list of scalars matching the elements of the structure returned by the corresponding C function call. In scalar context, however, the functions have been optimized to return the single scalar object that is needed for the calls in the Berkeley socket interface functions.

10.6.2. TCP Servers

Here is a simple server process that listens on a port specified as the first (and only) argument to the program. When a connection is made, the server process spawns a child process that accepts input and echoes back the characters:

```
use Socket;
use Sys::Hostname;

$SIG{'CHLD'} = 'IGNORE';          # don't wait() for children

$proto = getprotobyname('tcp')     or die "getprotobyname(): $!\n";
$addr  = gethostbyname(hostname()) or die "gethostbyname(): $!\n";
$saddr = sockaddr_in($ARGV[0], $addr);

socket(SOCK, PF_INET, SOCK_STREAM, $proto)
                                   or die "socket(): $!\n";
setsockopt(SOCK, SOL_SOCKET, SO_REUSEADDR, 1)
                                   or die "setsockopt(): $!\n";
bind(SOCK, $saddr)                 or die "bind(): $!\n";
listen(SOCK, SOMAXCONN)            or die "listen(): $!\n";

for ( ;; ) {
    $remote = accept(NEWSOCK, SOCK) or die "accept(): $!\n";
    last unless (fork());
```

```
        # parent doesn't fall out of loop
        close(NEWSOCK);
        ($port, $raddr) = sockaddr_in($remote);
        $hostname = gethostbyaddr($raddr, AF_INET);
        $inet = join(".", unpack("C4", $raddr));
        print STDERR "Connect from $inet($hostname), port $port\n";
    }

    # child process down here
    select(NEWSOCK); $| = 1;
    while (<NEWSOCK>) {
        print;
    }
```

Notice that the `sockaddr_in()` function has two opposite behaviors, depending on context. In scalar context, the function returns what C programmers refer to as a `struct sockaddr` (as shown in the TCP client example in section 10.6.1). In list context, however, the function disassembles a `sockaddr` structure and returns the port and address components. The address is in network byte encoding, and the octets have to be pulled out using the cumbersome `join(..., unpack(...))` syntax shown. Perl is not very programmer efficient when it comes to dealing with binary data.

`%SIG` is a per-process special variable that hides the semantics of the `signal(3)` system call. Instead of using the keyword `IGNORE`, you can supply instead a function reference:

```
use Socket;
use Sys::Hostname;

sub reaper {
    $pid = wait();
    $SIG{'CHLD'} = \&reaper;
    print STDERR "reaped child $pid\n";
}

$SIG{'CHLD'} = \&reaper;
# ... rest of code per previous example ...
```

10.6.3. Asynchronous Communication

Aficionados of network programming in C may at this point be wondering what happened to the `select(2)` system call. The call is, in fact, implemented in Perl and confusingly enough is also called `select()` despite the existence of a completely unrelated function with the same name.

One item that will be appreciated by C programmers is that Perl's assignment operator allows one to write

```
($found, $time_left) =
select($rout = $rin, $wout = $win, $eout = $ein, $timeout);
```

That is, the `$*out` variables first get assigned by their `$*in` counterparts and then get overwritten by `select()`, leaving the `$*in` variables untouched.

One item that will not be appreciated by C programmers is the lack of an `fhbits()` equivalent for constructing the `$*in` variables in the first place. The following code may be used for this purpose:

```
sub fhbits {
    my(@files) = @_;
    my($bitvec);

    foreach $filehandle (@files) {
        vec($bitvec, fileno($filehandle), 1) = 1;
    }
    return($bitvec);
}
```

This example once again demonstrates that Perl does not deal with binary data in anything like a graceful fashion.

Note that the `timeout` value in Perl's `select()` function is a floating-point value expressing seconds and fractional seconds. One may write

```
select(undef, undef, undef, 0.5);
```

to `sleep()` for finer granularities than 1 second. To have `select()` wait indefinitely write

```
$found = select($rout = $rin, $wout = $win, $eout = $ein, undef);
```

10.7. Formats

Highly developed interprocess communications APIs aside, Perl is first and foremost a text processing and manipulation language. One of the earliest sets of primatives in the Perl language includes those dealing with outputting tabular formatted data.

10.7.1. Basic Formatting

Here's a simple program that reads financial transactions from a tab-delimited file and prints them in tabular format with a running balance:

```
format top =
Chk No Date  Transaction           Amount      Balance
====== ====  ===========           ======      =======
.

format STDOUT =
@<<<<< @<<<< @<<<<<<<<<<<<<<<<<<< $@######.## $@######.##
$code, $date, $description,        $amount,    $balance
.

$balance = 0;
while (<>) {
     chop();
     ($code, $date, $description, $amount) = split(/\t/);
     $balance -= $amount;
     write;
}
```

`format` statements can be thought of as "pictures" of how the data will be formatted. The special `top` format is a header printed at the top of each page. (The number of lines per page is stored in the special variable `$=` and defaults to `60` but can be changed by assigning a different value to `$=`.) Each file handle may also have a format assigned to it—in this case, the program emits output on the STDOUT—which describes how each line of output should look. Fields that are to be replaced by a value are indicated with `@` markers followed by special characters indicating the length of left-adjusted character fields (`<`), right-adjusted fields (`>`), centered fields (`|`), or numeric fields with an optional decimal specifier (`#`), which are always right adjusted. All other characters (e.g., the `$` before the numeric fields) are literals. Following any format line containing an `@` specifier, there must be a line containing a comma-separated list of variables corresponding to the various replacement fields. `format` statements are terminated with a period on a line by itself. `format` statements may appear anywhere within a program.

The `write` statement is used to produce a line of formatted output as described by the format named after the appropriate file descriptor (the preceding example uses the implicit STDOUT). Programmers should take care never to mix `write` and `print` or `printf` statements, or the output of the program becomes garbled.

10.7.2. Special Variables and Dirty Tricks

As mentioned previously, the `$=` variable contains the number of lines per page of formatted output. This variable is specific to the currently selected file handle, so programmers are warned to be careful to use `select()` before modifying this variable when writing to file handles other than STDOUT. The special variable `$-` holds the current number of lines left on the page; the top of form can be forced by setting `$-` to `0`. `$%` is the current page number. An alternate header format name (instead of the default top) may be specified by setting `$^` to the name of the alternate format. Similarly, an alternate body format for a given file handle may be specified by setting `$~`.

Note that there is no special footer format. A somewhat kludgy solution can be created by watching the value of `$-`:

```
format first_header =
Transactions as of: @<<<<<<<<<<<<<<<<<<<<<<<<<<<<<<<<
                    $stamp


Chk No Date  Transaction            Amount       Balance
====== ====  ===========            ======       =======
.

format later_headers =
Chk No Date  Transaction            Amount       Balance
====== ====  ===========            ======       =======
.

format footer =
                             Page @##
                                  $%

.

format STDOUT =
@<<<<< @<<<< @<<<<<<<<<<<<<<<<<<<< $@######.## $@######.##
$code, $date, $description,        $amount,     $balance
.

$^ = 'first_header';
$stamp = localtime();

$balance = 0;
while (<>) {
     chop();
     ($code, $date, $description, $amount) = split(/\t/);
     $balance -= $amount;
     write;
```

```
        if ($- == 2) {
            $~ = 'footer';
            write;
            $~ = 'STDOUT';
            $^ = 'later_headers';
        }
}
```

Note the use of `$%` in the footer format, as well as the use of a different header format for the first page than for subsequent pages.

10.7.3. Lengthy Texts

Sometimes, a given string is too long to fit on a single line. Use the format field specifier `^` instead of `@` to produce wrapped text:

```
format message =
Date: @<<<<<<<<<<<<<<<<<<<<<<<  ^<<<<<<<<<<<<<<<<<<<<<<<<<<<<<<<<<<<<<<<
      $date,                    $body
From: @<<<<<<<<<<<<<<<<<<<<<<<  ^<<<<<<<<<<<<<<<<<<<<<<<<<<<<<<<<<<<<<<<
      $from,                    $body
To  : @<<<<<<<<<<<<<<<<<<<<<<<  ^<<<<<<<<<<<<<<<<<<<<<<<<<<<<<<<<<<<<<<<
      $to,                      $body
Subj: ^<<<<<<<<<<<<<<<<<<<<<<<  ^<<<<<<<<<<<<<<<<<<<<<<<<<<<<<<<<<<<<<<<
      $subject,                 $body
~~    ^<<<<<<<<<<<<<<<<<<<<<<<  ^<<<<<<<<<<<<<<<<<<<<<<<<<<<<<<<<<<<<<<<
      $subject,                 $body
.
```

Assuming appropriate values for the variables in the preceding format, the output might look like:

```
Date: Mon,  1 Dec 1997 14:49:57   Hal: We're still waiting for that
From: peter@pedant.com (Peter Sa  Perl chapter you promised us last
To  : hal@deer-run.com (Hal Pome  year. Don't make us call Msrs
Subj: your submission for the     Vinny, Vinny, and Vinny to come
      programming languages       and explain the situation to you.
      series                      We can assure you that you wouldn't
                                  enjoy it in the least. Your humble
                                  editor, Peter.
```

`^` fields consume characters from the given string until the string is exhausted (outputting blank lines if the string ends before the corresponding `^` field specifiers). The `~~` construct forces the format to keep outputting lines until all strings are exhausted.

CHAPTER 11

Python: An Object-Oriented Scripting Language

by Mark Lutz

This chapter introduces the Python programming and scripting language. As we'll see, Python is an exciting object-oriented language that is freely available on the Internet. Because it combines integration tools with a simple but powerful language, Python is useful in a wide variety of development roles and application domains. In fact, Python's target domains range from simple system utility scripts to advanced applications such as numerical programming and animation.

11.1. About This Chapter

Before we jump into details, here are a few words about this chapter's scope. Although Python is a comparatively simple language, we can't really do it justice in a single chapter. Instead, our goal here is to get a general feel for what Python is and take a first look at the language itself. More specifically, this chapter is composed of five parts:

- *Overview*: We'll start out with a high-level look at the language and its roles.
- *Tutorial*: Next, we'll move on to a more technical introduction to the language itself.
- *Integration*: We'll also discuss basic Python and C integration concepts and strategies.
- *Samples*: After that, we'll explore a collection of larger Python program examples.
- *Resources*: Finally, we'll wrap up with a look at popular Python packages and resources.

Beyond this chapter are a variety of Python information resources that can fill in details we'll finesse here. For instance, there are currently three Python books (with more on the way), online manuals and tutorials, and a vigorous Python support group on the Internet (see the references near the end). At the risk of being immodest, much of the material here parallels my book *Programming Python* from O'Reilly. Most of the topics in this chapter are covered in greater detail in the book.

11.1.1. About the Examples

Python is a dynamic, interactive language, and working along with the examples here can be a great way to learn the language. To fetch the latest release of Python, see the sources listed at the end of the chapter. Python is available in both binary and source-code form from online sites as well as the CD-ROMs accompanying Python books. Source code for the examples in this chapter will be made available online at my Web page: Point your browser to `http://rmi.net/~lutz`.

Most of the examples we'll see here are portable to all platforms Python runs on. Python is available for most major platforms (including UNIX, Microsoft Windows, and the Macintosh). Although the language itself is extremely portable, each target platform offers nonportable extensions that we'll try to avoid. Along the way, I'll point out platform-specific details as they arise. For reference, the examples here were tested on both Windows 95 and UNIX machines under Python Version 1.4 (and should work with later releases as well).

11.2. General Python Overview

If you're like most developers, one of the first questions you may ask when you hear about a new programming language or tool is what can I use it for? After all, programming languages are tools; although they can be interesting to study in isolation, their real utility lies in the context of applications.

Because of that, our first goal here is to address Python's roles and purpose. In this section, we'll briefly define Python, explore its history, peek at its best features, and look at how it's commonly used by real software developers. Some of this section is a very high-level overview, and you'll have to take it on faith until we see the language in action later. Naturally, technical language details matter too, and we'll get to them soon. But let's first address the why before we get around to the how.

11.2.1. What Is Python?

Because Python is a general-purpose language, arriving at a single all-encompassing definition isn't an easy task. What Python is depends much on how it is used. To some, Python serves as a programmable front end to libraries coded in a compiled language such as C or C++. For others, it takes the form of an embedded scripting language for customizing larger systems. Moreover, many programmers use Python as a stand-alone language, leveraging its library of precoded system interfaces. In terms of basic functionality, Python can be described in a variety of ways:

- *An object-oriented scripting language*—As we'll see, Python is a fundamentally object-oriented language. Its class system supports modern object-oriented development paradigms and makes Python ideal for use in object-oriented systems. Perhaps more importantly for a scripting language, Python's object model is surprisingly easy to use, yet it supports advanced object-oriented concepts such as operator overloading, multiple inheritance, and more.

- *A stand-alone rapid development tool*—Python provides both a conceptually simple language and rapid development-cycle turnaround. It is specifically optimized to support speed of development. In fact, many programmers find Python development to be orders of magnitude faster than other approaches. By combining development speed with integration tools, Python fosters radically faster development modes.

- *A next-generation extension language*—Like many scripting languages, Python programs can be both extended with modules coded in a compiled language such as C and can be embedded in a C program. Unlike many scripting tools, Python provides both integration with external components and a powerful object-oriented language. Because of this combination of utility, Python can address a wide range of problem domains.

- *A freely available, interpreted language*—By most definitions, Python is an interpreted language. More accurately, Python code is compiled to portable byte code that is run by a virtual machine. This scheme provides both fast turnaround after program changes and reasonable execution speed. Finally, Python is true freeware: Its source code is freely available, and it may be embedded in products without copyright constraints or fees.

Python can be classified as both a VHLL (very high-level language) and an OODL (object-oriented dynamic language). Although this puts Python in the same general category as languages such as Smalltalk and Eiffel, we'll see that Python has a unique flavor all its own. For instance, Python has a very practical orientation: Unlike some OO languages, Python was created by and for engineers interested in solving day-to-day programming tasks.

11.2.2. Some Quotable Quotes

Don't take my word for it: Some of the comments that have been made by Python programmers on the Internet speak volumes about the language's design. Although personal reactions vary, the following quotes are representative of the level of enthusiasm Python typically generates in newcomers:

- "Python looks like it was designed, not accumulated."—As we'll see, Python sports a refreshingly coherent design. Python's creator carefully balanced the need to support practical programming needs with the desire to avoid feature glut and complexity. The result is a simple language that scales well to support larger systems. Moreover, Python has a remarkably clear syntax: For many, its inherent readability makes it ideal for programs that may be reused or maintained by others.

- "Python bridges the gap between scripting languages and C."—As we'll also see, Python's design and implementation place it somewhere between compiled languages such as C and traditional scripting languages such as csh, Awk, and Perl. Python's syntax resembles languages like C (e.g., there are no $ variable prefixes), but its high-level programming tools and lack of compile and link steps are familiar to users of other scripting languages. In some sense, Python provides the best of both worlds: It supports scripting and embedding but doesn't ask programmers to abandon normal standards of development quality.

- "Python is the BASIC of the '90s."—Although Python is certainly being applied in real companies and products, many current Python users fall into the hobbyist category: They use Python because they want to, not because they have to. In fact, Python's popularity is largely due to a strong grass-roots following among engineers, similar in spirit to the support BASIC enjoyed in the early days of the PC revolution. Naturally, Python isn't a new-and-improved BASIC (it incorporates advanced programming tools such as exceptions, modules, and classes), but it generates similar excitement.

- "Python is as easy or as powerful as you want it to be."—Python programs can range in complexity from simple five-line scripts to complex object-oriented frameworks. Program complexity can be scaled for both the programmer's skill level and the problem at hand. For instance, Python supports OOP but does not impose it: Classes are an optional language tool. Programmers (not language designers) decide whether OOP, and other advanced Python tools, are warranted for each task.
- "Python: less filling, tastes great."—This quote will probably be more meaningful if you're familiar with American beer advertisements, but it underscores one of the central concepts in Python. If you've used other compiled, strongly typed languages such as C or C++, you'll find that Python eliminates much of the complexity inherent in traditional tools. In fact, some have called Python "executable pseudocode": Because of their simplicity, Python programs can more closely reflect the problems they are designed to solve.

Of course, some of these quotes will make more sense after we examine the language in more detail. For instance, some of Python's simplicity stems from its high-level built-in object types (lists, dictionaries, etc.) and the absence of type and size declarations in Python (objects are created dynamically and reclaimed automatically when no longer used). We'll expand on some of Python's technical features in a moment.

A More Formal Definition?: The following quote was seen on Python's Usenet newsgroup, `comp.lang.python`. Although perhaps more colorful than some, it's another reflection of the zeal common to many Python programmers:

> python, (Gr. Myth. An enormous serpent that lurked in the cave of Mount Parnassus and was slain by Apollo.) 1. any of a genus of large, nonpoisonous snakes of Asia, Africa, and Australia that crush their prey to death. 2. popularly, any large snake that crushes its prey. 3. totally awesome, bitchin' language invented by that rad computer geek Guido van Rossum that will someday crush the `$s` out of certain *other* so-called VHLLs.

11.2.3. A Python History Lesson

Python was created by Guido van Rossum in Amsterdam around 1990. Before Python, Guido worked on the ABC programming language and the Amoeba distributed operating system, and both of these influenced Python's design. For instance, Python was originally conceived as a scripting language for the Amoeba system, and it inherits ABC's usability study-inspired syntax features. But Python adds practical features to ABC, such as a C-like nature and integration with external C components. As we'll see later, Python borrows features from a variety of languages, including Modula, C, Icon, C++, and others.

Despite the proliferation of snake icons on book covers, Python is named after the BBC comedy series *Monty Python's Flying Circus*. According to Python folklore, Guido viewed various Monty Python videos at the same time he was busy inventing a new object-oriented language; the association naturally arose. This legacy tends to foster a generally humorous (and occasionally irreverent) flavor to the Python community. For instance, the standard labels `foo` and `bar` become `spam` and `eggs` in Python examples, and quotes from Monty Python skits pervade the Python culture (and documents such as this).

Python was first offered to the public domain in 1991, and a Usenet newsgroup devoted to Python first appeared in 1994 (`comp.lang.python`). Python now enjoys a growing international user community with a strong following in the United States, Europe, Japan, and Australia. To help manage some of its growth, a non-profit support organization has been established: the Python Software Activity (PSA). The PSA maintains Python's Internet sites and helps organize Python conferences. At this writing, the PSA is hosted by the Corporation for National Research Initiatives (CNRI), which also pays Guido's salary.

11.2.4. What Is Python Good For?

As you might expect, Python's general-purpose nature makes it applicable to more domains than we can list here. As a sampling, here's a quick look at some of the most common things people are using Python for today:

- *System utilities (shell tools)*—Python's standard interfaces to operating system tools make it ideal for writing portable system utilities. Among other things, Python supports UNIX tools such as sockets, regular expressions, and POSIX bindings. On Windows, Python also interfaces with COM, OLE, and more.

- *Graphical user interfaces*—Python's high-level nature and rapid turnaround are well-suited to GUI development. It comes with an object-oriented interface to the Tk GUI library, MFC, X11, and more. The Tk interface runs on X Windows, Windows, and the Macintosh, making it a portable GUI solution.

- *Internet scripting*—Python also comes with a full suite of Internet tools. It has support for CGI scripts, Web-browser applets, Web agents and crawlers, HTML generation, and more. Precoded library modules support most Internet protocols: FTP, URLs, HTTP, e-mail, and so on. On Windows systems, Python can also be used in conjunction with ActiveX scripting and Active Server Pages.
- *Database programming*—Object persistence is a standard part of Python: Programmers can save entire Python objects to a persistent store and retrieve them later. Moreover, Python offers interfaces to more traditional database systems, such as Oracle, Informix, Sybase, mSql, PostGres, ODBC, and others.
- *Component integration*—Because Python can be integrated with components written in compiled languages such as C and C++, many use Python as a glue language to control or extend application components. Wrapping libraries in a high-level language like Python makes them easier to use. Embedding Python in a C/C++ program opens up the system to customization without recompilation.
- *Rapid application development*—To Python programs, components written in Python and C look the same. This allows developers to implement in Python first and later move selected components to a compiled language such as C. This development mode is often called prototype-and-migrate: When used well, it can leverage both the development speed of Python and the performance advantages of C.
- *More specific domains*—Python is also being used in more specific application areas, such as numeric programming, artificial intelligence, image processing, distributed object systems (e.g., CORBA), and more. Although these are interesting applications, many are really instances of the component integration potential of Python. For example, Python numeric programming is implemented as compiled-language libraries integrated into Python for ease of use.

11.2.5. What Is Python Not Good For?

Naturally, no language can be optimized for every development need. Like most interpreted languages, Python sacrifices some performance in order to maximize development speed. Because of that, Python is not the ideal tool for implementation of time-critical components. For instance, compute-intensive image processing libraries are probably best coded in a compiled language such as C, C++, or Fortran.

Even in performance-critical domains, we can make use of Python's development speed. By implementing compute-intensive components in a compiled language and exporting them to Python, we get a system that's both easy to use and efficient. The numeric programming example mentioned previously is a perfect example of this approach to development.

Python is optimized for speed-of-development and designed for multiple-language systems: By adding it to the mix, we can make use of a rapid development language for our system interface and infrastructure while simultaneously achieving performance goals. Moreover, Python can be used to prototype demanding systems before investing the extra time needed to code critical components in C.

11.2.6. The Compulsory Features List

Another way to understand Python is by listing its major features. Table 11.1 summarizes some of the things people seem to like best about the language. It's by no means complete, and we'll fill in details on most of the table's entries later in this chapter. The point to notice here is that Python combines a wide variety of features in a single, relatively simple language. For many, the end result is a remarkably expressive and responsive language that can actually be fun to use.

TABLE 11.1. *Major Python features.*

Features	*Benefits*
No compile or link steps	Rapid development-cycle turnaround
No type declarations	Programs are simpler, shorter, and flexible
Automatic memory management	Garbage collection avoids bookkeeping code
High-level data types and operations	Fast development using built-in object types
Object-oriented programming	Code structuring and reuse, C++ integration
Extending and embedding in C	Optimization, customization, system glue
Classes, modules, exceptions	Modular programming-in-the-large support
A simple, clear syntax and design	Readability, maintainability, ease of learning
Dynamic loading of C modules	Simplified extensions, smaller binary files

Features	*Benefits*
Dynamic reloading of Python modules	Programs can be modified without stopping
Universal first-class object model	Fewer restrictions and special-case rules
Interactive, dynamic nature	Incremental testing and development
Parser/compiler present at runtime	End-user coding, programs can build programs
Access to interpreter information	Metaprogramming, introspective objects
Wide portability	Cross-platform systems without ports
Compilation to portable byte code	Execution speed, protecting source code
Built-in interfaces to external services	O/S, GUI, persistence, DBMS, regular expressions...
True freeware	May be embedded and shipped without copyright restrictions

Note that most of Python's features aren't new by themselves: It's really how Python combines features that make it what it is. For many, it seems to be the right mix of programming language concepts.

11.2.7. Python in the "Real World"

Naturally, Python is more than a collection of features. It has become a tool of choice for real programmers in real companies around the world. To get a feel for how companies apply Python for real development tasks, here's a sampling of some of the larger organizations in Python's current user base. This list is necessarily incomplete; check Python's Web site (described at the end of the chapter) for up-to-date information about other companies applying Python:

- *Surfing made easy (Infoseek, Four11)*—Many major Internet-related companies use Python in a variety of roles. For instance, Infoseek was an early adopter of Python in its Web-search systems.
- *Cockroaches and Pepsi jingles (Blue Sky animation)*—If you've seen the movie *Joe's Apartment*, you've seen Python at work: Python has been successfully applied as a scripting language for creating commercial-grade animation.

- *Blowing up the energizer bunny (the Alice VR system)*—The University of Virginia uses Python as the scripting interface for its virtual reality system, Alice. One Alice demo features the Energizer Bunny (along with methods to make it explode).
- *Rocket science (Lawrence Livermore Labs, NASA)*—Lawrence Livermore labs uses Python in numerical programming applications and sponsored a recent Python conference. Python is also applied at NASA in a number of ways.
- *Linux install tools (Red Hat)*—Anytime you install the Red Hat Linux system, you're using Python: portions of Red Hat's installation system are written in Python.
- *Distributed object systems (ILU, Hector)*—ILU and Hector both make use of Python in distributed object programming systems. ILU, from Xerox, is a CORBA-based system that provides bindings to Python's object model.
- *Finding the Grail, intelligent agents (CNRI)*—Besides Python, Guido van Rossum also created an extensible Internet and Web browser called (appropriately enough) Grail. It's written in Python and allows Python programs to define applets executed in the client (browser), much like Java. We'll take a look at Grail later in this chapter. CNRI also uses Python in research on intelligent agents for the Internet.

11.2.8. Apples and Oranges and Bananas and Coconuts

Finally, Python is often compared to other free (and not so free) languages, especially on Internet forums. Although language choice is often a matter of style, a brief comparison to similar tools can help point out some of Python's primary distinctions and some of the main reasons people choose to use it. Table 11.2 summarizes some of the most common arguments of Python proponents.

TABLE 11.2. *Python versus similar tools.*

Tool	*Python Advantage*	*Description*
Tcl	Power	Python is not just a string processor. It is a full-blown language with support for modules, OOP, exceptions, and more.

Tool	*Python Advantage*	*Description*
Perl	Coherence	Many find Python's syntax more readable and maintainable. Some also find Python to be less magical: fewer special variables, and so on.
Java	Simplicity, turn-around, freeware	Python's built-in objects, dynamic typing, and other features make it much simpler. Moreover, Python can be freely shipped with products.
C++	Simplicity, turnaround	Because Python is interpreted, it provides much faster turnaround. Further, Python avoids most of the complexity inherent in C++.
Smalltalk	Conventionality	In Python, `if` statements are not message-receiver objects: Python has a more conventional programming model.
Scheme	Conventionality	Python's syntax is closer to traditional languages such as C and Pascal. This can be especially important for end-user coding scenarios.

Naturally, your mileage may vary. Some of these distinctions reflect different design goals. For instance, Perl is optimized for text processing, C++ and Java are generally considered to be systems languages (not scripting tools), and Tcl is targeted more toward simple glue tasks than larger systems development.

It's also important to notice that programmers matter too: Although Python is deliberately designed to prevent unreadable code, there's nothing stopping us from writing it if we try. Moreover, having many languages to choose from can only be a good thing. In fact, support for multiple-language systems is one of the central concepts in Python: No language can satisfy all our needs at once.

Although I hope the next sections underscore some of Python's technical advantages, it's more important that programmers be empowered to pick and choose the best language for each task at hand. Python is a great language to have in your development toolbox, but it should not be the only one.

11.3. A First Look at the Language

So far we've been concerned with generalities. In this section, we're going to jump into a more technical introduction to Python. We'll first explore Python's arsenal of built-in object types and then move on to Python's basic statements and program structuring tools. Along the way, we'll also investigate Python's solutions to common object-oriented goals such as inheritance and composition. As a preview, here are the main topics we'll be studying in this section:

- Running Python programs
- Built-in object types
- Python statements
- Program structure
- Python's OOP model
- Python's first-class object model
- Built-in system interfaces

This section is roughly a Python tutorial. To illustrate basic concepts, most of the examples we'll see here are small and deliberately artificial and will be demonstrated at Python's interactive command prompt. Although this is a good way to introduce the language, it's not entirely representative of real Python development. We'll study more realistically scaled programs in a later section.

11.3.1. How to Run Python Programs

Before we jump into language specifics, let's first explore ways to run Python code. This section will help you get set up to work along with the examples. Python is available in both source-code form (which you compile locally) and in binary executable form (which runs out of the box). If you don't have access to a Python interpreter, consult the resources listed at the end of the chapter. If you're new to installation procedures, try seeking out a local administrator or other guru; Python books and manuals provide additional details.

11.3.1.1. Environment Variables

Assuming you have Python installed, you'll probably need to configure your environment for your local directory structure. On UNIX (and UNIX-like) systems, Python uses the shell environment variable `PYTHONPATH` as its module (source file) search path; you'll want to make sure PYTHONPATH includes all the directories that contain programs you want to load and run. In addition, to use the Tkinter GUI extension, which we'll meet later, you usually need to set Tcl-specific variables.

11.3.1.2. A Sample Startup Script

Listing 11.1 shows a simple csh script for UNIX that illustrates most configuration details.

LISTING 11.1. ***file:*** runpy.

```
#!/bin/csh
# Give this file executable privileges (chmod +x runpy).

# 1) Add path to command-line interpreter
set path = (/usr/local/bin $path)

# 2) Set python library search paths
# add your module file working directories to the list as desired
setenv PYTHONPATH\
.:/usr/local/lib/python1.4:/usr/local/lib/python1.4/tkinter

# 3) Set tk library search paths (for GUIs)
setenv TCL_LIBRARY /usr/local/lib/tcl7.4
setenv TK_LIBRARY  /usr/local/lib/tk4.0

# 4) Start up the interactive command-line
python
```

Note that this is for illustration purposes only; most users would probably put these settings in their system startup files (e.g., .cshrc, .kshrc) so they're always available, rather than run this script every time they run Python. Moreover, some of the settings may not be needed; if Python (and Tcl/Tk) is installed in the standard places, the standard library directories may be hard-coded in the executables, so you'd only need to add directories holding components you develop.

11.3.1.3. Program Execution Modes

If you tailor and run the preceding script, you'll find yourself at Python's interactive command line, where you can type Python statements and expressions. For instance, here's how we might start Python from a system shell and create a simple GUI interactively (more on GUI details later):

```
% runpy
Python 1.4 (Mar  6 1997)  [GCC 2.7.2]
Copyright 1991-1995 Stichting Mathematisch Centrum, Amsterdam
>>> from Tkinter import *
>>> w = Button(text="Hello", command='exit')
>>> w.pack()
>>> w.mainloop()
```

If you're set up correctly, and your version of Python supports the Tkinter GUI extension, you should get a simple one-button window on your screen after typing the preceding code. In all the examples in this chapter, commands typed at the system shell will be preceded by a `%` (e.g., `% runpy`). When we start Python, it prints a prompt when it expects you to type Python code: a `>>>` for normal code or a `...` for continuation lines when you're typing compound statements. Note that interactive listings are shown in boldface.

Python's interactive command line is a convenient place to experiment with the system and test program components. There are actually four ways to run Python code, and we'll use all of them in this chapter. Here's a brief summary of all four modes:

- *UNIX scripts*—On UNIX-like systems, a Python code file can be executed directly from the system shell, if it starts with a special comment line containing the path to the Python interpreter and the file is made executable. As we'll see later, it may access command-line arguments and environment settings. Listing 11.2 shows an example.

LISTING 11.2. *file:* `brian.py`.

```
#!/usr/local/bin/python
print 'The Bright Side of Life...'        # or "#!/usr/bin/env python"

% brian.py
```

- *Module files*—Python source files (modules) can also be executed by passing their names to the `python` executable directly on a shell command line. This mode works much like UNIX scripts (command-line arguments are passed to Python) but is a convenient way to start program files on platforms that don't support the `#!` line convention. Python module file names normally have a `.py` suffix; as we'll see in a moment, modules can also be run by importing them from another module:

```
% python spam.py -i eggs -o bacon
```

- *Interactive command line*—We saw this mode in a previous example: When we type `python` without any arguments, the interactive command line is started. From there, we can import modules, test built-in tools, start a debugging session, and so on. Python prints expression results in interactive mode:

```
% python
>>> print 'Hello world!'
Hello world!
>>> lumberjack = "okay"
```

- *Embedded code/objects*—Finally, Python code can also be run by another language. In this mode, the Python code can take the form of strings or objects and is run by calling functions exported by the Python runtime API. For instance, the following C example sketches how to run a Python assignment statement string from C. This is called embedding Python, a topic we'll explore later in this chapter. As we'll see, Python code can also be embedded in other Python programs; the Python parser and compiler are always available in any system that uses Python, whether it's coded in Python or C:

```
#include <Python.h>

main()
{
     Py_Initialize();
     PyRun_SimpleString("x = brave + sir + robin");
}
```

11.3.1.4. Platform-Specific Startup Details

Depending on which port you install, startup and configuration details may differ between UNIX, Windows, and Macintosh platforms. Programs might be started from a system command line or be launched by clicking on GUI devices. For instance, the PythonWin port for Windows provides a rich GUI environment, but other Windows ports provide just a simple command-line interface. Unfortunately, we can't cover many platform-specific details here; if you're using Python on a non-UNIX platform, see your port's documentation for more details.

11.3.2. Built-In Object Types

Now that we have a feel for how to launch Python programs, let's dig into some basic details about the language itself. In general, Python programs are composed of *modules*, which contain *statements* that create and process *objects*. From a bottom-up perspective, objects are the most fundamental building block, so we'll start our language exploration with this topic.

In terms of functionality, Python falls somewhere between languages like Lisp (that rely heavily on built-in tools) and languages like C++ (which rely on frameworks of user-supplied extensions). Python provides both powerful built-in objects and tools, as well as statements and APIs for adding new ones. When needed, Python lets us write arbitrarily sophisticated object-oriented frameworks.

For simple programs, Python's rich set of built-in tools is usually sufficient. Because common data types and tools are a standard part of the language, simple programs are fast to write in Python. Moreover, Python's built-in types usually serve as the fundamental components of user-defined extensions. Because built-in types use optimized implementations in Python, they are often more efficient than custom data structures or algorithms. Table 11.3 summarizes the basic built-in object types available in Python.

TABLE 11.3. *Basic built-in object types.*

Object Type	*Examples of Constants/Usage*
Numbers	`3.1415, 1234, 999L, 3+4j`
Strings	`'spam', "guido's"`
Lists	`[1, [2, 'three'], 4]`
Dictionaries	`{'food':'spam', 'taste':'yum'}`
Tuples	`(1,'spam', 4, 'U')`
Files	`text = open('temp', 'r').read()`

Let's look at each of Python's basic object types in more detail.

11.3.2.1. Numbers

As you might expect, Python provides the standard numeric object types found in most programming languages: integer, floating-point, and a variety ways to write number constants. In addition, Python provides a long integer type with unlimited precision, a set of built-in mathematical functions (e.g., `pow`, `abs`), and utility modules (e.g., `rand`, `math`). Beginning in Python 1.4, there is also support for complex numbers (syntax and libraries). Although it's not a standard part of the language, the Numeric Python extension turns Python into a high-performance numerical programming tool, with a matrix object, interfaces to numeric libraries, and more. Table 11.4 summarizes Python's standard numeric types.

TABLE 11.4. *Numeric constants.*

Constant	*Interpretation*
`1234, -24`	Normal integers (C longs)
`99999999L`	Long integers (unlimited size)
`1.23, 3.14e-10`	Floating-point (C doubles)
`0177, 0x9ff`	Octal and hex constants
`3+4j, 3.0+4.0j`	Complex number constants

If you're familiar with other programming languages, most of Python's numeric objects should seem straightforward. Python uses normal algebraic characters to build up expressions: + for addition, * for multiplication, and so on. In fact, Python provides most of C's familiar numeric operators: << shifts an integer's bits left, & performs a bitwise and operation, and so on. In mixed-type expressions, types are converted up just as in C (adding an integer and a floating-point number produces a floating-point result), and parentheses can be used to group subexpressions as desired.

Let's type a few expressions at the interactive command line to demonstrate basic number operations. First, we start the command line, assign variables to integers, and type a few basic expressions:

```
% python
>>> a = 3
>>> b = 4
>>> b / 2 + a
5
>>> b / (2.0 + a)
0.8
```

Here, things typed interactively follow the >>> prompt, and Python output appears on lines without the prompt. In Python, variables (and all other names) are created when we assign values (objects) to them, so we can create variables on-the-fly at the command line. Assignment usually happens when we use = statements as shown here, but some statements we'll see later assign to names too (imports, class and function definitions, etc.). When we type an expression at the interactive prompt, Python evaluates it and echoes the result back to the screen; statements have no result so there's no output from the interpreter.

Notice how the first expression produced an integer result (4 / 2 + 3 = 5); in Python, / is evaluated before +, just as in C. The second expression yields a floating-point result because we use 2.0 (a float) instead of 2 (an integer); mixed-type expressions always cast up to the more complex object type. We also used parentheses to change the order of evaluation, hence the result (4 / (2.0 + 3) = 0.8). As in C, Python integers can be treated like bit-strings too, but it's not as common in Python (because Python is a higher-level language, bit-twiddling isn't always as useful):

```
>>> x = 1
>>> x << 2
4
>>> x | 2
3
>>> x & 1
1
```

Finally, Python's long integer object type lets us use arbitrarily large integers; their size is limited only by the amount of memory in your machine. To get a long integer, we just suffix an integer constant with an `L`:

```
>>> 9999999999999999999999999999 + 1
OverflowError: integer literal too large
>>> 9999999999999999999999999999L + 1
10000000000000000000000000000L
```

Naturally, long integers incur some performance penalties, so normal integers are usually the more efficient choice. In general, Python integers and floats corresponding to C longs and doubles, in terms of efficiency and size.

> ***Operator Overloading: A Preview:*** As we'll see later, all of Python's numeric operators can be applied both to built-in numbers and to extensions coded in either Python or C that provide the proper numeric type protocols. In fact, we'll see later that extensions can overload most operations in the language: This includes the numeric operators here, as well as the operations applied to other data types later in this section. This will make more sense when we introduce classes and C types later; for now, as we look at the rest of Python's built-in object set, keep in mind that the operators we'll see are somewhat more general than the examples here suggest.

11.3.2.2. Strings

Naturally, using Python as a command-line calculator probably isn't the best role for an object-oriented programming language. Although Python numbers come in handy for many tasks, Python's compound data types are usually more useful. The simplest compound type in Python is the character string; in Python, strings are collections of characters, or more accurately, collections of one-character strings (there is no distinct character type in Python).

Python provides a variety of ways to write strings (single, double, or triple enclosing quotes), a set of operators for processing strings (`+` to concatenate, `[i]` to index, etc.), and a collection of utility modules for common string-processing tasks. For instance, the `string` library module provides functions similar to the standard C library, and the `regex` module supports regular expression parsing. Table 11.5 illustrates common string constants and operations.

TABLE 11.5. *Common string operations.*

Operation	*Interpretation*
`s1 = ''`	Empty strings
`s2 = "spam's"`	Double quotes
`block = """..."""`	Triple-quoted blocks
`s1 + s2, s2 * 3`	Concatenate, repeat
`s2[i], s2[i:j], len(s2)`	Index, slice, length
`"a %s parrot" % 'dead'`	String formatting
`for x in s2, 'm' in s2`	Iteration, membership

Strings take the form of a sequence of characters enclosed in quotes. Single and double enclosing quotes work the same; as line two in the table demonstrates, supporting both allows for embedding a quote in a string, without using backslash escape characters (e.g., '\"'). Triple quotes support blocks of text: The enclosed string can span multiple lines. The operators in the table are probably best illustrated with a few interactive examples. Let's start up the command-line prompt again:

```
% python
>>> 'abc' + 'def'
'abcdef'
>>> 'Ni!' * 4              # like "Ni!" + "Ni!" + ...
'Ni!Ni!Ni!Ni!'
```

Here, we first type a concatenation expression: The + operator returns a new string with its two operands joined. The * operator is much like concatenating a string with + multiple times: It returns a new string object that contains its left operand repeated the number of times specified by its right operand. Notice the operator overloading implied here already: + and * work on both numbers (add, multiply) and strings (concatenate, repeat). In fact, we'll see that all the string operators here can really be used on any ordered-sequence object type (lists, user-coded extensions, etc.):

```
>>> S = 'spam'
>>> S[0], S[-2]
('s', 'a')
>>> S[1:3], S[1:], S[:-1]
('pa', 'pam', 'spa')
```

Because strings are ordered collections, we can index individual characters by their offsets: In the second line of the preceding code, we fetch the item at the front with `S[0]` (at offset zero from the left). Python also lets us fetch items using offsets from the end: If an index is negative, it's taken to be the offset from the right. For instance, `S[-2]` fetches the second item from the end; Python adds the length of the string to the negative index to yield the referenced item's offset. For instance, `S[-2]` is the same as `S[len(S)-2]`, where `len(S)` returns the length of `S` (here, `4`). The net result is that the expression fetches the item at offset 2 from the left.

The third line illustrates slicing in Python. For any ordered collection, such as strings, an expression of the form `S[x:y]` extracts a contiguous section of the sequence, starting at offset `x` and continuing up to (but not including) the item at offset `y`. When the `x` and `y` limits are omitted, they default to zero and the length of the object:

- `S[1:3]` refers to all items from offset 1 through offset 2 (extract the second and third items).
- `S[1:]` is the same as `S[1:4]` (extract all items past the first).
- `S[:-1]` is the same as `S[0:-1]` or `S[0:(4-1)]` (extracts all items up to the last).

As we'll see in other examples, slicing turns out to be a powerful and general tool. Like concatenation and repetition, indexing and slicing both create new strings as their results, instead of changing the operand strings in place. In fact, strings can never be changed in-place (items cannot be appended, indexed items cannot be reassigned, and so on); to get a new string value, we need to create a new string, by applying string operator expressions and assignments:

```
>>> S = S + 'Spam!'
>>> S
'spamSpam!'
>>> 'That is %d %s bird!' % (1, 'dead')
That is 1 dead bird!
```

In the first line here, we extend `S` by concatenating and assigning, thereby creating a new string; if any other names were assigned to `S`'s prior value (`spam`), the concatenation here won't change their value out from under them. In Python nomenclature, we say that strings are *immutable*: They cannot be changed in-place. This allows for some interpreter optimizations and provides some integrity in our programs.

The third line demonstrates another powerful string operation: The `%` operator allows us to format strings much like the C library's `sprintf` function. Python replaces `%X` markers in the left operand with the string representations of objects in the right operand formatted according to the `%X` markers on the left. For instance, a `%d` marker converts an integer to a string, and %s specifies a string object conversion. The % operator supports all the usual C string formatting conventions, and like other string operations, returns a new string as its result.

11.3.2.3. Lists

Besides strings, Python provides a set of compound object types that are much more general. Lists are one of the most general. In Python, lists are ordered collections of objects, enclosed in square brackets. Items in a list are accessed by indexing with a numeric offset, much like C arrays; in fact, Python lists are essentially just arrays of object references.

Lists can contain any number of other objects, including numbers, strings, user-defined objects, and even other lists (to support arbitrary nesting). Moreover, lists can be changed in-place. They support some of the same operators as strings (e.g., + concatenates two lists, [x:y] extracts slices of lists) and provide additional operations for changing items in-place (e.g., L[x:y]=x). Finally, list objects also provide methods for list-specific processing: appending items, sorting lists in-place, and so on. Table 11.6 illustrates typical list operations and constants.

TABLE 11.6. *Common list operations.*

Operation	*Interpretation*
`L1 = []`	An empty list
`L2 = [0, 1, 2, 3]`	Four items: indexes 0..3
`['abc', ['def', 'ghi']]`	Nested sublists
`L2[i], L2[i:j], len(L2)`	Index, slice, length
`L1 + L2, L2 * 3`	Concatenate, repeat
`L1.sort(), L2.append(4)`	Methods: sort, grow
`del L2[k], L2[i:j] = []`	Shrinking
`L2[i:j] = [1,2,3]`	Slice assignment
`range(4), xrange(0, 4)`	Make integer lists
`for x in L2, 3 in L2`	Iteration, membership

This table is representative but not complete; lists support more methods and operations than we can cover here (see the resources at the end of the chapter for more details), but the table entries are typical. Notice that many of the entries are the same operations we just studied for strings. Lists also respond to indexing, slicing, concatenation, and repetition; these operations work the same on both strings and lists, but when applied to lists, the result is a new list object. An interactive example will illustrate:

```
% python
>>> [1, 2, 3] + [4, 5, 6]
[1, 2, 3, 4, 5, 6]
>>> ['Ni!'] * 4
['Ni!', 'Ni!', 'Ni!', 'Ni!']
```

Here, we first concatenate two lists; the result is a new list containing all the items in both. This is exactly like string concatenation, but lists contain any kind of object (not just one-character strings). As the second line shows, repetition (*) adds a list to itself, just as for strings. Indexing and slicing work the same too:

```
>>> L = ['spam', 'Spam', 'SPAM!']
>>> L[2]
'SPAM!'
>>> L[1:]
['Spam', 'SPAM!']
```

Here, we create a list of three strings and index and slice it. More generally, ordered sequence objects all respond to ordered sequence operations with similar results. This applies both to built-in objects as well as objects we code ourselves in Python or C. We'll return to this concept later. Unlike strings, lists also provide operations that change their contents in-place:

```
>>> L[1] = 'eggs'
>>> L
['spam', 'eggs', 'SPAM!']
>>> L[0:2] = ['eat', 'more']
>>> L
['eat', 'more', 'SPAM!']
>>> L.append('please')
>>> L
['eat', 'more', 'SPAM!', 'please']
```

In this interaction, we

- Assign to an existing index (replacing the object stored there with the new item)
- Assign to a slice (replacing all the objects in the slice with the new sequence)
- Call the list `append` method (inserting a new item on the end)

In general, lists can change, grow, and shrink on demand. We say that lists are mutable: We can change them without making a new copy. That makes them efficient for some kinds of processing but also open to side effects: If we change a list in-place, it changes the list for every name that is assigned to it. Sometimes that's what we want, but we need to be aware of the potential for list changes in larger programs (more on this later).

In practice, lists are one of the main tools used in Python programming; they're typically used anytime we need an ordered collection of objects. They're also commonly used in conjunction with Python's sequence iteration loop, the `for` statement; we'll explore statements in more detail later, but here's a preview:

```
>>> for x in L: print x,
...
eat more SPAM! please
```

In general, the `for` loop iterator also works on strings and every other ordered sequence object in Python.

11.3.2.4. Dictionaries

Lists are useful anytime we need to represent an ordered sequence collection, where an offset is sufficient for object retrieval. In many cases, we need more flexible retrieval mechanisms; Python's dictionary object addresses this role. In Python, dictionaries are collections of objects that are stored and retrieved by key, rather than by offset. In classical data-structure terms, dictionaries are essentially built-in hash tables (and in fact are implemented as such internally).

Syntactically, dictionaries take the form of *`key:value`* pairs, enclosed in curly braces. Items are indexed much like lists (`x[k]`), but the index takes the form of an arbitrary key object, not an integer offset. Keys in dictionaries can be any object that can yield a unique and unchanging identifier; string keys are common, but keys can also be any built-in or user-defined object whose value doesn't change (for instance, keys may be instances of classes and C types that implement hashing protocols). Table 11.7 introduces dictionaries.

TABLE 11.7. *Common dictionary operations.*

Operation	*Interpretation*
`d1 = {}`	Empty dictionary
`d2 = {'spam': 2, 'ham': 1, 'eggs': 3}`	Three items
`d3 = {'pork': {'ham': 1, 'brats': 2}}`	Nesting
`d2['eggs'], d3['pork']['ham']`	Indexing by key
`d2.has_key('eggs'), d2.keys()`	Methods
`len(d1)`	Length (entries)
`d2[key] = new, del d2[key]`	Changing

Once again, let's turn to a few interactive examples to demonstrate typical dictionary operations:

```
% python
>>> d2 = {'spam': 2, 'ham': 1, 'eggs': 3}
>>> d2['spam']
2
>>> len(d2)
3
>>> d2.keys()
['eggs', 'spam', 'ham']
```

In simple usage, we can write dictionary constants, index them, fetch their length (`len`), and retrieve a list containing the keys of all stored items. Like lists, dictionaries provide a set of methods (e.g., `d2.keys()`) for dictionary-specific operations.

Notice that indexing (in the second line) uses the same syntax we've been applying to strings and lists: `object[index]`, but for dictionaries the item in the brackets is a key, not an offset. There's no notion of order among the items stored in a dictionary; in fact, Python randomizes the order in which items are stored to provide optimized retrieval. Because of that, offsets don't make sense when using dictionaries. Here are a few more dictionary operations in action:

```
>>> d2['ham'] = ['grill', 'bake', 'fry']
>>> d2
{'eggs': 3, 'spam': 2, 'ham': ['grill', 'bake', 'fry']}
>>> del d2['eggs']
>>> d2
{'spam': 2, 'ham': ['grill', 'bake', 'fry']}
```

In this code, we make use of key assignment and deletion to change a dictionary in-place. Like lists, we can change a dictionary directly, without having to make an altered copy. In fact, we can add new entries to dictionaries by assigning to new keys; assigning to an out-of-bound index in a list raises an error.

Finally, here's a more realistic example of dictionaries in action: They're useful any time we want to associate information with a symbolic key. In the following, we make a three-item table of programming language creators, indexed by language name:

```
>>> table = {'Perl':    'Larry Wall',
...          'Tcl':     'John Ousterhout',
...          'Python':  'Guido van Rossum' }
...
>>> language  = 'Python'
>>> creator   = table[language]
>>> creator
'Guido van Rossum'
```

```
>>> for lang in table.keys(): print lang,
...
Tcl Python Perl
```

We're nesting simple strings here, but in practice, the value stored under each key might be a complex collection itself or a user-defined object. Python compound object types support arbitrary nesting.

Before we move on, there's something important to underscore here: Although dictionaries can be changed in-place (they're mutable), they don't support the sequence operations we applied to strings and lists. Because dictionaries are unordered collections, there's no notion of slicing (extracting sections), concatenation (an ordered joining), and so on. For instance, in the preceding example, we can use the `for` statement to iterate through a dictionary's keys list but can't iterate over the dictionary directly.

Technically, dictionaries are called mutable *mappings* in Python; they support key-based operations, instead of order-based operations. However, because mappings and sequences are both collections, they both respond to the `O[x]` indexing syntax (the index is an integer for sequences but any object for mappings), and both support the `len` built-in function (in both cases, it returns the number of items stored in a collection object).

11.3.2.5. Tuples

Like lists, tuples are another ordered collection object type in Python. They take the form of a sequence of objects (values) separated by commas and enclosed in parentheses. Tuples respond to most of the same operations as lists: `+` to concatenate, `[x:y]` to slice, and so on. Unlike lists, tuples cannot be changed in place: To alter a tuple, we need to make a new tuple object (a copy). In other words, tuples are immutable sequence objects.

Tuples may seem redundant given the Python list, but their immutability provides some degree of integrity because we can be sure a tuple won't be changed by another part of a program. Also unlike lists, tuples don't have any associated methods (because most methods change lists in-place). As we'll see later, some built-in operations use tuples too; for instance, function argument lists can be constructed dynamically at runtime as a tuple of values. Table 11.8 illustrates some commonly used tuple operations.

TABLE 11.8. *Common tuple operations.*

Operation	*Interpretation*
`()`	An empty tuple
`t1 = (0,)`	A one-item tuple
`t2 = (0, 1, 2, 3)`	A four-item tuple
`t2 = 0, 1, 2, 3`	Another four-item tuple
`t3 = ('abc', ('def', 'ghi'))`	Nested tuples
`t1[i], t1[i:j], len(t1)`	Index, slice, length
`t1 + t2, t2 * 3`	Concatenate, repeat
`for x in t2, 3 in t2`	Iteration, membership

Most of these are just the standard sequence operations we've already seen in action on strings and lists, so we won't demonstrate anything new here. Notice the fourth entry in this table: Where not syntactically ambiguous, tuples can be written without enclosing parentheses. Because of that convention, single-item tuples require a unique syntax, as shown in table entry two: a single item with a trailing parenthesis. Without this syntax, there would be no way to make a one-item tuple distinct from a normal expression.

11.3.2.6. Files

In Python, basic files are supported by the built-in `open` function: It creates a link to the operating system's file system and returns a file object, which exports methods that support common file processing tasks. Table 11.9 summarizes common file methods.

TABLE 11.9. *Common file operations.*

Operation	*Interpretation*
`output = open("/tmp/spam", 'w')`	Create output file
`input = open('data', 'r')`	Create input file
`input.read(), input.read(1)`	Read file, byte (return a string)
`input.readline(), input.readlines()`	Read line, lines list
`output.write(S), output.writelines(L)`	Write string, lines list
`output.close()`	Manual close (or when freed)

C programmers might notice that Python files created by the `open` function are really just a thin interface to C's `stdio` file system. Besides the `open` function shown here, Python also has built-in support for descriptor based files, DBM keyed files, persistent objects, and more. We'll see some of these later.

Unlike the types we've seen so far, there is no special syntax for file objects. Instead, the `open` function generates and returns an object. As we'll see later, this is exactly how extensions we code work too: We call classes to make instance objects and call C module functions to generate C type instance objects. The only difference here is that file objects are a standard type, built in to the language.

Files export methods (like lists and dictionaries) but don't respond to any operators; they're not really sequences or mappings. But extensions we write can respond to the operators we've seen earlier; in fact, Python strings, lists, dictionaries, and tuples are really just precoded C extension types with special object syntax. Anything that can be done with built-in types can be done with classes and C types that we code ourselves.

> ***Python Memory Management:*** Python uses a reference-count garbage collector scheme to reclaim objects once they are no longer needed by a program (i.e., not referenced from variables, data structures, or system components). The `close` method at the end of Table 11.9 can be used to manually close files. Because Python automatically closes files for you when they are garbage collected, `close` is usually optional except in special cases (e.g., to reopen an output file in the same process that creates it or to terminate a pipe connection).

11.3.2.7. And Everything Else

Because everything in Python is a Python object, our exploration of built-in types here is necessarily incomplete. Python's built-in type set includes the objects mentioned previously as well as larger language units and interpreter components, such as

- Functions
- Modules
- Methods
- Classes
- Byte-compiled code
- Stack tracebacks
- Type objects: `type(X)`
- The null object: `None`

In fact, everything is an object in Python—even object types themselves. The built-in `type(X)` function returns the `X` object's `type` object. This is a programming language feature usually called a *first-class* object model. We can assign variables and data structures to any sort of object we like without having to declare object types ahead of time. We'll explore some of the benefits of this generality later in this chapter.

Figure 11.1 shows how Python's built-in (intrinsic) types are related. Functions, methods, instances, and modules may all be implemented in Python or a C-compatible language. Internally, only functions have a distinct type for C implementations; bound methods *reference* a function, and as we'll see later, C extension modules and types really use the same mechanisms as Python built-in types.

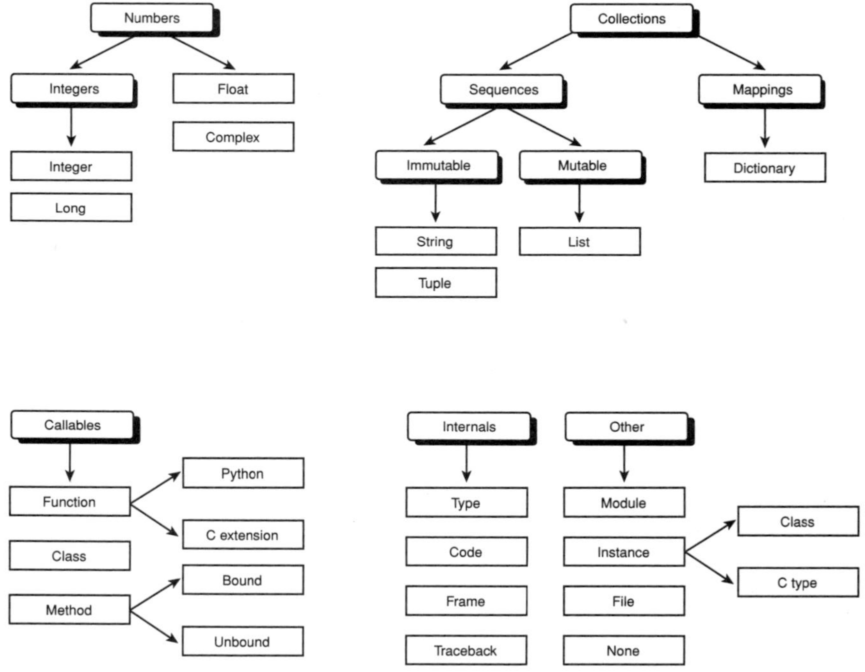

FIGURE 11.1. *Python type hierarchies.*

11.3.2.8. General Object Properties

Now that we've seen the basic built-in types, let's summarize some of their common properties:

- *Operation categories*. As we've seen, Python object types are generally classified as numeric (numbers), sequence (ordered collections), or mapping (keyed collections) and may be mutable (changeable in-place) or not. Objects share generic operation sets according to type categories (Table 11.10). As we'll see later, this applies both to built-in types, as well as types we implement as Python classes or C extensions.

TABLE 11.10. *Built-in type categories.*

Object Type	*Category*	*Mutable?*
Numbers	Numeric	No
Strings	Sequence	No
Lists	Sequence	Yes
Dictionaries	Mapping	Yes
Tuples	Sequence	No
Files	Extension	n/a

- *Generality.* Strictly speaking, Python lists, dictionaries, and tuples are both heterogeneous (can store any object type) and arbitrarily nestable (can store nested collections). Moreover, mutable types (lists and dictionaries) can be dynamically resized. Here's an example of the sort of nesting that built-in types support. Given the assignment

```
L = ['abc', [(1,2), ([3], 4)], 5]
```

  Python generates a tree of nested objects and assigns it as an object to name `L`. `L` embeds strings, sublists, numbers, and tuples. To access nested components, we string index operations. For instance, the integer `4` is accessed by `L[1][1][1]`.

- *Shared references.* One final note before we move on: We've made a point of specifying which object types are mutable and which aren't for a good reason. In Python, assignments always create references to objects: A variable is just a named reference to an existing object, and data structure slots are unnamed object references. Because of these semantics, assignments can sometimes generate shared references to the same object; changing one reference will change it for every reference:

```
>>> X = [1, 2, 3]
>>> L = ['a', X, 'b']
>>> D = {'x':X, 'y':2}
>>> X[1] = 'surprise'
>>> L
['a', [1, 'surprise', 3], 'b']
>>> D
{'x': [1, 'surprise', 3], 'y': 2}
```

  Here, there are three references to the shared list `X` (from `X`, nested in `L`, and nested in `D`). Changing one updates all three. Normally, this is exactly what we want; references make it possible to pass large data structures around a program without generating multiple copies. But we need to be aware of Python's reference-based assignment model when we change possibly shared mutable objects.

11.3.3. Statements and Programming

At the next level of complexity, Python programs are composed of statements, which create and process objects. In this section, we'll introduce Python statements: both basic imperative statements and statements used to construct larger program units. Because statements lead us to bigger programming concepts, let's first introduce some general Python development topics we'll explore along the way.

11.3.3.1. Python Syntax Concepts

If you're accustomed to languages like C and Pascal, there are two unique aspects of Python program syntax that will probably stand out immediately:

- *There are no braces or semicolons in Python.* Python detects the end of a nested code block using the indentation level of its statements, rather than `{}` or `begin/end` tokens. Moreover, statements usually end at the end of a line, so there's no need to terminate or separate them with a `;` (although continuation lines are supported). In effect, block and statement boundaries are detected automatically in Python. This policy avoids some programming problems (the classic "dangling `else`" problem goes away) and provides a sort of standardization for program layout. In fact, Python has been called the "what you see is what you get" of languages: As we'll see, its indentation-based syntax enhances readability.

- *There are no variable/type declarations in Python.* The other big surprise for many experienced programmers is the complete lack of type and size declarations in Python. In Python, variables (and object members) come into existence when assigned, without having to be predeclared. A name can be assigned to objects of many types: The type of the assigned object determines what a variable refers to, not static type declarations. This rule applies to everything that can be assigned in Python: simple variable names, data structure components, function arguments and return values, and so on need never be declared ahead of time and need never be limited to a particular data type. As we'll see, this adds flexibility to the language. For instance, a single implementation can often be applied to many kinds of objects.

11.3.3.2. Python Assignment Concepts

We'll look at the syntax for assignment statements later, but keep in mind that assignment actually comes into play in many contexts in Python: statements (`=`, `def`, `class`, `import`, `from`), function and method argument passing, `for` loop targets, and so on. Because assignment works the same everywhere it is applied, here are a few general notes on the meaning of Python assignments:

- *Assignments create object references.* In Python, assignment always creates a reference to an object. This holds true whether we're assigning an object to a simple variable name, assigning to a data structure component, passing function arguments, and so on. It's important to distinguish references from objects: Unlike some languages, Python assignment never copies the assigned value, and it's possible to generate multiple references to the same shared object.
- *Variables are created when first assigned but must exist when referenced.* As mentioned previously, names, object members, and some data-structure components come into existence the first time a program assigns a value to them. They don't need to be predeclared and may be assigned any type of object. Conversely, variables must have been already assigned when used in an expression. Python will raise an undefined name error if a program attempts to reference a variable that hasn't yet been assigned (rather than return some sort of default value). The rationale behind this policy is that it catches common coding errors, such as name misspellings.
- *Variables live in a name space.* We'll look at this in more detail in a moment, but as a preview, Python uses a simple lexical scoping rule to resolve names: Simple names are looked up by searching up to three scopes (local, global, built-in), and assignment to simple names always creates them in a local scope (unless they're declared global). For instance, variables assigned in a function are all local to that function call (and go away when the function exits), but names used in the function may also be global (in the enclosing module) or built-in (a Python-provided service). As we'll see, qualified name references (e.g., `object.name`) work differently: They create or look for an attribute in a specific object and might search multiple objects (when classes are used).

11.3.3.3. Python Programming Concepts

We won't have time to talk much about programming tools in this chapter, but here are a few odds and ends that you'll likely encounter very early in Python programming.

- *Program comments start with a* `#`. In Python programs, all the text starting with a `#` up to the end of the line is ignored (as long as the `#` isn't in a string constant). This provides a way to insert documentation into a program. The `#` can start anywhere on a line, even in column 1 to insert whole-line comments. Python also supports the notion of documentation strings: Roughly, a string constant at the start of a program unit (module, function, class) is associated with the object at runtime as its `_[hr]_doc_[hr]_` attribute. Documentation strings are essentially just comments that are available at runtime.
- *There are no compile/link steps in Python programming.* We'll expand on this when we study modules later, but in short, Python automatically compiles module files into portable byte code at runtime, when they are first imported. Because this compilation step is hidden, modules simply import other modules, without explicit compiles.
- *Debugger and profiler are imported modules.* Normally, Python responds to uncaught program errors by printing a message and stack trace. Python also provides a full debugger and profiler as standard library modules. They're both coded in Python (using interpreter hooks) and are used by importing and calling their exported functions. Python's debugger works much like standard C debuggers (e.g., `dbx`, `gdb`) but makes use of Python's dynamic nature. See other Python documentation sources for more details.

11.3.4. Simple Statements

Now let's move on to specific Python statements. The first set we'll see includes basic imperative statements for typical programming tasks: assigning names, calling functions, printing results, and selecting and repeating actions.

11.3.4.1. Assignment

We talked about assignment abstractly, but the `=` statement is its most concrete realization. In Python `=` statements, the target on the left is assigned a reference to the object on the right. If the target being assigned is a name that doesn't yet exist, the assignment creates it in the name space (scope) where the `=` statement appears.

Table 11.11 illustrates common variations of the `=` statement in Python: The second and third entries give the multiple assignment forms (targets on the left are paired with values on the right), and the last entry demonstrates the multiple target form (each target is assigned a reference to the rightmost object). Note that assignment is only a statement in Python (it can't be used as an expression as in C).

TABLE 11.11. *Assignment statement forms.*

Operation	*Interpretation*
`spam = 'SPAM'`	Basic form
`spam, ham = 'yum', 'YUM'`	Tuple assignment
`[spam, ham] = ['yum', 'YUM']`	List assignment
`spam = ham = 'lunch'`	Multiple-target

11.3.4.2. Expressions

Expressions are used as statements if they do something useful. The most common uses for expression statements are to call functions and methods that return no value (sometimes called procedures) and to print results at the interactive command-line prompt. Table 11.12 summarizes typical expression usage; note that boolean operators are typed out (`and` instead of C's `&&`), and comparisons may be strung together as a shorthand for range tests.

TABLE 11.12. *Common expression forms.*

Operation	*Interpretation*
`spam(eggs, ham)`	Function calls
`spam.ham(eggs)`	Method calls
`spam`	Interactive print
`spam < ham and ham != eggs`	Compound tests
`spam < ham < eggs`	Range tests

11.3.4.3. Printing Objects

The Python `print` statement is a convenient way to print an object's textual representation to the standard output stream (usually, to the screen where you started Python). Technically, `print` sends its text to the pre-opened `sys.stdout` file object: Programs can reset `sys.stdout` to a user-defined object that defines file methods (read, write, etc.) to intercept `print` statement text. Table 11.13 gives common print forms; note that adding a trailing comma suppresses the line feed normally inserted by print.

TABLE 11.13. `print` *statement forms.*

Operation	*Interpretation*
`print spam, ham`	Print objects to `sys.stdout`
`print spam, ham,`	Don't add line feed

11.3.4.4. `if` Selections

The `if` statement is Python's primary selection tool. Its form is typical of most programming languages: an `if` test, followed by one or more optional `elif` tests, followed by an optional `else`. Python executes the statements indented under the first test that evaluates to `true`, or the `else` block if all the tests evaluate to `false`. Here is a first example of `if` in its most complex form:

```
>>> x = 'killer rabbit'
>>> if x == 'bunny':
...     print 'hello little bunny'
... elif x == 'bugs':
...     print "what's up doc?"
... else:
...     print 'Run away!  Run away!...'
...
Run away!  Run away!...
```

Note that there is no `switch` or `case` statement in Python, but `if`/`elif` statements achieve the same effect. It's also possible to use dictionaries to perform multiway branching in Python: Indexing a dictionary is functionally equivalent to a `switch` statement, and a missing-key test is like a `switch` default clause:

```
>>> switch = { 'curly': 'good',
...            'moe':   'bad',
...            'larry': 'ugly'}            # like if/elif/elif/else
>>>
>>> if not switch.has_key('larry'):
...     print 'not found'
... else:
...     print switch['larry']
...
ugly
```

Truth, Equality, and Comparisons

The `if` introduces more general concepts we should say a few words about here. In Python, an expression's value is `true` if it evaluates to a nonzero number, or a non-empty data structure. For instance, `1`, `1.0`, `[1]`, and `spam` are all `true` values in Python. Conversely, `false` means zero, or an empty data-structure, so `0`, `0.0`, `[]`, `""`, and `None` are all considered `false`. The `if` example uses string equality as its tests: The `==` operator tests value equality as in C, but in Python, all comparisons are automatically applied recursively when data structures are compared, as deeply as needed to determine the comparison result. In the example, Python tests for equality of the string's characters, from left to right.

Compound Statement Syntax

The `if` statement is also the first compound statement we've seen. As mentioned earlier, Python associates nested statement blocks by noticing their indentation. For instance, all the statements indented with the same number of spaces or tabs under an `if` header line become the nested block of statements to be executed if the `if` test evaluates to `true`. If we have a simple statement, we can put it on the header line without indenting:

```
if x > y: print 'passed'
```

but complex bodies are indented under the header. In general, indentation can consist of any number of spaces or tabs as long as it's the same for all statements in a block. A program starts in column 1, and tabs count for enough spaces to move to the next column (a multiple of eight), but it's usually best not to mix spaces and tabs. As a rule of thumb, just indent your Python code as you'd do in any structured language such as C or Pascal, and the indentation rules take care of themselves.

11.3.4.5. `while` Loops

The `while` loop is Python's most general iteration tool. It works as you'd probably expect: The statements indented under the `while` header line are repeated until the test in the header line evaluates to `false`. For instance, an infinite loop in Python might look like this:

```
while 1:
    print 'Type Ctrl-C to stop me!'
```

The `while` loop's body isn't executed if the test is `false` initially. Python loops (`while` and `for`) can contain some special statements that only make sense in loops and work just as in C:

- The `break` statement jumps out of the closest enclosing loop.
- The `continue` statement jumps to the top of the closest enclosing loop.

In Python, loops can also have an associated `else` clause: When an `else` is indented at the same level as the `while` header line, the statements indented under the `else` are executed if the loop exited normally, that is, without running into a `break` statement. For instance, the following example uses `break` to exit a `while` loop when a factor is found. The loop `else` at the bottom is only run if the `break` isn't executed (i.e., when no factor was found). The loop `else` can often eliminate search result flag management:

```
x = y / 2
while x > 1:
    if y % x == 0:                          # remainder
        print y, 'has factor', x
        break                               # skip else
    x = x-1
else:                                       # normal exit
    print y, 'is prime'
```

11.3.4.6. `for` Loops

The Python `for` loop is a generic sequence iterator. It assigns a variable (or other target) to successive items in a collection and executes the statements indented under the `for` header for each item in turn:

```
>>> for x in ["spam", "eggs", "spam"]:
...     print x,
...
spam eggs spam
```

`for` can iterate over any sort of ordered collection object: lists (as shown here), strings, tuples, and instances of user-defined classes and C types that provide iteration protocol hooks (i.e., indexing operator overloading). Although `for` can be simulated with `while`, it automates index and counter management, so it is a much more convenient way to step though collections.

If we really need to code explicit counter/indexing loops in Python, we can do it with `for` too. The built-in `range` function generates a list of integers which we can iterate over with a `for`:

```
>>> range(5)
[0, 1, 2, 3, 4]
>>> for i in xrange(len(X)):
...     use X[i] here

>>> for i in range(4): print 'A shrubbery!'
...
A shrubbery!
A shrubbery!
A shrubbery!
A shrubbery!
```

`xrange` is like `range` but generates the list of integer indexes on demand, instead of all at once; it's useful when the range of values is very large.

11.3.5. Program Unit Statements

At the highest level of complexity, Python programs are composed of larger program-unit structures, which are created and managed by our last set of statements. Larger program units take a variety of forms:

- Functions: procedural units
- Modules: code/data packages
- Exceptions: errors and special cases
- Classes: new objects
- C modules: optimization, customization, integration

We'll look at statements used to manage the first four of these here; C modules look the same as Python modules, but we'll introduce them later in the chapter. In general, modules contain statements, which create and process objects. Some of the statements in this section generate objects for later use.

11.3.5.1. Functions

Perhaps the simplest program unit in Python is the function: a named block of statements that are executed by a call expression. As usual, functions allow us to code procedural components for later use and parameterize them by passed-in argument values.

In Python, functions are defined by the `def` statement. Unlike C, the Python `def` is an executable statement. It both creates a new function object and assigns that object to the function name used in the `def` header line. Typically, `def` statements appear at the top level of a program file to create functions used and exported by the file. But a `def` can actually appear anywhere a Python statement can (e.g., nested in another function); when executed, the new function object named by the header is created.

Let's look at a simple example of `def` at work. In the following, we define a function assigned to the name `intersect`:

```
def intersect(seq1, seq2):
    res = []                    # start empty
    for x in seq1:              # scan seq1
        if x in seq2:           # common item?
            res.append(x)       # add to end
    return res
```

This function accepts two arguments: When the function is called, `seq1` and `seq2` are assigned to the objects passed by the caller. Statements indented under the `def` header line are the function body; they are executed each time the function is called.

The function `intersect` returns a new list containing all items present in both of the sequences passed in: The `return` statement sends a value (`object`) back to the call as the result of the call expression. If no `return` is executed, a function returns the Python `None` object by default (Python's null value).

Here is our function in action, intersecting two strings and then a list and a tuple. Because we don't need to declare argument types, this function can take any sort of arguments. Because `for` and `in` are generic, this function can be used to process any kind of sequence object, even mixed types:

```
>>> s1 = "SPAM"
>>> s2 = "SCAM"

>>> intersect(s1, s2)              # strings
['S', 'A', 'M']

>>> intersect([1, 2, 3], (1, 4))   # mixed types
[1]
```

We call functions by listing arguments, if any, in parentheses after the function name (technically, after any expression that returns a callable object). The expression `intersect` yields a function object; adding parentheses forces it to be called.

Although not statements, Python functions can also be created anonymously by the `lambda` expression form. In the following, `lambda` and `def` have the same effect, but `lambda` lets us generate functions in expressions, so it can sometimes be convenient:

```
>>> def adder(x, y): return x + y
...
>>> t = lambda x, y: x + y
>>>
>>> adder(2, 4)
6
>>> t(2, 4)
6
```

`lambdas` are commonly used to create simple callback handler functions in GUI programming and in conjunction with Python's functional programming tools (e.g., implied iterations such as `map()`, `filter()`, and `reduce()`).

Arguments and Scopes

In Python, arguments are passed to functions by assignment, which we've seen always creates object references. In our previous function, `seq1` and `seq2` will reference the same objects passed by the call. Although this object sharing is open to side effects, it works much like C's argument rules in practice:

- Immutable objects (e.g., integers) are shared but can't be changed in place (like simple C types).
- Mutable objects (e.g., lists) are shared and may be changed in-place (like C array pointers).

Python does not pass arguments by aliasing names: `seq1` in the function is a new name local to the function, and reassigning it has no effect on the caller's names. As mentioned earlier, within a function

- Arguments, and all other names assigned in a function's body, are always considered local to the function, unless they are explicitly declared to be global within the function body with a statement of the form `global name`. Python stacks local names internally for fast access.
- Names that are used but not assigned in a function may be in one of three scopes: locals (the function call), globals (at the top level of the enclosing module), or built-in names (e.g., `range`, `open`). Global names need not be declared if they are only used in a function and not assigned.

Although `def` statements can be nested in another `def`, scopes don't nest in Python the way they do in Pascal. Name references always have access to at most three scopes, regardless of the nesting of the `def`.

Finally, although arguments are always passed by assignment, Python provides a variety of ways to match arguments in the call to argument names in the function header. Table 11.14 summarizes the matching modes that may be coded in function headers and calls.

TABLE 11.14. *Argument matching modes.*

Operation	*Location*	*Interpretation*
`def func(name):`	Function	Normal argument: matches any
`def func(name=value):`	Function	Default argument value
`def func(*name):`	Function	Matches remaining positional arguments
`def func(**name):`	Function	Matches remaining keyword arguments
`func(value)`	Caller	Normal argument: matched by position
`func(name=value)`	Caller	Keyword argument: matched by name

By default, passed arguments are matched to names in the header by position (left to right), but special syntax can be used to generalize the matching step:

- The function header can specify default values for unpassed arguments (`name=default`) and also collect extra positional arguments in a tuple (`*name`) and extra keyword arguments in a dictionary (`**name`). The `*name` and `**name` forms are similar in spirit to C's `varargs` feature but are based on high-level objects in Python (tuples and dictionaries).
- The function call can specify the name of the argument in the header that is to receive the passed value (`name=value`) and may pass either more or fewer arguments than the function expects: If it passes too few, defaults in the header are used, and if passes too many, the `*name` and `**name` arguments in the header are filled.

We'll use keyword argument matching to set configuration parameters in the Tkinter GUI API later.

11.3.5.2. Modules

In Python, everything lives in a module: a name space used to package logic and data for external use. Modules are the biggest program unit; they are created by writing Python source-code files, or C extensions, and are used by clients that import modules as a whole, import names from them, or reload modules dynamically. In simple terms, modules are just a place to define named objects to be used by other parts of a system; they are component partitioning tools.

In a nutshell, when a Python module is imported, Python locates the module's file by inspecting directories named on the `PYTHONPATH` environment variable. Once located, a module file is executed line-by-line (on first import). Some of the lines in a module create objects and assign them to names (`def`, `=`, `class`, `import`, etc.). Names assigned at the top level of the module file in this way become the module's exported attributes. Later imports don't rerun the module's code again but fetch the already loaded module object.

Let's look at a simple module in action. Suppose we use our favorite text editor to type a simple function definition in a text file called `hello.py` (see Listing 11.3).

LISTING 11.3. *file:* `hello.py`.

```
def printer(x):
    print x
```

This file is a full-fledged Python module. We can import it and call its function using either `import hello` or `from hello import...` statements:

```
% python
>>> import hello
>>> hello.printer('Hello world!')
Hello world!

>>> from hello import printer
>>> printer('Hello world!')
Hello world!

>>> from hello import *
>>> printer('Hello world!')
Hello world!
```

Here, we access the function from the interactive command line, but we can do the same from other module files, too. Although this is an artificial example, the basic ideas apply to realistically scaled modules as well: Clients simply import and use the names assigned at the top level of module files. Python handles dynamic loading and compilation details (discussed later) behind the scenes. C modules are similar in spirit, but C defines exports by registering C function pointers instead (C module details are presented later).

Writing module files is simply a matter of typing Python statements in a file with a `.py` name suffix. In fact, we've been creating a module all along: Code typed at the interactive command line is really added to a module called `__main__`; the only difference is that module files are a more permanent device, and expression results are echoed at the interactive prompt.

Using a module is straightforward, too: Table 11.15 summarizes module usage tools. The `import` and `from` statements are actually assignments, like `def`:

- `import` loads a module object (or fetches one already loaded) and assigns it to the module name.
- `from` imports a module and copies out its top-level names into the importing module.

When `import` is used, the importer fetches the entire module, so names in the module must be qualified to be used (e.g., `module.name`). With `from`, names are copied out, so they don't need to be qualified by the owning module's name (e.g., `name`). `from` simply assigns names in the imported module to names in the importing module; as for all assignments in Python, the names in the importing and imported modules initially share the same object.

`reload` is a built-in function that forces a module's source code to be reloaded and re-executed, in the existing module's name space. This re-execution replaces the module's top-level name values in-place. Recall that a module's code is only run when it is first imported; to force a module to be updated to reflect its new source code without restarting the program, we need to call `reload`. Where applicable, `reload` lets us change components of Python programs while they are running. `reload` is most useful with `import`; because `from` clients copy names, changes in the original module may have no effect.

TABLE 11.15. *Module access operations.*

Operation	*Interpretation*
`import mod`	Fetch a module as a whole
`from mod import name`	Fetch a specific name from a module
`from mod import *`	Fetch all top-level names from a module
`reload(mod)`	Force a reload of module's code

One special module trick to note: Because program files are sometimes run as scripts, too, Python sets a module's `__name__` attribute to the string `__main__` if and only if the file is being run as a script, instead of being imported by a client. This lets us write files that can both be run standalone and used as a component of a larger system:

```
def function(arg):
    action...                  # define exports

if __name__ == "__main__":
    function(1)                # only when I'm run as a top-level program
```

Module Compilation Semantics: Python compiles modules to byte-code files (.pyc suffixed) when they are first imported. Later imports use the existing byte-code version of a module, unless the corresponding module source code file has been changed since the last compilation to byte code. This byte-code compilation step serves as an automatic make-like dependency check and is entirely hidden from programmers: Python modules simply import and use services from other modules at runtime, without having to manage explicit compile/link steps.

11.3.5.3. Exceptions

In Python, exceptions are a high-level program control-flow tool. They are raised both by the interpreter to communicate unusual conditions to programs and by programs to communicate conditions and implement alternative control-flow models. From a functional perspective, they are similar to C's setjmp/longjmp constructs, but they take a much higher-level form in Python. In simple terms

- try statements catch exceptions.
- raise statements trigger exceptions.
- Python triggers built-in exceptions.
- User-defined exceptions are objects.

In their basic form, try statements specify a body to be executed, along with one or more except clauses that list exceptions to be caught and statements to execute if the named exception occurs. For instance, the following example wraps a function call in a try statement that catches the built-in IndexError exception (which lives in the built-in name scope):

```
def kaboom(list, n):
    print list[n]              # trigger IndexError

try:
    kaboom([0, 1, 2], 3)
except IndexError:
    print 'Hello world!'       # catch exception here
```

Here, when we call the `kaboom` function, it triggers the exception, and the `Hello world!` message is printed. The body of a `try` can contain any sort of statements; Python stacks exception handlers at runtime and executes the most recently entered matching `except` clause when an exception is raised. If no `except` clause matches, Python terminates the program and displays an error message and stacktrace with source-file information at the top level.

User-defined exceptions are an object. They may be classes and class instances (not discussed here) but are more commonly simple strings. For instance, the following example uses the `raise` statement to force the `MyError` exception to be raised:

```
MyError = "my error"
def stuff(file):
    raise MyError

file = open('data', 'w')    # open a file
try:
    stuff(file)             # raises exception
finally:
    file.close()            # always close file
```

This time, the `try` statement uses a `finally` clause instead of an `except`. The `finally` specifies a block of statements to always be executed on the way out, whether an exception is raised or not. If an exception does occur during the `try` block, Python executes the `finally` block and then reraises the current exception. Because of these semantics, the `finally` clause is a convenient place to code clean-up actions; in the example, we want to always close the file we opened, whether an error occurs in `stuff` or not.

`try` statements can also specify an `else` clause to be executed if no exception occurs while the `try` block is executing. In general, a variety of clauses can appear in a `try` statement, as summarized in Table 11.16.

TABLE 11.16. `try` *statement clauses.*

Operation	*Interpretation*
`except:`	Catch all exception types
`except name:`	Catch a specific exception only
`except name, value:`	Catch an exception and its extra data
`except (name1, name2):`	Catch any of the listed exceptions
`else:`	Run block if no exception raised
`finally:`	Always perform block

Exceptions are also bound up with the notion of error-handling in Python. As mentioned, the interpreter raises exceptions when it discovers errors, such as an out-of-bounds list index, non-existent dictionary key, syntax error (at import time), or type error (e.g., adding a string to a number). But some exceptions raised by the interpreter are not necessarily program errors; for instance, depending on the built-in tool used, end-of-file is sometimes communicated by an empty return value and sometimes by an exception. In the latter case, we detect end-of-file by embedding the file read operation in a `try` statement:

```
while 1:
    try:
        next = <read operation>
    except EOFError:
        break
    else:
        <process 'next' here>
```

One last note: When we raise exceptions ourselves, we can also pass an extra data item along with the exception to provide additional information. For instance, if we define a variable named `myexception` assigned to a string object, we can raise it as an exception in one of two ways:

```
myexception = "Error description"
raise myexception                # raise the exception
raise myexception, data         # pass extra information
```

When the second form is used, the extra `data` is a Python object that can be caught in an except clause that specifies both the exception name and a target for the data (the extra data defaults to `None` if not passed):

```
try:
    ...
except myexception, extrainfo:
    ...
```

11.3.5.4. Classes

As in C++, Python's `class` statement is its primary object-oriented programming (OOP) tool. In terms of program structure, classes always exist in a module. In terms of functionality, classes let Python programmers implement new object types in Python: Classes serve as templates for creating new objects. Classes may implement both data members and functional methods. They may also overload common Python operators and object operations to work on objects created from the class. Compared to other program units, classes support three unique concepts:

- *Multiple instances*—Like `def`, the `class` statement creates a class object and assigns it to the name in the class header. Unlike `def`, calling a class object generates a new class instance object. We can make as many instances of a class as we like: Each instance becomes a new name space, which inherits the names defined inside the class statement.
- *Customization via inheritance*—By listing other classes in the class header, Python programs define a subclass(superclass) relationship: Subclasses inherit names defined in their superclasses. Subclasses may also replace or extend names inherited from superclasses, in order to specialize inherited behavior. Superclasses are customized by subclassing them externally, rather than changing the superclass in-place.
- *Operator overloading*—By providing specially named methods, classes may intercept operators and apply them to class instances as desired. For example, if a class provides a method called `__add__`, it will be called whenever instances created from the class appear in `+` expressions (`X+Y`). Operator overloading allows classes to implement objects that integrate closely with Python's type model.

Let's take a concrete look at a simple Python class, to demonstrate basic concepts. In the following, we define a class called `FirstClass` with one method called `printer`:

```
class FirstClass:                    # class
    def printer(self, text):         # method
        print text
```

In Python, methods are simply nested `def` statements with a special first argument to accept the class instance object. Python automatically passes the instance object to the first argument (usually called `self`, by convention) so that the class can process the instance explicitly.

Much like modules and functions, the `class` statement introduces a new local scope: Statements that create (assign) new names inside a `class` statement generate class attributes. In `FirstClass`, because the method `def` statement is nested under the `class`, the `printer` function is assigned in the class's local scope and becomes an attribute of the class object. `printer` prints a passed-in object to the standard output stream:

```
>>> x = FirstClass()
>>> x.printer('Hello world!')
Hello world!
```

Here, we make an instance of `FirstClass` by calling it just like a function. Once we have an instance, we can call its methods by qualifying the instance with attributes inherited from the class: `x.printer` references the `printer` method in the class statement. When called, Python automatically passes the instance (`x`) to the `self` argument of `printer`. Internally, Python translates a method call `instance.method(args)` into a class method call of the form `class.method(instance, args)`. To better understand how the `self` is used inside methods, we need a bigger example:

```
class SecondClass(FirstClass):          # subclass
    def __init__(self, value):          # constructor
        self.name = value               # save in instance
    def printname(self):
        self.printer(self.name)         # inherited method

>>> x = SecondClass('Hello world!')
>>> x.printname()
Hello world!
```

This time, we create a subclass of `FirstClass`, called `SecondClass`: By listing a superclass in parentheses, the subclass inherits all the names defined in the superclass's `class` statement. Here, this means that `SecondClass`, and all instances created from `SecondClass`, will inherit the `printer` attribute defined in `FirstClass`. When we make a `SecondClass` instance and call its inherited `printname` method, `printname` calls `self.printer`, which refers to the `printer` method in `FirstClass`. In OOP terms, `x` is a `SecondClass`, which is a `FirstClass`: `x` inherits names from both `SecondClass` and `FirstClass`.

`SecondClass` also defines a constructor: When a class provides a method called `__init__`, Python calls it automatically each time an instance is created from the class, passing in the new instance object and any arguments passed to the class name. For example, in the `SecondClass` constructor, `self` is assigned the new instance object, and `value` is set to the `Hello world!` string. When it assigns `value` to `self.name`, it creates a `name` attribute in the instance object (`self`). Assigning to self attributes in this way generates per-instance state data: Each instance created from `SecondClass` will have its own `name` attribute.

In Python, the instance object is implied when calling methods outside the class but is always explicit inside the method itself. Methods must explicitly qualify the `self` argument to access instance data attributes. Unlike C++, there is no special, hidden scope for the class (`self` works like C++'s implied `this` pointer).

11.3.5.5. Python Scope Rules: The Whole Story

We'll return to more class concepts in a moment. Now that we've seen functions, modules, and classes, let's first summarize Python's scope and name-space rules. They turn out to be a central concept for both classes and modules. As we saw when studying functions, access to simple unqualified names (`X`) is arranged as follows:

- *Assignment:* `X = value`—Creates or changes names in the current local scope, unless global declarations are used to map names to the global scope (the enclosing module).
- *Reference:* `X`—Looks for names in the current *local* scope, then the current global scope (enclosing module), and then the built-in scope. The first appearance found is used.

For qualified name accesses (`object.X`), the name access rules depend on the object being qualified. For example, when qualifying a class instance object

- *Assignment:* `X.name = value`—Creates or alters the attribute name in the object being qualified.
- *Reference:* `X.name`—Searches for the attribute name in the object and then all accessible classes above it.

Qualifying simpler object types (e.g., modules) works the same, except references only search for attributes in the object itself; there are no other objects to inherit attribute names from. In some sense, both modules and classes are just name spaces: They are both places to define names to be exported. In classes, names may be found by searching superclass trees. This is just Python's definition of inheritance.

11.3.5.6. Name-Space Dictionaries

One of the main unifying concepts in Python is the fact that most name spaces are actually implemented as dictionaries behind the scenes. In fact, Python lets us access name-space dictionaries at runtime: Most objects with attributes export their name spaces in the built-in `__dict__` attribute.

For instance, given a module called `M`, the attribute `name` can be accessed either as `M.name` or by going through `M`'s name-space dictionary: `M.__dict__['name']`.

Qualification is the same as indexing a dictionary, both in terms of references and assignments. For instance, assigning to an attribute creates it if it doesn't exist, but referencing an undefined attribute raises an exception, exactly like dictionary accesses. Because of this equivalence, Python inheritance is really just a matter of indexing one or more dictionaries.

Because Python records all loaded modules in the user-accessible `modules` dictionary of the built-in `sys` module, we can actually get to `M.name` with any of these expressions:

```
M.name
M.__dict__['name']
sys.modules['M'].name
sys.modules['M'].__dict__['name']
sys.__dict__['modules']['M'].__dict__['name']
```

Naturally, `M.name` is considerably easier to type than most of these forms, but by exporting name-space components to programs, Python supports metaprogramming: writing programs that manage other programs. Not all objects export a `__dict__` attribute; for instance, some C extension types export their method and member names with different mechanisms. In general, Python programs can process name spaces using standard dictionary operations.

11.3.6. Python's OOP model

In the discussion on classes, we used very simple examples to demonstrate basic usage. Naturally, classes are designed for more than printing messages to the screen. In this section, we're going to talk more about object-oriented concepts such as inheritance and composition and show how they may be implemented in Python. We'll also introduce the notion of operator overloading and summarize a few other key class concepts.

11.3.6.1. OOP and Inheritance

We talked about inheritance earlier: In Python, it's really just a matter of searching for attributes in a tree of objects. Whenever a class instance object is qualified (`object.name`), Python searches for the attribute name in a number of objects' name spaces:

- *Instance*—The object being qualified
- *Class*—The class that the instance was created from
- *Superclasses*—All accessible superclasses above the instance's class

Inheritance hierarchies and names are defined in a variety of ways: Class attributes are generated by statements nested in `class` statements, instance members are created by assignment to instance attributes (`self.name=value`), and superclass hierarchies are defined by listing superclasses in parentheses in `class` headers. The net effect is a tree of name spaces: Because this tree is searched from the bottom up, lower definitions of a name can override higher (less specific) versions.

Listing 11.4 is a concrete example of attribute inheritance in action: the classic zoo-animal hierarchy coded in Python. The classes in the following `zoo` module define an inheritance hierarchy, which specializes the `speak` method in subclasses. For example, when we create a `Hacker` instance and call its `reply` method, the `reply` attribute is found by searching up to `Animal` (from the instance, to `Hacker`, to `Primate`, to `Mammal`, and finally to `Animal`). When `Animal.reply` calls `self.speak`, the `speak` name is found in `Primate`, by searching up from the instance.

LISTING 11.4. *file:* `zoo.py`.

```
class Animal:
    def reply(self):    self.speak()
    def speak(self):    print 'spam'

class Mammal(Animal):
    def speak(self):    print 'huh?'

class Cat(Mammal):
    def speak(self):    print 'meow'

class Dog(Mammal):
    def speak(self):    print 'bark'

class Primate(Mammal):
    def speak(self):    print 'Hello world!'

class Hacker(Primate):
    pass


% python
>>> data = Hacker()
>>> data.reply()
Hello world!
>>> from zoo import Cat, Hacker
>>> spot = Cat()
>>> spot.reply()
meow
```

The `Cat` instance follows a similar search for attribute names, but the inheritance path is one level shorter, and the `speak` name is located in `Cat` instead of `Primate`. This is an artificial example, but the notion of specialized attribute hierarchies can be used to construct and specialize arbitrarily complex systems. Notice the `pass` statement in `Hacker`: It's Python's empty placeholder statement and does nothing when run.

11.3.6.2. OOP and Composition

Another way to make use of classes is to embed class instances in a larger, composite object. If we call inheritance an *is a* relationship, composition may be considered a *has a* relationship: A controller object owns and controls other objects that represent the logical components of an application. Composition is perhaps the most common object-oriented design tool, besides inheritance itself.

Let's look at a simple example of composition at work. The `parrot` module shown in Listing 11.5 simulates the classic Monty Python `dead-parrot skit` with Python classes. It implements three `Actor` objects (a `Customer`, a `Clerk`, and a `Parrot`), which all inherit a `line` method and provide a specialized `says` method that returns the object's output string. The composite object, `Scene`, creates instances of all three `Actor` objects and calls their `line` methods in turn, when it receives an `action` call.

LISTING 11.5. *file:* `parrot.py`.

```
class Actor:
    def line(self): print self.name + ':', `self.says()`

class Customer(Actor):
    name = 'customer'
    def says(self): return "that's one ex-bird!"

class Clerk(Actor):
    name = 'clerk'
    def says(self): return "no it isn't..."

class Parrot(Actor):
    name = 'parrot'
    def says(self): return None

class Scene:
    def __init__(self):                    # constructor method
        self.clerk    = Clerk()            # embed some instances
        self.customer = Customer()         # Scene is a composite
        self.subject  = Parrot()

    def action(self):
        self.customer.line()               # delegate to embedded
        self.clerk.line()
        self.subject.line()


% python
>>> import parrot
>>> parrot.Scene().action()
customer: "that's one ex-bird!"
clerk: "no it isn't..."
parrot: None
```

Note that the `Scene` object doesn't do much on its own: It's mostly a container, which passes requests off to the three objects it creates and embeds. In practice, we might use this scheme to implement things such as GUI containers: The embedded objects could be buttons and labels, drawn automatically when the container is. Also notice that the embedded objects still use inheritance to specialize the output string, much like our `zoo` example earlier: Inheritance and composition are complementary tools.

11.3.6.3. Operator Overloading in Classes

So far, we've seen how to define and use basic class features: members, methods, and simple inheritance. Python classes support more advanced OOP concepts, such as operator overloading, constructors, and more. In Python, classes may overload operations and expression operators to work on their instances, by providing specially named methods. If defined, Python automatically calls a class's operator overloading method when the associated operation is performed on an instance of the class.

We've already seen one special method in action: the `__init__` constructor method. Let's look at another example that illustrates a few more. The following `Counter` class also provides a `__call__` method to intercept function calls to an instance, an `__add__` to overload the `+` operator to work on instances, and a `__repr__`, which returns a string to be used when instances are printed:

```
class Counter:
    def __init__(self, start):              # on Counter()
        self.data = start
    def __call__(self):                      # on x()
        self.data = self.data + 1
        return self.data
    def __add__(self, y):                    # on x + y
        return Counter(self.data + y)
    def __repr__(self):                      # on print
        return `self.data`


if __name__ == "__main__":          # self-test
    x = Counter(2)                  # __init__
    x = x + 4                       # __add__
    print x                         # __repr__, output: 6

    c1 = Counter(10)                # __init__
    c2 = Counter(24)                # __init__
    print c1(), c2(), c1(), c2()    # __call__, output: 11, 25, 12, 26
```

Table 11.17 summarizes a handful of representative operator overloading methods. There are many more, but the ones listed here are a sampling of what's available. Note that they all start and end with two underscores to make them distinct from names your class defines.

TABLE 11.17. *Typical operator overloading methods.*

Method	*Overloads*	*Called for*
`__init__`	Constructor	Instance creation: `X=C()`
`__add__`	Operator `+`	`X + Y`
`__repr__`	Printing	Print `X`
`__call__`	Function calls	`X()`
`__or__`	Operator `|`	`X | Y`
`__getattr__`	Qualification	`X.undefined`
`__getitem__`	Indexing	`X[key]`, iteration
`__len__`	Length	`len(X)`, truth tests
`__cmp__`	Comparison	`X == Y, X < Y`

Most of this table is self-explanatory, but the last few entries warrant examples of their own. The `__getitem__` method overloads indexing operations: `X[key]`, where `key` can be an offset (to support sequence type objects) or an arbitrary key (to implement mappings). But it can do more; the Python `for` loop works by repeatedly indexing the subject sequence object by successively higher indexes until an index exception is raised. Because of that, `__getitem__` can also be used to overload sequence iteration. Here's a simple example:

```
>>> class indexer:
...     def __getitem__(self, index):
...         return index ** 2
...
>>> X = indexer()
>>> for i in range(5): print X[i],
...
0 1 4 9 16
```

The `indexer.__getitem__` method is called each time the `X` instance is indexed and returns the square of the index passed in. The `__len__` method can similarly be used in more than one context. As we've seen, in Python, `true` means a nonzero number, or an empty data structure:

```
>>> L = []
>>> if not L: print "it's empty!"
...
it's empty!
```

Because of this, the `__len__` method not only overrides the `len` length built-in function, but also the results of truth testing, when applied to class instance objects. If it returns zero, the object is classified as `false`; in

Python, even truth can be overloaded. The __getattr__ method can be used to intercept accesses to undefined instance attributes:

```
>>> class empty:
...     def __getattr__(self, attrname):
...         return attrname + ' not supported!'
...
>>> X = empty()
>>> X.age
'age not supported!'
```

Hooks like this let us write programs that control the behavior of class instances. For example, we can write wrappers around real class instances, which delegate method calls to embedded objects according to the results of precondition tests. Finally, the __cmp__ method is called for all comparisons in Python; like the C library's strcmp, it returns a -1, 0, or 1, to designate a comparison result of less than, equal to, or greater than. Other special methods handle type conversions, index and attribute assignment, right-operand expressions, slicing, computing hash values, and more. In general, operator overloading lets us intercept most language operations and interpret them as appropriate for our classes.

11.3.6.4. Class Odds and Ends

There's more to Python classes than we have time to cover here. For instance, multiple inheritance is coded by listing more than one superclass in a class header and implemented as a depth-first, left-to right search through all accessible superclasses. Moreover, Python methods and members are all virtual and public in the C++ sense, but Python 1.5 introduced the notion of name-mangling to localize names to a class (attributes such as __X are automatically prefixed with the enclosing class's name). See Python books or reference manuals for further details. It's also possible to call class methods directly through their classes, and this gives rise to the pattern for extending (instead of replacing) methods in Python:

```
class Super:
    def method(self, args):
        # default behavior...

class Sub(Super):
    def method(self, args):         # replaces inherited method
        # extra behavior...
        Super.method(self, args)   # run inherited method explicitly
        # extra behavior...
```

This pattern is perhaps most commonly used for the __init__ constructor method: Because Python only finds and executes a single inherited __init__ method, subclasses must manually call superclass constructors from their own constructor, if needed.

11.3.7. Python's First-Class Object Model

As mentioned earlier, everything is a generic object in Python: Any object can be passed around and used generically, without having to know its data type ahead of time. This has some profound flexibility benefits and is one of the main reasons for Python's simplicity. In this section, we're going to explore a few benefits of Python's object model to highlight the flexibility of the language. Note: Don't confuse Python's first-class object model with Python's OOP support. In Python, everything is a first-class object, but only objects defined by classes support the notion of OOP objects (inheritance, etc.).

11.3.7.1. Functions Are Objects: Indirect Calls

As we saw earlier, the `def` statement is really just an assignment: It creates a new function object and assigns it to the function name in the header. The `class` and `import/from` statements work the same. As one result of these semantics, we can assign function objects to variables, store them in data structures, and even pass them to other functions to be called indirectly. Because function argument and return types are never declared in Python, it's possible to treat functions in a highly generic fashion.

For instance, let's define a simple function, `echo`, which just prints its single argument to the `stdout` stream. After the initial `def` statement, the name `echo` is bound to the new function object:

```
def echo(message):
    print message
```

There's nothing special about the name `echo`: We can just as easily assign the function object to another name (`x`) and call it as usual:

```
x = echo
x('Hello world!')
```

Similarly, we can pass `echo`'s value to a function that calls it indirectly (`indirect`). Passing function arguments is really an assignment, too:

```
def indirect(func, arg):
    func(arg)

indirect(echo, 'Hello world!')
```

Finally, it's just as easy to store the function object as an embedded component in a data structure (again, just Python assignment at work). In the following, we assign two references to our function object in tuples nested in a list and step through the list with a `for` loop, using the built-in `apply` function to call our function indirectly:

```
schedule = [ (echo, 'Hello!'), (echo, 'Ni!') ]
for (func, arg) in schedule:
    apply(func, (arg,))
```

These examples are somewhat artificial to demonstrate the notion of indirect function calls, but this has some practical uses, too. For instance, we can write file-scanner functions that apply a passed-in function to each line of a text file. Such a structure separates file interface logic from data processing functions.

11.3.7.2. Classes Are Objects: Factories

Because classes are objects at runtime, too, we can pass them to functions, store them in data structures, and so on, just as if they were integers or strings. One consequence of this is that it's possible to pass classes to functions that generate arbitrary kinds of class instance objects. Such functions are often called factories: utilities that generate objects generically.

In the next code segment, we first define a function called `factory`, which accepts a class object (`aClass`) and a list of one or more arguments to pass to the class's constructor (`args`); it uses the `*name` argument form to collect passed arguments in a tuple and calls the `apply` built-in function to invoke the class indirectly.

We also define two test classes (`Spam` and `Person`) and create instances of both by calling our factory function. The key point to notice is that the factory function can handle arbitrary passed-in classes here; as usual in Python, there's no need to declare the type of `aClass`. Because of that, a single factory function usually handles every sort of case we're likely to come across. Moreover, this pattern can be applied in many common contexts. For instance, we can define class test functions that exercise any class passed in:

```
def factory(aClass, *args):         # varargs tuple
    return apply(aClass, args)      # call aClass

class Spam:
    def doit(self, message):
        print message

class Person:
    def __init__(self, name, job):
        self.name = name
        self.job  = job

object1 =
           factory(Spam)
object2 = factory(Person, "Guido", "guru")
```

11.3.7.3. Methods Are Objects: Bound or Unbound

In Python, methods are first-class objects, too, just like functions and classes: They can be assigned to variables and passed around a program generically. Method objects come in two flavors:

- *Bound methods*—With an implied `self` instance object
- *Unbound methods*—Without an implied `self` instance object

Like simple functions, both can be processed generically, but bound methods have an associated instance object, and unbound methods don't. Python packages the `self` object with bound methods (they are essentially instance/method pairs), but we need to supply `self` explicitly when calling an unbound method object.

An example will make the distinction clearer. Suppose we make an instance of the `Spam` class called `object1`. When we extract a method of the instance (`object1.doit`), Python packages the instance (`object1`) along with the method function (`doit`) and returns a bound method object. Because the instance is implied (packaged in the object), we can call the bound method object later as though it were a simple function, without explicitly supplying a `self` instance object:

```
object1 = Spam()
x = object1.doit           # bound method object
x('hello world')           # instance is implied
```

On the other hand, if we ask for a method from the class instead of an instance (`Spam.doit`), there is no associated `self` instance, and Python returns an unbound method object. We can assign it to variables and call it generically later, too, but because this is a class attribute, we must supply the missing instance object explicitly in the first argument of the call:

```
t = Spam.doit              # unbound method object
t(object1, 'howdy')        # pass in instance
```

Naturally, there are many reasons for using both flavors of methods. For example, bound methods let us use object methods in any context that expects to find a simple function: Because the instance object is implied, either a function or bound method will do. We'll see this in action when we see how callbacks are registered in Tkinter GUIs later.

11.3.7.4. Modules Are Objects: Metaprograms

Finally, modules are first-class objects, too: When we import a module, Python creates a new module object and runs the file's code in the object's name space (or fetches an already loaded module object). But really, `import` and `from` statements are also assignments of objects to names. After we've imported a module, we can store it in data structures, pass it to functions, assign it to other names, and so on, just like functions, classes, methods, and everything else in Python.

As we've seen, we can also fetch module name spaces and process them as dictionaries (e.g., in browsers) and apply generic object tools to them. For instance, the function in Listing 11.6 makes use of the `exec` and `eval` built-ins to run strings of Python code that import and then fetch a module by name string. It also uses the `getattr` function to fetch an attribute by name string and the `apply` built-in to call it generically.

LISTING 11.6. *file:* `dynamic.py`.

```
def runFunction(moduleName, functionName, argsTuple):
    exec 'import ' + moduleName                   # import by string
    module = eval(moduleName)                     # fetch module object
    function = getattr(module, functionName)      # fetch attr of module
    return apply(function, argsTuple)             # call attr with args
```

The result is a module that is used to access other modules. Here it is in action, loading the `test.func` function with name strings and calling the function with an explicit argument's tuple:

```
% cat test.py
def func(op1, op2): return op1 + op2

% python
>>> from dynamic import *
>>> runFunction("test", "func", ("abc", "xyz"))
'abcxyz'
```

11.3.8. Common Built-In System Interfaces

Finally, let's conclude this language introduction section with something perhaps a bit more practical than the topics we've studied so far. As mentioned at the start of this chapter, Python has a distinctly practical flavor: It was developed to handle real programming chores. As an example of some of its pragmatic orientation, let's take a quick look at some of Python's most commonly used system interfaces.

The tools shown here are also representative of a vast collection of built-in library modules that come standard with Python. Built-in modules handle everything from formatting strings to fetching files over the Internet. In fact, for real programming tasks, Python's library modules are almost as important and useful as the language itself. We'll see more built-in tools in the next section, but the Python library reference manual provides a complete catalog of all the utility modules that come with Python.

11.3.8.1. Python Tools: sys

Python's built-in `sys` module contains a variety of tools. In general, `sys` is used to export interpreter-specific components for use in Python programs. For instance, we can access Python's module search path (initialized from `$PYTHONPATH`) as `sys.path` and get an identifier for the platform we're running on as `sys.platform`. The `sys` module is built-in (it's always available), but we must import it to access its attributes (exports) from a Python program:

```
>>> import sys
>>> sys.path
['.', '/usr/local/lib/python', ... ]
>>> sys.platform
'sunos4'
```

11.3.8.2. System Tools: os

The Python `os` module provides POSIX bindings for Python programs. Roughly, POSIX bindings are a set of standard system functions and tools, which are portable across most UNIX-like platforms:

- `os.environ` is a Python dictionary that contains shell environment variables; it can be both read and changed.
- `os.popen` spawns a shell command and returns a file object (a pipe) connected to the command's input or output streams.
- `os.system` runs a shell command without connecting to its data streams.
- `os.listdir` returns a list of file names in the current directory that match a name pattern.

The following session illustrates all of these tools; they each have direct counterparts in standard C libraries, so consult standard documentation for more details (e.g., man pages):

```
>>> import os
>>> os.environ['USER']
'mlutz'
>>> listing = os.popen("ls *.py").readlines()     # or win32pipe.popen
>>> for name in listing: print name,
...
cheader1.py
finder1.py
summer.py

>>> for name in listing: os.system("vi " + name)
...
>>> os.listdir(".")
['summer.out', 'summer.py', 'table1.txt', ... ]
```

Note that we can get a directory listing by spawning a shell command (`popen`) or via the `listdir` function. We also use `system` to start an editor (`vi`) from inside a Python program; `system` (and `popen`) can start any command we can type at the system shell.

11.3.8.3. File Globbing: `glob`, `string`

The built-in `glob` module provides a more general way to collect a directory listing from a Python program. Given a name pattern, `glob.glob` returns a list of all file names that match the pattern. For instance, if we pass in a `*.py` pattern string, we'll get a list of all Python source files in the current directory, which we can process with a `for` loop. The `glob` module is named for file name globbing (expansion) and acts much like directory listing in the system shell (e.g., the `ls` command in UNIX).

In the following example, we use this technique to rename all Python source files to uppercase-only names (e.g., `summer.py` becomes `SUMMER.PY`). The string module's `upper` function does the name conversion for us, and the POSIX `os.rename` function changes the file name in the file system:

```
>>> import glob, string, os
>>> glob.glob("*.py")
['cheader1.py', 'finder1.py', 'summer.py']

>>> for name in glob.glob("*.py"):
...     os.rename(name, string.upper(name))
...
>>> glob.glob("*.PY")
['FINDER1.PY', 'SUMMER.PY', 'CHEADER1.PY']
```

11.3.8.4. Arguments and Streams: `sys`

Last but not least, the `sys` module also provides access to arguments passed on command lines, as well as the standard UNIX `stdin`/`stdout`/`stderr` streams preopened for each process:

- `sys.argv` returns a list of strings, containing all the words used on the command line typed to start a Python program. It works exactly like the `argv` `char*` array in C `main` programs but takes the form of a list in Python.

- `sys.stdout` is a Python file object, connected to the C `stdout` stream. As usual, `sys.stdout` is a preopened file; writing to it using normal file methods sends text (a Python string) to the `stdout` stream, which is usually the terminal where the Python program was started (in fact, this is just how the `print` statement works internally). As you might expect, the standard input and error streams are also available, as `sys.stdin` and `sys.stderr`.

The following example illustrates both of these interfaces in action:

```
% cat play.py
#!/usr/local/bin/python
import sys
print sys.argv
sys.stdout.write("ta da!\n")

% play.py -x -i spammify
['play.py', '-x', '-i', 'spammify']
ta da!
```

11.3.9. Summary: Python Toolset Layers

We've seen quite a few details in this tutorial section. Despite the complexity, most of what we've studied can be summarized in simple terms because Python provides a layered approach to functionality. In fact, most of what we've seen can be grouped into one of the three main functionality categories in Python:

- *Built-ins: lists, dictionaries, strings, library modules, and so on*—High-level tools for simple, fast programming
- *Python extensions: functions, classes, modules*—For adding extra features and new object types
- *C extensions: C modules, C types*—For integrating external systems, optimizing components, customization

We'll move on to study the last of these three categories (C integration) in the next section. The main point to notice here is that Python provides both built-in objects and tools, as well as tools for extending the built-in tool set in either Python or C. For simple tasks, Python's built-in tools are often all we really need. When applications demand more complex solutions, Python also provides the tools needed to scale up: It supports development of systems that are both arbitrarily sophisticated and highly reusable.

11.4. Python/C Integration

Beyond the Python language itself, Python programs can also be used as components of larger systems, by integrating them with other languages. In more specific terms, Python programs can be both

- *Extended by* (call to) modules implemented in a language like C or C++
- *Embedded in* (run by) programs written in a language like C or C++

Extending is useful when we want to use existing libraries in Python or optimize components of Python programs. Embedding comes in handy when we want to support system customizations. Roughly, extending is implemented by registering function pointers to Python, and embedding is accomplished by calling functions in the Python runtime API. In practice, many systems combine extending and embedding techniques to implement callback-based architectures, export application specific interfaces to embedded code, and so on.

Integration is a big topic that we can't cover in detail here and requires some knowledge of C programming. Because it's also at the heart of Python's role as a scripting language, C integration is a crucial tool. Because of that, this section provides a brief introduction to basic extending and embedding concepts in Python, by demonstrating simple integration programs. See the Python documentation sources listed at the end of this chapter for further details on the concepts introduced here.

11.4.1. Extending Python in C

Functionally, C extension components serve as optimization and integration tools. They can take the form of C modules or C types. In general, C modules work like Python modules, and C types work like built-in types (e.g., lists, dictionaries) and make use of the same extending interfaces. The chief difference is that C extensions register functionality with C function pointers, rather than Python-coded attributes. C types are almost like Python classes (they support multiple instances and operator overloading), but there's no notion of inheritance in C types unless we provide Python wrapper classes for them.

11.4.1.1. A Simple C Extension Module

The simplest C extension component is the C module. The C source file in Listing 11.7 implements a C extension module for Python, called `environ`. It simply wraps the C library's `getenv` routine for use in Python programs. Such an extension isn't strictly needed in Python (as we've seen, environment variables are available in the `os.environ` dictionary, and Python 1.4 now exports `os.environ` changes to the system shell), but this example illustrates the general structure of extension modules. Because extension modules are written to fit a standard integration structure, they are straightforward to code; as we'll discuss later, they may also be generated automatically by integration tools such as SWIG.

LISTING 11.7. *file:* `environ.c`.

```
#include <Python.h>
#include <stdlib.h>

/* Functions */
static PyObject *                                  /* returns object */
wrap_getenv(PyObject *self, PyObject *args)        /* self not used */
{                                                  /* args from python */
    char *varName, *varValue;
    PyObject *returnObj = NULL;                    /* null=exception */

    if (PyArg_Parse(args, "s", &varName)) {        /* Python -> C */
        varValue = getenv(varName);                /* call C getenv */
        if (varValue != NULL)
            returnObj = Py_BuildValue("s", varValue);
        else
            PyErr_SetString(PyExc_SystemError,
                            "Error calling getenv");
    }
    return returnObj;
}

/* Registration */
static struct PyMethodDef environ_methods[] = {
    {"getenv", wrap_getenv},        /* name, address */
    {NULL, NULL}
};

/* Initialization */
void initenviron()                          /* this is called by Python  */
{                                           /* on first "import environ" */
    (void) Py_InitModule("environ", environ_methods);
}
```

When we compile this module and bind it with Python, it can be used in Python programs exactly like a module coded in Python: The exported `environ.getenv` C function is called as though it were a Python function. The C module handles all data conversion details:

```
% python
>>> import environ
>>> environ.getenv("USER")
'mlutz'
>>> environ.getenv("PYTHONPATH")
'.:/opt/local/src/Python-1.4/Lib'
>>> dir(environ)
['__doc__', '__file__', '__name__', 'getenv']
>>> environ.__file__
'./environ.so'
```

Like all C extension modules, this file is composed of three standard parts:

- *Module method functions*—We first define the C functions that we want to export to Python. The module file exports one function, called `wrap_getenv` in C. When called by Python, it receives a `self` argument (not used for modules), and an `args`—a Python tuple object containing the arguments passed by the Python caller. The C function converts arguments to C form with the `PyArg_Parse` function (`s` means string) and returns a result object to the Python caller. The `Py_BuildValue` function converts C data to Python objects. Python objects all have the generic type `PyObject*` in C, and most symbols in the Python API start with a `Py` prefix to avoid clashing with names in your C code.
- *Name-to-address registration table*—C modules register C functions to Python, by providing a table that maps name strings to C function addresses. Our module file performs the mapping in the `environ_methods` table. The function's name in Python appears on the left, and the C function address is stored on the right.
- *Module initialization function*—Finally, modules also provide an initialization function, which Python automatically calls when the module is first imported. Normally, initialization functions call the `Py_InitModule` function to initialize the module, but they may also perform other module-specific processing (e.g., initializing shared data structures, etc.). Our module's initialization function is called `initenviron`; notice that it is the only exported (nonstatic) symbol in this file. Python links to and calls it by name, so it must be called `initenviron`.

To bind this C module into Python, we compile it into object code and link it with Python libraries and object files. More specifically, C extension modules may be bound to Python statically or dynamically. In static binding, we add a line to the Python configuration file and rebuild Python itself:

1. Put (or link to) the source or object file in the `Modules` directory of the Python source tree.
2. Add a line to the `Modules/Setup` file in the Python source tree, like `environ environ.c`.
3. Remake Python by running a `make` command at the top level of its source tree.

When we use this strategy, Python's build procedure updates built-in module tables and links our module's object code into the Python interpreter. If we don't want to rebuild Python (or don't have access to its source code), we can usually add extensions using dynamic binding instead. In this approach, we

1. Compile our module into a sharable object file.
2. Put the object file in a directory named on the `$PYTHONPATH` environment variable.

This way, Python locates and loads our C module dynamically, when it is first imported. Dynamic binding is more flexible (there's no need to rebuild Python) and minimizes Python executable size (extensions are only loaded into a process when used). However, some of the details are platform-specific; for instance, sharable object files may take a variety of forms (`.so` files, DLLs, etc.).

11.4.1.2. C Extension Types

C modules are useful for integrating external libraries, optimizing components originally coded in Python, and implementing shared services (e.g., data structures). In terms of functionality, they serve the same purposes as Python modules. But Python also lets us define new data types in C, by writing C extension types. Like Python classes, C types support multiple instance objects and can overload type operations and operators (e.g., method calls, `+`).

C type instances are true first-class objects and can fully integrate with Python's object model. They may be stored in data structures, passed to functions, and so on. In short, C types let us implement new Python objects in C for efficiency. Unlike Python classes, C types don't currently support the notion of inheritance: We need to wrap C types in Python classes if we want to subclass and specialize them in Python.

Although it might not have been obvious, we've used C types already: In fact, every built-in Python object is implemented as a C extension type. Because of that, anything we can do with lists, dictionaries, numbers, and so on can be implemented in C types that we code and bind with Python.

Unfortunately, C extension types are relatively large in terms of code size, so we don't have time to look at a real example in this chapter. Instead, here are a few general comments about coding C types. Refer to the information resources at the end of this chapter for further details.

Like C modules, C types are coded according to a standard structure. They're typically composed of the following components:

- A C `struct` used to hold per-instance data (each instance gets a new `struct`)
- Instance method functions and registration table
- Functions to handle general type operations (creation, printing, qualification, etc.)
- Functions to handle specific type category operations (sequence/mapping/number)
- Type-descriptor tables (to register operation handler functions by pointers)
- A C extension module (functions, table, initializer), which exports an instance-creation function

Type instances are normally created by calling a function in a module exported by the C type file; this instance creation function is analogous to class constructors. We've seen this in action, too: The built-in `open` function creates a file type instance object, which we later qualify to access file methods. `open` is really a precoded C extension function in the automatically imported built-in names module.

Like classes, types can also overload operators and type operations; in C types, we store pointers to C handler functions in type descriptors, rather than code specially named methods. Like classes, each instance of a C type gets a new copy of a `struct`, which holds its state information. Class instances get new name-space dictionaries instead, but the effect is similar.

Finally, in C types, the only symbol exported to Python is the instance-creation module's initialization function; all other functionality must be accessed through a type instance object (and is reached through type descriptor tables). Like C modules, C types may be bound to Python statically or dynamically.

11.4.1.3. Wrapping C Extensions in Python

As mentioned, C types don't support inheritance themselves, but it's straightforward to augment them to support inheritance, by wrapping type instances in a Python class. In Listing 11.8, the Python class `CtypeWrapper` embeds an existing or new instance of an imported C type. The Python class doesn't do much on its own: It passes most operations off to the embedded C type instance (this is often called delegation). By defining a Python wrapper class, we can subclass to specialize the C type's behavior in Python: `Subclass` specializes a method exported by the C type using normal class inheritance rules. If we make an instance of the `Subclass`, `method` calls are resolved in the subclass, not the C type.

LISTING 11.8. *file:* `cwrapper.py`.

```
from Cextension import Ctype

class CtypeWrapper:
    def __init__(self, start=None):
        self._base = start or Ctype()       # embed/wrap C type object
    def __getattr__(self, name):
        return getattr(self._base, name)    # pass off attributes
    def __add__(self, other):
        return CtypeWrapper(self._base + other)    # operators

class Subclass(CtypeWrapper):
    def method(self, args):                 # specialize C type method
        CtypeWrapper.method(self, args)     # do superclass method
        # add specialized behavior here     # do extra operations
```

11.4.1.4. Python and Rapid Development

C extensions also turn out to be a key factor behind Python's role as a rapid prototyping and development tool. Because C extensions look just like Python components to their Python clients, it is possible to code a system in Python first and later move time-critical parts of it to C extensions for delivery. Clients of migrated components need not be updated to make use of the optimized C extensions.

This development paradigm is sometimes called "prototype-and-migrate." Because it combines Python and C, it leverages both Python's speed-of-development and C's execution speed. Because Python is a full-featured object-oriented language, developers don't need to sacrifice quality when prototyping in Python. Because Python is designed for mixed-language systems, systems don't need to be recoded in C all at once.

Naturally, this is just one possible way to make use of Python's hybrid systems support. Although prototyping can dramatically improve the development cycle, a deliberate split into Python front-end and C/C++ back-end components might make more sense for a given project. As for most development tasks, the best hybrid system design depends on an application's goals.

11.4.2. Embedding Python in C

As mentioned earlier, Python programs can both call C (extending), and be called by C (embedding), in whatever manner is appropriate for our needs. Although C modules and types provide a convenient way to extend Python with external components, it's also often useful to be able to run Python programs from a C program. For instance, we can support on-site customization of our systems by running embedded Python code at strategic points in a C application. Users can tailor the embedded Python code dynamically, without having to recompile the enclosing system and without having access to its source code.

Before we look at embedding examples, let's introduce some of the general concepts they will illustrate. Unlike extending, embedding is implemented by calling Python API functions, rather than coding to a standard module structure. In general, Python embedded programs can take a variety of forms, may be located by C in a variety of ways, and may use a variety of communication techniques to pass data to and from C. Common embedded code forms include strings, objects, and files:

- *Code strings*—Running expressions, statements
- *Callable objects*—Calling functions, classes, methods
- *Code files*—Importing modules, executing scripts

Embedded code may be located in a variety of ways:

- *Modules*—Fetching code from modules (on `$PYTHONPATH`)
- *Text files*—Fetching code from simple text files
- *Registration*—Letting Python pass code to a C extension module
- *HTML tags*—Extracting code from Web pages
- *Databases*—Fetching code from a database table

- *Processes*—Receiving code over sockets or streams
- *Construction*—Building code in C at runtime
- *Others*—System registries and so on

These categories aren't completely orthogonal. In common practice, code forms suggest location techniques (code sources). For example, callable objects usually originate from modules or explicit registration, but code string sources can take a number of forms: files, modules, registration, databases, HTML files, and so on. Code files only exist as files but may be imported like modules or run as scripts.

Regardless of how embedded code is represented and found, C usually must communicate information with Python programs: to pass in knowledge of the surrounding context (inputs) and to fetch results generated by Python (outputs). Again, the form of the embedded code determines the sort of communications techniques it may support. For instance, strings and objects support the strategies in Table 11.18.

TABLE 11.18. *Embedding communication techniques.*

Code Form	*Technique*	*Mode*
Objects	Function arguments	Input, output
Objects	Function return values	Output
Strings	Expression results	Output
Strings, objects	Global module-level variables: copy-in-copy-out	Input, output
Strings, objects	Exported C extension module get/set functions	Input, output
Strings, objects	Files, stdin/stdout streams, sockets, etc.	Input, output

When we call function or class objects, argument lists and return values provide a natural input/output mechanism, but module-level variables can make more sense for string inputs. In some scenarios, it may be appropriate to create a C extension module that the embedded Python code can import and use to communicate with the enclosing C layer. In general, Python code called from C can communicate with the caller in the same ways as code called from Python.

11.4.2.1. Running Simple Code Strings

The `PyRun_SimpleString` API function is probably the simplest way to run embedded Python code from C. It takes a C character string (a C `char*`) containing a Python statement and compiles and runs the string in the `__main__` module's name space. Because the string must be a statement, no return value is communicated to the C caller. Moreover, each string run this way shares the same module name space (module `_[hr]_main_[hr]_`). For some applications, simple strings are all that we need. The C file in Listing 11.9 demonstrates simple code string embedding.

LISTING 11.9. *file:* `main1.c`.

```
#include <Python.h>

main(argc, argv)
int argc;
char **argv;
{
     /* This is the simplest embedding mode.  */
     /* Other API functions return results,   */
     /* accept namespace arguments, allow     */
     /* access to real Python objects, etc.   */
     /* Strings may be precompiled for speed. */

     Py_Initialize();                  /* initialize python */
     PyRun_SimpleString("print 'Hello embedded world!'");

     /* use C extension module above */
     PyRun_SimpleString("from environ import *");
     PyRun_SimpleString(
             "for i in range(5):\n"
                  "\tprint i,\n"
                  "\tprint 'Hello, %s' % getenv('USER')\n\n" );

     PyRun_SimpleString("print 'Bye embedded world!'");
}

char *Py_GetProgramName() { return "main1";}
```

In this C program, C executes Python statements by calling the Python API (Python's parser/compiler is always present at runtime). The effect is as if the following is typed at Python's interactive command line:

```
print 'Hello embedded world!'
from environ import *
for i in range(5):
     print i,
     print 'Hello, %s' % getenv('USER')
print 'Bye embedded world!
```

Notice that the embedded code imports the C extension module we saw earlier. Embedded Python code has access to all Python services: built-in modules, C extensions we add, and Python modules we code. It's normal for embedded code to call C extensions like this; in fact, Python supports arbitrary language nesting. C can call Python, which can call C, which can call Python, and so on. In practice, C extensions are a convenient way to export application-specific information and tools for use in embedded Python code.

The C file contains a `main` function; when we compile it and link with Python libraries, we get an executable file called `main1`. Running this executable from the system shell produces the following output. Each time through the `for` loop, the embedded code uses our `environ` C module to fetch the value of environment variable `USER`:

```
% main1
Hello embedded world!
0 Hello, mlutz
1 Hello, mlutz
2 Hello, mlutz
3 Hello, mlutz
4 Hello, mlutz
Bye embedded world!
```

Techniques for building the executable from the C file vary per platform, but the makefile in Listing 11.10 illustrates a typical way to build systems that embed Python. It compiles the C file and links its object code with Python's four libraries and two configuration object files. This file uses the original Python source tree (where Python was built); in some installations, all the necessary Python include, library, and object files may instead be located in standard directories. On some systems, Python might also be packaged as a single library file (`.so`, `.dll`, etc.). You may also need to link in fewer or more libraries, depending on which extensions you've bound into your Python installation.

LISTING 11.10. *file:* `Makefile.main1`.

```
# make a simple C executable that embeds (calls) Python code

Cc = /opt/SUNWspro/bin/cc
PY = /opt/local/src/Python-1.4

PLIBS = $(PY)/Modules/libModules.a \
        $(PY)/Python/libPython.a \
        $(PY)/Objects/libObjects.a \
        $(PY)/Parser/libParser.a

POBJS = $(PY)/Modules/config.o $(PY)/Modules/getpath.o

main1: main1.o
       $(Cc) main1.o $(POBJS) $(PLIBS)\
                  -lsocket -lnsl -ldl -lm -o main1

main1.o: main1.c
       $(Cc) main1.c -c -I$(PY)/Include -I$(PY)/.
```

11.4.2.2. Calling Objects and Methods

In general, the Python runtime API lets C programs perform most of the same operations Python programs can. Let's look at how that API is employed in a typical embedding task: calling objects defined in external Python modules. Suppose a C program needs to create an instance of a Python class defined in a module file and call the instance's methods. In pseudo code, we want C to perform these steps:

```
import <module>
object = <module>.<class>()
result = object.<method>(..args..)
```

Listing 11.11 shows one way to perform these steps using built-in API calls. First, let's define the module file that C will access; as usual, this file should be on a directory listed in environment variable `$PYTHONPATH` if we want to import it (from Python or C).

LISTING 11.11. *file:* `module.py`.

```
class klass:
    def method(self, x, y):
        return "brave %s %s" % (x, y)    # run me from C
```

Now, let's write the C file that imports this module and calls its class. Most of the API functions it uses have a direct counterpart in the Python language (see the section on first-class module objects).

- `PyObject` is the C type of a Python object.
- `PyImport_ImportModule` imports a Python module, much like the Python `import`.
- `PyObject_GetAttrString` performs attribute qualifications (`X.name`).
- `PyEval_CallObject` calls any callable object (class, function, method), like the `apply` built-in.
- `Py_BuildValue` converts C data to Python form.
- `PyArg_Parse` converts Python data to C form.

To call a fetched object, C calls `PyEval_CallObject`, passing in a tuple of argument objects and getting a Python object pointer back as the function's result. To convert Python objects to and from C form, the `Py_BuildValue` and `PyArg_Parse` converters both use type format strings to direct the conversion process (e.g., `(ss)` means convert between two Python strings and two C `char*s`). Finally, `Py_DECREF` is used to decrement reference counts on Python objects exported to C (as mentioned earlier,

Python uses a reference-count garbage collector; we need to accommodate it when integrating C components). Listing 11.12 shows the complete program.

LISTING 11.12. *file:* `objects1.c`.

```
#include <Python.h>
#include <import.h>
#include <stdio.h>
char *Py_GetProgramName() { return "objects1"; }

main() {
  char *arg1="sir", *arg2="robin", *cstr;
  PyObject *pmod, *pclass, *pargs, *pinst, *pmeth, *pres;

  /* instance = module.klass() */
  Py_Initialize();
  pmod   = PyImport_ImportModule("module");
  pclass = PyObject_GetAttrString(pmod, "klass");
  Py_DECREF(pmod);

  pargs  = Py_BuildValue("()");
  pinst  = PyEval_CallObject(pclass, pargs);        /* call class() */
  Py_DECREF(pclass);
  Py_DECREF(pargs);

  /* result = instance.method(x,y) */
  pmeth  = PyObject_GetAttrString(pinst, "method");/* bound method */
  Py_DECREF(pinst);
  pargs  = Py_BuildValue("(ss)", arg1, arg2);
  pres   = PyEval_CallObject(pmeth, pargs);
  Py_DECREF(pmeth);
  Py_DECREF(pargs);

  PyArg_Parse(pres, "s", &cstr);                    /* convert to C */
  printf("%s\n", cstr);
  Py_DECREF(pres);
}
```

To make an executable program from this file, we link it with Python's libraries and object files as shown earlier. Recall that class instances are generated by calling a class like a function: To make a Python class instance from C, we import the class and call it. When we run the C executable from the command line, it imports the Python module file (`module.py`), creates an instance of class `klass` by calling it, and then calls the instance's `method` method, passing in two string arguments. C prints the returned string:

```
% objects1
brave sir robin
```

The `objects1` program works, but we've skipped an important detail to make it easier to understand: Normally, we should always check for errors after each `Py*` API call. To be safe, we also need to check for `NULL` pointer results and bad integer return codes, to detect errors raised by Python during API calls. A more complete version of `objects1` would look something like the file in Listing 11.13.

LISTING 11.13. *file:* `objects1err.c`.

```
#include <Python.h>
#include <import.h>
#include <stdio.h>

char *Py_GetProgramName() { return "objects1err"; }
#define error(msg) do { printf("%s\n", msg); exit(1); } while (1)

main() {
  char *arg1="sir", *arg2="robin", *cstr;
  PyObject *pmod, *pclass, *pargs, *pinst, *pmeth, *pres;

  /* instance = module.klass() */
  Py_Initialize();
  pmod = PyImport_ImportModule("module");
  if (pmod == NULL)
      error("Can't load module");

  pclass = PyObject_GetAttrString(pmod, "klass");
  Py_DECREF(pmod);
  if (pclass == NULL)
      error("Can't get module.klass");

  pargs = Py_BuildValue("()");
  if (pargs == NULL) {
      Py_DECREF(pclass);
      error("Can't build arguments list");
  }
  pinst = PyEval_CallObject(pclass, pargs);
  Py_DECREF(pclass);
  Py_DECREF(pargs);
  if (pinst == NULL)
      error("Error calling module.klass()");

  /* result = instance.method(x,y) */
  pmeth  = PyObject_GetAttrString(pinst, "method");
  Py_DECREF(pinst);
  if (pmeth == NULL)
      error("Can't fetch klass.method");

  pargs = Py_BuildValue("(ss)", arg1, arg2);
  if (pargs == NULL) {
      Py_DECREF(pmeth);
      error("Can't build arguments list");
  }
  pres = PyEval_CallObject(pmeth, pargs);
  Py_DECREF(pmeth);
  Py_DECREF(pargs);
  if (pres == NULL)
      error("Error calling klass.method");
```

```
    if (!PyArg_Parse(pres, "s", &cstr))
       error("Can't convert klass.method result");
    printf("%s\n", cstr);
    Py_DECREF(pres);
}
```

As you can probably tell from looking at the last example, embedding interfaces can become complex if we code each operation from scratch. We need to detect errors, handle reference count details, and recall API details. A better approach may be to wrap the built-in API in higher-level abstractions.

Here is one approach: To simplify common embedding tasks, the file `objects2.c` in Listing 11.14 uses the extended API functions presented in Chapter 15 of the book *Programming Python*. It performs the exact same tasks as the original `objects1.c` but is noticeably simpler (especially compared to the version with error-checking code). The extended API automates common embedding tasks such as reference count management, error checking, data conversions, and module access. It also supports debugging and reloading of embedded code and exports functions for running code strings and objects, accessing module-level variables, and so on.

LISTING 11.14. *file:* `objects2.c`.

```
#include <stdio.h>
#include "pyembed.h"
char *Py_GetProgramName() { return "objects2"; }

main () {
  int failflag;
  PyObject *pinst;
  char *arg1="sir", *arg2="robin", *cstr;

  failflag =
    Run_Function("module", "klass", "O", &pinst, "()") ||
    Run_Method(pinst, "method", "s", &cstr, "(ss)", arg1, arg2);

  printf("%s\n", (!failflag) ? cstr : "Can't call objects");
  Py_XDECREF(pinst);
}
```

The arguments to the `Run_Method` extended API function are arranged as follows:

```
status = Run_Method(pinst,  "method",        /* call pinst.method     */
                    "s",     &cstr,          /* result format/target */
                    "(ss)", arg1, arg2);     /* args format/sources? */
```

`Run_Function` is similar, but the first argument is a Python module name (functions are fetched from modules, and methods are associated with known objects). Errors trigger a nonzero return code. To build an executable from this file, we link it with Python libraries and object files, as well as the pyembed* files from *Programming Python.* We get the same results when the executable is run:

```
% objects2
brave sir robin
```

Whether we use the built-in or extended API tools to call objects, communication protocols are simple: C passes data as function arguments and receives results as function return values. Callable objects also have access to global (module) variables and may import C get/set extension functions, but normal function-call behavior provides a direct input/output mapping. Also note that we fetch objects from modules in the preceding examples, but they might also be located by registration techniques (described later).

11.4.2.3. Running Code Strings with Results and Namespaces

In the first embedding example, we called PyRun_SimpleString to run statements in the module __main__. Other API tools let us run code strings in a namespace of our choosing and receive the results of Python expression strings in C. In the example in Listing 11.15, we import the string module and run a Python code string in its namespace: upper('spam')+'!', which simply converts spam to uppercase letters and concatenates an !. The result comes back as a Python string object that we convert to C as before. There are only two new API tools to introduce here:

- PyModule_GetDict—Fetches a module's namespace dictionary (its __dict__)
- PyRun_String—Runs a code string in local/global namespace dictionaries

The PyRun_String function also takes a parsing mode flag: eval_input is used for expressions and file_input for statements. We can run either kind of code, but only expressions return useful results to C.

LISTING 11.15. *file* codestring1.c.

```
#include <Python.h>          /* standard API defs  */
#include <import.h>          /* PyImport functions */
#include <graminit.h>        /* parse-mode flags   */
#include <pythonrun.h>       /* PyRun interfaces   */

char *Py_GetProgramName() { return "codestring1"; }
void error(char *msg) { printf("%s\n", msg); exit(1); }
```

```
main() {
     char *cstr;
     PyObject *pstr, *pmod, *pdict;                  /* with error tests */
     Py_Initialize();

     /* result = string.upper('spam') + '!' */
     pmod = PyImport_ImportModule("string");        /* fetch module */
     if (pmod == NULL)                              /* for name-space */
         error("Can't import module");

     pdict = PyModule_GetDict(pmod);                 /* string.__dict__ */
     Py_DECREF(pmod);
     if (pdict == NULL)
         error("Can't get module dict");

     pstr = PyRun_String("upper('spam') + '!'",
                          eval_input, pdict, pdict);
     if (pstr == NULL)
         error("Error while running string");

     /* convert result to C */
     if (!PyArg_Parse(pstr, "s", &cstr))
         error("Bad result type");
     printf("%s\n", cstr);
     Py_DECREF(pstr);        /* free exported objects, not pdict */
}
```

If we build this C program and run it, we get the following results:

```
% codestring1
SPAM!
```

But as before, we can recode this example to be much simpler, by using the extended API functions from Chapter 15 of *Programming Python* (see Listing 11.16).

LISTING 11.16. *file:* `codestring2.c`.

```
#include "pyembed.h"
#include <stdio.h>
char *Py_GetProgramName() { return "codestring2"; }

main() {
     char *cstr;
     int err = Run_Codestr(
                     PY_EXPRESSION,
                     "upper('spam') + '!'", "string",
                     "s", &cstr);
     printf("%s\n", (!err) ? cstr : "Can't run string");
}
```

The `Run_Codestr` function handles most embedding tasks for us; we pass in a parse-mode flag, a code string, a module name (the namespace to run the string in), and a result format/target for expressions. The API returns

`-1` on errors. When we build an executable from this file, we run it just like `codestring1`:

```
% codestring2
SPAM!
```

The extended API also supports the notion of running code strings that don't have real associated modules (by providing a dummy module abstraction, rather than raw dictionaries). The preceding string examples are mostly straightforward, but here are a few general comments about running strings.

- *Namespaces for strings*—Notice that both of the preceding examples run the code string in the built-in `string` module's namespace. The `string.upper` function can be used without qualifying it by the module name because the code string executes in the module's scopes; `upper` is a global (module-level) name to code in the string. It's also possible to create new dictionaries to serve as code string namespaces, instead of importing modules. In fact, we can run strings without importing modules at all; each application component can create its own unique namespace dictionaries. This strategy lets us execute strings that have no associated module (for instance, strings stored in databases). Namespaces aren't usually as big an issue when calling objects because they have implicitly associated namespaces; for example, methods reside in an object and run in lexically determined scopes.

- *Code sources (location techniques)*—Also note that all the embedded code strings we've run in the examples have been string constants hard-coded into the C program, to keep the examples simple. But, in practice, they might be located using any of the techniques we outlined at the start of this section: fetched from module attributes (variables), loaded from text files named by environment variables, extracted from HTML pages, and so on. More generally, any source of C character arrays can be a source of Python code strings. Because strings are a very general code medium, they provide a great deal of flexibility when designing an integration structure. In contrast, callable objects are usually only fetched from module files or registered to C by Python code (discussed later).

- *Data communication techniques*—Finally, when we run code strings, there's no notion of passed arguments or return values (except for expressions). But global (module-level) variables provide a simple way to communicate with code strings. This strategy is sometimes called *copy-in-copy-out*: The enclosing C layer sets global Python variables to inputs, runs the embedded code string, and then fetches global variables that the string assigns as outputs. For instance, the following code makes use of the extended API to implement a copy-in-copy-out strategy; the code runs in the name space of module `validate`:

```
/* set input vars */
char *string = . . .
Set_Global("validate", "QUANTITY",  "i", quantity);
Set_Global("validate", "ORDERTYPE", "s", ordertype);

/* run code string */
status = Run_Codestr(PY_STATEMENT,
                     string, "validate", "", NULL);
if (status == -1)
    PyErr_Print();   /* stack traceback */
else {
    /* fetch output vars */
    Get_Global("validate", "QUANTITY", "i", &quantity);
    Get_Global("validate", "MESSAGES", "s", &messages);
}
```

Within the embedded Python string, names `QUANTITY` and `ORDERTYPE` refer to the inputs from C, and names `QUANTITY` and `MESSAGES` are assigned to send results back to C. Of course, this is just one way to communicate data `to/from` strings. For example, we might instead export C `get/set` functions to Python; see the communication options outlined at the start of this section.

11.4.2.4. Calling Registered Python Objects and Strings

Our final embedding example really has more to do with code sources than with its form. It's sometimes possible to let Python programs tell C which code it should run, rather than fetch objects from modules or run general strings. This is usually called registration: Python code calls a C extension to register code it should execute. The registered code itself may take the form of objects or code strings, but Python programs explicitly tell C what code is to be run for a given situation.

Under this scenario, C defines both a C extension module to provide registration hooks, as well as embedding code to run the registered code. In other words, registration strategies make use of both extending and embedding interfaces. The Python program that registers code to C typically runs on top: Python is extended by C, which in turn embeds Python. But C might also run registration code as an initial embedding step. An example will make this more concrete. The C file in Listing 11.17 defines

- A C extension module that exports a registration function to Python (`setHandler`)
- A `Route_Event` function that calls the registered Python object in response to events

When Python calls the `setHandler` function, C saves the passed-in Python callable object. Later, C calls the registered object whenever events occur. For illustration purposes, the C module also defines a `triggerEvent` function, which the enclosing Python layer calls to simulate events. Normally, the registered Python object might be called in response to events caught by the C layer. In traditional terms, the registered Python object becomes a callback function: C routes events to registered Python code.

LISTING 11.17. *file:* `cregister.c`.

```
#include <Python.h>
#include <stdlib.h>

/***********************************************/
/* 1) code to route events to Python object    */
/* note that we could run strings here instead */
/***********************************************/

static PyObject *Handler = NULL;     /* keep Python object in C */

void Route_Event(char *label, int count)
{
    char *cres;
    PyObject *args, *pres;

    /* call Python handler */
    args = Py_BuildValue("(si)", label, count);   /* make arg-list */
    pres = PyEval_CallObject(Handler, args);      /* run a call */
    Py_DECREF(args);

    if (pres != NULL) {
        /* use and decref handler result */
        PyArg_Parse(pres, "s", &cres);
        printf("%s\n", cres);
        Py_DECREF(pres);
    }
}

/*****************************************************/
/* 2) python extension module to register handlers   */
/* python imports this module to set handler objects */
/*****************************************************/

static PyObject *
Register_Handler(PyObject *self, PyObject *args)
```

```
{
     /* save Python callable object */
     Py_XDECREF(Handler);                     /* called before? */
     PyArg_Parse(args, "O", &Handler);        /* one argument? */
     Py_XINCREF(Handler);                     /* add a reference */
     Py_INCREF(Py_None);                      /* return 'None': success */
     return Py_None;
}

static PyObject *
Trigger_Event(PyObject *self, PyObject *args)
{
     /* let Python simulate event caught by C */
     static count = 0;
     Route_Event("spam", count++);
     Py_INCREF(Py_None);
     return Py_None;
}

static struct PyMethodDef cregister_methods[] = {
     {"setHandler",    Register_Handler},        /* name, address */
     {"triggerEvent",  Trigger_Event},
     {NULL, NULL}
};

void initcregister()                   /* this is called by Python  */
{                                      /* on first "import cregister" */
     (void) Py_InitModule("cregister", cregister_methods);
}
```

This C extension module is bound into Python statically or dynamically, using the normal techniques we saw earlier. Once bound in, Python can import it as usual to register objects and trigger events. In the Python file in Listing 11.18, each time Python calls `triggerEvent`, the previously registered function is called by C.

LISTING 11.18. *file:* `register.py`.

```
# handle an event, return a result (or None)

def function1(label, count):
    return "%s number %i..." % (label, count)

def function2(label, count):
    return label * count

# register handlers, trigger events

import cregister
cregister.setHandler(function1)
for i in range(3):
    cregister.triggerEvent()   # simulate events caught by C layer

cregister.setHandler(function2)
for i in range(3):
    cregister.triggerEvent()   # routes these events to function2
```

Running this Python program from the shell command line produces the following results:

```
% python register.py
spam number 0...
spam number 1...
spam number 2...
spamspamspam
spamspamspamspam
spamspamspamspamspam
```

Notice that registration is not tied to callable objects: The registered code can actually take the form of objects, code strings, or files. In fact, registration is really just a technique for telling C which code to run, by letting Python call through a C extension module. We could also let Python pass in strings of code and run them when events occur using the code string interfaces we saw earlier.

11.4.2.5. Comparing Embedding Techniques

Registration is a useful technique and can sometimes provide more control over code selection than importing modules or running strings fetched from files or other sources. Programs specify objects and strings to run directly, rather than rely on external linkage protocols. Moreover, some applications require finer granularity than modules can easily support. For instance, the Tkinter GUI API we'll see later uses a registration-based approach, to allow clients to associate callable objects with potentially many widget objects (user-interface devices) in a GUI structure. In such a scenario, registration may provide a more direct way to associate embedded code with objects in a hierarchy than other techniques (modules, etc.).

At the same time, registration adds an extra coding step, implies an application structure, and does not directly support dynamic reloading of embedded code:

- *Registration step*—Not only must Python programmers write code to handle calls from C, but they might also need to write additional code to register those handlers to a C extension module. In some cases, this extra programming step is trivial, but in others, fetching code from modules or other sources can eliminate the registration step altogether and may be a simpler approach.
- *Application structure*—Python registration code must be run before the code it registers. In most cases, this means that Python must run

as the top level of an application; for many systems, this isn't a realistic expectation. Alternatively, a top-level C layer can run the registration code with a separate, initial embedded code call. This adds complexity and requires an extra protocol for locating the registration code itself, which is no different from the problem of locating embedded code without registration. If C must be on top, registration may not buy us much simplicity.

- *Reloading embedded code*—Finally, explicit registration does not readily support dynamic code reloading because registered code normally has no associated module. The API function `PyImport_ReloadModule(module)` works like the Python `reload` function we saw earlier; when applicable, it can be used to reload embedded code dynamically, to allow for changes without stopping the enclosing program. As long as we always fetch code from modules each time it runs, it's straightforward to reload the enclosing module on demand. To arrange for reloading of registered code, we would also need to register a module name or object along with the Python code to be run and (for objects) applying indirect call techniques (like objects imported with `from` statements, a raw Python object held by C won't be updated if its module is reloaded).

Because the Python API is general, code forms, code sources, and communication techniques all represent tradeoffs. As usual, integration designs depend on an application's structure and requirements.

11.4.2.6. Building the Examples

Finally, the makefile in Listing 11.19 illustrates how the various examples in this section are built. It generates the embedding examples (C executables), as well as the two extension modules we've seen (`cregister` and `environ`). The embedding examples link the C `main` function with Python's libraries and object files. The two extension modules are built as dynamically loaded sharable object files, loaded on first import. This listing shows how to build C components in a mixed Python/C system, but here are a few things to note:

- Your makefile details will vary according to where Python is installed, which extensions are enabled in your installation, and so on. They may also vary slightly in future Python releases (e.g., a single `.a`).

- The extension module build details are specific to the Sun Solaris platform and produce `.so` files. On other systems, you may need to generate `.dll` or `.sl` files or use static linking techniques (change the `Modules/Setup` file and rebuild Python). See Python extension documentation for more details.
- The examples that make use of the extended API functions (e.g., `Run_Function`) also require the `pyembed*` files packaged with the book *Programming Python*; see the resources section for details.

LISTING 11.19. *file:* `Makefile.all`.

```
######################################################################
# Build all embedding examples: "make -f Makefile.all";
# also builds extension modules shareables (cregister, environ);
# be sure to set the Python search path to find imported modules:
# setenv PYTHONPATH .:/opt/local/src/Python-1.4/Lib
######################################################################

Cc = /opt/SUNWspro/bin/cc
PY = /opt/local/src/Python-1.4

# libs and objects from Python build tree
PLIBS = $(PY)/Modules/libModules.a \
        $(PY)/Python/libPython.a \
        $(PY)/Objects/libObjects.a \
        $(PY)/Parser/libParser.a

POBJS = $(PY)/Modules/config.o $(PY)/Modules/getpath.o

CLIBS  = -L/usr/lib -lsocket -lnsl -ldl -lm
CFLAGS = -c -g -I$(PY)/Include -I$(PY)/. -I$(APISRC)

# extended API files from "Programming Python" CD
APIMODS = pyembed0.o pyembed1.o pyembed2.o pyembed3.o pyembed4.o
APISRC  = ..

# targets
EXECS = main1 \
        objects1 objects1err objects2 \
        codestring1 codestring2
CMODS = cregister.so environ.so

all: $(EXECS) $(CMODS)

# [main1: run simple strings]
main1:
	$(MAKE) -f Makefile.main1

# [objects1: call objects]
objects1: objects1.o
	$(Cc) -g objects1.o $(POBJS) $(PLIBS) $(CLIBS) -o $@

objects1.o: objects1.c
	$(Cc) objects1.c $(CFLAGS)
```

```
# [objects1err: objects1 + error checking]
objects1err: objects1err.o
	$(Cc) -g objects1err.o $(POBJS) $(PLIBS) $(CLIBS) -o $@

objects1err.o: objects1err.c
	$(Cc) objects1err.c $(CFLAGS)

# [objects2: call objects via api]
objects2: objects2.o $(APIMODS)
	$(Cc) -g objects2.o $(APIMODS)\
				$(POBJS) $(PLIBS) $(CLIBS) -o $@

objects2.o: objects2.c $(APISRC)/pyembed.h
	$(Cc) objects2.c $(CFLAGS)

# [codestring1: run strings]
codestring1: codestring1.o
	$(Cc) -g codestring1.o $(POBJS) $(PLIBS) $(CLIBS) -o $@

codestring1.o: codestring1.c
	$(Cc) codestring1.c $(CFLAGS)

# [codestring2: run strings via api]
codestring2: codestring2.o $(APIMODS)
	$(Cc) -g codestring2.o $(APIMODS)\
				$(POBJS) $(PLIBS) $(CLIBS) -o $@

codestring2.o: codestring2.c $(APISRC)/pyembed.h
	$(Cc) codestring2.c $(CFLAGS)

# [extended api files: 0..4]
pyembed%.o: $(APISRC)/pyembed%.c $(APISRC)/pyembed.h
	$(Cc) $(APISRC)/pyembed$*.c $(CFLAGS)


###################################################################
# add the extension modules (cregister, environ) as dynamically
# linked modules; when first imported, they are located in a dir
# on $PYTHONPATH, and loaded into the process.
#
# Note: the code here is specific to Sun Solaris (SunOS 5); it may
# need to be tweaked to produce a shareable object file on your
# system.  Alternatively, these two modules can be bound into
# the 'python' executable statically (not dynamically), by adding
# lines to Modules/Setup like "cregister cregister.c", putting a
# link to the .c file in Modules (or the .o file), and remake'ing
# Python.  Static linking requires rebuilding Python itself, but
# is a more portable strategy.
###################################################################


cregister.so: cregister.c
	$(Cc) cregister.c $(CFLAGS) -DDEBIG -KPIC -o cregister.o
	ld -G cregister.o -o $@
	rm -f cregister.o

environ.so: environ.c
	$(Cc) environ.c $(CFLAGS) -KPIC -o environ.o
	ld -G environ.o -o $@
```

```
        rm -f environ.o

clean:
        rm -f *.o *.pyc $(EXECS) $(CMODS)
```

11.4.3. Other Integration Topics

Integration is a big topic, and we've glossed over most of the details here. But here's a quick look at some other key topics in Python/C integration programming.

11.4.3.1. Running Code and Module Files from C

We didn't see an example of this, but it's also possible to run external files of Python code from C: The `PyRun_File` and `PyRun_SimpleFile` functions execute entire files of code. They are analogous to the `PyRun_String` and `PyRun_SimpleString` interfaces we saw earlier. Because the code in Python modules is executed when they are first loaded, the import functions we saw earlier can be used to run module files as well. Modules files are located in a directory on the `PYTHONPATH` environment variable; for simple text files, we might define other environment variables that point to the files.

11.4.3.2. Error Handling

We've seen common error interfaces in the examples, but here are a few more details:

- *Sending error information to Python (extending)*—C extensions signal errors to Python by returning `NULL` pointers from C extension functions; when the function returns, the `NULL` causes an exception to be raised in the Python caller. C may also set the exception's name and extra data: the `PyErr_SetString(exception-object, message-string)` API function provides a simple way to set the exception raised by returning `NULL`.

- *Getting error information from Python (embedding, extending)*—Errors in embedded code are flagged by API call return values: `NULL` for pointer result functions or an integer status code. The enclosing C layer can use the `PyErr_Fetch` API function to extract the type and data of the exception Python raised. Note that API functions can fail when we're extending, too: For instance, the data converter functions can report errors when parsing argument lists. In these cases, we often simply return `NULL` without setting our own error information (because Python has already set the exception itself).

When an error occurs during a Python API function call, Python sets the current exception type and data before the API call returns. If we just want to display exception information, we can call another API function:

```
PyErr_Print();    /* show Python stack traceback on stderr */
```

Alternatively, we can fetch exception information from Python more directly. The file in Listing 11.20 defines a utility function that fetches, prints, and saves the most recently raised Python exception.

LISTING 11.20. *file:* `pyerrors.c.`

```
#include <Python.h>
#include <stdio.h>
char save_error_type[1024], save_error_info[1024];

PyerrorHandler(char *msgFromC)
{
     /* process Python-related errors */
     /* call after Python API raises an exception C detects */

     PyObject *errobj, *errdata, *errtraceback, *pystring;
     printf("%s\n", msgFromC);

     /* get latest python exception info */
     PyErr_Fetch(&errobj, &errdata, &errtraceback);

     pystring = NULL;
     if (errobj != NULL &&
        (pystring = PyObject_Str(errobj)) != NULL &&
        (PyString_Check(pystring))
        )
         strcpy(save_error_type, PyString_AsString(pystring));
     else
         strcpy(save_error_type, "<unknown exception type>");
     Py_XDECREF(pystring);

     pystring = NULL;
     if (errdata != NULL &&
        (pystring = PyObject_Str(errdata)) != NULL &&
        (PyString_Check(pystring))
        )
         strcpy(save_error_info, PyString_AsString(pystring));
     else
         strcpy(save_error_info, "<unknown exception data>");
     Py_XDECREF(pystring);

     printf("%s\n%s\n", save_error_type, save_error_info);
     Py_XDECREF(errobj);
     Py_XDECREF(errdata);          /* caller owns all 3 objects */
     Py_XDECREF(errtraceback);    /* already NULL'd out in Python */
}
```

To use this file, change the `error` macro in file `objects1err.c` to call the exported function:

```
#define error(msg) \
    do { PyerrorHandler(msg); exit(1); } while (1)
```

and add this file's object code to the link command in `Makefile.all`:

```
objects1err: objects1err.o pyerrors.o
        $(Cc) -g objects1err.o pyerrors.o\
                       $(POBJS) $(PLIBS) $(CLIBS) -o $@
```

Now, run the resulting `objects1err` executable without setting the `PYTHONPATH` environment variable to include the directory that contains the Python `module.py` in the test. The attempt to import the module from C fails as expected, and the resulting `NULL` return value triggers the new `PyerrorHandler` function, which prints a C message, along with the exception type and data set by Python's API:

```
% objects1err
Can't load module
ImportError
No module named module
```

Finally, if we just want to print an exception object, a single API call will usually suffice:

```
PyErr_Fetch(&errobj, &errdata, &errtraceback);
if (PyObject_Print(errobj, stdout, PRINT_RAW) != 0)
     err_clear();
...
```

Note that the extended API functions we used (e.g., `Run_Function`) exit as soon as any error is detected in a built-in API call. They all return a `-1` integer or `NULL` pointer to flag errors to callers and propagate the exception information set by the underlying built-in Python API.

11.4.3.3. Precompiling Code Strings into Byte Code for Speed

When we run code strings, Python normally needs to compile them into byte code first. In some applications that demand optimal performance, the compile step can be expensive, especially if the string is run repeatedly. For such cases, Python lets us precompile code strings into byte code objects, which we can run later. As usual, we implement this strategy with Python API functions:

```
PyObject*
Py_CompileString(char *string, char *filename, int parsemode)
```

compiles a code string into a Python code object (really, a `PyCodeObject*`). `filename` is only used for error reporting, and `parsemode` is the normal eval_input/file_input constant we used earlier (for compiling expressions and statements). The resulting byte code object can then be executed by passing it to the API function:

```
PyObject* PyEval_EvalCode(PyCodeObject *code,
                          PyObject *globalnsdict,
                          PyObject *localnsdict)
```

These two API functions are the C equivalents of the built-in compile and eval/exec Python tools. Note that code stored in files can usually be precompiled by importing the file once. Moreover, objects fetched from modules are already compiled by the time they're exported to C.

11.4.3.4. C++ Integration

Python is coded in portable ANSI C, so all the usual C/C++ integration concepts apply when mixing Python and C++. Python header files are all wrapped in extern "C" declarations, so they compile correctly when included by C++ files. Here are a few more details:

- When embedding Python in C++, the extern "C" declarations in Python header files are sufficient to allow C++ to link with and call Python API functions. Python's libraries normally don't have to be recompiled by the C++ compiler.
- When extending Python with C++, it's usually necessary to wrap functions to be called by Python in extern "C" declarations. This includes module initialization functions and (usually) all method functions. Moreover, if the main program is compiled as a C system, C++ global or static objects with constructors (initializers) might not work correctly. This isn't an issue if the main program is linked by C++. Initializer details may vary per compiler; see your compiler documentation for more details.

11.4.3.5. Interfacing with C Variables in Embedded Code

Extension modules are useful for accessing C functions from Python, but C variables cannot be called and normally require an extra wrapping layer to be used in Python. One way to implement the linkage is to export a C extension module with simple get/set functions for each C variable we want to export to Python:

```
import cvars          # import your C variable wrapper module
cvars.setX(24)        # set C X from Python
print cvars.getY()    # fetch C Y from Python
```

Alternatively, we can implement a variable interface extension type that overloads attribute accesses and provides a more Python-like interface to C variables:

```
import cvars              # import your C variable wrapper module
c = cvars.interface()     # make an interface object instance
c.X = (24)                # set attributes -> links to C variable
print c.Y                 # get attributes -> links to C variable
```

Each time the `interface` object is qualified, C intercepts the operation and maps it to the named C variables. Finally, if we can be sure embedded calls are non-reentrant, a copy-in-copy-out strategy may suffice as well. In abstract terms, to export C variables called `X` and `Y` to Python

1. C copies `X`s and `Y`s values to global variables in Python module `M`.
2. C runs embedded code in module `M`'s name space.
3. C fetches the final values of the Python global variables and copies them out to `X` and `Y`.

Under this scheme, the Python variables `X` and `Y` are `true` Python variables, which simply shadow their C counterparts while the embedded code runs.

11.4.3.6. Automatic Extension Tools

C integration is an inherently complex task but is relatively rare (compared to Python coding) and can be largely automated with auxiliary tools. Because C extensions follow a standard format, they support automatic generation especially well; embedding tasks may also be automated with extended APIs. Here's a quick overview of popular integration tools available to Python developers.

- The SWIG system uses C-type declarations and interface description files to generate complete Python interfaces to external C and C++ libraries. For C++, SWIG can generate both a C extension type that wraps exported methods, plus a Python wrapper (`shadow`) class that makes the C++ class appear as a true Python class (it may be subclassed and specialized in Python).
- The ILU system implements complete distributed-object systems from interface description files. ILU is based on the CORBA distributed object model. ILU objects can be implemented on a variety of platforms and in a number of programming languages; all interfacing details are automated.

- The abstract object-access API (file `abstract.h`) allows C programs to create and process Python objects generically, using the same operations available to Python programs (slicing, qualification, etc.). Like the extended API used earlier, the object access API is built on top of Python's built-in API.
- The extended API embedding functions we used in the examples (e.g., `Run_Function`) automate or simplify common embedded tasks: running code strings, calling objects and methods, accessing module variables, and so on. They also allow for embedded code debugging and reloading.
- The modulator tool is a Tkinter GUI that can be used to generate skeleton C extension modules and types. It inputs all relevant parameters (function names, type components) and produces correct C files that only need to have implementation-specific code segments (function bodies) inserted.
- Other tools support more specific integration models. For instance, the PythonWin package supports ActiveX/COM scripting on Windows platforms.

11.4.4. Summary: Integration Tasks

We've looked at a lot of examples in this section. Although we can't dig into API details further in this chapter, the examples should at least give you the general flavor of common integration structures. To summarize some of what we've seen, Table 11.19 describes the tasks that are typically performed when writing C extension modules. The first three entries are implemented by interacting with the Python API, and the last three have to do with the structure of an extension module and the way Python locates it.

TABLE 11.19. *Extension module tasks.*

Task	*Description*
Conversions	Converting Python data to/from C form
Error handling	Reporting, detecting, and propagating errors
References	Managing reference counts of exported Python objects
Registration	Mapping operation names to C function pointers
Initialization	Defining a function to be called on first import
Binding	Linking to Python libraries: statically or dynamically

As noted before, C extension types perform the same sorts of tasks, but the registration step is more complex: It involves filling out type descriptor structures in C. As we've seen, when Python is embedded, many of the same tasks are performed in C, but the last three entries in Table 11.19 don't apply:

- There's no notion of extension module registration or initialization.
- Binding takes the form of linking Python's libraries and object files with your `main` function.
- There's an extra step: initializing the Python runtime system itself.

For more details on C integration topics, consult the information sources at the end of this chapter.

11.5. Real Python Programs

Now that we've seen the basics, we're going to briefly study a handful of realistically scaled programs in this section (as realistic as space allows, at least). As mentioned before, real Python programs can range from short scripts composed of a few lines of code all the way up to huge frameworks and systems. Common practice usually falls somewhere in between, as illustrated by the examples here.

Part of our goal here is also to demonstrate common Python roles. The programs in this section are drawn from popular Python domains:

- Shell tools
- Graphical user interfaces
- Persistent objects
- Data-structure classes
- Internet scripts

Of course, this set isn't complete, and we can't cover any of these areas in great detail here. Again, refer to the information sources at the end of this chapter for more details about specific Python domains.

11.5.1. Shell Tools

One of the main roles Python plays is as a system utility programming language. In this domain, Python is used in roughly the same way as UNIX shells (csh, ksh), Perl, and Awk. Python's interactive nature and built-in system interfaces make it well-suited for writing system tools.

Many also find that Python's readability, and support for more advanced development paradigms, make it well-suited for writing maintainable, scalable system utilities. Moreover, Python's portability also means we can write shell tools that will run on a variety of platforms without changes.

11.5.1.1. Unpacking Files with Simple Scripts

To illustrate, here is a more or less typical task for a shell tool script. One way to combine a set of text files is to pass them to the UNIX `more` command. For example, suppose we want to package two text files, `t1.txt` and `t2.txt`, into a single text file called `t.more` for convenient transfers. The `more` command puts both files into the output file with a separator before each:

```
% cat t1.txt
Hello
Shell
% cat t2.txt
Tools
World!

% more t1.txt t2.txt > t.more
% cat t.more
::::::::::::::
t1.txt
::::::::::::::
Hello
Shell
::::::::::::::
t2.txt
::::::::::::::
Tools
World!
```

The file prefix/separator takes the form of a line of 14 colons (`::::::::::::::`), followed by a line with the original file name, followed by another line of colons. Now, suppose we want to extract the original files from a `more` command's output. The Python script in Listing 11.21 extracts multiple files from such an archive file; the `more` output file is either piped in on the system command line (`< file`) or passed in by name on the script's command line.

LISTING 11.21. *file:* `unmore1.py`.

```
#!/usr/local/bin/python
# unpack result of "more x y z > f"
# usage: "unmore1.py f" or "unmore1.py < f"
# uses simple top-level script logic

import sys
marker = ':'*14
```

```
try:
    input = open(sys.argv[1], "r")
except:
    input = sys.stdin
output = sys.stdout

while 1:
    line = input.readline()
    if not line:                               # end of file?
        break
    elif line[:14] != marker:                  # text line?
        output.write(line)
    else:                                      # file prefix
        fname = input.readline()[:-1]          # strip eoln ('\n')
        print 'creating', `fname`
        output = open(fname, "w")              # next output file

        line = input.readline()                # end of prefix
        if line[:14] != marker:
            print "OOPS!"; sys.exit(1)

print 'Done.'
```

This script doesn't introduce anything we haven't seen in this chapter. In short, the main `while` loop just scans the `more` output file line-by-line until end-of-file, writing normal lines to the current output file and resetting the current output file when a prefix sequence is detected. We can use our script to extract the two original files as follows:

```
% unmore1.py t.more
creating 't1.txt'
creating 't2.txt'
Done.
```

Either of the following commands will run our script, too: The first pipes the input file to the script's `stdin` stream, and the second invokes the Python interpreter explicitly (useful on non-UNIX systems):

```
% unmore1.py < t.more
% python unmore1.py t.more
```

11.5.1.2. Adding a Functional Interface

As coded previously, the `unmore1` script consists of top-level logic executed immediately when the script is executed. If the unpacking logic is something that may be useful outside this script, it may be a better idea to package it as a function, which external clients can import and reuse. To both package unpacking for clients, and invoke it in script mode, we can make use of the `_[hr]_name_[hr]_` trick we saw earlier: The module in Listing 11.22 works the same as the original but exports its utility as a function, instead of top-level code.

LISTING 11.22. *file:* `unmore2.py`.

```
#!/usr/local/bin/python
# unpack result of "more x y z > f"
# usage: "unmore2.py f" or "unmore2.py < f"
# packages unpacking logic as an importable function

import sys
marker = ':'*14

def unmore(input):
    output = sys.stdout
    while 1:
        line = input.readline()
        if not line:                              # end of file?
            break
        elif line[:14] != marker:                 # text line?
            output.write(line)
        else:                                     # file prefix
            fname = input.readline()[:-1]         # strip eoln ('\n')
            print 'creating', `fname`
            output = open(fname, "w")             # next output file
            if input.readline()[:14] != marker:
                print "OOPS!"; sys.exit(1)

if __name__ == '__main__':
    if len(sys.argv) == 1:
        unmore(sys.stdin)                         # unmore2.py < f
    else:
        unmore(open(sys.argv[1], 'r'))            # unmore2.py f
    print 'Done.'
```

This file can be run as a script just like the original version, but because we've bundled up its logic in a function, it may also be imported and called from other components:

```
% unmore2.py t.more
creating 't1.txt'
creating 't2.txt'
Done.

% python
>>> from unmore2 import unmore
>>> unmore(open("t.more", "r"))
creating 't1.txt'
creating 't2.txt'
```

11.5.1.3. Unpacking Files with an Application Framework

One last improvement: The preceding scripts work but are very specific to the task at hand. Because Python is a full-fledged object-oriented language, it's also possible to write application frameworks, which wrap common system interfaces for ease of use and automate typical shell tool tasks. For instance, the script in Listing 11.23 performs the same task as the simpler versions, but it does so by subclassing a generalized `StreamApp` superclass. `StreamApp` provides a number of precoded services for its clients:

- It hides (wraps) most system details.
- It provides a standard start/run/stop protocol for applications.
- It makes application instances act like input/output files.

The `UnmoreApp` subclass provides a `run` method to process the input stream and reads and writes itself to access the script's input/output streams. `StreamApp` automatically redirects read/write operations to files or streams, according to the command-line arguments used when starting an application.

LISTING 11.23. *file:* `unmore3.py`.

```
#!/usr/local/bin/python
# unpack result of "more x y z > f"
# usage: "unmore3.py -i f -v?" or "unmore3.py -v? < f"
# uses StreamApp class from "Programming Python" (appendix D)

from apptools import StreamApp
marker = ':'*14

class UnmoreApp(StreamApp):                               # app subclass
    def run(self):                                        # start/run/stop
        while 1:
            line = self.readline()
            if not line:                                  # end of file?
                break
            elif line[:14] != marker:                     # text line?
                self.write(line)
            else:                                         # file prefix
                fname = self.readline()[:-1]
                self.message('creating ' + `fname`)
                self.setOutput(fname)
                if self.readline()[:14] != marker:
                    self.exit("OOPS!")

if __name__ == '__main__': UnmoreApp().main()             # make/run an app
```

To start the application when this file is run as a script, we make an instance of the `UnmoreApp` class and call its imported `main` method. Note that because we're using an imported superclass here, we need to make sure it is in the `PYTHONPATH` directory list, too:

```
% setenv PYTHONPATH\
        ".:/pp/examples/other/framewrk:/usr/local/lib/python"
% unmore3.py -i t.more
creating 't1.txt'
creating 't2.txt'
```

The `-i` command-line flag is handled by the `StreamApp` superclass; we can also make use of a `-v` verbose flag, which triggers default superclass messages:

```
% unmore3.py -i t.more -v
UnmoreApp start.
creating 't1.txt'
creating 't2.txt'
UnmoreApp done.
```

As before, we may also pipe the input file in instead of giving its name, and we can make use of the unpacking class by importing it from other Python components:

```
% unmore3.py -v < t.more
... same output

% python
>>> from unmore3 import UnmoreApp
>>> app = UnmoreApp()
>>> app.setInput("t.more")
>>> app.main()
creating 't1.txt'
creating 't2.txt'
```

As usual under encapsulation, much of the action in this version happens in the superclass. This is what we want: Because `StreamApp` generalizes the notion of streams, clients can be made to process other kinds of streams (e.g., sockets, shared memory, etc.) by simply inheriting from more specialized superclasses. `StreamApp` is part of an application class framework presented in Appendix D of the book *Programming Python*. The application framework also defines classes that handle menu-based interaction, internal (string) stream redirection, and so on. See the resource section at the end of this chapter for more details.

11.5.2. GUI Programming

For many, Python's very high-level semantics, together with its fast turnaround after program changes, make it a natural for GUI development and prototyping. GUI programs in Python are fast to write because there's less for the programmer to manage. Just as important, it's easy to experiment with GUI alternatives in Python because the effects of program changes can be observed quickly (there are no compile/link steps). In some scenarios, it's even possible to change a GUI's behavior without restarting it at all: The `reload` function lets us incorporate modified program code at runtime.

To support GUI development, Python comes with a standard interface called Tkinter. Roughly, Tkinter is an object-oriented interface to the Tk GUI API, originally written for the Tcl language. Tk, and hence Python's Tkinter, are portable GUI solutions: Python GUI programs written using Tkinter are portable to X Window, Microsoft Windows, and the Macintosh. Moreover, Tkinter programs run with a native look-and-feel on all supported platforms. Other GUI options exist for Python (including MFC wrappers on Windows and WPY— portable MFC-like API), but Tk has become an industry standard, and Tkinter is the de facto standard for portable GUI development in Python.

11.5.2.1. The `Hello World` GUI Program in Python

Because Tkinter GUI programming is such a natural fit for Python, let's look at a few simple GUI programs that illustrate the flavor of the interface, and some of the benefits of wrapping it in an object-oriented language like Python. To use Tkinter, programs import widget classes and make instances to activate user-interface components. More complex GUIs are typically built by subclassing widget classes and embedding widget class instances in larger containers. Despite its scalability, simple things are simple in Tkinter. For instance, the `Hello World` GUI program in Python is straightforward (see Listing 11.24).

LISTING 11.24. *file:* `gui.py`.

```
from Tkinter import *                        # get widget classes/constants
Label(text="Hello GUI world!").pack()        # make/arrange a label widget
mainloop()                                   # show window, catch events
```

Despite its size, this is a fully functional Python/Tkinter GUI program. It simply

1. Imports widget classes from the Tkinter module.
2. Makes a `Label` widget attached to the default top-level window.
3. Arranges (`packs`) the widget inside its parent.
4. Calls the `mainloop` function to show the window and start catching GUI events.

Notice that we use a keyword argument to configure the Label's text string (`text=...`). In Tkinter, configuration options are typically set by passing keyword arguments to widget constructors. When we run this script file, we get the window shown in Figure 11.3. As the screen shot in the figure suggests, these examples were run on a Microsoft Windows 95 machine; they look slightly different on other platforms but have the same functionality. `gui1` is started like any other Python program (Tkinter is linked in):

```
% python gui1.py
```

FIGURE 11.3. *The* `gui1` *window.*

11.5.2.2. Adding Buttons, Frames, and Callbacks

Of course, we usually want our GUIs to do a bit more than display labels. The example in Listing 11.25 builds a window with a label and a button configured to call a function we provide whenever it is pressed. For buttons, the `command` keyword argument lets us register a Python callable object to catch the GUI event; in this case, we register the `callback` function in our script. Each time the button is pressed, a message line is printed to the `stdout` stream (normally, the window where we started the script).

LISTING 11.25. *file:* `gui2.py`.

```
from Tkinter import *                        # get widgets and constants

def callback():                              # define an event handler
    print 'hello stdout world...'

top = Frame()                                # attach widgets to container
top.pack()
Label(top,  text="Hello callback world").pack(side=TOP)
Button(top, text="press me", command=callback).pack(side=BOTTOM)
top.mainloop()
```

We also use an explicit parent for our widgets here: The label and button are attached to a new `Frame` container widget (`top`) and are arranged on its top and bottom sides. The `mainloop` function used to start the GUI is also a widget method (we get to it through `top` here). When we run this script, we get a one-button window, as shown in Figure 11.4:

```
% python gui2.py
hello stdout world...
hello stdout world...
```

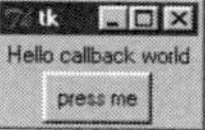

FIGURE 11.4. *The* `gui2` *window.*

In general, Tkinter works on a "what you build is what you get" principle: We define how the GUI looks by the order in which we attach widgets to frames and the packing options we use to configure them. For example, Figure 11.6 shows how `gui2` is built.

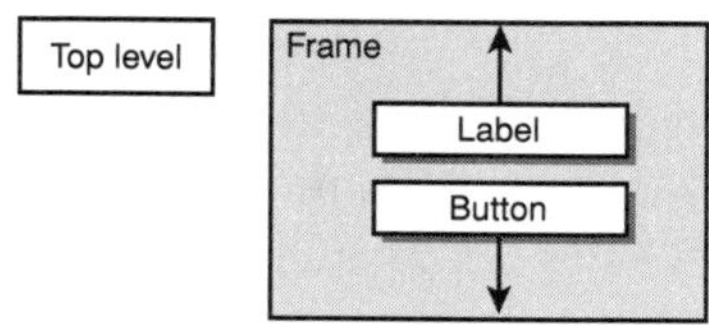

FIGURE 11.5. *Arranging widgets in frames.*

When we pass parents into widget constructors, Tkinter also takes care to internally cross-link parents to children. The result is an implicit tree of widget objects, like the one sketched in Figure 11.6. Note that this tree guarantees that widgets will be referenced (and therefore not garbage collected), even if we don't assign them to variables or members in our construction logic. For instance, in the preceding example, we create a `Label` and `pack` it in place without assigning it to a name; Tkinter adds the label to the internal widget tree and returns it to our program, but there's no need to retain another reference to the object.

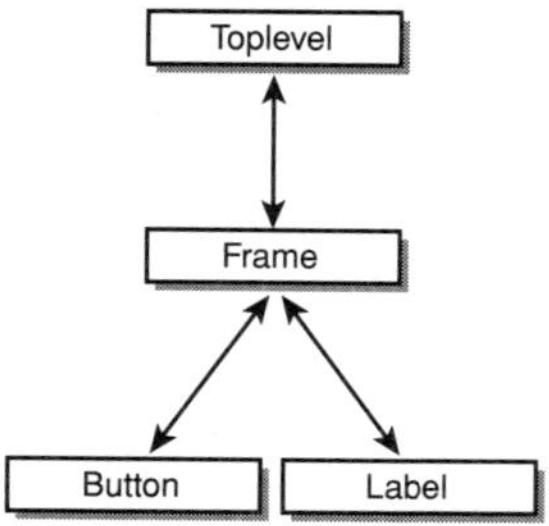

FIGURE 11.6. *Implicit widget object trees.*

11.5.2.3. Building GUIs with Container Classes

For more complex GUIs, we often need a more powerful organizational structure. As usual, Python classes provide the program structure we need. Not only do they help us organize our GUIs, but they support both specialization (by subclassing) and reuse (by attachment). A common way to employ classes in GUI programs is to organize a GUI as a subclass of the Tkinter `Frame` container widget. In the example in Listing 11.26, we define a `Hello` class, which is a specialized `Frame`. The GUI is built by attaching widgets to the `Frame` (i.e., to `self`), and event handlers take the form of bound methods of a `Hello` instance (of `self`).

LISTING 11.26 *file:* `hello.py`.

```
#!/usr/local/bin/python
from Tkinter import *                        # get widget classes

class Hello(Frame):                          # container subclass
    def __init__(self, parent=None):
        Frame.__init__(self, parent)         # do superclass init
        self.pack()
        self.make_widgets()                  # attach widgets to self

    def make_widgets(self):
        widget = Button(self, text='Hello', command=self.onPress)
        widget.pack(side=LEFT)

    def onPress(self):
        print 'Hi.'                          # write to sys.stdout

if __name__ == '__main__':  Hello().mainloop()
```

When we run this file, we get a one-button window again (Figure 11.7); as before, each time the button is pressed we see a new line on the `stdout` display (printed by the `onPress` method). The last line in the script creates a `Hello` instance and calls its `mainloop` method to display its `Frame` and start the event processing loop. When a `Frame` is displayed, all its attached children are displayed as well:

```
% hello.py
Hi.
Hi.
```

FIGURE 11.7. *The* `hello` *window.*

11.5.2.4. Reusing GUIs by Subclassing: Is A

Although this may seem like a complex way to pop up a button, the `Hello` class graphically demonstrates the power of OOP in Python. Because the GUI is a class, it's easy to tailor and extend it by defining a subclass. For instance, the example in Listing 11.27 defines a subclass that extends

Hello's make_widgets method (to add an extra button) and replaces Hello's onPress method (to print a different message). In OOP terminology, we say HelloExtender is a hello.Hello: It inherits and customizes existing methods.

LISTING 11.27. *file:* hellosub.py.

```
#!/usr/local/bin/python
from hello   import Hello                # get superclass to extend
from Tkinter import *                    # get Tkinter widget classes

class HelloExtender(Hello):              # specializes hello.Hello
    def make_widgets(self):              # extend superclass method
        Hello.make_widgets(self)
        mine = Button(self, text='Extend', command=self.quit)
        mine.pack(side=RIGHT)

    def onPress(self):
        print 'Greetings!'               # replace superclass method

if __name__ == '__main__': HelloExtender().mainloop()
```

Notice how the make_widgets method here first calls the inherited version by qualifying the superclass directly; all we're doing here is adding additional logic to the inherited version. Conversely, onPress completely overrides the inherited method.

When we run this file, we get an expanded GUI with two buttons (Figure 11.8). Pressing the original Hello button now prints Greetings! because we've replaced the callback method. Pressing the new Extend method calls a quit method inherited from Frame, which simply closes the GUI:

```
% python hellosub.py
Greetings!
Greetings!
```

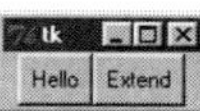

FIGURE 11.8. *The* hellosub *window.*

11.5.2.5. Reusing GUIs by Attaching: Has A

Naturally, we're using simple examples here to illustrate basics, but the concepts scale up to more complex GUI interfaces. When used well, subclassing lets us reuse already coded GUIs by defining how our needs differ. Another way to reuse GUI classes is to attach them to larger components. In the script in Listing 11.28, we define an outer Frame subclass (HelloContainer), which makes an instance of our original Hello class and attaches it to itself (to self). In OOP nomenclature, HelloContainer has a hello.Hello.

LISTING 11.28. *file:* `hellouse.py`.

```
#!/usr/local/bin/python
from hello   import Hello           # get class to attach
from Tkinter import *               # get Tk widget classes

class HelloContainer(Frame):
    def __init__(self, parent=None):
        Frame.__init__(self, parent)
        self.pack()
        self.make_widgets()

    def make_widgets(self):
        mine = Button(self, text='Attach', command=self.quit)
        mine.pack(side=LEFT)
        Hello(self)                  # attach a Hello frame to me

if __name__ == '__main__': HelloContainer().mainloop()
```

Running this file creates the window in Figure 11.9; we get two buttons again. This time, pressing the original `Hello` button prints the original `Hi.` message because we haven't overridden the `onPress` method: We're embedding objects here, not subclassing:

```
% hellouse.py
Hi.
Hi.
```

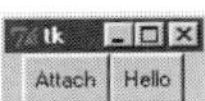

FIGURE 11.9 *The* `hellouse` *window.*

By embedding GUI class instances like this, we can build up arbitrarily complex GUIs. In fact, this is just an instance of the object-oriented composition idiom we introduced earlier: Larger objects can be constructed by embedding and controlling other objects. In Tkinter programming, composition is usually coded by passing parent widgets to embedded widget constructors; Tkinter maintains the object embedding links internally, but the effect is the same. By contrast, the prior example employed simple inheritance to specialize the GUI. Whatever route we take, Python's object-oriented support makes it easy to customize and reuse GUI code.

From an implementation perspective, Tkinter is just an example of Python's C integration tools at work: It uses both C extending and embedding. At the top, the Tkinter Python module is a class-based wrapper over a C extension module; the C extension module in turn wraps the underlying Tk library. When we register an event handler, the embedding API is used to call our registered object when the associated event occurs. Although the integration layers are normally hidden from Python programmers, Tkinter is an example of what's possible with an open, object-oriented scripting language like Python.

The preceding examples demonstrate Python's utility as a GUI programming language, but Tkinter is a much more full-featured API than the programs here suggest. For instance, Tkinter includes support for text browsers and editors, drawing canvases, image display, and common GUI devices such as list boxes, radio buttons, sliders, and so on. Unfortunately, we can't really delve into more API details here. See the bibliography at the end of this chapter for further reading.

11.5.3. Persistent Python objects

Besides files, Python provides a number of higher-level storage tools, including the following:

- Dbm files—Keyed-access files of strings
- Pickling—Object serialization (conversion to byte streams)
- Shelves—Keyed-access files of persistent Python objects
- Databases—Full-blown database system interfaces (Sybase, Oracle, etc.)

We don't have enough space to cover all of these here, but we'll take a quick look at shelves in action as a sample of what's available. Python shelves allow programs to store and fetch nearly arbitrary Python objects from a keyed-access file.

Internally, shelves are a combination of Dbm keyed-access files and Python's object serialization (pickling): Shelves take care of converting objects to and from byte streams when they are transferred to and from a Dbm file. To the shelve user, conversion details are hidden: Shelve exports a dictionary-like interface. An object is stored by assigning it to a shelve key and later fetched by indexing the shelve on the object's key. In fact, shelves look like dictionaries that must be opened.

Here's a first example of shelves at work. In the following session, we open a new shelve file called `mydbase` in the external file system and store two objects in it by assigning to keys (`brian`, `knight`). Notice that we're storing fairly complex data structures here; Python's pickler takes care to handle multiple appearances of the same object, circular objects, and so on:

```
% python1.4
>>> import shelve
>>> dbase = shelve.open("mydbase")
```

```
>>> object1 = ['The', 'bright', ('side', 'of'), ['life']]
>>> object2 = {'name': 'Brian', 'age': 33, 'motto': object1}
>>> dbase['brian']  = object2
>>> dbase['knight'] = {'name': 'Knight', 'age': None, 'motto': 'Ni!'}
>>> dbase.close()
```

Once we've stored objects, we can fetch them back by reopening the shelve and using normal dictionary operations on it. For instance, indexing a shelve fetches the object stored under that key:

```
% python1.4
>>> import shelve
>>> dbase = shelve.open("mydbase")
>>> len(dbase)
2
>>> dbase.keys()
['knight', 'brian']
>>> dbase['knight']
{'motto': 'Ni!', 'age': None, 'name': 'Knight'}
>>>
>>> for row in dbase.keys():
...     print row, '=>'
...     for field in dbase[row].keys():
...         print '  ', field, '=', dbase[row][field]
...
knight =>
   motto = Ni!
   age = None
   name = Knight
brian =>
   motto = ['The', 'bright', ('side', 'of'), ['life']]
   age = 33
   name = Brian
```

This example stores nested dictionaries to represent records (rows), with one key per field (column), but stored objects can be built arbitrarily. Because we can store native Python objects like lists, class instances, and dictionaries, shelves are a very flexible storage medium. They are processed with normal Python language operations, instead of a specialized database interface.

11.5.3.1. Storing Class Instances

One of the most useful kinds of objects to store in a shelf is a class instance: Python stores the instance's attribute dictionary, but not the associated class. When the instance is later fetched from the shelve, Python re-imports the class to re-create the instance. This lets us change a class to modify stored object behavior, without having to manually update all stored instances.

The net effect is that Python classes play the role of both records and programs in traditional data-processing terms. In the example in Listing 11.29, we store three `Person` class instances, using their names as shelve keys. Notice that the `Person` class has defaults for all constructor arguments; because Python re-imports and calls the class to re-create fetched instances, this is a default requirement for persistent class instances. (Python doesn't remember the original constructor arguments, but extra protocol can provide them.)

LISTING 11.29. *file:* `person.py`.

```
# a person object: fields + behavior
# class defined at outer level of file

class Person:
    def __init__(self, name = '', job = '', pay = 0):
        self.name = name
        self.job  = job
        self.pay  = pay                 # real instance data
    def tax(self):
        return self.pay * 0.25          # computed on demand
    def info(self):
        return self.name, self.job, self.pay, self.tax()


% python
>>> jerry = Person('jerry', 'dentist')
>>> bob   = Person('bob', 'psychologist', 70000)
>>> emily = Person('emily', 'teacher', 40000)

>>> import shelve
>>> dbase = shelve.open('cast')           # open a new dbm file
>>> for obj in (bob, emily, jerry):       # put objects in a shelve
>>>     dbase[obj.name] = obj
>>> dbase.close()

% python
>>> import shelve
>>> dbase = shelve.open('cast')            # reopen shelve file
>>> print dbase['bob'].tax()               # fetch 'bob' object
17500.0
```

11.5.3.2. The Pickling Interface

Finally, it's possible to use pickling without shelves if desired. The utility module in Listing 11.30 defines functions that save and load a passed-in object (`table`) to a flat file, using the pickling and unpickling interfaces directly. If we pickle a dictionary all at once in this fashion, we'll get functionality similar to that of a shelve.

LISTING 11.30. *file:* `mydbase.py`.

```
import pickle

def saveDbase(filename, table):
    file = open(filename, 'w')
    pickle.dump(table, file)      # pickle to file all at once
    file.close()
```

```
def loadDbase(filename):
    file = open(filename, 'r')
    table = pickle.load(file)      # unpickle from file all at once
    file.close()
    return table
```

Note: At this writing, there is a new `Cpickle` module, which replaces the original Python-coded `pickle` with a compatible version implemented in C. `Cpickle` is reportedly three or four magnitudes faster than the original pickler; because shelves use a pickle module to serialize objects, they can attain similar speeds.

11.5.4. Implementing Sets

One way to measure a language's power is to study common data-structure implementations. In Python, lists are built into the language, but extra set operations (union, intersection, etc.) are not. We can add this utility by extending lists with set-processing functions or set object classes.

11.5.4.1. Set Functions

If we approach set utilities in procedural terms, they can be naturally implemented as Python functions. We saw a simple intersection function when we discussed functions earlier; we'll add a union tool here. The intersection and union algorithms are surprisingly clear when coded in Python. Moreover, Python's dynamic typing means we only need to code the algorithms once to support a wide variety of object types. In the example in Listing 11.31, the set functions can be applied to any kind of sequence object types: lists, strings, tuples, class instances, C extension type instances, and even mixed types (e.g., to intersect a list and a tuple).

LISTING 11.31. *file:* `inter.py`.

```
def intersect(list1, list2):
    res = []                      # start with an empty list
    for x in list1:               # scan the first list
        if x in list2:
            res.append(x)         # add common items to end
    return res

def union(list1, list2):
    res = map(None, list1)        # make a copy of list1
    for x in list2:               # add new items in list2
        if not x in res:
            res.append(x)
    return res


% python
>>> from inter import *
>>> s1 = "SPAM"
>>> s2 = "SCAM"
```

```
>>> intersect(s1, s2), union(s1, s2)          # strings
(['S', 'A', 'M'], ['S', 'P', 'A', 'M', 'C'])

>>> intersect([1,2,3], (1,4))                  # mixed types
[1]
>>> union([1,2,3], (1,4))
[1, 2, 3, 4]
```

11.5.4.2. Set Classes

The preceding functions do the job, but it would be much more in the spirit of Python to implement sets as classes. Classes allow us to override Python operators and operations and allow clients to make multiple, independent set objects. They also better support extension and customization than simple functions. Like the preceding functions, the set class in Listing 11.32 can be used with any sequence types; we don't need a new set class for each sequence type to be supported.

LISTING 11.32. *file:* `set.py`.

```
class Set:
    def __init__(self, value = []):     # constructor
        self.data = []                  # manages a list
        self.concat(value)

    def intersect(self, other):         # other is a sequence
        res = []                        # self is the subject
        for x in self.data:
            if x in other:
                res.append(x)
        return Set(res)                 # return a new Set

    def union(self, other):
        res = self.data[:]              # copy of my list
        for x in other:
            if not x in res:
                res.append(x)
        return Set(res)

    def concat(self, value):            # value: list, Set...
        for x in value:                 # removes duplicates
           if not x in self.data:
                self.data.append(x)

    def __len__(self):          return len(self.data)
    def __getitem__(self, key): return self.data[key]
    def __and__(self, other):   return self.intersect(other)
    def __or__(self, other):    return self.union(other)
    def __repr__(self):         return 'Set:' + `self.data`


% python
>>> from set import Set
>>> x = Set([1,2,3,4])                # __init__
>>> y = Set([3,4,5])
```

```
>>> x & y, x | y                        # __and__,__or__,__repr__
(Set:[3, 4], Set:[1, 2, 3, 4, 5])

>>> z = Set("hello")                   # set of strings
>>> z[0]                                # __getitem__
'h'
>>> z & "mello", z | "mello"
(Set:['e', 'l', 'o'], Set:['h', 'e', 'l', 'o', 'm'])
```

11.5.4.3. Multiple Operands: *varargs

One more improvement here: We can make use of the Python *varargs feature to support multiple operands in our set functions. When an argument of the form *X appears in a function header, it receives all the remaining arguments passed by the caller in a tuple. We can apply this here to collect arbitrarily many operands (arguments) passed to intersect and union (see Listing 11.33).

LISTING 11.33. *file:* inter2.py.

```
def intersect(*args):
    res = []
    for x in args[0]:                  # scan first list
        for other in args[1:]:         # for all other args
            if x not in other: break   # this in each one?
        else:
            res.append(x)              # add items to end
    return res

def union(*args):
    res = []
    for seq in args:                   # for all args
        for x in seq:                  # for all nodes
            if not x in res:
                res.append(x)          # add items to result
    return res


% python
>>> from inter2 import *
>>> s1, s2, s3 = "SPAM", "SCAM", "SLAM"

>>> intersect(s1, s2), union(s1, s2)           # 2 operands
(['S', 'A', 'M'], ['S', 'P', 'A', 'M', 'C'])

>>> intersect([1,2,3], (1,4))
[1]

>>> intersect(s1, s2, s3)                       # 3 operands
['S', 'A', 'M']

>>> union(s1, s2, s3)
['S', 'P', 'A', 'M', 'C', 'L']
```

11.5.5. Internet Tools

As mentioned earlier, Python comes with a suite of Internet tools in its standard source library. In this section, we'll sample a few of the more common interfaces available but will really only scratch the surface; see Python's library reference manual for more details on Internet tools.

11.5.5.1. The FTP Module

An interface for transferring data with the FTP protocol is standard in Python. Provided your machine has support for Internet sockets, the Python `ftplib` module allows Python programs to perform remote FTP transfers. It supports both binary and text retrieve and store operations and handles all handshaking with the remote site automatically. Listing 11.34 shows an example of the Python FTP module in action; it fetches the Python source-code distribution file from Python's FTP site and unzips and untars it locally. If we add `os.system` calls to configure and make the unpacked Python directory, this script could be used to automatically download and build Python from its source code site.

LISTING 11.34. *file:* `getpython.py`.

```
#!/usr/local/bin/python
# A Python script to download Python source code

import os, sys
from ftplib import FTP                 # socket-based ftp tools
tarname = 'python1.4.tar.gz'           # remote/local file name

# fetch file
output = open(tarname, 'w')
ftp = FTP('ftp.python.org')            # connect to ftp site
ftp.login()                            # use anonymous login
ftp.cwd('pub/python/src')
ftp.retrbinary('RETR ' + tarname, output.write, 1024)
ftp.quit()
output.close()

# unpack it
os.system('gzip -d '  + tarname)
os.system('tar -xvf ' + tarname[:-3])  # and cd/config/make
```

11.5.5.2. Writing CGI Scripts

Python's CGI interface is one of its most commonly used Internet tools. CGI scripts are referenced from links in HTML pages and print HTML to display results in a browser, so you need to know something about HTML to understand CGI script operation. The basic concept is straightforward: Roughly, CGI scripts are stored on a server and automatically run by the server when a client (i.e., Web browser) fills in and submits a form. The CGI script extracts the form information by parsing the `stdin` stream (or fetching environment variables) and displays results in the client browser by writing HTML text to the `stdout` stream.

In Python, the built-in `cgi` module provides interfaces that handle data stream (and environment) parsing: Information entered in a form in the browser is accessible through a dictionary interface. At this writing, the basic CGI interface is the `FieldStorage` class. When an instance is created, Python reads the form contents from standard input or the environment and exports field values as dictionary entries. Here is an abstract example of how a typical Python CGI script might look:

```
print "Content-type: text/html"              # HTML text follows
print                                        # blank line: end headers
print "<TITLE>CGI script output</TITLE>"

import cgi
form = cgi.FieldStorage()
form_ok = 0
if form.has_key("name") and form.has_key("addr"):
    if (form["name"].value != "" and
        form["addr"].value != ""):
        form_ok = 1

if not form_ok:
    print "<H1>Error</H1>"
    print "Please fill in the name and addr fields."
    return
...
```

You might occasionally see a `FormContent` class in older Python CGI scripts as well. It represents a (now) outdated interface with similar functionality, but `FieldStorage` is the preferred scheme. Because `FormContent` is still supported for backward compatibility, here's a sketch of how the interface works:

```
import cgi
...
form = cgi.FormContent()          # parse input stream
if form.has_key("fieldname"):     # another dictionary interface
    data = form["fieldname"][0]   # index [0] fetches the field value
```

See Python's library reference manual for more details on the CGI interface module.

11.5.5.3. The Grail Web Browser in Action

Python scripts can also serve as applets: programs downloaded to and run on the client (browser) instead of the server. In a nutshell, applets extend the browser by adding new widgets (e.g., buttons, frames) with callback handlers that execute on the client. There are existing Python interfaces for popular Web browsers such as Netscape; in addition, there is a browser written entirely in and for Python called Grail. Grail uses Tkinter as the browser GUI API; in typical operation, it passes in the browser widget to applet class constructors, and applets extend the browser by using normal Tkinter GUI operations to attach new widgets to the parent (browser).

Listing 11.35 shows a simple example of Grail operation: The HTML file names a Python applet class to be downloaded and run, using the special `APP` tag. When the Grail browser processes this HTML file, it automatically downloads the `Question.Question` class and executes it on the client. The result is a new button in the browser, which changes its bitmap each time it is pressed.

LISTING 11.35. *HTML and applet files.*

```
<HEAD>
<TITLE>Grail Applet Test Page</TITLE>
</HEAD>

<BODY>
<H1>Test an Applet Here!</H1>
Click this button!
<APP CLASS=Question>
</BODY>

file: Question.py
# Python applet file: Question.py
# in the same location (URL) as the html file
# that references it; adds widgets to browser;

from Tkinter import *

class Question:                              # run by grail?
    def __init__(self, master):              # master=browser
        self.button = Button(master,
                             bitmap='question',
                             command=self.action)
        self.button.pack()

    def action(self):
        if self.button['bitmap'] == 'question':
            self.button.config(bitmap='questhead')
        else:
            self.button.config(bitmap='question')

if __name__ == '__main__':
    root = Tk()                          # run stand-alone?
    button = Question(root)              # master=Tk: top-level
    root.mainloop()
```

11.5.6. Things We Skipped

We've barely scratched the surface of Python domains in this short overview. For instance, we haven't said much about

- The sockets interface
- Many of Python's operating system interfaces
- Text processing: string splits/joins, regular expressions
- HTML generation tools
- Most of the widgets in the Tkinter API
- Numeric Python extensions
- The ILU (CORBA) interface
- ActiveX/COM PythonWin extensions
- The new jpython Python-to-Java compiler
- Functional programming tools: map, reduce, filter
- The new package imports in Python 1.5

For a quick look at some other popular Python applications and tools, see Appendix A in *Programming Python*, browse Python's reference manuals, or visit the Python Web site for a survey of other recent works and documentation sources.

11.6. Python Resources

Finally, we'll close this chapter with a few words about Python portability, a look at some prominent Python extensions, and a summary of resources where you can find more information about Python. Some of the information given here is only current as of this writing and is sure to change over time. The Python Web site is probably the best source to consult for up-to-date resource details.

11.6.1. Python Portability

The Python interpreter is written in highly portable ANSI C, so it is portable across a wide variety of platforms. A partial list of machines on which the interpreter runs today includes

- UNIX (most flavors, including Linux)
- Windows 3.1, 95, and NT

- MS-DOS
- Macintosh
- OS/2
- VMS
- NeXT
- Be OS
- Amiga, Atari ST

Python programs will run portably on all these platforms unchanged, provided they don't make use of any platform-specific extensions or tools. In general, the core Python language (types, syntax, etc.) works the same everywhere, but some system interfaces may not be supported across all platforms.

11.6.1.1. General Portability

Besides the interpreter itself, Python byte code is portable across platforms, and Python's Tkinter GUI API works on all major window systems.

- *Byte code*—As we've seen, Python programs are automatically compiled to byte code on import. Python byte code is a machine-independent representation, portable across platforms: byte code files (`.pyc`) generated on one platform can be executed by a Python interpreter on another platform, provided the compiling and executing interpreter versions are compatible, and the compiled program doesn't make use of platform-specific extensions not available in the executing machine.
- *Tkinter GUI API*—As we've also seen, Python programs written with the Tkinter GUI API run portably on X11, Windows, and Macintosh systems. Moreover, with the latest versions of Tk, Python Tkinter programs run with native look-and-feel on each target platform, without program changes. Tkinter provides a portable GUI solution on the three primary window systems in use today.

11.6.2. Platform Extensions

Beside the standard interpreter, Python ports on major platforms usually contain platform-specific extensions. For instance, UNIX ports provide full POSIX bindings, and Windows and Macintosh ports provide extensions that only apply to the underlying platform:

- *Windows ports*—The PythonWin port is perhaps the leading Windows-specific port for Python. It comes with extensions that support ActiveX scripting, the MFC framework, OLE and COM, dynamic loading of DLLs, Windows sockets, and more. PythonWin also comes with a basic GUI IDE (Integrated Development Environment), built on top of its MFC support. Other Python Windows ports that support the Tkinter GUI API are also available (see `http://www.pythonware.com`).
- *Macintosh ports*—The MacPython port comes in PowerPC and 68000 flavors and supports the AppleEvents API, as well as other Macintosh-specific tools.

Naturally, using platform-specific features limits a program's portability dramatically, but some applications can be specialized for a given platform. See Python's Web page and other documentation sources for more information on platform ports.

11.6.3. Major Python Packages

Besides tools that are shipped with the Python package, there is a rich collection of related tools and packages available on the Internet. Some of the most commonly used Python extensions include

- Tkinter—Tk GUI API (object-oriented)
- WPY—Portable MFC-like GUI API
- PIL—Python imaging library
- ILU—Distributed objects (CORBA)
- SWIG—C/C++ wrapper generator
- Grail—Python-based Internet browser
- Netscape plug-ins
- Numeric Python—Matrix object, numeric libraries
- Advanced GUI tools—Tix, Pmw, SpecPython, PyDebug, and so on

We've mentioned most of these earlier in this chapter. Like Python, most are freeware, and all are accessible from links documented at Python's Web site.

11.6.4. Information Resources

Finally, beyond this chapter is a variety of resources to help you learn more about Python programming: the Internet, books, articles, conferences, and training. Let's quickly summarize some of the places you can look for more information.

11.6.4.1. Internet Resources

Table 11.20 lists the most commonly used Internet locations for Python information. Python's Web site is usually the first stop: It has documentation (e.g., Python's reference manuals in HTML form), a news archive search engine, and links to a large collection of associated software and sites. Python's FTP site can be used to fetch Python binary or source-code packages, and the newsgroup is the most common meeting place for Python-related discussions and questions.

TABLE 11.20. *Online Python resources.*

Source	*Address*
Python's Web site	`http://www.python.org`
Python's FTP site	`ftp://ftp.python.org/pub/python`
Python's newsgroup	`comp.lang.python`
Author's Web site	`http://rmi.net/~lutz`
O'Reilly's Web site	`http://www.ora.com`
Python's support mail list	`python-help@python.org`
CompuServe Python forum	`go python`
German-language email list	(see `www.python.org`)

Note that Python can be found in binary or source-code forms and can also be found on CD-ROMs accompanying Python books. Other CD-ROM based distributions are being planned as this chapter is being written; check the Python Web page for details. The most recent release of Python is currently made available on Python's Web and FTP sites.

11.6.4.2. Python Books

Although Python's manuals do a good job documenting most details, books can often fill in the extra context that manuals cannot. At this writing, there are three published Python books, with two more on the way, and others being planned:

- *Programming Python*, by Lutz, from O'Reilly
- *Internet Programming with Python*, by Watters, Ahlstrom, and van Rossum, from MIS Press

- *Das Python-Buch*, by von Löwis and Fischbeck, from Addison-Wesley (German language only)
- *Instant Python Applications* (forthcoming), by Lundh, from O'Reilly
- *Programming Python* (forthcoming), Japanese language edition, by Lutz
- *Python Pocket Reference* (forthcoming), by Lutz, from O'Reilly
- *Learning Python* (forthcoming), by Lutz and Ascher, from O'Reilly
- Others still in the rumor stage: *Python for Windows* and others

One of the current books is only available in German (*Das Python-Buch*), and another is being translated to Japanese as this chapter is being written (*Programming Python*). Be sure to check Python's Web site for up-to-date book information; the PSA also maintains an online bookstore at the Python Web page, which sells Python-related books. Other useful documents include

- *Python's standard reference manuals*—The manuals are shipped in the Python source-code package and are also available online at Python's Web page in HTML and PostScript form. There are currently four manuals in the set: a tutorial, language and library references, and an extending guide.
- *Python source code*—The source code shipped with Python (library modules, demos, built-in extensions, etc.) also contains a wealth of information and hints for beginners; once you understand the basics, you can learn a lot of Python by simply scanning the Python library modules.
- *The Fairly Incomplete and Rather Badly Illustrated Monty Python Song Book*, Harper Collins—Of marginal relevance to be sure, but this and similar books provide a background in Python's namesake (*Monty Python's Flying Circus*). Such a background isn't strictly required for Python programming, but it can't hurt.

11.6.4.3. Recent Python Articles

Python has shown up in a variety of publications recently. Naturally, this list is doomed to be out-of-date soon, but as a sample, here are a few publications that have recently carried Python-related articles:

- *Linux Journal*, May 1997: "Python Update"
- *World Wide Web Journal*, April 1997: "Scripting Languages"

- *BYTE*, February 1997: "Core Technologies" section
- *Linux Journal*, February 1997: "Python CGI Programming"
- *Web Review*, January 3, 1997 (`http://webreview.com`)
- *Dr. Dobbs Sourcebook*, January/February 1997: "Hector, ILU"
- Chapter in *Handbook of Object Technologies* (forthcoming)
- Series in Japanese *Dr. Dobbs*

11.6.4.4. Python Conferences

To foster more direct interaction among Python users, the PSA sponsors regular Python conferences. To date, they have been biannual gatherings that may be held once a year in the future (see `www.python.org` for conference information). For instance, at this writing, the 6th International Python Conference is scheduled to be held in October 1997, in San José, but check Python's Web site for more recent conference schedules.

11.6.4.5. Python Training and Support

Finally, for a more interactive and intensive learning experience, formal Python training is also available. See `http://rmi.net/~lutz/training.html` for more details. At this writing, there is one known offering that provides a three-day, hands-on, on-site training course taught at your company or organization. Other training options are currently under discussion and may be available by the time you read this; see the URL I mentioned or check the Python Web page for updated details. Because training combines lectures, laboratory work, and close interaction with an expert, it can provide a quick start for a larger group of people. At this writing, there are also efforts underway to provide commercial support for Python (beyond what is available on the Internet). See Python's Web page for recent developments on this front.

Chapter 12

Little Music Languages

by Peter S. Langston

12.1. Introduction

Little languages are programming languages or data description languages that are specialized to a particular problem domain. In the last two decades, little languages have merged to support a multitude of tasks, ranging from complex statistical calculations to the construction of lexical parsers. Meanwhile, in the last decade and a half, a multitude of computer-controlled sound synthesis devices have become available. Unfortunately, there has been little overlap of these two development areas, and the software to support these new devices continues to be rudimentary at best.

This chapter describes a handful of little languages that were designed for music tasks. Some of them allow particularly dense encoding of musical material or specify music at a higher level of abstraction than notes, whereas others present musical data in a form that is easy for users to read and edit. In all cases, the representations are machine-readable and can be played on a sound synthesizer under computer control.

The areas of endeavor that involve computer software support can be broadly divided into three classes. First are those in which the problems to be solved are known at the outset, so a single program or suite of programs can be designed to provide all the necessary functions. Most financial programming tasks fall in this class (accounts payable, payroll, billing, etc.). Second are those areas at the other extreme, in which few of the problems and goals can be predicted in advance. Support for these areas must come in the form of general-purpose programming languages that make as few assumptions as possible about the problem goals and techniques. The familiar high-level programming languages (Fortran, PL/I, Pascal, Ada, etc.) address these areas.

The third class consists of those areas that fall in between the first two classes: areas in which enough is known in advance to make the use of general-purpose programming languages unnecessarily tedious, but in which too little is known to make monolithic does-everything-you'll-ever-want-to-do (DEYEWTD) systems possible. Software development often finds itself in this area.

Software support for tasks in this third class usually takes the form of one or more programs that "know" a little about the task area but make few assumptions beyond those that characterize the area. The term "little language" is often applied to such moderately general programs. Examples of little languages range from the program awk (which borders on being a general-purpose programming language; Aho, Kernighan, & Weinberger, 1979) through programs such as bc (Berkeley Software Distribution, 1994), lex (Levine, Mason, & Brown, 1992), and make (Feldman, 1979) to massive packages such as Finale (which borders on being a DEYEWTD; Coda, 1989).

Much of the development in software engineering in the past 15 years has been in the area of little languages; as Jon Bentley (1986) says, "Little languages are an important part of the popular fourth- and fifth-generation languages and application generators, but their influence on computing is much broader." Meanwhile, 1982 and 1983 saw two unusual and important events in the high-tech consumer electronics industry. First, representatives of consumer electronics companies agreed on a standard interface for connecting electronic musical instruments together called MIDI.[1] In this intensely competitive industry, where competing, incompatible standards abound (VHS/Beta, NTSC/SECAM/PAL, TIAA/NARTB, to name a few), this was indeed an unusual event. The second unusual event was the introduction of a keyboard synthesizer known as the Yamaha DX7. This was the first serious sound synthesizer to appear with a list price below $25 per oscillator. The DX7's low price was the result of mass-production of the large-scale integration circuit chips in it. Thousands of DX7s were sold, to the general amazement of the musical instrument industry. In the following years, consumer music manufacturers and products have proliferated, causing the cost of computer-controlled sound synthesis equipment to drop even lower. A common feature of these products, from the DX7 on, has been the inclusion of the MIDI communication interface. Whether the success of the MIDI standard was a result of the success of instruments like the DX7

[1]MIDI is an acronym for Musical Instrument Digital Interface.

or vice versa is a genuine chicken-and-egg question. But with 20/20 hindsight, it is obvious that neither would have been as successful without the other.

Along with the plethora of digitally controllable musical instruments has come a plethora of computer software to control, record, generate, and otherwise manipulate the digital data that these instruments read and write. Most of this software has been written for the hobbyist computers that have also been proliferating during this time. Unfortunately, these computers are equipped with relatively primitive operating systems having little or no real multitasking or data pipelining facilities. As a result, the available software is usually in the form of stand-alone programs that must try to be DEYEWTDs (sometimes failing to do even one thing well) and that cannot interface with other programs directly.

At Bellcore, where these languages were developed, we were lucky enough to have a large selection of powerful minicomputers running the UNIX operating system. Although little, if any, of the commercially available music software could be run on our systems, everything that would run on our systems could be interfaced with everything else. All we had to do was interface our computers to MIDI (Langston, 1989a) and then write all the software ourselves!

In the process of writing and using this music software, we found ourselves doing the same thing over and over again. So we started looking for ways to make the common tasks easier, and the little languages described in this chapter were born.

This chapter has two main sections: binary formats and ASCII formats. The binary formats are the order codes that the synthesizers execute to play music, their "machine language" as it were. Three binary formats are described in three subsections. These are the logical targets of little language compilers. The ASCII formats are the little languages. Eleven subsections describe eleven languages. Two further subsections describe particular programs that read and write specific little languages.

All of the ASCII formats but one were created by the current author. The remaining one (MA) was extended by him. Each format has one or more associated programs that process it; some convert to other formats and some perform transformations on the data; there are over 100 such programs in all (see Tables 12.1 and 12.2 at the end of the chapter). Although there is not room to give more than a one-line description of each of these programs, two of the programs are described in detail: One is a very general program (`mpp`) that is a preprocessor for all of the ASCII formats; the other program (`lick`) performs an unusual conversion on one of the ASCII formats.

This chapter concentrates on the following:

Binary Formats	
MIDI	Standard real-time synthesizer control language.
MPU	Standard time-encoded synthesizer control language.
SMF	Standard time-encoded synthesizer control and music description language.

ASCII Formats	
`mpp`	Music preprocessor program.
MA	ASCII time-encoded (low-level) synthesizer control language.
MUTRAN	Ancient melody description language.
MUT	Melody/harmony description language based on MUTRAN.
VMU	Melody/harmony/lyric description language based on MUTRAN.
DP	Drum pattern description language.
SD	Melody/harmony description language.
CCC	Accompaniment (chord chart compiler) description language.
CC	Harmonic structure (chord chart) description language.
GC	Guitar chord description language.
`lick`	Banjo improvisation generator program.
TAB	Stringed instrument music notation language.
DDM	Algorithmic composition language.

The generation of these little languages was not as monumental a task as it might have been for three reasons. First, a few other people with interests similar to ours have been most helpful either as collaborators or as sources and sinks for software efforts. These include Michael Hawley (1986), Gareth Loy, Daniel Steinberg, and Tim Thompson (Thompson, 1989, 1990). Second, the software tools available with the UNIX operating system make software development relatively easy. Third, creating a little language to support a class of activities is often only marginally more work than writing a program to perform an instance of those activities and is certainly a more rewarding (and therefore motivating) task.

The languages described here have made possible projects like the algorithmic music composition telephone demo (Langston, 1986) and the algorithmic background music generator called PellScore (Langston, 1990b) or IMG/1 (Langston, 1991), as well as dozens of other projects (Langston, 1988, 1990b, 1990c).

12.2. Binary Formats

The machine-readable formats that encode musical data specifically for use with synthesizers are binary formats and as such they are difficult (if not impossible) for humans to read directly. They were designed to specify the details of synthesizer actions in as dense a form as possible, often packing several fields into a single byte. Further, they depend on knowledge of prior data to evaluate following data; they cannot be interpreted from an arbitrary starting point in the middle of a sequence (unlike a tape recording that can be played from any point within a piece). An important limitation of these encodings is that, in order to save space and transmission time, assumptions were made about the kinds of events that would be recorded (e.g., pitches would be based on fixed chromatic scales), thereby making extensions to other sets of assumptions cumbersome at best.

Because of their density and the ready availability of synthesizers that read them, these formats may be the best choice for program output. All of the little languages described in this chapter have associated programs that convert them to at least one of these binary formats. A brief description of three of these binary formats is included here to provide an understanding of the range of events we can hope to control with our little music languages.

12.2.1. MIDI Format

MIDI was the result of a multivendor task force charged with designing a standard digital interchange protocol for sound synthesizers. It has been a resounding success. Virtually all sound synthesizer manufacturers now make their devices read or write MIDI format. Many other kinds of devices also use MIDI data to control their operation—mixers, echo units, light controllers, and so on. A whole industry exists to supply MIDI hardware devices and MIDI software. The authoritative description of the MIDI format is the MIDI 1.0 Detailed Specification, published by the International MIDI Association (1989).

MIDI is not a little language in the usual sense of the term; however, a description of it is included here because MIDI is the *lingua franca* of sound synthesizers. Any music representation that needs to be playable on modern sound synthesis equipment must be convertible into MIDI.

MIDI data are represented as a serial, real-time byte stream consisting of a sequence of messages representing synthesizer *events* such as note-start, note-end, volume change, or parameter selection. MIDI messages consist of one *status* 8-bit byte followed by zero, one, or two data bytes (except in the case of messages that start with a *system exclusive* status byte, which may have an arbitrary number of data bytes followed by an *end-of-exclusive* status byte). Status bytes have the high-order bit set, whereas data bytes have the high-order bit clear. The defined values for status bytes are shown in Figure 12.1.

MIDI COMMAND FORMATS		Status byte (hex)	Meaning	Number of data bytes	Effect on running status
Channel (n = 0–F) Message		8n	Key Off	2	8n
		9n	Key On	2	9n
		An	Polyphonic After Touch	2	An
		Bn	Control Change	2	Bn
		Cn	Program Change	1	Cn
		Dn	Channel After Touch	1	Dn
		En	Pitch Blend	2	En
System Message	Excl.	F0	System Exclusive	?	clear
	Common	F1	undef.	–	clear
		F2	Song Position Pointer	2	clear
		F3	Song Select	1	clear
		F4	undef.	–	clear
		F5	undef.	–	clear
		F6	Tune Request	0	clear
		F7	End of Sys. Excl.	0	clear
	Real Time	F8	Timing Clock (TCIP)	0	none
		F9	undef. (TCWME)	0	none
		FA	Start	0	none
		FB	Continue	0	none
		FC	Stop (TCIS)	0	none
		FD	undef. (clock to host)	0	none
		FE	Active Sensing	0	none
		FF	System Reset	0	none

FIGURE 12.1. *MIDI status bytes.*

MIDI describes *events* (e.g., hitting a key or moving a control) rather than notes. In order to encode a note, a pair of *events* must be specified—a *key-on* event and a *key-off* event. The MIDI standard defines key-on and key-off events as having two associated data bytes: a *key-number* (i.e., pitch) and a *velocity* (or loudness). Key-numbers range from 0 to 127 with 60^{10} representing middle C. In this chapter, we use the convention that middle C is `C3`[2] and the note one half-step below it is called `B2`. Thus 0 (zero) represents C in octave -2, or C-2, and 127^{10} represents G in octave 8, `G8`. Velocities range from 1 to 127^{10} in arbitrary units, with 1 being the slowest (quietest) and 64^{10} being mezzo-forte.

MIDI allows up to 16 channels of data to be multiplexed into a single stream by specifying a channel number in each status byte (with the exception of the system messages, which are global). Synthesizers can be configured to accept messages on a single channel or on all channels (*omni mode*).

To minimize the number of bytes transmitted, the MIDI specification allows the omission of a status byte if it is identical to the preceding status byte. Thus, a series of key-on events only requires the key-on status byte be transmitted for the first key-on event. This is called *running status*. To take advantage of running status, most synthesizer manufacturers allow a key-on event with a velocity of 0 to be used as a synonym for key-off. Therefore, the sequence `0x90 0x3c 0x40 0x3c 0x00` represents two events, a key-on event for a mezzo-forte middle C and a key-off event for middle C.

Listing 12.1 shows the MIDI data for a C major scale printed as ASCII equivalents for the binary data, one MIDI message per line with a comment appended. You may wonder why the MIDI data on the left and the comments on the right don't seem to jibe very well. Keep in mind that the MIDI data are shown in hexadecimal, as is common for printed versions of MIDI data, and although hexadecimal numbering starts at 0, synthesizer manufacturers often number *voices* (a.k.a. *programs* or *patches*) and channels starting with 1. Fortunately, the MIDI data encoding scheme was not designed for human consumption in any case.

---

[2]There is some confusion on this matter; the nomenclature that has been in use by musicians and scientists for many years designates middle C as `C4`. Unfortunately, the Yamaha corporation chose to use `C3` for middle C, and by dint of their importance in the market, many manufacturers have followed suit, leaving the industry split into two camps.

LISTING 12.1. *MIDI data for a C major scale.*

```
c5      7        select program (voice) 8 on channel 6
b5      4 7f     set foot controller value to 127 on channel 6
95     3c 40     C3 key-on, channel 6, vel-64 (mezzo-forte)
95     3c  0     C3 key-on with vel=0 => key-off
       3e 40     D3 key-on (note running status)
       3e  0     D3 key-off
       40 40     E3 key-on
       40  0     E3 key-off
       41 40     F3 key-on
       41  0     F3 key-off
       43 40     G3 key-on
       43  0     G3 key-off
       45 40     A3 key-on
       45  0     A3 key-off
       47 40     B3 key-on
       47  0     B3 key-off
       48 40     C4 key-on
       48  0     C4 key-off
```

MIDI data encoding represents real-time events; nothing in the MIDI data encode when an event is to occur; events happen immediately upon receipt of the data. For the purpose of slaving one synthesizer to another, this is perfectly adequate. When the first synthesizer makes a sound, the slave synthesizer also makes a sound; whatever controls the first synthesizer specifies the timing for both. However, this is not adequate when we want to store a performance in a file on a computer; something must encode the timing information with the MIDI data. For example, playing all the MIDI data in Listing 12.1 without any added delays takes about 12 milliseconds; each note sounds for 0.64 milliseconds (the time for the next 2-byte command to be received at a rate of about three bytes per millisecond). Either the MPU format or the SMF format can provide the needed timing information.

12.2.2. MPU Format

The MPU data format gets its name from an early hardware interface device manufactured by the Roland Corporation, the MPU-401. This device interconnects a computer and synthesizers, providing timing functions and other features such as tape synchronization and a metronome. Several companies make similar interfaces that implement the same protocols to take advantage of existing software.

The Roland MPU-401, when run in its "intelligent" mode, accepts time-tagged MIDI data, buffers them up, and spits them out at the times specified by the time tags. The time tags are relative delays indicating how many 120ths of a quarter note to wait before sending out the next MIDI data. Notice that the MPU's timing resolution is one 480th note. The maximum allowable time tag is 239_{10} (EF_{16}). Thus, a mezzo-forte quarter note of middle C immediately followed by a mezzo-forte sixteenth note of the G above it and then a forte C major chord lasting a dotted eighth note could be encoded by the binary data shown in Listing 12.2. The same data are shown, rearranged for readability and commented, in Listing 12.3.

LISTING 12.2. *Time-tagged MIDI data.*

```
00  90  3c  40  78  80  3c  00
00  90  43  40  1e  80  43  00
00  90  3c  56  00  40  56  00
43  56  5a  80  3c  00  00  40
00  00  43  00
```

LISTING 12.3. *Time-tagged MIDI data explained.*

```
time status key vel
 00    90    3c  40   delay 0, key-on, key 3c16=6010=C4, velocity 4016=6410
 78    80    3c  00   delay 7816=12010, key-off, key 3c16=6010=c4
 00    90    43  40   delay 0, key-on, key 4316=6710=G4, velocity 4016=6410
 1e    80    43  00   delay 1e16=3010, key-off, key 4316=6710=G4
 00    90    3c  56   delay 0, key-on, key 3c16=6010=C4, velocity 5616=8610
 00          40  56   delay 0, key-on, key 4016=6410=E4,velocity 5616=8610
 00          43  56   delay 0, key-on, key 4316=6710=G4, velocity 5616=8610
 5a    80    3c  00   delay 5a16=9010, key-off, key 3c16=6010=C4
 00          40  00   delay 0, key-off, key 4016=6410=E4 (running status)
 00          43  00   delay 0, key-off, key 3c16=6010=C4
```

The MPU also defines some of the unused MIDI status codes to represent time-related events not covered by the basic MIDI specification. Figure 12.1 includes annotations for these extra definitions. The value $F9_{16}$ is used to indicate the presence of a bar line and is called Timing Clock With Measure End (TCWME). The value FD16 is used to alert the host computer that a clock tick has occurred and is called Clock To Host. Two of the defined status codes are given modified meanings by the MPU to handle other time-related events. During recording, the value $F8_{16}$ Timing Clock is used in place of a time tag and without any MIDI data to indicate that the internal MPU clock has reached its maximum value, 240_{10}; this code is called Timing Clock In Play (TCIP). To represent a delay of 240_{10} clock ticks any other way would require four bytes.[3] Similarly, during playback, the MPU interprets TCIP as a delay of 240_{10} clock ticks. If an $F8_{16}$ is received after a time tag, it is treated as a no-op

[3]This will save space in stored files but will not save time in transmitting MIDI data, because timing bytes are never transmitted in the MIDI stream and even if they were, TCIP codes, by definition, only occur when there are no other data to be transmitted.

(no operation) with the delay specified by the time tag. In some cases, the value FC^{16} is treated like TCIP; it appears without a time tag when the MPU has been told to stop recording, but data are still arriving.

The MPU format for storing MIDI is the lowest common denominator for musical data storage in our system. All the little languages can be converted to MPU format, which then can be played (converted to sound) by the synthesizers.

12.2.3. SMF Format

Although MIDI was originally designed to let synthesizers be interconnected in performance (i.e., real-time) situations, the designers and users of MIDI quickly became aware of the need to save timing and other information with MIDI files. Toward this end, the standard MIDI file format (SMF) was established (MIDI, 1988).

The standard MIDI file format is far broader in scope (if not complexity) than the MPU format. To quote from the SMF proposal (International MIDI Association, 1988); "MIDI files contain one or more MIDI streams, with time information for each event. Song sequence, and track structures, tempo and time signature information, are all supported. Track names and other descriptive information may be stored with the MIDI data."

Listing 12.4 gives a fairly complete BNF grammar (Backus, 1960) for standard MIDI files. In this grammar, double-quote marks, '', denote ASCII quantities; square brackets, [], denote 2-byte quantities; double square brackets, [[]], denote 4-byte quantities; unenclosed hexadecimal numbers denote 1-byte quantities; and numbers separated by a colon, :, denote ranges. The <varnum> construct is a way of encoding unbounded numbers that the SMF specification calls *variable-length quantities*. In these, values are represented with 7 bits per byte, most significant bits first. All bytes except the last have bit 7 (the high-order bit) set. The <var data> construct is simply a <varnum> byte count followed by that many data bytes.

LISTING 12.4. *Partial BNF grammar for SMF format.*

```
<SMF file>          ::  <header chunk> <track chunks>
<header chunk>      ::  "MThd" [[6]] <format> <ntrks> <div>
<format>            ::  [0] | [1] | [2]
<ntrks>             ::  [0:65535]
<div>               ::  <ticks per beat> | <ticks per sec>
<ticks per beat> ::  [0:32767]
<ticks per sec>     ::  [-32768:-1]
<track chunks>      ::  <track chunk> | <track chunk> <track chunks>
```

```
<track chunk>      ::  "MTrk" <length> <trk events>
<length>           ::  [[1:4294967295]]
<trk events>       ::  <trk event> | <trk event> <trk events>
<trk event>        ::  <delta-time> <event>
<delta-time>       ::  <varnum>
<varnum>           ::  00:7F | 80:FF <varnum>
<event>            ::  <MIDI chan event> | <sysex event> | <meta-event>
<chan event>       ::  <status byte> <data> | <data>
<status byte>      ::  80:EF
<data>             ::  00:7F | 00:7F <data>
<sysex event>      ::  F0 <var data> | F7 <var data>
<var data>         ::  <varnum> 00:FF | <var data> 00:FF
<meta-event>       ::  FF <type> <var data>
<type>             ::  00:7F
```

SMF files consist of *chunks*. Each chunk is a sequence of data bytes with a header that identifies the chunk type and length. The SMF specification includes two chunk types: header and track.

Header chunks give global information about the file. `<format>` indicates whether there is more than one track data chunk and whether multiple track data chunks are sequential or simultaneous; `<ntrks>` is the number of track data chunks; and `<div>` specifies the units for the time tags in the track data (either in parts of a quarter note or seconds).

Track data chunks consist of a stream of time-tagged events. The events can either be MIDI channel events, system exclusive events, or SMF meta-events. MIDI channel events and system exclusive events are as defined in the MIDI spec (MIDI, 1989), whereas meta-events are new. There are 128 possible meta events; 15 of them are defined in *Standard MIDI Files 1.0* (MIDI, 1988), shown in Listing 12.5.

LISTING 12.5. *SMF meta-events.*

```
00 02  [0:65535]                         Sequence Number
01 <var data>                            Text Event
02 <var data>                            Copyright Notice
03 <var data>                            Sequence / Track Name
04 <var data>                            Instrument Name
05 <var data>                            Lyric
06 <var data>                            Marker
07 <var data>                            Cue Point
20 01 02:255                             MIDI Channel Prefix
2F 00                                    End of Track
51 03 [[0:16777215]]                     Set Tempo
54 05 00:17 00:3B 00:3B 00:1E 00:63      SMPTE Offset
58 04 00:FF 00:FF 00:FF 00:FF            Time Signature
59 02 -7:07 00:01                        Key Signature
7F <var data>                            Sequencer-Specific
```

Because these meta-events appear following a time tag, they have a location in time. This gives a temporal meaning to events such as End of Track beyond the (redundant) information that no more track data will appear. For more details on any of these meta-events, refer to *Standard MIDI Files 1.0* (MIDI, 1988).

12.3. ASCII Formats

Obviously, it would be arduous in the extreme to enter a piece of music in any of the binary formats. Some form of symbolic entry would be much more manageable, if less compact. An ASCII representation of the MIDI or MPU data would be a good starting point. It doesn't take much imagination to see a parallel between generating MIDI binary data and generating binary machine code data; in those terms, we're talking about using an assembler.

We describe a simple music assembler in section 12.3.2 on MA format. Such an encoding format, because it converts human-readable ASCII entities to compact binary entities on a one-to-one basis, is necessarily less dense than the output it generates, but it is completely general in that any possible binary output can be specified. As we move to higher levels of abstraction, the symbolic form becomes more dense and the output becomes less general. The graph in Figure 12.2 gives an approximate idea of the relationship between density of expression (measured by the number of notes encoded per byte) and generality (ease with which any legal binary output can be generated) for our little languages.

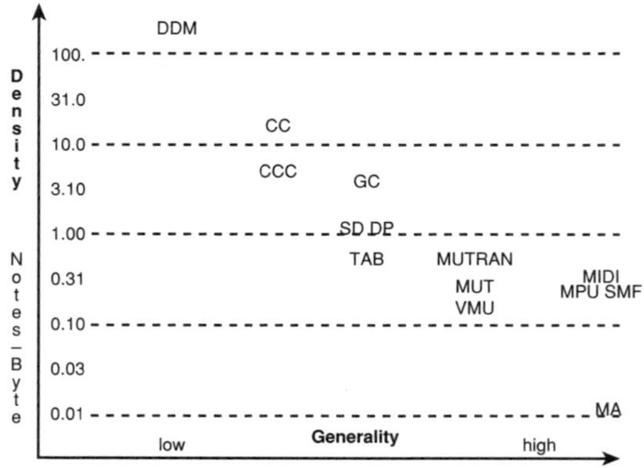

FIGURE 12.2. *Density versus generality for little music languages.*

With these "higher-level" languages, it is important to target the specific problem domain so that the smaller range of possible outputs match those required. Several specification formats, each targeted for a specific domain, are presented here.

Some constructs are common to all of the little languages; these have been separated out and implemented by a music preprocessor called `mpp`. Several keywords appear in many but not all of the languages and may have different meanings in each language. To save space (and tedium), when a keyword appears for the first time, it will be explained fully; later uses of it will only explain the differences. Comment lines, for instance, are described under `mpp` and not mentioned again. Table 12.1 at the end of this chapter shows all the keywords and the places in which they are used.

Our description of ASCII formats will start with the preprocessor `mpp` and then go on to the simple assembler followed by the other formats and programs.

12.3.1. mpp

The program `mpp` implements ASCII data file control constructs used to specify logical sections, repeats, and so on in a piece of music. Input data lines are passed to the output as specified by control lines. Five functions are provided by `mpp`: comment stripping, conditional inclusion of sections, looping over repeats, defined symbol replacement, and skipping (ignoring) input.

The `-c` option inhibits stripping comment lines and blank lines from the input. The default action is to strip out all lines beginning with `# ` (i.e., sharp sign followed by a space) and all lines consisting of just a newline character.

The command line `-s` argument can be used to specify which *section* or *sections* will be generated; sections may be numbered with arbitrary non-negative integers. Note that a series of sections can be generated by specifying a list of section numbers. Section numbers may be separated by commas or blanks; ranges of section numbers are specified by the first and last section numbers (inclusive) separated by a hyphen.

Control lines consist of one or more fields. A field is either a sequence of non-whitespace characters separated from others by whitespace or two or more such sequences enclosed in double quotes (`''`). Control lines begin with a keyword field and may contain one or more argument fields.

Any input line not recognized as a control line is considered a data line and is passed through unchanged. The various control line formats and their meanings are

`# anything`	Any line beginning with a sharp sign (a.k.a. number sign, pound sign, octothorpe, hash mark, scratch mark, or the bottom right button on a touch-tone keypad) followed immediately by a space or tab character is considered a comment and is not passed through to the output unless the `-c` option has been specified.
`#ALLRPTS`	The following input is applicable to all repeats at the current nesting level (the default). The `#ALLRPTS` control is not used to end repeats; `ENDRPT` does that.
`#ALLSECTS`	The following input is applicable to all sections (the default). The `#ALLSECTS` control can be used to end sections started by `#NOTSECT` and `#ONLYSECT`.
`#DEFINE symbol value`	Replace all occurrences of the first (`symbol`) field with the contents of the second (`value`) field. Defined symbols are replaced immediately after the line is read and before any other processing. Replacements will only take place if the entire field in the file matches the symbol field. Forward references are permitted.
`#DOSECT#[#]...`	Act as if the following arguments had appeared prefixed with `-s` on the command line. This functions much like a subroutine call. The following three command lines are equivalent: `#DOSECT 1 2 3`, `#DOSECT 1-#`, `#DOSECTS 1,2-3`. `DOSECTs` may be nested, but beware of recursion.
`#ELSE`	See `IFNEXT`.
`#ENDIF`	See `IFNEXT`.
`#ENDRPT`	End the current set of repeats and unstack one level of repeat nesting.
`#ENDSKIP`	See `SKIP`.

`#IFNEXT # [#] ...` The following arguments are section numbers. The data between an IFNEXT and an ENDIF or ELSE will be included in the output if one of the specified sections will be the next one output. This is often a convenient way to specify first and second endings that depend on which section will follow. When an ELSE is encountered, it negates the result of the preceding IFNEXT test. IFNEXTs may not be nested, so there is no ELIF construct.

`#INCLUDE` Interpolate the contents of the named file (the argument) here. The file will not be read if mpp is currently skipping input because of section, repeat, or skip requirements (thus control lines in the included file that might logically end the skipping will not do so).

`#NOTRPT #[#] ...` The following input should appear in all repeats (at the current level of repeat nesting) *except* those listing as arguments.

`#NOTSECT #[#] ...` The following input should appear in all sections *except* those named in the arguments.

`#ONLYRPT #[#] ...` The following input should only appear in those repeats (at the current level of repeat nesting) listed as arguments.

`#ONLYSECT #[#] ...` The following input should only appear in those sections listed as arguments.

`#REPEAT #` Begin a repeated section (ended by a matching #ENDRPT). The section will be included the number of times specified as an argument. Repeated sections may be nested up to eight deep.

`#SKIP` Any data or controls between this and the first ENDSKIP encountered are ignored. SKIP/ENDSKIP may not be nested and take precedence over all other controls. This is largely a debugging aid.

The order of precedence (high to low) among the various control lines is skips (SKIP/ENDSKIP), then sections (ALLSECTS/NOTSECT/ONLYSECT), then ifs (IFNEXT/ELSE/ENDIF), then repeats (REPEAT/ALLRPT/NOTRPT/ONLYRPT/ENDRPT), followed by all others. Pairs from one group should not span members of a group with higher precedence; for example, it is a mistake to have NOTSECT appear between REPEAT and ENDRPT.

The example in Listing 12.6 demonstrates the use of the repeat and section controls. `mpp` is commonly used as part of a pipeline of commands. In makefiles or shell command files, the section (s) argument is often defined separately so that it can be specified in just one place and used in many (see "`Make`—A Program for Maintaining Computer Programs" [Feldman, 1979] for a description of `make` and makefiles). Listing 12.7 shows part of a makefile used to assemble a piece. After `make foo` has been executed, the file `foo` will contain the merged MPU data for sections 0,1,2,5,3,0,1,2,4 (in that order) from the various source files.

LISTING 12.6. *Example of sections and repeats with* `mpp`.

```
% cat xyz             % mpp -s0,2,1 xyz     % mpp -s1,2 xyz
a-a-a-a-a-a-a-a-a     a-a-a-a-a-a-a-a-a     f f f f f f f f f
#NOTSECT 1            b-b-b-b-b-b-b-b-b     b-b-b-b-b-b-b-b-b
b-b-b-b-b-b-b-b-b     c-c-c-c-c-c-c-c-c     c-c-c-c-c-c-c-c-c
#REPEAT 3             d-d-d-d-d-d-d-d-d     d-d-d-d-d-d-d-d-d
c-c-c-c-c-c-c-c-c     c-c-c-c-c-c-c-c-c     c-c-c-c-c-c-c-c-c
#NOTRPT 2             c-c-c-c-c-c-c-c-c     c-c-c-c-c-c-c-c-c
d-d-d-d-d-d-d-d-d     d-d-d-d-d-d-d-d-d     d-d-d-d-d-d-d-d-d
#ENDRPT               e-e-e-e-e-e-e-e-e     e-e-e-e-e-e-e-e-e
e-e-e-e-e-e-e-e-e     f-f-f-f-f-f-f-f-f     f-f-f-f-f-f-f-f-f
#ALLSECTS             b-b-b-b-b-b-b-b-b     g-g-g-g-g-g-g-g-g
f-f-f-f-f-f-f-f-f     c-c-c-c-c-c-c-c-c
#ONLYSECT 2           d-d-d-d-d-d-d-d-d
g-g-g-g-g-g-g-g-g     c-c-c-c-c-c-c-c-c
                      c-c-c-c-c-c-c-c-c
                      d-d-d-d-d-d-d-d-d
                      e-e-e-e-e-e-e-e-e
                      f-f-f-f-f-f-f-f-f
                      g-g-g-g-g-g-g-g-g
                      f-f-f-f-f-f-f-f-f
```

LISTING 12.7. *Makefile fragment using* `mpp`.

```
FOOSECTS=-s0-2,5,3,0-2,4
foo:      foo.b.tab foo.g.gc foo.v.m
          mpp $(FOOSCTS) foo.b.tab | tab2mpu >bass
          mpp $(FOOSCTS) foo.g.gc | gc2mpu >guitar
          mpp $(FOOSCTS) foo.v.vmu | vmu2mpu >voice
          merge bass guitar voice >$@
```

12.3.2. MA Format

MA format started as a disassembled listing of MPU format. The program `da` reads MPU data and produces an ASCII version with annotation. Listing 12.8 shows the MA data for the familiar Westminster Cathedral half-hour chime sequence followed by a single super "bong." (Normally the bong would not follow the sequence rung on the half hour, but its inclusion gives a pleasant resolution and the hours sequence would have taken too much space.) Everything to the left of the semicolon is MPU data; everything to the right is explanatory comment. The column of decimal numbers gives the absolute timing in beats (quarter notes).

LISTING 12.8. *MA format listing of* the *Westminster chimes.*

```
0 98   3e 40 ;    0.000   0 kon    [ 62]=64   D3 key on
   c   3e  0 ;    0.100   1 koff   [ 62]=0    D3 key off
  e4   42 40 ;    2.000   2 kon    [ 66]=64   F#3 key on
   c   42  0 ;    2.100   3 koff   [ 66]=0    F#3 key off
  e4   40 40 ;    4.000   4 kon    [ 64]=64   E3 key on
   b   40  0 ;    4.092   5 koff   [ 64]=0    E3 key off
  e5   39 40 ;    6.000   6 kon    [ 57]=64   A2 key on
   c   39  0 ;    6.100   7 koff   [ 57]=0    A2 key off
  e4   3e 40 ;   12.000  10 kon    [ 62]=64   D3 key on
   c   3e  0 ;   12.100  11 koff   [ 62]=0    D3 key off
  e4   40 40 ;   14.000  12 kon    [ 64]=64   E3 key on
   c   40  0 ;   14.100  13 koff   [ 64]=0    E3 key off
  e4   42 40 ;   16.000  14 kon    [ 66]=64   F#3 key on
   c   42  0 ;   16.100  15 koff   [ 66]=0    F#3 key off
  e4   3e 40 ;   18.000  16 kon    [ 62]=64   D3 key on
   c   3e  0 ;   18.100  17 koff   [ 62]=0    D3 key off
  e4   32 40 ;   24.000  20 kon    [ 50]=64   D2 key on
   0   26 40 ;   24.000  21 kon    [ 38]=64   D1 key on
   c   32  0 ;   24.100  22 koff   [ 50]=0    D2 key off
   0   26  0 ;   24.100  23 koff   [ 38]=0    D1 key off
```

There are two ways to turn MA format into MPU format. The program `ra` (re-assembler) inverts the effect of `da`, but because the same information is multiply embedded in the MA output (appearing on both sides of the semicolon in one form or another), a decision must be made as to which value to use. `ra` chooses to believe all the information to the left of the semicolon except the time-tag value; this it escalates from the absolute timing value to the right of the semicolon. The logic for this will become apparent in the next paragraph. The program `axtobb` (ASCII hex to binary bytes) inverts the effect of `da` by only paying attention to the data to the left of the semicolon. (As a matter of fact, `axtobb` treats any characters other than `0-9`, `a-f`, `A-F`, tab, and space as the start of a comment that extends to the end of the line.)

When a small change is needed in an MPU file, the simplest approach is to convert the file to MA format, edit the ASCII file with any text editor, and then convert the file back with either `ra` or `axtobb` as appropriate. The most common editing operations are deleting and inserting commands. For these operations, `ra` will usually be the reassembler of choice because the absolute time values on unaffected lines would still be accurate. In situations where whole sections need to be moved forward or backward in time, changing the first and last time tags and then reassembling with axtobb is considerably easier than changing the time values on every affected line.

In much the same way that we can use existing ASCII text editors to manipulate MPU files by converting to and from MA format, other ASCII software tools can be used. For example, to make a copy of the file foo.mpu with all the program change (voice change) commands deleted, we might search for the mnemonic that da uses for program change, porgc:

```
da foo.mpu | grep -v " progc " | ra >foo.mpu.copy
```

Similarly, we could try to delete all key-on and key-off data for channel three with

```
da foo.mpu | grep -v "^.[0-9] [89]2 " | ra >foo.mpu.copy
```

However, if foo.mpu contained commands using running status, they would be left in and would appear on some other channel (or no channel at all). The command midimode (and many others) can be used to ensure each command has a status byte, and then a pipeline such as

```
midimode <foo.mpu | da | grep -v "&..[89]2 " | ra >foo.mpu.copy
```

would work. As it turns out, there are specific commands to perform most of these editing operations on the MPU data directly, but, when you come up with a need that nothing else quite fills . . . .

There are other situations in which MA format can be particularly useful; you may need a graceful way to create some MPU commands inside a command stream. For instance, the following line could appear either in a shell command file or in a makefile (Feldman, 1979):

```
(echo "0 c0 4 0 b0 4 0" | axtobb; cat foo.mpu) >foonew.mpu
```

This line will create the file foonew.mpu, containing the commands to select voice 5 on channel 1 and then set the foot controller to 0 on that channel, followed by the contents of foo.mpu. Another use for MA format is as the output of a program written in a restricted programming language, such as awk (Aho et al., 1979) or a command line interpreter such as csh. MPU data contain many zeroes, and as far as awk is concerned these are NULS; NULS are used to terminate strings and cannot be generated as output. Listing 12.9 shows an awk program that uses MA format to generate all 128 possible key-off commands on channel 1 and a shell program that does a slightly different version of the same thing.

LISTING 12.9. *Using MA format to turn all notes off.*

```
% cat x.awk
BEGIN   { for (i=0; i<128; i++) { printf "0 80 %x 00, i } exit }
% awk -f x.awk | axtobb >alloff.1

% cat x.sh
for s in 0 1 2 3 4 5 6 7; do
           for u in 0 1 2 3 4 5 6 7 8 9 A B C D E F; do
                   echo "0 90 $s$u 0" | axtobb
           done
done
% sh x.sh >alloff.1
```

The MA format is general in that it can express anything that MIDI or MPU format can express; its strength is that it is composed of ASCII characters and can be generated by even the simplest program (or language). Its biggest drawback is that it is unnecessarily detailed for many uses and not easy to decipher. It only "knows about" MIDI and MPU codes, it doesn't "know" anything about music.

12.3.3. The MUTRAN Family

Two recent languages derive many aspects of their design from a music specification language and compiler written by the current author more than a quarter of a century ago. This language, called MUTRAN, has survived in one form or another with little change.

One of the fundamental problems that any scheme for transcribing music on a computer must solve is that of specifying pitches and durations in an easily editable form. Aside from being representable in bits and bytes, the encoding needs to be easy to learn, compact, and comprehensive. Even the standard, handwritten or printed music notation scheme only partly meets these goals. It has a long history, however, and is already understood by most people interested in reading or writing music. Unfortunately, normal music notation is a continuous, two-dimensional notation and is not readily converted to the quantized, linear form that digital computers impose. Rather than base its representation on the written score, MUTRAN took as its model the musician's verbal description of a piece—a description that is inherently linear (although not necessarily quantized). MUTRAN's character-based conventions for specifying pitches and durations, aside from being representable in bits and bytes, are easy to learn and compact (but limited). In an attempt to remedy its limitations, other languages have adopted and expanded on MUTRAN notation.

The following three sections describe the original MUTRAN and its direct descendants MUT and VMU. Later sections also refer to the note formats described here.

12.3.3.1. MUTRAN

MUTRAN format got its name from a program I wrote in the mid-1960s. The MUTRAN program was designed to read music scores encoded on punched cards and produce a program that, when executed, would cause the CPU (an IBM 1620) to create radio frequency interference that sounded like music on a nearby AM radio. Recognizing this program to be a compiler, I named it after the only other compiler I had ever used—Fortran. (MUTRAN itself was written in machine language; I had not yet encountered assemblers!)

Although the MUTRAN program has not survived, the data encoding scheme has, and with minor revisions it has been used as a basis for several other formats. This section is provided so descriptions of other formats may refer to it to define the basic MUTRAN characteristics, allowing their descriptions to focus on particular aspects or differences. Because of the absences of any known MUTRAN compiler, this descriptions is, for the most part, in the past tense.

MUTRAN data consisted of data records and control records. Data records consisted of a sequence of encoded notes, with an arbitrary number of notes on each 80-column card. Typically, each data record contained a phrase, measure, half-measure, or other consistent time length.[4] Control records began with an asterisk in column 1 followed by a keyword and other parameter fields.

Data records contained notes with time value information, separated by blanks. MUTRAN notes were encoded according to the simple BNF grammar in Listing 12.10. Note that all alphabetic characters were uppercase; keypunches had only uppercase. Octave numbers were the so-called "scientific" numbering; `C4` for middle C and `B3` for the pitch one half-step below it. The time value (`<tval>`s) represented *w*hole, *h*alf, *q*uarter, *e*ighth, *s*ixteenth, *t*hirty-second, and sixty-fourth (*f*ast) notes, respectively.

[4]This rather fastidious convention had some serendipitous repercussions. The musical score for an extremely abstract movie was produced by shuffling a deck of cards containing C. P. E. Bach's *Sofegietto* and playing the resulting jumble of single-measure phrases. The soundtrack was a great success.

LISTING 12.10. *Ancient MUTRAN note grammar.*

```
<Mnote>             :: <pitch><duration>
<pitch>             :: <notename><octave> | <rest>
<notename>          :: <letter> | <letter><accidental>
<letter>            :: 'A' | 'B' | 'C' | 'D' | 'E' | 'F' | 'G'
<accidental>        :: <sharp> | <flat>
<sharp>             :: '+' | '+' <sharp>
<flat>              :: '-' | '-' <flat>
<rest>              :: 'R'
<octave>            :: '0' | '1' | '2' | '3' | '4'
                     | '5' | '6' | '7' | '8' | '9'
<duration>          :: <tval> | <tval><tmod>
<tval>              :: 'W' | 'H' | 'Q' | 'E' | 'S' | 'T' | 'F'
<tmod>              :: <dot> | <let>
<dot>               :: '.' | '.' <dot>
<let>               :: 'T' | '3' | '5' | '7' | '9'
```

There were relatively few control record keywords. There were TITLE and COMMENT records, but they were ignored.[5] QUARTER records specified the number of quarter notes per minute (in the same way that metronomes are marked). The TIME control record allowed global scaling of tempo; the nominal TIME value was 100, and setting it to 200 played the piece twice as fast. Finally, MUTRAN needed to know when to stop and the END record provided that information.

The first measure of J. S. Bach's *Well-Tempered Clavier, I, Prelude no. 11* (in 12/8 time) contains two voices; Listing 12.11 is a straightforward MUTRAN version.

LISTING 12.11. *Sample of early MUTRAN from the Well-Tempered Clavier.*

```
*TITLE J.S. BACH WELL-TEMPERED CLAVIER, I, PRELUDE NO. 11
*COMMENT UPPER PART
F5S C5S A4S G4S A4S C5S F4S A4S C5S E-5S D5S C5S
D5S B-4S F4S E4S F4S B-4S D4S F4S A4S C5S B-4S A4S
*COMMENT LOWER PART
F3E A3E C4E A3E F3E A3E B-3E D4E B-3E F2Q RE
```

MUTRAN, in an effort to reduce keypunch effort (and to economize on cards), was content to let everything but the <notename> default to the previous value, so the same two parts would more likely have been encoded as in Listing 12.12.

[5] After all, what's a language without comment records?

LISTING 12.12. *Denser sample of MUTRAN from the Well-Tempered Clavier.*

```
*TITLE JSBACH WELL-TEMP-CLAV, I, NO 9
*COMMENT UPPER PART
F5S C A4 G A C5 F4 A C5 E- D C D B-4 F E F B- D F A C5 B-4 A
*COMMENT LOWER PART
F3E A C4 A3 F A B- D4 B-3 F2Q RE
```

The original MUTRAN compiler only handled single melodic lines; there is only so much you can do with stray radio interference from a machine whose memory cycle time was about 5 microseconds. However, MUTRAN made a hit on a local TV news program when it played the Bach double violin concerto with a human violinist. The violinist later commented that MUTRAN "kept unrelenting time"; given her own particularly sweet and carefully produced violin tone, it was probably the nicest thing she could think of to say.

12.3.3.2. MUT

MUT format (sometimes called modern MUTRAN) is a recent version of the ancient MUTRAN language. This format is a dense, easy-to-read notation scheme for instrumental music. (There is no provision for lyrics; see VMU format for that.) MUT is easy to transcribe, and programs exist to convert it into data that can be played directly on most sound synthesizers.

Modern MUTRAN format (still) consists of data lines and control lines. Each data line begins with an instrument or voice name and contains a sequence of notes for just the instrument. Control lines begin with a sharp sign (#) followed by the keyword and, in some cases, one or more parameters. Control lines specify control changes to take place after preceding lines and before following lines of data. The data lines are arranged such that time proceeds left-to-right, top-to-bottom (i.e., reading order) independently for each instrument (unless #BAR or #SYNC controls intervene). Most programs consider it an error if the accumulated durations of all voices are not equal when a #BAR control is encountered.

MUT notes are encoded according to a simple BNF grammar similar to that for MUTRAN. Listing 12.13 gives the complete grammar. A quick comparison with the grammar in Listing 12.10 reveals that this format has not changed very much in 30 years.

LISTING 12.13. *Modern MUTRAN note grammar.*

```
<Mnote>          :: <pitch><duration>
<pitch>          :: <notename><octave> | <rest>
<notename>       :: <letter> | <letter><accidental>
<letter>         :: 'A' | 'B' | 'C' | 'D' | 'E' | 'F' | 'G'
<accidental>     :: <sharp> | <flat>
<sharp>          :: '#' | '#' <sharp>
<flat>           :: 'b' | 'b' <flat>
<rest>           :: 'R'
<octave>         :: '-2' | '-1' | '0' | '1' | '2' | '3'
                 |  '4'| '5' | '6' | '7' | '8'
<duration>       :: <tval> | <tval><tmod>
<tval>           :: 'w' | 'h' | 'q' | 'e' | 's' | 't' | 'f'
<tmod>           :: <dot> | <let>
<dot>            :: '.' | '.' <dot>
<let>            :: 't' | '3' | '5' | '7' | '9'
```

Octave numbers are as defined earlier in the MIDI section; `C3` is middle C and `B2` is one half-step below it. The time values (`<tval>`s) represented *w*hole, *h*alf, *q*uarter, *e*ighth, *s*ixteenth, *t*hirty-second, and sixty-fourth (*fast*) notes, respectively. The time modifiers have the standard meanings. The modifier . multiplies the duration by 1.5; .. multiplies the duration by 1.75, and so on. The modifiers `t` and `3` multiply the duration by 2/3; `tt` and `33` multiply the duration by 4/9, and so on. Modifiers `5`, `7`, and `9` multiply the duration by 4/5, 6/7, and 8/9, respectively. (This should be extended to allow modifiers of the form `m:n` such that `t` is equivalent to `3:2`.)

Data lines must begin with a whitespace-delimited name that has been defined by appearing in the most recent `#VOICES` control line. Following the name are an arbitrary number of notes in MUT format with | (vertical bar) characters interspersed to indicate measure boundaries (bar lines).

The effect of a vertical bar is identical to that of the `#BAR` control except no synchronization checking is done. Thus, the two examples in Listing 12.14 are truly identical (because a single voice can't have synchronization problems with itself).

LISTING 12.14. *Equivalent MUT representations.*

```
bass     A0q   A1q   C#1q   C#2q  |  D1q   D2q   B0q   E1q   |


bass     A0q   A1q   C#1q   C#2q
#BAR
bass     D1q   D2q   B0q    E1q
#BAR
```

MUT format allows control lines to be defined as needed; many of them will be ignored by any particular program. Commonly used control keywords include

`#ARTIC #.#[#.#]...`	The ARTIC control specifies the articulation with which the notes are to be played. An argument of 1.0 makes the notes connected (*legato*), whereas an argument of 0.25 makes the notes sound for only the first quarter of their time value (*staccato*). If there are fewer arguments than voices, the last argument will be used for the extra voices; thus, a single argument will set the articulation for all the voices, but they can all be set individually if necessary. The default value is usually 0.8 (for all voices).
`#BAR`	A measure ends here. No arguments are used. In scoring programs, a bar line is generated; in programs that produce MPU data, a Timing Clock with Measure End code is generated. In most programs, a check is made to ensure that all voices are in synchronization (have equal cumulative durations).
`#CHAN #[#]...`	The control assigns to the various voices (default is channel 1). A decimal number argument in the range 1 to 16 is expected for each voice.
`#METER ##`	The METER control has two arguments that are the numerator and denominator (respectively) of the time signature. For example, `METER 3 4` would specify waltz time. These are used primarily by scoring programs.

`#SOLO` *`v1 [v2]...`*

This control specifies coarse volume information for each voice. A single character argument, chosen from the following list, is expected for each voice (separated by whitespace):

- `-` This voice is silent (key velocity = 0).
- `S` This voice is soft (key velocity = 21).
- `M` This voice is of medium volume (key velocity = 64).
- `L` This voice is loud (key velocity = 106).
- `#` A decimal argument selects velocity explicitly [0..127].

Note that `S`, `M` and `L` divide the velocity range into three roughly evenly spaced levels, whereas `-` mutes the voice entirely. The name `SOLO` was chosen as a reference to the solo buttons on a mixing console.

`#SYNC`

When this control is encountered, all voices will be synchronized, aligning with whichever voice has the greatest cumulative duration at the moment. Thus, following a section with particularly tricking tempo by a `#SYNC` control will assure synchronization (before the `#BAR` check occurs).

`#TEMPO #`

The `TEMPO` control expects a single, numeric argument representing the number of quarter notes per minute (equivalent to metronome settings).

`#TITLE` *`the title of the piece`*

The `TITLE` control is used by programs that give some special handling to the title of the piece (e.g., scoring programs).

`#TRANS #[#]` The `TRANS` control is used to specify transpositions for scoring. An argument is required for each voice. The transpositions are expressed in scale steps; thus `-7` would transpose down an octave.

`#VOICES name1 [name2]...` The `VOICES` control defines the number of voices and associates a name with each one. Each voice is represented by an argument that can be any combination of characters. Whereas scoring programs will use the names provided here when printing part scores, other programs may need this control to determine how many voices are involved. Therefore, this control should precede all data and any controls that expect an argument per voice.

It should be noted that the music preprocessor, `mpp`, defines keywords to handle conditional inclusion of sections, repeats, and file inclusion for languages like MUT. See section 12.3.1.

The first measure of *Prelude No. 11* in the *Well-Tempered Clavier* could be expressed in modern MUTRAN as shown in Listing 12.15. The choice of `left` and `right` as voice names is purely arbitrary. Voice names may contain any non-whitespace characters and may be up to 31 characters long, although it is convenient to keep them shorter than a tab stop (eight characters).

LISTING 12.15. *Sample of modern MUTRAN from the Well-Tempered Clavier.*

```
#TITLE J.S. Bach Well-Tempered Clavier, I, Prelude no. 11
#VOICES left    right
# first measure
right   F4s C4s  A3s G3s A3s C4s F3s A3s C4s Eb4s D4s C4s
left    F2e      A2e     C3e     A2e     F2e      A2e
right   D4s Bb3s F3s E3s F3s Bb3s D3s F3s A3s C4s Bb3s A3s
left    Bb2e     D3e     Bb2e     F1q              Re
#BAR
```

Listing 12.16 shows a shell command file that generates nine measures of reggae rhythm section consisting of guitar on channel 3, bass on channel

15, and drums on channel 2. The output is MUT data. The command `pick1` simply chooses one of its arguments (randomly) to output. The argument will be followed by a line feed unless the `-n` option is specified.

LISTING 12.16. *Shell command file to generate reggae in modern MUTRAN.*

```
echo "#VOICES    HIHAT    TIMBALE  SNARE    BD     G1    G2     G3    BASS"
echo "#CHAN      2        2        2         2      3     3      3      15"
echo "#SOLO      7        5        7         8      5     5      5       4"
echo "#ARTIC     0.1      0.1      0.1       0.1    0.2   0.2    0.2   1"
for key in E A E A A A E A; do
     echo "HIHAT   Rq A2h A2q"
     echo -n "TIMBALE "
     pick1 -n "Rh" "Rh" "Rh" "C4h" "Rq C4qt C4et" "C4q Rqt C4et"
     pick1 -n " C4q" " C4qt C4et" " C4qt C4st C4st" " Rqt C4st C4st"
     pick1 " Rq" " Rq" " C4q" " C4qt C4et" " Ret C4et C4et"
     echo -n "SNARE   "
     pick1 "Rh Db2h" "Rh Db2h" "Db2h Db2h" "Rh E2h" "Rh E2h" "E2h E2h"
     echo -n "BD         "
     pick1 "Rh A1h" "Rh A1h" "Rh Ab1h" "Rq Rqt Ab1et Ab1h"
     if [ "$key" = "E" ]; then
          echo "G1        Rq B2qt  B2et  Rq E3qt  E3et"
          echo "G2        Rq E3qt  E3et  Rq G#3qt G#3et"
          echo "G3        Rq G#3qt G33et Rq B3qt  B3et"
          echo -n "BASS     E3qt "
          pick1 "E3et E3qt E3et E2qt Rht" "E2q E3et E2q Rq"
     else
          echo "G1        Rq C#3qt C#3et Rq B2qt  B2et"
          echo "G2        Rq E3qt  E3et  Rq D#3qt D#3et"
          echo "G3        Rq A3qt  A3et  Rq F#3qt F#3et"
          pick1 -n "BASS   Rq A2et " "BASS    Rq A2et " "BASS     A2ht "
          pick1 "Ret C#3et D#3q B2q" "A3et A2et B2q D#3q"
     fi
     echo "#BAR"
done
echo "HIHAT C3w:TIMBALE E2w: BD A1w; BASS E2w: #SYNC" | tr ":" "\012"
```

It is hard to appreciate how effective this little shell program is without tinkering with it and hearing the results. By specifying alternative material for the timbale, snare drum, and bass parts, we've added enough variation to break up the potential repetitiveness while ensuring that all possible sequences sound good.

By lengthening the list in the `for key in...` line, longer pieces can be composed. Adding more clauses to the `if` statement would allow greater harmonic variety. If you added `if` clauses for many other chords and changed the `for key in...` line to read:

```
for key in $*; do
```

you would have a little language of your own for generating reggae accompaniments.

12.3.3.3. VMU

VMU format is an earlier variant of MUTRAN format. It is particularly well-suited to notation of multipart scores with lyrics (e.g., four-part harmonizations) and is generally designed to be easy for humans to read and edit, although it is not as dense as MUT format. Filters exist to produce printed scores (both full and individual parts) from VMU format and to play VMU files on MIDI-equipped sound synthesizers (as well as some other, non-MIDI devices).

Like MUT format, VMU format consists of control lines and data lines; control lines comprise an initial keyword followed by arguments. The control keywords are almost identical to those in MUT; they are

`#ARTIC #.# [#.#]...`	Same as MUT.
`#BAR`	Same as in MUT.
`#CHAN #[#]...`	Same as in MUT.
`#CPQ #`	This control expects a single argument that sets the number of "clocks per quarter" note. This value must be chosen such that every note encountered can be represented by an integral number of clocks; for example, the presence of eighth notes requires that CPQ be a multiple of 2; dotted quarters require CPQ to be divisible by 3; eighths *and* dotted quarters require CPQ to be a multiple of 6, and so on. Fortunately, this complicated control is only required for output to Votrax PSS speech synthesizers and is ignored by all other known programs.
`#METER ##`	Same as in MUT.
`#SOLO v1[v2]...`	Same as in MUT.
`#TEMPO #`	Same as in MUT.
`#TITLE the title of the piece`	Same as in MUT.
`#TRANS #[#]...`	Same as in MUT.
`#VOICES name1 [name2]...`	Same as in MUT.

In addition to these, programs may define controls for their own use. It is recommended that such controls consist of the number sign followed immediately (with no intervening whitespace) by uppercase characters. `mpp`, the music preprocessor, defines several useful macro controls; see the description of `mpp`.

Unlike MUT format, data are arranged such that time proceeds downward with each part represented by a column of data. The first column is the lyric and either contains one of the special symbols `-` or `/` or any string of characters containing no whitespace. `-` is understood by most programs to be a placeholder and indicates that there is no associated lyric and often no sound at all (rests are a good example). `/` is understood by most programs to be a placeholder and indicates that although there is no associated lyric, there is some sound produced (e.g., instrumental sounds, especially drums). All columns but the first contain notes encoded in the format used by modern MUTRAN (described in section 12.3.3.2) with `-` added as a silent (durationless) placeholder.

Listing 12.17 is the beginning of the file `tbp.vmu`, which contains a simple example of VMU format. The control lines at the beginning establish general parameters for the various programs that may be used to process the file. Scoring programs will title the piece as indicated, assign names to the four parts, and show the bass and baritone voices transposed up an octave (7 steps). Programs that generate sound will set the tempo to 150 beats per minute, make the soprano voice louder than the rest, and put each voice on the specified MIDI channel (if MIDI or MPU output is being generated).

LISTING 12.17. *Example of VMU format.*

```
#TITLE  Teddy Bear's Picnic
#VOICES Bass    Bari    Tenor   Soprano
#CHAN   1       2       3       4
Pic     D3q     D3q     D3q     D3q
-nic    D3q     D3q     G3q     B3q
time    C#3q    E3q     G3q     A#3q
for     D3q     G3q     G3q     B3q
#BAR
ted     C3qt    E3qt    G3qt    E4qt
-dy     B2et    E3et    G3et    B3et
bears   G2q     G3q     B3q     D4q
-       Rqt     Rqt     Rqt     Rqt
the     D3et    D3et    G3et    B3et
lit     C#3qt   E3qt    G3qt    A#3qt
-tle    D3et    G3et    G3et    B3et
#BAR
```

```
ted      C3qt   E3qt   G3qt   E4qt
-dy      B2et   E3et   G2et   B3et
bears    G2qt   G3qt   B3qt   D4qt
are      G2et   D3et   G3et   B3et
hav      C3et   G3et   C4et   E4et
-ing     D3et   F#3et  B3et    D4et
a        B2et   D3et   G3et    B3et
love     C#3qt  D#3qt  F#3qt   A#3qt
-ly      D3et   E3et   G3et    B3et
#BAR
day      F#3qt  A3qt   B3qt    D4qt
to       F3et   G#3et  A#3et   Db4et
-day     E3h    G3q    B3q     C4h
-ay      -      F#3q   A3q     -
-        Rq     Rq     Rq      Rq
#BAR
```

12.3.4. DP

DP format allows particularly dense encoding of drum rhythms in a notation that is similar to that commonly used by drummers. As a result, it is easy to read. It can be edited on any ASCII terminal, and programs exist to play it on most drum machines or synthesizers that can make drum sounds.

Drum patterns are commonly printed in a notation loosely based on common practice notation ("normal" music notation). A staff line is provided for each instrument, and the usual shapes or specific variations of them are used to denote time values with dynamic markings about the staff or below the notes.

To adapt this format for computer use, the dynamic markings replace the notes and spacing indicates timing, not unlike the layout on most drum machines. This works well for percussion instruments that ignore note durations (i.e., the time between MIDI key-on and key-off events), but when this format is used for duration sensitive instruments, it is worth knowing that durations are set to the current quantum (see `#QUANT` control) multiplied by the current articulation (see #ARTIC control).

DP control lines include an initial keyword possibly followed by arguments. The control keywords are

`#ARTIC#.#`	Same as in MUT except only one argument is used to set the durations of all notes generated.
`#BARLEN #`	This control specifies the number MPU clocks per measure. The default is `#BARLEN 480`.

`#GAIN channel/key multiplier`

The GAIN control allows global modification of key velocities on an instrument-by-instrument basis. The first argument identifies an instrument (see the description of channel/key in the discussion of data formats). The second field is a multiplicative factor to be applied to every key velocity for this instrument. The default value for all possible channel/key combinations is `#GAIN chan/key 1.0`.

`#QUANT timevalue`

A single argument specifies the duration associated with each note symbol. The argument may be a decimal number or one of `whole`, `half`, `quarter`, `eighth`, or `sixteenth`. `#QUANT 16` makes each note or rest a sixteenth note long. `#QUANT 8` is the default.

`#ROLL char vel rate`

This control defines special pattern characters to represent multiple drum hits (e.g., for snare rolls). Three arguments are required. The first is the pattern character being defined (should not be `0`, `1`, `2`, `3`, `4`, `5`, `6`, `7`, `8`, `9`, or `-`). The second argument is the velocity for the strokes in the roll encoded as `0` through `9` (see description of data lines). The last argument is the rate at which the strokes should be repeated, using the same scheme as the argument for `#QUANT`. For example, the character `~` can be defined to produce thirty-second notes with a MIDI key velocity of 28 by the following:

```
#ROLL     ~ 2 32
```

If used in a section with `#QUANT 8` specified, four notes will be generated for each `~` symbol in the pattern. The `#TUPLE` control provides another approach to drum rolls.

`#SYNC`

The data for each instrument is buffered up as an independent stream with its own clock. Thus, each instrument can be represented by several consecutive input lines and, when output, all the instruments will be merged, each starting at time zero (the beginning). Sometimes, however, you want to flush the buffering and resynchronize the instrument clocks (e.g., when a piece is too long to fit in the buffers in its entirety). When the SYNC control is encountered in the input, all buffered data is output and the clocks for all instruments are set to the highest clock value so far. This allows an instrument that only appears late in a piece to be synchronized with the other instruments without having to be represented by rests throughout the entire beginning of the piece. It also allows very long pieces to be processed without overflowing the buffers.

`TUPLE` *`char vel mult`*

The TUPLE control defines special pattern characters to represent drum hits at a rate faster than the current #QUANT setting. Three arguments are required. Like #ROLL, the first is the pattern character being defined; (should not be 0, 1, 2, 3, 4, 5, 6, 7, 8, 9, or -). Unlike $ROLL, the second argument is the actual MIDI velocity for the notes, encoded as 1 through 127. The last argument is the rate multiplier for the repeated strokes; if the argument is 5, then five notes will be generated for each symbol. For example, the character = can be defined to produce notes with a velocity of 56 at double the current rate with the following line:

```
TUPLE = 56  2
```

If used in a section with #QUANT 8 specified, two sixteenth notes will be generated for each = symbol in the pattern.

The controls defined for the program mpp are useful in DP files. In particular, the #DEFINE control can be used to associate symbolic names with channel/key pairs and the #INCLUDE control can be used to refer to libraries of such symbol definitions.

DP data lines require two fields (separated by whitespace): a channel/key field and a pattern field. Any further files are ignored as comments.

The channel/key field defines the instrument to be played and consists of a channel number (in decimal), a slash, and a key number (in hexadecimal, decimal, or as a note name, such as Eb3). 5/0x3d, 5/51, and 5/C#3 are all equivalent formats for specifying key 61_{10} on channel 5. This field may be specified using a symbolic name specified earlier in a #DEFINE line (if mpp preprocesses the file).

The pattern field is formed from the digits 0 through 9, the character -, and any #ROLL or #TUPLE pattern characters defined. The digits represent key velocity with the generated velocities being 1, 14, 28, 42, 56, 71, 85, 99, 113, and 127 (going from 0 to 9). A minus character, -, represents silence.

Listing 12.18 is an example of eight measures of a Latin samba rhythm coded in DP format. There are hundreds of different variations of the samba; this one is a classic variation known as "Samba Batucada" from Birger Sulsbruck's excellent book (1982). Note that only four measures are written out; the mpp repeat controls (#REPEAT 2 and #ENDRPT) are used to double the length. For illustration purposes, some of the drums have been defined in mpp #DEFINE lines. Typically, they would all be defined in a separate file referenced with the mpp #INCLUDE control line. A comparison with the standard notation for this drum pattern (which requires a full page in Sulsbruck's book) will demonstrate the efficiency and readability of this format.

LISTING 12.18. *DP format for Samba Batucada.*

```
#DEFINE  Surdo    2/-x32   (TOM2)
#DEFINE  Caixa    2/49     (SD2)
#DEFINE  Pratos   2/Db3    (CHINESE (cymbal))
#REPEAT  2
#        1 2 3 4 1 2 3 4 1 2 3 4 1 2 3 4
Surdo    70-46--570-46--570-46--570-46--5
2/56     64546454645464546454645464546454   Chocalho (SHAKER)
2/51     7-7-7-77-7-7-77-7-7-7-77-7-7-77-   Tamborim (RIM1)
4/71     72267226722672267226722672267226   Pandeiro (TAMBO)
Caixa    63636336363636636363633636363663
4/73     6---6---6--66-6-6---6---6--66-6-   Caixeta (TIMBL)
4/75     6-----336-----436-----436-----33   High Agogo (AGOGH)
4/74     --336----6-36-----436----6-36---   Low Agogo (AGOGL)
4/0x4d   --7------5--------6------5------   High Cuica (CUICH)
4/0x4c   4---54-4---45-4-4---54-4---45-4-   Low Cuica (CUICL)
Pratos   6------------70-6------------70-
#ENDRPT
```

12.3.5. SD

Files in SD format contain melodic information expressed as "scale-degrees." SD format is designed to be easy for humans to read and edit and is particularly well-suited to notation of melodies that only use notes from a particular seven-note (or fewer) scale. Most tonal (as opposed to atonal) music meets this criterion. It is common among musicians to describe notes or melodies in terms of scale degrees, partly because of its compactness ("5" is quicker to say than "B flat"), partly because its key independence avoids problems for musicians playing transposing instruments, and partly because it seems more natural to focus on the function of the note in the key rather than on its absolute pitch. The SD format shares all these advantages.

SD format consists of control lines and data lines arranged such that time proceeds from left to right in equal-sized steps with each part represented by one or more lines of data. SD control lines comprise an initial keyword followed by arguments. The control keywords recognized are

`CODING` *`symbols`*	The `CODING` control associates symbols with scale degrees. It defines 21 symbols; 7 for scale degrees with downward motion guaranteed; 7 for scale degrees with shortest motion guaranteed (the usual symbols); and 7 for scale degrees with upward motion guaranteed. The default coding definition is equivalent to `#CODING abcdefg12345676ABCDEFG`. Thus, `a`, `!`, and `A` are equivalent except that although `1` will select the root (first degree) of the current scale that is closest to the last note, `a` will choose the root below the last note, and `A` will choose the root above the last note. See also the `#INIT` control and the description of the `^` and `v` data characters (in the discussion of the note field) for other ways of controlling the direction of motion.

`#INIT note[note]`	This control specifies the initial pitch associated with each voice in MUTRAN timeless note format, which consists of a pitch class and an octave number (e.g., `C3` for middle C). Because data in SD format may specify choosing the direction of motion that yields the shortest jump from the previous note, there must be a previous note from which to measure. At the beginning of the piece, there is no previous note; `#INIT` specifies an imaginary previous note. `#INIT` can also be used in the middle of a piece to force large jumps up or down (also see the description of the note field).
`#METER ##`	Same as in MUT.
`#QUANT timevalue`	Same as in DP.
`#SCALE note[note]...`	The `SCALE` control defines the pitch classes associated with the (up to) seven scale degrees. It is followed by a comma-separated list of pitch classes in either numeric or symbolic form (`0=C`, `1=C#`, . . . `11=B`). The default scale is a C major scale, that is, `#SCALE C,D,E,F,G,A,B`.
`VOICES name1 [name2]...`	Same as in MUT.

In addition, any control line not mentioned (i.e., a line starting with a number sign followed by other, non-blank characters) is allowed as part of the input and is passed through to the output unchanged (thereby allowing controls such as `#ARTIC`, `#BAR`, `#CHAN`, `#CPQ`, `#SOLO`, `#TEMPO`, `#TITLE`, and `#TRANS` to be passed to programs that read VMU format). Further `mpp`, the music preprocessor defines several useful macro controls; see section 12.3.1.

SD data lines require two fields (separated by whitespace): a voice name field and a note field. Any further fields are ignored as comments. The voice name field defines the voice with which to associate the note field data and consists of a name that must have already appeared in the preceding `#VOICES` control line.

The note field is composed of any non-whitespace characters. Specifically, these include the symbols defined in the `#CODING` control line, the tie character (`(`), the three special symbols `|`, `^`, and `v`, and finally, all other non-whitespace characters. The tie character (`(`) lengthens the previous note by the `QUANT` duration. The character `|` is a placeholder and is ignored; unlike any other character, it takes no time. It is often convenient to use `|` to demarcate measures (for readability). The character `^` revises the program's idea of the last note played for this voice upward by one octave, thus ensuring that the next note will be interpreted an octave higher than it would otherwise. Note, however, that the `^` takes time and generates a rest. The character `v` revises the program's idea of the last note played for this voice downward by one octave, thus ensuring that the next note will be interpreted an octave lower than it would otherwise. The `v` also generates a rest. All other non-whitespace characters represent rests; the most common choice is to use minus, `-`, but some people prefer the period (`.`).

Listing 12.19 is a simple example of a three-voice scale-degree encoded harmony. The comment line gives the chord structure in scale degrees (`1` = tonic, `4` = subdominant, `5` = dominant) with periods marking the quarter-note beats in the eight measures. To move this piece to another key would only require changing the `#SCALE` and `#INIT` lines.

LISTING 12.19. *"Departure Tax" in SD format*

```
#TITLE  Departure Tax
#VOICES Al      Bob     Cy
#SCALE  G,A,B,C,D,E,F#
#INIT   F#3     A3       C4
#   1 . . . 1 . . . 5 . . . 4 . 5 . 5 . . . 5 . . . 1 . . . 4 . 5 . |
Cy  45565(5434516543217-7(7717617(--34454(4323456542311-1(1117617(--|
Bob 23343(3212354321765-5(5565465(--12232(2171234327165-5(5565465(--|
Al  71111(1757132176542-2(2232132(--57777(6545712175543-3(3332132(--|
```

Because the three parts in "Departure Tax" consist entirely of notes that lie in the scale and almost all the notes have the same duration (eighth notes), SD format is especially appropriate. The few quarter notes are handled by tying two eighth notes together with the tie symbol (`(`).

Figure 12.3 is a representation (in standard music notation) of the VMU format output generated by running the SD example in the previous figure through the program `sd2vmu`. The VMU format output was then run through an `awk` program, `vmu2p.awk`, which produced a `pic` file that uses a set of standard macros to print music. There is no "music font" in this example; everything is drawn. Both the treble clef and the quarter rest, for example, are spline curves. The `pic` file was then massaged by hand to beam the notes and add chord symbols (`vmu2p.awk` doesn't know about them yet).

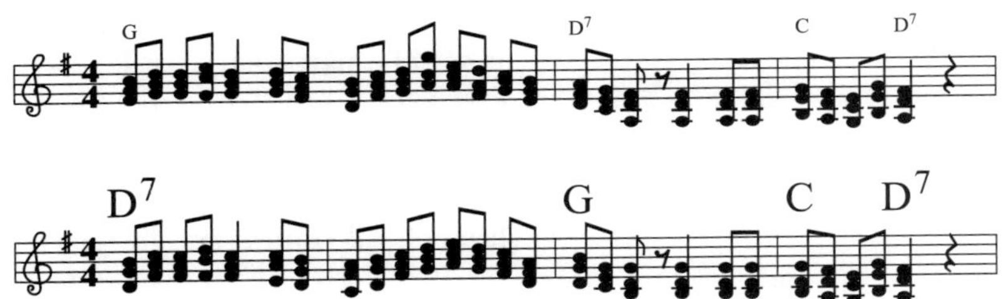

FIGURE 12.3. *Output from SD data in Listing 12.19.*

12.3.6. CCC

Chord charts are a succinct way of expressing the harmonic structure of a piece of music. Files in CCC format are ASCII-encoded chord charts arranged to be read and edited by humans and computers alike. Because the CCC format mimics the chord charts used by musicians, little special training is required to enter CCC data, and the programs that convert CCC files to other formats can be used to give quick auditory feedback for editing.

The format for chord charts includes control lines and data lines; CCC control lines are distinguished by an initial keyword. Keywords include

`#ARTIC` *`style`*

Same as in MUT except in addition to the numeric arguments, three symbolic style arguments are defined: staccato, normal, and legato. Staccato makes each chord last 1/4 of the time between chords. Legato makes each chord last the entire time between chords and does not retrigger any notes it doesn't have to; for example, if two succeeding chords both have `C4` as the low note, then `C4` will not be resounded, just held. Legato will not hold from one input line to the next, however. `#ARTIC normal` (the default) and `#ARTIC 0.8` are equivalent.

`#CHORD` *name note...*	This control defines the individual notes in a particular chord. The *name* field is just that; it can be any collection of characters except `/` or whitespace characters. Thus `C`, `Cm`, `Cm7(b9)`, and `ugly_Zappa_mess` are all legal chord names (but do remember that these will be the names you use in the chord sequences later in the file). Chord names may be up to 15 characters long. The *note* fields can be in any one of three formats: decimal, hexadecimal, or MUTRAN timeless note format (described in section 12.3.8); for example, `60`, `x3c`, `x3C`, `X3c`, `X3C`, and `C3` are all equivalent. Octave numbers may range from –2 to 8, although notes below `C#-2` and above `G8` are not allowed. Use `#` for sharp and `b` for flat.
`#QUANT` *timevalue*	Same as in DP except the setting of quantum defines the length associated with each chord. `#QUANT quarter` (the default) and `#QUANT 4` are equivalent. A fractional value is also permissible; `#QUANT 1.5` will make each chord have the duration of a whole note triplet.
`#SPEED` *timevalue*	`#SPEED` is a synonym for `#QUANT`.

Any line that is not recognized as a control line (does not begin with `#`) is treated as a data line containing chords to be played. Chord names must be separated from each other by whitespace characters (i.e., tabs or spaces) and will be interpreted left to right, top to bottom. The special chord name `/` is taken to mean the last chord played.

Listing 12.20 is an example of a simple chord chart. Unlike this simple example, however, many chord charts require dozens of chords. A simple expedient is to create files that contain only `Chord` commands and use the `mpp #INCLUDE` command to refer to them. Standard files exist for block piano chords and for guitar chords. Once again, the functions provided by the music preprocessor program, `mpp`, are useful in CCC files (note the `#REPEAT`/`#ENDRPT` construction in the example).

LISTING 12.20. *"Empty Bed Blues" in CCC format.*

```
# Empty Bed Blues
#CHORD   C       C4 E4 G4 C5
#CHORD   C7      C4 E4 G4 Bb4
#CHORD   F       C4 F4 A4 C5
#CHORD   G7      D4 F4 G4 B4
#QUANT   quarter
#ARTIC   staccato
#REPEAT 8
C  /  /  C7      F  /  G7   /
C  /  G7 /       C  /  C7   /
F  /  /  /       F  /  G7   /
C  /  /  /       C  /  /    /
G7 /  /  /       F  /  G7   /
C  /  F  /       C  /  G7   /
#ENDRPT
```

12.3.7. CC

CC format is an extension to CCC format to allow it to be used for generating complex accompaniments as well as melodic lines. Like CCC, this format uses both control lines and data lines. The format for data lines is identical in the two formats; however, the control lines are different. The control keywords used in CC format are

`#CHORD` *`name class transpositions`* The `#CHORD` control defines harmonic structure by reference to a structure type and a list of (transposition) transformations to be carried out on it. The `name` field is any collection of characters except whitespace characters (the special name `/` is disallowed). As in CCC format, `C`, `Cm`, `Cm7(b9)`, and `ugly_Zappa_mess` are all legal chord names. The `type` field selects from a small repertoire of harmony structures, `tri` for major and minor triads, `dom7` for dominant seventh and other four-note harmonies, `aug5` for harmonies with an augmented fifth, and `dim5` for harmonies with a diminished fifth. The `transpositions` field consists of 12 comma-separated signed integers that indicate the transposition for each of the 12 pitch classes.

`#PART` *name*	The `#PART` control line can be used to indicate something of the phrase structure of the piece. The *name* can be any sequence of non-whitespace characters. Typically, the name will either describe the function within the piece (e.g., `verse`) or the generic pattern from which the following chords are derived (e.g., `turnaround3`). Accompaniment generation and melody generation programs may use this information to deduce intermediate level structure.
`#QUANT` *timevalue*	Same as in CCC.
`#STYLE` *name*	This control is used to choose among the different composition algorithms. Accompaniment generators and melody generators endeavor to produce output that matches the harmonic data and fits the style specified here. As of this writing, ten styles are defined: `bebop`, `bluegrass`, `boogie`, `classical`, `march`, `mozart`, `samba`, `sequence`, `swing`, and `tonerow`. About 25 more styles are planned.

Any line that does not start with a sharp sign is treated as a data line containing chords to be played. Chord names must be separated from each other by whitespace characters (i.e., tabs or spaces) and will be interpreted left to right, top to bottom. The special chord name `/` is taken to mean the last chord played.

Listing 12.21 shows a CC file generated by the program IMG/1 (Langston, 1990b, 1991) to specify a one-minute long swing composition to be played at a tempo of 128 beats per minute. The `# Title` line contains the creation date expressed in seconds since midnight, Jan. 1, 1970 GMT (used to seed the random number generator for creation of the chord chart).

LISTING 12.21. *CC format chord chart created by IMG/1.*

```
# Title 621791525
#STYLE  swing
#INCLUDE        "/u/psl/midi/etc/accagc.cc"
#QUANTUM        quarter
#PART Igrva
Bb  /   Bo  / Eb   / F7   / Bb  /  Bo  / Eb  / F7  /
#PART Igrvb
Bb  /   Bb7 / Eb   / Gb7  / Bb  /  F7  / B   / F7  /
#PART Igrva
Bb  /   Bbo / Cm   / F7   / Bb  /  Bbo / Cm  / F7  /
#PART Igrvb
Bb  /   Bb7 / Eb   / Eo   / Bb  /  Cm  F7 Bb / /   /
#PART Igrb
D7  /   Am7 / D7   / D7   / G7  /  /   / Dm7 / G7  /
C7  /   C7  / C7   / C7   / Cm7 /  /   / F7  / /   /
#PART Igrva
Bb  /   Bbo / Cm   / F7   / Bb  /  Bbo / Cm  / F7  /
#PART Igrvb
Bb  /   Bb7 / Eb   / Eo   / Bb  /  F7  / Bb  / /   /
```

No #CHORD lines appear in this file; the file mentioned in the #INCLUDE line contains #CHORD definitions that describe the transformation from the key of C to all the appropriate chord harmonizations. Listing 12.22 is an excerpt from /u/psl/midi/etc/accagc.cc containing all the #CHORD lines referenced in the chord chart in Listing 12.21.

LISTING 12.22. *Excerpt from an* #INCLUDE*d CC file.*

```
#          name      type      transpositions
#CHORD     Am7       dom7      -3,-3,-3,-3,-4,-3,-3,-3,-3,-4,-3,-3
#CHORD     Bb        tri       -2,-2,-2,-2,-2,-2,-2,-2,-2,-2,-2,-2
#CHORD     Bb7       dom7      -2,-2,-2,-2,-2,-2,-2,-2,-2,-2,-2,-2
#CHORD     Bbo       dom7      -2,-2,-2,-2,-3,-2,-2,-3,-2,-2,-3,-2
#CHORD     B         tri       -1,-1,-1,-1,-1,-1,-1,-1,-1,-1,-1,-1
#CHORD     Bo        dom7      -1,-1,-1,-1,-2,-1,-1,-2,-1,-1,-2,-1
#CHORD     C7        dom7      0,0,0,0,0,0,0,0,0,0,0,0
#CHORD     Cm        tri       0,0,0,0,-1,0,0,0,0,-1,0,0
#CHORD     Cm7       dom7      0,0,0,0,-1,0,0,0,0,-1,0,0
#CHORD     D7        dom7      2,2,2,2,2,2,2,2,2,2,2,2
#CHORD     Dm7       dom7      2,2,2,2,1,2,2,2,2,1,2,2
#CHORD     Eb        tri       3,3,3,3,3,3,3,3,3,3,3,3
#CHORD     Eo        dom7      4,4,4,4,3,4,4,3,4,4,3,4
#CHORD     F7        dom7      5,5,5,5,5,5,5,5,5,5,5,5
#CHORD     Gb7       dom7      6,6,6,6,6,6,6,6,6,6,6,6
#CHORD     G7        dom7      7,7,7,7,7,7,7,7,7,7,7,7
```

The definitions for Bb, B, Cm, and Eb are based on triad harmony—that is, based on the first (tonic), third (mediant), and fifth (dominant) scale degrees. For Bb, everything is transposed down a whole-step from the C major prototype. The harmonization will be based on Bb, D, and F (a whole-stop down from C, E, and G), and an (C major-based) accompaniment that uses an A note will be transposed to use a G note in its place. For Cm, only the third and sixth are transposed down a half-step from the C major prototype. The harmonization will be based on C, Eb, and G and an accompaniment that uses an A note will be transposed to use an Ab note in its place.

All the other definitions in Listing 12.22 are based on four-note dominant seventh harmony. The definitions for `Bb7`, `C7`, `D7`, `F7`, `Gb7`, and `G7` are simple transpositions of the `C7`-based harmony in the prototype. The definitions for `Am7`, `Cm7`, and `Dm7` are transpositions that flat the third and sixth of the `C7`-based harmony in the prototype.

With this simple mechanism, a small collection of prototypes (four per style) can be used to provide hundreds of harmonic structures. The program `acca` uses chord charts in the CC format, and these harmonic structure definitions to assemble complete accompaniments (e.g., bass, guitar, and drums) from a small set of canned prototypes. Similarly, the program `accl` uses CC format chord charts to define harmonic structure within which it composes melody lines and harmonizations.

12.3.8. GC

Files in the GC format give specific instructions on providing guitar-like accompaniment (although they can also be used to provide other kinds of chording accompaniment as well). GC separates the specifications of the harmonic structure and the rhythmic structure of an accompaniment. This allows independent experimentation with either aspect.

Programs exist to convert this format to synthesizer data that encode the specified accompaniments. There are also programs that use GC data to define the harmonic structure of an original instrumental solo. See the following sections on the `lick` program for an example.

Basic to the understanding of GC format is the concept of a "picking pattern." Picking patterns are sequences of events that occur at evenly spaced times within the basic time interval. The basic time interval, set by the `#QUANT` control, is the time allotted to each line of GC data. Each event is a part of the chord to be played at the specified time. Events are specified by reference to the fields in a data line; thus `1` represents the note in the first data field, `2` represents the note in the second data field, and `1-99` represents all the notes in all the fields of the data line.

For example, a common guitar pattern called "split" (or sometimes "boom-chuck") involves hitting a low string (the "bass note" or "boom") on the first count and then strumming the upper strings (the "chord" or "chuck") on the second count. The whole pattern would take two counts. This pattern could be specified by `#PICK split 1 2-99`. Note that `2-99` effectively means the notes in all the data fields except the first one. Thus, a data line such as `A1 E2 A2 C#3 E3` would generate a boom-chuck of A major chord.

In fingerpicking patterns, the basic time interval might be subdivided into four counts with a single string being played on each count (e.g., `#PICK fingers 1 4 2 3`). At any time, the current picking pattern determines how many counts the basic time interval represents.

Although the picking pattern governs the onset of notes, their duration (and thus their stopping time) is determined by the length of their subdivided time interval and the "articulation" with which they are being played. An articulation of 1 will cause notes to be sustained through their entire time subdivision, making them contiguous, with no intervening silence. An articulation of 0.5 will make silences between the notes that are as long as the notes themselves. Values larger than 1 may also be useful; for example, if `#PICK split` is played with an articulation of 2, the bass note and chord will overlap each other.

GC control lines begin with a keyword and may contain arguments separated by whitespace. The various keywords and their meanings are

`#ARTIC #.#[#.#]...` This control requires one or more parameters to specify the duration of notes as a fraction of the time allotted to each part of the chord. If more than one parameter is given, then they will be used in rotation, starting with the first. It is common to specify as many articulation parameters as there are subdivisions in the current picking pattern. The following controls set the rotation back to the first: `#ARTIC`, `#MULT`, `#PICK`, `#QUANT`, `#SPEED`, `#STYLE`. Note that articulations greater than 1 can cause notes to hang over the end of the time allotted to each input line except the last. If `#PICK split` and `#ARTIC 2 2` have been specified, the chord notes will last halfway through the next pattern up until the end when there will be no next pattern to overhang.

`#BARLEN #`

Same as in DP.

`#CHORDTONES name note[,note]...`

This control is used by programs wanting to know the harmonic structure of the piece (see the description of `lick` for an example). Two parameter fields, separated by `<space>` or `<tab>`, are required. The first field is a chord "name" and may be any combination of ASCII characters not including whitespace characters. The second field is a comma-separated list of pitch classes in either numeric or symbolic form (`0 + C, 1 + C#, ... 11 + B`).

`METER ##`

Same as in MUT except the time signature will be used to reset `BARLEN` (based on 120 clocks per quarter notes) and the `METER` parameters can be fractional.

`#MULTIPLICITY #`

This control requires a parameter to specify the number times each following chord is to be played. The MULTIPLICITY control greatly shortens pieces containing long sequences of repeated chords. `#MULT` is a synonym for `#MULTIPLICITY`.

`#PICK name[#]...`

The `PICK` control requires a name parameter and has optional parameters. If it appears with just a name parameter, it invokes an already defined picking pattern. If it appears with further parameters, it defines (or redefines) the named picking pattern. Each optional parameter is either a number or a range of numbers (separated by a hyphen) indicating the notes to be played; `1` represents the first note on the data line; `2-99` represents all the notes on the line except the first; and so on. The number of optional parameters defines the interval subdivision for the pattern. A common picking pattern is defined by #PICK AltBass 1 3-99 2 3-99, which means that a piece with #QUANT set to 2 will generate four eighth-note time subdivisions.

#QUANT *timevalue*

Same as in DP except the duration being defined is that for a line of data. If #QUANT 4 is specified, the time interval represented by a line of input data is a quarter note. Changing picking patterns will change how this interval is subdivided, but not its overall length. The QUANT argument may be a floating-point number; thus #QUANT 2.667 will give dotted quarter notes (approximately).

#SCALE *note[,note]...*

This control is used by programs wanting to know the scalar structure of the piece. It is followed by a comma-separated list of pitch classes in either numeric or symbolic form (0 + C, 1 + C#, ... 11 + B). For example, the line #SCALE 0,Db,2,3,4,F,F#,G,Ab,9,10,B. would define a chromatic scale.

#SPEED *timevalue*

SPEED is a synonym for QUANT.

#STRUM *#.#*

STRUM sets the delay (in quarter-notes) between notes played in a chord. If STRUM is set to 0.025 (a fortieth of a quarter note) and a six-note chord is played, the first note will be played one fortieth of a quarter note ahead of the second and a thirty-second note ahead of the last (five fortieths of a quarter note). The first note will be played early enough that the last note comes out on the beat. See the description of #PICK for additional information.

`#STYLE` *name*	This control is a convenient way to specify the accompaniment figure to be used; it invokes a predefined style. This control will set picking pattern, strum value, articulation values, and velocity values to those defined by the style.
`#STYLEDEF` *name*	This control defines a style. It requires a single name parameter by which the style will be invoked. The style that is defined includes the current picking pattern, strum value, articulation values, and velocity values. A typical usage is to create a separate file containing the definitions of several styles and then include it in data files with the music preprocessor `#INCLUDE` statement.
`#VELOCITY#[#]...`	This control requires one or more decimal parameters to specify the key velocity with which each part of the chord will be played. If more than one parameter is given, then they will be used in rotation, starting with the first. The `#MULT`, `#PICK`, `#QUANT`, `#SPEED`, `#STYLE`, and `#VEL` controls set the rotation back to the first (`#VEL`, `VOLUME`, and `VOL` are all legal synonyms for `#VELOCITY`). The key velocity parameters may range from 1 to 127; a common default is 64. If the `PICK` pattern has metric subdivisions, then specifying multiple key velocity parameters may be particularly useful; for example, `#VEL 80 48 48` will accent the first beat of each waltz pattern.

Any line that begins with a sharp sign but is not recognized as a control line is considered a comment. Further, any line beginning with a sharp sign followed by a space (i.e., `# `) will *never* be recognized as a control line and will thus *always* be considered a comment line.

In addition to the controls listed here, the controls defined for the program `mpp` are useful in GC files. For instance, files containing a large repertoire of style definitions can be referenced with the `mpp` `#INCLUDE` control.

GC chord lines consist of notes encoded in MUTRAN "timeless" format (without time values) separated by spaces or tabs. Listing 12.23 give the BNF for the timeless note format.

LISTING 12.23. *BNF for MUTRAN timeless note format.*

```
<note>          :: <snote><octave> | <rest>
<snote>         :: <letter> | <letter><accidental>
<letter>        :: 'A' | 'B' | 'C' | 'D' | 'E' | 'F' | 'G'
<accidental>    :: <sharp> | <flat>
<sharp>         :: '#' | '#' <sharp>
<flat>          :: 'b' | 'b' <flat>
<rest>          :: 'R' | '-'
<octave>        :: '-1' | '0' | '1' | '2' | '3' | '4'
                        | '5' | '6' | '7' | '8' | '9'
```

Note that the character `-` functions differently from the way it does in VMU format where it acts as a silent placeholder with no duration; in GC format, it is a synonym for `R` and effectively has duration.

Listing 12.24 is a fragment of a bluegrass backup guitar-chord file. The first few statements define a picking pattern and the other elements of a style that is called `AltDrive` in one of the standard GC library files. The last data line in this fragment introduces a rest that lasts for one and a quarter beats (a half note per line minus the dotted eighth duration of the D3).

LISTING 12.24. *Example of GC format.*

```
# Pecusa Waltz, (c) psl 6/87
#PICK   alt     1   3-99  2   3-99
#ARTIC          1.5 1.8 1.5 1.8
#VEL            64  80  64  80
#STRUM  0.0125
#METER  4 4
#SCALE  7,9,10,0,2,3,5,6
#QUANT  2
#CHORDTONES     Gm      7,10,2
G2 D3   Bb3 D4 G4
G2 D3   Bb3 D4 G4
#CHORDTONES     Adim    3,6,9,0
Eb3 C4  C4 Eb4 Gb4
A2 Gb2  C4 Eb4 Gb4
#CHORDTONES     Gm      7,10,2
G2 D3   Bb3 D4 G4
G2 Bb2  Bb3 D4 G4
#CHORDTONES     D7      2,6,9,0
D3 A2   A3 C4 F#4
D3 -    -  -  -
```

12.3.8.1. `lick`

The `lick` program produces banjo improvisations to fit a specified set of chords expressed in the GC format. It implements a technique that uses specific information about the mechanics and common practices of five-string banjo playing to compose instrumental parts that follow a specified chord progression and are particularly suited to (i.e., easy to play on) the banjo.

The five-string banjo is one of the few musical instruments claimed to be of American design. Even so, it is clearly related to African instruments formed from a gourd, a stick, and one or more gut or metal strings. Figure 12.4 is a schematic diagram of the American five-string banjo.

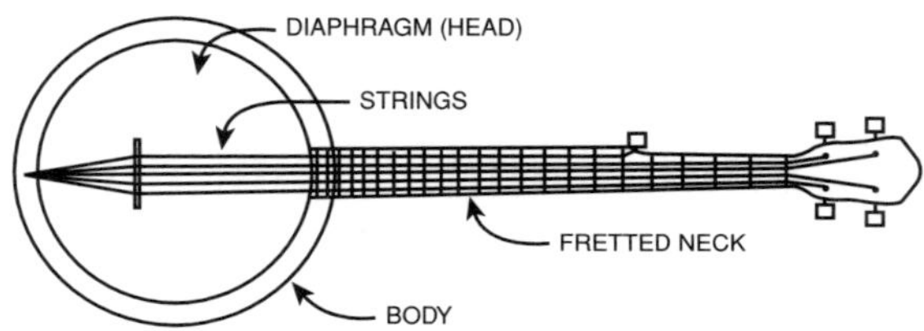

FIGURE 12.4. *Five-string banjo.*

The five-string banjo is commonly played in one of two ways, "Clawhammer style" in which the strings are struck with the tops of the fingernails on the right hand and plucked with the pad of the right thumb and "Scruggs style" (named after Earl Scruggs, the first popularizer of the style) in which the strings are plucked with the thumb and first two fingers of the right hand, usually wearing metal or plastic plectra (picks) on all three fingers. In both styles, the left hand selects pitches by pressing the strings against the fingerboard, causing the metal frets in the neck to stop the strings at specified points that produce chromatic pitches; this is called "fretting" the strings.

The `lick` program simulates Scruggs-style playing. In this style, the right hand typically follows a sequence of patterns. The most common of these patterns are eight notes long and consist of permutations of the three playing fingers. It is uncommon for the same finger to be used twice in a row because it is easier and smoother to alternate fingers. A common pattern is the "forward roll": thumb, index, ring, thumb, index, ring, thumb, ring (or `T I R T I R T R`). Many banjo parts are composed of only two or three basic patterns artfully arranged to allow the melody notes to be played.

The mechanics of banjo playing impose certain restrictions on the sounds that can be produced. At most, five distinct notes can be produced at once and certain note combinations cannot be produced at all. Sequences of notes on the same string will be slower and sound different from sequences that alternate between strings, and so forth. Much of the sound that we associate with the banjo is a necessary result of these constraints. `lick` generates a large number of possible solos and then uses these constraints to judge which of the solos is the most "banjo-like" (i.e., easy to play on the banjo).

`lick` produces both MPU format output files that can be played by the synthesizers and "tablature" files that can be read by humans (and also by machines; see the description of TAB format).

Listing 12.24 in the previous section shows the beginning of the guitar chord file for "Pecusa Waltz" in GC format. Figure 12.5 shows the `lick` output for the chords in Listing 12.24 converted to standard music notation (via VMU format and `pic`) from the MPU format output. The chords for this piece are somewhat atypical for five-string banjo music,[6] but even when constrained to use only "forward rolls" for a right-hand pattern (as in this example), the result is quite credible.

FIGURE 12.5. *"Pecusa Waltz"* `lick` *output.*

The algorithmic music composition demo, narrated by two voice synthesizers named "Eedie & Eddie" (Langston, 1986), involves composing music for listeners who call in through the public telephone network. Eedie & Eddie's demo uses `lick` to compose banjo improvisations for two different pieces (one in the "long" version of the demo and one in the "normal" length demo). The fragment shown here came from an instance of the "normal" length demo. The banjo improvisations seem to get the most enthusiastic listener reception of all the composition techniques used in the telephone demo.

[6]Nor is it typical for a piece in 4/4 to be called a waltz, but . . . .

12.3.9. TAB

Tablature is a musical notation system. According to the *American Heritage Dictionary, Second College Edition*, tablature is "an obsolete system of notation using letters and symbols to indicate playing directions rather than tones." Tablature (often called "Tab" colloquially) is in common use today by teachers of stringed musical instruments, especially in folk or popular music. When a piece requires playing the G above middle C, there is only one way to play it on a piano, but there are five ways on the banjo, at least six ways on the guitar (counting harmonics), and many more ways on the pedal steel guitar, all with different timbral characteristics, decay, and so on.

In the attempt to simulate the playing of an instrument on which there is such a choice, knowing how the sounds are produced allows greater realism in the generated notes (e.g., letting "open" strings ring longer or letting a string ring until it is used for another note). Further, tablature can be transcribed in an ASCII format quite easily.

The major change required to make tablature easy to transcribe is "turning it sideways" so that it reads top-down instead of the conventional left-to-right. Each string is represented by either a number, indicating the position at which the string is fretted or stopped, a left parenthesis, indicating a held note (essentially a tie), or a vertical bar to indicate that the string is not played. The strings are usually numbered from 1 on the right (the guitar string with the highest pitch) increasing to the left. The left-most string in guitar tab would be the sixth string (the string with the lowest pitch). Thus a C major scale on the guitar could be notated as shown in Listing 12.25.

LISTING 12.25. *C major scale in TAB format for guitar.*

```
#TUNING E1 A1 D2 G2 B2 E3
T        |  3  |  |  |  |
I        |  (  0  |  |  |
M        |  (  2  |  |  |
T        |  |  3  |  |  |
I        |  |  |  0  |  |
M        |  |  |  2  |  |
I        |  |  |  |  0  |
M        |  |  |  |  1  |
```

Note that the initial C note, played on the fifth string, is held through the following two notes by the ties (`(`) in the second and third lines. The optional letters at the left indicate the finger used to pick the string—`T` = thumb, `I` = index, `M` = middle, `R` = ring, and `P` = pinky.

Control lines comprise an initial keyword possibly followed by arguments. TAB format files can have other information embedded in them for the programs that take them as input. For instance, almost all programs require the `#TUNING` control.

The common control keywords are (in alphabetical order)

`#ARTIC #.#` Same as in MUT except only one argument is used to set the durations of all notes generated.

`#BARLEN#` Same as in DP.

`#CHAN #[#]...` This control assigns channels to the strings (default is usually channel 1). A decimal number argument in the range 1 to 16 is expected for each string.

`#METER # #` Same as in GC.

`#NUT # [#]...` This strange control expects an argument per string that defines the string length. The most common example of an instrument that would need something other than the default (all zeros) is the five-string banjo, which has one string, (the fifth string) shorter than the rest. A five-string banjo piece would probably have, at the beginning

```
#TUNING G4 D3 G3 B3 D4
#NUT    5  0  0  0  0
```

`#QUANT` *`timevalue`* Same as in DP except the argument specifies the number of tablature lines per measure and can be fractional; thus `#QUANT 1.5` would make triplet whole notes (i.e., three tablature lines will take two measures' time).

`#SPEED` *`timevalue`* `SPEED` is a synonym for `QUANT`.

`#TUNING # [#]...` This control assigns pitches to the strings and is often used to determine how many strings are involved. A pitch name or decimal number argument is expected for each string, separated by whitespace. A guitar in standard tuning would be represented by either of

```
#TUNING E2 A2 D3 G3 B3 E4
#TUNING 40 45 50 55 59 64
```

Note that the "sixth" string—that is, the lowest pitched string—is at the left, as if you were facing the guitar while it is being held with the neck pointing up.

`#VELOCITY #` Same as in GC except a single numeric argument specifies the MIDI key velocity to use for each note played.

In addition to these, programs may define controls for their own use. It is recommended that such controls consist of the number sign followed immediately (with no intervening whitespace) by uppercase characters. In particular, the controls defined for the music preprocessor `mpp` are useful in tab files.

12.3.10. DDM

Files in DDM format contain probabilistic instrument descriptions for programs that use a composition technique called "stochastic binary subdivision." Because this technique can be used to generate pieces of arbitrary length from a single file, this format could, in theory, be considered infinitely compact. Of course, the music generated by these routines can become boring in a finite amount of time, but even so, a great deal of useful musical output can be generated from quite a small DDM file.

Stochastic binary subdivision was originally designed to create drum patterns but was later extended to create melodies. The library routine `sbsd()` generates a single measure of drum pattern or melody by generating a set of simultaneous patterns and then combining them. Its input is a list of instruments (which may be different kinds of drums or different notes for a pitched instrument) with associated parameters defining such characteristics as MIDI channel, loudness, and minimum note resolution. In brief, the algorithm does the following. For each participating instrument, an interval of time starting with one measure is recursively subdivided into two equal parts with a musical event (e.g., a drum strike or a musical note) being placed at each subdivision. This continues until the program decides, based on the density probability and minimum resolution for that instrument, that the subdivision has gone far enough. The subdivision process is carried out independently for each instrument and then the results are combined using a priority structure that only allows one instrument's event to happen at a particular moment.

The library subroutine `sbsdinit()` reads instrument parameters from an instrument description file (typically with a file name ending in `.ddm`) and creates an internal data representation to drive the `sbsd()` routine. Instrument description files contain instrument lines and control lines. Instrument lines have the format

```
Channel/Key#  Dens:Up-beat:Res:Dur:Vel  Comment
```

The parameter fields in the instrument lines have the following meanings:

`Channel` — The MIDI channel. The channel number specified (1 to 16 in decimal) here will determine the channel over which the output for this instrument is sent.

`Key#` — Although melodic synthesizers associate key numbers with pitches (e.g., middle C is 60, the B below it is 59, etc.), drum synthesizers associate key numbers with instruments. The association is specific to each synthesizer or drum machine; Yamaha drum machines usually use 45 for the bass drum and 52 for the snare drum while synthesizers that conform to the General MIDI instrument specification (MIDI, 1991) use 36 and 38 (respectively) for them. To generate melodic output, this parameter should be either a MIDI key number in the range 13 to 127 (C#-1 to G8) or a scale delta in the range -12 to 12. The effect of scale deltas is discussed later in this section. The `Key#` can be specified as hexadecimal (prefixed with `0x`), decimal, or by note name, such as `Bb3`.

`Dens (Density)` — At each step in the recursive subdivision, a pseudorandom decision is made as to whether to subdivide further. This parameter defines the probability that subdivision will occur. Density is expressed as a percentage; a value of 0 assures no subdivision, whereas a value of 100 guarantees subdivision at every level (until stopped by `Resolution`).

`Up-beat` — If `Up-beat` is `D`, the musical event will be placed at the beginning of each time subdivision; if `Up-beat` is `U`, the musical event will be placed at the first time when a subdivision did not occur. Thus, two instruments that only differ in the `Up-beat` parameter will have different fates; if, for instance, they both have `Density` set to zero, one will generate a note on the first beat of the measure (the down beat), and the other will generate a note in the middle of the measure (the up beat in a two-beat world).

`Res (Resolution)` — To avoid the possibility of endless subdivision, and to allow a small degree of level-sensitive control over the `Density` parameter, `Resolution` defines the time length at which no further subdivisions will be allowed to occur. It is expressed in fractions of a measure; for example, a `Resolution` of `4` represents a quarter note.

`Dur (Duration)`	Most drum synthesizers use only the key-down events (onsets) of notes and ignore the key-up events, thereby ignoring the duration. Some, however, use both. Setting `Duration` to a value greater than `0` will give the note a duration of that many sixty-fourth notes; for example, `24` will make a dotted quarter-note duration. It is perfectly legal for `Duration` to be larger than `64/Resolution`; however, any note that is generated before the `Duration` has expired will end the note early.
`Vel (Velocity)`	The speed with which a key is pressed down is called its velocity. Most synthesizers use this information to control loudness. The range of legal values for `Velocity` is 1 (vanishingly quiet) to 127 (mezzo forte).
`Comment`	Any text past the `Velocity` field is considered comment and ignored.

Listing 12.26 shows the file `drum.ddm` as used in an algorithmic music composition telephone demo (Langston, 1986). Because the bass drum definition appears first and it has `Up-beat` specified as `D`, it will always play the downbeat (beat 1) of the measure. Because it has `Resolution` set to `2` (half note), it will only be able to play on beats 1 and 3 of the measure. Because it has `Density` set to `80%`, it will play on the third beat 80 percent of the time. Because the snare drum has the same parameters as the bass drum except for `Up-beat`, it will play on beats 2 and 4 80 percent of the time and on the third beat 4 percent of the time (the snare drum tries 20 percent of the time, but 80 percent of the time the bass drum already has it).

LISTING 12.26. *DDM file for telephone demo.*

```
# Eedie's basic drum rhythm
2/45    80:D:2:0:96      Bass drum
2/52    80:U:2:0:96      Snare drum
2/57    80:D:8:0:127     Closed hi-hat
2/51    50:U:8:0:64      Rim shot
2/48    50:D:8:0:80      Tom-tom
2/54    40:U:8:0:64      Hand clap
2/55    40:U:8:0:64      Cowbell
2/59    67:U:8:0:80      Open hi-hat
2/62    80:D:8:0:72      Ride cymbal
2/57    80:D:16:0:96     Closed hi-hat
```

Figure 12.6 is a notated form (produced via VMU format and `pic`) of eight measures of drum rhythm generated from the file in the preceding listing. The specified probabilities were realized, for the most part. Of the five measures generated (not counting the three measures that were repeats), the bass drum played on the third beat in 4—that is, exactly 80 percent of the time. The snare drum played on beats 2 and 4 for 100 percent of the time and never played on the beat 3 (it only had one chance).

FIGURE 12.6. *Sample output from* the *DDM file in Listing 12.26.*

DDM format can also be used to generate melodies. If an instrument's `Key#` is specified as a number less than or equal to 12, it is considered a scale offset rather than an absolute key number. The value given as `Key#` can also be a negative number. Thus the output becomes a series of relative scale motions. Both types of specification (relative and absolute) can be intermixed. Indeed, the relative specifications need some absolute value to start with; in the absence of anything else, the starting point defaults to middle C.

Two controls are implemented to facilitate relative motion:

`#SCALE`*`note[,note]...`*	The *`#SCALE`* control defines the pitches that can be generated. It is followed by a comma-separated list of pitch classes in either numeric or symbolic form (`0 + C, 1 + C#, ... 11 + B`). Any relative motion will be interpreted in accordance with the specified scale. The default values form a dodecaphonic (12-tone) scale.
`#LIMITS` *`low, high`*	The *`#LIMITS`* control line contains two comma-separated decimal numbers that are taken to be the low and high limits for pitches generated by relative motion (this avoids subsonic and supersonic notes). The default values of `C-2` and `G8`.

A DDM file that uses relative motion is shown in Listing 12.27. This file is similar to the one used in the algorithmic composition telephone demo to generate Eedie's scat solo. The `#SCALE` line defines an A blues pentatonic scale (with the added flat 5) and the `#LIMITS` line cuts off notes below `C1` and above `C4`.

LISTING 12.27. *DDM file for melody generation.*

```
#SCALE  A,C,D,Eb,E,G
#LIMITS C2,C5
1/A3 50:D:2:32:64   A above middle C, mezzo-forte
1/E3 50:D:4:16:56   E above middle C, mezzo-piano
1/+2 35:D:8:8:48    up two scale steps, piano
1/-2 35:U:8:8:48    down two scale steps, piano
1/+1 60:D:16:4:72   up a scale step, forte
1/-1 65:U:16:4:64   down a scale step, mezzo-forte
1/0  33:U:8:8:60    repeat previous note, mezzo-piano
```

Figure 12.7 shows eight measures of music generated from the file in Listing 12.27. Note that the program repeated each measure it had generated; the default is to allow at most one repeat of each measure (see the description of the `-r` option).

FIGURE 12.7. *Sample output from* `the` *DDM file in Listing 12.27.*

Also note that all the lines request durations that are only as long as their minimum resolutions (i.e., `Resolution * Duration = 64`). Because most instruments will not subdivide down to their minimum resolution, there will be some rests in the output (not a bad idea for something that is to be sung).

In addition to the `#SCALE` and `#LIMITS` control lines, the `#DEFINE` and `#INCLUDE` control lines of `mpp` make reference to libraries of drum definitions convenient. Definitions of `Channel/Key#` symbols set up for use with DP format will work with DDM files as well.

Stochastic binary subdivision programs recognize several command-line options to control the generation process:

`-b#` Generate the specified number of measures (bars). The number of measures is treated as an unsigned number, so if `-b-1` is specified, a virtually infinite number of measures will be produced (actually only 2^{32}-1).

`-debug` Print an ASCII version of the generated pattern on the standard output instead of sending MIDI output there. In this graphic output, the results of the subdivision for all instruments is shown. It differs from the normal MPU format output in that the MPU output can contain no more than one instrument event at each sixty-fourth note (selected by precedence criterion from among those instruments that generated a note at a time), whereas the ASCII output shows all the subdivisions generated. When `-debug` is specified, the random number seed is also printed on `stderr`.

`-vmu` Generate output in VMU format on the standard output, instead of sending MPU output there. The VMU format output represents the same notes that would be in the MPU output except that all notes are associated with MIDI channel 1. When `-vmu` is specified, the random number seed is also printed on `stderr`.

`-r` Set the maximum number of repeats allowed to the specified number. If the maximum number of repeats, `N`, is greater than 1, then each time a measure is generated, a repeat count is also generated. The choice is made from a uniform distribution ranging from `0` to `N-1`. The default is `-r2` (i.e., each measure could appear twice).

`-2` Set the random number seed to the specified value. Without this argument, the random number seed is set to the number of seconds that have elapsed since midnight, January 1, 1970 plus the process ID of the current process (the process ID is added to avoid having two runs within the same second produce the same output). Setting the random number seed allows reproducibility.

12.4. Summary

We have described 16 "little languages" to perform tasks relating to music. Tables 12.1 and 12.2 give control keyword usage and a list of programs for these languages. The diagram in Figure 12.8 shows most of the language interconversions for which programs exist.

TABLE 12.1. *Control keyword usage.*

Keyword	*Used in . . .*									
# (comment)	mpp	mut	vmu	dp	sd	ccc	cc	gc	tab	ddm
#ALLRPTS	mpp									
#ALLSECTS	mpp									
#ARTIC		mut	vmu	dp		ccc		gc	tab	
#BAR		mut	vmu							

continues

TABLE 12.1. *Continued.*

Keyword	*Used in . . .*									
#BARLEN				dp				gc	tab	
#CHAN		mut	vmu						tab	
#CHORD						ccc	cc			
#CHORDTONES								gc		
#CODING					sd					
#CPQ			vmu							
#DEFINE	mpp									
#DOSECT	mpp									
#ELSE	mpp									
#ENDIF	mpp									
#ENDRPT	mpp									
#ENDSKIP	mpp									
#GAIN				dp						
#IFNEXT	mpp									
#INCLUDE	mpp									
#INIT					sd					
#LIMITS										dmm
#METER		mut	vmu		sd			gc	tab	
#MULTIPLICITY								gc		
#NOTRPT	mpp									
#NOTSECT	mpp									
#NUT									tab	
#ONLYRPT	mpp									
#ONLYSECT	mpp									
#PART							cc			
#PICK								gc		
#QUANT				dp	sd	ccc	cc	gc	tab	
#REPEAT	mpp									
#ROLL				dp						
#SCALE					sd			gc		ddm
#SKIP	mpp									
#SOLO		mut	vmu							
#SPEED						ccc		gc	tab	
#STRUM								gc		
#STYLE							cc	gc		

Keyword	*Used in . . .*					
`#STYLEDEF`					gc	
`#SYNC`	mut		dp			
`#TEMPO`	mut	vmu				
`#TITLE`	mut	vmu				
`#TRANS`	mut	vmu				
`#TUNING`						tab
`#TUPLE`			dp			
`#VELOCITY`					gc	tab
`#VOICES`	mut	vmu		sd		

TABLE 12.2. *Little music language tools.*

Program	*Input*	*Output*	*Description*
`acca`	CC	MPU	AMC of stylized accompaniments
`accl`	CC	MPU	AMC of stylized melody lines
`adjust`	MPU	MPU	MMF to retime a piece from a click track
`allnotesoff`	cla	MPU	UTG MIDI commands to clear stuck notes
`axtobb`	MA	MIDI, MPU, SMF	Assemble MIDI/MPU/SMF files
`bars`	MPU	MPU	MMF to cut and paste measures
`bbriffs`	CLA	MPU	AMC using the "riffology" technique
`bbtoax`	MIDI, MPU, SMF	MA	Convert MIDI/MPU/SMF, files to MPU assembler
`bs`	CC, mouse	CC, MPU	AMCGI of video background music
`ccc`	CCC	MPU	Chord chart compiler; produce accompaniments
`ccc2gc`	CCC	GC	Convert chord charts to guitar chord files

continues

TABLE 12.2. *Continued.*

Program	*Input*	*Output*	*Description*
`ched`	MPU	MPU	Graphic editor for MPU data
`chmap`	MPU	MPU	MMF to map MIDI channels
`chpress`	cla	MPU	UTG MIDI channel aftertouch
`cntl`	cla	MPU	UTG MIDI continuous controller messages
`cntlseq`	cla	MPU	UTG sequences of controller of aftertouch messages
`countin`	MPU	MPU	MMR to trim leading silence intelligently
`da`	MIDI, MPU	MA	MIDI/MPU disassembler
`ddm`	DDM	VMU, MPU	AMC of drum rhythms and melodies
`ddmt`	mouse	DDM, MPU	AMCGI of drum rhythms and melodies
`dp2ma`	DP	MA	Convert drum pattern files to MPU assembler
`dp2mpu`	DP	MPU	Convert drum pattern files to MPU data
`dx7but`	cla	MPU	UTG Yamaha DX7 button pushes
`dx7tune`	cla	MPU	UTG DX7 tuning commands
`ekn`	cla	CC, MPU	AMC for network testing
`fade`	mouse	MPU	Graphic MIDI mixer controller
`filter`	MPU	MPU	MMF to invoke filters on parts of an MPU data stream
`fract`	MPU	MPU	AMC MMF to perform fractal interpolation
`gc2ma.awk`	GC	MA	Convert guitar chord files to MPU assembler

Program	*Input*	*Output*	*Description*
`gc2mpu`	GC	MPU	Convert guitar chord files to MPU assembler
`grass`	CC	MPU	AMC of bluegrass music
`inst`	cla	MPU	UTG MIDI program change commands
`invert`	MPU	MPU	MMF to perform pitch inversion
`julia`	cla	MPU	AMC based on Julia sets
`just`	MPU	MPU	MMF to quantize timing
`keyvel`	MPU	MPU	MMF to manipulate key velocities
`kmap`	MPU	MPU	MMF to remap MIDI key numbers
`kmx`	mouse	MPU	Graphic MIDI patch bay controller
`libnote`	text	text	Maintain descriptions of voice libraries
`lick`	GC	MPU, TAB	AMC of banjo solos
`mack`	MA	text	Check MPU assembler files for errors
`mecho`	MPU	MPU	MMF to delay and echo selected MIDI data
`merge`	MPU	MPU	MMF to combine MPU data streams
`mfm`	MPU	MPU	Graphic wavesample editor/generator
`mg`	MIDI	MIDI	Read raw MIDI through MPU-401
`midimode`	MPU	MPU	MMF to defeat "running status"
`mirbut`	cla	MPU	UTG Ensoniq Mirage button pushes
`mirpar`	MPU	MPU	Graphic interface to get/set Ensoniq Mirage parameters

continues

TABLE 12.2. *Continued.*

Program	*Input*	*Output*	*Description*
`mirset`	MPU	MPU	Get/set Ensoniq Mirage parameters
`mixer`	mouse	MPU	Graphic MIDI mixer controller front end
`mixer_sa`	mouse	MPU	Graphic MIDI mixer controller, stand-alone
`mixplay`	MIDI, MPU	/DEV/MPU	Combine MIDI and MPU data and play it
`mjoin`	MPU	MPU	MMF to join over-lapped notes
`mkcc`	cla	CC	AMC chord chart gen-erator
`mozart`	cla	MPU	AMC based on the musical dice game
`mpp`	*	*	Music file preprocessor
`mpu2midi`	MPU	MIDI	Convert MPU to untimed MIDI
`mpu2pc`	MPU	MPU	Calculate pitch change track from MPU data
`mpu2smf`	MPU	SMF	Convert MPU to SMF
`mpu2vmu`	MPU	VMU	Convert MPU data to VMU format
`mpuartin`	MIDI	MIDI	Read and filter raw MIDI from MPU-401
`mpuclean`	MPU	MPU	MMF to condense MPU data
`mpumon`	MPU	MA	Split MPU data stream into MPU and MA streams
`mustat`	VMSTAT	MPU	Audio operating sys-tem monitor
`mut2mpu`	MUT	MPU	Convert MUT files to MPU data
`mut2vmu`	MUT	VMU	Convert MUT files to VMU files
`muzak`	text	MPU	Convert ASCII text to notes
`notedur`	MPU	MPU	MMF to manipulate note durations

Program	*Input*	*Output*	*Description*
`numev`	MPU	text	Provide statistics about an MPU file
`p01`	grammar	MPU	AMC based on 0L system grammars
`pbend`	cla	MPU	UTG MIDI pitch-bend commands
`pbendseq`	cla	MPU	UTG interpolated sequences of MIDI pitch-bend commands
`pharm`	MPU	MPU	MMF to add parallel harmonization
`phonemes`	text	text	Converts ASCII text to ASCII phoneme codes
`play`	MPU	/DEV/MPU	Play MPU data through the MPU-401
`pseq`	cla	MPU	AMC of logo sound sequences
`ra`	MA	MPU	Assemble MPU assembler files
`record`	/DEV/MPU	MPU	Input interface to MPU-401
`retro`	MPU	MPU	MMF to generate retrograde melody
`rpt`	MPU	MPU	MMF to repeat sections of MPU data
`rtloop`	MPU	MIDI	Convert MPU to timed MIDI (in real time)
`scat`	MPU	DT	Convert MPU data to scat for voice synthesizer
`sd2vmu.awk`	SD	VMU	Convert SD files to VMU files
`select`	MPU	MPU	MMF to extract specified events from MPU data
`sing`	MPU	DT	Generate voice commands from MPU data and phonemes

continues

TABLE 12.2. *Continued.*

Program	*Input*	*Output*	*Description*
`sinst`	cla	MPU	UTG MIDI program change and sample data
`slur`	MPU	MPU	MMF to substitute pitch-bend for key-off/on
`smf2mpu`	SMF	MPU	Convert SMF data to MPU data
`stats`	MPU	text	Provide statistics about an MPU file
`sustain`	MPU	MPU	MMF to convert sustain pedal to note duration
`sxmon`	MIDI	MA	Monitor system-exclusive MIDI data from MPU-401
`sxmpu`	MIDI, MPU	MIDI, MPU	Send/capture MIDI system-exclusive dumps
`sxstrip`	MPU	MPU	MMF to strip system-exclusive commands
`tab2mpu`	TAB	MPU	Convert tab files to MPU data
`tempo`	MPU	MPU	MMF to change tempo
`tmod`	MPU	MPU	MMF to apply a tempo map
`tonerow`	cla	MPU	AMC of 12-tone sequences
`transpose`	MPU	MPU	MMF to transpose pitches
`trim`	MPU	MPU	MMF to remove silent beginnings and endings
`tshift`	MPU	MPU	MMF to shift MPU data in time
`txeld`	MIDI	MPU	Load voice/performances into TX/DX edit buffer
`txget`	MPU	MIDI	Read voices/performances from TX/DX synths

Program	*Input*	*Output*	*Description*
`txload`	MIDI	MPU	Load and try TX/DX voices
`txportamento`	MIDI	MPU	Set portamento parameters in TX/DX synths
`txput`	MIDI	MPU	Store voices/performances in TX/DX synths
`txvmrg`	MIDI	MIDI	UTG 32-voice TX816 dumps from 1-voice dumps
`umecho`	MIDI	MIDI	Loop back MIDI data through a serial port
`ump`	MPU	MIDI	Convert MPU data to MIDI through a serial port
`unjust`	MPU	MPU	MMF to add random variation `to timing`
`vegplot`	MIDI	SUN	UTG plots of DX7/TX7/TX816 envelopes
`velpat`	MPU	MPU	MMF to apply a velocity pattern to key-on events
`vget`	MPU	MIDI	Read voices from DX7/TX7/TX816
`vmod`	MPU	MPU	MMF to apply a dynamic (volume) map
`vmu2mpu`	VMU	MPU	Convert VMU files to MPU data
`vmu2mut`	VMU	MUT	Convert VMU files to MUT files
`vmu2p.awk`	VMU	PIC	Convert VMU files to `pic` macros for scoring
`voxname`	MIDI	text	UTG names for DX7/TX7/TX816 voices
`vpr`	MIDI	text	UTG parameter listings from DX7/TX7/TX816 voices

continues

TABLE 12.2. *Continued.*

Program	*Input*	*Output*	*Description*
`vput`	MIDI	MPU	Store voices in DX7/TX7/TX816

Abbreviations used in the table:

AMC	Algorithmic music composition
AMCGI	Algorithmic music composition with a graphic interface
CLA	Command-line arguments
DT	Commands for the DecTalk DTC01 speech synthesizer
MMF	MPU to MPU filter
MOUSE	Graphic input
SUN	Suntools graphic output
TEXT	General ASCII text
UTG	"Utility to generate"

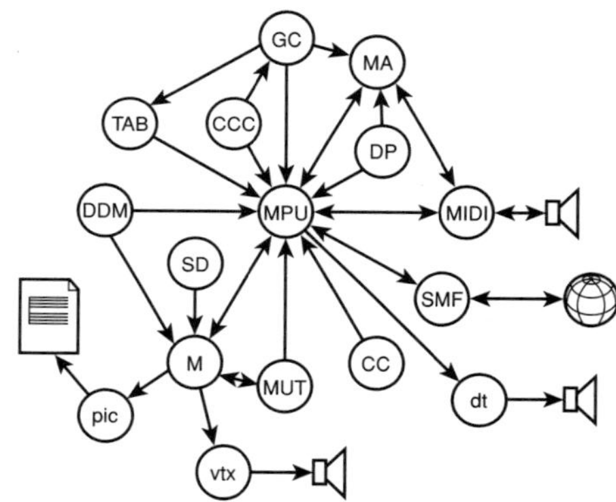

FIGURE 12.8. *Little language conversion flow.*

In Table 12.3, letter codes appearing in the Strengths column refer to noteworthy advantages of the entry, whereas codes appearing in the Lacks column indicate important features lacking.[7] In particular, the `E` code appearing in both columns for CC is meant to indicate that although a large style repertoire is possible, only a few styles have been implemented so far.

Table 12.3 lists the languages along with standard file name endings, related formats, and some strengths and weaknesses for each. In this table, `pic` refers to macros for music printing using the `pic` troff preprocessor, vtx

[7]Thus, code `D` is taken for granted and only appears if it is lacking.

refers to data for the Votrax PSS speech synthesizer, and dt refers to data for the ecTalk DT01 speech synthesizer. Table 12.3 shows little language characteristics but does not show several little languages that, although not designed with music in mind, have proven extremely helpful in music projects (including the implementation of little languages themselves and the creation of music project documentation). Were these not already generally known by the computing community, they would have been described here. Most notable among these are `awk` (Aho et al., 1979), make (Feldman, 1979), `pic` (Kernighan, 1984), sh (BSD, 1994), and tbl (Lesk, 1976).

TABLE 12.3. *Little languages characteristics.*

Little Language	*File Type*	*Converts Directly To*	*Strengths*	*Lacks*
CC	`.cc`	MPU	A, B, C, E, F	E, H
CCC	`.ccc`	MPU, GC	A, B, F	E
DDM	`.ddm`	MPU, VMU	A, B, C	F, H
DB	`.dp`	MPU, MA	A, B, F	H
GC	`.gc`	MPU, MA, Tab	A, B, F	H
MA	`.ma`	MPU, MIDI	B, F, H	A
MIDI	`.midi`	MPU, MA	A, G, H	B, C, F
MPU	`.mpu`	MIDI, MA, VMU, SMF, dt	A, G, H	B, C, F
MUT	`.mut`	MPU, VMU	A, B, F	H
MUTRAN	?	IBM 1620 binary	A, F	D
SD	`.sd`	VMU	A, B, F	H
SMF	`.mf`	MPU	G, H, I	B, C, F
TAB	`.tab`	MPU	B, F, I	H
VMU	`.vmu`	MPU, `pic`, vtx	B, F	H

Abbreviations used in the table:

A	Dense; compact encoding of date
B	Easily edited by ASCII text editors
C	High-level conceptual description
D	Processing software exists
E	Large style repertoire
F	Easily read (understood) by human musicians
G	Standard; allows communication with other software
H	General; expresses anything expressable with MIDI
I	Encodes subtleties beyond keyboard capabilities

12.5. Acknowledgments

The bulk of the work described in this chapter was carried out while the author was a researcher in the Software Engineering Research group at Bell Communications Research, Inc. (Bellcore) in Morristown, N.J.

An earlier version of much of the material in this chapter appeared in a paper titled "Little Languages for Music" (Langston, 1990a), which appeared in the Spring 1990 issue of the USENIX journal *Computing Systems*.

Gareth Loy of UCSD and Michael Hawley of NeXT Computers (at Lucasfilm at the time) provided initial version of the MPU kernel device driver and generally shared music software with us (e.g., Gareth's disassembler program, da, has been the helpless subject of many hours of code mutilation).

Gary Haberman provided critical feedback on the music tools and the music they produced along with numerous practical suggestions. Brian Redman provided the impetus for trying to get voice synthesizers to sing harmony.

I also want to thank Al Aho, Jon Bentley, and Brian Kernighan, whose pursuit and popularization of the little language idea has given many people useful tools and a name for what they are doing.

Finally, I'd like to thank Dr. John Hancock of the Reed College Chemistry Department for encouraging early computer work such as the development of the MUTRAN language and for being aware, even way back then, that computers were wasted on accounting and payroll tasks.

12.6. References

Aho, A. V., B. W. Kernighan, and P. J. Weinberger. 1979. AWK—A pattern scanning and processing language. *Software Practice & Experience* 9:267–280.

Backus, J. W. 1960. The syntax and semantics of the proposed International Algebraic Language of the Zurish ACM—GAMM Conference. *Proceedings of the International Conference on Information Processing, UNESCO, Paris*, 1959, R. Oldensbourg, Munich; Butterworths, London, 1960, pp. 125–132.

Bentley, J. 1986. Programming pearls. *Communications of the ACM* 29(8):711–721.

Berkeley Software Distribution. 1994. *4.4 BSD user's reference Manual.* Sebastopol, CA: O'Reilly & Associates and the USENIX Association.

Coda Music Software. 1989. *Finale encyclopedia.* Bloomington, MN: Coda Music Software.

Feldman, S. 1979. Make—A program for maintaining computer programs. *Software Practice & Experience* 9:255–265.

Hawley, M. 1986. MIDI music software for UNIX. *Proceedings of the USENIX Summer '86 Conference,* Atlanta, GA.

Kernighan, B. W. 1984. PIC—*A graphics language for typesetting.* AT&T Bell Laboratories computing Science Technical Report No. 116.

Langston, P. S. 1986. (201) 664-2332 Eedie & Eddie on the wire, an experiment in music generation. *Proceedings of the USENIX Summer '86 Conference,* Atlanta, GA.

Langston, P. S. 1988. *Six techniques for algorithmic composition.* Bellcore Technical Memorandum #ARH-013020.

Langston, P. S. 1989a. *Getting MIDI from a Sun.* Bellcore Technical Memorandum #ARH-016282.

Langston, P. S. 1989b. *UNIX MIDI manual.* Bellcore Technical Memorandum #ARH-015440.

Langston, P. S. 1990a. Little languages for music. *Computing Systems* 3(2):193–288.

Langston, P. S. 1990b. *PellScore—An incidental music generator.* Bellcore Technical Memorandum #ARH-016281.

Langston, P. S. 1990c. UNIX MIDI tools. *Software—Practice & Experience* 20(S1).

Langston, P. S. 1991. IMG/1—An incidental music generator. *Computer Music Journal* 15(1):28–39.

Lesk, M. E. 1976. *TBL—A program for setting tables.* Bell Laboratories Computing Science Technical Report #49.

Levine, J. R., T. Mason, and D. Brown. 1992. *lex & yacc* (2nd ed.). Sebastopol, CA: O'Reilly & Associates.

The International MIDI Association. 1988. *Standard MIDI files 1.0.* Los Angeles: Author.

The International MIDI Association. 1989. *MIDI 1.0 detailed specification, Document version 4.1*. Los Angeles: Author.

The International MIDI Association. 1991. General MIDI ratified by MMA and JMSC. *The IMA Bulletin* 8(5).

Sulsbruck, B. 1982. *Latin American percussion.* Copenhagen, Denmark: Den Rytmiske Aftenskoles Forlag.

Thompson, T. J. 1989. *Keynote—A language for musical expressions.* AT&T Bell Laboratories Technical Report.

Thompson, T. J. 1990. *Keynote—A language and extensible graphical editor for music.* Proceedings of the USENIX Winter '90 Conference, Washington, D.C.

INDEX

A

B

C

D

E

F

G

H

I

J

K

L

M

P

Q

R

S

T

U

V

W-X

Y-Z